THINKING AND LEARNING SKILLS

Volume 2:

Research and Open Questions

Edited by

Susan F. Chipman and **Judith W. Segal**
National Institute of Education

Robert Glaser
University of Pittsburgh

LAWRENCE ERLBAUM ASSOCIATES, PUBLISHERS
1985   Hillsdale, New Jersey   London

Lawrence Erlbaum Associates, Inc., Publishers
365 Broadway
Hillsdale, New Jersey 07642

Library of Congress Cataloging in Publication Data

Main entry under title:

Thinking and learning skills.

  Bibliography: p.
  Includes index.
  Contents: v. 1. Relating instruction to research—
v. 2. Research and open questions.
  1. Learning.   2. Cognition in children.   3. Education
—Research.   I. Segal, Judith W.   II. Chipman, Susan F.
III. Glaser, Robert, 1921–
LB1060.T48   1985   370.15′23   84-25878
ISBN 0-89859-164-3 (set)
ISBN 0-89859-165-1 (v. 1)
ISBN 0-89859-166-X (v. 2)

Printed in the United States of America
10 9 8 7 6 5 4 3 2

Contents

Problem Solving

Intelligence and Reasoning

**The Generality and Specificity
of Cognitive Skills**

**Learning and Development in the
Acquisition of Cognitive Skills**

Preface

Robert Glaser
University of Pittsburgh

Currently, two streams of endeavor offer promise for improving school effectiveness in developing students' higher cognitive capacities. One of these is represented by the increased interest of school districts, colleges, and universities in identifying ways to help their students build the cognitive skills that enable them to learn and think effectively. What can be done, they ask, beyond teaching the fundamentals of reading, writing, arithmetic, and subject-matter knowledge, to enable students to use their skills and knowledge for effective problem solving, reasoning, and comprehension? The second stream is apparent in recent scientific advances in the study of intelligence, human development, problem solving, the structure of acquired knowledge, and the skills of learning.

This confluence of renewed educational interest and modern scientific investigation offers a challenging opportunity to attack the problem of "passive knowledge"—knowledge that students receive and express, but cannot use effectively for thinking and learning. Schools have not been well enough equipped for this task. Older theories of learning focused on simpler forms of learning and did not provide understanding of higher cognitive processes. Educational practices based on those theories resulted in improved instruction for fundamental skills; less emphasis was given to exercising thinking and problem-solving abilities in the course of schooling. Today, however, educators, educational researchers, developmental psychologists, and cognitive scientists are designing school programs and conducting investigations on understanding and problem solving in mathematics and science, comprehending and reasoning with text material, study skills and abilities to learn, and the role of memory organization in the acquisition of knowledge. These processes of human cognition and learning are being studied with particular attention to how conditions that foster them might be built into the materials, methodologies, and environments for learning and schooling.

In recognition of this potential, scientists at the National Institute of Education (NIE), Susan Chipman and Judith Segal, proposed the conference on which these volumes are based. Their goal was to examine educational practices and scientific investigation concerned with students' abilities to understand, reason, solve problems, and to learn. The plan for the conference was to bring together cognitive researchers, program developers, and teachers of cognitive skills to provide mutual advice and to discuss their theories, findings, and recommendations. In this way, a rich array of current work could be assembled that would be available for educators and researchers. In addition, the conference could provide information to NIE that would assist in identifying needs for future research.

The conference took place at the Learning Research and Development Center (LRDC) of the University of Pittsburgh, one of the major research and development centers funded by NIE, engaged in both basic and applied research on the relevant issues. Organizing the conference called for close collaboration between LRDC and NIE. Chipman and Segal at NIE and Michelene Chi and Robert Glaser of LRDC formed the initial planning committee. Conference contributions were carefully structured. Each chapter in these volumes was especially requested to fulfill a particular function. The aspirations and rationale for the conference are well described in Chipman and Segal's introductory chapter, "Higher Cognitive Goals for Education." They point out that whereas schools appropriately make the basic skills of reading, writing, and mathematics a high priority, skills in learning, reasoning, and general problem solving—including the more sophisticated aspects of reading and mathematics—are less emphasized or neglected. Thus, the burgeoning research on cognition fills an important need: to understand and describe these skills with the precision that would make it possible to teach them and assess their acquisition. The related practical requirement is to design instructional programs that successfully teach these higher cognitive skills.

These volumes, like the conference sessions, are organized by a classification of cognitive skills into three groups: intelligence and reasoning, knowledge acquisition, and problem solving. Although we recognize that there are features common to these areas, as well as important relations between them, these categories serve present purposes in reflecting attention to the three central themes of conference discussions.

While each of the editors has been concerned with both volumes, Volume 1 is particularly Judith Segal's contribution, and she introduces it. In Volume 1 she attempts to bring theory and practice into close perspective. Programs that have been implemented in schools are described by their developers. These programs encompass the range of approaches to cognitive skills instruction from which practitioners can currently choose. Their diversity offers readers a basis for exploring the advantages and limitations of different approaches to instruction. The developers describe the theories and assumptions underlying their programs, discuss the specific skills they are seeking to instill, offer examples of typical instructional methods and materials, and discuss the effectiveness of their programs.

In three invited essays, leading cognitive psychologists analyze the instructional programs presented. Their contributions look carefully at the ideas and practices recommended. They examine the assumptions built into the programs about the nature, development, and acquisition of thinking and learning skills; comment on the relationship of these assumptions to research findings and current theory; review evaluation data on these programs and discuss the problems of evaluation; and suggest additional ideas for research and further questions for exploration.

In the final section of Volume 1, we are fortunate to include chapters by educators who have implemented programs of instruction in cognitive skills in different settings. They comment on current efforts and describe impressions and results from their own experiences.

Volume 2 displays the guiding hand of Susan Chipman, who also has written an introduction to it. This volume contains a representative sample of contemporary research on cognitive skills and considers research issues and open questions that indicate future research directions. The papers she has brought together here exhibit the rich variety of theory and methodology currently being brought to the study of thinking and learning by cognitive scientists. Each major topical area—knowledge acquisition, problem solving, and intelligence and reasoning—includes perspectives from developmental psychology and from the study of cultural influences on human learning.

Reflected here is an issue prominent throughout the conference—the question of the generality or domain specificity of problem-solving and learning skills. Early seminal research emphasized the important common characteristics of problem solving in various task environments, but it is not obvious that these common characteristics can be treated as general, teachable skills. General skills may develop slowly and naturally out of much specific experience, and perhaps problem-solving skills can best be taught in the context of the acquisition of particular domains of knowledge. Many other fundamental research issues appear in Volume 2, including questions about the influences of learning, development, and social background on the acquisition of cognitive skills, and about the necessity for adapting instruction to the prior experience, knowledge, and skill level capabilities of students. Developmental differences also receive special attention in this volume.

The conference at LRDC was an exhilarating experience for those who attended, as we hope these volumes will be for those who peruse and study them. We have attempted to address a wide audience, and the conference and the resulting volumes should help to strengthen a community of interest that cuts across the boundaries separating basic researchers, program developers, and classroom teachers. These volumes should enlarge that community, helping to accelerate an integration of the efforts of all those concerned with guiding students in becoming more independent, effective learners and problem solvers throughout their lives.

Research on the training of cognitive skills is, as these volumes attest, a high priority in education—one supported by growing public interest and scientific advances. Few other educational possibilities beckon us to apply our energies and exploratory talents as much as this one does. Teaching thinking and the ability to learn have been long-term aspirations for schools, and now progress has occurred that brings these goals within reach. Our task is to produce educational environments where knowledge and skill become objects of interrogation, inquiry, and instruments for learning so that as individuals acquire knowledge, they also acquire cognitive abilities to think, reason, and continue learning.

There are many acknowledgments to be made in producing a work as extensive as this, and we would like to express our thanks to all who contributed to the success of the conference and to the production of these books. Karen Locitzer shouldered the responsibility for all the conference arrangements. Michelle von Koch handled the technical editing with Helen Craig's invaluable assistance. Emilee Luckett at NIE provided vital secretarial support for Chipman and Segal throughout the process of conference planning, writing, and editing. The conference was enriched by others who do not appear as authors, particularly Richard Anderson, Joseph Psotka, and Virginia Shipman, who made important contributions.

Robert Glaser

Higher Cognitive Goals for Education: An Introduction

Susan F. Chipman
Judith W. Segal
National Institute of Education

In a rapidly changing technological environment, it is difficult to predict what knowledge students will need or what problems they will have to solve 20 years from now. What they really need to know, it seems, is how to learn the new information and skills that they will require throughout their lives. These general skills are prominent among the characteristics employers say they would like to see in the youth they hire (Chatham, 1982). Clearly, much of the value of education for students' later lives comes from whatever general thinking and learning skills have been acquired along with the specific knowledge that schools impart. Quite appropriately, schools place the highest priority on skills with very general applicability: reading, writing, and mathematics. However, skills in learning, reasoning, and general problem solving—including the more sophisticated aspects of reading and elementary mathematics—are neglected by the schools.

An Evident Need

Even in the earliest grades, teachers direct students to a lesson or reading assignment with instructions to learn information, concepts, or skills. Little is said to the child about how to go about learning. Recent research focused on reading has shown that explicit instruction in strategies for effective thinking and learning rarely occurs in classrooms (Beck, 1983; Durkin, 1984; MacGinitie, 1984). Similarly, it is assumed, or hoped, that repeated attempts to learn or to solve problems will automatically result in improvement of general ability to reason or solve problems; little is taught about ways of going about solving the problems.

The central research problem in this area is still to understand and to describe these skills with the precision that would make it possible to measure them.

Nevertheless, Jencks (1978) has argued that it is the complex skills, not the basic skills, that are deteriorating. NAEP (National Assessment of Educational Progress, 1981) does report that the problem with student writing seems to rest in the quality of thinking and organization rather than in the mechanics. There is general agreement that reading comprehension, not decoding, is the most important problem area in reading instruction today. Repeated assessments have shown that students' mathematics problem-solving performance is much less satisfactory than their computational skill (NAEP, 1983). Instructors at the college level, especially in community and open admissions colleges, complain that students have great difficulty managing and evaluating their own learning efforts. Students agree: On the SAT questionnaire (College Entrance Examination Board [CEEB], 1981) students rate study skills as the skill area in which they feel the greatest need for assistance. Not surprisingly, the recent CEEB effort (1982) to define basic competencies for college entrance includes competencies in general reasoning, problem formulation and solution, studying, and general learning skills. Many of these competencies, of course, are not well defined. Current emphasis on measuring competencies and training for the competencies measured may be creating a still more unfavorable environment for the development of these more complex competencies that we do not yet know how to measure.

Research (Dansereau, Long, McDonald, & Actkinson, 1975) indicates that even good students know very little about techniques they might use to remember better the material they are studying. Nonetheless, one way successful students and more educated persons differ from the less successful and less educated is that they are likely to know and use learning techniques more sophisticated than rote repetition (Weinstein, 1978). For example, only good readers at the 12th-grade level are able to adjust their style of reading to the purposes for which they are reading (Smith, 1967). Although it would be difficult to set minimum competency standards for learning skills, it is clear that there is room for improvement: Even good students have a limited repertoire of such skills, and others have fewer still.

There is good reason to try to improve the characteristics of individual students as learners. Most commonly, educational research attempts to improve instructional techniques in general or in specific subject matter areas. Dansereau (1978) points out, however, that research at the college level indicates that truly different methods of instruction—lecture, discussion, reading, computers—have negligible effects on student performance, whereas there are large individual differences in student performance. Although carefully developed and researched instructional materials may enhance achievement of particular educational or training goals, such materials will never be available to meet all the needs of individuals. Only a few high priority subjects are likely to receive the necessary research and development investment, and learning about developing topics such as the frontiers of technology requires an independently active learner. It does make sense, therefore, to invest in the alternative strategy of improving learners, rather than simply improving instructional materials.

An Opportunity for Genuine Improvement

Because explicit instruction in thinking and learning skills has received little attention in the schools, it is likely that large improvements are possible. It is much easier to improve instructional outcomes in a new or neglected area than to achieve significant improvements in instructional methods that have undergone decades or centuries of evolutionary improvement by trial and error. Furthermore, there is reason to believe that increased efforts in this area hold promise for ameliorating the persistent problem of unequal school success for the diverse social and ethnic groups that make up our society. A recent investigation of the delivery of study skills instruction (USDE, 1982) indicated the rarity of serious school programs of study skills instruction and revealed that students, parents, and school staff all believe that these skills are learned primarily in the home. Unlike teachers and school administrators, however, most parents and students were unable to explain what is meant by study skills. Educational practice has evolved in relation to the surrounding culture, particularly the subcultures from which both educators and those participating most fully in schooling traditionally have come. Therefore, educational practice is grounded in tacit assumptions about the skills and knowledge students bring to school and about the supplementary assistance and training provided at home. Detailed observations are beginning to show that the forms of help with school work available at home vary dramatically in quality and quantity (Chall & Snow, 1982; Varenne, Hamid-Buglione, McDermott, & Morison, 1982). Obviously, students whose parents know what is meant by study skills are advantaged.

There is some evidence from cross-cultural psychological research that techniques for learning schoollike material are culturally influenced. For instance, Westerners and non-Westerners differ in the use of rote, associative forms of learning typical of less successful students here as opposed to the use of a more complex, organized, and strategic form of learning typical of more successful students (Scribner & Cole, 1976). Within our own society, parallel ethnic or socioeconomic differences in the use of such strategies may exist (Glasman, 1968; Jensen, 1969). In laboratory studies, parents' ways of directing children's behavior vary among social classes and ethnic groups (Wertsch, 1978). A plausible form of parental guidance—nonspecific encouragement to figure out reasons for events—has been shown to produce moderately lasting effects on the systematicity of problem solving in young children (Richards & Siegler, 1981). One suspects that such guidance would be differentially distributed across social groups and that its compounded effects over many years could be substantial.

Furthermore, parents cannot transmit skills that they themselves have not had the occasion to develop and practice in their own occupational and social situations (Ogbu, 1978). Consequently, there is reason to suggest that the omission of explicit training in thinking and learning skills from the school curriculum may be one reason why social class and cultural backgrounds are now so strongly predictive of school success. Among the research papers of Volume 2, some represent nascent efforts to examine the relation in our society between culture and cognitive function.

New Conceptions of Intellect

Cross-cultural cognitive research has been one influence contributing to a reconceptualization of human intelligence that is now in progress (Hunt, 1983; Sternberg, 1979, 1982). What in the past has been seen as innate cognitive ability or aptitude for learning may turn out to be largely a matter of opportunity to acquire skills critical for success in the school environment. Most people recognize that traditional measures of "intelligence" or IQ reflect experience and environmental opportunity as well as other factors. However, the fact that these measures were designed to classify individuals and to predict school performance has hindered progress in understanding either what was important in school performance itself or what really is important about differences in environmental experience. For example, many people would define intelligence as ability to learn. Most intelligence tests, in fact, measure how much people have learned from their general experience. Therefore, it has long been a puzzle in differential psychology why individuals with high IQs show little superiority in basic ability to learn (Tyler, 1965). It may be that the critical differences in intellectual functioning rest on the organization and management of our basic learning ability. Although it is likely that there are constitutional aspects to individual intellectual differences, Pellegrino and Glaser (1982) have found that both specific knowledge relevant to the test items and memory management strategies that might be learned or trained are important determinants of performance on intelligence test items.

We are not the first to suggest that there might be a need for systematic training to improve learning and thinking skills. Indeed, efforts to train and strengthen mental powers have a very long history (Mann, 1979). In 1706, John Locke said: "The business of education is not to make the young perfect in any one of the sciences, but so to open and dispose their minds as may best make them capable of any, when they shall apply themselves to it." Alfred Binet (1909), whose theoretical investigations of intellectual functioning initiated the technology of intelligence measurement, was himself convinced of the possible benefits of "mental orthopedics." In these volumes, we sample the curricular and theoretical research resources that are now available to work toward those long-standing educational goals.

At this descriptive level, it may sound as if we are talking about facts that have always been known. Because we are talking about the importance of self-knowledge and self-control of learning and problem-solving strategies, that is partially true. If an analysis is correct, skilled learners should recognize it as corresponding reasonably well to their own thinking. The critical difference is that modern research techniques take the descriptions to a level of precision and detail that is making it possible to communicate these strategies to those who do not already know them as well as to those who do know them. For example, there is little use in instructing students to identify the main ideas in material they are studying and to concentrate on them—a commonsense strategy—if students are unable to identify the main ideas. In fact, even many college students find it difficult to isolate the important points in texts (Brown & Smiley, 1978) and therefore cannot profit from study skill advice at that level. Training that is informed by current research, however, can overcome that obstacle (Brown & Day, 1983; Day, 1980). Rereading an earlier effort to summarize what was known about "learning about learning" (Bruner, 1966), one is struck both by the constancy of the general descriptions of intellectual skills and by the great progress in applicable specific knowledge of cognition.

A Renewed Challenge for Educators

In summary, the development of higher cognitive skills that enable students to be independent learners and independent, creative, problem-solving users of their knowledge has always been a very important goal for educators. There is evidence, however, that explicit instruction in these skills is rare and that students' mastery of them is frequently inadequate. Furthermore, there is reason to believe that improved instruction in such skills might help to overcome persistent socio-economic and cultural differences in the outcomes of education. Today, our long-standing aspirations for education can draw upon new resources provided by the recent, rapid growth of research into cognitive function, including developing reconceptualizations of intelligence or intellectual ability. Today, educators are being challenged to strive for excellence in their students' development— the higher goals of learning, thinking, and problem-solving skills as well as basic computational and decoding skills (National Commission on Excellence in Education, 1983). The cover article of the January, 1983, *New York Times Education Supplement,* "Teaching to Think: A New Emphasis," (Maeroff, 1983) illustrates the widespread concern and the growing educational response to this challenge.

RESOURCES TO MEET THE CHALLENGE

In these volumes, we have brought together a rich sample of the resources that educators may call upon to meet this renewed challenge. They are resources of two kinds. There are educational programs that have already been developed to teach learning, thinking, and problem-solving skills. The first of these volumes samples such programs, discussing both their relation to research understanding of cognitive functions and issues of practical implementation. A second kind of resource is the rich and growing body of modern cognitive research that will provide the foundation for new approaches to the teaching of cognitive skills. The remaining volume samples this research, touching upon both the analysis of the major skills and key open questions that surround the teaching of cognitive skills.

Research on cognitive skills and practical educational efforts to teach cognitive skills interlock in a complex way. Educators' goals are frequently more ambitious and broader in scope than the topics on which researchers have focused their analytic efforts. Yet, educators' conceptualizations of the skills they are attempting to teach are frequently derived from the efforts of previous generations of researchers. Both draw upon their own and others' introspective intuitions about the nature of learning, thinking, and problem-solving skills as one source of inspiration for their work. Thus, educational programs embody both the practical wisdom of gifted teachers and the theoretical understanding of intellectual functioning that prevailed at the time they were developed. New theoretical understanding of cognitive skills may suggest a reformulation of educational goals and provide considerable guidance for instruction, but the artful contributions of gifted teachers and curriculum developers also are needed to realize those goals. An important feature of Volume 1 is the set of analysis papers that were designed to foster the relationship between research and educational practice in cognitive skills training, drawing out the lessons that each enterprise has to offer the other. The authors were asked to analyze the presuppositions and educational activities of the programs in relation to research understanding of the skill domain in question, but they were also asked to identify important educational goals that seem to have been neglected as subjects of research.

Defining and Describing the Higher Cognitive Skills

For both research and practice, the issues of definition and description of complex learning, thinking, and problem-solving skills remain absolutely central. Past and present research focuses on these problems of definition—for example, on identifying the processes and strategies that good text comprehenders, good students, and effective problem solvers use. In educational practice, better understanding is needed so that we can measure the presence of these skills, set them as goals for instruction, devise reasonable methods of training, and evaluate the effectiveness of training. As our discussions of educational programs show, current understanding is generally insufficient to permit convincing evaluation of programs with respect to their claims to develop complex cognitive skills. Although the emphasis in Volume 1 is on the discussion of programs intended to develop general cognitive skills, the same problems in measuring efficacy exist for the more ambitious goals of traditional curricula. Today, striving to develop complex cognitive skills requires an element of faith from educators, but the price of excessive skepticism is likely to be the certainty of limited educational accomplishment.

As yet, there is no comprehensive and universally accepted theory capturing complex human intellectual functions in a single conceptual framework. For purposes of discussion, we have divided the general thinking and learning skills that are the subject of these volumes into three major areas: (1) knowledge acquisition, (2) problem solving, and (3) such very basic cognitive skills as approaching tasks in an organized, non-impulsive fashion, or drawing simple logical conclusions. Nevertheless, we recognize that there are common features to all these skills, and important relations among them. This can be seen in even the briefest of descriptions. In discussing knowledge acquisition, A. Brown (1980) characterized the key cognitive skills as: knowing when you know, knowing what you know, knowing what you need to know, and knowing the utility of taking active steps to change your state of knowledge. In problem solving, these skills include analyzing the problem, searching related knowledge, planning possible attempts at solution, keeping track of progress, and checking results against the overall goal or more immediate goals. The distinction between acquiring knowledge and making flexible use of that knowledge to confront new situations is helpful, but it cannot be sharply drawn. Especially when it comes to taking steps to improve one's state of knowledge, there is a problem-solving aspect to learning. And operational methods for problem solving are a kind of knowledge that one must acquire. In our third category, we have risked grouping together very disparate mental functions—elemental mental processes that form a part of many complex skills (cf. Sternberg's chapter) and very general self-control or self-management strategies that are also applicable in a wide range of situations (cf. Baron's chapter). Most of human experimental psychology contributes to our understanding of elemental mental processes. For the readers of these volumes, a relatively new research focus—metacognition, the study of individuals' knowledge of, awareness of, and control of their own cognitive processes—is most critical. Metacognitive sophistication—the deliberate and reasoned deployment of cognitive resources and strategies—is the goal of much cognitive skills training. Whether that is a reasonable goal and, if so, what instructional process is likely to achieve the goal is something we may learn from research on metacognition.

In the preceding paragraph, we provided first steps in the characterization of the elusive general cognitive skills that are the subject of these volumes. As a further introduction, we provide only brief summaries of the understanding of these skills that is emerging from research. These themes are elaborated throughout these volumes, first in the analysis chapters of Volume 1 and then in the research chapters of Volume 2, each of which gives a detailed view of some aspect of cognitive skill.

Knowledge Acquisition

How people acquire and add to complex bodies of knowledge is poorly understood, in spite of recent dramatic advances. Many years ago, Bartlett (1932) demonstrated that what a person remembers from a text or a drawing depends on previous general knowledge as much as on the material itself. More recent research in both cognitive psychology and artificial intelligence (Schank &

Abelson, 1977; Winograd, 1972) has demonstrated that general knowledge is required to make sense of even simple sentences and texts; careful analysis shows that a great deal is left out, taken for granted. Anderson (1978) and others have been very active in showing the many ways that the reader's background knowledge or general expectations for a text affect its interpretation and what is remembered. Work towards explaining more precisely how such knowledge affects understanding and memory for information continues.

In addition, readers have knowledge about the general form of texts themselves—about, for example, the parts that can be expected in a story. Bartlett also demonstrated that such knowledge is part of our cultural heritage, that stories drawn from an unfamiliar culture are extremely difficult to recall. Although simple stories have received most attention from researchers, it is obvious the same point applies to literary genres in general. In addition, researchers are beginning to recognize and analyze the characteristic forms of other kinds of texts such as science textbooks or popular science articles.

Understanding the Skills of Comprehension.   The crucial question about the skill of comprehension is how the reader makes use of such knowledge in comprehending a text. One interesting conjecture (J. S. Brown, Collins, & Harris, 1978) is that comprehension of a story involves divining the plan and purpose behind the actions in the story. We understand the actions in a story because they fit plans that we ourselves might be able to generate. Brown and his colleagues suggested that a wide range of comprehension skills have this common characteristic—seeking to place the elements into a plan or purpose that makes sense for the whole. Another example they gave is comprehending a mathematical proof: To make sense of it you have to know that particular sequences of steps are intended to do something. That is, they form a larger conceptual unit that has a particular function in the proof.

These researchers are making progress in explaining what it is to "know what it is you know and what it is you need to know." You could know that you have to come up with a plan behind a text that makes it reasonable for everything that is there to be there. You could know that if certain things don't fit, then you still have a need to find some hypothesis that will make them fit. In the case of a simple story, it has been possible to observe skilled readers formulate a general plan for the entire story even before the main narrative begins (Olson, Duffy, & Mack, 1980). A surprising statement is recognized immediately as the introduction to the climactic event, and readers are able to predict that it will involve the character who has not been mentioned since the beginning of the story. (Otherwise, why would he have been there?)

Aids to Comprehension and Memory.   Much less is known about the process of acquiring complex knowledge, like that presented in school and college textbooks, than is known about the comprehension of simple stories. As for stories, there may be characteristic expository patterns that good students can use to structure the information being presented, to identify the important points, and so on. Rather extensive attention (Mayer, 1979; Reder, 1980) has been given to the effect of such devices as advance organizers, interpolated questions, and elaborations of content upon memory for texts. The results of this research have been sometimes positive, sometimes negative, apparently because it was not founded on a theory that could describe the relation between particular questions, for example, and the content of the text. Techniques for characterizing the structure and content of texts in a reliable, consistent, and detailed manner are now available and may lead to more reliable techniques for assisting students' learning. On the other hand, the demonstrated important effects of the reader's prior knowledge on both comprehension and memory suggest limits to what can be achieved with an approach based on the text design alone.

Traditional Study Techniques. Traditional study skills techniques seem to have been informed by the same ideas that led to the instructional research on text design, with the important difference that the student is to supply the questions and elaborations and to derive an advance organizer from a quick skimming of the text. In effect, the student is asked to act as his or her own instructional designer. It is not at all obvious that we should expect students to be able to do this, or that their efforts would be any more consistently effective than those of instructional researchers. Indeed, evidence for the effectiveness of traditional study techniques is limited (Anderson, 1980). Not surprisingly, extensive training in supporting skills such as the identification of main ideas seems to be required in order to achieve sucess with a study technique such as outlining (Barton, 1930). Brown (1980) has observed that underlining key points is an effective study technique for those who use it spontaneously, but not for others who are induced to use it. It seems likely that traditional analyses of study skills are too superficial and insufficiently detailed to be instructionally useful. Although research to date suggests that time-consuming study techniques like elaboration and imagery, self-questioning, and outlining are no more effective than simple reading and rereading (Anderson, 1980), more serious investigation of the relationship between these techniques and the rapid, seemingly automatic comprehension processes of skilled readers is needed. Obviously, the quality of what students are doing when they read and reread varies a great deal. Research should be done to determine whether overt study techniques can be used to improve the quality of covert processes in students' later reading to study.

Characterizing States of Knowledge. A current trend in research on human knowledge is detailed description and contrasting of the knowledge of experts and novices in a particular field of endeavor. The scope of investigation in this research is much greater than that concerned with the mastery of and memory for brief passages of text. It has been facilitated by systems of notation in which concepts and their relations are represented as complex networks in a computer memory. The hope is that such systems may help us analyze students' states of knowledge, diagnose problems, direct instruction, and evaluate the effect of instruction upon the state of knowledge. Perhaps such work will lead to sensitively adapting computer-tutors. Characteristic patterns of information—of relations among concepts—can also become learning tools for the student (see chapters by Dansereau, Rissland, Jones).

Nevertheless, the formulation of a theory concerning the way in which knowledge develops from the novice to the expert form remains an important challenge for the future. Norman (1978) has provided an evocative, intuitively appealing description of the changes in knowledge as learning occurs: accretion, restructuring, tuning. By analogy to comprehension, one might speculate that the restructuring of knowledge involves an attempt to achieve an organization that conforms to some as yet unarticulated ideal.

The first stage of systematic analysis—introspective analyses of the process of learning new subject matter—is just now beginning. At this time, research on the learning of realistically complex bodies of knowledge demonstrates the incredible detail and complexity of relationships in the specific subject matter knowledge that experts have (cf. Rissland's chapter) and the importance of previous knowledge to the acquisition of new knowledge. But there are also tantalizing hints of more general tactics and strategies in learning that more effective students may use. The image of the student as instructional designer may have some value for suggesting the nature of learning and study skills that facilitate mastery of entire domains of knowledge, entire college courses.

Problem Solving

A Characterization of Problem-Solving Processes.   The scientific study of problem-solving behavior began early in this century when Gestalt psychologists undertook systematic descriptive and experimental studies. They found that sometimes a problem solution appears to be a sudden event, which Kohler (1927) called insight. By studying people trying to solve very difficult problems, however, these researchers were able to see and describe steps in the problem-solving process: First, the problem is recognized and defined; then there is a phase of exploration in which the elements of the situation and their relationships are examined; next the problem is analyzed, the information gathered is organized and structured, and a plan is formulated; and finally, the problem is attacked and an overall solution occurs. Obviously, much is unexplained in this account. What is meant by analysis? How does solution occur? The Gestalt psychologists thought of the information gathered as making up a perceptual field with built-in structural stresses and strains. As relations are considered or interpretations are varied, the perceptual field will suddenly restructure, they concluded, leading to a solution.

This is a rather vague theory. Nevertheless, these researchers were able to demonstrate that there were internal mechanisms of thought—even when problem solvers could report only sudden insight—that could be affected by various factors that the experimenter manipulated. Maier (1931), for example, influenced the likelihood of insight by delivering various verbal or visual hints. Other research showed that people could become stuck on the idea that a particular object had only a certain function—"functional fixedness." Similarly, a history of success with one method of solution tends to blind the problem solver to simpler approaches that would work in a particular case and would be seen by someone without that history (Luchins, 1942).

Instructional Implications.   The research did make major advances in the understanding of problem solving. Many of the findings could be translated into advice for problem solvers: for example, telling them to attempt redescriptions of situations, to break down fixed ideas about the form that must accomplish a given function, or about the function of particular objects or materials. Indeed, this research is the basis of most current attempts to teach problem solving. Research did not advance beyond those rather general descriptions, however, and consequently there was a lengthy fallow period in problem-solving research.

A New Theoretical Approach.   Research on problem solving revived with the pioneering work of Newell, Shaw, and Simon (1957), who began to work with computer simulations of problem-solving processes. When you can write a computer program that explores a problem, analyzes the relation between the goal and the present state, evaluates means of solution, and forms a plan, then your theory is no longer vague. The problem-solving performance of such programs can be impressive, and they are being developed to model human performance in an increasing number of subject matter domains like geometry (Greeno, 1982). Models of expert and novice problem solvers have been used to gain insight into the underlying difference in their skill (Simon & Simon, 1978). One interesting suggestion of this line of study is that novices in a field may show more evidence of control and general problem-solving skill than experts, for whom solutions seem to come automatically. Perhaps general problem-solving knowledge is most important during the acquisition of new skills and knowledge.

Efforts to simulate the performance of problem solvers at differing stages of learning resulted in a class of computer models called production systems (Simon & Newell, 1971). Productions consist of conditions of application, and of operations that occur if the appropriate conditions are met. The conditions of application are altered as a result of experience. Productions can be combined as a result of successful experience to yield more complex productions, and thus the appearance of automatic solution. One can easily see how fixation on a particular method of solution, as well as other observed features of problem-solving behavior, would develop in such a system.

New Instructional Implications.   The influence of this theoretical approach to problem solving is now appearing in practical instructional efforts. In science and mathematics instruction, we are discovering that too little attention has been given to instruction in the conditions of application, to identifying when it is appropriate to apply a method of solution. Production system models tend to highlight the importance of specific knowledge and specific practice with particular kinds of problems, as opposed to general problem-solving skill. On the other hand, they also hint at the way experience might be designed to produce "general" problem-solving behavior, as a result of long experience. Research computer simulations have provided a set of concepts and a vocabulary that makes it possible to talk about problem solving in more concrete and better defined terms: control processes, memory capacity, conditions of application, etc. These concepts are beginning to influence the design and content of instruction.

Computer simulation studies of problem solving have concentrated on puzzle problems that can be described and worked out in symbols. Whereas, recent efforts to understand problem-solving in physics have begun to point out the importance of other representations of problems. Appropriate uses of schematic drawings or images—and skill in translating between verbal descriptions, drawings, and mathematical expressions—are critical to successful problem-solving performance. Perhaps this work is providing a more systematic version of the Gestalt theorists' exhortations to look at problems in new perspectives, a new explication of some instructional goals in problem solving.

Metacognition: Skills of Cognitive Control and Management

In both knowledge acquisition and problem solving, the vital importance of control of cognitive activities, of self-awareness, and self-management of cognitive activity is evident. The student must be alert to failure of comprehension in order to take corrective action. The problem solver must monitor progress toward a goal. Baron (1978) has suggested that there may be a number of very general "central" strategies that are desirable in the intellectual functioning of both children and adults. As possible examples of such strategies, he suggested: imposing limits, defining tasks into chunks that are appropriate to the person's capacity; subject organization, appropriate grouping, categorization, etc., of materials; checking, the use of multiple solution techniques to verify problem solutions. Although these strategies sound general, much specific knowledge may be required to display them. Considerable familiarity with a task may be required in order to judge its demands on capacity. Checking with multiple methods of solution requires knowing multiple methods of solution.

Indeed, Brown (1980) has suggested that metacognition—conscious awareness of and control of cognitive processes—emerges only as knowledge and skills in a particular domain become quite well developed. Perhaps it is not surprising, then, that developmental psychologists who study universal novices have given the most explicit research attention to people's awareness of thinking processes and to their knowledge about the workings of their own and others' minds. Some developmental theorists, working within the Piagetian tradition, postulate a fifth stage of intellectual development occurring in adulthood that would incorporate general, overarching comprehension of one's own intellectual functions (Arlin, 1975; Commons, Richards, & Kuhn, 1982; Fischer, 1980). Unfortunately, most research on metacognitive development is focused on rote-learning skills in quite young children (Brown, 1980; Flavell, 1977). It has not been common, for example, to query adults about their knowledge of problem-solving strategies in concert with investigations of their problem-solving performance. Gradually, the developmental research is broadening to examine the metacognitive aspects of a wider range of cognitive functions such as comprehension of instructions (Markman, 1979), selective attention (Miller & Weiss, 1982), or simple problem solving (Richards & Siegler, 1981).

Despite the limited scope of this research, it provides a number of observations that are important for cognitive skills training. Both children and adults may verbally display knowledge of effective learning techniques that they do not apply when confronted with a learning task (Brown & Barclay, 1976). It is equally true that they may not be able to articulate knowledge that they can readily put into action at appropriate times (Brainerd, 1973). Obviously, those who articulate insights about the way they go about solving problems or inventing mathematical proofs (Polya, 1945), or who describe the characteristic structure of literary genres, are exceptional individuals. This casts doubt on the prevalent approaches to cognitive skills instruction that rely heavily on verbal descriptions of strategies. Verbal instruction may be useful for older persons who already have the implicit knowledge to understand what is meant by the strategies, but not useful for those who need to learn them. On the other hand, children can learn to talk to themselves to pace their actions at critical points (Meichenbaum, 1978). Markman (1979) has found that first- to third-grade children's ability to evaluate inconsistencies in instructions was improved by asking them to demonstrate the instructions or by having them view others' partial demonstrations. This is another encouraging indication that it may be possible to teach these metacognitive skills.

OPEN ISSUES

The discussion of metacognition touched upon three unresolved issues that are of critical importance for anyone interested in education of the higher cognitive skills. These are the final 3 topics of Volume 2.

The Generality or Specificity of Cognitive Skills

The idea that there are very general learning or problem-solving skills is an attractive one. In essence, it is the idea that these volumes are meant to explore. It holds the promise of greater efficiency and longer lasting value for our educational efforts. It gives us an alternative view of what we might mean by general intelligence. But it is an unproven idea. General skills may not exist. That is, even though we might characterize an individual as using a particular strategy such as means–ends analysis in a variety of different problem domains, it might be that the individual must learn that strategy separately for each domain. There may be no deep psychological unity to the strategy across domains. A more likely hypothesis is that general skills must be built on the foundation of skills that have developed to an advanced state in at least one and probably more than one specific domain. The significance of this issue for the theory of human intellectual functions is obvious, but its practical importance is equally great. Some advocate teaching general cognitive skills and strategies as a separate school subject. Others believe that this is an emphasis that should be incorporated into the teaching of specific school subjects.

The Teachability of Cognitive Skills

Even if learning, thinking, and problem-solving strategies, whether general or specific, are shown to exist, it might not be possible to teach them directly. Perhaps they must spontaneously emerge as a consequence of substantial experience. At the very least, it should be possible to select and design experience to result in a more rapid and complete emergence of such skills. Probably more explicit instruction can be helpful as well. For example, we need to understand more about the value of verbal labels for cognitive activities and of conscious, deliberate control of cognitive activity. On the other hand, we need also to understand how verbal labels can be made meaningful to a wide range of students so that they evoke the desired cognitive activities. We need to understand how effortful, conscious, and deliberate patterns of cognitive activity can be taught in such a way that they will be transformed into efficient, automatic patterns. Volume 2 samples work that provides a promising beginning to the enterprise of teaching complex cognitive skills.

Developmental Differences

Whether young children and adults are fundamentally different learners remains an open theoretical question. Certainly, complex learning and problem-solving skills are found predominantly in older individuals. Some believe, however, that very sophisticated cognitive skills can be developed by quite young children in domains that they happen to know well or that are restricted in the content that must be mastered. Such domains might serve as a foundation for the development of widely applicable general cognitive skills.

It is more likely that older individuals will have developed the implicit concepts needed to understand abstract, verbal approaches to cognitive skills instruction. On the other hand, both older students most in need of help and younger children probably have similar needs for more concrete, intensive instruction. They may need training to develop the mental processes that make up strategies, not simply training to use processes that they have already mastered. They may need to learn to recognize and distinguish among their own mental processes as well as to learn the verbal descriptions that theorists and program developers use to talk about those processes. Cognitive skills training cannot be the same for all students and must adapt to the characteristics of the learner. Because of the practical importance of these issues for educators, a section of Volume 2 is devoted to them, and chapters on developmental studies appear in the major skill sections of Volume 2 as well.

A CLOSING AND OPENING WORD

These open questions beckon to researchers exploring the powers of the human mind. Theirs is an adventure we invite you to share in these volumes. It is an adventure shared and renewed in the life of each developing individual who experiences the unfolding of the intellect to encompass more and more of experience. The powers of the human mind are amplified, we hope, as the creative intellectual insights of one generation become the common self-knowledge of the next. Educators make that hope a reality by shaping the insights of exceptional thinkers or the hard won conclusions of analytic research into effective instructional experiences. In doing so, the teacher is privileged to share students' delight in their developing competence and to increase the number who experience it. Minds become capable of dealing with the future by mastering the insights and inventions of the past. The challenge to all who have contributed to these volumes, and to all who read them, is to bring about that translation from research into the thinking minds of our students.

ACKNOWLEDGMENTS

This introduction is partially based upon research area plans which were developed for the Basic Cognitive Skills program at the National Institute of Education, where Susan Chipman has been Assistant Director for Learning and Development and Judith Segal has been a senior staff member of that division. Just as it introduces this volume, a version of the research area plans was provided to the authors as an introduction to the purpose of the conference and of these volumes. Joseph Psotka and Rosalind Wu also contributed to versions of those plans and thus to this introduction. Although the National Institute of Education supported this work, the views expressed herein are the authors' own and do not necessarily reflect the official policy or position of the National Institute of Education. Chipman is now with the Office of Naval Research.

REFERENCES

Anderson, R. C. Schema-directed processes in language comprehension. In A. M. Lesgold, J. W. Pellegrino, S. D. Fokkema, R. Glaser (Eds.), *Cognitive psychology and instruction*. New York: Plenum, 1978.

Anderson, T. H. Study strategies and adjunct aids. In R. J. Spiro, B. C. Bruce, & W. F. Brewer (Eds.), *Theoretical issues in reading comprehension*. Hillsdale, N.J.: Lawrence Erlbaum, 1980.

Arlin, P. Cognitive development in adulthood: A fifth stage? *Developmental Psychology, 1975, 11,* 602–606.

Baron, J. Intelligence and general strategies. In G. Underwood (Ed.), *Strategies of information processing*. New York: Academic Press, 1978.

Bartlett, F. C. *Remembering*. Cambridge: Cambridge University Press, 1932.

Barton, W. A., Jr. *Outlining as a study procedure*. New York: Columbia University Bureau of Publications, 1930.

Beck, I. L. Developing comprehension: The impact of the directed reading lesson. In R. Anderson, J. Osborn, & R. Tierny (Eds.), *Learning to read in American schools: Basal readers and content texts*. Hillsdale, N.J.: Lawrence Erlbaum Associates, 1983.

Binet, A. *Les idees modernes sur les enfants*. Paris: Ernest Flammarion, 1909.

Brainerd, C. J. Order of acquisition of transitivity, conservation, and class inclusion of length and weight. *Developmental Psychology, 1973, 8,* 105–116.

Brown, A. L. Metacognitive development and reading. In R. J. Spiro, B. C. Bruce, W. F. Brewer (Eds.), *Theoretical issues in reading comprehension*. Hillsdale, N.J.: Lawrence Erlbaum Associates, 1980.

Brown, A. L., & Barclay, C. R. The effects of training specific mnemonics on the metamnemonic efficiency of retarded childen. *Child Development, 1976, 47,* 70–80.

Brown, A. L., & Day, J. D. Macrorules for summarizing texts: The development of expertise. *Journal of Verbal Learning and Verbal Behavior, 1983, 22,* 1–14.

Brown, A. L., & Smiley, S. S. Rating the importance of structural units of prose passages: A problem of metacognitive development. *Child Development, 1978, 48,* 1–8.

Brown, J. S., Collins, A., & Harris, G. Artificial intelligence and learning strategies. In H. F. O'Neil (Ed.), *Learning strategies*. New York: Academic Press, 1978.

Bruner, J. (Ed.). *Learning about learning: A conference report*. Washington: U.S. Government Printing Office, 1966.

Chall, J., & Snow, C. *Families and literacy: The contribution of out-of-school experiences to children's acquisition of literacy*. Final Report on NIE–G–80–0086. Harvard Graduate School of Education, December 22, 1982.

Chatham, K. M. Employment practices with entry-level workers. *Research Brief*. Far West Laboratory, San Francisco, CA, December 1982.

College Entrance Examination Board. *National college-bound seniors*. Produced by the Educational Testing Service, Princeton, New Jersey, 1981.

College Entrance Examination Board. *Preparation for college in the 1980s: The basic academic competencies and the basic academic curriculum*. (1982, undated).

Commons, M. L., Richards, F. A., & Kuhn, D. Systematic and metasystematic reasoning: A case for levels of reasoning beyond Piaget's Stage of Formal Operations. *Child Development, 1982, 53,* 1058–1069.

Dansereau, D. The development of a learning strategies curriculum. In H. F. O'Neil, Jr. (Ed.), *Learning strategies*. New York: Academic Press, 1978.

Dansereau, D. F., Long, G. L., McDonald, B., & Actkinson, T. R. Learning strategy inventory development and assessment (AFHRL–TR–FS–40, contract F41609–74–C–0013). Brooks Air Force Base, Texas, 1975.

Day, J. D. *Training summarization skills: A comparison of teaching methods.* Unpublished doctoral dissertation, University of Illinois, 1980.

Durkin, D. Do basal reader manuals provide for reading comprehension instruction? In R. Anderson, J. Osborn, & R. Tierney (Eds.), *Learning to read in American schools.* Hillsdale, N.J.: Lawrence Erlbaum Associates, 1984.

Fischer, K. W. A theory of cognitive development: The control and construction of hierarchies of skills. *Psychological Review,* 1980, *87,* 447–531.

Flavell, J. H. *Cognitive development.* Englewood Cliffs, N.J.: Prentice-Hall, 1977.

Glasman, L. D. *A social-class comparison of conceptual processes in children's free recall.* Unpublished doctoral dissertation, University of California, 1968.

Greeno, J. Forms of understanding in mathematical problem solving. In S. G. Paris, G. M. Olson, & H. W. Stevenson (Eds.), *Learning and motivation in the classroom.* Hillsdale, N.J.: Lawrence Erlbaum Associates, 1982.

Hunt, E. On the nature of intelligence. *Science,* 14 January 1983, *219,* 141–146.

Jencks, C. The *wrong* answer for schools is: (b) Back to basics. *Washington Post,* February 19, 1978.

Jensen, A. R. IQ and scholastic achievement. *Harvard Educational Review, 39,* Winter 1969.

Kohler, W. *The mentality of apes.* New York: Harcourt, Brace, 1927.

Luchins, A. S. Mechanization in problem solving. *Psychological Monographs.* 1942, *54*(6), Whole No. 248.

MacGinitie, W. H. Readability as a solution adds to the problem. In R. Anderson, J. Osborn, & R. Tierney (Eds.), *Learning to read in American schools.* Hillsdale, N.J.: Lawrence Erlbaum Associates, 1984.

Maeroff, G. I. Teaching to think: A new emphasis. *The New York Times,* January 9, 1983, Education Winter Survey (Sec. 12), p. 1.

Maier, N. R. F. Reasoning in humans II: The solution of a problem and its appearance in consciousness. *Journal of Comparative Psychology,* 1931, *12,* 181–194.

Mann, L. *On the trail of process: A historical perspective on cognitive processes and their training.* New York: Grune & Stratton, 1979.

Markman, E. Realizing that you don't understand. *Child Development,* 1979, *50,* 643–655.

Mayer, R. E. Can advance organizers influence meaningful learning? *Review of Educational Research,* 1979, *49,* 371–383.

Meichenbaum, D. Teaching children self-control. In B. Kahey & A. Kazdin (Eds.), *Advances in child clinical psychology* (Vol. 2). New York: Plenum Press, 1978.

Miller, P. H., & Weiss, M. G. Children's and adults' knowledge about what variables affect selective attention. *Child Development,* 1982, *53,* 543–549.

National Assessment of Educational Progress. *Reading, thinking and writing: Results from the 1979–80 National Assessment of Reading and Literature.* Report No. 11–L–01, October 1981.

National Assessment of Educational Progress. *The third national mathematics assessment: Results, trends and issues.* Report No. 13–MA–01, Education Commission of the States, Denver, Colo. April 1983.

National Commission on Excellence in Education. *A nation at risk.* Washington: U.S. Government Printing Office, 1983.

Newell, A., Shaw, J. C., & Simon, H. A. Empirical explorations of the logical theory machine: A case study in heuristics. *Proceedings of the Joint Computer Conference,* 1957, 218–230.

Norman, D. A. Notes toward a theory of complex learning. In A. M. Lesgold, J. W. Pellegrino, S. D. Fokkema, & R. Glaser (Eds.), *Cognitive psychology and instruction.* New York: Plenum, 1978.

Ogbu, J. *Minority education and caste: The American system in cross-cultural perspective.* New York: Academic Press, 1978.

Olson, G. M., Duffy, S. A., & Mack, R. L. Knowledge of writing conventions in prose comprehension. In W. J. McKeachie (Ed.), *Learning, cognition, and college teaching*. San Francisco: Jossey-Bass, 1980.

Pellegrino, J. W., & Glaser, R. Analyzing aptitudes for learning: Inductive reasoning. In R. Glaser (Ed.), *Advances in instructional psychology* (Vol. 2). Hillsdale, N.J. Lawrence Erlbaum Associates, 1982.

Polya, G. *How to solve it*. Princeton, N.J.: University Press, 1945.

Reder, L. The role of elaborations in the comprehension and retention of prose: A critical review. *Review of Educational Research*, 1980, *50*, 5–53.

Richards, D. D., & Siegler, R. S. Very young children's acquisition of systematic problem-solving strategies. *Child Development*, 1981, *52*, 1318–1321.

Schank, R., & Abelson, R. P. *Scripts, plans, goals and understanding*. Hillsdale: N.J.: Lawrence Erlbaum Associates, 1977.

Scribner, S., & Cole, M. Etudes des variations sub-culturelles de la memoire semantique: Les implications de la recherche inter-culturelle. *Bulletin de Psychologie*, 1976, 380–390.

Simon, H. A., & Newell, A. *Human problem solving*. Englewood Cliffs, N.J.: Prentice-Hall, 1971.

Simon, D. P., & Simon, H. A. Individual differences in solving physics problems. In R. Siegler (Ed.), *Children's thinking: What develops?* Hillsdale, N.J.: Lawrence Erlbaum Associates, 1978.

Smith, H. K. The responses of good and poor readers when asked to read for different purposes. *Reading Research Quarterly*, 1967, *3*, 53–84.

Sternberg, R. J. The nature of mental abilities. *American Psychologist*, 1979, *34*, 214–230.

Sternberg, R. J. (Ed.), *Handbook of human intelligence*. Cambridge: Cambridge University Press, 1982.

Tyler, L. E. *The psychology of human differences* (3rd ed.). New York: Appleton-Century-Crofts, 1965.

U.S. Department of Education, Division of Management Systems Development, Organizational Performance Service, Office of Management. *Study skills instruction: A service delivery assessment*. December 1982.

Varenne, H., Hamid-Buglione, V., McDermott, R. P., & Morison, A. *The acquisition of literacy for learning in working class families*. Final Report on NIE–G–400–79–0046. Teachers College, Columbia University, 1982.

Weinstein, C. Elaboration skills as a learning strategy. In H. F. O'Neil (Ed.), *Learning strategies*. New York: Academic Press, 1978.

Wertsch, J. W. Adult–child interaction and the roots of metacognition. *Quarterly Newsletter of the Institute for Comparative Human Development*, 1978, *1*, 15–18.

Winograd, T. *Understanding natural language*. New York: Academic Press, 1972.

Introduction to Volume 2: Research Trends and Their Implications

Susan F. Chipman
National Institute of Education[1]

This second volume samples the research insights that provide the foundation for new approaches to instruction in thinking and learning skills, and identifies directions for future research that will enhance that foundation. The last 20 years have seen a renaissance of serious scientific investigation of human intellectual capacities, research that is, as yet, reflected in only a few educational innovations. We hope that the new conceptualizations of human learning and thinking that appear in the chapters of this volume will capture educators' imagination and inspire instructional innovations to improve students' cognitive capacities. For we believe that instruction is a separate and distinct creative endeavor, by no means a straightforward application of the products of research. Research changes the nature of the conceptual framework within which that creativity is exercised, and the outlines of a new conceptual framework are emerging.

This set of chapters is also addressed to researchers and potential researchers so that the contrast between what has been learned and what we would like to know may inspire them to further explorations of human intellect. The rebirth of research into human cognition has produced rich resources from which we sample here; we anticipate still more from a mature science that is ready to address the complexity of realistic educational goals.

In this volume, research contributions that were often motivated by different or more limited questions are organized around the topics and issues germane

[1]Current affiliation: Office of Naval Research. The opinions expressed herein are the author's own and do not necessarily represent the official policy or position of the National Institute of Education or of the Office of Naval Research.

to the teaching of cognitive skills. By redefining the goals of inquiry in this way, we hope to raise new and different questions that will result in future research more thoroughly covering the issues that arise when one attempts to teach cognitive skills. To highlight the relationship between research and major educational goals, the research contributions in the first half of this volume have been grouped around three major aspects of human intellectual performance: knowledge acquisition, problem solving, intelligence and reasoning. In each of these topic areas, attention is given to developmental research and to research concerned with cultural influences upon cognition, because developmental and cultural variations in human learners and performers represent a challenge to be met by any truly general cognitive theory.

Cutting across these topical domains of inquiry are major issues for research that organize the second half of the volume into three sections: To what extent are cognitive skills general, to what extent specific? To what extent are younger and older learners and thinkers alike, to what extent different? To what extent, and by what means, can the skills of learning and thinking be taught?

Finally, the volume concludes with two contributions by authors who were asked to respond to the Conference on Thinking and Learning Skills as a whole. Robert Glaser was asked to respond from his perspective as a psychologist of learning and instruction. Jerome Bruner was asked to respond from the perspective of a developmental psychologist. Their responses differ in other respects also: Glaser emphasizes the promise of current research in leading the way to deliberate, designed instructional experiences that will create expertise, whereas Bruner discusses the possibility that spontaneous playfulness may be an essential root of flexible, thoughtful intellectual skill.

This introduction constitutes a third response, emphasizing the identification of questions that merit future research attention. Some of these questions were raised by the authors of the research chapters themselves; other questions were identified by the authors contributing discussion chapters. Still others reflect the personal opinions of this author. These volumes provided all of us the occasion to consider what research can now tell us about the teaching of cognitive skills and to reflect upon what more we would like to learn in the future.

THREE ASPECTS OF INTELLECTUAL PERFORMANCE

Knowledge Acquisition

The label given to this section presents a formidable challenge to researchers. How do people acquire the substantial bodies of knowledge represented by school subjects, college courses, professional expertise? This question unfolds into several related subquestions. How can we best characterize the knowledge that people have? Are there instructional techniques to facilitate its acquisition? Do individuals have strategic approaches to knowledge acquisition that facilitate their learning?

The opening chapter by Lynne Reder is representative of current research that is germane to school learning. Unlike earlier research on learning in highly simplified tasks, Reder's work investigates the mastery of the content of a section of a typical college text. Reder (1980) had reviewed similar research on learning from text and found inconsistent results, which seemed to stem from a disregard for the relationship between study aids and the structure of the text. Reder and Anderson's use of text summaries in a series of experiments is one way of attending to the structure of text because summaries, of course, contain the important points of the text. In contrast to the inconsistency of previous research, the results of these experiments have consistently favored summaries over elaborated texts, despite considerable variation in the experimental conditions of study and testing. Yet, the amounts of material being learned are relatively small and the acquired knowledge is tested in restricted ways—just as it often is in school.

In the chapter by Carl Bereiter and Marlene Scardamalia, strategies used by students to cope with school tests are discussed and contrasted with more challenging uses of previously acquired knowledge such as writing school compositions. Their work raises questions about which form of instruction might make knowledge truly useful in a wide range of situations. Perhaps elaborated presentations of information, richly interconnecting concepts, would fare better when measured against the criteria of usefulness in complex tasks than they do in simple tests of recall such as those Reder used. It would be premature to conclude that summaries should replace our textbooks!

In another contribution to this section, Anderson Franklin suggests that the utility of categories as a device for remembering information may depend on a high degree of familiarity with the categories. Extensive research demonstrates that categorizing lists of words is an effective strategy for increasing the amount of information that can be remembered. However, cultural and developmental differences in the use of categorization are often reported. The degree of match or mismatch between the categories in a memory test and the salient categories that organize the knowledge possessed by members of a particular cultural group may explain the observed cultural differences. (In a later chapter, Michelene Chi gives a similar account for developmental differences in the use of categories.)

These three chapters underscore the need to learn more about the way that knowledge is organized in memory. We need that understanding to guide our investigations of how knowledge is most effectively acquired and used. The chapter by Edwina Rissland exemplifies work that is addressing that aspect of the study of knowledge aquisition. She analyzes the overall structure of knowledge in a particular field, mathematics, and thus begins to meet the challenge of dealing with the full complexity of human learning. As an expert in mathematics, Rissland presents hypotheses concerning the fundamental organization of mathematical knowledge. The psychological validity of those hypotheses has not yet been tested. Has she correctly characterized the knowledge that an expert mathematician has? Other recent work by Chi, Feltovich, and Glaser (1981) on knowledge of mechanics illustrates the methods that can be used to provide an empirical foundation for such characterizations of expert knowledge. In future research, the combination of expert analysis with empirical confirmation will provide us with a firmer understanding of the organization of expert knowledge.

Questions that Merit Future Research.   Given a characterization of a mature knowledge structure—something that we are nearly ready to achieve in at least some areas of physics and mathematics—it is natural to ask, "What is the most efficient way to acquire that knowledge, or to teach it?" Anecdotal evidence such as that provided by Rissland and by Dansereau (Volume 1) indicates that students find it useful to be told about the structure of knowledge.

Information about the organization of knowledge in a field may provide a clearer definition of the student's task, a set of blanks that must be filled in. It remains to be demonstrated, however, that such information truly is helpful, and to discover what circumstances are necessary in order to make it helpful.

Questions about the utility of structural information are special cases of a more general instructional question: Given that we have a defined structure, how do we present the information most effectively? In particular, we need to understand how individuals acquire higher levels of conceptual organization such as those that have been demonstrated in experts' knowledge of physics. Can they be directly taught or must they emerge from extensive experience with lower level concepts? Or is there some way to facilitate their emergence by structuring the student's experience?

All these questions are intertwined with another that has become salient in recent research: What is the relation between knowledge about one's knowledge and the knowledge itself? One may alter that relationship by providing students with a high-level characterization of the knowledge structure; that is, some proposed instructional innovations would provide students with information about the characteristics of knowledge in a field that is ordinarily possessed by only a few insightful experts.

The foregoing questions presume situations of instructional design, where the structure of knowledge that is desired as a goal of instruction may be known. Equal attention should be given to situations of individual acquisition, where the structure of knowledge is likely to be unknown, at least to the student. The latter is more common because the complete analysis of any subject matter would represent a very large investment. Can we characterize effective learning strategies for learning tasks on this scale? Are there ways to recognize key generalizations and important points when they are presented? Are there clues to their interrelationships? Are there effective ways for students to track and organize such information as they identify it? Perhaps effective students are importing a general framework for knowledge from some other area that they have previously mastered, which provides the equivalent of the structural information that Rissland or Dansereau would provide. Researchers may well need an analysis of the structure of knowledge in a particular domain in order to study these questions, but it is probably most important to understand how students can proceed effectively when the structure of knowledge is unknown to them.

Whether knowledge is the result of careful instructional design or of an individual effort to acquire it, there are important questions about the later accessibility of that knowledge, about the flexibility of access to that knowledge, and about its usability in a context other than the one in which it was acquired. What characteristics of the final state of knowledge or of the process of acquistion predict the flexible utility of knowledge? Answering these questions will require a more imaginative and multidimensional approach to the assessment of knowledge than has been typical in the past. However, analyses of knowledge structure should provide a stronger foundation for assessments than has been available in the past.

Problem Solving

The second section of this volume is concerned with problem solving, the use of previously acquired knowledge and skill to deal with new situations. Research exploring human problem-solving performance contributes to a richer understanding of the diverse kinds of knowledge that learners must acquire. It is common to think of knowledge as a static collection of concepts and their relationships. However, the study of problem solving points up the importance of procedural knowledge, "how-to" knowledge about the actions or operations that are possible in order to transform the problem situation. Until recently, problem-solving research was primarily concerned with procedural knowledge, with understanding how people operate within a formal characterization of a problem once it has been achieved (cf. Polson & Jeffries, Volume 1). As was true for research on knowledge acquisition, the chapters in this section reflect the movement of researchers to more realistic and complex tasks. Currently, the emphasis is upon understanding how a problem is characterized and framed, upon how the problem situation does or does not make contact with potentially relevant formal knowledge that the person has acquired. These research questions are not new; they were the primary concerns of the Gestalt psychologists who investigated problem solving in the 1930s and 1940s. But the questions are being revisited with greater precision and more powerful theoretical tools.

The chapter by Bert Green, Michael McCloskey, and Alfonso Caramazza describes what happens when students are presented with very simple qualitative physics problems in which the primary challenge is to recognize the applicability of major physics principles. The results demonstrate that a major part of the students' task is to learn how to translate problem situations into the terms of the physical theory they have been taught, to learn how to recognize instances of the theoretical concepts. Such critical recognition and translation skills usually are not taught explicitly. Jill Larkin's research provides further insight into the process of translating a problem statement into the terms of a physical theory. Experts do not simply translate physical problem situations into the mathematical equations of the theory; instead, she contends, much of the problem-solving work goes on within what she calls the "scientific representation" of the problem. Today, it is already clear that a major part of the task of the science student is to master these scientific representations, scientific ways of thinking about problem situations. It is equally clear that a major part of the task of the researchers of science learning is to uncover and characterize these scientific representations, for most of them have never been made explicit and codified.

The processes of problem analysis and characterization, of encoding, become even more salient when one studies the problem solving of children. Real physical problem situations provide a rich diversity of information that the problem solver might work with. We select some of that information as the basis for our problem-solving efforts and neglect other aspects of it. For reasons that are still a matter of theoretical debate, children have a more limited capacity to encode information about a problem situation than do adults, and their selection of information may differ as well. The research reported in the chapter by Robert Siegler shows that the aspects of the problem situation that are encoded by the learner limit the possibility that the learner has of learning from particular experiences. Again, the process of selecting or neglecting information about a problem situation is something that we tend to be unaware of. Therefore, we tend to omit teaching this aspect of problem-solving skill.

One possible explanation for adults' ability to encode more information is that extensive experience has provided adults with well-learned patterns that effectively reduce the amount of information to be held in mind. In his chapter, Richard Duran discusses another, perhaps closely related, source of limitations in the processing of problem information—limited English proficiency. He suggests that the processing demands of an unfamiliar language may interfere with gathering all the information in a problem statement and detecting all the important relationships among problem statements. In some cases also, successful problem solution may depend on a felicitous verbal restatement of the problem that will be less accessible to a person of low linguistic proficiency. Duran's chapter is more a statement of research questions than of answers because the exploration of cognitive processes in bilingual persons is only beginning. Because these populations permit the separation of cognitive characteristics that are normally yoked together—general intelligence, developmental maturity, linguistic proficiency—the future pursuit of such research promises valuable insights for general cognitive theory as well as practical applications in bilingual education.

In the final contribution to this section, James Greeno provides a discussion of the relationships that exist between practical efforts to train problem-solving skill and both past and present research. Based upon this discussion, he makes several suggestions for new directions for both research and educational practice. His emphasis is upon research that might provide a reconciliation of the view and evidence that problem-solving skill can be very general, with the view and evidence that problem-solving skill is often very specific. He also suggests the expansion of problem-solving research to the analysis of real-life decision-making processes.

Questions that Merit Future Research.   Attempts to address the complexity of real life in problem-solving research are certain to lead to continued emphasis upon the processes of information seeking and selection that are already so prominent in these chapters. The development of effective methods for exploring these processes is a high priority for future research. Yet, the link with past research on well-structured problem domains like mathematics or puzzle problems will be maintained. The function of encoding processes and of scientific representations is to transform amorphous problem situations into well-structured problems that can be solved by processes like those psychologists have studied in mathematical and puzzle problem solving. This observation points to one way in which the debate concerning specificity and generality might be reconciled by the outcome of future research. As has been found for the solvers of puzzle problems (cf. Polson & Jeffries, Volume 1), beginning physics students work with the superficial features of problems. The scientific representations that Larkin describes can be seen as bringing superficially diverse problems within the scope of the relatively general problem-solving methods provided by physical theory. The physical theory, in turn, links problems to the very general methods provided by mathematics.

On the other hand, experienced problem solvers often do not employ general methods. The same research by Larkin is one of many indications that the investigation of thinking processes within representations other than the logical/mathematical—such as visual or kinesthetic imagery—will be an important direction for future research in human problem solving. For example, Larkin has shown that the successful solution of some physics problems requires the ability to draw or image diagrams of the physical situation, making inferences about relationships in the drawing or mental image.

Intelligence and Reasoning

Success in acquiring new knowledge or in using knowledge to solve problems must depend on the appropriate use of very fundamental mental abilities or processes. In the first of the five chapters of this section, Robert Sternberg sketches the framework of a complete theory of intelligence. He describes major categories of fundamental mental processes that require investigation and specification. Like the parts of a hi-fi system processing sound, the fundamental mental processes of Sternberg's theory are called components. Extensive experimental studies of performance in a wide variety of tasks will be required to give substance to this skeletal theory. For example, Sternberg and his associates have done the experimental work to show that highly overlapping sets of processes are used in analogical, serial, and classification reasoning tasks. Sternberg suggests that executive control processes—which he calls metacomponents—are most critical in intellectual performance and in intellectual development.

Throughout Sternberg's chapter, he interestingly compares his theory with the views that Feuerstein (see Volume 1) developed from extensive experience working to correct deficits in intellectual performance. Feuerstein's account also gives prominence to executive control processes. It appears that these processes are the modern theorists' counterpart to the notion of general intelligence that emerged from earlier psychometric theories, but the validity of that comparison has not yet been explored. Reconciliation of new information-processing models of cognitive performance with earlier psychometric accounts is a continuing challenge for researchers.

The chapter by Edward De Avila and Sharon Duncan considers one of the exceptional cases—bilingual children—that challenges well-entrenched psychometric habits like measuring "verbal ability" to indicate intellectual capacity. Such cases point out the need for a more fundamental theory of intellectual capacity than we now possess. The study reported in this chapter was primarily concerned with measures of cognitive style, which have been advanced as explanations of cultural differences in school performance and as candidates for the general aspect of cognitive performance (cf. Baron, this volume).

The next two chapters in this section exemplify investigations of more specific aspects of intellectual capacities—one logic and the other metacognition in reading. Ellen Markman investigated the ability to judge the quality of one's own comprehension and/or the comprehensibility of the message. Such capacities seem absolutely central to competent intellectual performance, essential to the control of intellectual efforts to achieve the desired results. Many have attempted to teach a direct self-questioning strategy—"Do I understand this?"—to enhance such metacognitive capacities. However, Markman challenges the assumptions of such instruction, suggesting that judgments of comprehension and comprehensibility might be nearly automatic by-products of other cognitive activities. For example, if a reader is engaged in constructive comprehension processes that generate predictions about what the text will say next, the failure of those predictions may indicate comprehension problems; that is, metacognition might be a phenomenon that emerges as processing becomes more complex, not something that can properly be viewed as a separate "metacognitive component" or function. The distinction has important instructional implications: Markman's view would suggest teaching students to be active in making predictions about the material they are reading rather than teaching a strategy of self-questioning about the adequacy of comprehension.

Logic is the most venerable candidate for the status of a fundamental component in human thinking, and the teaching of logic is the longest standing example of efforts to improve the quality of human thinking. In his chapter, Philip Johnson-Laird reports research investigating the mental processes that people actually use to deal with logical tasks. Reminiscent of the work on physics problem solving discussed earlier, Johnson–Laird's research has uncovered the mental models that people employ in thinking about logical problems. He suggests that teaching strategies for working effectively with these models—such as trying to construct models for counterexamples to the asserted conclusion— may be more helpful than instruction in formal logic.

In her response to the chapters of this section, Ann Brown ranges widely over issues raised in this entire volume, giving particular emphasis to the issue of generality versus specificity in cognitive skills and to the issue of the teachability of cognitive skills. Like many of her fellow authors, she emphasizes the importance of self-management. She reminds us of Binet's original conception of intelligence as something that can be taught, and she makes a specific proposal about the effective design of instruction in cognitive skills. It should, she believes, combine instruction in task-specific strategies with a metacognitive level of instruction dealing with such issues as recognizing when specific strategies are appropriate.

Questions that Merit Future Research.   The specific mental processes that contribute to intellectual performance are many and diverse, and all are worthy of study. But the investigation of "metacomponents"—the management of one's processing resources—now should be a major focus of research. Although the consensus is that these processes are key elements in performance, it is still a major issue whether they can be viewed meaningfully as separate functions or whether they are just a manifestation of extensive knowledge. Deciding when to use a particular strategy or problem-solving technique typifies a self-management function that we might attempt to teach, but it may be that this apparent "skill" represents the accumulated learning of many very specific conditions over a long period of time. Do many individuals exist who have mastered all the components of intellectual tasks but fail to combine them effectively into overall performance? Finding such individuals would be one form of evidence for separate metacognitive skills.

The relation of metacognitive capacities to traditional conceptions of general intelligence calls for further investigation, as do the mutual relations to other information-processing concepts like memory capacity. Investigating the intellectual development of children may be helpful in this endeavor because metacognitive capacities appear to emerge with development; indeed, developmental psychologists have been giving more attention to metacognition than have other investigators of cognition.

Characterizing metacognition as the management of one's cognitive resources suggests that it might be helpful to teach about cognitive capacities and limitations. Is there a way to teach useful knowledge about mental capacities? Is this a way to develop "metacomponents," to make students more effective managers of their cognitive resources? These are matters for future exploration.

MAJOR RESEARCH ISSUES IN COGNITIVE SKILL

The next three sections of this volume are devoted to major issues that arise in the discussions of each major aspect of intellectual performance: the relative generality or specificity of cognitive skills; the possibility of fundamental change in the nature of cognitive skill in the course of individual cognitive development; the possibility of teaching general intellectual skills.

Generality or Specificity of Cognitive Skill

The idea that general problem solving or learning skills can be developed is extremely attractive. The robustness of the concept of general intelligence as a predictor of a wide range of intellectual performances implies that there is some generality in cognitive capacities, whether or not those capacities are subject to instructional improvement. On the other hand, recent research has frequently indicated that cognitive skills are extremely specific. Studies of expert performance have shown the vital importance of large amounts of specific knowledge, rather than of general ability or general problem-solving strategies. Problem solvers have been shown to fail to transfer acquired skills to formally identical problems (cf. Polson & Jeffries, Volume 1). Usually, students apply learning strategies only to the particular situation in which they were trained. This has cast doubt upon the wisdom of trying to teach general cognitive skills, as opposed to teaching skills embedded in the specific subject-matter domains in which they are to be used.

The first two chapters of the four in this section are efforts to characterize what might be general in cognitive skill. David Perkins provides an explicit statement of the assumptions that he believes underlie the various approaches to training cognitive skills. Intellectual competence, he says, is viewed as consisting of a few general cognitive control strategies plus specific knowledge of particular domains. Perkins discusses some of the difficulties with this point of view, notably the difficulty people have in learning the strategies and in knowing how and when to apply them. Often, that seems to require specific knowledge. As a means of resolution to the tension between the general and the specific, Perkins suggests that we attempt to define very general classes of tasks with fundamental similarities that permit the use of common strategies. He suggests "inductive arguments" or "designs" as examples of such broad categories.

In the next chapter, Jonathan Baron attempts to characterize the components of intelligence that might be considered fundamental and general, as well as potentially modifiable. He reviews the evidence that many of the fundamental elements of intellectual performance—speed of processing, memory capacity, etc.—cannot be modified by practice. In an earlier paper on the same subject, Baron (1978) had identified several general strategies—such as search for related cases or checking one's work—as possible fundamental components of intelligence. In this chapter, he discusses the difficulty of defining such strategies or measuring their presence and questions whether the different instances of such strategies are really the same. He concludes by considering the possibility that a cognitive style of reflectivity might be an example of a fundamental component of intelligence. Baron thinks of cognitive styles as being akin to motives or habits that affect the likelihood of acquiring and using more specific strategies. But the reader finds that De Avila and Duncan's results (this volume) are not encouraging about the explanatory value of cognitive style: Defining general cognitive skills remains a major challenge.

Some of the doubts that Perkins and Baron express about the existence of general cognitive strategies are brought into focus in the chapter by John Hayes. Even in those areas of human achievement that are most commonly attributed to ability, inspiration, and genius—music and painting—Hayes has shown that years of intensive study and practice precede the production of outstanding work. Specific knowledge is very important indeed. He points out that large numbers of specific strategies appear in courses that attempt cognitive skill training, such as his own book, *The Complete Problem Solver* (1981). He discusses failures to generalize problem solving but also formulates the hypothesis that people generalize according to the major categories of experience: objects, events, actions, etc. He suggests that generalization will not occur across these major category boundaries. This hypothesis suggests some guidelines that might be used in pursuing Perkins' agenda of mapping out the domains within which "general" strategies might be taught.

The final chapter in this section, by Donald Meichenbaum, draws upon a rich empirical and clinical background in its discussions. Meichenbaum supports the view that metacognitive or executive control skills are key goals for cognitive training, citing the fact that many different populations of children in difficulty have been characterized as lacking in such skills. Furthermore, he argues that the teaching of such executive strategies has been critical in successful efforts to obtain transfer of more specific skill training. Meichenbaum asserts that a number of general problem-solving strategies—self-interrogation, self-checking, analyzing tasks and proceeding sequentially, matching strategies to task demands—

have been successfully taught, but he also emphasizes the care that must be taken to ensure the acquisition of a truly general skill rather than a rigid, rote habit tied to specific training materials.

Questions that Merit Future Research.   The conclusion to be drawn from this section is not that cognitive skills are either general or specific. Instead, the consensus seems to be that one must deliberately train and develop the generality of cognitive skills. Without that effort, even skills that were intended to be relatively specific are likely to prove excessively, disappointingly specific. Characterization of the major domains of human cognitive tasks is emerging as an important step in understanding how generalization of skill might occur and how it might be fostered. These hypotheses should be pursued and tested.

There is some promise that quite general skills in the self-management of cognitive function can be taught. Future work should aim at specifying what those skills are, and identifying the conditions that maximize their generality. For it is evident that instructional efforts can easily go astray and end up teaching empty limited rituals of a new kind. As such general skills are specified, it will be important to explore their relationship to earlier conceptions of intelligence. In particular, the suggestion that individuals differ in the ease with which wide-ranging generality of cognitive skills is achieved should be explored.

Developmental Differences in Cognitive Skill

Developmental differences in cognitive skill are among the most obvious individual differences that can be explored. For example, there appear to be important developmental differences both in the generality of cognitive skills and in metacognition—awareness of and deliberate control of cognitive processes. Research suggests that talking to young children about learning, thinking, or problem-solving processes may not be very fruitful. Yet, such talk is the predominant method of cognitive-skills training today. It is likely that programs for younger children must be designed differently from programs for adolescents and adults. Special attention to the question of cognitive development is needed also because this is a time of crisis in developmental theory. There has been a loss of faith in the once dominant view that younger and older children, or adults, display fundamentally different kinds of thinking. Today, many believe that developmental change could be explained by the same processes of knowledge acquisition that we observe in adults, that apparently fundamental changes in cognitive function emerge from accumulated knowledge. On the other hand, the presumption that a theory of cognitive skill can be formulated without special attention to developmental differences should not go unchallenged.

The opening chapter of this section by Michael Krupa, Robert Selman, and Daniel Jaquette is very strongly influenced by the Piagetian view of human development. The authors describe "stages" in the types of scientific explanation that children use to account for phenomena. They found considerable commonality in the progression of explanations across different domains of science, but the stage of explanation offered depended on the particular domain. The classic Piagetian logical reasoning tasks evoked more advanced performance than some of these science tasks and less advanced performance than others. Thus, this research joins the growing body of evidence that places the classic Piagetian tasks as simply some of many possible tasks, not critical indices of a wide-ranging, uniform style or level of thinking. Yet, the similarity of intellectual progressions within different domains remains compelling. The issue is whether it is truly "developmental" in nature or whether one would observe the same progression when an adult is learning about an unfamiliar domain.

Michelene Chi, the author of the next chapter in this section, has set out to challenge some of the most thoroughly supported generalizations about young children's cognitive functioning, especially in the area of memory. She has examined situations in which a young child happens to know a great deal about a particular subject, and she has been able to demonstrate children performing in unexpectedly "advanced" ways. One example is the use of taxonomic categories in memory. Generally, young children do not use taxonomic categories to organize information that they remember, but Chi has found some instances in which individual children do use taxonomic categories. Chi suggests that taxonomic categories are what emerge as salient after one knows a great many facts and interrelationships within a domain. In summary, Chi's research provides considerable evidence that sheer amount of knowledge may be the key factor differentiating younger and older learners.

Susan Carey's chapter is a penetrating theoretical discussion of the possible interpretations that can be given to the notion that children think in ways fundamentally different from the ways that adults think. She considers a wide range of experimental evidence bearing upon these notions, as well as purely theoretical arguments. Carey concludes that the acquisition and reorganization of domain-specific knowledge probably accounts for most of the cognitive differences between 3-year-olds and adults. Characterizing how that knowledge is acquired and how it comes to be reorganized is an amply challenging problem for developmental researchers. However, she also acknowledges that there are some kinds of knowledge that cut across many domains and therefore could have widespread effects on cognitive functioning. Mathematical knowledge is one example. Metacognitive knowledge of concepts like hypothesis, experiment, and confirmation, which can be used to systematize the exploration of phenomena, is another example, although we have little evidence that it actually does make a great difference. This, too, is an important issue for future research.

Warren Simmons takes a similar position toward the understanding of cultural, subcultural, and ethnic differences in cognitive performances. Like Chi, he has shown that commonly observed comparative patterns of categorization performance can be reversed by working with domains that are more or less well known to the groups being studied. He argues that one must understand the task demands that a culture makes upon the individual in order to understand the patterns of cognitive performance that emerge. He finds that most present attempts to characterize the aspects of the environment that influence cognitive functioning— income level, years of parental education—are extremely inadequate. Theories of development that are in fact conditioned upon the particular circumstances of the researcher's cultural environment do not have the generality that they claim. More seriously, the resulting misinterpretations of observed differences in performance, as indicating fundamental differences in intellectual potential, can have real and damaging consequences for peoples' lives.

In her response to the chapters of this section, Rochel Gelman provides a partial correction to the revolution in thinking about cognitive development that she herself has helped to create. Gelman is well known for demonstrating unexpected cognitive capacities in young children. Yet, here she characterizes some of the ways young children differ from mature learners. Although researchers have demonstrated that children have many fundamental cognitive capacities they were once thought to lack, Gelman points out the importance of the fact that special, simplified tasks were necessary to reveal that competence. Older children demonstrate such competencies with ease, across a wide variety of situations. Gelman further points out that the phenomena of cognitive development are success stories in accomplishing what many practitioners of cognitive-skills training would like to do—producing generalization of trained skills and developing metacognitive control strategies. She suggests that studying how these successes come about may help educators to emulate them. On the other hand, these natural and nearly universal forms of learning may be intrinsically different from school learning. That possible difference, of course, is one of the traditional arguments for pursuing developmental psychology as distinct from learning psychology.

Questions that Merit Future Research.   There are distinct parallels between commonly observed developmental differences in cognitive function and the individual differences that are of concern to educators. In older individuals, more sophisticated functions are commonplace, though not universal. Studying how that developmental change comes about and what environmental circumstances seem to favor it may yield useful insights for educators. In particular, a focus on the way in which the "fundamental" capacities become more generally applicable is likely to be helpful. Similarly, the idea that skills that are initially bound to a particular context and sequence of activity later become available for flexible use should be explored. How does that come about, if it does?

Feuerstein's notion of *mediated learning experiences* provides an important hypothesis concerning the nature of critical environmental differences that should be sought. One may find that cultural or individual differences in the development of cognitive capacities are accompanied by differences in the characteristic patterns of communication between children and the adults surrounding them. For example, one can easily imagine that metacognitive capacities would be enhanced by parents who characteristically discuss the reasoning processes that they are using to cope with the problems they confront.

Carey's speculative conclusions about the nature of the intellectual differences between young children and adults suggest an entire research agenda that might confirm or disconfirm them. In pursuing that agenda, we would learn much more about the nature of cognitive growth and about the likely limits of our ability to enhance that growth. For example, it would be interesting to compare children and adults learning subjects that are new to them. Does an adult go through the stages that Selman et al. describe when learning about a new scientific domain? Or can we describe ways that adults use their prior knowledge to form analogies and learn more efficiently? Can we identify kinds of knowledge that do have very widespread effects on thinking? How rapidly do such general effects occur and how extensive are they?

Teaching Cognitive Skills

The last section of this volume presents three rather diverse approaches to the teaching of cognitive skills. The earlier chapters by Meichenbaum and Brown also devote considerable attention to the teaching of cognitive skills, as does the chapter by Bransford, Arbitman-Smith, Stein, and Vye in Volume 1.

Robbie Case presents a methodology for teaching particular, quite specific cognitive skills to advance performance considerably beyond the level one ordinarily finds in a child of a given age. Essentially, tasks are redesigned to fit the memory constraints that seem to limit younger performers. Case also acknowledges the importance of automatizing subskills used in the task so that memory demands are minimized. Indeed, many would attribute the apparent changes in memory capacity with age to increasing automaticity of important skills. According to Case, it can often be shown that later, more sophisticated strategies for dealing with tasks require keeping track of more information in memory. Thus, although the skills that Case teaches are quite specific, in contrast to the aspirations expressed in these volumes, his analytic perspective may be helpful in understanding why developmental differences in metacognitive strategies are observed. Children may not have sufficient processing capacity to both do the task and think about the way they are doing it.

In contrast, Marlene Scardamalia and Carl Bereiter have been trying to teach skills that are necessarily quite general because the tasks where they are employed—like writing a school composition—are themselves quite general and ambiguously specified. They attempt to train "self-regulatory mechanisms," information-processing skills, or executive functions such as checking, planning, and evaluating. Two techniques are used. One is to provide particular procedural routines, supported by external aids that reduce the processing burden on the student. The other is to make the goal of the task more concrete and definite than it ordinarily is. There is preliminary evidence that these aids do improve the level of performance. In addition to improving performance with the use of aids, the hope is that students will, with practice, internalize the procedures that the aids foster and become independent of those aids.

Whether or not that occurs, the procedures are still relatively specific. To illustrate this point, it may be helpful to mention what might be considered general skills to deal with the same problems. A student might be taught, for example, that memory capacity is a problem in many tasks, and that it is a good idea to develop one's own procedures or aids to get around the problems that limited memory creates. Thinking creatively about the meaning of the goal for a task is a general skill that many cognitive-skill programs have attempted to foster. It is quite different from providing a helpful redefinition of the goal for the student.

In his chapter, Allan Collins argues that Socratic tutors are attempting to teach such very general skills. They do so by systematic questioning that guides the desired patterns of thought, and by modeling thinking skills such as the forming of hypotheses, their testing, and the generation of counterexamples. Again, the central premise of the method is that students will come to internalize the procedures that are at first externally aided and/or modeled by the teacher. The teaching methods Collins describes seem to be very similar to the teaching approaches recommended in the most significant programs attempting to teach thinking and problem-solving skills. The nature of these methods and the validity of the premises upon which they are built need much more serious research attention.

In her response to the chapters of this section, Mary Carol Day suggests that the teaching of cognitive skills is itself one of the compositional tasks that Scardamalia and Bereiter describe; that is, as we gain experience in the effort to teach cognitive skills, our conceptions of what we are attempting to teach will change. She suggests also that all the skills discussed in these chapters are somewhat specific, that more general skills are required in order to decide when to invoke these more specific skills. Despite the very great differences in these three approaches, she finds that they have a major common feature: the provision of external support for what is eventually to become an internal cognitive ability. Clearly, this process of internalization of cognitive processes is something that requires serious research investigation in the future.

Questions that Merit Future Research.   There is a need to examine what teachers in apparently successful programs of cognitive-skills training are doing, with the same degree of care that Collins gave to the analysis of Socratic tutoring. There seems to be a common thread of providing an external control structure, later to be internalized. Does this approach really work? Are there conditions that favor the successful internalization of such processes? Might there be a better way to create an internal control structure? Recognizing that this is the goal of one's instructional efforts may suggest new approaches to achieve that end. In particular, the relative specificity of what is now being taught suggests that one might attempt to teach students to design their own control structures, to think about how a task might be effectively done. In general, there seems to be a need to take the process of instruction in cognitive skills seriously as a subject of research, to bring it out of the realm of unexamined practice.

CONCLUDING PERSPECTIVES

Several clear themes emerge from these discussions as the major new challenges to researchers. In Robert Glaser's interpretation, the importance of rich, domain-specific knowledge to thinking is one of the most salient lessons: Views of learning and problem solving that ignore specific content must be superseded by theories that incorporate the role of complex knowledge. By analyzing the structure of knowledge in particular domains and studying the most effective means of instructing, learning, and using knowledge in relation to that structure, researchers can arrive at such new theories.

Today, the metacognitive skills displayed in the management of one's cognitive resources seem to be the major candidates for truly general intellectual skills. Testing the psychological reality of those putative skills must be a high priority for research. Jerome Bruner agrees, and he makes the provocative suggestion that spontaneous intellectual play is what fosters the acquisition of metacognitive insight. In play, he argues, one learns about the possible results that can be obtained, freed from obsessive concern to reach a particular goal.

Future research must maintain a balance between instruction and learning. The activities of effective teachers need closer examination, and principles of more effective instructional design may be discovered. Effectively sharing the achievements of our human cultures is the essence of education. Ultimately, however, the activities of learners determine the outcome of education. Discovering the circumstances that foster effective learners—whether that means carefully designed instruction or the encouragement of intellectual play—is the goal of this research. We want students to share what is known. But we also want them to challenge the unknown and bring it into the realm of the known, learning what no one else has ever known.

REFERENCES

Baron, J. (1978). Intelligence and general strategies. In G. Underwood (Ed.), *Strategies in information processing*. London: Academic Press.

Chi, M. T. H., Feltovich, P. J., & Glaser, R. (1981). Categorization and representation of physics problems by experts and novices. *Cognitive Science, 5*, 121–152.

Hayes, J. R. (1981). *The complete problem solver*. Philadelphia: The Franklin Institute Press.

Reder, L. (1980). The role of elaboration in the comprehension and retention of prose: A critical review. *Review of Educational Research, 50*, 5–53.

Knowledge Acquisition

1 Techniques Available to Author, Teacher, and Reader to Improve Retention of Main Ideas of a Chapter

Lynne M. Reder
Carnegie-Mellon University

PREFACE

It is difficult to imagine how one could avoid feeling self-conscious when writing a chapter about techniques to improve the writing of chapters. Indeed, without discipline and willpower, one could easily become so inhibited that the chapter would never be written. An easy escape from such an embarrassment would be an early disclaimer stating that all ideas on the improvement of chapter writing are tentative; that because the ideas are in the formative stage no attempt will be made to practice what is preached. In that way, immediate evaluation of the effectiveness of the suggestions is precluded.

I will not take the coward's way out. This chapter is an experiment in the usefulness of some of the notions presented, viz., the instructions to authors on how to make main points more memorable. For this reason, the structure of this chapter seems unusual, e.g., the same headings are repeated throughout the chapter, as ideas are restated with more elaboration. However, even if this endeavor fails, it is possible that there is some worth in the ideas; I simply may not be very good at executing my own suggestions. At the end of the chapter, a summary version of the chapter is included like those used in experiments described in this chapter. The summary and text forms of this material allow for experimental comparison of which form produces better learning and retention.

ABSTRACT

This chapter is concerned with possible devices to improve the communication of ideas of the author to the prospective reader. Most of the proposed ideas are intended for the author to incorporate into plans for writing a chapter; however, some points suggest techniques the reader could employ when reading a text, and there are also suggestions that a teacher could use to improve a student's learning from the available material.

A brief review is given of some of the past work on how to improve retention of the important ideas from a text. This research is largely concerned with the effects of advance organizers as well as questions posed before and after reading. Two theoretical explanations are offered for the effectiveness of the various manipulations—the Focus Hypothesis and the Elaboration Hypothesis. Arguments along with empirical data are offered to bolster each position.

A series of experiments is described that indicates that people learn the central ideas of a chapter more effectively when they read a summary version than when they read the original, embellished text. These data argue for the focus interpretation. Other data suggest that elaborations aid retention. An attempt is made to reconcile these somewhat contradictory findings.

It is suggested that the elaborations provided by the reader are often more effective than those provided by the author. This is due to the inherent value of integrative processing (i.e., being forced to generate one's own embellishments) and due to the poor quality of many author-provided elaborations. An implication of this notion is that authors should provide better embellishments of the central ideas or skip writing embellishments at all. It is also suggested that authors present their ideas in a top-down fashion, repeating them more than once, each time giving more detail. The ideas in this chapter are presented several times, each time with more detail.

RESEARCH ON HOW TO IMPROVE RETENTION OF PROSE

For several decades, much of the research on improving reading comprehension has looked at the effects of adjunct aids, especially adjunct questions, that is, aids that are not part of the text itself. Ausubel, in the early 1960s, studied how *advance organizers* stimulate cognitive structures to improve retention of a passage. This work was extended by other investigators to look at other aids to comprehension, especially the use of pre and postquestions, also known as *priming questions*.

Experiments using priming questions manipulate when the questions are asked relative to the passage being read and vary the overlap between these questions and the criterion test questions. Readers do better on test questions if they are given priming questions first, so long as these questions are not totally irrelevant to the criterion questions. If the two sets of questions are exactly the same, subjects do better when given the priming questions before reading the passage. Otherwise, they are better off when the priming questions come after reading the passage.

Theoretical Explanations for the Effectiveness of Adjunct Aids

The two most obvious hypotheses to account for the effectiveness of adjunct aids are the Elaboration Hypothesis and the Focus Hypothesis. The former states that priming questions stimulate the reader to *elaborate* relevant parts of the passage and this causes redundant propositions to be stored in memory. Redundancy will be useful if the original statements are forgotten because they can be reconstructed from the redundant embellishments stored. The second hypothesis states that priming questions cause a person to *focus* attention on the important, central ideas. This facilitates rehearsal of the important information, which is thereby strengthened for better retention.

Support for the Elaboration Hypothesis.   This hypothesis is supported by biases observed in memory: distortions of recall and selective recall of certain portions of a passage, as well as uneven susceptibility to intrusions and incorrect recognition (false alarms). These biases are affected by factors that affect elaboration, such as prior knowledge, orienting instructions, topic sentences, or special information about a passage.

Support for the Focus Hypothesis.   The predominant analyses of text structure represent the information hierarchically and stipulate that the important ideas of a passage are represented higher in the hierarchy with details below them. Access to the information in a hierarchy is top-down. Because search starts at the top in this model, retrieval of a main idea could not be helped by knowing details. The reader must divide study time between the important ideas and details that do not help memory for the main points. Details also hurt memory for main points by distracting the reader from focusing on the main points and by making it more difficult to identify the main points.

A large number of experiments were conducted (Reder & Anderson, 1980) that indicated that people learn better by reading summaries of textbook chapters than by reading the original. Subjects read some topics in the original form, others in a summary form that was roughly one-fifth the original length. With retention intervals of 20 minutes, 30 minutes, 1 week, and 6 to 12 months, summaries were consistently at an advantage on true-false tests and on short-answer tests. Summaries were superior both for questions directly taken from the text and for inference questions that required the subject to combine facts that had been studied. Subjects learned new, related material better in a transfer task if the original material had been learned in summary form. Reaction time differences showed the same pattern as percentage of questions answered correctly. Summaries maintained their superiority even when the main points in the text were underlined.

Resolution of Apparent Inconsistencies—or What Does All This Mean?

There is a great deal of literature that supports the elaboration hypothesis. The experiments mentioned previously appear to favor the Focus Hypothesis in that embellished main points found in texts are not as well remembered as summaries that focus attention on just the central ideas. However, these results are not necessarily inconsistent.

Texts are not simply elaborated collections of main points. Some of the details in texts are irrelevant to the central ideas and interfere with them. They compete for study time, distract the reader from the important points, etc. There is evidence from other experiments that author-provided elaborations are not as effective at promoting memory as subject- or reader-provided elaborations.

This does not necessarily mean that a chapter could not be written that promotes better retention of the central ideas than a summary. An author should be better able to provide accurate, diverse, and interesting elaborations to the reader. The usefulness of elaborations has been shown to depend primarily on whether or not they help *constrain* the interpretation of the main point. Author-provided, constrained elaborations should be at least as good as subject-provided elaborations.

A text should also allow for distributed practice of each main point, by repeating the main ideas at spaced intervals. An optimal organization might be a top-down structure where the reader first gets an overview of the important ideas and then successively is presented with the ideas in more detail. This can partly replace the PQ4R method that students should use for normal texts. This method advocates six phases for studying a chapter: *Preview* the material, make up *Questions* about each section, *Read* each section carefully, *Reflect* on the text as it is being read, *Recite* back the information contained in a section, and *Review* the entire chapter, recalling the main points after completing it. This chapter provides the preview (abstract and first pass summary) for the reader. It does not provide the questions, although a potentially better version of this chapter might include questions for thought too. The reader, however, must still reflect for him or herself. In the following sections, the ideas discussed so far are given in more detail.

RESEARCH ON FACTORS AFFECTING
COMPREHENSION OF PROSE

There has been a great deal of work describing those aspects of prose or texts that are best remembered (e.g., Crothers, 1972; Kintsch, 1974,1977; Mandler & Johnson, 1977; Meyer, 1975; Schank, 1975; Thorndyke, 1977). Much of this work has focused on specifying grammars for stories or texts. This research predicts what aspects of stories or paragraphs are considered important and are best remembered. Investigations have continued to try to determine why certain parts of a text are better remembered than others. For example, Meyer (1975) had found that *height* of a paragraph within a passage, as she defines it, is correlated with probability of recall; recently, she and others have attempted to understand why this is so. Britton, Meyer, Simpson, Holdredge, and Curry (1979) found that height of a paragraph within the hierarchical description of a passage was not correlated with reading time nor with ability to perform a secondary task. Therefore, they argue that the effect of paragraph height is in the ability to retrieve the input, not in selective attention during acquisition. On the other hand, Walker and Meyer (1980) found that the probability of a reader integrating various assertions in a text (i.e., drawing inferences) is partly a function of the height of the paragraph that contains the assertions. This indicates that height predicts different processing during reading.

Related research has tried to predict what aspects of natural reading matter take longest to read and what parts are best remembered, (e.g., Carpenter & Just, 1980; Miller & Kintsch, 1980). Both groups of researchers would claim that readability is an interaction of the reader's processing strategies and the text. Other research has been concerned with determining those factors necessary to achieve normal comprehension and retention of prose, (e.g., Adams & Bruce, 1980; Bransford & Johnson, 1973; Britton, Holdredge, Curry, & Westbrook, 1979; Collins, Brown, & Larkin, 1977; Dooling & Lachman, 1971; Morris, Stein, & Bransford, 1979). Some of the notions put forth include the importance of prior knowledge to comprehension and the ability to identify the referents of the passage. For example, abstract passages are much better recalled when an elaboration such as a descriptive title or picture is presented just before reading the passage. However, elaborations help only when they are precise, that is, to better remember the sentence, "The group felt sorry for the fat man but could not help chuckling about the incident," one should also study the precise elaboration, "The fat man had gotten stuck in the cave," rather than the imprecise elaboration, "The fat man had made a fur hat." The reader must be able to elaborate the input using concepts already available in memory. There must be a good correspondence between the knowledge the author assumes of the reader and what the reader actually knows before reading the passage.

RESEARCH ON HOW TO IMPROVE
RETENTION OF PROSE

The concern of this chapter, however, is not on determining those aspects of texts that are normally remembered best, nor on isolating those aspects of text that are critical to normal processing. Rather, the goal of this chapter is to develop ways to actually *improve* retention of those aspects of a document that are deemed important by author, teacher, or student. There is evidence that students have a great deal of difficulty determining what aspects of a passage are important and retaining those aspects the speaker/writer wants the student to remember. Kintsch and Bates (1977) found that students' memory was equally good (or poor) for details and main points of a lecture.

There has been a considerable amount of research on the goal of improving the reader's ability to comprehend a passage. Most of this work has been concerned with adjunct aids, especially adjunct questions. Perhaps the most influential work concerned with improving the retention of a passage was that of Ausubel. Ausubel (1960) claimed that *advance organizers* stimulate available *cognitive structures* (i.e., meaningfully organized information in memory) or help build new structures to facilitate the anchoring of new, incoming ideas. He wanted to show that giving the reader a preview of the content leads to better comprehension and retention. An example of his task is to give subjects a passage before the critical passage. The passage either contains subsuming concepts of the critical passage or is essentially irrelevant to it. He predicted that prior exposure to subsuming concepts or *anchors* would facilitate retention. Ausubel found data to be consistent with these notions to some extent (e.g., Ausubel & Fitzgerald, 1962); however, it was noted that an advance organizer's usefulness interacts with many other variables such as previous knowledge and verbal ability.

Although many researchers agree that Ausubel's work provided interesting speculations that stimulated others to pursue similar questions, he has been criticized for lack of appropriate experimental controls and lack of objective measures of his stimulus variables (see Frase, 1975). It is difficult to test the notion that previous exposure to high-level concepts of a passage will improve retention of lower level concepts when no procedure for evaluating the structure of a passage has been proposed. Gagné and Wiegand (1970) are an example of investigators who put Ausubel's conclusions into doubt. They found that improvement in retention due to Ausubel's advance organizers may have involved facilitation in retrieval, not in encoding or acquisition. This possibility was suggested by the finding that recall was improved even when the related topic sentence was not given until just before the test. Britton, Meyer, Hodge, and Glynn (1980) also argue that the effect of textual importance on recall may be in retrieval rather than in acquisition. This is inconsistent with Ausubel's argument that improvement results from the ability to embed the information in preexisting structures.

The investigation of the use of adjunct aids in the comprehension of prose has been continued by a number of investigators. The major thrust of this research has been on the effect of adjunct or priming questions on text comprehension (see R. C. Anderson & Biddle, 1975 and Rickards, 1979 for extensive reviews). The paradigm that is used involves subjects receiving priming questions about the passage either before, during, or after reading the text. Their performance is compared with subjects who do not receive priming questions. A test is used to measure comprehension of a passage. Experiments also vary the extent of overlap between the priming questions and the criterion test questions. Some experiments involve giving subjects orienting directions other than questions, such as, "Pay attention to the following aspects of the passage" or "Underline all instances of the following."

From this research, a number of conclusions can be drawn that are summarized here. First, people perform better on criterion tests if previously given orienting instructions or priming questions regarding the text. The benefit of priming questions is comparable for groups asked priming questions prior to the relevant material and for groups asked priming questions after the relevant material in the text, so long as the criterion question taps the same information as the priming question. However, if the criterion question is different than the priming question, then the postquestion group (those asked a priming question *after* the relevant information) perform better. Presumably, when readers are given the questions before the passage, they search out the answers in the text and ignore all other information; if questions are given afterwards, only the review and rehearsal processes are affected.

Second, the extent of benefit depends in part on the overlap between the orienting directions and the criterion test. For example, Frase (1975) gave subjects learning directions such as, "Pay attention to the number of rotations of Mars around the sun that occur in one year." Control subjects were given no directions. Experimental subjects did slightly worse than control subjects on questions irrelevant to the directions (52% correct vs. 57% correct). However, the experimental subjects did much better than controls on questions relevant to the orienting instructions (76% vs. 57%). So, *overall*, there is a clear advantage for asking relevant priming questions.

Priming questions do more than indicate what is important; they force readers to process the text in a certain way. This is clear from results of experiments where critical aspects of the text were directly highlighted (in a box) at study. Bruning's (1968) study found that this method of highlighting was not nearly as effective as forcing subjects to *review* material by asking them to answer a particular question. The conclusion that providing information may not be as effective as forcing subjects to retrieve it themselves has been encountered before. Bobrow and Bower (1969) found that providing the mnemonic to relate a pair of words was not nearly as effective as asking subjects to provide one themselves.

Frase (1967) suggested that priming questions cause subjects to review the relevant aspects of the passage. This review process probably involves more than merely stating the critical information in the question or answer because highlighting the critical information was so much less effective. Indeed, McGaw and Grotelueschen (1972) found that the information does not need to be directly tested. In their study, when a question *reminded* subjects of information present in the text, without either stating the information in the question or demanding it as an answer, subjects later recalled that fact better than a comparable fact unrelated to the priming question. For example, the question, "The surveying ship which recovered starfish . . . was exploring a route for a cable from Faroe to _____," aids recall of "The surveying ship _____, which recovered . . . ". Just mentioning the ship caused subjects to review the relevant information.

The reason that priming questions in studies mentioned earlier only helped some questions and not always new test questions is probably due to the nature of the overlap between questions. In fact, Reder (1979) and Watts and Anderson (1971) both conducted experiments in which priming questions helped some new questions and not others, depending on the type of question or the type of relation between priming and test questions.

It seems clear that merely asking a question will not produce improved performance. The question must force the subject to process relevant aspects of the text in useful ways. Watts and Anderson (1971), for example, found that subjects do better on a posttest about passages they read if they had been asked immediately after reading each passage a question that forced them to "integrate" the material (i.e., apply a principle in the passage to a new example). On the other hand, subjects do even worse on the posttest if asked a low-level question (name the scientist associated with the principle) than if asked no question at all.

Britton, Piha, Davis, and Wehausen (1978) also investigated why readers perform better when priming questions are asked after the relevant information. They found that on the pages immediately following a priming question, subjects' *cognitive capacity* is more efficiently used. They claim that efficient use of cognitive capacity maps onto the slower response times obtained in a secondary and simultaneous task of detecting clicks while reading. In other words, immediately after a priming question that asks about prior information, subjects are slower to detect clicks while continuing to read than they are to detect clicks when asked irrelevant questions or no questions. They argue that the allocation of the increased use of cognitive capacity is for more elaborative processing rather than for "literal comprehension."[1]

---

[1]This, they claim, is because word recognition and grammatical calculation do not require cognitive capacity. However, Britton, Westbrook, and Holdredge (1978) found that cognitive capacity usage was greater with easy texts than with difficult ones. This result is the opposite of what one would have originally expected. They suggested that with very difficult texts readers simply give up careful processing and are more easily distracted.

Mayer (1975) compared pre, post, irrelevant, and no questions on level of surprise and ability to answer critical test questions. He concluded that post-questions create a "set concerning the goals of instruction" (p. 168), because subjects in the postquestion condition were much less surprised by the critical test questions. Gagné and Rothkopf (1975) also found that providing subjects with goal-descriptive directions improved performance on goal-relevant test elements so long as the goal directions were given all at once rather than dispersed throughout the text.

THEORETICAL EXPLANATIONS FOR EFFECTIVENESS OF ADJUNCT AIDS

There are two alternative notions that can explain the results discussed previously. The first is that advance organizers, priming questions, etc. *stimulate elaboration* of relevant parts of the passage. The second is that orienting directions cause a person to *focus attention* on the important central ideas. Allowing the subject to know what to focus attention on facilitates *rehearsal* of the important information, which is thereby strengthened for better memory. The first explanation I call the Elaboration Hypothesis and the second the Focus Hypothesis. Before describing research that attempts to determine which view is more accurate, I expand upon the differences between these two views.

THE ELABORATION HYPOTHESIS

The Elaboration Hypothesis should be distinguished from the Focus Hypothesis in that rather than assuming that the subject rehearses and strengthens the exact facts in a text, it assumes that the advance organizers cause subjects to create redundant interconnection and continuations. In this way, if one fact is lost, it can be reconstructed from other embellishments in memory.

The idea that elaborations are critical to memory has been proposed elsewhere (e.g., J. R. Anderson, 1976; J. R. Anderson & Reder, 1979, Reder, 1976, 1979). We have proposed that experimental manipulations intended to affect what has been called *depth of processing* have their powerful effects upon memory performance by changing the *number* and *type* of elaborations stored. Similarly, adjunct aids such as orienting questions and directions have their effect by causing the reader to create more relevant elaborations concerning the material of interest.

One might ask why extra elaborations are important to retention of the ideas in a passage. One might also wonder why orienting directions should affect the number of elaborations generated. To answer these questions, it is necessary to articulate my view of the nature of the representation of information in memory. I assume that long-term memory is a network of interconnected propositions and that when a person reads a passage new propositions are added to this memory network. Any particular encoded proposition is fragile. There is a significant chance that the reader will not be able to activate the presented proposition at test. So, if a person's memory for the tested idea rested only upon the minimal, original set of propositions, poor memory would be the result. However, if the person encoded multiple propositions that were partially redundant with the to-be-remembered information, he or she would have a much better chance of recalling it at time of test.

Experimental Support for the Elaboration Hypothesis

The provision of strong empirical support for the Elaboration Theory is difficult because the theory implies that an experimenter has poor ability to manipulate the amount and direction of elaboration. Nonetheless, there are a number of experiments concerning selectivity in memory for prose that are consistent with an elaboration-plus-reconstruction viewpoint. If subjects have more ability to make certain types of elaboration than others, or if subjects are directed to make certain elaborations rather than others, one should see better memory for material consistent with the preferred elaboration, and more distortion of material in the direction of preferred elaboration. In the classic study conducted by F. C. Bartlett (1932), subjects from pre-World War I England studied an Indian story, "The War of the Ghosts." Bartlett obtained what he interpreted as systematic distortion of the material in the direction of the knowledge of his subjects. This distortion took the form of additions to the material that made the story more consistent with the world view of his subjects, deletion of inconsistent information, and transformations of inconsistent information to make it more consistent with prevailing beliefs.

There has been a long history of debates (e.g., J. R. Anderson & Bower, 1973; Gould & Stephenson, 1967; Spiro, 1975) over the extent to which Bartlett's subjects were really misremembering and the degree to which they were knowingly confabulating in response to perceived task demands. It seems that, at least to some degree, subjects are aware of their distortions and are able to assign lower confidence to these than to veridical recalls. However, this debate misses an important point: The behavior of subjects in Bartlett's task is typical of prose processing. Normally, the reader does not make distinctions between what was actually read in a passage and what is a plausible inference. With most stories, the inferences made are plausible extensions of the story and are not distortions. It was Bartlett's clever story selection that served to highlight the elaborative behavior of subjects.

Sulin and Dooling (1974) and Dooling and Christiaansen (1977) showed that subjects are more likely to falsely recognize statements that are consistent with a famous person as having been presented when the passage is described as being about that person than when the same passage is said to be about a fictitious person. These distortions can occur as a reconstructive process or as an encoding process. Subjects make more thematic false recognitions if they are told the famous name prior to reading the passage, but they still make them if told this information immediately after reading the passage. When told the name just prior to the test, they make still fewer errors, but more than if not given this bias. The difference in errors among the three conditions is probably due to differential elaboration.

Bower (1976) reports an interesting experiment looking at the effect of prior information on subjects' memory for a passage. Subjects were given a story that consisted of episodes. Half the subjects were given prior information that would suggest an unusual interpretation of some of the subpassages, such as that the main character (a college co-ed) had just found out that she was pregnant. The story follows the heroine through five episodes: making a cup of coffee in the morning, visiting a doctor, attending a lecture, going shopping in a grocery store, and attending a cocktail party. The meaning of these episodes can be very different depending on whether or not we view the heroine as pregnant. Subjects given the interesting interpretation intruded many more inferences appropriate to the pregnancy theme. However, they also recalled more facts from the story. This result is what would be expected if subjects had used the information about pregnancy to elaborate. These elaborations should make the text information more redundant and introduce additional inferences.

Hayes (1977) has found a similar correlation between number of intruded inferences and overall memory for text. Hayes and his colleagues tried to find out what mechanisms allow some people to remember more than others. They pretested subjects on their memory for various historical facts and then classified them as those who remember a lot of history and those who do not. The subjects were then given a fictitious historical passage to read. The same subjects who knew more veridical history performed better on a test of the fantasy history passage. Subjects were also asked to free recall the passage that they had read. Not only did the subjects with better history-memory recall more; they also recalled many elaborations that were not asserted. These elaborations were not simply paraphrases of the passage nor were they simple inferences. The subjects classified as having poor memory for history offered almost no elaborations. From this finding, Hayes conjectured that embellishing the input with elaborations promotes better retention.

Schallert (1976) indirectly provided evidence consistent with the notion that elaborations help retention and that the amount of elaboration generated can be influenced by instruction. Subjects were given ambiguous passages that were either biased by prior information or were not biased. She found that subjects in the biased group remembered more information consistent with the bias than those who did not receive prior information. She also introduced a depth-of-processing manipulation in which subjects either processed the sentences at a *shallow* level (counting four-letter words in the passage) or at a *deep* level (rating for ambiguity). Biased subjects were more likely to remember consistent information when they were processing the material at the semantic level. It is reasonable to assume that subjects would be generating more elaborations under semantic-orienting instructions (see J. R. Anderson & Reder, 1979), and that elaborations are responsible for the bias found in recall. Therefore, one would expect to find a greater bias in recall for the deep-processing group. In other words, Schallert's data support the notion of elaborative processing in comprehension because of the interaction of mode of processing and bias.

Brown, Smiley, Day, Townsend, and Lawton (1977) conducted a study with children that supports the elaboration theory by showing that the types of elaborations generated can be manipulated and that generating more elaborations improves recall. The study indicates that if teachers provide students with background knowledge, students are likely to remember more of the material presented to them. In the Brown et al. study, children in various grades were presented with information about either a fictitious tribe called the Targa or people from Spain. Those who learned about the Targa were told either that the tribe consisted of Eskimos or desert Indians. A week later all groups read a story about a young boy from the Targa tribe, and no mention was made about what they had studied the preceding week. Of those receiving relevant background information, intrusions and biases in interpretations of ambiguous sentences were consistent with the orientation given earlier. More important, those subjects in the Spanish control recalled significantly less of the veridical material. The usefulness of the background material was evident at all age levels. However, not only did older children recall significantly more veridical information; they recalled significantly more elaborations (had more intrusions) consistent with the background material. In other words, both recall and number of elaborations increased with age.

Owens and Bower (1977) conducted a study that indicates how perspective on a passage can affect memory for the input. Other studies discussed earlier manipulated prior knowledge about concepts in the passage or manipulated the focus of attention by the questions asked during reading. This study was more subtle in that the first few lines of the story caused the reader to identify with one character or the other, depending on which character was introduced first. Mishaps were described in the story without specifying who was to blame for them. On a subsequent recognition test, subjects were asked to judge which statements were presented in the story. Subjects were much more inclined to inaccurately recognize (i.e., false alarm to) a statement that imputed blame for the mishap to the character with whom they did not identify, and much less likely to false alarm to statements putting fault on the character with whom they did identify. Similar results have been obtained by Abelson (1976) and R. C. Anderson and Pichert (1977). These results are consistent with the notion that readers elaborate material in a fashion that is consistent with their wishes, prejudices, or perspective. And there is, of course, some tendency to confuse elaborations with presented input.

The Watts and Anderson (1971) result described earlier, that subjects do best on a posttest if asked integrating questions and worst if asked low-level questions, is consistent with the elaboration notion. When subjects were asked no questions, they probably had more time to generate useful elaborations than when asked the low-level question, the name of the scientist, which had nothing to do with the point of the principle. Integrating questions encourage elaboration, because the answers require complicated thinking about the passage. The no-question condition produces an intermediate amount of elaboration and an intermediate recall performance.

Rothkopf (1972) conducted a study, the results of which are consistent with this view. In this study, subjects read material at their own rate and they would read slower those passages for which they were given priming questions. They probably were attending (thinking, elaborating) more to the relevant information in primed passages.

In a study of mine (Reder, 1976, 1979), I manipulated more directly the amount of elaboration given to prose material. An earlier study of mine indicated that subjects have very good memory for the sentences used in the same experimental stories. So the dependent measure chosen was the *speed* with which subjects can make judgments about a story, not the accuracy. The task demanded of subjects was to judge the plausibility of statements rather than their verbatim accuracy, which seems more representative of everyday tasks.

In these studies, the plausibility of the test sentence (with respect to the story being queried) affected plausibility judgment time even when the item had been explicitly presented. When the test sentence had been primed earlier by asking the subject to answer a related question while reading the story, there was also a plausibility effect. The decision times were faster for test items that had previously been presented or primed than for those not so treated, suggesting that the manipulations had an effect. However, because there was a large effect of statement plausibility for explicit and primed statements, it seems that people do not always first search for a specific fact in memory. Rather, they may often try to answer questions simply by computing plausibility.

Just as the number of relevant elaborations is postulated to affect *retention* of the input, it is also thought to affect the *speed* of retrieval of relevant information. This notion is based on the assumption that searching through memory for relevant information takes time and that the greater the proportion of relevant to irrelevant information, the faster a useful or relevant fact can be found; hence, faster reaction times occur with more elaborations. (See Reder, 1976, for a fuller discussion.)

FOCUS HYPOTHESIS

There are fewer theoretical arguments that can be made in support of the Focus Hypothesis as an explanation for why priming questions help. Instead, the arguments are, for the most part, made on an intuitive level. The thrust of the argument is that when trying to master the important points of a text, the more clutter that is included in the reading, the harder it will be for the reader to attend to what is important. The adjunct aids remind the reader of what to attend to and what to ignore. Following are arguments for the Focus Hypothesis.

A number of cognitive scientists have proposed theories of the structure of text (e.g., Crothers, 1972; Frederiksen, 1975; Kintsch, 1974; Kintsch & van Dijk, 1975; Mandler & Johnson, 1977; Meyer, 1975; Rumelhart, 1975; Thorndyke, 1977), and these analyses suggest that certain facts are more likely to be retained. The predominant analysis of text has structured the propositions or idea units hierarchically where the more central or important propositions are represented higher in the hierarchy, with details subordinate to the main points in the memory representation.

Assuming that hierarchies are searched in a top-down manner, access to details depends on getting the main points, but there would be no dependence of main points on details. Therefore, details cannot help one remember the main points because access to the details is contingent on recovering the main points. Consistent with this view, investigations of these representations have found that propositions higher and more central in these hierarchies are better recalled, more accurately recognized, and more rapidly verified (e.g., Kintsch, 1974; Kintsch & van Dijk, 1975; Meyer, 1975).

Studying an unfocused text means that readers have to time-share in their concentration between the main points and the details rather than devote all their attention to the central ideas.

Because details cannot help memory for the main points, this is wasted study time. It is also more difficult to extract the important points if they are embedded in details. Both B. J. Bartlett (1978) and Kintsch and Bates (1977) obtained data consistent with this view.

Experimental Support for Focus Hypothesis

In order to determine whether the Focus Hypothesis or the Elaboration Hypothesis is a more reasonable explanation of the research on the benefits of adjunct aids, John Anderson and I performed a series of experiments comparing learning from texts with learning from summaries of texts. Following is a brief review of some of the experiments and results reported in Reder and Anderson (1980).

Experiments 1 and 2.   In the first two experiments, college subjects studied one introductory chapter from a college text in its original form and studied the other in summary form. Examples of introductory college texts chosen as experimental materials were *An Introduction to Descriptive Linguistics* by Gleason (1967, pp. 1–13), and *The Geography of Modern Africa* by Hance (1975, pp. 5–20). The texts did not require that the student have prior knowledge of that content area. Summaries were written for the chapters. These summaries were roughly one-fifth the length of the originals. The questions we chose to ask the subjects could all be answered on the basis of the summaries. In the first set of experiments, the questions were true–false and half the trues and half the falses could be answered by retrieving a simple assertion provided in the summary. The other half of the questions required that the reader combine statements presented in the summary. The former type are called *direct* questions; the latter, *indirect* questions.

The summaries were written to restate the main points in as compact a fashion as possible. The section headings of the original text were kept, but no paragraph structure or interstitial material was maintained. Each sentence started a new line. Each subject studied both the linguistics material and the Africa material, one in the original text form and the other in the summary form. Subjects in Experiment 1 studied the text for 20 minutes and the summary for 20 minutes. Some subjects complained that 20 minutes was not sufficient time to read the text; so in Experiment 2, subjects were given 30 minutes to study each type of material.

Immediately after studying each topic, subjects were tested with 16 statements, 4 indirect true, 4 indirect false, 4 direct true, and 4 direct false as defined earlier. Another 16 statements of the same types were tested 1 week later. Of the 32 questions, the selection of 16 for the immediate test was randomly determined for each subject. Questions were presented on a computer terminal. Using computer methodology meant that we could surreptitiously collect reaction times from the onset of the statement until the subject responded true or false. The computer also allowed us to run multiple subjects in parallel.

The pattern of results is essentially identical for the 20- and 30-minute (study time) versions of the experiment. Subjects performed less than 2% better with 10 extra minutes. Because no other differences were observed, we describe the data of these two experiments together.

Table 1.1 presents the data as a function of study form (summary vs. text), delay (immediate vs. 1 week later), and question type (direct vs. indirect). In both experiments, the summary condition was significantly better (10%) than the text study form. Subjects also responded more accurately immediately than at a delay. The advantage of summary was not affected by delay. There was an interaction of question type and study form, such that subjects answered direct

TABLE 1.1

Accuracy and Latency Performance on Questions From Experiments
1 and 2 As a Function of Type of Question, Type of Study, and Delay

| | Proportion correct | | | |
| | Immediate | | Delay | |
	Summary	Text	Summary	Text
Direct	.839	.651	.718	.607
Indirect	.752	.707	.700	.647

questions better than indirect questions when the material was studied in summary form but answered indirect questions better than direct questions when the material was learned in the original text form. However, indirect questions were still answered better for material learned in summary, i.e., there was a clear main effect of type of study over and above the interaction. Subjects also responded faster in the summary conditions.

Experiment 3.   Experiments 1 and 2 found that when summary and text material were given equal study time, there was a clear advantage for summaries. One might wonder whether memory for prose would be more resistant to forgetting if initial acquisition were equated. With this in mind, we ran a third experiment giving subjects only 15 minutes to study the summaries and 45 minutes to study the text. In other respects, the procedures and materials were identical with the first two experiments. In the immediate test condition, the difference between summary and text was reduced to only 2.5% as compared with 11.7% in Experiments 1 and 2. Although there was still a slight advantage for material studied in summary form, this effect was not significant. There was a significant effect of delay on retention; however, the expected interaction of delay with type of study was not present. Moreover, the nonsignificant difference in retention favored summaries rather than prose.

In Experiments 1 and 2 it was noted that there was an interaction between type of question asked and study form. In those experiments, the interaction seemed to diminish slightly with delay. In the current experiment, the interaction was only present in the immediate condition; the effect disappears in the delayed condition. Indirect questions were not answered as well as direct questions for material studied in text form either.

Experiment 4.   The data do not support the notion that the reason details are included in a text is to enable readers to better retain the central points of a passage. Conceivably a more subtle benefit might accrue with the inclusion of details. Details provide the reader with a richer, more elaborate structure of the knowledge base and perhaps this elaborated structure helps the reader to acquire *subsequent information* better. This hypothesis can be tested by looking at whether there is an improvement in learning a set of facts when other related facts learned previously were acquired either through text form or summary form.

In this experiment, new materials were used that could easily be split in half so either half (first or second) could be learned in either form (text vs. summary). The overall performance for each half of each topic studied in summary form was superior to that studied in text form. Further, subjects did better when both halves were studied in the same form, regardless of whether it was text or summary. In answer to our major question, we found no advantage for learning material in the second half by studying the first half in prose form. If anything, there was a slight advantage here too for having learned the earlier material in summary form. Overall then, not only does one learn information better when it is studied in summary form; there is some indication that one acquires new information better when prior related material has been studied in summary form.

Experiment 5. Having been unable to find an advantage for prose in any circumstance, we made one last attempt to see if perhaps the long-range retention of prose might not be superior to retention of summaries. We brought back as many subjects as we could from Experiments 1, 2, and 3. The original three experiments had been performed from January through May of 1977, whereas the retention tests were administered from November 1977 through May 1978. Thus, the delays varied from 6 to 12 months. We constructed new true–false questions on the same chapters and verified with pilot subjects that these too were answered at chance levels by those who had not studied the material.

Even at a delay of up to 1 year, there was still some advantage for the summary condition. There was an interaction between study form and delay such that the advantage of summaries declined over time. Also, the difference between the text condition and the summary condition was not significant at the longest delay. These last two results may be attributed to a floor effect. Both groups approached chance performance at the longest delay.

Conclusions and Theoretical Interpretations

The data from a number of experiments have been summarized, all of which argue that learning material from summaries is at least as good as reading the original text. People's ability to recognize important facts about a topic is superior when the information is learned in summary form, and acquisition of new material is better (measured by one's ability to answer questions) if information learned earlier on a related topic was learned by reading a summary.

Our initial expectation had been that the embellishments would improve retention because they provide a redundant coherent structure. Apparently, helping subjects focus attention and avoid having to share study time between main points and details is a more effective way to aid learning.

WHAT DOES ALL THIS MEAN?

Although much of the literature I reviewed argued for the Elaboration Hypothesis, the set of experiments summarized in this paper seems to point to the Focus Hypothesis. Because the two hypotheses have been described as antithetical, it would appear that the results are inconsistent. If one assumed that the original text version is an elaborated version of the summary condition, the Elaboration Hypothesis would imply that subjects would perform better with the original chapters than with the abbreviated summaries. Just the opposite result was found.

The advantage of the summary condition is not inconsistent with the Elaboration Hypothesis because it is overly simplistic to characterize the original text as just an elaborated version of the summary. Some of the extra material in the text is not really elaboration, but rather irrelevant to the main points. Also, it may be that author-provided elaborations tend not to be as effective as reader-provided elaborations. If the preceding points are correct, even if reader-generated elaborations are at some advantage, one should be able to construct an elaborated text that will be at least as memorable as a summary, and in some ways more memorable.

The notion that author-provided elaborations are not as effective as reader-generated elaborations is not new. Bobrow and Bower (1969) demonstrated that subjects learned paired associates better when they were forced to generate a mnemonic to connect them than when they were given a verbal mediator provided by the experimenter. This has also been demonstrated by Rohwer (Rohwer & Ammon, 1971; Rohwer, Lynch, Levin, & Suzuki, 1967; Rohwer, Lynch, Suzuki, & Levin, 1967). Presumably it is the constructive process itself, the generation of the connection, that is valuable, rather than the reader's mnemonics. Bobrow and Bower provided data consistent with the view that it is the search, the deep processing, that is critical, more so than the appropriateness of the connection. On the other hand, Stein and Bransford (1979) showed that the precision of the elaboration is more critical than other factors. The elaboration must *constrain* the proposition. The precision of self-generated elaborations can be affected by prompting. This in turn affects retention. Nonetheless, self-generated elaborations tend to be more precise (useful) for the reader than author generated, unless care is taken in the construction of author-generated details.

The fact that subjects are better off providing their own elaborations and that author-provided details are often interfering rather than useful does not preclude the possibility of constructing a chapter that would be at least as effective as a summary of a chapter. An author should be better able to provide useful elaborations of the main points. Those elaborations should seem as relevant as what the reader can generate and they certainly could be more accurate, diverse, and interesting. The embellishments could potentially be much more educational as well as more redundant. Stein and Bransford's (1979) results indicate that author-provided elaborations can be as effective as subject-generated ones.

Another reason the summary condition was superior to the original text version was due to the phenomenon of spaced versus massed practice. When the experimenter equates for total study time, the subject learns faster when the amount of time allocated to learn a specific fact is distributed across several trials with intervening practice on other items. Massed practice is less efficient, both in learning verbal material (see Glenberg, 1976 or Hintzman, 1969 for a review) and in learning a new physical skill such as tennis or skiing. When subjects read the original text, they had time to read through the material only once; with the much shorter summaries, subjects could go back and re-read the information several times with spaced practice. Recently, Anderson and I (Reder & Anderson, 1982) tested the notion that the advantage of summaries was due to spaced practice on the important ideas rather than the absence of details. We found that both the absence of details and distributed practice contributed to improved knowledge acquisition. This result of better learning with spaced practice implies that an optimally written chapter would present the main ideas several times, distributed throughout the text. For example, the author might first give an overview or summary of the material to be covered, then present it again with more embellishment, and close the chapter with another long summary. These techniques have been used by many authors; however, the summaries tend to be short in that they do not cover every important point.

An optimal organization might be a top-down structure where the reader first gets an overview of the important ideas and then successively is presented with these ideas with more and more detail. Newspaper stories tend to be written in this fashion so that people can read to the level of detail that interests them. Textbooks might be more interesting to the student if they too were written in such a fashion.

A top-down organization could replace for the reader some of the work that is required by the PQ4R method of Thomas and Robinson (1972). That technique for improving retention of normal texts involves the reader *Previewing* or surveying the chapter, then making up *Questions* about each section, then *Reading* each section, trying to answer the questions, and *Reflecting* on the text in the process, *Reciting* the information in a section when finished, and finally *Reviewing* the chapter, recalling its main points when the chapter is finished. Of course, the central feature of the PQ4R method is its question-generation and question-answering property. A top-down organization does nothing to help influence the depth-of-processing as the PQ4R's question properties do. A top-down organization aids the reader by offering previews and reviews. Perhaps still better designed text could also provide questions for the reader to answer and spur the reader into generating questions of his or her own.

REFERENCES

Abelson, R. P. (1976). Script processing in attitude formation. In J. S. Carroll & J. R. Payne (Eds.), *Cognition and social behavior*. Hillsdale, NJ: Lawrence Erlbaum Associates.

Adams, M., & Bruce, B. (1980, January). *Background knowledge and reading comprehension* (Tech. Rep. No. 13). Urbana: University of Illinois, Center for the Study of Reading.

Anderson, J. R. (1976). *Language, memory, and thought*. Hillsdale, NJ: Lawrence Erlbaum Associates.

Anderson, J. R., & Bower, G. H. (1973). *Human associative memory*. Washington, DC: Hemisphere Press.

Anderson, J. R., & Reder, L. M. (1979). An elaborative processing explanation of depth of processing. In L. S. Cermak & F. I. M. Craik (Eds.), *Levels of processing in human memory*. Hillsdale, NJ: Lawrence Erlbaum Associates.

Anderson, R. C. & Biddle, W. B. (1975). On asking people questions about what they are reading. In G. H. Bower (Ed.), *The psychology of learning and motivation* (Vol. 9). New York: Academic Press.

Anderson, R. C., & Pichert, J.W. (1977, April). *Recall of previously unrecallable information following a shift in perspective* (Tech. Rep. No. 41). Urbana: University of Illinois, Center for the Study of Reading. (ERIC Document Reproduction Service No. ED 142 974).

Ausubel, D. P. (1960). The use of advance organizers in learning and retention of meaningful verbal material. *Journal of Educational Psychology, 51*, 267–272.

Ausubel, D. P., & Fitzgerald, D. (1962). Organizer, general background and antecedent learning variables in sequential verbal learning. *Journal of Educational Psychology, 53*, 243–249.

Bartlett, B. J. (1978). *Top-level structure as an organizational strategy for recall of classroom text*. Unpublished doctoral dissertation, Arizona State University.

Bartlett, F. C. (1932). *Remembering: A study in experimental and social psychology*. Cambridge, England: Cambridge University Press.

Bobrow, S., & Bower, G. H. (1969). Comprehension and recall of sentences. *Journal of Experimental Psychology, 80*, 455–461.

Bower, G. H. (1976, September). *Comprehending and recalling stories*. Division 3 Presidential Address presented at the meeting of the American Psychological Association, Washington, DC.

Bransford, J.D., & Johnson, M. K. (1973). Considerations of some problems of comprehension. In W. G. Chase (Ed.), *Visual information processing*. New York: Academic Press.

Britton, B. K., Holdredge, T. S., Curry, C., & Westbrook, R. D. (1979). Use of cognitive capacity in reading identical texts with different amounts of discourse level meaning. *Journal of Experimental Psychology: Human Learning and Memory, 5*, 262–270.

Britton, B. K., Meyer, B. J. F., Hodge, M. H., & Glynn, S. (1980). Effects of the organization of text on memory: Test of retrieval and response criterion hypotheses. *Journal of Experimental Psychology: Human Learning and Memory, 6*, 620–629.

Britton, B. K., Meyer, B. J. F., Simpson, R., Holdredge, T. S., & Curry, C. (1979). Effects of the organization of text on memory: Tests of two implications of a selective attention hypothesis. *Journal of Experimental Psychology: Human Learning and Memory, 5*, 496–506.

Britton, B. K., Piha, A., Davis, J., & Wehausen, E. (1978). Reading and cognitive capacity usage: Adjunct question effects. *Memory and Cognition, 6*, 266–273.

Britton, B. K., Westbrook, R. D., & Holdredge, T. S. (1978). Reading and cognitive capacity usage: Effects of text difficulty. *Journal of Experimental Psychology: Human Learning and Memory, 4*, 582–591.

Brown, A. L., Smiley, S. S., Day, J. D., Townsend, M. A. R., & Lawton, S. C. (1977). Intrusion of a thematic idea in children's comprehension and retention of stories. *Child Development, 48*, 1454–1466.

Bruning, R. H. (1968). Effects of review and testlike events within the learning of prose material. *Journal of Educational Psychology, 59*, 16–19.

Carpenter, P. A., & Just, M. A. (1980). A theory of reading: From eye fixations to comprehension. *Psychological Review, 87*, 329–354.

Collins, A., Brown, J. S., & Larkin, K. M. (1977, December). *Inference in text understanding* (Tech. Rep. No. 40), Center for the Study of Reading.

Crothers, E. (1972). Memory structure and the recall of discourse. In R. O. Freedle & J. B. Carroll (Eds.), *Language comprehension and the acquisition of knowledge*. Washington, DC: Winston.

Dooling, D. J., & Christiaansen, R. E. (1977). Episodic and semantic aspects of memory for prose. *Journal of Experimental Psychology: Human Learning and Memory, 3*, 428–436.

Dooling, D. J., & Lachman, R. (1971). Effects of comprehension on retention of prose. *Journal of Experimental Psychology, 88*, 216–222.

Frase, L. T. (1967). Learning from prose material: Length of passage, knowledge of results and position of questions. *Journal of Educational Psychology, 58,* 266–272.

Frase, L. T. (1975). Prose processing. In G. H. Bower (Ed.), *The psychology of learning and motivation* (Vol. 9). New York: Academic Press.

Frederiksen, C. H. (1975). Representing logical and semantic structure of knowledge acquired from discourse. *Cognitive Psychology, 7,* 371–458.

Gagné, E. D., & Rothkopf, E. Z. (1975). Text organization and learning goals. *Journal of Educational Psychology, 67,* 445–450.

Gagné, R. M., & Wiegand, V. K. (1970). Effects of superordinate context on learning and retention of facts. *Journal of Educational Psychology, 61,* 406–409.

Gleason, H. A. (1967). *An Introduction to descriptive linguistics* (pp. 1–13). New York: Holt, Rinehart, & Winston.

Glenberg, A. M. (1976). Monotonic and nonmonotonic lag effects in paired-associate and recognition memory paradigms. *Journal of Verbal Learning and Verbal Behavior, 15,* 1–16.

Gould, A., & Stephenson, G. M. (1967). Some experiments relating to Bartlett's theory of remembering. *British Journal of Psychology, 58,* 39–49.

Hance, W. A. (1975). *The geography of modern Africa* (pp. 5–20). New York: Columbia University Press.

Hintzman, D. L. (1969). Apparent frequency as a function of frequency and the spacing of repetitions. *Journal of Experimental Psychology, 80,* 139–145.

Kintsch, W. (1974). *The representation of meaning in memory.* Hillsdale, NJ: Lawrence Erlbaum Associates.

Kintsch, W. (1977). On recalling stories. In M. Just and P. Carpenter (Eds.), *Cognitive processes in comprehension.* Hillsdale, NJ: Lawrence Erlbaum Associates.

Kintsch, W., & Bates, E. (1977). Recognition memory for statements from a classroom lecture. *Journal of Experimental Psychology: Human Learning and Memory, 3,* 150–159.

Kintsch, W., & van Dijk, T. A. (1975). Recalling and summarizing stories. *Languages, 40,* 98–116.

Mandler, J. M., & Johnson, N. S. (1977). Remembrance of things parsed: Story structure and recall. *Cognitive Psychology, 9,* 111–151.

Mayer, R. E. (1975). Forward transfer of different reading strategies evoked by test-like events in mathematics texts. *Journal of Educational Psychology, 67,* 165–169.

McGaw, B., & Grotelueschen, A. (1972). Direction of the effect of questions in prose material. *Journal of Educational Psychology, 63,* 586–588.

Meyer, B. J. F. (1975). *The organization of prose and its effect on recall.* Amsterdam: North-Holland.

Miller, J. R., & Kintsch, W. (1980). Readability and recall of short prose passages: A theoretical analysis. *Journal of Experimental Psychology: Human Learning and Memory, 6,* 335–354.

Morris, C. D., Stein, B. S., & Bransford, J. D. (1979). Prerequisites for the utilization of knowledge in the recall of prose passages. *Journal of Experimental Psychology: Human Learning and Memory, 5,* 253–261.

Owens, J. E., & Bower, G. M. (1977, August). *Character point of view in text comprehension and memory.* Paper presented at the meeting of the American Psychological Association, San Francisco.

Reder, L. M. (1976). *The role of elaborations in the processing of prose.* Unpublished doctoral dissertation, University of Michigan.

Reder, L. M. (1979). The role of elaborations in memory for prose. *Cognitive Psychology, 11,* 221–234.

Reder, L. M., & Anderson, J. R. (1980). A comparison of texts and their summaries: Memorial consequences. *Journal of Verbal Learning and Verbal Behavior, 19,* 121–134.

Reder, L. M., & Anderson, J.R. (1982). Effects of spacing and embellishments on memory for the main points of a text. *Memory and Cognition, 10*, 97–102.

Rickards, J. P. (1979). Adjunct postquestions in text: A critical review of methods and processes. *Review of Educational Research, 49*, 181–196.

Rohwer, W. D., Jr., & Ammon, M. S. (1971). Elaboration training and paired-associate learning efficiency in children. *Journal of Educational Psychology, 62*, 376–383.

Rohwer, W. D., Jr., Lynch, S., Levin, J., & Suzuki, N. (1967). Pictorial and verbal factors in the efficient learning of paired-associates. *Journal of Educational Psychology, 58*, 278–284.

Rohwer, W. D., Jr., Lynch, S., Suzuki,N., & Levin, J. R. (1967). Verbal and pictorial facilitation of paired-associate learning. *Journal of Experimental Child Psychology, 5*, 294–302.

Rothkopf, E. Z. (1972). Structural text features and the control of processes in learning from written materials. In R. O. Freedle & J. B. Carroll (Eds.), *Language comprehension and the acquisition of knowledge*. Washington, DC: Winston.

Rumelhart, D. E. (1975). Notes on a schema for stories. In D. G. Bobrow & A. M. Collins (Eds.), *Representation and understanding: Studies in cognitive science*. New York: Academic Press.

Schallert, D. L. (1976). Improving memory for prose: The relationship between depth of processing and context. *Journal of Verbal Learning and Verbal Behavior, 15*, 621–632.

Schank, R. C. (1975). The structure of episodes in memory. In D. G. Bobrow & A. M. Collins (Eds.), *Representation and understanding: Studies in cognitive science*. New York: Academic Press.

Spiro, R. J. (1975, October). *Inferential reconstruction in memory for connected discourse* (Tech. Rep. No. 2). Urbana: University of Illinois. (ERIC Document Reproduction Service No. ED 136 187).

Stein, B. S., & Bransford, J. D. (1979). Constraints on effective elaboration: Effects of precision and subject generation. *Journal of Verbal Learning and Verbal Behavior, 18*, 769–777.

Sulin, R. A., & Dooling, D. J. (1974). Instrusions of a thematic idea in retention of prose. *Journal of Experimental Psychology, 103*, 255–262.

Thomas, E. L., & Robinson, H. A. (1972). *Improving reading in every class: A sourcebook for teachers*. Boston: Allyn & Bacon.

Thorndyke, P. W. (1977). Cognitive structures in comprehension and memory of narrative discourse. *Cognitive Psychology, 9*, 77–110.

Walker, C. H., & Meyer, B. J. F. (1980). Integrating different types of information in text. *Journal of Verbal Learning and Verbal Behavior, 19*, 263–275.

Watts, G. H., & Anderson, R. C. (1971). Effects of three types of inserted questions on learning from prose. *Journal of Educational Psychology, 62*, 387–394.

APPENDIX: SUMMARY OF "TECHNIQUES AVAILABLE TO AUTHOR, TEACHER, AND READER TO IMPROVE RETENTION OF MAIN IDEAS OF A CHAPTER"

Preface

• Writing a chapter on how to write a good chapter makes the author self-conscious.

• The text form of this chapter attempts to follow my prescriptions for how a chapter should be written.

- The summary and text forms of this material allow for experimental comparison of which form produces better learning and retention.

Research on Factors Affecting Comprehension of Prose

- There has been much research trying to specify those parts of text that are best remembered.

- Much of this research has been concerned with developing text grammars.

- The *height* of an idea in a tree structure representation is the best predictor of recall.

- Other research has tried to predict how long it takes to read different parts of a text and what parts are best remembered.

- The prior knowledge of the referents of a passage has been shown to be critical to comprehension.

Research on How to Improve Retention of Prose

- This chapter is less concerned with the normal processing of prose and more concerned with how to *improve* the typical retention of text material.

- Much research has been done on how adjunct aids, especially adjunct questions, can improve retention.

- The most influential work was that of Ausubel on the effects of advance organizers.

- He believed giving the reader a preview of the contents of a passage leads to better comprehension and retention of the passage.

- Although Ausubel's ideas stimulated further research, he was criticized for lack of appropriate experimental controls.

- For example, Ausubel believed that advance organizers improve acquisition of the passage; others suggested the improvement may be in retrieval.

- Further work on adjunct aids centered on the effects of priming questions on text comprehension.

- The general paradigm involves giving subjects priming questions on the text prior to the criterion test.

- The priming questions can be asked before reading the passage, after reading each paragraph or several paragraphs, or immediately after reading the passage.

- The adjunct questions can be identical to the criterion test questions, closely related to the test questions, or irrelevant to the test questions.

- Several general conclusions can be drawn from this line of research:
  We perform better when given adjunct test questions.
  The extent of benefit depends partly on the overlap between the priming questions and criterion questions.
  Performance is slightly better on relevant questions if these questions are asked before the text than if asked after; however, overall performance, especially performance on test questions not primed by the adjunct questions, is better if the priming questions are asked *after* the passage has been read.

- Priming questions do more than indicate what ideas are important; they force the reader to review relevant aspects of the passage.

- Priming questions must force the reader to process relevant aspects of the text in useful ways; distracting questions hurt performance.

- Investigations of why people perform better when given priming questions have found that readers more "efficiently use their cognitive processing capacity" after such questions.

- Questions asked after the text create "a set concerning the goals of instruction." Questions in other positions do not.

Theoretical Explanations for the Effectiveness of Adjunct Aids

- There are two alternative explanations for the effectiveness of adjunct questions and orienting instructions.

- The Elaboration Hypothesis states that priming questions stimulate *elaboration* of relevant parts of the passage.

- The Focus Hypothesis states that priming questions cause a person to *focus* attention on the important, central ideas.

The Elaboration Hypothesis

- More processing of the input, caused by adjunct aids, results in additional, related, or redundant interconnections and continuations.

- By having redundant propositions, if one fact is lost, it can be reconstructed from other elaborations in memory.

- Memory is a network of interconnected propositions, and any given connection is fragile. Therefore redundancy is important.

Experimental Support for the Elaboration Hypothesis

- Although it is difficult to experimentally manipulate the amount and direction of a person's elaborations, there is data consistent with the elaboration-plus-reconstruction position.

- Some of this data is in the form of better memory and more distortions consistent with the view of the material that subjects are encouraged to adopt or the view consistent with their prior knowledge. Subjects should have poorer memory and fewer distortions for aspects of inconsistent material.

- F. C. Bartlett's (1932) classic study showed consistent distortions of an Indian story by his British subjects to make it more consistent with their world view.

- Sulin and Dooling showed that subjects are more likely to falsely recognize statements that are consistent with a famous person as having been presented when the passage is described as being about that person than when the same passage is said to be about a fictitious person.

- When subjects read about a set of events that is given an interesting interpretation (e.g., the heroine is worried about being pregnant), they recall more facts from each set of events but also have more intrusions (consistent with the interpretation) than subjects given no interpretation.

- The Elaboration Hypothesis predicts the result that, with an interesting interpretation of a passage, there will be more veridical recall, due to more redundant embellishment of the input and also more thematically consistent intrusions.

- People make more thematically consistent intrusions when they have more time for deep processing or elaboration.

- Providing children with relevant background information improves their retention of a story and increases the number of consistent elaborations recalled. Amount of veridical recall and number of elaborations intruded increases with age.

- When people are asked no questions about a passage, they later perform better than if asked a low-level question, and worse than if asked an integrating question. Low-level questions inhibit readers from making their own elaborations; integrating questions encourage the most useful elaborations.

- There is evidence that people read passages slower when given priming questions, so that they can think more deeply about the relevant information and perhaps generate more relevant elaborations.

Focus Hypothesis

- The Focus Hypothesis states that adjunct aids let a person know what to attend to. This facilitates *rehearsal* of the important information, which is thereby strengthened for better memory.

- It is more difficult to appreciate what the important ideas are if they are embedded in details. Adjunct aids help the reader to recognize the important ideas.

- The more clutter of details in a passage, the more difficult it is to devote attention to the central ideas.

- The predominant analyses of text structure stipulate that the important ideas are represented higher in a hierarchy with details below them; the hierarchies are said to be searched in a top-down manner so access to main ideas cannot be helped by knowing details.

- Consistent with this analysis, investigations of text structure have found that propositions represented higher in the hierarchy are better recalled, more accurately recognized, and more rapidly verified.

- Studying details takes time away from studying main points; because details cannot help memory for main points, they hurt learning of the important ideas.

Experimental Support for the Focus Hypothesis

- Following is a summary of a series of experiments (Reder & Anderson, 1980) comparing learning from texts with learning from summaries of texts. Texts can be thought of as main points plus embellishments, whereas the summaries only introduce (and hence focus on) the main points.

Experiments 1 and 2

- Summaries were written for two introductory college texts that were roughly one-fifth the length of the originals.

- True–false questions were constructed that could be answered from the summaries; half the questions were asked immediately after study and half were asked a week later.

- In Experiment 1, subjects had 20 minutes to read the summary of one chapter and 20 minutes to read the other chapter; in Experiment 2 they had 30 minutes.

- The data were essentially identical for 20 and 30 minutes of study.

- Subjects performed approximately 10% better in the summary than in the text condition. Although people do better immediately than at a delay, the summary advantage is not affected by delay.

Experiment 3

- An attempt was made to equate initial learning for the text and summary conditions to see if text would be remembered longer. Subjects studied the original text for 45 minutes and the summary for only 15.

- With this modification in procedure, the initial difference in test performance was reduced to 2.5% from 11.7% in the earlier experiments.

- Text material was not better remembered at delayed tests.

Experiment 4

- Because details do not help people retain the main points, perhaps they enrich the knowledge base to facilitate *subsequent* learning.

- Chapters and summaries were divided in half, so that subjects could study the first half in text or summary form and study the second half in text or summary form. They were tested on each half separately.

- There was no advantage on the second half of learning the first half in text form; if anything, there was a slight advantage of having learned the first half in summary form.

Experiment 5

- In a final attempt to find an advantage for the original text form, subjects from the first three experiments were brought back 6 months to 1 year later and further tested on what they studied earlier.

- At this long delay, there was still some advantage for the summary condition.

Conclusions and Theoretical Interpretations

- This initial expectation had been that embellishments of main points would improve retention by providing a redundant coherent structure. However, texts seem not to do this.

- Apparently, reading a summary that helps subjects focus attention and avoid having to time-share between main points and details is a more effective way to aid learning.

What Does All this Mean?

- Much of the literature reviewed previously argued for the Elaboration Hypothesis, although the set of experiments just summarized *seems* to favor the Focus Hypothesis.

- These results are not necessarily inconsistent. It is overly simplistic to characterize the original text as just an elaborated version of the summary.

- Some of the text details are irrelevant to the main points and may only interfere.

- There is evidence that author-provided elaborations tend to be less effective than reader-provided elaborations.

- Although most author-provided details may be irrelevant and interfering, and though subjects may typically be better off providing their own elaborations, one could still conceivably construct a chapter that would be at least as effective as a summary.

- The usefulness of elaborations really depends on whether they help *constrain* the interpretation of the main point. Author-provided *constrained* elaborations can be as good as subject-provided elaborations.

- The author should also be better able to provide accurate, diverse, and interesting elaborations.

- A text that allowed for spaced or distributed practice of each main point would also help.

- An optimal organization might be a top-down structure where the reader first gets an overview of the important ideas and then successively is presented with the ideas in more detail. Newspaper stories are written this way so that people can read to the level of detail that interests them.

- This can partly replace the PQ4R method that students might use to improve retention of normal texts: Preview, Question, Read, Reflect, Recite, and Review.

2 Cognitive Coping Strategies and the Problem of "Inert Knowledge"

Carl Bereiter
The Ontario Institute for Studies in Education

Marlene Scardamalia
York University

Alfred North Whitehead (1929) decried what he called "inert ideas"—propositional knowledge that the student could express but not use. Whitehead declared that the central problem of all education was "the problem of keeping knowledge alive, of preventing it from becoming inert." His view of this problem was essentially a cognitive one; that is, he saw the problem as residing, not in the knowledge itself, considered epistemologically, but in the way this knowledge was represented in the student's mind. The "parroting" problem has long been recognized, the problem of students learning propositions by rote that were intended to be meaningful. But Whitehead saw beyond that to recognize that propositions could be comprehended and still constitute inert knowledge.

Whitehead took a large view of the sources of this problem, but, mainly, he found them in the fragmented character of the curriculum and the lack of active application, which together resulted in "the passive reception of disconnected ideas." In other words, Whitehead saw the problem of inert knowledge to arise from the way knowledge is presented to students and from the kinds of operations they are asked to perform on it. In this, also, Whitehead was in tune with contemporary cognitive notions. We think, in fact, that among educational philosophers Whitehead is particularly good reading for "cognitivists," because he shares their basic view, while considerably enriching and humanizing it.

Much of current cognitive research in education is serving to provide a theoretical basis for Whitehead's intuitions. Thus we are coming to understand more explicitly what connectedness and unconnectedness of knowledge mean psychologically and to know more about the effect that different kinds of processing have on the way knowledge is encoded and on its subsequent availability for use.

In this chapter, however, we want to go back to the "inert knowledge" problem and add a different dimension to it, one that Whitehead does not seem to have

65

treated and that may have some novelty within the current scientific context as well. The dimension is a cognitive-developmental one. We want to suggest that children may early in their school careers develop certain cognitive coping strategies that prove to be powerful enough that they continue in force and override educational efforts to get students to encode knowledge in certain ways and to perform certain operations on it. Accordingly, efforts to solve the "inert knowledge" problem may fail if they deal only with how knowledge is presented to students and what they are asked to do with respect to that knowledge. Unless direct attention is given to the coping strategies children bring to knowledge-use tasks, those strategies may defeat instructional intentions.

This is a very speculative matter at present, but there is abundant evidence from one area, expository writing, to suggest the matter is worth attending to. In this chapter, we draw on that body of evidence to develop, as far as we can, the implications of one particular coping strategy.

The plan of the chapter is as follows: The next section describes an important class of knowledge-use activities of which expository writing is one member. In the section after that, we identify a performance limitation of children that forces them to develop a special strategy for coping with the knowledge-access demands of expository writing. In the subsequent section, we develop a model of a coping strategy we call "knowledge telling" and present evidence supporting it as a description of actual cognitive behavior in students. In a final section, we discuss how school practices may not only allow this strategy to survive but even encourage it, and the effect that this may have on how knowledge is initially encoded. This chapter stops short of dealing with ways of changing cognitive coping strategies in children, because that is the topic of a companion chapter (Scardamalia & Bereiter, this volume).

EXPOSITORY WRITING AS A PARADIGM TASK FOR KNOWLEDGE USE

To say that knowledge is inert is to say that it is seldom put to use in those situations where it is potentially applicable. Research on "insight" problems (e.g., Duncker, 1945; Maier, 1930) revealed many instances of people failing to solve problems because some critical item of knowledge available to them was not brought into play. Although these special instances are relevant to the general topic, logic problems and concrete puzzle problems are not very good paradigms for everyday problems of knowledge use. They typically involve very small amounts of relevant information. Typically, moreover, the solver is forbidden to make unrestricted use of knowledge resources. In the familiar problem of getting cannibals and missionaries across a river in a small boat, for instance, it is quite out of the question to draw on one's knowledge of alternative means of crossing a river. We may describe problems of these contrived kinds as occupying knowledge-restricted problem environments. By contrast, real-life problems, of the kind to which we must attend if we are concerned about inert knowledge, are problems that occupy knowledge-unrestricted problem environments. The problem, that is, imposes no limits on the knowledge that may be brought to bear on it. Furthermore, the problem as encountered often gives little suggestion as to what knowledge may be relevant to solving it, and so the likelihood of solving it will depend much more on the characteristics of one's knowledge and of one's means for accessing it.

Even the simplest real-life problem, such as deciding where to go on a holiday, opens up vast areas of knowledge as potentially relevant. Identifying what knowledge is relevant and gaining access to it become an important part of real-life productive thinking. It is also characteristic of real-life productive thinking that the relevant knowledge is sufficiently diverse that it cannot be accessed efficiently by a top-down search. Thus, the knowledge relevant to deciding where to go on a holiday is not all accessible by starting with one's highest level knowledge about holidays and working down until appropriate specific items of knowledge have been found. Some knowledge may be "filed" under geography, some under finances, some under current events, and some may be episodic. Successful thinking will therefore require flexible access (Brown & Campione, 1981) to long-term memory stores. To the extent that people have fixed access, dependent on very specific cues, it will be difficult for them to make use of stored knowledge in coping in a flexible forward-and-backward manner with the kinds of mental tasks normally encountered in real life.

Most school tasks, however, do not pose the kinds of knowledge access demands that the tasks of everyday life do. Even when a test or homework assignment is high in Bloom's hierarchy of cognitive demands, its knowledge demands are generally confined to retrieving information dealt with in the particular course. (Fairness in grading more or less requires this.) This knowledge, moreover, is likely to be organized in a way that facilitates search—if not organized hierarchically, at least organized into learning episodes that will have some logical sequence to them. One might go farther and say that the conscientious teacher *conspires* to see to it that there is a congruity between the way students encode knowledge on acquisition and the retrieval requirements of course assignments and tests. "Teaching for the test" is an epithet applied to going to the extreme in this effort, but testing for what was intended to be taught is considered a virtue.

At the end of this chapter, we speculate on the consequences of this affinity between encoding and retrieval in school instruction. There is, however, one kind of school task where this affinity is not so close, and where, accordingly, the knowledge-retrieval demands are somewhat closer to those found in out-of-school life. This is the task of expository writing, as represented in term papers, "projects," opinion essays, and other writing assignments that are not precisely bounded as to the range of knowledge that it is appropriate to draw upon.

Expository writing, if it is not simply a disguised recall task, is a good example of problem solving in a knowledge-rich domain. Consider the primary-grade Canadian child setting out to do a paper on Canada. The task space is knowledge rich in that the child has a wealth of potentially usable knowledge of many different kinds and may rapidly acquire more by "research." Given that, for a person growing up in Canada, *Canada* is such an inclusive concept that it would subsume a large part of the child's stored experience, a top-down search is not likely to be adequate. As to whether expository writing requires problem solving, it is clear that for expert writers it does (Flower & Hayes, 1980). Expert writers put much of their planning effort into elaborating constraints, setting subgoals, and, as composition proceeds, reevaluating and adding to these. However, because writing is also an "ill-structured" task, in which the end state is largely defined by the writer, one cannot say that the task *demands* forward and backward processing in the sense that missionary and cannibal problems do—in the sense that an inadequate executive strategy will, with high probability, lead to an impasse, halting progress short of the goal. In this respect, expository writing is, again, like many other real-life tasks. Whereas planning a holiday may involve accessing varied stores of knowledge in the course of working forward and backward in relation to goals, it is possible to go at the task with simpler, forward-acting strategies, drawing only on spontaneously recalled (i.e., associatively cued) knowledge. The result will not be failure to reach a decision, but only a suboptimal decision that may nevertheless be sufficient.

Expository writing, therefore, is a normal school task that has about it many of the properties of everyday life uses of stored knowledge. Study of children's composing processes may thus give us insights into how accessible their knowledge is for use on such tasks and what kinds of strategies they employ for bringing it into use.

When knowledge access is studied in any practical context, the inquiry inevitably spreads across the boundary between memory and problem solving. This is inevitable because whenever the task environment does not provide sufficient cues for directing memory search, a person must carry out some intermediate analysis to determine what information is required, and this is by definition problem solving. Accordingly, in the discussion that follows, we do not presume to separate the problem-solving aspects of composition from the knowledge-access aspects but instead will try to draw from the area of their overlap such insights as are particularly applicable to questions of promoting knowledge acquisition in school.

Problems in Knowledge Access During Writing

With children in the elementary grades, "thinking of what to write" looms as an enormous problem from beginning to end of the composing process. They report this in interview studies (Keeney, 1975), and they reveal it behaviorally in a number of ways. When they stop writing, having produced an essay of less than 100 words on a large topic, their usual explanation is that they can think of nothing more to say. Yet it takes very little prompting to reveal that they have much more potentially usable knowledge (Bereiter & Scardamalia, 1982). Up through grade 6, protocols of children planning aloud consist of almost nothing but content generation (Burtis, Bereiter, Scardamalia, & Tetroe, 1983). Perhaps the most striking indication of the immensity of the content-search problem for children is the extent to which they seize on any procedural device offered, regardless of its putative purpose, and exploit it as a source of prompts to aid knowledge retrieval. This was true, for instance, when we gave them sentence openers like "On the other hand . . ." and "Another reason is . . . ," which were intended to provoke a more considered choice of discourse elements to use in composing. Instead, children seemed to use them simply as prods to memory, even though none of the sentence openers actually suggested any particular content. (See Scardamalia & Bereiter, this volume for a discussion of these procedural devices and how they functioned.)

Let us consider what kind of knowledge retrieval problem we are dealing with here. The student has either selected a topic within some broad category or the teacher has assigned one. In either event, the topic is presumably one about which the student has ample available knowledge. In most of our research, we have assigned opinion essay topics in the form of questions—e.g., "Should students be able to choose the subjects they study in school?"—questions on which students, even if they do not already have well-formed opinions, could be assumed to have plenty of knowledge on which to base an opinion.

The topic, however, does not normally serve as a sufficient cue for retrieval of all this knowledge. Opinion essay topics like the preceding one appear to serve primarily as cues for constructing a sentence of the form, "I think X because Y." In the most primitive compositions of primary-grade children, this sentence may constitute the entire composition. Finding an item of information to fill the slot Y requires a memory search, but evidently this search is adequately cued by the already-selected X and the topic question. At least, we never find children who are at a loss for a reason to fill slot Y, although it will sometimes be one that seems to have slot filling as its only virtue.

In developing a text beyond this point, there are two main ways that may be observed. One appears to come about through extending the discourse schema. The child may give another reason for X, or may shift to, "But I also think P because Q," or in the rare cases may explicate the link between X and Y. Once having set out these few additional discourse elements, however, the child is likely to declare he or she has nothing left to say.

The other way of developing the text is to take off on a new theme introduced in Y. If the first sentence is, "I think winter is the best time of year because you can make snowmen," the child may go on for several sentences telling about snowmen. Having exhausted that topic, however, the child will then declare the composition at an end. It is not clear whether such shifts represent abandoning a discourse schema and going off on free association, or whether they represent shifting to a different schema—to a factual essay schema. We should mention that the uncertainties on these points are not the result of having only looked at children's compositions and made guesses about what was going on mentally. We have had children compose aloud (Burtis et al., 1983; Tetroe, Bereiter, & Scardamalia, 1981), but what comes out in thinking-aloud protocols is too close to what appears on paper to shed much light on subtle questions like the present one.

In both ways of developing text, however, one is struck by the local nature of the knowledge search. It is as if the child, by a rather chancy process, locates one item of knowledge in memory and then does all the rest of the memory search in the neighborhood of that one item. Is this phenomenon peculiar to test-like writing situations? We can't venture to say, but one is reminded of de Bono's injunctions to think laterally (see Volume 1) and of the strategies employed in synectics (Gordon, 1961) to dislodge people from the content node first brought to mind by a problem. There seems to be a common human tendency to select a knowledge store first and then carry out searches within it, rather than to carry out goal-directed searches both among and within knowledge stores. In the next two sections, we look at evidence suggesting why that might be so.

Metamemorial Search.   Given the abundant evidence on how reading comprehension is influenced by knowledge the reader brings to the text (e.g., Anderson, 1978), it has seemed reasonable to suppose that the same might apply to composition—that various parameters of the written output might be influenced by the writer's knowledge of the subject. This is one of those hypotheses that in the extreme case (having some knowledge versus no knowledge whatsoever of the topic) is trivially true, and so there is a problem of identifying a range within which the hypothesis is potentially interesting.

In an effort to get at a realistic range of knowledge availability, Scardamalia, Bereiter, and Woodruff (1980) interviewed children in grades 4 and 6 and asked them to identify topics about which they knew quite a bit and topics about which they knew little. The first finding, and the one perhaps most germane to the present discussion, is that the children found this very difficult to do. We had originally planned to elicit five topics of each kind, in order to have some flexibility in selecting actual topics for composition. But most children could not produce that many. Each child planned aloud and wrote a composition on one "high-knowledge" and one "low-knowledge" topic. In planning, they generated more items of content on the "high-knowledge" topic, and when asked to name items of information about the topic that they would *not* include in their compositions, they named more of them too. But the differences, though statistically significant, were small. A third of the children could not name a single item of information on *either* kind of topic that they would not wish to include in a composition. Many of the younger children, in fact, were baffled by the question and indicated they could not imagine thinking of something about a topic and then not wanting to use it—another indication of how large the content-search problem looms for children. The compositions the children actually produced on these "high-knowledge" and "low-knowledge" topics, however, were not discriminable on any of six dimensions that we evaluated.

Children's apparent difficulty in locating topics they know much or little about suggests a failure to search memory at a high level. In any mental tasks of the kind we are dealing with in this chapter, it seems important to be able to inventory, at a high level, one's knowledge resources.

To turn back to our planning-a-holiday example, inventorying knowledge on hand is important because it will permit a consideration of the kinds of information you might draw on in planning, and because it may indicate gaps in knowledge that need to be filled before planning can proceed. If you are not free to do research, you might rule out a place like the Azores, for instance, as a possible destination, simply on grounds that a preliminary survey indicated you didn't know enough about them to make an intelligent decision. Such memory searches, we can be sure, are not exhaustive. That would be altogether impractical in any knowledge-rich domain. It also seems unlikely that they would take place by sampling, although we can't be certain (cf. Landauer, 1975). It *seems* that what we are able to do is look down from different high-level memory nodes and make rapid global assessments of the knowledge subsumed under them—how much there is, how complete it is, how likely it is to contain material relevant to the task at hand.

Let us accept the premise that skilled adults are able to do something functionally equivalent to this "looking down from a node." Whether the actual process is anything like that or whether it is, for instance, more like spinning the dial of a multiband radio to get a general idea of the amount and kind of activity on a particular band, we cannot speculate, although it seems a matter worth speculation. (The most relevant speculations we know of come from Bransford, McCarrell, Franks, & Nitsch, 1977. Although the "feeling of knowing" or FOK phenomenon is obviously relevant to the issue, all the research we are aware of deals with FOK for specific items following retrieval failures. See Gruneberg, 1978.)

To distinguish this high-level memory search from the normal kind, we may call it *metamemorial search*. Although not wishing to contribute to metapollution, we think the term is appropriate. The search yields knowledge about knowledge. It does not yield knowledge for direct use in the task at hand. It seems likely, however, that metamemorial search does more than yield knowledge. It probably also serves a priming or attuning function (Bransford et al., 1977), boosting the accessibility of those memory stores judged potentially usable.

In another paper (Bereiter & Scardamalia, 1982), we have tried to make the case that, within the language realms, metamemorial search is peculiar to composition. It is not normally required in conversation and so it is not learned by children through their oral language experience. It is not needed because of the rich cueing of memory provided by conversational exchange and because the unpredictable course of topic shifts in conversation makes it impractical to carry out extended searches of memory. The same argument can be extended to other productive thinking activities. The need for metamemorial search arises when one is understanding an extended course of solitary directed thought. When thinking goes on as a joint activity, people can start out cold and activate each other's knowledge stores through the spontaneous effect of things they say. Developing ability at sustained thought, however, would seem to require just what written composition requires—active approach to one's own memory, which includes identifying and activating knowledge stores that one intends to draw on.

How might children learn to do this? Valerie Anderson devised a simple instructional technique that appears to induce a practical inventorying and activating of memory stores. The technique consists simply of having children produce, in advance of writing on a topic, a list of words they think they might use in the composition. In an experimental test, after 12 hours of practice in various genres, this treatment was shown to double the overall output of words in compositions and to triple the number of uncommon words, which we took as an index of content variety (Anderson, Bereiter, & Smart, 1980).

The treatment could be termed brainstorming, but evidently not any kind of brainstorming will do. In earlier pilot work, Robert Sandieson had tried having children list ideas, in typical brainstorming fashion. But children seemed to find generating content in this way about as hard as ordinary writing and, in fact, they frequently slipped into ordinary writing, simply putting down continuous text in list form. As we see it, the trick is to get children to address their memory stores at a suitably high level. With a procedure in which they wrote down whole ideas, they slipped from metamemorial search down to a direct search for details of content. But seemingly, by limiting the task to putting down single words, this "downsliding" (Collins & Gentner, 1980) is avoided and the children stick to accessing relatively high-level nodes.

The Anderson et al. experiment suggests that it may be fairly easy to teach children ways of attaining more flexible access to their memory stores, so that they can retrieve a greater variety of task-relevant knowledge. This would be a worthwhile accomplishment, but it does not ensure a goal-directed search of memory that would enable children to retrieve the particular items of knowledge needed to serve a particular purpose. To do that requires that memory search be carried out under the direction of a problem-solving strategy. In the next section, we consider a composing strategy that enables students to avoid the more problematic aspects of memory search.

The Knowledge-Telling Strategy

The reader may have had an experience that both of us recall having had as students. In an essay examination, you discover that you don't have the knowledge necessary to answer one of the questions. Instead of leaving the question blank, you write down whatever you do know about the topic of the question, even though it in no way constitutes an answer. When the examination paper is returned, you are surprised to find that your response received a middling mark, whereas you had expected at best a charity point or two.

From later experience as markers of examination papers, we can understand why such bluffing passes without condemnation. It is only doing deliberately what many students do unwittingly as a standard mode of response. They produce information that is on the topic and that is influenced by the form of the question, so that the response has a kind of genre appropriateness as well as topical appropriateness. But it doesn't answer the question; that is, it doesn't achieve the intended goal of explaining such and such, specifying the difference between this and that, or whatever the question might demand. Instead, it *tells what the writer knows* within a domain demarcated by key words in the question and by the question's general form. Accordingly, we call the strategy that gives rise to this type of response the *knowledge-telling strategy.*

We explicate a first approximation model of this strategy and indicate how the strategy circumvents the difficulties of knowledge search described previously. The general phenomenon illustrated in examination writing has been recognized from other viewpoints. Flower's (1979) characterization of "writer-based" prose is compatible with the model we sketch. "Writer-based" prose, according to Flower, is dominated by the way knowledge is represented in the writer's own memory instead of being shaped to the needs of the reader who will be trying to take this knowledge up. Britton, Burgess, Martin, McLeod, and Rosen (1975) have identified "expressive" writing as a kind of writing directed by internal needs and developmentally prior to "transactional" writing, which is writing directed toward external objectives. Similarly, Graves has noted what he calls "all about" writing, in which children record whatever information comes to mind about a composition topic (Graves & Giacobbe, 1982).

Analyses of thinking-aloud protocols have been valuable in revealing what poor writers *don't* do that expert writers do. Mainly, they do not, to nearly so great an extent as experts, elaborate goals or consider actions in relation to goals (Flower & Hayes, 1980). That much is certainly consistent with the brief characterization we have already given of a knowledge-telling strategy, but it leaves it still unknown how such a strategy actually works.

In Figure 2.1 we present a rough model of knowledge-telling strategy—rough in the sense that it describes a process that could generate products having the main attributes we see in examination papers and student essays. We first explicate the model and later indicate evidence suggesting its fit to reality. It may be noted at this point, however, that parts of the process are assumed to go on unconsciously and therefore are not to be apparent in writers' self-reports.

The knowledge-telling strategy requires that two things be extracted from an essay examination question or writing assignment. One is a set of descriptors drawn from key lexical items in the assignment, and the other is information to guide the choice of a schema for the text to be produced. These schemata would be comparable to story grammar schemata, representing such discourse forms as explanation, thesis and defense, comparison and contrast, etc. Their precise nature need not concern us here, nor need we assume invariance across persons or genres (Bereiter & Scardamalia, 1982). We do assume, however, that they provide general types of elements to be used in discourse, that some of these elements may be necessary and some optional, and that some may be reusable in the same discourse and some may not be (like concluding statement).

Discourse generation is set in motion when STM (short-term memory) is examined for an element that matches the selected schema requirement and the

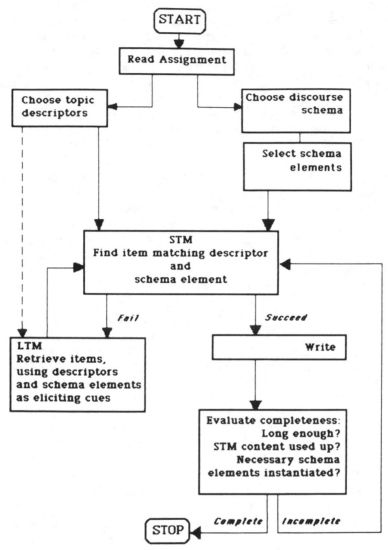

FIG. 2.1.   A model of the knowledge-telling strategy as applied in expository writing.

descriptor (or chunked descriptor set). One might suppose that at the start nothing would be in STM waiting to be tested. That may often be the case, but we assume (as suggested by the broken line in Fig. 2.1) a more direct route from descriptors to long-term memory (via the limbic system, if one choose) that may already have produced spontaneous recall of revelant material to STM. This would be especially likely if the descriptor happened to have emotion-laden associations. If, however, no match to requirements is found in STM, new items are retrieved from LTM (long-term memory). Both the descriptors and the schema elements will serve as cues for retrieval. (For evidence that schema elements can serve as cues for content retrieval, see Bereiter, Scardamalia, Anderson, & Smart, 1980; Paris, Scardamalia, & Bereiter, 1980). When an item has been found that matches both descriptors and schema element, it is translated into text, and the process repeats until the text is judged finished.

Figure 2.1 does not show what happens if search of LTM keeps failing to bring forth a matching item. Different recourses are available, and we have seen evidence of each one being used. One is to choose a new schema element, another is to go back to the assignment and search for additional descriptors (Flower & Hayes, 1980, note this as a common practice of novice writers when stuck), and another is to mine what one has already written for eliciting cues.

On first inspection, it may not be obvious why this would be called a model of an immature or inadequate strategy. In fact, the strategy is adequate for many school tasks. It is well suited to writing assignments of the "What I Did on My Summer Vacation" or "An Interesting Character" type and also to essay examination questions like the old college literature standby, "Discuss the use of such-and-such in the work of so-and-so." These are assignments in which key words, together with contextual clues as to the desired genre, are sufficient to make the model work. The model will work even better if the topic is one that evokes strong associations, or if the teacher has taken the trouble through prewriting activities to prime relvant stores in long-term memory. Then the ready flow of material to STM will ensure fluent and sometimes quite coherent and expressive writing.

What the knowledge-telling strategy lacks, however, is any provision for goals. (This shows up in Fig. 2.1 at the bottom of the chart, with the rather paltry sct of criteria for testing whether the discourse is finished; lacking goal attainment as a standard of completeness, only technical criteria can be used.) The lack of procedures for testing content against goals means that this strategy is inadequate for any task of the kind defined at the beginning of this chapter—tasks that require backward as well as forward processing and for which strategically directed assessing of different knowledge stores is required.

The model shown in Fig. 2.1 depicts an "ideal" strategy. One would expect real subjects to show greater or lesser amounts of goal-directed processing tied into the basic knowledge-telling scheme. But a variety of findings suggest to us that the model as shown is not a bad approximation to the actual behavior of many school-age children. First, there is the absence of goal-related planning in their thinking-aloud protocols, even when they have been provided with a video-taped model and cues for thinking about goals (Burtis et al., 1983). Second, there is evidence that production can be influenced by controlling the choice of schema elements (Paris et al., 1980). Third, there is the lack of internal constraint in their texts, even though they can detect its lack in other texts. One sentence is typically as deletable as another (Scardamalia, Cattani, Turkish, & Bereiter, 1981). This lack of interconnectedness is consistent with a forward-acting, serial-generative process like the one modeled. Fourth, there is all the evidence cited in the preceding section about the primacy of the content-search problem. The knowledge-telling strategy is a sort of no-frills system for digging out usable content and getting it down on paper as efficiently as possible. Finally, there is the remarkable disinclination of children to make other than cosmetic revisions of text (Nold, 1981; Scardamalia & Bereiter, 1983). The model shown in Fig. 2.1 contains no provisions for revision, but, what is more to the point, there is no apparent function that substantive revision could have in the model unless the whole model were overhauled to incorporate goal directedness.

The model seems to fit a variety of observables parsimoniously and not to be incompatible with any observations we are aware of. For purposes of advancing the present argument, we need not press the issue of the model's validity any farther than that. Accordingly, we proceed to the final section, where we treat this model as describing a disquieting type of school outcome.

THE ROLE OF KNOWLEDGE TELLING IN KNOWLEDGE ACQUISITION

Viewed pragmatically, the most interesting thing about the cognitive strategy depicted in Fig. 2.1 is that it is virtually worthless for any purpose other than getting through certain kinds of school assignments. There are few instances in real life where telling what you know, within a few topical and discourse constraints, is called for. Sustaining small talk with a taciturn partner is one. Serving as a witness is another. Both instances are revealing, in that they involve suspending the usual purposefulness of discourse. In both cases it is intentionality at the semantic level that is suspended—in one case because the construction of meaning is subordinated to fluency, and in the other because (if the witness is being fully cooperative) intentionality is turned over to the questioner. In all normal forms of discourse—and this applies to private monologue as much as to communicative expression—there is problem solving or goal directedness of some sort that requires that knowledge be sought and manipulated in ways that the knowledge-telling strategy does not provide for. We can therefore justly say that knowledge that can only be brought into use through the knowledge-telling strategy is inert knowledge in Whitehead's sense.

This out-of-school uselessness is not by itself deplorable. Schooling, being a very special enterprise, is entitled to demand skills that are of no use elsewhere, provided they have instrumental value in promoting learning that is of use elsewhere. (As an example, one might think of the skills children are sometimes taught in grouping and regrouping popsicle sticks—skills of no value in themselves, but instrumental in some methods of teaching arithmetic.) Our concern about the knowledge-telling strategy is that it appears to be seriously counterproductive within the school context—not just useless but harmful. How harmful, though, we cannot really tell, and we must speculate with caution.

A simple knowledge-telling strategy is obviously a poor strategy for writing, but it may be capable of refinement, without radical change, to the point where it reliably produces at least mediocre writing (Bereiter & Scardamalia, 1983).

Whereas the knowledge-telling strategy is surely something for teachers of writing to be concerned about, it is not as a writing strategy per se that it seems most worrisome. It is more worrisome as a strategy that, if students use it "across the curriculum," may come to influence very broadly how they manipulate and perhaps even how they encode propositional knowledge.

The possibilities for a knowledge-telling strategy to have an effect on the actual encoding of knowledge are twofold. The first has to do with what is sometimes glamorously referred to as "language as a way of knowing" (Nystrand, 1977). When we think of knowledge stored in memory we tend, these days, to think of it as situated in three-dimensional space, with vertical and horizontal connections between sites (Wickelgren, 1979). Learning is thought to add not only new elements to memory but also new connections, and it is the richness and structure of these connections that would seem, as Whitehead said in his own way, to spell the difference between inert and usable knowledge. On this account, the knowledge-telling strategy is educationally faulty because it specifically avoids the forming of connections between previously separated knowledge sites. An intriguing extension of this idea comes from Gazzaniga and LeDoux (1978), who hypothesize that not all memory contents are internally connectable, so that the mind may have to form relationships among memory contents by observing their manifestations in the integrated external behavior of the organism (see also Luria, 1973, p. 31). In other words, the way the mind gets to know itself is not altogether different from the way it gets to know other minds. To the extent this is true, expository writing and similar forms of expression have an even more vital role to play in knowledge acquisition than even the most ardent advocates of the rhetoric of invention (e.g., Young, Becker, & Pike, 1970) have supposed. Knowledge telling, on this account, would be severely limiting to the growth of knowledge because it only externalizes mental content that already is easily amenable to internal connection.

The other way in which the knowledge-telling strategy may influence knowledge acquisition is through a social route. This is the route whereby the instructional system adapts to the cognitive strategies of the student rather than the reverse. (Presumably both kinds of adaptation must go on in any self-maintaining social system.) What we are suggesting, in brief, is that over the years school practices for presenting, reviewing, and assessing knowledge may have accommodated to students' cognitive coping strategies so that finally what is taught is what the knowledge-telling strategy is equipped to handle—and that is, precisely, inert knowledge.

Consider the folllowing list of school practices, each quite justifiable in its own right, yet each of which in some way plays into the knowledge-telling strategy and quite inadvertently encourages its persistence:

1. Testing only on content taught in the course.
2. Reviewing by identifying superordinate categories of the specific items called for on the examination thus priming those knowledge stores that will serve for knowledge telling.

3. Presenting test items in an order corresponding to the temporal sequence of topics in the course, which is a boon to those who store course content episodically.

4. Teaching concepts in hierarchically ordered fashion. (Who could object to this? But it does mean that recall cued by descriptors will suffice, without the need for goal-directed search.)

5. Phrasing test items to specify the discourse schema as in compare and contrast questions.

6. Referring to course content by its temporal connections (what we studied last week, etc.).

7. Assigning long course papers calling for assembling knowledge on a single topic such as women's rights, the Industrial Revolution, Captain Cook, etc. (Clearly an opportunity for integrating knowledge, but also an assignment tailor made for knowledge telling.)

8. Teaching topic outlining and procedures for putting content items on separate note cards and arranging them, which is valuable for some writers, but permits purely formal arrangements of items without need to have a goal.

9. Assigning topics that "turn students on" and therefore provoke a ready flow of spontaneously recalled content.

10. Using "prewriting" activities—films, discussions, interviews, and the like—to activate knowledge stores or provide fresh new knowledge for students to draw on in writing.

11. Giving passing marks to students who don't actually address presented problems but who "show that they learned something in the course."

Let us repeat, these are all justifiable practices and some are virtually indispensable. Our only point is that they are all compatible with a knowledge-telling strategy. One would be hard put to come up with a comparable list of instructional practices that make it rough on students who use this strategy. Thus, it is not unreasonable to conjecture that these school practices have survived at least in part because they accommodate the cognitive coping strategies of students. But to the extent that school practices simply accommodate, they defeat their intended educational purposes and become practices for instilling inert knowledge.

One danger of attributing to children general coping strategies that defeat educational efforts is that it can easily slip over into blaming the child for educational shortcomings. When someone attributes to children a naive strategy for doing balance beam problems, there is no implication that the child really ought to know better. But when one attributes to them a general strategy that subverts teachers' efforts to confront them with intellectual challenges, then one is dangerously close to implying that children are mentally lazy and refuse to be educated.

We want to make it clear that no such implication is meant or endorsed. We see the knowledge-telling strategy being carried out by children who, as far as we know, have the best of intentions and think they are giving their best to the educational enterprise. They did not develop the knowledge-telling strategy as a way to avoid work but as a way to do work that, without such a strategy, would have been beyond them. Knowledge telling is not a conscious strategy and they have no reason or means to evaluate it. Because it goes on working, they go on using it; that's what one expects of adaptive organisms. But its effectiveness is all in the short run, whereas in the long run, it is bound to be a losing strategy. Children cannot be expected to know this, and so it is the responsibility of educators to know this and try to do something about it.

REFERENCES

Anderson, R.C. (1978). Schema-directed processes in language comprehension. In A. M. Lesgold, J. W. Pellegrino, S. D. Fokkema, & R. Glaser (Eds.), *Cognitive psychology and instruction* (pp. 67–82). New York: Plenum Press.

Anderson, V., Bereiter, C., & Smart, D. (1980). *Activation of semantic networks in writing: Teaching students how to do it themselves.* Paper presented at the meeting of the American Educational Research Association, Boston.

Bereiter, C., & Scardamalia, M. (1982). From conversation to composition: The role of instruction in a developmental process. In R. Glaser (Ed.), *Advances in instructional psychology* (Vol. 2, pp. 1–64). Hillsdale, NJ: Lawrence Erlbaum Associates.

Bereiter, C., & Scardamalia, M. (1983). Does learning to write have to be so difficult? In A. Freedman, I. Pringle, & J. Yalden (Eds.), *Learning to write: First language, second language* (pp. 20–23). New York: Longman Inc.

Bereiter, C., Scardamalia, M., Anderson, V., & Smart, D. (1980). *An experiment in teaching abstract planning in writing.* Paper presented at the meeting of the American Educational Research Association, Boston.

Bransford, J. D., McCarrell, N. S., Franks, J. J., & Nitsch, K. E. (1977). Toward unexplaining memory. In R. Shaw and J. Bransford (Eds.), *Perceiving, acting, and knowing: Toward an ecological society* (pp. 431–446). Hillsdale, NJ: Lawrence Erlbaum Associates.

Britton, J., Burgess, T., Martin, N., McLeod, A., & Rosen, H. (1975). *The development of writing abilities* (pp. 11–18). London: Macmillan Education.

Brown, A. L., & Campione, J. C. (1981). Inducing flexible thinking: A problem of access. In M. Friedman, J. P. Das, & N. O'Connor (Eds.), *Intelligence and learning.* (pp. 515–529). New York: Plenum.

Burtis, P. J., Bereiter, C., Scardamalia, M., & Tetroe, J. (1983). The development of planning in writing. In G. Wells & B. M. Kroll (Eds.), *Explorations in the development of writing* (pp. 153–174). Chichester, England: Wiley.

Collins, A., & Gentner, D. (1980). A framework for a cognitive theory of writing. In L. W. Gregg & E. Steinberg (Eds.), *Cognitive processes in writing.* (pp. 51–72). Hillsdale, NJ: Lawrence Erlbaum Associates.

Duncker, K. (1945). On problem solving. *Psychological Monographs, 58* (5, Whole No. 270).

Flower, L. (1979, September). Writer-based prose: A cognitive basis for problems in writing. *College English, 41*(1), 19–37.

Flower, L., & Hayes, J. R. (1980). The cognition of discovery: Defining a rhetorical problem. *College Composition and Communication, 31*(2), 21–32.

Gazzaniga, M. S., & LeDoux, J. E. (1978). *The integrated mind.* New York: Plenum Press.

Gordon, W. (1961). *Synectics: The development of creative capacity.* New York: Harper & Row.

Graves, D.H., & Giacobbe, M. E. (1982). Questions for teachers who wonder if their writers change. *Language Arts, 59,* 495–503.

Gruneberg, M. M. (1978). The feeling of knowing, memory blocks and memory aids. In M. M. Gruneberg & P. Morris (Eds.), *Aspects of memory* (pp. 186–209). London: Methuen.

Keeney, M. L. (1975). *An investigation of what intermediate-grade children say about the writing of stories.* Unpublished doctoral dissertation, Lehigh University, Bethlehem, Pennsylvania (Order No. 76–5091)

Landauer, T. K. (1975). Memory without organization: Properties of a model with random storage and undirected retrieval. *Cognitive Psychology, 7,* 495–531.

Luria, A. R. (1973). *The working brain: An introduction of neuropsychology.*London: Penguin Books.

Maier, N. R. F. (1930). Reasoning in humans: I. On direction. *Journal of Comparative Psychology, 10,* 115–143.

Nold, E. W. (1981). Revising. In C. H. Frederiksen, & J. F. Dominic (Eds.), *Writing: The nature, development and teaching of written communication* (pp. 67–79). Hillsdale, NJ: Lawrence Erlbaum Associates.

Nystrand, M. (1977). *Language as a way of knowing: A book of readings.* Toronto: The Ontario Institute for Studies in Education.

Paris, P., Scardamalia, M., & Bereiter, C. (1980). *Discourse schemata as knowledge and as regulators of text production.* Paper presented at the meeting of the American Educational Research Association, Boston.

Scardamalia, M., & Bereiter, C. (1983). The development of evaluative, diagnostic, and remedial capabilities in children's composing. In M. Martlew (Ed.), *The psychology of written language: A developmental approach* (pp. 67–95). London: Wiley.

Scardamalia, M., Bereiter, C., & Woodruff, E. (1980). *The effects of content knowledge on writing.* Paper presented at the meeting of the American Educational Research Association, Boston.

Scardamalia, M., Cattani, C., Turkish, L., & Bereiter, C. (1981). *Part–whole relationships in text planning.* Paper presented at the meeting of the American Educational Research Association, Los Angeles.

Tetroe, J., Bereiter, C., & Scardamalia, M. (1981). *How to make a dent in the writing process.* Paper presented at the meeting of the American Educational Research Association, Los Angeles.

Whitehead, A. N. (1929). *The aims of education.* New York: Macmillan.

Wickelgren, W. A. (1979). Chunking and consolidation: A theoretical synthesis of semantic networks, configuring in conditioning, S–R versus cognitive learning, normal forgetting, the amnesic syndrome, and the hippocampal arousal system. *Psychological Review, 86*(1), 44–60.

Young, R. E., Becker, A. L., & Pike, K. E. (1970). *Rhetoric: Discovery and change.* New York: Harcourt, Brace, & World.

3 The Social Context and Socialization Variables as Factors in Thinking and Learning

Anderson J. Franklin
The City College and The Graduate School
of the City University of New York

Researchers in thinking and learning place importance on models representing general processes of learning. As a result, many studies aim to substantiate the validity of assumptions and hypotheses within these models. I believe that the consequence of this orientation has been the neglect of population characteristics as major variables in model building. Such population characteristics include ethnicity, sex, age, and concommitant social contexts. This phenomenon is illustrated by research reports that treat subject characteristics as incidental to the formulation of hypotheses. It is my contention that another perspective on thinking and learning would emerge from both a more serious theoretical inclusion of population characteristics and the development of models based upon observation of behavior within its natural, social context. Stated simplistically, I am advocating that we develop models of thinking and learning as they are manifested in populations rather than study how populations manifest our models of thinking and learning. Making this conceptual shift is not easy. Likewise, the testing of universal hypotheses and the building of research designs is more problematic in this conceptual framework.

In an effort to move toward this conceptual shift, my research derives materials and hypothesized outcomes from the observation of mnemonic processes operating in the natural daily activities of inner-city adolescents. I selected a social context for analysis that reflects the unique culture and socialization experiences of black inner-city youth. By social context, I mean those social settings in which conditions of interaction consistently yield a prescribed set of behaviors. For me, this became the informal settings for youth such as school hallways, street corners, discos, pizza parlors, etc., where the form of communication entails facility in the use of slang. The use of slang is an essential aspect of socialization into the peer group. From my observation, the dynamics of using slang manifest many of the issues we are trying to explore with our models of memory. Certainly word association, code switching, encoding, storage, retrieval, short- and long-term memory can be recognized as activities engaged in by youth employing this communicative style. I became interested in exploring how slang, within given social contexts, affects research on fundamental cognitive processes.

In psychology, basic research in memory includes the study of verbal learning processes. The greater ability to use class membership of words during learning is considered representative of acquired higher order learning skills. In his well-publicized *Harvard Educational Review* article (1969) and other published papers (e.g., Jensen & Frederiksen, 1973), Jensen has argued that lower class and/or black people "have" less organizing capacity than their middle-class, white counterparts. It is presumed that black children apply relatively more "level I," that is, rote memory, skills to basic recall tasks. Relatively small performance differences between randomly constructed and categorizable lists, plus relatively little semantic clustering in recall by black children, constitute the evidence for this conclusion. Jensen's interpretation of the significance of free recall data has not gone unchallenged. However, the challenges have not been as effective as they should be because they have stayed within the general traditions of standard work in the development of memory. They have not taken account of important issues that enter into intergroup or cross-cultural comparisons (see Cole, Gay, Glick, & Sharp, 1971, Chapters 4 and 7).

In their book on *Culture and Thought,* Cole and Scribner (1974) note "that a major source of group differences is in the ways of classifying the world that characterize a given cultural group" (p. 99). Central to the verbal-memory task is the group's (or individual's) perception of those attributes and rules that determine class membership. A major unwarranted assumption in all the comparative studies of memory is that category norms elicited from college students are representative of adolescents from social groups not generally found in the college population (Jensen & Frederiksen, 1973; Mensing & Traxler, 1973; Schultz, Charness, & Berman, 1973). In view of the extensive evidence of lexical and syntactic differences among subcultures in the United States (e.g., Cazden, John, & Hymes, 1972; Dillard, 1972; Hall & Freedle, 1973), the use of published norms for comparative studies represents a glaring violation of good research principles. There is abundant evidence to show that word frequency affects recall; yet no provisions are made for assuring equivalence of word frequency across groups, nor for assuring that items within categories are equally related to the category names. In fact, in the absence of any directly relevant data, it seems most reasonable to assume that different groups (e.g., Blacks, Chicanos) do *not* have the same lexical structure. Before basing conclusions about the differential existence of higher order cognitive capacities on differences between categorizable and noncategorizable lists and on the amount of category clustering, equivalence of materials is an absolutely necessary starting point.

The studies described here are aimed at providing more *valid* data upon which to base statements about ethnic and social class differences in mnemonic skills. The present series of studies was undertaken to first develop category norms for black and white adolescent populations and to then use those norms to form sociolinguistically equivalent lists that could be employed to assess group differences in recall and clustering. When words and categories that are more familiar to black students are included on a recall task, an advantage for blacks over whites in recall and clustering may well result. The first experiment in this series was designed to test this hypothesis by incorporating category instances elicited from black adolescents into a recall list administered to black and white high school students.

We started our investigation by collecting data from 9th and 12th graders on the composition of 25 common categories found in existing category norms (Postman & Keppel, 1970). In this and subsequent studies, subjects were selected from New York area high schools to represent four population groups: black lower class, black middle class, white lower class, and white middle class. Educational opportunity (private vs. public education) also varied.

In our analysis of these data, we were concerned with several points. First, we wanted to establish the group norm for each group—e.g., the relative frequency with which each category member occurs in response to the category name. Second, we were concerned with replicating the work of Jensen and Frederiksen, using stimulus materials tailored to each group. Specifically, we constructed categorizable and noncategorizable lists for each subject group based upon their responses to the category names. By using content variations in materials, we were able to determine whether performance varies correspondingly. Moreover, by sampling different adolescent age levels, the contention that development is stabilized during this period could be empirically tested. These issues represent the major common concern of the verbal-memory experiments described in the following sections. Each experiment provided additional information in this regard by incorporating slight modifications in one or more variables or procedures.

EXPERIMENT 1[1]

As mentioned before, the purpose of this experiment was to test the hypothesis that an advantage for blacks over whites in recall and clustering would be found when using words and categories that had been generated (or standardized) by black students.

---

[1]Experiments I and III were also reported in Boykin, A. W., Franklin, A. J., & Yates, J. F. (Eds.), *Research directions of black psychologists.* New York: Russell Sage Foundation/Basic Books, 1979.

Method

Subjects.   Subjects in the recall test were 34 adolescents living in the New York metropolitan area. Of these, 17 were black students attending an alternative high school set up in an impoverished area of Brooklyn to accommodate students with poor school performance or unacceptable social behavior in their regular schools. This black sample included 9 females and 8 males with an average age of 18. All black students were placed in the 10th or 11th grade, although the work assigned to them was drawn from the entire range of the normal high school curriculum.

White subjects were drawn from the 11th grade of an integrated parochial school for girls located in central Manhattan. Their average age was 16 years. All white subjects were female.

Materials.   To provide a set of category instances that would be specifically tailored to the experiences and categories of urban black adolescents, 75 black teenagers were interviewed in their neighborhoods in central Brooklyn. With each subject in this separate sample, the experimenter went through a list of categories assumed to be high in interest and familiarity for black adolescents and then asked for five instances of each category. The use of slang terms was encouraged. The three categories for which the greatest commonality was obtained for exemplars (dances, soul food, drugs) were selected for use in the recall task. These categories and five commonly cited instances for each composed the Black categories that made up half of the recall list.

The other half of the recall list consisted of the five words most frequently given by college students in response to each of three categories from the Battig and Montague (1969) norms that have been widely used in previous free recall experiments. These category instances, which are referred to as Standard categories, appear along with the Black category items in Table 3.1.

Five randomized orders of the recall list were constructed with the sole restriction that no two items from the same category appeared contiguously in the list. Subjects in Experiment 1 were presented with a different ordering of the list on each recall trial.

Procedure.   Subjects were informed that they were participating in a study of memory, that they would be given a list of words to remember and recall in any order they liked, and that the experimenter would go through the list and test their recall a total of five times. The recall list was presented orally at a rate of approximately 2 seconds per word. After the experimenter had read the complete list, the subject verbally recalled as many words as he or she could remember. The procedure was repeated for a total of five trials.

TABLE 3.1
Conceptual Categories and Member Items

BLACK CATEGORIES		
I Drugs	*II Dances*	*III Soul Food*
smoke	bump	chicken
coke	latin	greens
ups	grind	corn bread
downs	robot	chittlins
acid	truckin'	ribs

STANDARD CATEGORIES		
IV Tools	*V Utensils*	*VI Clothing*
drill	spoon	shirt
axe	plate	hat
saw	cup	socks
file	glass	pants
hammer	pan	shoes

Results

Measures of interest were number of words recalled and level of categorical clustering, as indexed by z-scores (Frankel & Cole, 1971). A preliminary comparison of scores for male and female students within the black sample indicated that the sexes did not differ (at the $p < .05$ level) in either number of words recalled ($t(15) = 0.26$) or amount of clustering ($t(15) = 0.40$). Consequently, scores for black males and females combined were compared to those of white females in all subsequent analyses.

An analysis of variance conducted on the scores for the full 30-item list showed a steady improvement in recall over trials ($F(4,128) = 35.50$) as displayed graphically in Fig. 3.1. The recall advantage of black students over white students did not attain significance overall ($F(1, 32) = 1.66$). However, there was a significant interaction between race and trial with black students' recall improving more over trials than that of white students ($F(4, 128) = 4.37$).

A comparable analysis on the z-scores measuring categorical clustering indicated that black students clustered more than white students ($F(1, 32) = 9.63$), clustering increased over trials ($F(4, 128) = 12.43$), and the increase in organization over trials was greater for blacks than whites ($F(4, 128) = 3.02$). The graphic display of these scores in Fig. 3.2 shows that by the final recall trial, black students were obtaining clustering scores that were more than double those attained by white students.

In order to check whether the deficit of white students in clustering (and, to a lesser extent, in recall on later trials) was confined to the Black categories, t-tests were used to compare performance on the two halves of the list (Black

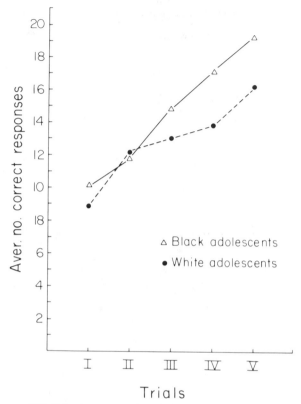

FIG. 3.1   Average number of correct responses per trial.

categories and Standard categories). The mean total recall and clustering score for each type of category by ethnic group are shown in Table 3.2. As is evident from an inspection of the means, white students' level of recall was not better for Standard than for Black categories, (t (32) = 0.92). Although whites' clustering scores appeared somewhat higher for Standard than for Black categories, this difference was not significant (t (32) = 1.56). Similar comparisons conducted on the black students' scores showed no differences between Black and Standard categories in recall (t (32) = 1.23) or clustering (t (32) = 0.71) scores. Sublist score comparisons between races showed that blacks clustered significantly more than whites on the Black (t (32) = 3.58) but not the Standard (t (32) = 1.76) categories.

Correlations between level of recall and amount of clustering showed a strong relationship for blacks in both Black (r = .83) and Standard categories (r = .54). White students' clustering and recall were not positively related for Standard categories (r = .20) or Black categories (r = .08).

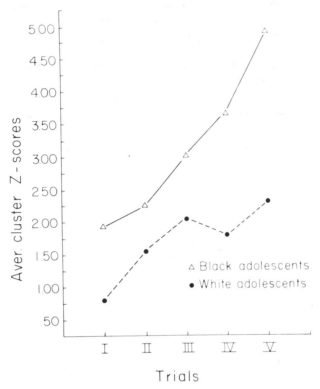

FIG. 3.2   Average cluster z-scores per trial.

Discussion

When a list containing items selected for their categorical relatedness for black adolescents was used in a recall task, white adolescents showed a marked deficit in categorical clustering. Applying Jensen's logic to the results of this study

TABLE 3.2
Mean Recall and Clustering Over Five Trials, by Race and Category Type

| | Black Students n = 17 | | White Students n = 17 | |
	Mean Recall	Z-Scores	Mean Recall	Z-Scores
Black categories	39.24	3.11	34.00	.29
Standard categories	34.24	2.38	31.00	1.00

without regard for the list derivation procedure would lead to the conclusion that the white adolescents in the present sample were deficient in terms of conceptual ability. Clustering, the index of conceptual performance (or Level II intelligence) used in Jensen's earlier work, was greater in the recall of black teenagers with poor academic records than in the recall of white parochial school students. However, any conclusions about differences in conceptual ability are clearly unwarranted because many of the list items were probably more familiar and categorizable for blacks. The most important implication of these results is that the outcome of such experiments is going to depend on the particular materials selected and the congruence of those materials with subjects' conceptual categories.

A cautionary note to be kept in mind when considering group differences in clustering scores is that the categorical clustering scores per se do not reveal the particular strategies a group of low clusterers is using. Jensen had interpreted low clustering scores as evidence that subjects are learning a list in a rote or purely associative manner. However, it is also possible that subjects with low categorical clustering scores are organizing the list according to conceptual structures other than those built into the list and measured by the experimenter. In support of this hypothesis, Scribner (1974) has shown that if free recall organization is measured both in terms of categorical clusters and in terms of personal groupings used by individual subjects when asked to sort the recall items, the latter measure often reveals more organization in subjects' recall than does the former. The probably unfamiliarity of many of the Black category instances for the white subjects in the present study raises the question of whether white students were trying to organize their recall along some other lines. In the present case, however, measures of idiosyncratic groupings (Pellegrino's 1971, index of intertrial repetitions) failed to reveal any consistency in the patterns of word groupings in white students' recall over successive trials.

An unanticipated finding was the possibiity that the presence of a certain proportion of unfamiliar categories on the list apparently depressed whites' tendency to apply adequately organizational processes even to familiar categories. Previous recall studies using partially categorizable lists (Forrester & King, 1971; Steinmetz & Battig, 1969) had concentrated on demonstrating that recall was greater for the categorizable than for the noncategorizable portion of the list and had not explored the possibility that the presence of some noncategorizable items may impede organization of categorizable ones. Such an effect would be important within the context of evaluating ethnic-group differences in clustering and recall, because the whites' predicament in Experiment 1 may be analogous to that faced by children of nonwhite ethnic groups when they are given lists drawn from standard categories. Many of the list items and categories are probably familiar to them, but some may be unfamiliar, which may result in impaired performance with the list as a whole. Drawing conclusions on the basis of differences in clustering or recall for groups whose relative familiarity with the list items is unknown becomes particularly hazardous in light of the possibility of such "half-categorizable" list effects. Experiment 2 was conducted to obtain clearer evidence for the hypothesis that the presence of some noncategorizable items on a list would impede organization of categorizable items.

EXPERIMENT 2

The performance of the white adolescents in Experiment 1 was consistent with the hypothesis that a certain proportion of items on a recall list that cannot be readily assigned to familiar categories will hinder a subject's performance with those items on the list that he or she *can* easily categorize. However, there was neither direct evidence that the Black category instances were noncategorizable for the white students in Experiment 1 nor the necessary control condition to establish whites' clustering level for an all-categorizable list. To get a clearer test of this "half-categorizable" list hypothesis, standard category norms were used to create a mixed list, half of which was categorizable and half of which was not. Recall on the categorizable portion of the mixed list was expected to be poorer and to show less organization than performance on the same set of items embedded within an all-categorizable list.

Method

Subjects.   In order to test for organization effects with a sample similar to that developed with the standard category norms, 40 white college-age students were employed as subjects in the recall task.

Materials.   Three 30-item recall lists were developed. The All-Categorizable list contained five frequent responses for each of six Battig and Montague categories (birds, occupations, spices, weapons, geography, and kitchen appliances). Two Mixed lists were constructed, each containing 15 randomly selected items without any category overlap and 15 items from three of the categories included on the All-Categorizable list. (One Mixed list contained the categories *occupations, spices,* and *weapons*; the other included *birds, geography,* and *kitchen appliances*).

Procedure.   Subjects received five study-test trials on one of the two types of list using the same procedure as in Experiment 1. Twenty subjects received the All-Categorizable list and then received each of the Mixed lists.

Results

Mean recall and clustering scores over five trials for the categorizable items on the Mixed and All-Categorizable lists are displayed in Table 3.3. (All recall scores in Table 3.3 are means for three categories in order to obtain comparability between the All-Categorizable and Mixed list scores and to allow for easy comparison with the data on Black sublist recall in Table 3.2.) The performance of college students in this experiment parallels that of the white students tested in Experiment 1. The differences in mean recall for categorizable items on the two list types fails to reach significant (t (38) = 1.5, $p < .10$), but the difference in clustering is significant (t (38) = 2.63 < .01). The mean z-score for categorizable items is almost twice as large when the items are contained within an All-Categorizable list as when they are in a Mixed list. The relationship between clustering and recall is strong when the items are contained within either type of list ($r = .82$ for both All-Categorizable and Mixed lists). As expected, recall for the noncategorizable items on the Mixed lists was less than that for categorizable items (t (19) = 2.97, $p < .01$), averaging 6.49 out of 15 for the two Mixed lists.

Discussion

The performance of college-age subjects with a mixed list in Experiment 2 was similar to that of the white adolescents in Experiment 1. It thus seems reasonable to infer that the presence of a large proportion of items for which categories are not readily available will impair the organization of items for which the subject does have convenient categories. This mixed-list effect could stem from the fact that the subjects are less likely to become aware of the categorical nature of these items if the other list items are noncategorizable, either because they decide to devote more study time to the more difficult, noncategorizable items in a mixed list or experience other disruptions in the organization process itself. Regardless of the source of the effect, these results underscore the importance of insuring that *all* items and categories on a free recall list are equally consonant with the experience and conceptual structures of different subject groups if their clustering in recall is to be interpreted as an index of organizational activity.

TABLE 3.3
Recall, Clustering, and Recall-Clustering Correlations for
Categorizable Items in the All-Categorizable and Mixed-List
Conditions

Group	$\bar{X}$ Recall for Categorizable Items (possible = 15)	$\bar{Z}$	$r_{x,z}$
All-Categorizable List	8.72	1.54	0.82
Mixed List	7.32	0.66	0.82

EXPERIMENT 3

Evidence for the hypothesis that the sociolinguistic appropriateness of recall items affects recall clustering was obtained in Experiment 1. In that study, half the items on the recall list were category instances elicited from black adolescents, and the other half of the list consisted of items from standard category forms. Black adolescents showed more clustering on this list than white adolescents, and the trend extended even to the standard category items that should have been very familiar to the white students. This finding was interpreted as an indication that the presence of some unfamiliar category items on a recall list (by virtue of being ethnospecific to black adolescents) depressed the whites' attempts to organize even familiar category instances. The present investigation was designed to extend the evidence for effects of ethnospecificity on recall and clustering and to test the generality of the finding that the presence of some unfamiliar items would disrupt performance with familiar ones.

This experiment expands upon the conditions used in the previous study by including several additional permutations in the development of the word lists. Lists were developed from black, white, or standard norms forming lists that were either all "black," "white," or "standard," or "black–white," "black–standard," or "white–standard." The rationale behind this modification was that group by list interactions should generalize to these lists as well if the main hypothesis is correct.

Another minor modification in the recall procedure was incorporated into the design to determine if the expected group differences were a function of storage or retrieval difficulty. After the fifth trial, subjects were given category labels and tested once again for recall on a sixth trial. If no significant improvements could be demonstrated, either storage or retrieval difficulty could be involved, offering no insight into the problem. However, if subjects improved their recall after cuing, retrieval processes would be indicated.

Method

Subjects. Eighty subjects were selected from a parochial school for girls located in New York City. Half the subjects were black and half were white, with each racial group being composed of equal-sized samples drawn from the lower (9th and 10th) and upper (11th and 12th) grades. The mean ages for the two grade-level groups were 14.8 and 17.0 years for the black subjects and 14.9 and 16.9 for the whites.

Materials. In order to develop recall materials expressly tailored for each ethnic group, a separate sample of 109 girls (one-third black) from the same school were given a questionnaire asking them to name the first five items that came to mind for each of six taxonomic categories. Results of the survey were analyzed separately for blacks and whites, and categories showing the largest degree of group consensus with the five most popular exemplars were identified as Black and White categories, respectively. These categories were used subsequently in composing some of the recall lists. The White recall list (WW) contained the high consensus members of the six categories from the white students' questionnaire responses. The Black list (BB) contained three high-consensus categories from the black students' responses in the present survey and three categories of items elicited from black adolescents in Experiment 1. The Black/White (BW) list contained three of the categories appearing on the Black list and three from the White list. A fourth list was based entirely on items from standard category norms (Battig & Montague, 1969), making this Standard list (SS) similar to those used in many previous recall studies. The final list contained three of these standard categories and three categories from the White list (WS). This White/Standard list (WS) was designed to be analogous to the Black/Standard list used in Experiment 1. This list allowed a test of the hypothesis that, like the white students in the earlier study, black students would show less clustered recall for standard category items when they were part of a mixed list, half of which was tailored to a different ethnic group's sociolinguistic experience. Each recall list contained a total of 30 items, five from each of six categories.

Procedure.   Six recall trials on one of the five lists were individually administered to each subject. The word list was read out loud by the experimenter at the rate of about 2 seconds per word and in a different random order on each study trial. After each list presentation, subjects were asked for immediate verbal recall. At the conclusion of the fifth trial, subjects were asked to name all the categories they had noticed on the recall list. The experimenter then gave the subjects the names of all six categories before administering the sixth recall trial.

Results

Recall and Clustering on Trials 1–5:   Recall was scored for both number of words recalled and recall organization, as measured by the z-score index of categorizal clustering (Frankel & Cole, 1971). A 5 by 2 by 2 analysis of variance was performed on these data with List, Grade, and Race as between-subjects factors and Trials as a within-subjects factor. The result of the recall and organization analyses closely paralleled each other and are discussed together. Each F statistic was evaluated for significance at p. less than .05.

A main effect of list was found for both recall (F $(4,60)$ = 3.26) and organization (F $(4,60)$ = 3.80). The basic source of this effect appeared to be the generally inferior performance on the sociolinguistically mixed BW list, which produced significantly lower recall than the WW (t (14) = 2.89) or the BB list (t (14) = 2.66) and less clustering than the WW (t(14) = 3.53) or WS list (t (14) = 2.50). There was no difference overall between black and white students on either recall or organization (F's (1,60) = 2.83 and 3.52, respectively). Nor did either List by Race interaction attain significance (F's (4,60) = 2.02 and 1.49), contrary to expectation. Older subjects showed more recall and organization than younger ones (F's (1,60) - 13.45 and 8.91 on recall and clustering, respectively) and this age difference did not vary with race (F's (1,60) < 1 and = 2.58). There was a significant Grade by List interaction for both recall and clustering (F's (1,60) = 3.59 and 3.77). Considerable improvement with grade occurred for the SS list, whereas none was found for the BB or BW list. Performance on the other lists showed intermediate levels of improvement with age. There was also a significant Grade by List by Race interaction in recall (F(4,60) = 2.70) but not organization (F(4,60) = 1.32), reflecting somewhat different patterns of list improvement with grade for the two races.

Performance improved over the five recall trials in terms of both number of words recalled and clustering (F(4,240) = 87.21 and 24.66). The extent to which organization increased over trials varied with lists (F(16,240) = 1.75), with the BW list showing little improvement over five trials. The increase in number of words recalled did not vary with list (F(16,240) = 1.33).

Sublist Analysis.   Previous research had suggested that the effect of having sociolinguistically tailored categories on a recall list would depend on the nature of the total list. Specifically, the amount of organization subjects display on the list may depend on whether the entire list is familiar and easily categorizable for them or whether some portion of it is relatively unfamiliar and difficult to categorize (e.g., tailored to a different cultural group's experience, cf. Franklin & Fulani, 1979). To see if the present data contained any such effects, separate analyses were performed on those categories that appeared on both the "mixed" BW list and on one of the sociolinguistically "pure" lists (either BB or WW). The BW list was composed of the categories *black leaders, soul food,* and *black musicians* from the BB list and the categories *national leaders, musicians,* and *dances* from the WW list. A Duncan Multiple Range Test was employed at the $p < .05$ level for all group comparisons. White students did better in recall on the common white categories when they were contained within the pure WW list than when they were part of the mixed BW list. Black students, on the other hand, did equally well on the common black categories whether they were part of the BB or the BW list. Looking at both types of common categories, black students recalled more words from black categories than from white ones, whereas white students showed the opposite performance pattern. Hence, this analysis of a portion of the recall data provides some support for the hypothesis that list recall and compatibility of items with subjects' sociolinguistic experience are related.

Similar comparisons can be made for the standard categories contained on both the SS and the WS lists (tools, utensils, clothes). The hypothesized outcome was that black students' organization and recall of the standard category items would be better when they were embedded in the SS list than when they were part of the WS list, which presumably contained some category items that were relatively less familiar for blacks. As predicted, blacks showed recall on the common standard category items when they were part of the SS list. White students did not show this effect, as expected, in light of the fact that both white and standard categories should be highly familiar for them. The clustering results for blacks were inconsistent with predictions, however; blacks' clustering of standard categories was not reduced in the WS condition.

Effects of Providing Category Labels.   The effect that providing subjects with the category labels prior to the sixth study trial had on their clustering and recall was assessed in separate analyses of variance, with List, Grade, Race, and Trials (Trial 5 or Trial 6) as factors in the design. Clustering and recall were higher overall on trial 6 ($F(1,60) = 54.08$) for organization and ($F(1,60) = 30.60$) for recall with the improvement between trials 5 and 6 varying by list in clustering only ($F(4,60) = 5.75$), and with the SS list showing the greatest increase. Of course, some improvement in recall and clustering would be expected after an additional study trial even if category labels had not been provided; nevertheless, the slope of the function relating clustering to trial clearly changed after category labels were provided. The pattern of recall results was similar. When subjects were interviewed about how they remembered the words, 51% of all subjects reported using categories; 37% of the black subjects claimed using categories in contrast to 65% of the white subjects.

Discussion

The study's results offered mixed support to the original research hypotheses. It seems clear that lists designed to be differentially ethnospecific will elicit varying recall and clustering levels. However, these effects do not consistently vary with race in any straightforward, simple manner. The analysis of common categories in the Black, White, and Black/White lists gave some support for the ethnospecificity hypothesis. Black students did better on black categories and white students on white ones. However, white students did as well as black students on black category items when they were part of the Black list, and analysis of the full set of study results failed to confirm the presence of a List by Race interaction.

The results were likewise equivocal in supporting the hypothesis that a group's recall of familiar categories would be impaired if those categories were part of a list that contained relatively unfamiliar items also. The recall performance of white students on white categories contained within the Black/White list was poorer than their performance on the White list; similarly, the black students indicated poorer recall for standard categories within a Standard/White as compared to a Standard list. These findings conform to the hypothesis. However, black students did equally well with black categories whether they were part of a Black/White or a homogeneous Black list.

Perhaps the lack of clear-cut results stems from the fact that categories for each cultural group were chosen for their degree of within-group consensus rather than on the basis of the size of group *differences* in familiarity with the items. The underlying assumption was that the most familiar and sharply defined categories for one group would be less familiar to the other. This outlook may be too simplistic. Ethnospecificity is a relative concept rather than an absolute one. Clearly, cultural *sharing* exists among black and white adolescents just as culture-specific experiences do. Some evidence of such sharing was demonstrated by a few items common to both the black and white high-consensus categories (specifically, *Walt Frazier* in the athlete and black athlete categories; *chicken* in the food and soul food categories; *ups* and *downs* in both groups' drug category; and *bump* in both dance categories). Moreover, black students are familiar with the national leaders contained in the white students' leader category, and white adolescents are familiar with the black musicians included on the Black recall list.

The generally poor performance of both racial groups on the Black/White list could be attributed either to its sociolinguistically "mixed" character or to its many proper names (potentially causing interference, or organization into fewer categories, either of which could account for reduced recall).

An unexpected finding was the poor performance on the Standard list in the lower grades. One could argue that this list was simply less unusual or less related to personal interests and experience than the others. However, it did produce the best performance in the upper grades. The marked improvement with grade on performance with the Standard list was more striking among black students but occurred among whites as well. Although inclination to organize items into taxonomic categories in such tasks has been associated with formal education (Cole, et al., 1971; Greenfield & Bruner, 1969), previous research led to the expectation that this tendency would be well established by the ninth grade. Determination of whether or not this apparent increase in the use of taxonomic categories in recall over the high school years is a genuine phenomenon requires further research.

EXPERIMENT 4

The purpose of this study was to replicate the basic study using improved controls for elicitation with fewer list conditions. The elicitation procedures were made sensitive to Grade by Race differences in order to more fully reflect experimental group characteristics. Also, the elicitation techniques used were more comparable to techniques employed in other elicitation studies, which used questionnaire-type formats. Because most classification normative data is collected from college students and word frequency lists, such as Thorndike and Lorge's (1944), which involve word frequencies for primary grade children and adults, there is very little data on high school populations. With the many variables influencing category clustering, the question of whether an adolescent population would generate different classification norms from previous studies, and whether there would be any differentiation in norms across ages or between black and white adolescents became the basis for this study. The empirical question was whether developmental and sociocultural differences would emerge in responses to standard and nonstandard taxonomic categories.

Method

Subjects.   The subjects were 108 high school students: 27 white 12th graders, 27 black 12th graders, 27 white 9th graders, 27 black 9th graders. The white subjects were from a parochial school that was 99% white in population. The black subjects were from a city public school with a 99% black population.

Materials.   Some of the categories selected were taken from previous norm studies such as Shapiro and Palermo (1970) and Battig and Montague (1969). Some of the categories chosen were ones the experimenter felt would generate cultural differences, e.g., types of dinner foods and types of dances. Some of the categories were universal, generating high-frequency norms, e.g., types of animals and kinds of tools.

Procedure.   Each subject was given a booklet containing 29 categories; two categories were listed on each page, and all pages in each booklet were randomized. The following instructions were read aloud by the experimenter: "Name five different things that belong in the following categories. Use one word only. Example, 'A beverage: coffee, tea, milk, soda, and beer.'" The task was self-paced but had to be completed within a 45-minute class period.

Results

Responses were tallied separately for each group. No attempt was made to separate different forms of the same word (e.g., singular or plural). Synonymous words were tallied the same way as any other response. An index of commonality (IC) was calculated by dividing the five most frequent instances by the total number of responses for all categories. This calculation shows the degree of consensus for all categories.

There were no major developmental differences between ninth and 12th graders or between racial groups on the top five instances for each category. Many categories have a few word instances that differ from group to group, but this was more a function of level of commonality index rather than an absence from subjects' lexicon.

Discussion

The consistency in responses for both adolescent populations by grade and by ethnic group strengthens the assumption of developmental uniformity of instances for conceptual categories. This typing phenomena starts early, with no significant modification during the adolescent phase of development.

Norms generated in this study were consistent with both groups and uniform with previous normative studies, in spite of contrasts between school environments. The white students attended an upper middle-class, highly structured parochial school, whereas the black students attended an overcrowded, loosely structured and frequently noisy public school.

Further inquiry suggests that additional research is needed on the associative strength of classification norms for different populations and its impact on the organization of memory. If the task had been conducted outside the school environment, would there be any differentiation in norms generated between ethnic groups? Did the environment stimulate the use of standard norms instead of norms that might be culturally influenced and verbalized in everyday speech? Moreover, in producing words for the experimental task, black subjects were impeded in part by their intrusive, noisy school environment, spelling deficiencies, and low task motivation. This brings into question the efficacy of group survey as a method for a task of this nature.

EXPERIMENT 5

The fifth experiment was capitalized on the norms collected in Experiment 4, which were used to develop free recall lists for black and white adolescents that were equated in terms of appropriateness and specifically tailored to each group's best defined categories. The design included giving separate samples from each racial group the other group's list so that the performance of different groups on the same list (with appropriateness varying) could be compared as well as performance on different lists with appropriateness controlled.

Method

Subjects.   Sixty 12th graders enrolled in the same high schools participating in Experiment 4 were used in Experiment 5. Of these, 20 were girls attending the white parochial school, 20 were girls in the regular curriculum at the black public school, and 20 were girls participating in the college-bound program at the same black public school. This latter group was included because their educational achievement and curriculum was more comparable to that of the white students attending parochial school, yet they presumably shared the same cultural background as their public school peers.

Materials.   Two 30-word lists, one derived from the norms of 12th graders in the black public school and one from 12th graders in the white parochial school, were devised for use in the recall task. The five most frequently cited instances from six categories with very high IC ratings were placed on each group's list with an effort to equate the mean IC for the two lists. The mean IC for the categories selected for the Black list (based on the data of black 12th graders) was .63 and the corresponding index for the White list was .62. Table 3.4 contains a listing of the categories and items selected for the two recall lists based upon each group's respective achieved level of commonality index.

It should be noted that the criteria used in selecting list items yielded quite similar lists from the black and white norms. Four of the six categories are the same for the two lists, and within these common categories, 16 of 24 words are identical. Overall then, over half the words on each recall list also appeared on the other. However, lists were based upon the six categories with the highest commonality index for each ethnic group separately, under the assumption that this list structure was primary in the lexicon of the group. Five randomized word orders were generated to be used on the five recall trials, with the restriction that no two words from the same category appear successively.

Procedure.   The recall task was individually administered to each subject. Students were told that they were participating in a study on memory and that the experimenter was interested in how many words they could remember from a list that would be read to them a total of five times. The experimenter read the words at a rate of about 2 seconds per word and asked for verbal recall after each complete reading of the list. Each subject received a random sequence of the five word orders. Recall was recorded on tape for later transcription.

Results

The total number of words recalled over five trials and the average z score indicating degree of categorical clustering were computed for each subject. A 2 by 3 by 5 analysis of variance, with List and Student Group as between-subjects factors and Trials as a within-subjects factor, was run on each of the response measures. The results of these analyses included significant main effects for Student Group and Trials on both recall and clustering ($F(2,54) = 6.75$ and 8.73, respectively). The significant group effect stemmed from the relatively poor performance of the black students in the regular school program. Recall

TABLE 3.4
Categories and Items from the Two Recall Lists

WHITE LIST

Fruits	Instruments	Liquors	Religions	School Subjects	Relatives
orange	guitar	whiskey	Protestant	math	mother
pear	flute	rum	Moslem	English	sister
apple	piano	scotch	Catholic	religion	aunt
grape	drum	vodka	Hindu	history	cousin
banana	organ	gin	Jewish	science	uncle

BLACK LIST

Fruits	Instruments	Tools	Religions	Sports	Relatives
banana	piano	pliers	Christian	basketball	sister
apple	drum	wrench	Moslem	football	mother
orange	trumpet	screwdriver	Catholic	tennis	cousin
strawberry	guitar	hammer	Baptist	baseball	uncle
grape	flute	saw	Jewish	track	aunt

and clustering increased over trials ($F(4,216) = 15.75$ and 3.68), and the extent of this increase did not vary by Student Group list. Neither the main effect of list nor any of the interactions attained significance.

Discussion

Contrary to expectation, black public school students did not show as much recall and clustering as white parochial school students when given materials designed to be as appropriate for them as the white students' were for that group. Black public school students in the college-bound program did, however, recall as proficiently as white students. One interpretation of these findings is that the educational experiences offered in the regular track of a crowded black urban high school do not foster the memory skills needed to apply the structures in one's semantic memory to a recall task in the same way that experiences in a disciplined white parochial school or a special college-bound program.

Before accepting the recall and clustering differences as genuine evidence for group differences in propensity to use conceptual structures in a recall task, however, one should critically examine the assumption that the black list used in the present experiment was valid as reflection of the conceptual structures of the black students in the regular track as the white list was for parochial school students. One cause for reflection is the similarity in content of the lists generated from the category norms despite obvious differences in everyday lexicon, interests, and cultural experiences between students at the two schools. A more objective cause for concern grows out of the experimenter's observations during the category elicitation study of Experiment 4. Black high school students did not appear to be comfortable with and fully engaged in the task at hand. Despite urging from the experimenter, some students appeared to be unmotivated, and others expressed a reluctance to write items they were not sure they could spell correctly. The reactions of black students in this relatively formal, school-like elicitation procedure contrasted sharply with those of adolescents from similar backgrounds in an earlier investigation (Experiment 1). In the earlier study, black teenagers were interviewed informally and individually in their neighborhoods and gave responses verbally rather than in writing. They appearaed more willing to think of items in the informal interview, responded more spontaneously, and gave more slang or "street" terms as responses. It is the difference between the items elicited from black adolescents by these two procedures that raises the most serious question about whether the more formal elicitation procedure used in the present experiment and in previous research with college students is really tapping the dominant conceptual structures of black teenagers.

The differences between the types of items elicited under the two procedures can be most unequivocally demonstrated by examining the most frequently given items for the two categories that were included in both elicitation studies— *dances* and *drugs*. When adolescents were interviewed individually in their neighborhoods, the most frequently cited dances were *bump, robot, truckin'*, *grind*, and *twist*. Black 12th graders asked to write instances of dances in a classroom setting, on the other hand, gave such "high-brow" dances as *waltz* and *ballet* among their five most frequent responses. Similarly, whereas teenagers interviewed on the street gave *smoke, acid,* and *dope* as their most frequent responses in the drug category, black students tested in school gave the more "proper" terms for the same drugs, *marijuana, LSD,* and *heroin* instead. Category elicitation may be yet another area of behavior where black students appear to have a certain understanding of what is accepted or expected in school and to modify their behavior accordingly. There appear to be more differences between the responses given by black adolescents in the two different contexts than there are between blacks and whites tested in the same context. Concern that the categories in the Black list used in Experiment 5 might not really reflect the semantic memory content of black adolescents led to a follow-up study in which a recall list containing some of these informally derived black "street" category items was administered.

EXPERIMENT 6

Method

Subjects.   From the three school populations used in Experiment 4—regular black public school, black public school college bound, and white parochial school—three groups of ten 12th graders served as subjects. All were female.

Materials.   The recall list (Black Street list) consisted of six items each from five categories developed from informal interviews with black adolescents conducted in conjunction with an earlier comparative recall study (Franklin & Fulani, 1979).

Procedure.   The recall task was individually administered in the same manner as in Experiment 5.

Results

The recall and clustering scores for the Black Street list were combined with those from the previous experiment and one-way analyses of variance performed on the recall and clustering scores for the groups defined by the various combinations of student type and list. (The combined analysis appeared justifiable because the length and structure of the Black Street list was isomorphic with those of the other two lists, the subject samples were from the same populations, and the testing was carried out within the same academic term.) The major result of interest from this analysis was that black public school, regular track students with the black street list recalled as many words as white parochial school students with the white list. Black regular track students also appeared to cluster somewhat more with the black street list than with the black list but the difference was not significant. Black students' clustering on the Black Street list still fell below the level of white students on the White list.

Discussion

The results of Experiment 6 suggest that efforts to develop a maximally appropriate list for black regular track high school students through the norming procedure of Experiment 5 were not entirely successful. The fact that a list developed from informal interviews produced superior recall for those students suggests that the formal elicitation procedure is not optimal for tapping the content of their semantic memory. The formal procedure may not be optimal for white adolescents either, and the question of whether racial groups would differ in recall on group-tailored lists generated through some other procedure remains open.

CONCLUSIONS

The most noteworthy finding revealed in these studies is the relationship between familiarity with content material and performance in recall and categorical clustering. White subjects' recall and clustering appeared less prominent when items selected for their conceptual relatedness for black adolescents were included in word lists. Furthermore, recall and clustering scores for black subjects increase as their familiarity with the items on the list increases. This is illustrated by their performance improvements from Experiment 5 to Experiment 6, where word lists were more distinguishable for black and white groups. The analyses within and across experiments are consistent in that list recall improves when the items are compatible with the subjects' sociolinguistic experience.

Race or sex per se did not appear related to recall, clustering, or item generation. Also age differences were not found in the elicitation task. However, grade and educational background was associated with recall and clustering. In several instances, college-bound blacks and white subjects had equal recall on White lists. Furthermore, on all tasks, performance of black and white subjects enrolled in the integrated parochial school was more often equivalent than that of subjects enrolled in segregated schools. These findings indicate that equivalence in educational background leads to greater equivalence in performance. The obvious advantage of integrated schooling and equitable exposure is made more obvious by these findings.

Recall and clustering differences were more apparent between ethnic groups when items were derived from individualized elicitation procedures than when the formal (booklet) group elicitation procedures were used. It is assumed that the informal surveys were more reflective of environmental differences because subjects were more relaxed and cooperative in the informal task, and because a one-on-one format may be more conducive than booklets to itemizing slang terms.

Finally, the Jensen hypothesis was clearly questioned by the results of these studies. The demonstration of a relationship between Level II thinking (clustering) and familiarity with items easily draws his conclusions into doubt because word familiarity was a variable Jensen neglected to control.

Implications: The Social Context as the Arena for Basic Research

This series of studies on the sociolinguistic relevancy of verbal learning tasks is only one attempt at formulating research by originating hypotheses that are based on the experiences of the subject populations. There are a number of investigators who are advocating this approach in the study of learning. The October 1979 Special Issue of the *American Psychologist* on Psychology and Children contains noteworthy articles on this point. When we consider the multitude of social situations in which people make daily transactions, numerous factors are uncovered that contribute to the shaping of their behavior. In considering the processes of learning and thinking, I believe that these social factors are major agents in mediating cognitive development. At present, there is no coherent theory that adequately takes into account the impact of variables within the social context on learning and thinking. Such a theory would explicate how thinking and learning are shaped by a socialization process within each cultural group. I review briefly five primary social contexts that are major settings for socialization experiences and that in my judgment, have an affect on how learning and thinking develop. Each of these domains is a potential area for empirical studies. These suggestions are offered as recommendations for research and funding, particularly when the goals are to comprehend the school performance of adolescents. They are the family, peer groups, school, community, and the individual.

In my opinion, we have not fully understood the role of the family in the development of learning and thinking. Some of the major questions that come to mind are: What is the effect of parent–child interaction over school work on learning and thinking? What role does parental motivation and behavior have in fostering achievement? What is the influence of role-model identification on educational motivation and achievement? What is the influence of sibling interaction and identification on motivation and achievement? What are the roles of extended family networks and family traditions? Certainly in contemporary times one needs to understand the impact on educational motivation of family economic stress. A related question is the impact of socioeconomic status (SES), which remains dubious and elusive as a research variable because in practice SES classification is based upon family income and educational level, with little regard for the influence of family values and behavior.

Peer groups provide another major social context in which experiences can shape the processes of learning and thinking. In my research I attempted to use only one aspect of the peer context; that is, slang, which is an important mode of verbal communication. However there are many other ways in which peer groups might affect learning and thinking processes. For example, there is still insufficient information on how peer interaction affects educational motivation and achievement. During adolescence, peer-group membership becomes a prime objective in that it helps to fulfill social interests and to develop identity. Honor clubs in school stimulate positive peer identification. They are intended—at least implicitly—to indirectly influence the learning and thinking processes and, subsequently, achievement. It would be interesting to have a series of in-depth systematic studies examining the effect of peer-group socialization on individual learning strategies.

The school is a third major setting for peer-group interactions and it is a primary social context from which many studies have evolved. No other social context can equal it in research attention about learning and thinking processes. By definition, the school setting is the logical place to explore the development of cognitive processes, but it is not the only context.

The community is an ambiguous concept but it must not be ignored in attempts to describe how the learning and thinking processes develop. There is certainly evidence to indicate that students from high-income communities with considerable school resources have a better performance record than the students of the average inner-city school with limited resources. On the other hand, studies for the New York City Board of Education have shown that effectively administrated schools in the inner city can have a better than expected achievement record. This suggests that more research should be directed to examining the characteristics of achieving and nonachieving schools. For example, what are the characteristics of the community or of other significant support systems of the achieving school? Although this is a rather broad area of proposed research, I still contend that understanding of the most basic elements of the learning and thinking processes should be based on the analysis of such a social context, at least to a greater extent than it currently is.

I also propose the *individual* as a fifth "context" that mediates these critical cognitive processes. The literature has not definitively explained the linkage between motivation and learning processes. In school settings we are repeatedly confronted with the way the socioemotional state of the individual students affects learning and performance. More and more programs are beginning to adopt a psychoeducational approach to the management of students' school performance. We are still ignorant of the way many other individual psychological processes affect the process of learning and thinking.

In conclusion, it is my opinion that the background factors comprising the social contexts are insufficiently considered in research projects on learning and thinking processes. The development of learning and thinking in the individual are shaped by an elaborate network of social learning contingencies; ability and performance must be understood within that framework. The process of socialization contains many variables whose consequences for basic cognitive processes are still unknown. Cross-cultural research in cognition suggests that different ethnic groups perceive and use information according to the traditions of learning for that specific society. Some of the same research issues can be raised for the culturally pluralistic society of the United States. What complicates such investigations into the relationship between socialization and cognitive processes in this country is the factor of acculturation. For example, the inconsistent findings in the studies reported here probably resulted from the fact that the backgrounds and social experiences of the black subjects varied considerably, reflecting the complexity of the acculturation process. However, if we propose to study the learning and thinking processes of inner-city students—many of whom are black and Hispanic or from a diverse collection of immigrant groups—and if we propose to develop educational intervention programs to facilitate and enhance learning, we should formulate our research and intervention programs by considering the characteristics of learning and thinking as manifested by the indigenous populations.

ACKNOWLEDGMENTS

This research was supported by a a grant from the Ford Foundation and the facilities of the Rockefeller University with research assistance from Michael Cole, Lenora Fulani, and Linda DeJesus.

REFERENCES

Battig, W. F., & Montague, W. E. (1969). Category norms for the verbal items in 56 categories: A replication and extension of the Connecticut category norms. *Journal of Experimental Psychology Monograph, 80* (3, Pt. 2).

Cazden, C., John, V., & Hymes, D. (Eds.) (1972). *Functions of language in the classroom.* New York: Teacher's College.

Cole, M., Gay, J., Glick, J., & Sharp, D. (1971). *The cultural context of learning and thinking.* New York: Basic Books.

Cole, M., & Scribner, S. (1974). *Culture and thought.* New York: Wiley.

Dillard, J. L. (1972). *Black English: Its history and usage in the United States.* New York: Random House.

Forrester, W. E., & King, D. J. (1971). Effects of semantic and acoustic relatedness on free recall and clustering. *Journal of Experimental Psychology, 88,* 16–19.

Frankel, F., & Cole, M. (1971). Measures of category clustering in free recall. *Psychological Bulletin, 76,* 39–44.

Franklin, A. J., & Fulani, L. (1979). Cultural content of materials and ethnic group performance in categorized recall. In A. W. Boykin, A. J. Franklin, & J. F. Yates (Eds.) *Research directions of black psychologists.* New York: The Russell Sage Foundation/Basic Books.

Greenfield, P. M., & Bruner, J. S. (1969). Culture and cognitive growth. In D. Goslin (Ed.), *Handbook of socialization theory and research.* New York: Rand McNally.

Hall, W. S., & Freedle, R. (1973). *Towards the identification of cognitive operations in standard and nonstandard English usage* (ETS RB 73-18). Princeton, NJ: Educational Testing Service.

Jensen, A. R. (1969) .How much can we boost I.Q. and scholastic achievement? *Harvard Educational Review, 39,* 1–123.

Jensen, A. R., and Frederiksen, J. (1973). Free recall of categorized and uncategorized lists: A test of the Jensen hypothesis. *Journal of Educational Psychology, 65,* 304–312.

Mensing, P. M., & Traxler, A. J. (1973). Social class differences in free recall of categorized and uncategorized lists in black children, *Journal of Educational Psychology, 65,* 378–382.

Pellegrino, J. W. (1971). A general measure of organization free recall for variable unit size and internal sequential consistency. *Behavior Research Methods and Instrumentation, 3,* 241–246.

Postman, L., & Keppel, G. (1970). *Norms of word association.* New York: Academic Press.

Schultz, T. R., Charness, M., & Berman, S. (1973). Effects of age, social class, and suggestion to cluster on free recall. *Developmental Psychology, 8,* 57–61.

Scribner, S. (1974). Developmental aspects of categorized recall in West Africa. *Cognitive Psychology, 6,* 475–494.

Shapiro, S. I., & Palermo, D. S. (1970). Conceptual organization and class membership: Normative data for representatives of 100 categories. *Psychonomic Monograph Supplements, 3,* (11, Whole No. 43).

Steinmetz, J. I., & Battig, W. R. (1969). Clustering and priority of free recall of newly learned items in children. *Developmental Psychology, 1,* 503–507.

Thorndike, E. L., & Lorge, I. (1944). *The teacher's word book of 30,000 words.* New York: Bureau of Publication, Teachers College, Columbia University.

4 The Structure of Knowledge in Complex Domains

Edwina L. Rissland
University of Massachusetts

INTRODUCTION

Objectives

Learning, teaching, and understanding are complex tasks in complex domains like mathematics. Any teacher or student knows that there is rich complexity to the subject of conic sections or continuity. Knowing such domains demands much more than knowing formal statements of definitions, theorems, and proofs: It demands knowing examples, methods, exercises, pictures, graphs, and diagrams; rules of thumb; metaphors and analogies; folksy or informal formulations of ideas; a sense of what is important; a sense of what should follow what. This complexity exists whether the purpose is to learn or to teach.

One objective here is to present a conceptual framework in which to describe and understand knowledge in complex domains. Another is to show how such a framework can aid teaching and learning in them.

There are several underlying themes. First, understanding a domain requires a great familiarity with its connections. Polya and Szego (1972) said eloquently:

There is a similarity between knowing one's way about town and mastering a field of knowledge: from any given point one should be able to reach any other point. One is even better informed if one can immediately take the most convenient and quickest path from the one point to the other. If one is very well informed indeed, one can even execute special feats, for example, to carry out a journey by systematically avoiding certain forbidden paths which are customary—such things happen in certain axiomatic investigations.

There is an analogy between the task of constructing a well-integrated body of knowledge from acquaintance with isolated truths and the building of a wall out of unhewn stones. One must turn each new insight and each new stone over and over, view it from all sides, attempt to join it on to the edifice at all possible points, until the new finds its suitable place in the already established, in such a way that the areas of contact will be as large as possible and the gaps as small as possible, until the whole forms one firm structure. (p.viii)

Second, being aware of what one knows and how one comes to know it are important ingredients of expertise. Clarification and explication of the process of knowing enable one to be a smarter student or teacher, as Papert and others have often pointed out (Papert 1971, 1980).

Thus, we are engaged in *espistemology,* the study of knowledge. The epistemology of complex domains includes the study of their content, structure, representation, and use. There are many dimensions and levels of epistemology. There is study of the domain itself, for example, through analysis of its content and structure. There is the epistemology of one domain with respect to different conceptual frameworks and the epistemology of one compared with another with respect to the same framework. There is the epistemology of epistemologies, that is, the study and comparison of frameworks.

In this chapter, we discuss not only the epistemology of particular domains, but, more importantly, also a general epistemological framework. Our approach reflects concerns and methodologies from cognitive science and artificial intelligence (AI). Important contributions of AI are the tools of information processing and knowledge representation (Feigenbaum & Barr, 1981; Winston, 1977). To be able to use them, not only should we have the knowledge, but also we should know what we want to do with it.

Our analysis is based upon the experience of the author and others as teachers and learners. The structural notions presented here seem natural to students. Several students, e.g., in calculus, have found that using such notions helps to give them understanding that is different from that of acquiring a large bag of tricks. Our conceptual framework is currently being applied to investigations in learning and understanding probability (Myers, 1980), discrete mathematics for computer science, and high school mathematics (Davis, 1979).

One of the themes running through our work is the importance and interaction of examples with other knowledge such as concepts and results. The role played by examples in the evolution of mathematical concepts is beautifully described by Lakatos (1976). Examples play a critical role in learning and concept formation by machines (Lenat, 1976; Winston, 1975a) as well as people (Collins & Stevens, 1979; Polya, 1965). Examples can also be a very effective means of presenting new technical ideas (Wegner, 1980).

Of course, attention to and understanding of the topic of heuristics and its role in discovery are due to Polya. His well-known books are full of insight (e.g., Polya, 1965); they also provide many examples of the kind of knowledge we wish to explicate further.

Structure and Representation

In this chapter, we distinguish between "structure" and "representation." *Structure* is something inherent in the knowledge domain that can be teased out by examination of the domain and how it is used. *Representation* is the way in which we encode the knowledge and structure.

We can see structure, or different aspects of it, when we examine the domain. The structure discerned is clearly influenced by our purposes, expectations, and point of view (Bruner, 1973; Kuhn, 1970). For instance, if we work with situation-action rules, such rules will jump out as we examine a domain (e.g., Greeno, 1978). With different purposes, we emphasize different aspects. For instance, if our purpose is to study logical development, we attend to deductive aspects like definitions, theorems, and proofs; if our purpose is to study expository style, we attend to rhetorical structures. In this chapter, our purpose is to understand the knowledge better, to improve our skills as teachers and learners, and to enhance our understanding of understanding.

Often there are many ways to represent the same knowledge; the one chosen depends on our preferences and purposes—on what we are going to use such knowledge for. For instance, researchers in logic and theorem proving often use the predicate calculus. We choose the representation scheme that best suits our purposes; "best" in the sense of conceptual clarity, ease of encoding or use. For instance, representation schemes like "frames" (Minsky, 1975), "scripts" (Schank & Colby, 1973), "schemata" (Rumelhart & Ortony, 1977), and "semantic nets" (Brachman, 1979; Quillian, 1968) make it easy to encode clustering, typing, and connectivity.

An underlying viewpoint in our approach is that chunking of knowledge is very important. In fact, what might distinguish an expert from a novice is the kind and degree of chunking used in thinking about a domain. As one becomes more expert, one is able to use bigger chunks, more encompassing and general. For instance, the expert mathematician sees a proof as a coherent whole, perhaps with substructure (Rissland, 1978a), whereas the novice may see only the succession of individual proof steps. The novice's view is very *local*; the expert's can be *global* as well. Experts can switch the level of description easily and naturally.

This pattern is also found developmentally: Young children often cannot summarize a story; they retell it line by line; older children can present a synopsis. Adults often use more global organizations like "scripts" (Schank & Abelson, 1977).

A CONCEPTUAL FRAMEWORK

Structure: Items, Relations, and Spaces

There are several kinds of structure in the knowledge of complex domains like mathematics:

1. Strongly bound clusters of information: for example, the statement of a theorem, its name, its proof, a diagram, an evaluation of its importance, remarks on its limitations and generality. In this chapter, we call such clusters *items*.

2. *Relations* between items: for example, the logical connections between results, such as *predecessor* results on which a result depends logically and *successor* results that depend on it.

3. Sets of similar types of items related in similar ways: for example, proven results and their logical dependencies. Such a set of items and relations constitute a *space* as, for instance, a *Results-space*.

What distinguishes a "space" from a "set" is the prominence of the relations. The structure of a complex domain like mathematics contains not just one but many spaces, each of which describes a different aspect of knowledge. In mathematics, for instance, as found in lectures and textbooks, (e.g., Rudin, 1964), there are spaces of:

Results: lemmas, propositions, theorems, corollaries, etc., related by *logical dependency,* i.e., how one result is deduced from others.

Examples: illustrative situations and cases related by *constructional derivation,* i.e., how one is built from others.

Concepts: formal ideas like definitions, and informal ones like heuristic principles related by *conceptual dependency,* i.e., how one concept is defined or presented in terms of others.

Exercises: exercises and unresolved conjectures related by how one exercise is generated from others, e.g., as a subproblem that would contribute to solution of a larger problem.

Procedures: procedures and methods related by *procedural dependency,* i.e., how one procedure is composed of or depends on others, as in program subroutines.

Strategies: control methods, doctrines, or heuristics related by how one strategy engenders or contributes to the practice of others.

Goals: goals and purposes related through dependencies of super and subgoals, i.e., how one goal engenders or contributes to the attainment of others.

In our freedom to use many spaces, we have departed somewhat from the usual semantic net approach in AI because we use many nets, i.e., spaces, simultaneously. Each space represents a different "cut" through the domain. In summary, if the same type of relation can be seen in a set of items, we can describe it as a space.

Mathematical Knowledge

Although all the aforementioned spaces, and probably others, would be needed to construct an exhaustive epistemological framework for describing complex domains in general, a significant part of the knowledge in domains like mathematics and computer science can be captured in the following spaces: Results, Examples, Concepts, Exercises, and Procedures.

Results.   The set of approved results and their logical dependencies constitute Results-space. For instance, in plane geometry (Jacobs, 1974), the "Isosceles Triangle Theorem," which states that if two sides of a triangle are equal, so are the angles opposite them, depends logically on the side–angle–side postulate which is used in its proof; a corollary result depending on this theorem states that an equilateral triangle is equiangular.

Examples.   An important aspect of examples is that one builds examples from other examples. The relation of constructional derivation emphasizes this and allows the collection of examples to be coherently organized. For instance, in order to show that not all second-degree equations represent conic sections, one can *modify* the example of the equation of a circle $x^2 + y^2 = 4$ to $x^2 + y^2 = -4$. Thus, the second example item would *point back* to the first, and the first would *point forward* to the second.

Another instance of the construction of examples is the derivation of the example $y = x \sin x$ near the origin from the reference examples $y = -x$, $y = x$, and $y = \sin x$, by squeezing the oscillations to occur between the lines $y = x$ and $y = -x$ (See below).

The generation of examples is an interesting study in itself (Gelbaum & Olmstead, 1964; Rissland, 1980; Steen & Seebach, 1970).

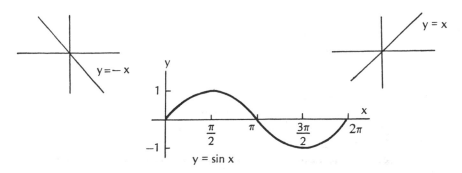

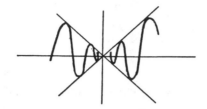

Concepts.   Concepts include formal and informal ideas. A formal idea is a precisely stated notion like a *definition,* e.g., the familiar "epsilon–delta" definition of continuity given in calculus. An example of an informal idea is the *paraphrase* of continuity as "not lifting the pencil from the paper." It is not a bona fide mathematical definition, but it is an idea that is frequently used. Informal ideas also include individual heuristics of two types: megaprinciples and counterprinciples. A *megaprinciple* is a "big" idea that is either an informal truth, such as "Continuous functions have no gaps or breaks," or suggests a good line of attack, such as "Try factoring the polynomial into linear factors." A *counterprinciple,* on the other hand, summarizes troublesome points or offers a warning, like "Be careful about dividing by quantities that might be zero" or "Don't forget to calculate the new dx."

Concepts can be related by dependencies of definition or pedagogy. A definition can be *definitionally dependent* on another if it uses the other in its formulation; for instance, the limit definition of continuity uses the concept of "limit." *Pedagogical dependency* is more subjective: It reflects our feeling that one concept should be learned or introduced before another. Some authors map out the conceptual dependencies of topics and chapters in their books (e.g., Dunford & Schwartz, 1958; Royden, 1963).

Exercises.   Exercises play an important role in helping a student. They can be related in several ways, as in the use of the solution or method of one exercise to pose or solve another. For instance, solving the cubic equation, $x^3 - 1 = 0$, involves solving the quadratic equation, $x^2 + x + 1 = 0$. More complicated, and often subtle, relations between exercises are found in higher level mathematics courses like real analysis.

Procedures.   In many domains, like computer science and applied mathematics, there are large collections of methods and procedures. Procedures can be related by the dependency of one procedure on another. This relation is important in analyses of skills like arithmetic, where for instance addition is a predecessor skill for multiplication (Davis & McKnight, 1979). The ordering is often related to student "bugs" (Seely–Brown & Burton, 1977).

The dependencies can be used to organize procedures hierarchically. For instance, the procedure to find the roots of a cubic equation like the one given previously is composed of the procedures to factor it $(x - 1) (x^2 + x + 1)$, and then to pick off one root, 1, by observation, and, finally to compute the other two by using the quadratic formula. For more complicated cubic equations, the solution procedure might include trying to guess a root, which itself involves procedures, and then proceeding as before.

Representation-graphs.   The dependency relations in the spaces allow us to treat the spaces as directed graphs where the nodes represent items and the arrows the relations between them; the direction shows the inherent predecessor–successor ordering. In this way, we have several graphs: *results-graph, concepts-graph, examples-graph,* etc.

Thinking of the spaces as directed graphs is a useful conceptual aid, because it allows us to picture them easily and from the picture to discern connections and the overall complexity of the domain. In fact, the use of the word "space" is itself an aid, because it calls to mind a mathematician's idea of space with its notions of coherence and distance. The graphs are a way to picture the representation spaces that represent the structure of the domain; the graphs themselves are not a part of the domain.

Structure: The Notion of Dual

An item is related to other items in its representation space through the space's dependency relations. In addition, an item is related to items in the other spaces. The notion of *dual* concerns these *interspace* relations.

As an illustration, consider results, examples, and concepts, which together constitute a large part of the knowledge in many mathematical domains. Results are connected to examples and concepts as well as to other results. The dual items of a result include: (1) the examples motivating and illustrating it and (2) the concepts needed to formulate it and those derived from it.

Similarly, examples and concepts are connected to items outside their spaces. The dual items of an example include: (1) the results illustrated by it and proving things about it and (2) the concepts illustrated and suggested by it. The dual items of a concept include: (1) results leading to its formulation and those proving things about it and (2) examples motivating and illustrating it.

Examples, results, and concepts also have dual items from the spaces of procedures, goals, exercises, etc. Exercises are closely tied to the procedures, examples, concepts, and results used in their solution and those that the exercise illustrates and affords practice with. In many high school texts, the relations between exercises and worked-out examples are particularly close.

Strategies, goals, and procedures are often strongly connected because the strategies are dual to the goals that they are useful for achieving; the procedures are ways to implement or carry out the strategies. In programming, this is often called "pragmatics" as compared with the syntax and semantics.

Thus each item is related to certain items from the other spaces: We call the set of those items its *dual*. Duals themselves have structure: Some dual items tend to precede the item in teaching and learning, others succeed it. For instance, motivating examples for a result come before the result; other examples, like those showing the limitations of the result (e.g., that the converse is not true) come after it. Thus, we can distinguish *pre* and *post* duals. These of course may depend on pedagogical and cognitive style.

The power of the dual notion is that it allows us to associate items that might not be closely related with regard to in-space relations. For instance, two concepts might be widely separate in concepts-space (e.g., because they are taught many chapters apart) but closely related in the dual sense, in that they share many examples. An important part of understanding is building up such associations; assigning exercises that draw on seemingly distant concepts is a way to help students establish such dual relations.

Taxonomies

Another important component of knowledge is the knowledge that not all items serve the same function in learning and understanding. For instance, experts (teachers and learners) know that certain perspicuous ("start-up") examples provide easy access to a new topic, that some ("reference") examples are quite standard and are always exhibited as illustrations, and that some examples are anomalous and don't seem to fit into one's understanding.

We can develop a taxonomy of items based upon how we use them to learn, understand, and teach a domain. In discussing concepts-space, we have already mentioned different kinds of concepts. Briefly, some important taxonomic classes of items are:

1. Results
   a. *basic* results: basic, first proved results.
   b. *key* results: major, frequently used results.
   c. *culminating* results: goal results.
   d. *transitional* results: intermediate logical stepping-stones.
   e. *technical* results: results establishing technical details.
2. Examples
   a. *start-up* examples: perspicuous, easily understood and presented cases.
   b. *reference* examples: standard, ubiquitous cases.
   c. *counter* examples: limiting, falsifying cases.
   d. *model* examples: general, paradigmatic cases.
   e. *anomalous* examples: exceptions and pathological cases.

3. Concepts
   a. *definitions:* formal definitions and specifications.
   b. *informal paraphrases:* informal formulations.
   c. *megaprinciples:* "big" ideas like certain heuristics.
   d. *counterprinciples:* heuristic warnings.

One can also distinguish kinds of procedures, exercises, and goals. Such a taxonomy is not an inclusive classification because an item can serve more than one role; for instance, some start-up examples become reference examples as one learns more in the domain. It is also surely not an exhaustive one.

Worth Ratings.   Not all items are of equal importance. One can use a *worth rating,* such as a scheme of *'s (as in the Michelin guidebooks):

*	An interesting item, worth noticing.
**	An important item, worth a "stop."
***	A very important item, worth a "detour."
****	An extremely important item, worth a "journey" in itself.

The worth rating and the taxonomy are related in that certain classes tend to be worth more than others; culminating results tend to have three and four-star ratings, whereas technical or transitional results might not even rate one star.

Just as items can be given a worth rating, so too can relations. For instance, the dual relations of examples to a given result probably have varying degrees of worth and importance: A telling counterexample, say to the converse of a theorem, is probably much more important as a dual example than an example that is just another instance of the theorem. Tagging the relations provides a way of describing the worth of an item relative to another item. Thus in addition to the "global" worth of an item with respect to the entire knowledge domain, items can have "local" relative worth. In this way, for instance, a one-star example that is usually not very important can be recognized as very important in relation for a particular item.

Context

In describing a domain, we must also include contextual information such as assumptions about what domains precede it and which items can be taken as known or axiomatic; these might be culminating results of a predecessor domain. Also important is the state of knowledge of the learner in studying the domain, e.g., prerequisite skills and material.

In mathematics the "same" set of items can be studied in several mathematical contexts or *settings:* One can study operators in finite dimensional vector spaces (i.e., matrices) or in Hilbert space or in normed linear spaces. The settings themselves can be organized into a space with a generality relation or what AI researchers refer to as "is-a" or "ako" ("a kind of") hierarchies.

Because our purpose in this chapter is to concentrate on a domain within a given context, we do not dwell upon the influence of setting other than to say that it is important. We keep our discussion localized to one context.

Representation Frames

In our representation of an individual item we included the kinds of information just described. We use the "frame" format (Minsky, 1975) to represent an item each of whose facets or subparts is represented in a "slot" of the frame. Slots can contain declarative, procedural, or relational information. In the following discussion, slot names occur in capital letters.

Items have a NAME, like "continuity." The CLASS of an item is its taxonomic class. The WORTH slot contains an evaluation of worth, perhaps in terms of zero to four stars. Its SETTING is the context in which it is valid or presented.

An item can be presented in more than one way: as a declarative STATE-MENT, in terms of its derivation or PROCEDURE, or by a PICTURE or diagram. For instance, the declarative statement of an example states what the example exemplifies; its procedural aspect describes its construction; its picture is a schematic diagram or plot or kinetic sequence of pictures. The declarative aspect of a result is a statement of its hypotheses and conclusions (e.g., in "if–then" form); its procedural aspect is its proof. A concept can be stated declaratively or in terms of a procedure that implements it or that provides a way to test whether an item is an instance of it. For instance, the "derivative" can be defined in terms of limits or in terms of differentiation procedures. The declarative aspect of a procedure is a statement that says what it does; its procedural aspect is its code. The declarative aspect of an exercise is the problem statement; the procedure could be its solution.

Relational information is encoded in slots containing pointers to other items. IN-SPACE pointers point BACK to predecessor items and FORWARD to successors. DUAL-SPACE pointers point to dual items.

The pointers, or sets of pointers, themselves have structure. We have already mentioned the pre- and post- distinction for dual pointers and that pointers can also have worth ratings. Pointers can also be partitioned into clusters of dual items that can be thought of as a group bound to the item (e.g., a cluster of examples varying slightly only in their numerical values) or sets of predecessor items that are sufficient to derive the item (e.g., when there may be more than one way to derive a proof from other proved results).

An item can have REMARKS such as NOTA BENE's (NB) and CAVEATS, which point out particularly noteworthy or critically limiting things about the item. An item might have PRAGMATIC data telling what the item is good for. In addition, an item has PEDAGOGICAL information regarding how and when to present it, like materials needed for a demonstration of it, or leading questions to ask about it; BIBLIOGRAPHIC data like references to books, articles, films; APPLICATIONS data pointing to real-world applications. OTHER data might include historical remarks.

AN EXAMPLE

In this section, we map out and discuss a section of a high school algebra text introducing the important notion of "function." This extended example illustrates how one can distil the ingredients of knowledge from a standard mathematics text and represent them in the conceptual framework developed in the previous sections.

It should be said that in extracting this topic for illustration we lose some of its richness; it will seem shallower and less connected than it would in the context of the entire text or course. However, even in the few pages of text examined, there is a surprising amount of material.

The examples are taken from a widely used text, Dolciani, Wooton, Beckenbach, and Sharron (1968). Our example deals with the topic of functions and relations (Sections 4–1 and 4–2). It assumes background about sequences of real numbers, which was covered in the previous chapter.

Section 4–1 begins with a discussion of the example of the negative, odd integers, which can be thought of as constructed from the important reference example of the odd integers: -1, -3, -5, . . . , 1-2n, . . . Using this example, the authors introduce the notion of "pairing" and "ordered pair"; the third number in the sequence is paired with -5, through the formula 1-2n, which evaluates to -5 for $n = 3$, and, of course, by simple counting.

The authors then define the concepts of "coordinates," "components," and "equality of ordered pairs." Equality of ordered pairs is then illustrated with (3, -5) = (3, 1-2*3). Inequality is illustrated with (3, -5) $\neq$ (-5, 3). Thus the first pairs serve as an illustration (postdual example) to the "equality of ordered pair" concept; the second, a derivate of the first, as a limiting counterexample.

The discussion returns to the primary topic of functions:

> Sequences are special examples of an important mathematical concept, called a *function*. A **function** is any pairing of the members of one set (the domain) with the members of another set (the range) so that each member has *exactly one* partner in the range. Thus, the infinite arithmetic sequence -1, -3, -5, . . . is a function whose domain is {the positive integers} and whose range is {the negative odd integers}. (p. 149)

Thus, using the negative odd integers as a start-up example, the authors have introduced the definition of function. If we were to fill in representation frames for the negative odd integers example and the function concept (as presented so far), they would be:

NAME: Odd negative integers
CLASS: start-up
SETTING:

DECLARATIVE STATEMENT: This example introduces the concept of function through the concept of ordered pair.

PROCEDURAL STATEMENT: $a_n = 1 - 2n$

IN-SPACE POINTERS: BACK: Odd integers
                              FORWARD:

DUAL-POINTERS: PRECONCEPTS: Sequence
                          POSTCONCEPTS: Ordered pair, Function

---

(Note that into the frame we are entering only the knowledge presented in the text. Putting in additional knowledge that reflects our own understanding is quite a different exercise.)

NAME: function
CLASS: definition
WORTH: ***
SETTING:

DECLARATIVE STATEMENT: A *function* is any pairing of the members of one set (the *domain*) with members of another set (the *range*) so that each member has exactly one partner in the range.

IN-SPACE POINTERS: BACK: Ordered pair
                              FORWARD:

DUAL-POINTERS: PREEXAMPLES: Odd negative integers
                          POSTEXAMPLES:

NB: Each member of the domain has *exactly one* partner in the range.

(We have set the worth at three stars because Dolciani et al. have used the word "important.")

To build a complete representation, we would also need to create frames for the concepts of "ordered pair," "coordinate/component," and "equality of ordered pairs." The frame for "ordered pairs" would have a PREEXAMPLES DUAL pointer to the "negative odd integers" example which was used to motivate it; it would have FORWARD IN-SPACE pointer to the concept "coordinate/component," which in turn would have a FORWARD pointer to the concept "equality of ordered pairs," which would point BACK to "coordinate/component," which in turn would point BACK to "ordered pair." Next, the terminology of *value* and *belong to* is explicated. We have the following statement which the authors italicize for emphasis: "Thus, you can think of a function as a *set of ordered pairs in which different ordered pairs have different first coordinates*" (p.150). This paraphrase can be thought of as the first variation on the theme of function; we could represent it as a concept which follows from the function concept and *inherits* its slot values (unless otherwise noted) by *default* from its predecessor, the "function" concept. Alternatively, in our representation frame, we could introduce a slot for PARAPHRASE.

Next, we begin to acquire some procedural knowledge about functions: "One way to specify a function is to show its ordered pairs in a table with the members of the domain name in one column (or row) and the corresponding values of the function in another column (or row)" (p.150). A simple example illustrates the function table idea:

Domain Element	Function Value
−1	−1
−2	−1
3	1
4	1

Note that the authors are combining the first few integers, particularly + 1 and -1, with a sprinkling of minus signs, to generate an example. One could say that this is an instance of the heuristic of "using plus and minus one's" for generating examples.

Next comes a nota bene remark on the preceding example and the function concept: "Notice that this function does not have a different value corresponding to each different member of its domain" (p.150). This NB deserves comment and encoding as a counterprinciple, which we could name the "not necessarily one-to-one" counterprinciple or CP (not necessarily one-to-one). It is closely connected with the "exactly one" NB of the "function" concept, which also is acquiring the status of a counterprinciple, which we name CP (exactly one). As the authors state in their teacher's manual: "This is a good place to make sure that students understand that although each element of the domain of a function is paired with exactly one element in the range, there is no restriction as regards . . . an element in the range." The preceding function table example is then re-presented as an example of specifying a function by a set of ordered pairs: {(-1, 1), (-2, -1), (3,1), (4,1)}.

The section's start-up example (negative odd integers) is further used to illustrate the table procedure. It is also used to introduce specification of a function in terms of a formula and the use of a function symbol:

The formula $a_n = 1 - 2n$, $n \in$ {the positive integers} provides a compact way to show pairings in the sequence and suggests a convenient way to indicate function pairings in general. However, let us replace the symbol a_n with the *function symbol* $a(n)$, read '*a* of *n*' . . . (p. 150).

At this point there is another warning to the teacher: "Be sure that students do not call the formula a function. The formula does, however, *specify* or *define* a function over (in this case) {the positive integers}" (p.150). This is really another counterprinciple, which we name CP (formula vs. function).

To update our function frame, we would now add the function table and formula information to the PROCEDURAL STATEMENT slot, another example pointer, and pointers to the CP (not necessarily one-to-one), CP (exactly one), and CP (function vs. formula) counterprinciples.

We now come to "Example 1," the first explicitly labeled example, the standard reference example of the absolute value function over the domain of the real numbers. A discussion of the implicit definition of the domain, i.e., the domain of definition, is repesented briefly.

From these remarks, we also learn that the tacit *setting* for all the discussion is the real numbers, R. "Also, it is argued that *the domain, unless otherwise specified, consists of those real values of x for which the formula provides a unique real value of f*" (p. 151). This "agreement" is illustrated with the function $f(x) = 1/x^2$.

Note that the authors have begun to use the letter "f." This seems unremarkable to anyone who has studied functions; it is part of the tacitly held knowledge that "f's," "g's," and "h's" are often used for functions, and "a's" for sequences. Furthermore, the second function ($1/x^2$), whereas not explicitly derived from the first ($|x|$), is not unrelated to it, because the absolute value function can be defined in terms of the square root.

Thus, the authors are really using examples coming from a cluster of examples around the x^2 example. This knowledge is not explicitly present in the section of text under examination but is present in the larger fabric of algebra and mathematics in general. The connections probably help to make the discussion more coherent, at least to the authors and the teachers.

Example 2 is, in fact, the important reference example x^2, which is ubiquitous in discussions about functions, polynomials, parabolas, etc. The example is presented as: $h = \{(x, h(x)) : h(x) = x^2\}$. It is used as an illustration of the concepts of function, domain, range, and domain of definition; thus its frame would have predual pointers to these concepts and their frames would have postdual pointers to it.

The next example, Example 3, is a counterexample serving to differentiate between the concept of "set of ordered pair" and "function." It can also be thought of as a counterexample to highlight the "exactly one" counterprinciple or nota bene remark (NB) of the function concept: "Let g be the set of all ordered pairs of real numbers such that $g = \{(x, y) : xy^2 = 1\}$" (p. 151). (Notice the use of second power again.)

This counterexample for "function" serves as a start-up example for "relation," which is then defined in terms of the "ordered pair" concept. This concludes Section 4–1.

Thus at the conclusion of the text of this first section on functions, we have several elements in Examples- and Concepts-spaces, and none in the others (although we have begun to build up knowledge of procedures, like graphing, which could be represented as procedure-items when they acquire "critical mass"). We have spent most of the discussion on the "function" concept and a large part on the "negative odd integers" example.

Thus, in a very few pages (three, to be exact), we have established the "function" concept.

In a high school text, exercises play an important role. The exercises for Section 4–1 are used to provide the student practice with the new concepts. Thus they serve mostly a dual role. A few harder exercises (in group "C") serve as nice introductions to other topics by encouraging the student to discover new knowledge.

The exercises are organized according to the concepts that they treat: i.e., by dual relations to concepts. In other sections, the exercises are often dual to examples in the sense that they ask the student to work through an example or procedure.

In the second section on functions (4–2), the authors begin by discussing the notion of "mapping," introduced with an example of mapping in the everyday sense. This notion is then pulled into the function discussion: "You can think of any function as a mapping of its domain into its range" (p. 154). Thus the authors have introduced the second important variation of the function concept, which we could call the "function as mapping" megaprinciple.

The important schematic of the "mapping diagram" quickly follows. Thus the procedures of making a function table and a mapping diagram are linked. Next comes the graphing procedure: "Another way of picturing a function depends on the fact that ordered pairs of real numbers can be graphed in a plane " (p. 154).

Domain   Range

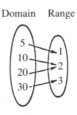

There is next a digression about graphing and coordinate systems. Before giving examples, the authors state the graphing procedure for a function and the definition of "graph": "To picture a function in the coordinate plane, plot the graphs of all the ordered pairs of the function. The set of points obtained is called the *graph* of the function." Note that the "graph" concept has been defined procedurally as the result of the "graphing procedure."

Drawing a graph is illustrated with Example 1 of Section 4–2: $1 - |x|$, which is closely related to Example 1 of Section 4–1 the absolute value function $f(x) = |x|$.

Before Example 2, $g:x \rightarrow 3x - 5$, $x \in \{1,2,3,4\}$, the authors introduce another way of representing a function as a "mapping statement" that involves the use of the arrow. Example 2 is not particularly noteworthy, except that once again it is built around the integers 1,2,3,4.

Example 3, $L = \{(x,y) \mid x = 4\}$, is used as a counterexample to distinguish between the "function" and "graph" concepts. It is dual to "exactly one" counterprinciple. It is also an example for the "relation" concept. Its graph, which lies on a vertical line, gives a pictorial representation for the "exactly one" CP.

The oral exercises for this section are quite nice, because they exercise both the mapping diagram and graph representations for functions. Included are examples that are not functions. There are several "favorite" reference examples for the concepts of one-to-one, onto, bijection, continuity, differentiability, etc. For instance, the graphical exercises (nos. 5–16) contain: (1) a function composed of other functions (#9); (2) a function with a "jump" discontinuity (#10); (3) a graph that is a well-known figure, but not a function, i.e., a circle (#11); (4) a step function (#13); (5) a nonfunction of "x," but a function of "y" (#15); (6) an absolute value function, $-|x|$ (#12); and the absolutely standard parabola $y = x^2$ (#14).

Thus in two short sections there has been a tremendous amount of knowledge clustered about the function concept.

Although it is not reasonable to expect anyone to analyze or map out all of a mathematics text in this detailed a fashion, it is useful to examine a section or two in this way to highlight the amount of knowledge that is presented or tacitly assumed, and the degree of interconnectedness of it. Such an exercise also serves to highlight the complexity of the task of learning and understanding new knowledge.

IMPLICATIONS FOR TEACHING AND LEARNING

In addition to representing the knowledge contained in textbooks, the conceptual framework can be used to organize what we know about a subject. The process of filling in the frames prompts us to recall and clarify knowledge. It can also help structure and represent lessons, which, for instance, could be thought of as a sequence of frames.

The framework can be used explicitly to help students understand or explore a domain; for instance, by asking them to map it out or fill in frames. The frame implicitly contains questions to be asked about an item (e.g., "How important is it, and why?"). Students, at least at the college level, enjoy the mapping process and find it helpful to their acquisition of understanding (e.g., when reviewing the subject). In some ways the mapping process is more important than the representation finally produced. Exercising their knowledge by directing their attention to important items and relations gives focus to their efforts at synthesis. Using specific questions that probe and prompt understanding, such as found in Rissland (1978b), gives the students a way to *actively* pursue understanding, a process often expected to happen magically.

Thus the framework suggests new homework and test questions, like those to probe dual connections (e.g., "Give two examples of this concept: a standard case and a not so nice case."). Students are not asked to give enough examples, much to their detriment because generating examples forces them to understand the concepts, results, etc. involved. One can encourage them to explore duals in another way by asking why two items, e.g., theorems, are related (even though they are found in different chapters). Such questions will encourage students to become active investigators.

For teachers, the conceptual framework offers guidance in choosing items for presentation. For instance, knowing that some examples are better than others for introducing a concept encourages one to look for such a "start-up" example to introduce a new concept. Knowing about the knowledge encourages one to tell others about it. It is easier to share one's knowledge if one has a way of talking about it. It also reminds one to tell students important learning and understanding heuristics that one often forgets to mention because they are so thoroughly assimilated. For instance, instead of hoping that the students will come to recognize an example as a standard, why not tell them it is a "reference," which they should think of as an old friend to be used to test out conjectures and new definitions.

Thus, a conceptual framework for knowledge in complex domains can help organize old knowledge and direct exploration of new. By knowing about knowing, one can be more expert in learning and teaching.

ACKNOWLEDGMENTS

This work is supported in part by NIE grant G–80–0096. Any opinions, findings, conclusions, or recommendations expressed in this chapter are those of the author and do not necessarily reflect the views of the U.S. government.

REFERENCES

Brachman (1979). On the epistemological status of semantic nets. In N. V. Findler (Ed.), *Associative networks: Representation and use of knowledge by computers*. New York: Academic Press.

Bruner, J. S. (1973). *Beyond the information given*. George Allen & Unwin.

Buchanan, B. G., & Headrick, T. E. (1970). *Some speculation about artificial intelligence and legal reasoning* (Memo AIM 123). Stanford: Stanford University, Computer Science Department.

Collins, A., & Stevens, A. (1979). *Goals and strategies of effective teachers*. Cambridge, MA: Bolt, Beranek, & Newman.

Davis, R. (1979). *Detailed description of mathematical behaviors that demonstrate understanding*. Curriculum Laboratory, University of Illinois, Urbana, IL, 61801.

Davis, R. B., & McKnight, C. C. (1979). *The conceptualization of mathematics learning as a foundation of improved measurement* (Development Report No. 4, Final Report HEW NIE/G 76 0085). Urbana: University of Illinois, College of Education, The Curriculum Laboratory.

Dolciani, M. P., Wooton, W., Beckenbach, E. F., & Sharron, S. (1968). *Algebra 2*. Boston: Houghton Mifflin.

Dunford, N., & Schwartz, J. T. (1958). *Linear operators, Part 2: Spectral theory*. New York: Interscience.

Feigenbaum, E. A., & Barr, A. (Eds). (1981). *The handbook of artificial intelligence*. Los Altos, CA: William Kaufman.

Gelbaum, B. R., & Olmstead, J. (1964). *Counterexamples in analysis*. San Francisco: Holden–Day.

Greeno, J. G., (1978). Understanding and procedural knowledge in mathematics instruction. *Educational Psychology, 12,* 262–283.

Jacobs, H. R. (1974). *Geometry*. San Francisco: W. H. Freeman.

Kuhn, T. S. (1970). *The structure of scientific revolutions* (2nd ed.). Chicago: University of Chicago Press.

Lakatos, I. (1963). Proofs and refutations. *British Journal for the Philosophy of Science, 1963, 14,* 1–25, 120–139, 221–245, 296–342. Also published by London: Cambridge University Press, 1976.

Lenat, D. B. (1976). *AM: An artificial intelligence approach to discovery in mathematics as heuristic search* (Stanford AI Lab Memo AIM–286). Stanford: Stanford University.

Minsky, M. L. (1975). A framework for representing knowledge. In P. Winston, *The psychology of computer vision*. New York: McGraw Hill.

Myers, J. L. (1980). *Structure and process in learning probability*. Proposal to the National Institute of Education. Amherst: University of Massachusetts.

Newell, A., & Simon, H. A. (1972). *Human problem solving*. Englewood Cliffs, NJ: Prentice–Hall.

Papert, S. A. (1971). *Teaching children thinking* (LOGO Memo 2). Cambridge, MA: MIT, Artificial Intelligence Laboratory.

Papert, S. A. (1980). *Mindstorms*. New York: Basic Books.

Polya, G. (1965). *Mathematical discovery* (Vol. 2). New York: Wiley.

Polya, G., & Szego, G. (1972). *Problems and theorems in analysis I*. New York: Springer–Verlag.

Quillian, M. R. (1968). Semantic memory. In M. L. Minsky, *Semantic information processing*. Cambridge, MA: The MIT Press.

Rissland, E. L. (1972a). *The structure of mathematical knowledge* (Tech. Rep. No. 472). Cambridge, MA: MIT, Artificial Intelligence Laboratory.

Rissland, E. L. (1978b). Understanding understanding mathematics. *Cognitive Science, 2*.

Rissland, E. L. (1980, May). Example generation. *Proceedings of the Third National Conference of the Canadian Society for Computational Studies of Intelligence*. CIPS, 243 College Street,

Toronto, Ontario, M5T 2Y1.

Royden, H. L. (1963). *Real analysis* (2nd ed.). New York: Macmillan.

Rudin, W. (1964). *Principles of mathematical analysis* (2nd ed.). New York: McGraw–Hill.

Rumelhart, D. E., & Ortony, A. (1977). Representation of knowledge. In R. C. Anderson, R. J. Spiro, & W. E. Montague (Eds.), *Schooling and the acquisition of knowledge.* Hillsdale, NJ: Lawrence Erlbaum Associates.

Schank, R. C., & Abelson, R. P. (1977). *Scripts, plans, goals, and understanding.* Hillsdale, NJ: Lawrence Erlbaum Associates.

Schank, R. C., & Colby, K. M. (1973). *Computer models of thought and language.* San Francisco: W. H. Freeman.

Seely–Brown, J. A., & Burton, R. R. (1977). *Diagnostic models for procedural bugs in basic mathematical skills* (Report No. 3669). Cambridge, MA: Bolt, Beranek, & Newman.

Steen, L., & Seebach, J. (1970). *Counterexamples in topology.* New York: Holt, Rinehart & Winston.

Wegner, P. (1980) *Programming with ADA: An introduction by means of graduated examples.* Englewood Cliffs, NJ: Prentice–Hall.

Winston, P. H. (1977). *Artificial intelligence.* Reading, MA: Addison–Wesley.

Problem Solving

5

The Relation of Knowledge to Problem Solving, with Examples from Kinematics

Bert F. Green
Michael McCloskey
Alfonso Caramazza
The Johns Hopkins University

Applications of cognitive psychology to science education have recently concentrated on classical physics. Studies have been made in several laboratories of the differences between novices and experts in their ability to solve problems in the physics of motion (Chi, Feltovich, & Glaser, 1981; Clement, 1978, 1982; Larkin, McDermott, Simon, & Simon, 1980). In our own work (Caramazza, McCloskey, & Green, 1981; McCloskey, Caramazza, & Green, 1980), we were struck by an important fact that must be faced by any cognitive account of how persons learn classical mechanics, as this branch of physics is called. Students do not come to the study of mechanics with a blank slate. They come with prior experience and with a good practical understanding of how objects move. They usually have some idea about the general principles underlying that motion. Unfortunately in most cases they are not quite right, and in many cases they are quite wrong.

This simple fact surprised us; we were amused by the bizarre answers students gave to seemingly simple problems. We were startled to find a student who thought that a pellet impelled through a curved tube would continue in a curved path when it emerged from the tube. And we smirked when we were told that a pendulum bob whose supporting cable broke would continue along its original path briefly and then fall perpendicularly, "when gravity took over." We were sobered to discover that such responses are not flukes —nearly half the students we tested had these or similar misconceptions about simple motion. These results are not unique. Clement (1978) had observed similar misconceptions at the University of Massachusetts, Champagne, Klopfer, and Anderson (1980) had found them at the University of Pittsburgh, Gunstone and White (1981) found them in Australia, and Viennot (1979) has found very similar results in France. (We were unaware of Viennot's work until very recently; it predated ours and reached similar conclusions.)

A little reflection suggests that "commonsense" views of motion should be expected. People got around in the world and devised successful transportation systems long before Galileo and Newton formulated the basic principles of classical mechanics. And a great many of our contemporaries manage very nicely without the straight news. After all, it is possible to play catch without being able to explain the ball's trajectory. It is also possible to drive a car without understanding acceleration. Today, most cars have two foot pedals—a "go" pedal and a "stop" pedal, with a hand lever to select forward or backward. That is all a driver ordinarily needs to know about acceleration. Most drivers interpret the accelerator as a speed control, because on a flat dry road it is nearly perfectly correlated with speed. Once in a while a driver gets the opportunity to try to control a car on icy pavement, but this is commonly considered to be a special condition involving abnormal behavior, and besides the driver is not likely to be in a mood for thoughtful contemplation of the experience. Friction is not considered in most naive accounts of motion. Indeed, we ourselves are not commonly aware that only balance and friction keep us from sliding out of our chairs onto the floor.

Motion is not the only phenomenon about which untutored people have misconceptions. Electricity is profoundly misunderstood. Anderson (1980) finds that the source-sink model of electrical power is popular. In this model, power flows from the source to the consumer, or from the outlet to the lightbulb, in the same way that water flows from pipes. Carey (1982) finds that people do not easily distinguish between heat and temperature. In the field of electronic computers, misunderstanding is vast.

Children encounter motion, electricity, heat, and even computers long before they have a chance to get formal science education. Curious children ask adults, most of whom have misconceptions, so the children's questions are not answered correctly, and the misconceptions persist as a kind of folklore. Thus, every science teacher must face the prospect that their students have serviceable misconceptions. Yet the prototypical science course ignores all preconceptions and presents the science de novo, as if it were a new branch of mathematics. Unfortunately, psychology can provide little guidance. Learning research has mainly been concerned with original learning, not unlearning or relearning. It is now generally agreed that old information does not decay in memory, but rather that later information interferes with access to the earlier information. But this consensus rests on research with word lists, not with highly structured information. Thus basic theoretical issues in the psychology of learning need as much attention as the practical matters of how to provide effective science education.

The present research does not address the psychological problems directly. It merely attempts to delineate the nature of people's misconceptions about motion, so that physics teachers will have a clearer view of their problem.

EMPIRICAL STUDIES OF MOTION CONCEPTS

In our first study of motion concepts, a questionnaire was answered that included two sets of qualitative problems. One set concerned horizontal circular motion with no consideration of gravity; the second set concerned acceleration due to gravity. A group of 50 students answered these problems. Four of the horizontal-motion problems are shown in Fig. 5.1, along with their correct answer (A, C, E, & G). Three variants of A are not shown.

Four of the vertical motion problems are shown in Fig. 5.2. Several students have now been interviewed exhaustively about their responses to these problems, and to some adjunct problems invented as the need arose in the interviews. Their responses reinforce earlier speculations about the nature of their confusions.

Problems About Circular Motion

The first set of problems consider circular motion in a horizontal plane. In three of those shown (Fig.5.1, A, C, & E), pellets or balls are impelled through curved channels; in the fourth, a tethered ball is being swung. In the first three problems, the student is to draw the path of the object as it emerges from the channel, "ignoring air resistance." In the fourth problem, the tether breaks; the ball's subsequent path is required. In all cases the correct answers are straight lines in the direction of the momentary velocity. But a surprising number of students provided curved paths. Curvature was evident in half of the paths drawn by students with no formal instruction in physics, one-third from students with one high school physics course, and one-eighth from students with one or more college courses.

According to Newton's first law, the law of inertia, every object continues in a state of rest or of uniform motion in a straight line unless acted upon by a net applied force. The responses suggest that subjects know the law of inertia in a vague way. As one subject put it, "Once a body starts in motion it tends to keep making that same motion until something else acts on it." The subject was not clear about what was meant by motion, because circular motion obviously qualified.

But there is more to it than misinterpretation of inertia. Somehow the object is imbued with a memory for past events, just like a tossed coin that "is due to come up heads" after four successive tails. If the coin can remember, why not the moving ball? Moreover, in some cases the circular paths tend to straighten, over time. The curvature dies out with distance from the channel, and the

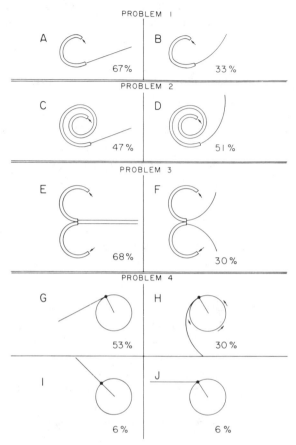

FIG. 5.1.   Typical responses to problems involving horizontal motion.

curvature is initially greater for the spiral than for the C-shaped tube. The protocols also indicate, for some subjects, that the object will not only straighten out, but it will stop. This response is rare and may be sensitive to context, for if we had put our tubes out in space, the stopping may have been avoided.

Problems About Gravity

The second series of problems shifted attention from the law of inertia to Newton's second law, $F = ma$. We used the trajectories of falling objects in the problems that tested understanding of the acceleration due to gravity. We asked one question about an object dropped from an airplane and four questions about a pendulum bob that suddenly became disconnected. Responses to the pendulum questions were readily classified and are most revealing. As shown in Fig.5.2

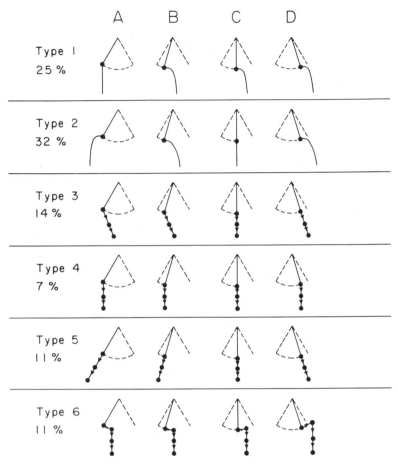

FIG. 5.2.   Typical responses to the pendulum problem.

(from Caramazza et al., 1981), about a quarter of our subjects, Type 1, respond correctly. Persons of Type 2 gave responses that have the trajectories right, but the initial velocities wrong. The Type 3's are wrong about both the initial velocities and the trajectories. The trajectories may indicate that gravity was seen as producing a velocity, not an acceleration. Type 4 respondents completely ignore the initial velocity, which is seen as having stopped when the tether broke. Type 5 subjects may have gotten confused about centrifugal force, supposing it to be dominant when the string breaks. Type 6's responses are the pure impetus responses. The object has an impetus that takes it along its course briefly, then the impetus dissipates, and gravity "takes over." When asked to draw the path of an object dropped from a plane, some of these subjects draw an inverted L; they indicate that the object initially moves in the direction of the plane, then gravity "takes over" and the object falls straight down. Another popular response to the airplane problem is a straight line trajectory similar to the Type 5 responses prevously mentioned. One subject said, "Nothing falling from an airplane drops straight down, but the reason why is because of air resistance." When asked to show what would happen in a void, the inverted L was drawn.

Probably the subjects who drew the curved trajectories had at least a general idea about acceleration due to gravity. We cannot be completely sure, for some subjects also drew parabolas for the horizontal path, with respect to the fixed ground, of an object thrown horizontally from a train traveling straight, at uniform velocity; the gradually straightening paths observed earlier may simply be instances of the ubiquitous parabola. Still, these subjects are able to adjust their responses to the falling objects in accordance with different starting conditions.

The responses tend to be consistent, indicating that they are driven by some kind of knowledge structure, however faulty. Indeed, many of the responses to these and later problems indicate a view of motion consistent with the medieval, pre-Galilean theory of impetus. According to the impetus theory, the action of an external force upon a body imparts to that body its own internal force, called impetus. Impetus is a property of that body, like its heat or weight. Impetus is the property that causes the body to move. In most versions of the theory, impetus is consumed as the object moves, and gradually dissipates, like heat. The object then either comes to rest, if on a surface, or falls straight down, if not supported. (Later sophisticated impetus theorists held that an external force was needed to change the impetus.) That the curves straighten could mean that impetus is invoked only for curved motion, and that as impetus dissipates straight line motion is the major factor. Or the motion could be the result of two kinds of impetus—with different rates of decay. In any case, the impetus theory is a useful guide for many practical situations and may well be the natural theory that rational, untutored people reach as an explanation of motion.

Of course the theory is wrong in detail, but people seldom observe their environment with enough care to notice the discrepancies. For example when a baseball player hits a foul fly ball into the stands, spectators know pretty well where it will drop. But a surprising number of fans do not seem to realize that the ball will hit their eager hands with nearly the same velocity as it had at the crack of the bat. Luckily, they seldom catch the ball. Those who do learn a valuable lesson.

Incidentally, Champagne et al. (1980) identified their subjects' beliefs as Aristotelean, rather than as an impetus belief. In both views, any motion requires a force. In the Aristotelean view, the medium in which the motion occurs transmits a continuing force from the original impeller to the object. In the impetus view, the force producing the continual motion resides in the body, as the impetus. There are several versions of the impetus theory, and there are several kinds of erroneous beliefs among our subjects. But all impetus theories hold that impetus is a property of the object. This seems to be our subjects' view. Many subjects are confused about the effect of the medium on the object but none indicated a belief that the medium transmitted the needed continuing force. We make a point of this philosophical distinction not to demean Aristotle, but to give as clear as possible a picture of the observed misconceptions. In our view it is not enough to know that a student is wrong, the teacher needs to know in what way the student is wrong.

Interviews

To gain a richer appreciation of the variety of misconceptions about motion, interviews were conducted with 13 college students, 4 of whom had had no formal physics instruction, 3 of whom had one course in high school; the remaining 6 had one or more college courses.

The results (McCloskey, 1983) show that most of the students held some form of naive impetus conception of motion. In this view, the initial force imparts an impetus to the object itself. But impetus gradually dissipates, which is why objects slow down and stop if they encounter another external force. The interviews revealed individual variants of the general impetus notion. In some, impetus must dissipate below some critical value before another force can have any effect on the object, whereas in other variants, two forces can combine impetus. Many variants admit curvilinear impetus, as indicated by the expected curved path in the ball and string problem; that is, objects moving in a curved path are expected to continue curving when there is no external force—the impetus in the object is of the curved variety. Generally, the curved aspect is more transient than the movement itself, for the path is expected to straighten, gradually.

Dynamic Visual Displays

All our work discussed so far has involved verbal problems supported by static diagrams. What if a simulated display showed the students the movements that they predict? Or what if the subject could see a variety of different movements, all but one of which is wrong? It seemed plausible that they would then be able to pick out the correct movement, or to recognize incorrect motion. So we programmed a minicomputer to display dynamic simulations of the ball and string, the pendulum, the curved tube, and the bomb falling from the plane. We showed these simulations to students, in various controlled experiments.

Alas, the results are unequivocal. Motions that are predicted, but that are physically impossible, nevertheless "look" perfectly believable. There is nothing especially compelling about the visual information. Showing the dynamic displays had virtually no effect on the subjects' judgments. We agree with the subjects; we can attest that a ball that continues curving as it emerges from the curved tube looks perfectly normal.

RELATION TO COGNITIVE PSYCHOLOGY

The work described here is a small part of a growing body of information about student misconceptions. In the field of motion, Trowbridge and McDermott (1980, 1981) showed that adults have trouble with the concepts of velocity and acceleration. Piaget (1970) reported that movement and speed are poorly understood by children. Champagne, Klopfer, and Gunstone (1982) found that many college students believe that objects fall at a constant speed. Clement (1978) has described a number of problems with which students have difficulty.

A cognitive account of the problem-solving behavior of students must rest on a description of their knowledge about motion. Scientific knowledge is of two sorts, knowledge of certain facts, principles and laws, and knowledge of procedures for applying the relevant factual knowledge to the problem situation. This is equivalent to the philosophical distinction between "knowing that" and "knowing how." Students must know *that* force equals mass times acceleration and must know *how* to determine the force acting on a body and the nature of the acceleration, if any.

Information about procedural knowledge has been obtained through a comparison of novices and experts solving problems (e.g., Bhaskar & Simon, 1977; Chi et al., 1981; Larkin & Reif, 1979; Larkin et al., 1980; Novak & Araya, 1980). Larkin et al. report that experts work forward from the quantities given in the problems to the desired unknown, whereas novices work backward from the unknown to the givens. Also experts can quickly categorize a problem (e.g., "Oh, that's an energy problem.") and have a standard procedure for dealing with each category of problem. By contrast, the nonexpert, like most of the subjects in our experiments, tries to retrieve factual and procedural knowledge relevant to the problem and then somehow constructs an answer from the retrieved data. If no data are retrieved from memory, the student lowers the criterion of relevance and tries again. Usually, several bits of knowledge are retrieved, and the student fits them together somehow. Collins, Warnock, Aiello, Nelleke, & Miller (1975) said it persuasively:

It does not trouble people much that their heads are full of incomplete, inconsistent, and uncertain information. With little trepidation they go about drawing rather doubtful conclusions from their tangled mass of knowledge, for the most part unaware of the tenuousness of their reasoning. The very tenuousness of the enterprise is bound up with the power it gives people to deal with a language and a world full of ambiguity and uncertainty. (p. 383)

The way that our subjects deal with the tangled bits of knowledge that they retrieve is not clear. Those who answer the curved tubes correctly and quickly apparently look for "motion," obtain the procedure "find forces and velocities," determine that the force is 0, and the velocity is unspecified. "Motion, no force" in turn yields Newton's first law, and they respond appropriately. Others keying on "circular motion" may find "centrifugal force," "angular momentum," and other bits of no use. Some may find a vague version of the law of inertia.

The retrieved information might either be a general principle or law, or it could be a specific experience. In the detailed interviews, subjects generally explain their responses in terms of general principles. In only a few cases is a specific experience or an example reported. Probably, if both principles and experience are retrieved, principles are preferred. But the characteristics of the situation—college professors talking to college students about obviously idealized problems—may seem to demand justification by general principles. It may be significant that the subject who referred most to specific experiences was a middle-aged lawyer, not a student.

It is possible that students *do* recall specifics but readily abstract generalities from examples. In any case, students mostly report general principles. For example, one of our subjects thinks that a swiftly moving object, when it encounters a cliff, will continue in a straight line and then fall straight down, "when gravity takes over." That is reminiscent of the coyote in the Roadrunner cartoon. But the resemblance was not volunteered. Only the general principle was enunciated.

Nearly all our subjects recalled some form of the law of inertia. Their difficulty was in knowing the details. About half did not know that it prescribed motion in a straight line. Most of the interviewed respondents did not know that it prescribed uniform motion. Many thought that all objects slow down and stop, if not acted upon by an outside force.

In the problems that involve gravity, the nature of gravity found many interpretations. Some merely retrieved the notion that gravity pulls things straight down. The nature of the pull was not clear. Some seem to understand that gravitational motion accelerates. Others thought gravity imparted a steady velocity. Some interpreted gravitational acceleration to mean that the pull of gravity was stronger close to the ground than way up in the air. One person held this belief so strongly that, given a choice between being hit on the head by an object dropped from 1 inch above the head or one dropped from 10 feet above the head, the subject opted for the 10-foot drop.

When two forces are acting on an object, a procedure must be evoked to effect some kind of resolution. Some subjects chose an average or compromise, in the manner of vector resolution. Others chose a dominance procedure, in which the stronger force acts alone, whereas the weaker force has no effect. We must be careful here, because the second force in these problems was usually gravity, which may be unique for these students. The fact is that some students thought that an object moving horizontally in the presence of gravity—the pendulum, the object dropped from a plane, and various objects propelled off various cliffs—would first exhibit horizontal motion and then fall straight down. This result requires the decaying impetus view of the horizontal motion and the dominance procedure for dealing wth competing components of velocity.

Some of the interviewees distinguished between a ball that was thrown (horizontally) off a cliff and a ball that was carried at a constant velocity to the edge of the cliff and let go. The carried object underwent what might be called passive motion, which apparently doesn't gather any impetus, because those objects were expected to fall straight down. By contrast, the thrown or impelled objects were seen as traversing parabolas, or inverted L's, having acquired impetus. The parabola indicates vector resolution; the inverted L represents the dominance view.

Some subjects correctly applied the technique of vector resolution but did not know that the vectors represented instantaneous velocities. They interpreted the vectors as trajectories. Others interpreted acceleration as velocity.

One reason for the difficulty most people have in interpreting natural motion may be that they have trouble idealizing. This would be especially the case when the ideal case is not normal, or prototypic, but is profoundly abnormal, such as the ideal of frictionless motion. People usually reserve their simplest explanations for the most commonly observed events, leaving the complications for the rare events. Thus, a surface offering an excess of friction is "sticky," a surface providing relatively little friction is "slippery." It takes expert instruction to accept the view that infinite slipperiness is ideal. Similarly, a container without any air or other content is not empty; it is viewed as containing a vacuum. This difficulty is quite natural. People view the world in terms of categories. Usually the prototypical category member is also the norm or mode. The prototypic chair has a seat, a back, and four straight legs. Most chairs are like that. But the prototypic motion is probably a throw, as in tossing a ball, or a fall, as in a dish knocked off the table, or even worse, a ride, as in a moving automobile. None is anywhere near the Newtonian ideal. Students must be taught that an extreme is really ideal. It does not come naturally.

A related problem is the human penchant for distorting truth in order to fit it into one's existing presuppositions. This is more of a problem when the truths are value laden, as in the political arena, but it is also a general cognitive problem. A student of the impetus persuasion might, upon encountering Newton's first law, decide that this meant that impetus did not die out but was permanent. Well, isn't that good enough? It will serve in many cases. But it could fail in Clement's spaceship problem, in which a ship in interstellar space is "drifting" in a path depicted as left to right across the page. At a certain point, a rocket on the object's side is turned on for a brief finite time, providing a force perpendicular to the path (toward the bottom of the paper, say). A believer in permanent impetus might choose the popular response of a straight line toward the lower corner of the page while the rocket is firing, returning to a left-to-right horizontal path when the rocket ceases, whereas in fact there is no return. The ship continues along the path followed while the rocket was active.

THE SIGNIFICANCE OF MISCONCEPTIONS
FOR INSTRUCTION IN SCIENCE

Of what use are characterizations of popular misconceptions? In our view, teachers must address the popular views as a part of instruction in the scientifically correct view. Cognitive psychologists now believe that very little is forgotten. New information either overlays or modifies old information. It is easy to overlay an incorrect law of inertia by the correct one. The other two postulates of motion can be treated in the same way. Will that suffice, or should the students be told why, or in what sense, their naive postulates are inadequate?

If old ideas neither die nor fade away, the teacher cannot simply say, "Forget all your preconceptions about motion and learn new principles." The student cannot follow that advice. If the student merely learns the new information of Newton's laws—then when he meets an unfamiliar problem, both the new and the old facts are likely to be retrieved. To prevent the old information from being used, the misconceptions must be altered in some way, by demonstrating their falseness. Because the misconceptions are the products of years of everyday experience, it seems to us that a good way to solidify the correct information and to show the error in the misconceptions is to require students to explain everyday natural phenomena in terms of the correct fundamental principles. It would probably be better for students to do it themselves rather than to hear about it, but they need careful guidance so that in the process of developing the correct explanations they make as few errors as possible. A fine example of this strategy is described by Minstrell (1980), who actively confronts the misconceptions about forces and motion, and whose students show long-term retention of the correct view.

Another possibility is to provide better experiences. On the assumption that misconceptions like impetus come from incomplete or incorrect perceptions of common events, complete accurate perception might help the student to accept the new concepts. For example, acceleration is not readily appreciated. A slow motion (possibly animated) display could show how gravity affects falling objects. A display that could be controlled by the student would be especially attractive. The student could then watch the effect of different gravities: Earth, moon, Jupiter, or some hypothetical space station.

Of course one function of laboratory experiences is to provide such insights. But another function of the lab that usually accompanies science courses is to teach scientific method and lab techniques. It is important to impart an appreciation of how science proceeds, and why precise measurements are necessary. Unfortunately for the content, method and technique are usually paramount and the students may fail to appreciate the facts being rediscovered, because they are concentrating on the methods. It seems important to use laboratory exercises both to display methods and also to provide insights.

In summary, physics courses should be designed in the knowledge that students do not correctly understand motion before the course and may cling to the various "commonsense" views that they have used all their lives, even after the course.

ACKNOWLEDGMENTS

This research was supported by NSF Award No. SED 7912741 in the Joint National Institute of Education-National Science Foundation Program of Research on Cognition Processes and the Structure of Knowledge in Science and Mathematics.

Any opinions, findings, conclusions, or recommendations expressed herein are those of the authors and do not necessarily reflect the views of the National Science Foundation or the National Institute of Education.

REFERENCES

Anderson, B. (1980, February). *Pupils' understanding of some aspects of energy transfer.* Department of Educational Research, University of Gothenberg, Box 1010, 26 Molndal, Sweden.

Bhaskar, R., & Simon, H. A. (1977). Problem solving in semantically rich domains. An example from engineering thermodynamics. *Cognitive Science, 1,* 193–215.

Caramazza, A., McCloskey, M., & Green, B. F. (1981). Naive beliefs in sophisticated subjects: Misconceptions about trajectories of objects. *Cognition, 9,* 117–128.

Carey, S. (1982). When heat and temperature are one. In D. Gentner & A. L. Stevens (Eds.), *Mental models.* Hillsdale, NJ: Lawrence Erlbaum Associates.

Champagne, A. B., Klopfer, L. E., & Anderson, J. H. (1980). Factors influencing the learning of classical mechanics. *American Journal of Physics, 4,* 1074-1079.

Champagne, A. B., Klopfer, L. E. & Gunstone, R. F. (1982). Cognitive research and the design of science instruction. *Educational Psychologist, 37,* 31-53.

Chi, M. T. H., Feltovich, P. J., & Glaser, R. (1981). Categorization and representation of physics problems by experts and novices. *Cognitive Science, 5,* 121-152.

Clement, J. (1978). *Formula-centered knowledge vs. conceptual understanding in physics* (Tech. Rep. No. 1). Amherst: University of Massachusetts, Conceptual Development Project, Department of Physics and Astronomy.

Clement, J. (1982). Students' preconceptions in introductory mechanics. *American Journal of Physics, 52,* 66–71.

Collins, A., Warnock, E. H., Aiello, Nelleke, & Miller, M. L. (1975). Reasoning from incomplete knowledge. In D. G. Bobrow & A. Collins (Eds.), *Representation and understanding.* New York: Academic Press.

Gunstone, R. F., & White, R. T. (1981). Understanding of gravity. *Science Education, 65,* 291-299.

Larkin, J., McDermott, J., Simon, D. P., & Simon, H. A. (1980, June). Expert and novice performance in solving physics problems. *Science, 208,* 1335-1345.

Larkin, J. H., & Reif, F. (1979). Understanding and teaching problem solving in physics. *European Journal of Science Education, 1,* 191-203.

McCloskey, M. (1983). Naive theories of motion. In D. Gentner & A. L. Stevens (Eds.), *Mental models.* Hillsdale, NJ: Lawrence Erlbaum Associates.

McCloskey, M., Caramazza, A., & Green, B. F. (1980). Curvilinear motion with absence of external forces: Naive beliefs about the motion of objects. *Science, 210,* 1139-1141.

Minstrell, J. (1980). *Explaining the "at rest" condition of an object.* Unpublished manuscript, Mercer Island High School, Mercer Island, Washington.

Novak, G. S., Jr., & Araya, A. A. (1980). Research on expert problem solving in physics. *Proceedings of the First Annual National Conference on Artificial Intelligence.* Stanford, CA: Stanford University.

Piaget, J. (1970). *The child's conception of movement and speed.* London: Routledge & Kegan Paul.

Trowbridge, D. E., & McDermott, L. C. (1980). An investigation of students' understanding of the concept of velocity in one dimension. *American Journal of Physics, 48,* 1020–1028.

Trowbridge, D. E., & McDermott, L. C. (1981). An investigation of students' understanding of the concept of acceleration in one dimension. *American Journal of Physics, 49,* 242-253.

Viennot, L. (1979). Spontaneous reasoning in elementary dynamics. *European Journal of Science Education, 1,* 205-221.

6 Understanding, Problem Representations, and Skill in Physics

Jill H. Larkin
Carnegie-Mellon University

Aristotle wrote in *The Art of Rhetoric:*

> All men endeavor to criticize or uphold an argument, to defend themselves or accuse. Now, the majority of people do this either at random or with a familiarity arising from habit. But since both these ways are possible, it is clear that matters can be reduced to a system, for it is possible to examine the reason why some attain their end by familiarity and others by chance; and such an examination all would at once admit to be the function of an art.

To paraphrase, all individuals endeavor to solve problems, some at random and some with skill arising from understanding. An examination of why some have this understanding and others do not is clearly the function of psychology. Indeed, as Richard Young points out (Young, 1982), Aristotle's "technical theory of art" has many similarities to theories of skill in modern rhetoric, and I think also in cognitive psychology. His central premise is that skill is not a mysterious commodity that can be merely fostered but not taught; but on the contrary it is analyzable, knowable, and teachable.

If we believe that skilled problem solving is a rational process, then we must believe that experts see in a new problem something that is familiar, something that cues use of already stored knowledge. Thus Aristotle speaks of the familiarity of habit. It is this process of making a new situation familiar that I call "understanding" the situation. The subject of this chapter is how the understanding of scientific problems occurs, how this understanding functions in problem solving, and how the understanding processes of experts and novices may differ. I also speculate on how we might teach scientific understanding.

NAIVE UNDERSTANDING

To make the discussion more concrete, consider the following problem in elementary mechanics:

A toboggan of mass m starts from rest at a height h above a valley down a perfectly slippery hill. As shown in Fig. 6.1, the toboggan then moves up over a hill with a circular cross section of radius R and a top crest located a distance y above the valley floor. What is the height h if the toboggan just barely leaves the snow surface at the top of the circular hill?

What happens when an individual reads and understands this problem? To work on the problem, the solver must convert the string of words with which he is presented into some internal mental representation that can be manipulated in efforts to solve the problem. Understanding the problem then means constructing for it one of these internal representaions. A useful and powerful representation corresponds to a good understanding, whereas a fragmented or limited representation corresponds to a poor understanding. In current theories of problem solving, internal mental representations are constructed of entities and relations between them. I distinguish between several kinds of understanding based on the nature of the entities used in the internal representation of the problem. Most people probably construct for the preceding problem what I call a naive representation, composed of entities related to familiar situations. Figure 6.2 suggests elements in such a representation. The concept of moving (like Schank's P-TRANS, Schank & Abelson, 1977) is central. Three locations are mentioned, and for each there are attributes of the motion, such as starting from rest, moving fast, or the roller-coaster sensation of just skimming the top of a hill. A more adequate reflection of how people represent this problem would be much more complex and would certainly be different for different individuals.

The important point is that, although I call it naive, this every-day representation of the problem is not trivial and constructing it depends on a lot of preexisting knowledge about toboggans and other things (e.g., roller coasters).

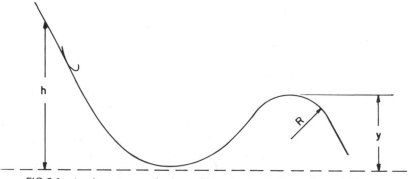

FIG.6.1   An elementary mechanics problem: A toboggan on a slippery hill.

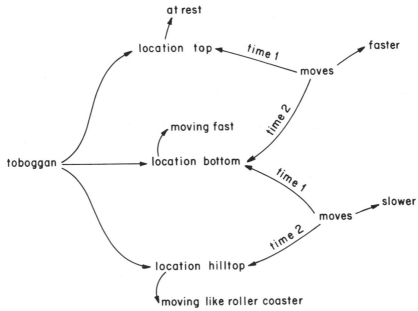

FIG. 6.2   A naive representation for the toboggan problem.

The importance of rich, intensely structured knowledge in understanding all prose is being explored intensively in the development of computer-implemented language understanders (Schank & Abelson, 1977) and in studies of how people understand stories (Rumelhart, 1975). In this chapter, I am concerned less with this naive understanding than with the special kind of understanding that comes from the knowledge possessed by individuals trained in science.

SEMANTICS OF UNDERSTANDING PROBLEMS

The message of the work previously discussed is that understanding English prose is not primarily a matter of grammatical syntax but very importantly involves knowledge that the understander brings to the situation. A Martian with good English grammar and a dictionary would have appreciable difficulty understanding physics problems (without some knowledge of physics).

To explore further the semantics of naive understanding of physics problems, I have developed a computer-implemented understanding system, called ATWOOD, that operates on a set of 22 fairly difficult problems from an introductory mechanics course.[1] The goal is to specify, by writing it in a computer

---

[1]These problems were collected and developed by Michelene Chi and Paul Feltovich, who generously allowed me to use them.

program, the knowledge that is required to understand a set of physics problems. The program processes the string of words comprising a physics problem and constructs for it an internal representation consisting of entitities (e.g., balls, planes, pulleys) and relations between them (e.g., touches, rolls-on). The program effectively constructs representations for 15 of the 22 problems. Thus its knowledge is *sufficient* for constructing representations for those problems. Experiments, described later in this chapter, suggest that, in fact, ATWOOD constructs representations that are rather similar to those constructed by knowledgeable human beings.

ATWOOD has some rudimentary knowledge about what is important in physics problems. Specifically it recognizes objects (e.g., blocks, planes, ropes, pulleys) and constructs for them mental entities that are central to its representation of the problem. It also recognizes attributes (e.g., velocity, height) and values and attaches nodes for these entities to objects and attributes, respectively. Fig. 6.3 shows one of the problems that ATWOOD understands and the semantic net it built. (A device involving two objects of roughly comparable mass, connected by a cord over a pulley, is called an Atwood machine. ATWOOD derives its name from its facility with problems involving such devices.)

Essentially ATWOOD has schemata that describe what information (e.g., objects, attributes, values) are important in physics problems, and what relations

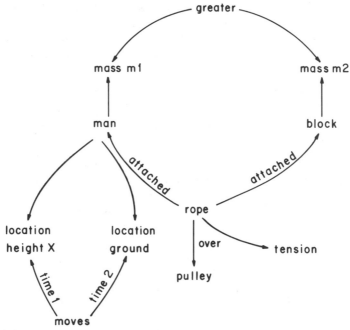

FIG.6.3   Semantic net built by ATWOOD for the problem in Table 6.1.

between such entities are legal. For example, it knows that a quantity does not have more than one symbol, and that a rod has only one length, although a spring may have more than one. It also has rudimentary knowledge of how objects are connected, for example, that ordinarily a rope is attached to two objects, and a pulley will have a rope over it. Thus the computer program ATWOOD has in it, written down in a programming language, part of the knowledge I believe is important to skilled human solvers of physics problems.

ATWOOD has strikingly little knowledge of English syntax. It does recognize sentence breaks and tags the first object encountered in a sentence as the subject. If it later encounters a pronoun, it assumes the pronoun refers to the subject of the most recent sentence. When it encounters a sentence break, ATWOOD considers all previously constructed nodes in its semantic net as "dead"; that is, nothing further can be attached to them, unless the node is reinstated, either through a pronoun, or through a repetition. But subject to this small amount of grammatical knowledge, ATWOOD simply processes one word after another. When it recognizes a word, it constructs a corresponding entity node and fits the node into the existing semantic net for the problem, following the knowledge of "legal" relations in physics problems outlined previously. ATWOOD has been run on a total of 22 problems. A total of 294 different words and symbols appear in those problems, and ATWOOD processes 98 of them. The rest are simply ignored.

The semantic nets built by ATWOOD were judged for acceptability by rough criteria that nothing in the net should be wrong, and that the information in the net should be sufficient to solve the problem. By these rough criteria ATWOOD built successful nets (i.e., successfully understood) 15 out of the 22 problems it processed. The problems for which ATWOOD was unsuccessful fall into two categories, with one problem appearing in both categories. First, ATWOOD was very successful in problems involving more than one object of the same kind (e.g., two blocks, two disks, etc.). The reason is clearly that syntactic cues are very important in distinguishing which of several objects is being referred to, and ATWOOD currently has far too little knowledge of syntax. (The problem is identical to the difficulties of the UNDERSTAND program in processing anaphoric references in the problems it encountered that involved multiple objects [monsters, globes, etc.], Hayes & Simon, 1974.) The three remaining problems for which ATWOOD was unsuccessful are wholly different from the rest; they came not from the ordinary problem section of the textbook, but from a section labeled "Questions." For example, the following problem was among them: A block of mass m, hangs from a cord C, which is attached to the ceiling. Another cord D, is attached to the bottom of the block. Explain why if you jerk suddenly on D it will break, but if you pull steadily on D, C will break. Such problems require more sophisticated understanding processes than typical problems such as that in Table 6.1, because the salient physical attributes of the objects are not mentioned.

TABLE 6.1
Problems Statements Reconstructed by Expert and Novice Subjects

---

Expert

A man of mass m_1 climbs to a height x on a rope connected to a block of mass m_2 over a pulley. The mass of the man equals the mass of the block. What is the tension in the rope?

Novice

A man of mass m_1 is standing on the ground holding a rope that passes through a pulley and has a mass of block m_2 attached to the other end of it. The block is resting on the ground and the man is holding the rope a height of x from the ground. The mass of the man equals the mass of the block. What is the tension of the rope when the man tries to lift the block, i.e., pulls on the rope?

The main goal in building ATWOOD is to use it as a vehicle to explore how human beings of varying degrees of experience understand problems. ATWOOD can build respectable semantic representations for traditional physics problems using relatively few of the words from the problem. If ATWOOD's processes are in any way analogous to human processes it should be possible for a human reader who has knowledge of what is important in physics problems (i.e., an expert) to understand a reduced problem statement that contains *only* the words that ATWOOD processes. Because ATWOOD's understanding is so heavily based on its schematic knowledge of how physics problems are constructed, these reduced problems should be almost unintelligible to a novice solver who does not possess such schemata. We have begun work in this direction, although the data reported here are very preliminary, coming from one expert and one novice working with problem versions corresponding to a preliminary version of ATWOOD.

To test the preceding ideas, a *reduced* problem form was prepared to correspond to each of the 15 problems and successfully processed by ATWOOD. The reduced form contained just those words processed by ATWOOD and excluded those that ATWOOD ignored. The reduced problem for the original problem shown in Fig. 6.3 reads:

Man mass m1 ground height x rope pulley block mass m2.

Mass man mass block.

Tension rope.

Two subjects were exposed to (these) reduced problems. The "expert" had considerable experience in solving physics problems (although he had not recently seen problems similar to the ones considered here). The "novice" had studied no physics since a single high-school course about 10 years earlier. Both subjects were told: Your task is to write what you think the original problems said. Don't spend more than about 5 minutes on any one problem. The problems constructed by these subjects were scored simply by noting whether or not they differed in substance from the original problem, i.e., whether solving the constructed problem would be different in any way from solving the original.

By that criterion, the expert correctly reconstructed 10 and the novice 2 of the 15 reduced problem statements. The 5 problems misconstructed by the expert involve verbs (e.g., compresses, slides, lowers) that ATWOOD does not currently process. Clearly these verbs are essential to an understanding of how objects interact, and a new version of ATWOOD is being built to handle them.

The problem statements reconstructed by the expert and novice subjects for the problem in Fig. 6.3 are shown in Table 6. The expert's version is just barely incorrect, probably because of ATWOOD's failure to process the verb "lowers." The novice's version is almost complete nonsense.

These preliminary results suggest that understanding of even elementary physics problems can be based very much on knowledge of how entities are related in physics problems. Thus for an expert a problem is intelligible from only a fraction of the words in the original problem statement. The same reduced statement is unintelligible to a novice. The expert understands a problem both because of general skills for processing English prose and considerable schematic knowledge of what entities are important in a physics problem and how they fit together. In contrast, the novice must try to understand the problem on the basis of general abilities for processing prose. Clearly direct investigation of how much of standard problem statements are understood by novices is needed.

SCIENTIFIC UNDERSTANDING

The kind of understanding just described involves simply building some internal representation of the important entities and relations in a text segment. As we have seen, this kind of understanding is far from trivial and involves a great deal of knowledge about what kind of entities and relations are important. However, it is still not sufficient to solve problems. As pointed out by Hayes and Simon and implemented in their UNDERSTAND program, understanding for problem solving must involve additional processing to develop "operators," things that act on a solver's current representation in order to produce new information. The action of these operators is what ultimately produces enough new information to lead to the answer. For example, in the Tower of Hanoi isomorphs used by Hayes and Simon, a problem understander must construct some representation of move (or change) operators, together with constraints on when moving or changing an entity is legal (Hayes & Simon, 1974, 1976, 1977).

In solving physics problems, the operators involved are physics principles in relations that allow the generation of new information from existing information.

Solving a problem consists of applying a sequence of these principles until the desired information is generated. This is unlike the situation with puzzles in which principles are usually already part of the solver's knowledge. (For example, he might have studied them in a textbook.) The difficulty is increased in that the operators in physics as usually taught and used by expert solvers, often do not act directly on naive problem representations. For example, both the toboggan and the atwood-machine problems discussed earlier can be solved through some combination of the following main principles:

The total force on a system is equal to its mass times its acceleration.

The total energy is conserved for a system on which no nonconservative forces act.

But a naive representation for these problems, e.g., one constructed by ATWOOD or by a novice solver (see Fig. 6.3), does not contain any forces or energies or systems. These entities are physics entities. They can be added to a problem representation only by a solver who has special knowledge of how to construct them from those appearing in a naive problem representation. I use the term scientific representation for representations that include entities such as systems and forces that appear in some scientific discipline (physics) but not in the naive understanding of untrained individuals.

Fig. 6.4 shows hypothesized scientific representations for the toboggan and atwood-machine problems. The representation for the atwood-machine problem is, in fact, very similar to representations built by PH632, the physics problem solver built by John McDermott and myself and intended to replicate major steps of the work of an expert solver (McDermott & Larkin, 1978, pp. 156–164).

The scientific representation is more abstract than the naive representation, in that many entities in the naive representation correspond to one scientific entity. For example, any object or collection of objects can be a system. Any contact (or other interaction) between systems can be characterized as a force. Abstraction is central, I think, and key to making unfamiliar problems familiar. Two problems with very different naive representations can have identical scientific representations. Thus if one has the knowledge to solve one of them in its scientific representation, the other problem becomes trivial. For example, the scientific (energy) representation of a freely moving pendulum is identical to the scientific representaion given in Fig. 6.4 for the toboggan moving down the hill.

Abstraction, of course, comes in varying degrees. For example, the physics problem-solving program ISAAC, developed by Novak, uses as its main problem representation something between my naive and scientific representations (Novak, 1976, 1977, Novak & Araya, 1980). The entities in ISAAC's representations are idealized real-world objects, for example, perfectly rigid levers and non-compressable supports. ISAAC does not construct a more abstract physical representation involving entities like torques that do not correspond to real-world

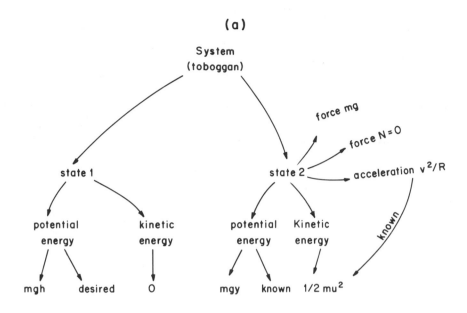

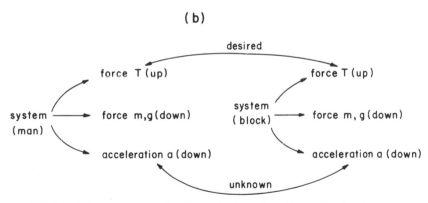

FIG.6.4   Scientific representations for (a) the Atwood-machine and (b) the toboggan problem.

objects. Instead its operators act directly on the collection of idealized objects to generate sets of equations.

Once a scientific problem representation (like the one in Fig. 6.4) is constructed, it is relatively easy to imagine how operators reflecting knowledge of physics could act to produce equations needed to find desired values or expressions. For example, for the toboggan problem a full statement of the principle of conservation of energy is: If a system goes from one state to another, and no work is done on it, then the energy of the initial state equals the energy of the final state. This statement provides a template for an equation that can be written using expressions or values for the initial and final energies of the toboggan, entities that appear in the relevant scientific representation (see Fig. 6.4). The resulting equation, $mgh = \frac{1}{2}mv^2 + mgy$, provides a large part of the solution of the toboggan problem.

To distinguish the equations used to solve the problems from the scientific understanding of the problem discussed earlier, I call these equations the mathematical representation of the problem. Mathematical representations are still more abstract than scientific representations. In other words, one entity in a mathematical representation, e.g. an equation in a particular form, can characterize scientific representations for several different problems. A striking example is an alternating-current circuit with capacitance and inductance. Compared with the pendulum and the toboggan problems considered earlier, this situation has a very different naive representation, and a substantially different scientific representation, but an identical mathematical representation.

EXPERT-NOVICE DIFFERENCES

I have described this sequence of problem representations (naive, scientific, mathematical) with the aim of stating and supporting with evidence the following hypothesis: The central difference between expert and novice solvers in a scientific domain is that novice solvers have much less ability to construct or use scientific representations. The most easily interpreted evidence is that of Chi, Feltovich, and Glaser (1981). They find that, when asked to sort physics problems into categories, inexperienced solvers use categories corresponding to what I call a naive representation of the problem. Specifically their categories corresponded to objects mentioned in the problem such as wheels or inclined planes. In contrast, experienced solvers sorted problems according to what I call a scientific representation, with categories corresponding to force problems or energy problems.

A second source of evidence is the puzzling but now repeatedly documented finding that when generating equations expert solvers tend to work "forward," starting with equations that mostly involve known quantities, whereas novices work "backward" starting with an equation involving the desired quantity (Larkin, 1980a; Larkin, 1982; Larkin, McDermott, Simon, & Simon, 1980). For example, the computer-implemented problem solver ABLE, in its more ABLE and less ABLE forms, produces problem solutions with principles applied in an order characteristic of more and less experienced human solvers (Larkin, 1980a).

For example, Table 6.2 shows the order in which ABLE would apply principles to solve the toboggan problems.

In the novice solution, typically the first principle involved would be one involving the desired quantity h (italicized in Table 6.2). Because this equation introduces an unknown quantity U_i (the initial potential energy of the toboggan), U_i becomes a desired quantity and cues the access of some principle involving it, here $E_i = U_i$, the total energy of a system equals the sum of its individual energies. The remainder of the principles in the novice column are produced by this search procedure. Italics indicate a currently desired quantity. This strategy is a general means–ends strategy applied to a mathematical representation of the problem. Each quotation is compared with the desired final state of the problem (an equation involving h and only known quantities). Deviations from this desired final state are reduced by substituting.

The typical expert order for using principles is very different. Principles are invoked when they can be used to find a new quantity. For example, in Table 6.2 because m and the gravitational constant g are known, the principle $F_g = mg$ can be used to find the gravitational force, i.e., express it in terms of known quantities. Once F_g is known, $F = F_g$ "finds" the value of the total force F. Underlining indicates newly found quantities. Similarly throughout the solution process experienced solvers seem to work forward in what is called elsewhere a knowledge development strategy (Larkin, 1980a, Larkin, et al., 1980, Simon & Simon, 1978).

These results have seemed puzzling because the backward strategy seems more intelligently directed toward the goal of finding the desired quantity. However, this is the case only if one imagines the problem being solved in its mathematical representation. Then the only cue as to what would be a useful equation is whether or not that equation would contribute directly to finding the

TABLE 6.2
Order of Principles Applied in Typical Expert and Novice Solutions
to the Toboggan Problem

Novice	Expert
$U_i = mgh$	$F_g = mg$
$E = U_i$	$F = F_g$
$E_i = E_i$	$F = ma$
$E_f = U_i + K_i$	$a = v^2/R$
$U_f = mgy$	$K_f = \frac{1}{2}mv^2$
$K_f = \frac{1}{2}mv^2$	$U_f = mgy$
$a = v^2/R$	$E = K_f + U_f$
$F = ma$	$E_i = E_f$
$F = F_g$	$E_i = U_i$
$F_g = mg$	$U_i = mgh$

desired quantity. In that representation, the means–ends strategy observed in novices is probably the best strategy available.

In contrast, if the problem is solved in the scientific representation (see Fig. 6.4), the first principles assessed are those that use entities in the naive representation to construct entities in the scientific representation, for example, $F_g = mg$ and $U_i = mgh$, relations that produce entities central to the scientific representation (forces and energies) from entities central in the naive representation (masses and heights). Major principles act to relate quantities that are known or desired in the scientific representation.

Detailed study of novice problem solutions (Larkin, 1980a) also reveals that they experience unusual difficulty with the principle: The total force on a system is equal to the sum of the individual forces on it. Indeed, in 22 solutions produced by 11 novice solvers for two moderately difficult problems in mechanics, this was the only principle consistently misapplied. I suspect that this difficulty arises because, in the naive representation used by novice solvers, forces do not appear explicitly. Thus they are easily omitted or misinterpreted.

Further evidence for the importance of a scientific representation in the problem-solving processes of experts comes from two detailed studies of experts solving more difficult problems. In one study 6 subjects, graduate students or professors in physics, solved a single difficult problem in mechanics (Larkin, 1977). Protocols from these subjects were analyzed considering only the initial section, before any equation was written, presumably before the subject began working with a mechanical representation of the problem. With the exception of one subject (who became thoroughly confused and never solved the problem), each subject considered one or more possible scientific representations. For example, one subject considered the *forces* in the problem and then changed to a representation involving the *virtual works* in the problem. If a subject discarded a possible representation, he or she did so without ever writing an equation. If the subject used a selected scientific representation to write a corresponding mathematical equation, he or she was then always successful in using that representation, and the associated equation, to solve the problem correctly. Two subjects considered just one scientific representation. Within seconds after reading the problem these subjects made a statement like, "I know how to do this one, it's virtual work." These subjects thus recognized from the immediate naive problem representation (or perhaps even from the word strings) what scientific representation would be appropriate. But note that they identified a scientific representation (e.g., virtual work), and not a mathematical representation, an equation.

A second detailed study involved a single expert subject solving five moderately difficult mechanics problems (Larkin, 1980b, McDermott & Larkin, 1978, pp. 156–164). Our aim was to develop a computer-implemented problem-solving system that would take steps analogous to those seen in the protocols of our expert subject. This particular subject was very articulate and complete in his descriptions. The protocols are clearly divided into sections that represent reasoning about the naive representation (blocks and strings); sections involving forces (scientific representation); and sections involving mathematics. Thus, in building a system to produce solutions analogous to his, we were required to consider explicitly these different kinds of representations and to build in capabilities for constructing and using them.

A final set of data that fits with the hypothesis stated previously comes from Clement and his colleagues (Clement, Lochhead, & Soloway, 1979). They find that a large number (47%) of entering engineering students do not solve the following problem correctly: Write an equation using the variables S and P to represent the following statement: "There are 6 times as many students as professors at this university. Use S for the number of students and P for the number of professors." (A hint, "Be careful: Some students put a number in a wrong place in the equation," had no significant effect, increasing the percentage of correct solutions by only 3–5%.)

The student solvers apparently do not have difficulty with mathematical representations; over 90% of them can reliably solve simple equations. And many clearly indicate that their naive representation of the problem is correct, making statements like, "There's six times as many students, which means it's six students to one professor."

I think what causes errors like these is translating directly from a correct naive representation, six students to one professor, to an incorrect mathematical representation, $6S = P$. What may be lacking is an intermediate (scientific) representation of how the *number* of students is related to the *number* of professors in the situation described. Clement and his colleagues address this issue by asking students to use an active operation to solve the problem, specifically to write a BASIC computer program to find the number of professors from the number of students. Writing the program encourages construction of an intermediate (scientific) representation which is reflected by students' statements, for example, "If you want to even out the number of students to the number of professors, you'd have to have six times as many professors."

TEACHING SCIENTIFIC UNDERSTANDING

I have recently been discussing with individuals teaching university-level basic sciences what topics cause particular difficulties in these courses. Throughout these discussions I have been struck that these topics seem to be characterized by a need for what I have called a scientific representation. I give two examples.

The first chapters in a physics book are usually concerned with measurement and with motion, specifically with relating different descriptions of motion such as distance, velocity, and acceleration. These quantities all appear in naive representations; position and speed of an object are certainly part of one's ordinary observations of it. Beginning physics students first encounter serious difficulties when they meet the quantity force, a quantity that is not part of our ordinary naive representation of situations, at least in the way that physicists use the term.

In beginning organic chemistry, students are often given a description of chemicals combined under specified conditions and asked what chemicals will be produced. Being able to answer such questions would apparently require memorization of vast numbers of reaction equations. How else could one know that ethyl acetate, in the presence of sodium hydroxide, water, and heat, reacts to form sodium acetate, and then in the presence of hydrogen chloride to form acetic acid? Students of organic chemistry apparently do spend large amounts of time, often with "flash cards," memorizing reactions that describe the naive representation of the problem—the representation that involves the chemicals one would see or measure directly. Watching skilled organic chemists perform a similar task, however, makes it clear they use very different procedures that have little to do with memorized individual reactions. They abstract from the chemicals appearing in the reaction certain important features (e.g., bond angles, reactivity of various sites). These abstracted features tell them how the chemical entities involved could react. They make the original problem, which might have been novel, something familiar. In this way, they are able to predict what particular chemicals will be produced.

Why do we have so little success, in these and other situations, in teaching students to use scientific representations? I think a main reason may be that these representations are not recognized or taught explicitly. For example, the problem solution in Fig. 6.5 comes from a textbook (Bueche, 1980) that actually does an extraordinarily good job in describing the complete solutions to problems. Furthermore, the scientific representation used for this problem, a representation in terms of forces, is one of the few that actually has a well-established notation for it. Yet the impression one gets in reading the sample solution is that the equations are what is important, i.e., that one goes directly from the original statement of the problem (naive representation) to the equations (mathematical representation).

Fig. 6.6 shows a section on addition reactions from an organic chemistry textbook (Solomons, 1978). As a "student" I find the grouping together of examples of addition reactions helpful. I also note, although it is pointed out only in passing, that the hydrocarbons participating in the addition reactions are always doubly bonded. But what other molecules can participate in addition reactions? On the basis of this section of text, my only solution would be to do what real students seem to do, i.e., to memorize a list of compounds that can participate in addition reactions.

What could we do to teach better scientific understanding? We really know very little about the details of learning in complex domains, so these comments must necessarily be speculative. However, it seems to me worth attempting the

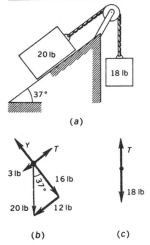

(a)

(b)   **(c)**

How large would the friction force
have to be if the system were to remain at rest?

In figure 5.12 the friction force between the block and plane
is 3.0 lb. Find the acceleration of the system and the tension
in the rope.

Reasoning Let us first decide which way the system
would move if the friction force were zero. The free-body
diagrams are shown in parts (b) and (c). As shown in part
(b), the component of the 20-lb weight pulling down the incline is 12 lb. This force would tend to pull the 18 lb weight
upward. However, this latter block is pulled downward by
an even larger force, 18 lb, and so it will actually fall. We see
then that the block on the incline will move up the incline.
The 3-lb friction force will tend to oppose this motion, and
so it is directed down the incline.

Referring to part (c), we can write $F = ma$ by using the direction of motion as positive and recalling that $m = W/g$,
where $g = 32$ ft/s^2 in this case. Therefore

$$18 - T = \tfrac{18}{32}a$$

Similarly for the situation shown in part (b)

$$T - 12 - 3 = \tfrac{20}{32}a$$

where the units in these equations should be supplied by the
student. Adding the two equations yields

Placing this value in either of the equations gives

$$T = 16.6 \text{ lb}$$

FIG.6.5   Solution to a problem as presented by a physics textbook. (From Bueche,
1980. Reprinted with permission.)

development of instruction that would make explicit to students how to construct
and use the scientific representations that experts use.

In some cases this explicitness may merely involve better instruction in how
to do something that experts do overtly. For example, in constructing a force
representation for a problem experts often draw what is called a "free-body"
diagram. Such a diagram uses labeled arrows of varying lengths to represent the
rough directions and magnitudes of all the forces acting on a system. For the
student who may not be able to keep the entire representation in his or her head,
this use of a specified external notation can be very helpful. What is needed
then is more extensive instruction in how to construct and use this readily visible
representation.

In other cases teaching students to use a scientific representation may be more
difficult, because experts do not use an explicit overt symbolism for this representation. In that case it may be necessary to invert such a symbolism to ease
the students entry into using this representation, Gordon (1980) has brought
together elements of a representation for features important in reacting organic

The most characteristic reaction of compounds containing multiple bonds is an *addition reaction*. When a reagent X-Y *adds* to a carbon-carbon double bond, X becomes attached to one atom of the double bond and Y to the other. The double bond changes to a single bond.

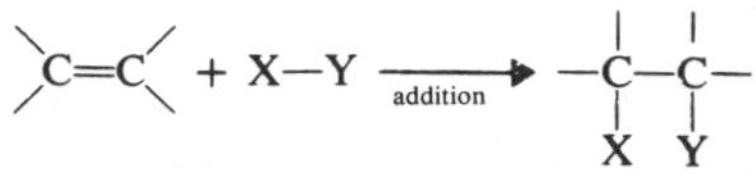

$$\begin{array}{c} \diagup \\ C=C \\ \diagup \end{array} + X-Y \xrightarrow[addition]{} \begin{array}{c} | \quad | \\ -C-C- \\ | \quad | \\ X \quad Y \end{array}$$

A specific example is the addition of hydrogen bromide to ethene.

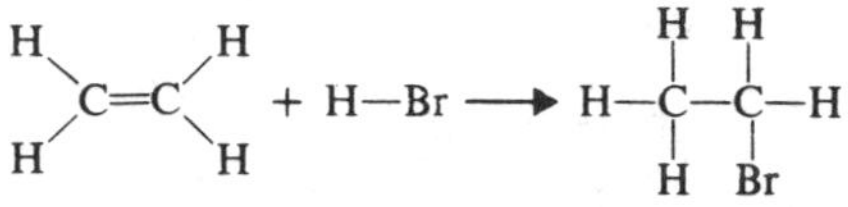

$$\begin{array}{cc} H \diagdown \quad \diagup H \\ C=C \\ H \diagup \quad \diagdown H \end{array} + H-Br \longrightarrow \begin{array}{c} H \quad H \\ | \quad | \\ H-C-C-H \\ | \quad | \\ H \quad Br \end{array}$$

Bromoethane

The reagent that adds may also be a symmetrical reagent, as in the addition of bromine to ethene.

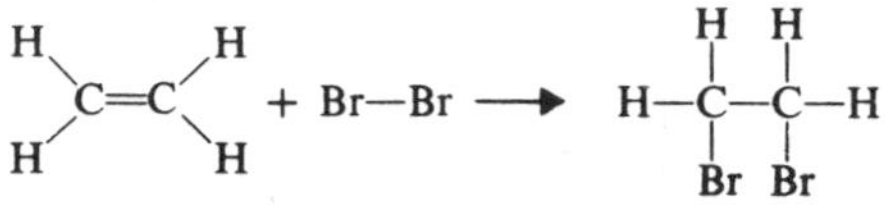

$$\begin{array}{cc} H \diagdown \quad \diagup H \\ C=C \\ H \diagup \quad \diagdown H \end{array} + Br-Br \longrightarrow \begin{array}{c} H \quad H \\ | \quad | \\ H-C-C-H \\ | \quad | \\ Br \quad Br \end{array}$$

1,2-Dibromoethane

Further examples of addition reactions of both symmetrical and unsymmetrical reagents to ethene are shown below.

$$CH_2{=}CH_2 + Cl_2 \longrightarrow CH_2ClCH_2Cl \quad \text{1,2-Dichloroethane}$$

$$CH_2{=}CH_2 + HCl \longrightarrow CH_3CH_2Cl \quad \text{Chloroethane}$$

$$CH_2{=}CH_2 + HI \longrightarrow CH_3CH_2I \quad \text{Iodoethane}$$

$$CH_2{=}CH_2 + HOH \xrightarrow{H^+} CH_3CH_2OH \quad \text{Ethanol*}$$

Propene shows the same addition reactions. If the adding reagent is symmetrical only one product can result:

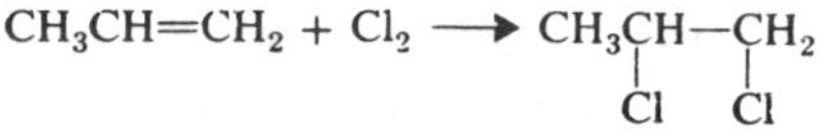

$$CH_3CH{=}CH_2 + Cl_2 \longrightarrow \begin{array}{c} CH_3CH-CH_2 \\ | \quad | \\ Cl \quad Cl \end{array} \quad \text{1,2-Dichloropropane}$$

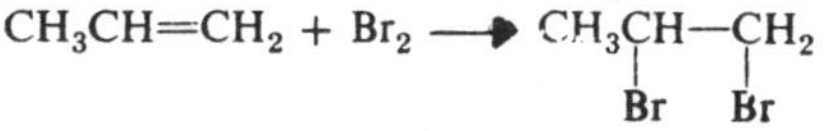

$$CH_3CH{=}CH_2 + Br_2 \longrightarrow \begin{array}{c} CH_3CH-CH_2 \\ | \quad | \\ Br \quad Br \end{array} \quad \text{1,2-Dibromopropane}$$

FIG.6.6   A set of related reactions described in a textbook on organic chemistry. (From Solomons, T.W.G. [1978]. *Organic chemistry*. Reprinted by permission of John Wiley & Sons, Inc.)

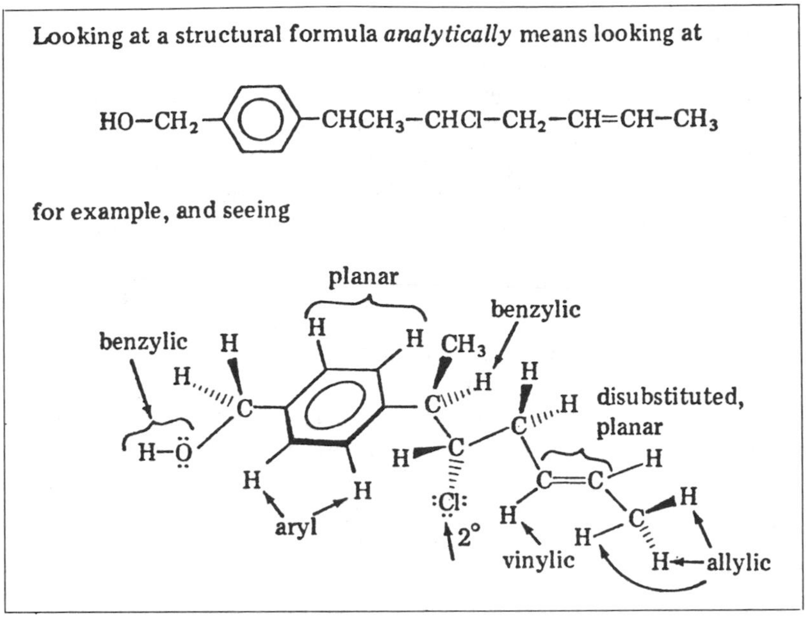

FIG.6.7 Scientific representation of an organic molecule. (From Gordon, J.E. [1980]. *How to succeed in organic chemistry.* Reprinted by permission of John Wiley & Sons, Inc.)

molecules. For example, Fig. 6.7 shows a representation of a molecule showing its bond angles. What is needed in addition to exhibiting this representation to the student is some systematic instruction in how to construct such representations, and how to use them in predicting what products will be produced in a reaction.

SUMMARY

Powerful problem solving is impossible without understanding. A useful definition of understanding is that it is the processing of the original problem presentation to construct a meaningful internal representation that can be manipulated by the solver in order to produce the desired result. As in many models for human information processing, I describe such internal representations as semantic nets, or sets of internal symbols for entities connected by relations.

The nature of the entities in the representation are crucial in determining how problem solving proceeds. Specifically, untrained individuals seem to produce what I call a "naive" representation, composed of entities familiar to everyday life. In contrast, individuals trained in a science can produce problem representations composed of entities that have special powerful meanings in the science. For example, many physics students understand problems in terms of the physical objects mentioned (e.g., toboggans, wheels), whereas skilled physicists understand the same problems in terms of physics entities (e.g., forces, momenta).

The kind of representation used is crucial to solving problems, because it determines the kind of operators that can act to produce new information. A solver working with a naive representation of a physics problem, a representation that contains no forces, is exceedingly unlikely initially to consider using force principles and may be prone to errors in finding forces. On the other hand, if a scientific representation involving forces has been constructed, the use of these principles becomes straightforward.

I have argued on the basis of various evidence that a central difference between expert and novice problem solvers is the extent to which they can use these specialized scientific representations. I describe in this chapter a variety of empirical work supporting the premise that this difference in representation is a major source of the different performance of experts and novices in technical problem solving. This evidence includes: (1) the categories into which solvers sort problems. Novice categories correspond to important entities in the immediate naive representation of the problems. Expert categories correspond to entities important in scientific (physical) representation; (2) the order in which principles are applied;. Novices select principles on the basis of a mathematical means–ends strategy. Experts use first those needed to develop a scientific representation; (3) detailed study of the processes of skilled solvers. Skilled solvers working on difficult problems spend a lot of time developing and testing possible scientific representations. Once a scientific representation is constructed, the mathematical solution proceeds rapidly.

Finally, I have speculated and suggested, with two examples, why students so often fail to acquire the use of scientific representations, and how we might begin to teach better the use of such representations. In some cases (e.g., the "force" or "free-body" diagrams use in mechanics), such instruction is made easier by the fact that good notations for scientific representations already exist. In many more cases, the first task may be to invent such a notation. In all cases, however, it remains to design reliable instruction in how to construct and use scientific problem representations.

ACKNOWLEDGMENTS

This work was supported by NIE–NSF grant number 1–55682. My thinking about these issues owes much to the members of the Working Group in Physics, in particular, Herbert and Dorothea Simon, James Greeno, and John McDermott. Thanks are due to Diane Mierkiewicz for comments on an earlier draft.

REFERENCES

Aristotle. (1959). *The "art" of rhetoric* (John Henry Freese, Trans.). Cambridge, MA: Harvard University Press.

Bueche, F.J. (1980). *Introduction to physics for scientists and engineers.* New York: McGraw–Hill.

Chi, M. T. H., Feltovich, P. J., & Glaser, R. (1981). Categorization and representation of physics knowledge by experts and novices. *Cognitive Science, 5,* 121–152.

Clement, J., Lochhead, J., & Soloway, E. (1979). *Translating between symbol systems: Isolating a common difficulty in solving algebra word problems* (Tech. Rep.). Amherst: The University of Massachusetts, Cognitive Development Project, Department of Physics and Astronomy.

Gordon, J. E. (1980). *How to succeed in organic chemistry.* New York: Wiley.

Hayes, J. R., & Simon, H. A. (1974). Understanding written task instructions. In L. W. Gregg (Ed.), *Knowledge and cognition.* Hillsdale, NJ: Lawrence Erlbaum Associates.

Hayes, J. R., & Simon, H. A. (1976). The understanding process: Problem isomorphs. *Cognitive Psychology, 8,* 165–190.

Hayes, J. R., & Simon, H. A. (1977). Psychological differences among problem isomorphs. In N. J. Castellan, G. R. Pisoni, & G. R. Potts (Eds.), *Cognitive theory.* Hillsdale, NJ: Lawrence Erlbaum Associates.

Larkin, J. H. (1977, July). *Problem solving in physics* (Tech. Rep.). Berkeley: University of California, Group in Science and Mathematics Education.

Larkin, J. H. (1980a). Enriching formal knowledge: A model for learning to solve problems in physics. In J. Anderson (Ed.), *Cognitive skills and their acquisition.* Hillsdale, NJ: Lawrence Erlbaum Associates.

Larkin, J. H. (1980b). Skilled problem solving in physics: A hierarchical planning approach. *Journal of Structural Learning, 6* (4), 121–130.

Larkin, J. H. (1982). The cognition of learning physics. *American Journal of Physics, 49,* 534–541.

Larkin, J. H., McDermott, J., Simon, D. P. & Simon, H. A. (1980). Models of competence in solving physics problems. *Cognitive Science, 4,* 317–345.

McDermott, J., & Larkin, J.H. (1978). *Representing textbook physics problems.* The Canadian society for computational studies of intelligence. Toronto: University of Toronto Press.

Novak, G. S. (1976). *Computer understanding of physics problems stated in natural language.* Unpublished doctoral thesis, University of Texas at Austin.

Novak, G. S. (1977). Representations of knowledge in a program for solving physics problems. *International Joint Conference on Artificial Intelligence, 5,* 286–291.

Novak, G. S., & Araya, A. A. (1980). *Research on expert problem solving in physics* (Tech. Rep. NL–40). Austin: The University of Texas, Department of Computer Sciences.

Rumelhart, D. E. (1975). Notes on a schema for stories. In D. G. Bobrow & A. Collins (Eds.), *Representation and understanding.* New York: Academic Press.

Schank, R., & Abelson, R. (1977). *Scripts, plans, goals, and understanding.* Hillsdale, NJ: Lawrence Erlbaum Associates.

Simon, D. P., & Simon, H. A. (1978). Individual differences in solving physics problems. In R. Siegler (Ed.), *Children's thinking: What develops?.* Hillsdale, N.J.: Lawrence Erlbaum Associates.

Solomons, T. W. G. (1978). *Organic chemistry.* New York: Wiley.

Young, R. E. (1982). Concepts of art and the teaching of writing. In J. J. Murphy (Ed.), *The Rhetoric tradition and modern writing.* New York: Modern Language Association.

7 Encoding and the Development of Problem Solving

Robert S. Siegler
Carnegie-Mellon University

Why do older children solve problems more successfully than younger children; why do experts solve problems more successfully than novices; why do normal children solve problems more successfully than retardates? In all cases, the answer has much to do with the way that people within the two groups represent the problems in memory, that is, with how they encode them.

Many sources of evidence converge on the view that encoding is a crucial part of problem solving and of cognition in general. Consider first an anecdotal example using reactions to art and music. When an especially innovative piece is first seen or heard, it is common for critics and the general public to experience it as not making sense, as being chaotic, and as being impossible to recall in any detail. With increased exposure to the piece and to related ones, and with increased knowledge about them, people often cease to view such innovations as strange; instead, the creations may be hailed as works of genius. Such changes in encoding can be produced by exposure to the particular work but can also be produced through less directly relevant experience. Bernard Levin, a British critic, commented that when he heard the premiere performance of Bartok's Concerto for Violin and Orchestra, early in Bartok's career, neither he nor other critics could make sense of it. When he heard the piece's next performance in England, almost 20 years later, it seemed eminently musical. Levin's explanation was that he "had come to hear the world with different ears" (*London Daily Telegraph*, June 8, 1977).

Expert problem solving has been found to be associated with extremely sophisticated encoding. De Groot (1966) found that a chess grandmaster could often select within a few seconds the correct move in a chess configuration. His research indicated that an important component of the grandmaster's skill was the ability to recognize almost immediately configurations of chess pieces and types of moves that might be appropriate given such configurations. Chase and Simon (1973) demonstrated that this did not imply that the grandmaster simply had better memory for chess configurations in general. They briefly presented chess masters and nonmasters with arrangements of chess pieces and then asked them to reproduce the arrangements. Some of the configurations were well organized and others consisted of haphazardly placed pieces. The chess masters were far superior in reproducing the well-arranged configurations, but there was no difference between the two groups in ability to reproduce the disorganized placements. Thus, the experts' superior encoding seemed to be at the level of organized configurations rather than at the level of individual pieces. In a similar demonstration, Chi and Glaser (1979) showed that physicists encoded physics problems in terms of general principles (e.g., a Conservation of Energy problem), whereas undergraduates encoded the problems in terms of more particular details (e.g., a blocks-on-an-inclined-plane problem).

The importance of encoding in basic perceptual and memorial processes also has been amply demonstrated. Garner (1974) summarized research indicating that performance on numerous classic psychological tasks (e.g., discrimination, paired-associate learning, memory scanning) was dependent on the difficulty of encoding the stimuli and distinguishing the encodings once they were in memory. Wickens (1972), in his research on release from proactive inhibition, found that shifts in the contents of some but not all dimensions were associated with increases in recall and recognition; he attributed this to the subjects' encoding some but not all possible dimensions on his task. Similarly, Neisser (1967) proposed that many but not all the dimensions present in any given stimulus are represented internally.

Recently, my colleagues and I have been studying children's problem solving. The research has focused on three aspects of this topic: children's existing knowledge of the problems, their response to instructional experiences that might advance their knowledge, and the basic processes that presumably underlie developmental differences in existing knowledge and in learning. Encoding has emerged as a particularly important process in accounting for why older children are better able than younger children to learn new material. The research is described in the following sections.

THE RULE-ASSESSMENT APPROACH

I developed the rule-assessment approach so that I could study children's strategies for solving Piagetian problems involving concepts such as conservation, proportionality, time, speed, and distance. Such problems are simple compared to many of the tasks that are studied with adults. Individual items differ along a few well-defined dimensions, and relatively simple solution formulas exist that are sufficient to yield correct answers to all possible items. Children often find these problems quite difficult, however, and prove resistant to seemingly reasonable instructional efforts. Therefore, these Piagetian problems have generated a huge research literature in developmental psychology. The goal of the rule-assessment approach was to assess children's reasoning in the several years between when they first knew anything about the problems and when they mastered them. The rule-assessment approach is based upon five assumptions:

1.   Children's conceptual understanding progresses through a regular sequence of qualitatively discrete rules.

2.   These rules are ordered in terms of increasing correlation with the correct rule in environments that the children encounter. Children will not adopt a new rule that is less correlated with the correct rule than the rule that they are already using.

3.   The effectiveness of a learning experience that aims at helping a child to use the next rule is largely determined by whether the learning experience discriminates the child's existing rule from the more correct rule. If the learning experience does not discriminate between the two rules, the child will continue to use his original rule. If the learning experience does discriminate between the two rules, the child will either adopt a more advanced rule or enter into a rule search state in which he is unsure which rule is correct.

4.   A major reason why children do not immediately adopt the correct rule for all concepts and why they have difficulty in learning is inadequate encoding of the correct rules' component dimensions. Understanding of concepts frequently requires integration of several component dimensions. Inadequate encoding of one or more of them can restrict children's ability to learn the concept (as can lack of knowledge of the appropriate method for combining the dimensions).

5.   Inadequate encoding may be caused by lack of knowledge of a dimension's importance or lack of perceptual salience relative to other dimensions of the situation that the concept is to be applied in. Increasing a child's knowledge of a dimension's importance or increasing a dimension's perceptual salience can lead to improved ability to learn, which in turn can lead to improved knowledge.

The research that we have done to test this model of conceptual development has a cyclical flavor. First, we develop means for determining what children already know about a concept; the rule-assessment method that we have used for this purpose is described later. Next, we use these assessments of existing knowledge to predict children's ability to learn new information about the concept. If the assessments of existing knowledge fail to adequately predict what learning occurs, this indicates that we need to develop more comprehensive assessments of the children's initial knowledge. These more comprehensive assessments typically include direct measures of the children's encoding. We then examine the usefulness of the new assessments in predicting when learning will occur and what form it will take.

Central to this approach is a methodology for determining which rule an individual child is using. The basic strategy that has been used is to formulate problem types that yield distinct patterns of correct answers and errors for children using different rules. To date, this error-analysis methodology has been applied to studying children's rules on 11 tasks: the balance scale, projection of shadows, probability, fullness, conservation of liquid quantity, conservation of solid quantity, conservation of number, speed, time, distance, and the Tower of Hanoi (Klahr & Robinson, 1981; Siegler, 1976, 1978, 1981; Siegler & Richards, 1979; Siegler & Vago, 1978). The next two examples illustrate how the approach works and how it can be used to study the relationship between existing knowledge, learning, and encoding.

Children's Understanding of Balance Scales

Existing Knowledge.   The first context in which we applied the rule-assessment methodology was the balance-scale task. The apparatus for this task is shown in Fig. 7.1. On each side of the balance's fulcrum are four pegs on which metal weights can be placed. The balance's arm can tip left or right or remain level, depending on how the weights are arranged. However, a lever (not shown in Fig. 7.1) can be set to hold the arm motionless. The task is to predict which (if either) side would go down if the lever were released.

The first step in applying the rule-assessment methodology to the balance-scale task was hypothesizing the rules that children might use. Siegler (1976) suggested that children would use one of the four rules illustrated in Fig. 7.2. Children using Rule I consider only the number of weights on each side of the fulcrum. If they are the same for the two sides, the children predict that the scale will balance; otherwise they predict that the side with the greater weight will go down. Children using Rule II base their judgments exclusively on the amount of weight if the two sides have different amounts of weight, but if their weights are equal, they also consider the distances of the weights from the fulcrum. Children using Rule III always consider both the amount of weight and the distance of the weights from the fulcrum. They consistently answer correctly

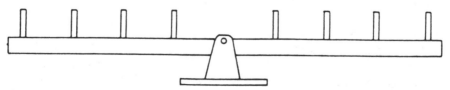

FIG. 7.1.   The balance scale.

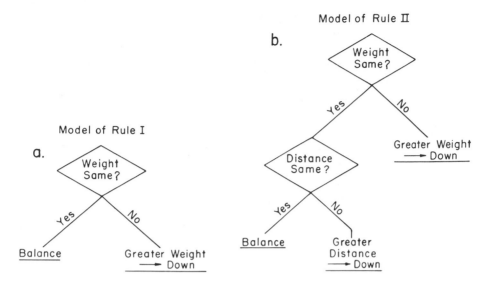

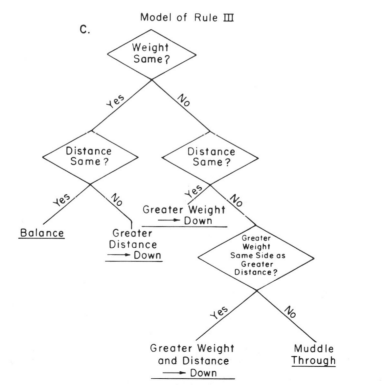

FIG. 7.2.   Decision tree model of rule for performing balance-scale task. From Siegler (1976, pp. 484–485); used here with permission.

Model of Rule IV

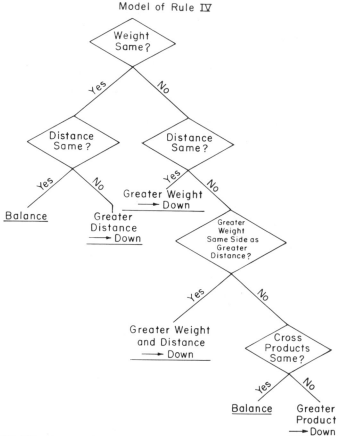

FIG. 7.2.   (*continued*)

when the weights, distances, or both are equal on the two sides of the fulcrum. However, they do not have any set decision rule for situations in which one side has more weight and the other side has its weight further from the fulcrum. In such situations, they can only muddle through or guess. Finally, children using Rule IV always consider both weight and distance dimensions, use the sum-of-cross-products formula when one side has more weight and the other side more distance and therefore answer all types of problems consistently correctly.

The next step in using the rule-assessment approach was to determine which, if any, of these rule models accurately characterized children's knowledge about balance scales. Six types of problems were generated on which children using different rules would generate distinct patterns of performance. The problem types, which are illustrated in Table 7.1, were: *balance problems,* with the same configuration of weights on pegs on each side of the fulcrum; *weight problems,* with unequal amounts of weight equidistant from the fulcrum; *distance problems,*

TABLE 7.1
Number of Children Using Each Rule on Balance-Scale Task—
Predictions Criterion
(from Siegler, 1976, Experiment 1, A Priori Condition)

| Age | Rule | | | | Unclassifiable |
	I	II	III	IV	
5–6	9	0	0	0	1
9–10	1	4	2	1	2
13–14	1	4	4	0	1
16–17	0	4	5	1	0

with equal amounts of weight different distances from the fulcrum; *conflict-weight problems,* with one side having more weight, the other side having its weight farther from the fulcrum, and the side with more weight going down; *conflict-distance problems,* with one side having more weight, the other side more distance, and the side with more distance going down; *conflict-equal problems,* with the usual conflict between weight and distance cues and the two sides balancing.

As illustrated in Fig. 7.3, the different rules lead to different response patterns on these six problem types. Children using Rule I would always predict correctly on balance, weight, and conflict-weight problems and would never predict correctly on the other three problem types. Children using Rule II would generate the same pattern of performance except that they would solve distance problems. Children using Rule III would invariably be correct on all three nonconflict problem types and would perform at a chance level on the three types of conflict problems. Children using Rule IV would solve all problem types.

To the extent that young children use the simpler rules and older children the more complex ones, these descriptions imply distinct developmental patterns for each of the six types of problems. Most interesting, perhaps, is the predicted developmental decrement in performance on conflict-weight problems. Young children, using Rules I and II, should consistently get these problems right, whereas older ones, using Rule III, should muddle through on them and be correct only one-third of the time. Performance on distance problems should show the most dramatic developmental increment, from below-chance performance in children using Rule I to 100% correct performance in children using the other three rules. To the extent that the rule models are accurate characterizations of children's knowledge, these patterns should hold for all items within a problem type, regardless of the particular numbers of weights that are used or the placements of the weights.

We have adopted a quite rigorous criterion for rule usage. Saying that a child used Rule I or Rule II or Rule IV indicates which of the three possible responses he or she should make on each item: left side down, right side down, or balance.

FIG. 7.3

Predictions for Percentage of Correct Answers and Errors for Children Using Different Rules—Balance Scale Task

Problem-Type	Rule			
	I	II	III	IV
Balance	100	100	100	100
Weight	100	100	100	100
Distance	0 (Should say "Balance")	100	100	100
Conflict-Weight	100	100	33 (Chance Responding)	100
Conflict-Distance	0 (Should say "Right Down")	0 (Should say "Right Down")	33 (Chance Responding)	100
Conflict-Balance	0 (Should say "Right Down")	0 (Should say "Right Down")	33 (Chance Responding)	100

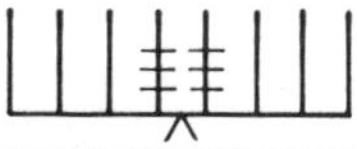

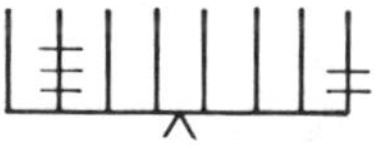

Note. From "Three Aspects of Cognitive Development" by R. S. Siegler, *Cognitive Psychology,* 1976, *8*, 481-520. Copyright 1976 by Academic Press. Reprinted by permission.

In order for the child to be said to be using a rule, he or she would need to answer at least 80% of the items in accord with the predictions of that rule. The likelihood that a random responder would be misclassified as using a rule by this criterion is less than one chance in five million.

In the first study using the rule-assessment approach (Siegler, 1976; Experiment 1), we examined 5-, 9-, 13-, and 17-year-olds' existing knowledge about balance scales. In the experimental condition of interest here (the a priori condition), children were simply presented 30 test items without feedback.

As shown in Table 7.1, the rule models fit the predictions of more than 80% of children of each age. Five-year-olds most often used Rule I, 9-year-olds most often used Rules II or III, and 13- and 17-year-olds most often used Rule III. Few children of any age used Rule IV. Children's explanations of their choices closely paralleled their predictions; 80% of the children were classified as using the same rule by predictions and explanations criteria.

In addition, the expected developmental patterns across groups were present (Table 7.2). On conflict-weight problems, the percentage of correct answers declined from 98% among 5-year-olds to 46% among 17-year-olds. This trend was consistent across the conflict-weight items. The percentage of correct answers declined on each of them, but on none of the items corresponding to any other problem type. The percentage of correct answers rose most dramatically on the distance problems, from 5% correct among the 5-year-olds to 78% correct among the 9-year-olds and 95% correct among the 17-year-olds. Here, too, performance was very consistent; the developmental increment on all the distance problems was greater than that observed on any item of the other problem types. Thus, the experimental results supported both the particular rules as characterizations of children's knowledge about the balance scale and the rule-assessment methodology as a technique for determining what children know.

TABLE 7.2
Developmental Trends Observed and Predicted on Different Problem
Types on Balance-Scale Task (Siegler, 1976, Experiment 1)[a]

| | Age | | | | |
Problem Type	5–6	9–10	13–14	16–17	Predicted Developmental Trend
Balance	94	99	99	100	No change—all children at high level
Weight	88	98	98	98	No change—all children at high level
Distance	9	78	81	95	Dramatic improvement with age
Conflict weight	86	74	53	51	Decline with age—possible upturn for oldest
Conflict distance	11	32	48	50	Improvement with age
Conflict balance	7	17	26	40	Improvement with age

[a]Percentage of problems predicted correctly.

Learning About Balance Scales.   The rule-assessment approach was next used to investigate the relationship between children's existing knowledge of balance scales and their ability to learn more about them. The issue of greatest interest concerned possible developmental differences in learning above and beyond differences in initial rule usage. The issue can perhaps be most clearly posed as a hypothetical question: If two children of different ages, but with identical task-specific initial knowledge, were presented the same learning experience, would they emerge with the same final knowledge of the task? There was nothing in the rule models that suggested that any developmental differences would be found. On the other hand, older children often seem more adept in learning new material when neither they nor younger children seem to have had directly relevant prior experience. Thus, it was difficult to anticipate whether such developmental differences in learning would appear.

The experimental strategy that was used to study these isues was a pretest-training-posttest design. First, 5- and 8-year-olds were pretested to assemble groups of children of different ages who used the same initial rule (Rule I). Then, the children were provided 16 feedback trials. On each of these, they saw a balance-scale configuration of weights on pegs, predicted which way the arm would tilt when the lever was released, and then observed as the lever was released and their prediction was confirmed or disconfirmed. One or 2 days later, they were given a no-feedback posttest to determine the effects of the experience.

The instructional manipulation in this experiment was the type of feedback problems that children were given. There were three distinct types of problems: distance problems, conflict problems, and control problems. The rule-by-problem-type analysis provided a method for classifying each of these with regard to the child's existing level. Distance problems were solvable by Rule II but not by Rule I. They were viewed as being one step beyond the learner's level. Conflict problems included a mixture of conflict-weight, conflict-balance, and conflict-distance items. Because such problems are not understood even qualitatively until Rule III, they were classified as being at least two steps advanced. Balance and weight items served as the control problems. These could be solved by Rule I; thus, they were not at all advanced from the children's original level.

The results were largely as anticipated for both 5- and 8-year-olds in the control and distance problems conditions. Children of both ages in the control group made very little progress, most continuing to use Rule I. Children of both ages in the distance problems group made considerable progress, most advancing to Rule II.

The patterns of results diverged considerably from expectations, however, in the conflict problems condition. As stage theorists would have predicted, younger children made no progress; they either continued to use Rule I or could not be classified as using any rule. Older children, however, derived greater benefits from exposure to conflict problems than from exposure to any other type of training; most advanced to Rule III. This finding indicated that there were differences between older and younger children that were relevant to learning but that were not captured by the rule assessments.

The Encoding Hypothesis.   In hopes of understanding why older and younger children responded differently to conflict problems, we decided to examine in detail the performance of a few individual children. Each of these children was presented pretest, conflict training, and posttest experiences identical to those received by children in the previous experiment. The only difference was the addition of impromptu questions by the experimenter. Videotapes were made of the sessions to allow repeated scrutiny of all the children's behavior.

Several of the protocols suggested what was to us a surprising finding. Five-year-olds appeared to totally ignore the distance dimension; that is, they appeared to view the two piles of weights only in terms of their number of weights, without any attention to the weights' distances from the fulcrum. If such limited encoding was occurring, it might well explain why the young children in the conflict problem condition had difficulty learning that a difference in distance could more than compensate for an opposing difference in weight.

In order to test the validity of this encoding hypothesis, it was necessary to measure encoding independent of the predictive knowledge tapped by the rule assessments. Chase and Simon's (1973) reconstruction paradigm suggested a means by which this could be done. A series of 16 balance-scale configurations of weights on pegs was presented to 5- and 8-year-olds. After each configuration was displayed for 10 seconds, it was hidden from sight, and the child was asked to reproduce the arrangement on a second, identical balance scale.

An advantage of this approach was that it allowed independent assessment of encoding on the weight and distance dimensions. A child could place the correct number of weights on each side of the fulcrum, could place the weights the correct distance from the fulcrum, could do both, or could do neither. If the encoding explanation was correct, it would be expected that 8-year-olds, who had benefited from the conflict problems, would encode both weight and distance dimensions, 5-year-olds, who had not benefited, would encode weight but not distance.

In Experiment 3A of Siegler (1976), the encoding task was presented to 10 five-year-olds and 10 eight-year-olds. The children were shown each of 16 arrangements for 10 seconds apiece. Then the initial arrangement was hidden and the children asked to "make the same problem" by placing weights on the pegs of a second, identical, balance scale. After the encoding task, children were presented the usual predictions posttest.

As shown in Table 7.3, the pattern of results was entirely consistent with the encoding hypothesis. Five-year-olds were much more accurate in encoding weight (51% perfect reproductions) than distance (16%). Eight-year-olds were similarly

TABLE 7.3
Percentage of Correct Encodings on Balance Sheet Task
(Siegler, 1976, Experiment 3)

	5-year-olds		8-year-olds	
Experiment	Weight Encodings	Distance Encodings	Weight Encodings	Distance Encodings
3A	51	16	73	56
3B	54	9		
3C	54	19	64	73
3D	52	51	72	76

accurate on the two dimensions (73% vs. 56% correct). These differing patterns were also evident at the level of individual children's encoding. Here and throughout Experiment 3, an arbitrary criterion of at least four more correct answers on one dimension than the other was adopted as the standard of differential encoding on the two dimensions. By this standard, seven of the 10 five-year-olds in Experiment 3A would be said to encode the dimensions differently versus two of 10 eight-year-olds. The particular criterion that was adopted made little difference. For example, all the 5-year-olds categorized as encoding differently made at least seven more correct reproductions on the weight than on the distance dimension. These differing patterns of encoding can be contrasted with the very similar predictions performance of the older and younger children; both groups consistently used Rule I.

Gelman and Gallistel (1978) demonstrated that young children's counting performance often appears much more advanced if we accept near misses as demonstrating understanding, rather than demanding completely correct performance. What if we consider near misses in encoding? In this instance, at least, to do so had little effect. Near errors were defined as trials on which one side was reproduced correctly and the other side was wrong by one weight (peg), or as trials on which an initial equality was preserved and each side was wrong by one unit. Far errors were defined as all more divergent mistakes. By these criteria, 5-year-olds made more than three times as many far errors on the distance as on the weight dimension (37% of all trials vs. 10%), whereas 8-year-olds made virtually the same number of far errors on the two dimensions (5% on distance, 4% on weight). Thus, even the more liberal scoring criterion did not yield evidence that the younger children were encoding distance accurately.

One possible interpretation of the Experiment 3A findings was that young children did not encode the distance dimension because they lacked sufficient time. This possibility was easy to test. In Experiment 3B, a group of 10 five-year-olds was given 15 rather than 10 seconds to encode. Otherwise, the procedure was identical to that previously described.

As shown in Table 7.3, the manipulation made no difference; again, 5-year-olds correctly encoded weight far more often than distance (54% vs. 9%). Of the 10 children, 8 were classified as encoding differently on the two dimensions. The children usually indicated that they were done before the 15-second period was over (if they did this, they were immediately allowed to reproduce the arrangement on the other balance scale). Thus, the lack of time interpretation could be rejected.

Another possibility was that 5-year-olds might not have understood the instructions; that is, they might have interpreted the charge to "make the same problem" as meaning only that they should place the correct number of weights on each side. Therefore, in Experiment 3C the instructions given to the 10 older and 10 younger children were made more explicit. Children were told directly that they should "watch closely to see how the weights are set on the pegs—how many there are on each side and how far from the center the weights on each side are."

Being explicit about what the children should encode did not result in large changes in their performance (Table 7.3). Five-year-olds encoded weight correctly on 54% of trials versus 19% correct encodings on distance. Eight-year-olds encoded weight correctly on 64% of trials versus 73% correct distance encodings. Of the 10 younger children, 8 had at least four more correct encodings on the weight than on the distance dimension, versus 2 of the 10 older ones. Therefore, telling children what to encode was not sufficient to allow them to encode both weight and distance.

In Experiment 3D, children were provided instruction in both what and how to encode. They were told first to count the disks on the left side of the fulcrum, then to count the number of pegs those disks were away from the fulcrum, then to rehearse the result (e.g., "three weights on the fourth peg"), then to repeat the procedure on the right side, then to rehearse both results together (e.g. "three weights on the fourth peg and two weights on the third peg"), and then to produce the arrangement described by these statements. The experimenter and child together performed seven practice trials using this strategy, with the child taking increasing responsibility for executing it. Finally, the child was given the usual 16 encoding trials, followed by the predictions posttest.

This instructional procedure, unlike the others, substantially changed 5-year-olds' encoding. As shown in Table 7.3, they now encoded weight correctly on 52% of trials and distance on 51%. None of them could be classifield as encoding the two dimensions to different extents. In addition, the type of errors that the 5-year-olds made changed. Where previously almost half their encoding errors on the distance dimension were far errors, now fewer than 20% were. This brought the 5-year-olds' errors on the distance dimension in line with those that they had made previously on the weight dimension and with those that the 8-year-olds had made previously on both dimensions. Now for both age groups on both dimensions, the large majority of errors were close misses.

The improved encoding performance of the 5-year-olds was not accompanied by improvements in their predictions performance; the majority of both older and younger children continued to use Rule I. This set the stage for a direct test of the encoding hypothesis. If the reason that 5-year-olds had not benefited from the conflict problem instruction in Experiment 2 was that they did not encode distance and if they now encoded distance, then they should now benefit from experience with the conflict problems. This prediction was tested in Experiment 3E.

The children who participated in Experiment 3D were brought back to the experimental room either 2 or 3 days afterward to participate in Experiment 3E. First they were given the standard posttest to determine how the feedback problems had affected their knowledge.

Experience with conflict problems now improved the performance of 5- as well as 8-year-olds. Virtually all children adopted a rule more advanced than Rule I. The majority adopted Rule III. Older children showed somewhat more improvement than younger ones, but, at the minimum, reducing the differences in encoding substantially reduced the differential responsiveness to experience previously observed. Thus differential encoding seemed at least partially to explain the differences between 5- and 8-year-olds' ability to learn.

Factors Underlying the Development of Encoding.   These findings on the importance of encoding raised the question, why does encoding improve between 5 and 8 years? Siegler and Long (described in Siegler & Klahr, 1982) suggested two possible explanations for the findings: improved memorial capabilities and improved knowledge bases.

First consider the memorial explanation. To encode weight and distance correctly, a child would need to store four numbers and their associated referents: the number of weights on the left side, the number of pegs those weights were from the fulcrum, the number of weights on the right side, and the number of pegs those weights were from the fulcrum. Faced with such a substantial memory burden, 5-year-olds may have elected to encode only the information that seemed most essential, information about weight (Case, 1978).

The second possibility concerned children's knowledge about what features were important on balance scale problems. Five-year-olds may simply not have known that distance was important in reproducing the original configuration. In a prior experiment (Siegler, 1976, Experiment 3C, see earlier), 5-year-olds had been told that both weight and distance dimensions were important, and this did not improve their performance. Nonetheless, it remained possible that the message had not gotten through and that emphasizing the point more strongly would produce improvements.

Manipulating the memorial demands of the encoding task was quite easy. Rather than presenting the task in the usual way, with a screen blocking the child's view of the original balance scale, the task was presented without any screen present. Thus, the child could look back and forth as often as necessary and simply copy the original arrangement of weights on pegs.

Manipulating the amount of information provided about the task was also straightforward. The instructions were made very directive and repetitive. Children were told three different times that both weight and distance were important dimensions, and they needed to tell the experimenter what the important dimensions were until they were right three times consecutively.

Thus, the children were presented the encoding task under one of the four factorial combinations of standard or low memory demands and standard or detailed instructions. As shown in Table 7.4, there were three basic findings. First, the results replicated the original ones; given the standard memory demands and instructions, 5-year-olds encoded weight much more accurately than distance, whereas 8-year-olds encoded the dimensions equally accurately. Second, the older chidren's encoding of the two dimensions was similar under all experimental conditions, whereas the younger children's encoding was more comparable under conditions of low memory demands and informative instructions than under other circumstances. Finally, it seemed that the reduced memory demands aided younger children's encoding of weight and distance approximately equally, while the detailed instructions were especially useful in promoting their encoding of the distance dimension. Thus, although memorial limitations are likely important in limiting 5-year-olds' absolute level of correct encoding, knowledge about what features are important may be the largest factor accounting for the differences between their weight and distance encoding.

Encoding as a Limit on Adolescents' Learning.   One of the surprising findings that has arisen in research on the balance scale is the rarity of the Rule IV strategy among adolescents and adults. Before we performed the first study of this task, we were almost dissuaded from including high school juniors and seniors; the headmistress of the school assured us that these students had already encountered the balance scale twice in their high school science classes and that

TABLE 7.4
Percentage of Correct Encodings on Balance-Scale Task Under
Different Memorial and Instructional Conditions

Age	Dimension	Condition			
		Simple Instructions		Detailed Instructions	
		High Memory Demands	Low Memory Demands	High Memory Demands	Low Memory Demands
5 years	Weight	36	68	63	79
	Distance	3	30	42	66
8 years	Weight	66	89	78	94
	Distance	75	87	78	99

they knew all there was to be known about it. It was fortunate that we persisted. Only 10% of the juniors and seniors used Rule IV spontaneously. Only 20% induced it from feedback problems of their own design (Siegler, 1976, Experiment 1). The question arose: What was preventing the adolescents from learning Rule IV?

There seem to be two likely points in the induction process at which difficulty might arise: in encoding the balance scale as a quantitative problem, and in choosing the correct algebraic equation from among the many possible ones. To use Rule IV, it is necessary to combine the weight and distance dimensions into a single mathematical equation. Realizing that distance can be quantified in exactly the same way as weight and that both can be combined within a single equation could be quite difficult. Even once this realization is made, however, determining which of the many possible algebraic formulas is correct may be an imposing task. In particular, it would seem to demand some relatively rapid means for disconfirming large numbers of incorrect hypotheses. If, due to memory limitations, a given trial could be used to check only a few possibilities, it might take many trials before the correct solution was identified (Levine, 1966).

Each of these hypothesized sources of difficulty suggested an experimental manipulation. First, if encoding the balance scale as a quantitative problem was a stumbling block, then highlighting the quantitative nature of the task would seem likely to be beneficial. Therefore, in the quantified encoding condition, rather than simply asking adolescents on each trial, "What do you think will happen," the experimenter asked, "Three weights on the third peg versus two weights on the fourth peg; what do you think will happen?"

Second, if choosing among the possible hypotheses was a problem, then providing external memory aids would seem likely to be helpful. In the external memory condition, adolescents were provided a sheet of paper with schematic representations of each problem and its outcome. The problems were revealed one by one, with the representations of all previous problems remaining visible. Thus, each time subjects in the external memory condition generated a new hypothesis, they could check its consistency with all the previous outcomes.

In the experiments, 13-year-olds and college students were first given a pretest to guarantee that they did not already know Rule IV. Then they were presented with a sequence of 18 balance-scale feedback problems under one of four conditions: external memory aids and quantified encoding, only external memory aids, only quantified encoding, or neither quantified encoding nor memory aids. Finally, they were given the standard balance-scale posttest.

As shown in Table 7.5, both external memory aids and quantified encoding helped both 13-year-olds and college students, but in somewhat different ways. The majority of college students were able to adopt Rule IV given either external memory aids or quantified encoding. By contrast, 13-year-olds required both types of aids in order to discover the most advanced rule; neither alone was sufficient. In all conditions, the college students made their last error earlier in

TABLE 7.5
Percentage of Children Using Rule IV under Different Memorial and
Encoding Conditions

Condition	Age	
	13-Year-Olds	17-Year-Olds
External memory & encoding	80	80
External memory	20	70
Encoding	10	80
Neither	0	20

the feedback set, suggesting more rapid learning. One interpretation of this finding is that college students are more familiar with quantitative solution formulas than 13-year-olds are. Given the memory aid, they quickly see the possibility of encoding quantitatively and of testing alternative formulas to predict which side goes down. Given the quantified encoding, they quickly infer the possibility of a quantitative solution algorithm and start testing potential ones. The 13 year olds, less familiar with quantitative solutions to physical problems, require both types of prompts to adopt this strategy.

Children's Understanding of Time

Existing Knowledge of Time. Another concept on which I have studied the interaction between children's existing knowledge and their ability to learn is the concept of time. My first experiment in the area (Siegler & Richards, 1979) was intended to assess existing knowledge of time. The task was quite similar to Piaget's (1969) cars problem. Children were shown two parallel electric-train tracks, each with a locomotive on it. The two locomotives could start at the same or different points, could stop at the same or different points, and could travel the same or different distances. They could start at the same or different times, could stop at the same or different times, and could travel the same or different total times. Finally, they could travel at the same or different speeds.

On the basis of Piaget's (1969) descriptions, children were expected to use one of three rules on this task. Rule I children would base their judgments on where the cars stop; whichever car stopped farther ahead would be said to have traveled for the longer time. Rule II children would judge similarly if the two trains stopped at different points but would choose the train that started farther back if the trains stopped at the same point. Rule III children would judge in terms of starting and stopping times; in other words, they would use the correct approach.

In order to test these hypothesized rules, it was necessary to formulate problem types that would yield discriminative patterns. The six problem types that were chosen are shown in Table 7.6. These yielded distinct patterns for the rules corresponding to each of the seven physical dimensions along which the trains' activity could vary: time of travel, distance traveled, speed, end point, end time, beginning point, and beginning time. A child responding consistently on the basis of any one of the seven dimensions would answer differently on at least two of the six problem types than a child responding on the basis of any other dimension. Note that in order to limit the problems' difficulty, the two trains always either started simultaneously or stopped simultaneously.

The procedure followed in the experiment was quite simple. Participants of four ages—5-year-olds, 8-year-olds, 11-year-olds, and adults—were each presented problems of the types shown in Table 7.6. No feedback was given at any time.

The data were essentialy in accord with expectation. Five-year-olds most often chose the train that ended at the point further down the track, 8- and 11-year-olds tended to choose the train that traveled the greater distance, and adults chose the train that traveled the greater total time.

Table 6
Specific Response and Percentage of Correct Answers
Predicted by Each Rule for Each Problem Type —
Time Concept Task (Siegler & Richards, 1979)

Problem Type		Rule I	Rule II	Rule III
1				
Train A.	0 —————— 6	A longer	A longer	A longer
Train B.	2 ————— 6	100	100	100
2				
Train A.	0 —————— 9	Equal	A longer	A longer
Train B.	0 ——— 5	0	100	100
3				
Train A.	0 ——— 9	A longer	A longer	A longer
Train B.	4½ ——— 9	100	100	100
4				
Train A.	0 —— 6	B longer	B longer	B longer
Train B.	0 ——— 5	0	0	100
5				
Train A.	0 ——— 6	A longer	A longer	A longer
Train B.	0 —— 4	100	100	100
6				
Train A.	0 ——— 5	B. longer	B longer	A longer
Train B.	2 — 5	0	0	100

Acquiring New Knowledge About Time.   The next question was whether we could use these assessments of children's existing knowledge about time to predict their ability to acquire new information about it. In particular, would the findings that young children relied on end point cues and older childer on distance cues allow prediction of the type of feedback problems that would advance their understanding?

First, 5- and 11-year-olds with the desired initial knowledge states were selected: 5-year-olds who relied on the end point cue and 11-year-olds who relied on the time cue. Then children of each age were presented feedback problems. These problems differed in whether they discriminated time from end point and/ or distance. The meaning of a problem discriminating one dimension from another was that answers based on the two dimensions would differ (e.g., distance would be discriminated from time if the train that traveled the shorter distance also traveled the longer time, because reliance on the time cue would lead to choosing one train and reliance on the distance cue would lead to choosing the other). The meaning of a problem not discriminating one dimension from another was that judgments based on the two dimensions would be identical (e.g., distance would not be discriminated from time if the train that traveled the longer distance also traveled the longer time, because reliance on either cue would lead to choosing the same train.)

Thus, in Siegler (in press; see also Richards, 1982), some children received feedback problems on which both distance and end point cues were discriminated from time; some received problems on which distance but not end point was discriminated; some received problems on which end point but not distance was discriminated; and some received problems on which neither distance nor end point were discriminated.

As in the balance-scale experiments, the results on the time concept demonstrated that the effectiveness of learning experiences is a joint function of children's initial knowledge and the particular dimensions(s) that are discriminated by the learning experience. First, consider the performance of 5-year-olds, for whom discrimination between time and end point was hypothesized to be critical. Those 5-year-olds who were given problems that did not discriminate end point from time continued to use the End Point Rule; 14 of the 20 children who were given such feedback problems used the rule on the posttest. Those 5-year-olds who were given feedback problems that discriminated end point from time shifted away from Rule I; only 3 of the 20 continued to use it. Whether or not the problems discriminated distance had no effect on the 5-year-olds' performance.

Now consider the performance of the 11-year-olds, for whom discrimination between time and distance was hypothesized to be critical. Here, the greatest effects of feedback were seen in the number of children adopting Rule III. Of those 11-year-olds who saw distance discriminated from time, 10 of 20 adopted this most advanced rule. Of those who did not see distance discriminated from time, only 4 of 20 shifted to it. Whether or not the problems discriminated end point had no effect on the 11-year-olds' performance. Thus, knowing the child's initial rule allowed prediction of which types of learning experiences would be effective and which types of learning experiences would not be.

Perhaps the most intriguing finding of this experiment concerned the relative benefits of demonstrating that (1) all rules but the correct one were incorrect; versus demonstrating that (2) the children's existing rule was incorrect but not demonstrating the incorrectness of a more advanced but still erroneous alternative. The relevant data were provided by regression analyses of the performance of the four groups of 5-year-olds. Children in two groups (the control and distance discriminating groups) received feedback that did not disconfirm their existing formula, Rule I; they therefore continued to use it. Children in a third group (the end point discriminating group) received feedback that indicated the incorrectness of their existing Rule but left open the possibility of the more advanced but still flawed Distance Rule; they began to rely on the distance dimension. Children in the fourth group (the distance and end point discriminating group) received feedback that demonstrated the incorrectness of both their existing Rule (Rule I) and the Rule they would ordinarily adopt next (the Distance Rule); they simply became confused, not relying heavily on any apparent rule.

The education implication of these findings would seem to be that it may sometimes be more desirable to teach toward an intermediate instructional goal than to teach directly toward the final goal. If we possess information about the precise source of children's difficulty, we can shape teaching procedures to directly address the problem. It may be more efficient to address these difficulties one at a time as they arise than to try to attain the ultimate instructional objective in one step.

Encoding and Inference Processes on the Time Concept. We were quite surprised that even among the 11-year-olds who were given distance discriminating feedback problems, only one-half learned the Time Rule. This led us (Richards, 1982; Siegler, in press) to consider exactly how children might solve the task. Recall that the problems involved either both trains starting at the same time or both trains stopping at the same time. This meant that all items could be solved by reliance on two rules: (1) If two events start at the same time and one ends later than the other, then the event that ended later lasted for more time; and (2) if one event starts before another and they end at the same time, then the event that started first lasted for more time.

What would children need to do to use these rules? A task analysis indicated that they could determine which train traveled for the longer time by (1) encoding which train started first (2) encoding which train stopped last and (3) drawing the appropriate inference based on the encoded information. This suggested that children's difficulty might lie either in not encoding the appropriate information or in not drawing the appropriate inference.

In order to examine these possibilities, it was necessary to develop means for assessing encoding and inference processes independent of children's judgments of time. To assess encoding, children were presented problems in which the trains' activities were as previously described. Instead of the children invariably being asked which train traveled for the longer time, however, this question was posed only on 9 of the 27 trials. On the other 18, the children were asked either which train started first (or whether they started at the same time) or which train stopped last (or whether they stopped at the same time). The order of questions was randomized so that children could not anticipate which type of information to focus upon; they would need to take in all three, just as they needed to be on the original task.

It was found that children frequently erred on the encoding as well as on the total time questions. Error rates were 24% on beginning time, 16% on ending time, and 31% on total time questions.

The next goal was to assess children's understanding of the inference rules. The same children whose encoding had been tested were brought back the next day and presented two written questions: "If the red and blue trains started at the same time and the blue train stopped last, which one would have gone the greater amount of time (or would they have gone for the same amount of time)?" "If the red train started first, and the red and blue trains stopped at the same time, which train would have gone the greater amount of time (or would they have gone for the same amount of time)?" This procedure eliminated all encoding problems, because the questions as written included the desired encodings.

Such abstract inference questions proved more difficult to answer than might have been anticipated. The 11-year-olds erred on 25% of the inference items. This suggested that lack of knowledge of the correct inference rules as well as inadequate encoding may have contributed to children's difficulty in solving the time problems.

These possible sources of difficulty were further probed by examining the effects of teaching children more sophisticated encoding and inference skills. The experiment utilized a 2 (encoding instruction: present or absent) by 2 (inference instruction: present or absent) factorial design. Encoding instruction involved telling the 11-year-old subjects to identify aloud at the beginning of each trial the train that started first (or to say that the trains started at the same time) and to identify aloud at the end of each trial the train that stopped last (or to say that they stopped at the same time). Inference training involved telling children the solutions to the abstract inference problems previously used to test knowledge of the inference rules. After the manipulation(s), children in each group were presented the previously described items testing encoding of beginning time, encoding of ending time, and judgments of total time.

The results of this experiment provided additional evidence that both encoding and inference processes constitute important sources of difficulty in solving these problems. The encoding manipulation by itself improved children's encoding of both beginning and ending time relationships but did not improve their performance on the total time problems. Inference training by itself had little effect on encoding but led to somewhat improved performance on the total time problems. Encoding and inference training together greatly improved children's encoding and their performance on the total time problems. In this last condition, the overall error rates were below 5% on total time, beginning time, and ending time problems. Of the 16 children, 15 met the criterion for using the time rule.

Like the balance-scale results, these findings on the time concept indicate that instruction in encoding, together with other types of instruction, can aid children's learning. Superficially, the balance-scale and time findings differ in the type of instruction that was found to be useful in combination with encoding; however, this difference may mask a deeper similarity. Inference training involved directly teaching children an algorithm for solving the time task; feedback training consisted of problems that allowed induction of such an algorithm for the balance scale. The overarching principle may be that one effective way to promote intelligent behavior is to call attention to the important dimensions of problems and then either explicitly or implicitly indicate the algorithm by which the dimensions are to be combined. At this very general level, the present conclusion resembles past analyses of such classic psychological tasks as discrimination learning (e.g., Zeaman & House, 1963) and concept learning (e.g., Haygood & Bourne, 1965). The present approach goes beyond these previous ones, however, in using assessments of existing knowledge to predict the usefulness of alternative instructional approaches.

WHY IS ENCODING DIFFICULT?

We have seen that inadequate encoding is frequently associated with difficulty in solving problems, and also that instruction that leads to more adequate encoding can lead to greater ability to learn new problem-solving approaches. Why is encoding difficult? Why don't people perceive problems accurately from the beginning? Part of the reason, we believe, is the necessity of fitting encoding to the demands of the particular task. There is no invariably optimal encoding approach to take, as limited cognitive resources need to be divided among a potentially infinite number of dimensions that could be encoded in any situation.

Consider the diversity of ways in which a person's encoding can fail to match the demands of a task. Perhaps the simplest way is that a relevant dimension is simply not encoded. This type of failure emerged in the study of 5-year-olds' encoding of the balance scale. Distance, which is causally related to the workings of the balance, was not encoded. When the children were taught to encode distance, they were better able to learn Rule III. Similar results emerged in a study of 3-year-olds' encoding of balance-scale configurations. They were found to not encode either weight or distance; when instructed in how to encode weight, their ability to learn Rule I improved (Siegler, 1978). Wickens (1972) also provided examples of failures to encode dimensions in his work, on release from proactive inhibition.

A related difficulty is encoding stimuli on a qualitative level, when quantitative encodings are necessary. An example of this emerged in the study of adolescents' learning of balance-scale relationships. In order to learn Rule IV, it is necessary to encode both weights and distances in quantitative terms (e.g., three weights on the second peg on the left versus four weights on the first peg on the right) rather than solely in qualitative terms (e.g., more weights on the left, more distance on the right). Presenting 13- and 17-year-olds with the quantitative encodings helped them learn Rule IV, a rule that they had great difficulty in learning when the quantitative encodings were not provided.

Just as important as failure to encode a relevant dimension, however, is encoding of unnecessary dimensions or of dimensions that interfere with performance. Weir (1964) reported numerous studies of probability learning in which preschoolers' performance was superior to that of elementary and high school students. On the probability problems that he presented, there was no determinate answer; the best that could be done was always to guess the side that was most often correct. Weir suggested that this was exactly what the preschoolers' encoding entailed. Older children, by contrast, encoded numerous features of the series of trials that were irrelevant to the solution. For example, they might note spurious regularities in cycles of seven trials. This encoding of features that were unrelated to the solution led them to be correct less often than the younger children.

The 5-year-olds' inadequate encoding of the balance scale might be interpreted as due to their focusing too sharply on one dimension (weight) to the exclusion of other relevant dimensions. It is also possible, however, to focus not sharply enough on the relevant dimensions. Hagen (1972) provided a number of illustrations of this in describing his work on selective attention. Older and younger children were presented pictures and asked to focus on particular parts of them. Later, they were either asked to recall the parts they had focused upon or parts on which they had not been asked to focus. Older children remembered much more than younger ones about the material on which they had been asked to focus, but younger children remembered as much and sometimes more about the material that had not been the central focus. Hagen suggested that much of the deficit that young children show in recall is due to overly broad encoding.

Numerous other problems can also arise in encoding. Encoding can be at a lower level than is optimal; for example, Chi and Glaser (1979) found that expert physicists encoded physics problems in terms of general principles, whereas novices encoded them in terms of details of the particular problem. Inadequate cognitive resources can be devoted to encoding; for example, Sternberg and

Rifkin (1979) found that older children's superiority in solving analogy problems could be traced to their taking longer in the initial encoding stage. Finally, an encoding can simply be wrong; jokes and riddles provide many examples in which the initial story leads the listener down the garden path so that he encodes the material in a way that proves to be incongruous with the outcome.

Inadequate encoding, then, can involve many distinct difficulties: omitting a dimension or encoding too many dimensions, encoding a given dimension at too detailed a level or not in enough detail, or simply producing the wrong representation. There is no single best way to encode, but rather any number of best ways that depend on the demands of the particular task. This same statement might be made about problem solving: the optimal problem-solving approach is also highly dependent on the demands of the task. Even tasks that are formally isomorphic are often solved very differently if their surface forms are different (cf. Hayes & Simon, 1976). This suggests that beyond instruction in a few general techniques, such as means–ends analysis, there is not going to be any simple way to make people better problem solvers. Rather, instruction in problem solving may best be accomplished by assessing people's existing knowledge in particular domains, by shaping their encoding to the demands of more advanced levels of knowledge, and by presenting them with learning experiences consonant with their encoding and existing knowledge. Seen from this perspective, much of the task of education in problem solving may be to identify the encoding that we would like people to have on specific problems, and then to devise instructional methods to help them attain it.

REFERENCES

Case, R. (1978). Piaget and beyond: Toward a developmentally based theory and technology of instruction. In R. Glaser (Ed.), *Advances in instructional psychology.* (Vol. 1) Hillsdale, NJ: Lawrence Erlbaum Associates.

Chase, W. G., & Simon, H. A. (1973). The mind's eye in chess. In W. G. Chase (Ed.), *Visual information processing.* New York: Academic Press.

Chi, M. T. H., & Glaser, R. (1979, April). *Encoding process characteristics of experts and novices in physics.* Paper presented at the annual meeting of the American Educational Research Association, San Francisco.

de Groot, A.D. (1966). Perception and memory vs. thought: Some old ideas and recent findings. In B. Kleinmuntz (Ed.), *Problem solving: Research, method and theory.* New York: Wiley.

Garner, W. R. (1974). *The processing of information and structure.* Potomac, MD: Lawrence Erlbaum Associates.

Gelman, R., & Gallistel, C. R. (1978). *The child's understanding of number.* Cambridge, MA: Harvard University Press.

Gibson, E. J. (1969). *Principles of perceptual learning and development.* New York: Appleton–Century–Crofts.

Gibson, J. J. (1966). *The senses considered as perceptual systems.* Boston, MA: Houghton Mifflin.

Hagen, J. W. (1972). Strategies for remembering. In S. Farnham–Diggory (Ed.), *Information processing in children.* New York: Academic Press.

Hayes, J. R., & Simon, H. A. (1976). The understanding process: Problem isomorphs. *Cognitive Psychology, 8,* 165–190.

Haygood, R. C., & Bourne, Jr., L. E. (1965) Attribute- and rule-learning aspects of conceptual behavior. *Psychological Review, 72,* 175–195.

Klahr, D., & Robinson, M. (1981). Formal assessment of problem-solving and planning processes in preschool children. *Cognitive Psychology, 13,* 113–148.

Levine, M. (1966). Hypothesis behavior by humans during discrimination learning. *Journal of Experimental Psychology, 71,* 331–336.

Neisser, U. (1967). *Cognitive psychology.* New York: Appleton–Century–Crofts.

Piaget, J. (1969). *The child's conception of time* (A. J. Pomerans, Trans.). New York: Ballantine.

Richards, D. D. (1982). Children's time concepts: Going the distance. In W. J. Friedman (Ed.), *The developmental psychology of time.* New York: Academic Press.

Siegler, R. S. (1976). Three aspects of cognitive development. *Cognitive Psychology, 8,* 481–520.

Siegler, R. S. (1978). The origins of scientific reasoning. In R. S. Siegler (Ed.), *Children's thinking: What develops?* Hillsdale, NJ: Lawrence Erlbaum Associates.

Siegler, R. S. (1981). Developmental sequences within and between concepts. *Monographs of the Society for Research in Child Development,* Whole No. 189.

Siegler, R. S. (in press). Five generalizations about cognitive development. *American Psychologist, 38.*

Siegler, R. S., & Klahr, D. (1982). When do children learn? The relationship between existing knowledge and the acquisition of new knowledge. In R. Glaser (Ed.), *Advances in instructional psychology* (Vol. 2). Hillsdale, NJ: Lawrence Erlbaum Associates.

Siegler, R. S., & Richards, D. D. (1979). Development of time, speed, and distance concepts. *Developmental Psychology, 15,* 288-298.

Siegler, R. S., & Vago, S. (1978). The development of a proportionality concept: Judging relative fullness. *Journal of Experimental Child Psychology, 25,* 371–395.

Sternberg, R. J., & Rifkin, B. (1979). The development of analogical reasoning processes. *Journal of Experimental Child Psychology, 27,* 195–232.

Weir, M. W. (1964). Developmental changes in problem-solving strategies. *Psychological Review, 71,* 473–490.

Wickens, D. D. (1972). Characteristics of word encoding. In A. W. Melton & E. Martin (Eds.), *Coding processes in human memory.* Washington, DC: Winston.

Zeaman, D., & House, B.J. (1963). The role of attention in retardate discrimination learning. In N. R. Ellis (Ed.), *Handbook of mental deficiency: Psychological theory and research.* New York: McGraw–Hill.

8 Influences of Language Skills on Bilinguals' Problem Solving

Richard P. Duran
Educational Testing Service

Developing effective programs for training cognitive skills that contribute to academic achievement will require sensitivity to the diverse characteristics of program trainees. Among those in the U. S. population who might benefit from such programs are persons from non-English language backgrounds. In 1976 it was estimated that one person in eight in the United States came from a background where a language other than English was spoken at home. About 10% of school-age children (6–18 years old) had such a background (NCES, 1978a). The educational attainment of children from non-English backgrounds is low relative to that of the populace as a whole. For example, children in grades 5–12 from language minority backgrounds who usually spoke a non-English language were more than three times as likely to be one or more grades below the grade levels expected for their ages than were children from English language backgrounds (NCES, 1978b). Restricted educational attainment level among persons from non-English language backgrounds is not limited to primary and secondary school-age children. For example, a review of higher education attainment data and research on Hispanics by Duran (1983) cites evidence that lack of English language familiarity inhibits college admission and success in college for adults from non-English backgrounds.

It is unlikely that limited facility in English is the sole factor inhibiting the educational attainment of persons from non-English speaking backgrounds. Associated socioeconomic disadvantage is certainly important. Nonetheless, the effect of lack of familiarity with English on academic functioning is a major problem in need of analysis. Attention to ways cognitive training may benefit non-English background persons will require a foundation based on an understanding of how bilingualism affects cognition. An important step toward building this foundation is a clearer understanding of how current cognitive science research might contribute to the study of bilinguals' problem-solving skill in each of their two languages. The purpose of this chapter is to pursue this goal. The main issue under analysis is how we might develop models of information-processing behavior that capture how problem-solving behavior is affected by skills in each of two languages.

Problem Solving, Verbal Ability, and Language Proficiency

Psychometricians have long recognized a connection between performance on tests of verbal skill and performance on tests of general cognitive ability. Measures of verbal skill are strongly predictive of a wide range of problem-solving and reasoning performances. Of course, the application of these general findings to bilingual persons is no simple matter. Cognitive psychologists and psychometricians have used the term *verbal ability* to refer broadly to language skills. In contrast, researchers in the area of bilingualism and language assessment traditionally have used the term *language proficiency* to denote familiarity with a language system. Although the terms are related, the connotations are different. Language proficiency usually refers to elemental skills in controlling the basic phonological, morphological, lexical, and grammatical units of a standard variety of a language. Language proficiency is seldom applied in reference to the language skills of a native speaker of a language; instead, it usually refers to the language skills of a person who does not manifest native-like skills. The term verbal ability tends to refer to a continuum of skills in a language that are manifest in native speakers. However, recent efforts to extend proficiency assessment to the measurement of more complex and advanced forms of proficiency tend to break down this distinction. Advanced levels of language proficiency seem to be a manifestation of a single, underlying language factor called *integrative proficiency* (Oller, 1979). This refers to the coordination of multiple language skills in the service of performing everyday pragmatic tasks with language. Oller's research has found that scores on tests designed to measure integrative proficiency correlate highly with performance on tests of general cognitive abilities.

Nevertheless, it is obvious that measures of language skill do not have precisely the same significance for bilinguals as indicators of cognitive ability, nor would one expect them to predict problem-solving performance in the same way or for the same reasons. Typically, a person will manifest stronger familiarity and proficiency in one language than in another. Relatively few persons come to demonstrate equal strength and fluency in more than one language system, and this implies that most bilinguals do not attain native-like proficiency in at least one of their languages. Still, it may be presumed that there is an overlap in language skills across two languages and that a single language-skill factor may exist; that is, problem-solving performance in a bilingual individual may be affected by specific language skills in the language in which the problem is presented, by general linguistic, comprehension, or representaion skills that are mostly independent of the particular language being used, and by nonlinguistic cognitive abilities that benefit from the cognitive functions exercised in becoming bilingual. Consequently, a general language-skill factor probably is not refined enough to capture how ability in a language affects performance on problem-solving tasks. Performance on tasks presented in a particular language cannot be predicted in information-processing detail from a single measure of proficiency in that language. Both a refined description of language proficiency and a good analysis of the way different aspects of language proficiency interact with the information-processing demands of problem-solving tasks are required in order to understand the problem-solving performance of bilinguals. It is necessary to specify more carefully what modality of language and linguistic code is involved, and how specific recognition and transformation of a linguistic code affects performance of steps in a particular problem solving task. These matters are taken up in more detail in the remainder of the chapter following brief discussions of efforts to characterize the language skills of bilinguals and the general nature of problem-solving tasks.

Describing the Language Skills of Bilinguals

An essential perspective on bilingualism is a linguistic one that deals with the description of and contrast between the formal structures of two languages and how this contrast may affect the development of bilingualism and skill in two language systems. Personal and psychological characteristics of a language learner, such as age and cognitive level of development, must also be taken into account. An excellent recent review of these issues is provided by Hakuta (1982).

According to Hakuta, an adequate psychological account of language acquisition by bilinguals ought to be able to capture how an individual develops, interrelates, and maintains models of two separate language systems. Because language systems exist outside of a single individual, the similarities and contrasts between two language systems predetermine some of the problems (or even advantages) that a language learner faces in acquiring a second language. The following list is given by Hakuta (1982, p.24), as an example of some major structural variables that differ or are similar across language systems: (1) position (postposition/preposition), (2) branching direction (left branching/right branching), (3) word order variability (rigid word order/free word order), (4) dummy subject (has no dummy subjects/has dummy subjects), (5) object–verb order (verb–object/object–verb), (6) agreement (has no subject–verb agreement/has agreement), and (7) passivization (has no passives/has passives).

Hakuta suggests that languages cluster together in terms of their realization of general structural variables such as those listed. He also suggests that the psychological process of acquiring a new language reflects the contrast in features between a new language and old language as well as the strategies and processes that thus help in acquiring the new language. The foregoing discussion is relevant to the study of bilinguals' problem-solving ability in each of two languages. In effect, bilinguals' skill in utilizing a new language or a less familiar language will depend on the degree to which the new language has been acquired. Difficulties that a bilingual has in a new language may reflect knowledge of a more familiar language and the extent to which a knowledge of a new language has become independent of the more familiar language. In the long run, if we wish to understand how knowledge of a less familiar language constrains problem solving in that language, we need to work from a linguistically powerful model of persons' knowledge of two language systems.

As part of this research goal, we will also need to know a lot about language-use strategies employed by bilinguals in working verbal problem-solving tasks in a less familiar language. The range and types of strategies that may occur is large; just a few are mentioned here. For example, bilinguals who are very weak in one language may mentally translate information from a less familiar language to a more familiar language. Another example: when encountering words that are unfamiliar in one language, bilinguals might substitute for them the meanings of words from another language. The basis for the substitution may be a judgment that the unrecognized word is equivalent to a word found in the other language, or else that the unrecognized word has the same etymology as a word in the other language.

Transfer of knowledge of language structure from one language system to another is likely to be most noticeable in production of speech or writing. Awkward or incorrect syntax and word usage in writing or speech may reflect a strategy of transferring structures and word knowledge from one language to another. Although infelicities in production of a less familiar language may reflect knowledge of another language system, it is also possible that infelicities are evidence of generalization strategies helpful in learning to use a new language. An erroneous use of a generalization strategy, for example, occurs when a language learner encounters a novel linguistic situation and tries to apply a grammatical rule that applies some, but not all, of the time in a new language. In English a classic example of this occurs when the suffix "-ed" is inappropriately appended to a verb root to form the past tense of a word, as in "speaked" or "breaked." Generalization strategies are necessary in all language learning; still, such strategies may result in erroneous description or interpretation of problem-solving information in a less familiar language.

Bilingualism also has significant social and cultural dimensions, affecting not only the varieties of the two languages that persons acquire, but also the situations and circumstances that accompany preference for use of one language versus another, including the possiblity of intermixing codes. The sociocultural aspects of bilingualism are a significant determinant of how fluent a person becomes in each of two languages. These topics are discussed briefly in the concluding section.

A General Characterization of Problem-Solving Processes

In further elaborating ways in which familiarity with two language systems may affect problem solving, it is helpful to outline an overview of problem-solving behavior consistent with an information-processing description of cognition. The second step is to isolate some information-processing behaviors that may show the influence of language familiarity on overall problem-solving performance. Next, relevant findings from existing research are used to illuminate the issues introduced.

Formal problem-solving situations, such as those encountered in academic settings, may be partitioned into three interactive sets of activities: *problem input, problem representation and conceptual solution,* and *physical execution of solution steps language production.* Problem input refers to a person's initial perception and interpretation of information in the physical environment defining a problem-solving circumstance. The second activity, problem representation and conceptual solution, refers to the purely mental acts that a person undertakes in solving problems. The third set of activities, physical execution of solution steps, refers to behavioral acts performed by a person in working with problem information in the external physical environment; some of these acts result in physical proof of a completed, correctly or incorrectly solved problem. In this chapter, concern for the third step is restricted to speech or writing in problem-solving contexts. The three sorts of problem-solving activities mentioned are not necessarily sequential, though for very simple problems they might be. By segregating these activities, we can distinguish ways in which language processing may be implicated in problem solving.

In information-processing accounts of problem solving, such as those advocated by Newell and Simon (1972) and others, the primary concern is with how problem representation and conceptual solution occur and are organized. In the Newell and Simon account, problem-solving behavior requires a clear idea of the conceptual state of affairs defining a problem, the conceptual state of affairs conforming to a solved problem, and the conceptual operations that are legitimate in creating intermediate problem states on the path to a solution. These three constraints on conceptual problem representation and solution fulfill in part Newell and Simon's notion of what constitutes a well-structured problem. Another aspect of a well-structured problem includes a match between conceptual problem information and states of affairs in the problem's physical or real-world task environment. This latter aspect of problem solving is responsible for guiding the physical execution of problem-solving steps and the production of language as required.

Conceptualization and solution of a problem is said to occur in a problem space or mental scratch pad in short-term memory that represents problem information. Thus, solution of a problem is affected critically by a person's ability to formulate a valid and tractable mental representation of a problem and its demands. A person's knowledge that is relevant to constructing a problem space is a key element in problem solving. A second key element is the mental resources that he or she may exercise in executing the mental operations required in problem solving. Availability of cognitive resources such as speed in information processing, short-term memory capacity for problem information, and capacity to maintain and direct immediate attention for problem information are important indicators of problem-solving ability that may be sensitive to language-processing skills.

A central issue for discussion in this chapter is the effect of language skills on problem-solving behavior and the concurrent links between overt measures of problem performance and cognitive processes. Overt measures of problem performance such as correctness of problem solution, speed in arriving at a solution, and sequence of actions and verbalizations enroute to solution of a problem need to be linked to reasonably explicit models of how language proficiency may affect not only overt behavior but also covert information-processing behavior. One valuable approach to these issues is to analyze performance on problem-solving tasks in terms of task structure and requirements and in terms of linguistic skills needed to meet task demands. The next section cites research evidence on how language skills after bilinguals' performance of the three key problem-solving activities: problem input, problem representation and conceptual solution, and language production.

Bilingualism Research Findings

Problem Input. Problem input is a receptive process by which a problem solver acquires information about problems; it is obviously dependent on skill in decoding and understanding the linguistic description of a problem and its accompanying instructions. For bilinguals we expect that verbal problem information would be easier to decode and understand in the more familiar language. Bilinguals should be faster and more accurate readers in a more familiar language than in a language in which they are less proficient; also, they ought to be better at comprehending oral speech and at making phonemic discriminations in a more familiar language. If we were able to control for similarity of bilinguals' and monolinguals' familiarity with a problem domain and for differences in other individual characteristics across these two groups, we would expect that monolinguals would likely be more efficient in decoding verbal problem information in their single language than bilinguals in this same but less familiar language.

The bilingualism research literature does provide findings that support the foregoing hypotheses. Lambert (1955) found that bilinguals showed slower reaction times to simple oral instructions in a less familiar versus more familiar language. Subjects in this study were instructed to press one of a number of keys, coded by a color and digit number, when told to do so in one language versus another. In this study, within-subject differences in response speed were not studied in relation to degree of assessed proficiency in the less familiar language. Dornic (1977), using a task somewhat similar to Lambert's and a within-subject research design, found that bilinguals performed more slowly in a less familiar language than in a native language. He found evidence that differences across languages in reaction time to oral instructions decreased as self-judgments of proficiency level increased in the less familiar language.

Attention to bilinguals' efficiency in recognizing language has led to concern for the structure of their semantic memory. The major issue has been whether bilinguals maintain one or two separate memory systems for word meanings. Contemporary cognitive theory would suggest that the conceptual knowledge referred to by words is stored in a single long-term memory system, regardless of the language in which words are input. An alternative to this view is that bilinguals maintain separate memory systems for the meaning of words in each language. Thorough reviews of research in this area are provided by McCormack (1977), Dornic (1977), and Lopez (1977). Results of studies tend to support the hypothesis of a single semantic memory system for words from two languages. Some of the major results are summarized succinctly by Dornic (1977) as follows:

> By far the largest amount of the bilingual memory research to date has given support to the common-store hypothesis. Kolers (1966b) was the first to demonstrate the "bilingual equivalence effect" (i.e., that translation equivalents behave as old items) in short-term memory. Kintsch (1970) observed false recognitions of translation equivalents, and Kintsch and Kintsch (1969) found interlingual interference in pair-associate learning. Young and Saegert (1966) and Young and Webber (1967) observed that associations formed in one language can interfere with, or facilitate, the formation of new associations in another language. Young and Navar (1968) demonstrated interlingual retroactive inhibition: they showed forgetting in one language to occur as a function of associations formed in the other language. Lopez and Young (1974) found positive transfer effects to be uniform both between and within languages. In a novel type of bilingual memory experiment, MacLeod (1976) using the "savings method" as a measure of long-time retention, also provided support for the common-store theory. (p.21)

One interesting approach to the question of bilinguals' semantic memory organization has been based on a monolingual word-recognition paradigm developed by Meyer and Schvaneveldt (1971). The latter investigators simultaneously presented pairs of word-like stimuli to monolingual subjects via a tachistoscope; the task of subjects was to respond "Yes" or "No" depending on whether *both* stimuli were words or not. It was found that correct "Yes" responses were faster for words that were semantically related (e.g., "doctor-nurse") than for words that were not obviously related (e.g., "doctor–chair"). This effect is interpreted to reflect the association of meanings among words in semantic memory. Words that are related are recognized faster because, once a single word has been recognized, access to its semantic associates is heightened. This facilitation is an effect of the organization of memory for word meanings and not only of ability to recognize that letters are appropriately combined to form a word.

Palij (1980) in a recent study found a semantic facilitation effect in a mixed French–English bilingual version of the Meyer–Schvaneveldt word–recognition task. In this task subjects were simultaneously presented with a word in one language and another word that was sometimes in the other language. Subjects were faster at recognizing word pairs in different langues when the words from different languages had meanings that were highly related. An earlier study by Meyer and Ruddy (1974) reported a similar finding with mixed English and German words. These results support the hypothesis that word meanings in different languages are represented by the same underlying system of semantic memory. Citing Hines (1978), Palij suggests that evidence for a single-store model of bilingual semantic memory may be further refined if consideration is given to perceptual word-recognition strategies that are language specific. Varying the orthographic and phonological difficulty of words may lead to differences in performance on a paired word-recognition strategies that are language specific. Varying the orthographic and phonological difficulty of words may lead to differences in performance on a paired word-recognition task. Speed of performance on mixed language versions of the Meyer–Schvaneveldt word-recognition task may be affected by bilinguals' word decoding efficiency in each language and not only by the presence or absence of an obvious semantic association among words.

Bilinguals' relative efficiency in decoding words in either language apparently has not been the objective of recent cognitive research. Research of this sort may be significant for cognitive training research on improving reading, because automaticity in decoding is known to be an essential skill affecting reading comprehension. For example, automaticity in decoding words presumably affects the availability of processing resources for establishing and recognizing linkages between relatively distant propositions represented in a text (Kintsch & Vipond, 1979). It would be valuable to investigate how lack of automaticity in word decoding in a less familiar language detracts from bilinguals' ability to comprehend semantic information as measured in a more familiar language. An appropriate study of this phenomenon would need to be informed by knowledge about the phonological and morphological structure of words in two languages. This would be necessary because efficiency of decoding skills in each language would have to be analyzed in terms of ability to recognize the elementary meaning constituents of words and their graphemic/phonological realization. The previous discussion of Hakuta (1982) suggests that a model of decoding skills in a less familiar language might have to allow for strategies in decoding that originate from knowledge of reading in the more familiar language. Such an allowance would clearly be needed for understanding the reading capabilities of persons who are of low proficiency in a new language.

It is conceivable that training of word decoding reading skills in a new language might be possible on the basis of perceptual recognition exercises designed to automate bilinguals' correct recognition of morphological and phonological word structures. This possibility is discussed in more detail in the concluding section of the chapter.

The previous discussion has concerned bilinguals' efficiency in recognizing words and word meanings in a less familiar language. Attention is now turned to bilinguals' efficiency in recognizing sentence and text-length materials. It is difficult to separate reading efficiency as a purely input process in verbal problem solving from conceptual utilization of verbal information in problem solving. This is because performance in reading is always influenced by the contextual demands of reading and because measurements of reading efficiency may accordingly require persons to do some problem solving with language in order to generate performance measures. For the moment, however, attention remains on reading efficiency for sentence-length materials where problem solving is kept at a minimum; this is more in line with a focus on input processing of language, rather than problem solving as a conceptual process affected by linguistic skills.

The conclusion that bilinguals read sentence-length materials slower in a less familiar versus more familiar language has long been established in research on bilingualism (e.g., see Kolers, 1966a; and Macnamara & Kellaghan, cited in Macnamara, 1967). The importance of efficiency in reading comprehension in a less familiar versus more familiar language for foreign students' schooling has also been investigated. Angelis (1982), for example, has found that graduate foreign students in business and engineering judge that limits in reading efficiency pose among the most serious linguistic difficulties for students. Despite occasional forays in the area, not too many comprehensive studies of bilinguals' reading efficiency have yet been done from a contemporary information-processing perspective.

One strategy for proposing and beginning such research might start by replicating well-known monolingual sentence verification experiments on bilingual subjects. The objectives of such research would be to study what linguistic and task characteristics affect bilinguals' ability to recognize and utilize semantic information in one language versus another. For example, I have examined Hispanic bilinguals' performance on Spanish and English versions of the Clark and Chase (1972) sentence verification task. In this task subjects were presented with sentence–figure pairs in each language and asked to determine whether they matched. Sentences were presented first, followed by figures. Sentences were very simple, such as "Star above Plus" or "Star not above Plus"; figures were of a form such as $^*_+$ or $^+_*$. The subject's task was to respond true or false as quickly as possible. Previous research by Clark and Chase (1972) has confirmed that speed in decision making in this task can be explained by an explicit information-processing model describing the linguistic structure of sentences, the correspondence between sentence forms and figures, and the decision-making steps required.

Table 8.1 from Duran's study displays data on bilinguals' performance on the Clark and Chase sentence verification task. The table gives mean reaction times in milliseconds for giving a *correct* decision. The table also displays mean reading time for affirmative and negative sentences and the difference in mean reading time for affirmative and negative sentences within each language. Decision and reading times were independently measured. The task was administered using an Apple II microcomputer.

The decision time results shown in Table 8.1 are congruent with previous monolingual studies of performance on this task (Carpenter & Just, 1975; Clark & Chase, 1972). Subjects' fastest reaction times in each language occurred when they needed to make decisions on the basis of an affirmative sentence. In both languages, when the input was an affirmative sentence, subjects were faster at making a correct true decisions versus correct false decisions.

Subjects' mean reaction times for making correct decision when the input was a negative sentence were slower than correct mean decision times for affirmative sentences. The results for English were just as theory predicted: subjects were slightly faster at correctly responding false rather than true in this situation. In Spanish when subjects were presented a negative sentence, they were slightly faster in making a correct true decision as opposed to a correct false decision. Although the latter result shows an inversion in the magnitude of mean reaction times that does not conform to the Chase and Clark theoretical model for this task, it is nonetheless a result that is sometimes found among monolinguals. Hunt and MacLeod (1978) and MacLeod, Hunt, and Mathews (1978) have found that correct false decisions were faster than correct true decisions when subjects used a spatial imagery strategy for working the sentence verification task in question. Thus, there may be a meaningful account of why performance in Spanish does not mirror performance in English. It may be that subjects are more prone to using a spatial imagery strategy in Spanish, their less familiar language, as opposed to English, their more familiar language. This possibility, of course, can be substantiated only on the basis of further research, but it suggests that variations in language skill could result in important differences in the internal representation that becomes the basis for problem-solving efforts.

One of the most interesting aspects of the data of Table 8.1 is that it suggests that subjects take the same amount of time to make correct decisions for affirmative sentences regardless of the language of input. This result is consistent with a theoretical view that the mental representation of the meaning of a sentence

TABLE 8.1
Sentence Verification Task: Latencies for Correct Responses[a]

Correct Response	English Stimulus				Spanish Stimulus			
	STAR ABOVE PLUS		STAR NOT ABOVE PLUS		ESTRELLA ESTA ARRIBA DE CRUZ		ESTRELLA NO ESTA ARRIBA DE CRUZ	
	True	False	True	False	True	False	True	False
Average decision latency	860.98	1256.13	1735.05	1615.20	845.21	1201.36	1375.23	1475.17
Average reading time	1325.90		1849.23		1815.40		2345.17	
Difference in reading times within language	523.33				529.77			

[a]Latencies are in milliseconds, $N = 49$.

is represented cognitively in a propositional or other nonlinguistic format. Thus, the reaction times for affirmative sentences is the same because the same mental representation of sentence meaning is being tapped. This interpretation does not seem as plausible for negative sentences across Spanish and English; the reaction times show more dissimilarity across language and decision type.

Reading speed data given in Table 8.1 are also provocative to interpret. Average reading time in Spanish is longer than average reading time in English for each sentence type. This is not unexpected, given that the Spanish sentences contain more words and more syllables per word and also because the college subjects studied were more proficient in reading English than Spanish (as assessed by independent tests of reading comprehension in each language). These factors contributed, no doubt, to faster reading of English as opposed to Spanish. It is interesting to note that within each language it took subjects almost exactly one-half second more time on the average to understand a negative versus affirmative form of a sentence. This result suggests the possibility that very similar linguistic encoding strategies were at work in understanding affirmative and negative sentences across the two languages.

Research such as the foregoing is valuable because it helps pinpoint explicit ways in which bilinguals' recognition and simple understanding of language is affected by the language of problem presentation. On the basis of such research, we can understand ways in which efficiency in language comprehension can be expected to vary and not vary on the basis of differential familiarity with two languages. Attention now turns to effects of linguistic familiarity on complex problem solving.

Conceptualization and Mental Solution.   The solving of complex problems may be affected by language familiarity in two basic ways. First, extending from the discussion on input processing of language, the appropriateness and sophistication of the mental model of a problem will be directly related to quality of comprehension of a problem statement, which in turn is based on a person's familiarity with the language system used to input a problem. Secondly, there may be a need to rely on knowledge of language during conceptual problem solving that goes beyond the original need to understand a problem as it is originally stated. Thus, conceptual problem solving may be affected by familiarity with a language. The basic question addressed here is the following: In what ways may bilinguals vary in their conceptual problem-solving activities given their degree of familiarity with two languages?

This research question has not been investigated intensively in bilingualism research despite its importance, though there are some classic investigations to note. Macnamara (1967), as part of a series of 22 studies of English–Irish bilinguals' mathematical skills, found that bilinguals performed better on mechanical arithmetic problems involving no verbal materials than on verbal arithmetic problems in their non-native language, Irish. When bilingual subjects were compared to monolingual subjects, they performed at a similar level on mechanical arithmetic problems but more poorly on verbal mathematics problems. Macnamara (1967) concluded that the observed pattern of results was "probably due to the fact that in mechanical math the student is simply required to carry out an arithmetic operation indicated by an arithmetic symbol, whereas in tests of problem [i.e., verbal] arithmetic he is required to read and interpret prose passages," (p.122, bracketed material added for clarification).

Macnamara believed that ability to understand individual sentences in a problem statement was inadequate to account for differences in problem solving such as those mentioned. Macnamara and Kellaghan (cited in Macnamara, 1967) investigated whether bilinguals' understanding of the subparts of a verbal problem equally well in two languages would be followed by an equivalent success rate in solving a problem completely in two languages. The verbal problems used were based on everyday knowledge. The study involved 341 sixth-grade Irish children who were native speakers of English but who had received instruction in both Irish and English. Subjects were divided into two groups; one group was presented with problems only in English and the other group received problems only in Irish. The results show that understanding the meaning of individual sentences in a problem (as measured by an ability to answer very simple questions about their meaning) did not lead to an equal success rate in solving all problems presented in two languages. The study found that a smaller proportion of subjects succeeded in solving some problems completely in Gaelic than they did in English, despite the fact that only the performances of subjects who understood the sentences equally well in both languages were compared. Recall that comprehension was gauged by the ability to answer simple questions about the meaning of sentences; a more demanding standard of comprehension might have been needed.

In a very recent study, Mestre, Gerace, and Lochhead (1980) investigated Hispanic engineering students' ability to convert linguistic statements of very simple verbal algebra problems in either of their two languages into equations. The results suggested that the balanced bilingual subjects showed equal facility in converting verbal problems into equations across their two languages and, further, that they tended to make similar types of errors across two languages. In addition, however, bilinguals were found to perform more poorly on the task than a comparision group of monolingual English subjects. For both monolingual and bilingual English groups, success in representing verbal problems as equations were significantly predicted by reading comprehension proficiency in each language, with this relationship being noticeably stronger for bilinguals than for English monolinguals.

I (Duran, 1979, 1981) investigated similarities in the performance of adult Hispanic bilinguals on four matched Spanish–English tests of logical reasoning. Factor analytic study of the tests that were administered had led to the conclusion that the tests identified the same underlying cognitive factor in their English versions (Ekstrom, French, & Harman, 1976; French, Ekstrom & Price, 1963). The results of this study indicated that subjects performed similarly on translation versions of the same tests in two languages, though they performed more poorly in the language they were least proficient in. The evidence supported the possibility that bilinguals were applying similar abilities in working highly related reasoning problems in two languages, but that reading comprehension ability in each language moderated performance in each language. Also found were substantial correlations between reading-comprehension test scores in any one language and logical-reasoning test scores in the other language for both Spanish and English. These results suggest that there are skills or abilities common to reading comprehension and to the solution of reasoning problems that are quasi-independent of a language required for problem solving, as discussed earlier in this chapter.

Language Production. The impact of ability to produce language in solution of complex problems has received only limited attention in the cognitive bilingualism literature. Two issues seem apparent. First, there is the question of the ability of bilinguals to encode information in language in order to communicate such information publicly, as may be required in a problem-solving task. A second issue concerns the quality of the language produced in these circumstances. The second concern is essentially about the intelligibility of language; this intelligibility may be influenced both by skill in encoding thought into language and also by the ability of a bilingual to modulate speech and writing in ways that conform to the phonology and orthography of a language. Overlaying both issues are discourse skills that determine the effectiveness of communication giving a setting, activity, and purpose for communication.

As with analysis of bilinguals' input capabilities with language, there is no clean separation between bilinguals' ability to conceptually solve problems and ability to produce appropriate language as required by problem solving. Especially in complex problems, a clear verbal formulation of the problem may be an important part of the thinker's representation and solution process. The examples of research discussed briefly here do not derive from information-processing psychology, but they suggest future research that might be undertaken from that perspective. The two problem contexts considered are writing on essay topics and answering questions in a psychiatric interview.

Studies of the English composition skills of persons with a bilingual background suggest that errors in composition can reflect not only lack of familiarity with English but also lack of skill in organizing a composition to convey required information. Errors of the former sort have been studied, e.g., by Herrick (1981), with Mexican–Americans writing in English. Herrick noted that his informants made errors that showed clear transfer of knowledge of Spanish into English. Some errors had an authentic orthographical origin, for example, English words such as "comfort" would be spelled as "confort," stemming from the Spanish word *confortable* of the same meaning. Other sorts of writing errors showed transfer of phonology from Spanish to English. For example, an incorrect phrase such as "I used to leave here when I was younger" might reflect a substitution for "live" based on pronunciation. Herrick diagnosed that incorrect writing errors of this sort arise because some Hispanics may pronounce the English "living" as "leaving" because in Spanish, *i* is pronounced like the English *ea* in leave. Randle (1981) studied the writing problems of Mexican–Americans from Spanish language backgrounds. She found that awkward rhetorical organization, lack of clarity of expression, and other shortcomings in discourse structure limited the quality of their English essays. These later errors were as notable as errors that appeared to stem from inappropriate transfer of Spanish structures to English. Randle suggested that to improve writing skills of bilingual children production of whole essays, where the objectives and purposes of writing guide the writing behavior, should be stressed. In her opinion, emphasis on eliminating grammatical errors and spelling errors and improving vocabulary does not accomplish enough in training bilingual children to write entire essays well.

Another example of how problem solving may be affected by bilinguals' fluency in a language focuses on speech behavior in psychiatric diagnosis. Marcos and Trujillo (1981), psychiatric practitioners reviewing their own work in this area, found that Spanish-dominant patients were often diagnosed inappropriately if their psychiatric interviews were conducted in English rather than Spanish. They found that patients, when asked questions in English, spoke more slowly and evidenced less skill in diction and less coherent development of their thoughts than in Spanish; this occurred despite the therapeutic context of interaction. One interesting observation of Marcos and Trujillo was that some Spanish-dominant patients evidenced more gestures and motor movements while speaking in English than in Spanish. Marcos and Trujillo suggested that such accentuated movement is indicative of stress when operating in a less familiar language; the gestures and movements indicated the exercise of deliberate motor strategies to assist in communicating meaning and to control the physical execution of speech. Dornic (1977) has suggested that information-processing models of bilinguals' language behavior should take into account the stress load or perceived difficulty of performing language tasks. Attentional demands required to comprehend or produce a language, as well as allocation of physical and mental resources to performance of language-related tasks may affect the pool of cognitive resources (e.g., memory and attention) that can be used during problem solving in a language.

Summary and Discussion

This overview of bilinguals' problem solving indicates that degree of ability to solve problems in a less familiar language can often be traced to fairly specific behaviors involving language processing and its impact on cognition. Training of biinguals' cognitive skills will need to be informed by the development of an extensive body of research findings such as those discussed in this chapter. Further information-processing research on bilingualism appears to be a very important route to refining our understanding of these issues. At present, much bilingualism research on cognition is unsophisticated, and it seldom draws on information-processing paradigms for research. This chapter suggests that it is possible to join research on bilingualism with research on information processing, though this task requires extensive expertise in linguistics and language assessment as well as in cognitive psychology.

In order to inform cognitive training of bilinguals, bilingual cognitive research must take an integral, programmatic approach. Subjects' language familiarity and proficiency must be analyzed along with the linguistic and nonlinguistic demands of problem-solving tasks, as well as research studies capable of describing how language familiarity specifically affects problem solving must be designed. Also, studies of bilinguals should always be informed by the particular profiles of bilingualism present in subjects. Bilinguals with knowledge of the same two language systems are not all alike in terms of their familiarity with the two language systems; equal familiarity across all domains of language use is extremely rare. Our ability to specify how language familiarity affects problem solving in a less familiar versus more familiar language depends on an accurate assessment of dual language capabilities.

Ideally, language capabilities should be assessed at two different levels. General proficiency in each of two language systems may be assessed by means of integrative proficiency tests that require coordination of multiple modalities of language use. Results of such tests are useful in describing the global abilities of persons in each language; such results may further be used in establishing hypotheses about the impact of gross differences in proficiency on problem solving. A second level of language proficiency in need of assessment is ability to utilize the particular language modalities and language codes that are involved in criterion problem-solving tasks. This level of assessment is important in accounting for explicit ways in which language familiarity may affect problem solving. With appropriate experimental designs, measurement of this sort of language proficiency can be accomplished as part of the examination of performance on criterion problem-solving tasks involving language.

A second procedure for improving bilingualism research from an information-processing perspective is to develop a task analysis model of performance on criterion problem-solving tasks. This chapter suggested the very general strategy of partitioning an account of problem solving on tasks into problem input, conceptual representation and solution of a problem, and verbal (or other) output of problem-solving behavior.

Well-known experiments in psycholinguistics involving word recognition and sentence verification can be used to study how language familiarity may or may not affect problem-solving performance across two language systems. Many paradigms or experimental procedures in cognitive research have a detailed account of information processing in carrying out tasks and of influences of information processing on task performance. Performance of bilinguals in each of their two language systems on information-processing tasks can be used to isolate differences and similarities in problem-solving behavior across two language systems. Although discovery of such effects in interesting theoretically in its own right—e.g., verification of the validity of existing monolingual-based theories, it may also be useful in generating ancillary measures that are helpful in studying bilinguals' performance on more complex tasks that share some processing requirements with the more elementary experimental tasks.

High-level problem-solving tasks involving rich semantic interpretation of problem materials, inference making, and extensive flexible use of metacomponents in thinking are not usually amenable to simple information-processing modeling. Nonetheless, language familiarity effects on problem solving on such tasks may be assessed if appropriate task analysis and problem-solving models are used. Most interesting and complex problem-solving tasks require sophistication in how problem-solving information is interpreted, represented, and manipulated. One important question for future research is whether bilinguals are capable of adopting and manipulating as sophisticated a representation of a problem when a problem is input via a less familiar language. Evidence that bilinguals are capable of more sophisticated problem solving in one language versus another for the same type of problem would lead to further questions. Going beyond evidence of differences in problem representation and resulting problem-solving performance, we should be able to conduct research to tell how language familiarity specifically resulted in differences in problem representation and solution.

As the foregoing discussion illustrates, more frequent use of within-subject research designs may enhance bilingual research. Within-subject designs allow us to compare individual bilinguals' problem-solving efficiency in one language versus another. This helps control for background and personal variables, which would be difficult if not impossible to control for in group-comparison research designs. As such, the reliability and precision of data—such as reaction times— are enhanced by use of designs comparing within-subject performance across two languages.

The question of how bilingualism research might be made useful for cognitive training is not premature altogether. An interesting example of a program for cognitive training that could be implemented with bilinguals is given by the reading research of Frederiksen (Frederiksen, Warren, Gillote, & Weaver, 1982). The objective of the Frederiksen work is to assess and train monolinguals in word decoding efficiency at different levels of text understanding. Training is administered via microcomputer games that challenge subjects to sharpen and speed up their ability to detect letter clusters in target words, to pronounce words quickly and accurately, and to detect appropriateness of word meaning in the context of sentences. Although the results so far of this training are complicated, evidence has emerged that suggests that training is effective in improving skills at each level of processing examined and that training may improve general reading skills outside of training contexts.

It is conceivable that a program of training such as that pursued by Frederiksen could be extended productively to bilingual trainees. The procedures proposed by Frederiksen might be used to teach non-English native speakers how to recognize and understand words more effectively in English. The particular letter and word stimuli chosen for training could be selected so as to sharpen discrimination and speed of discrimination of word features in English that otherwise might be confused with word features stemming from knowledge of a particular non-English language.

In the case where bilinguals are not skilled readers in their more familiar language, training of reading skills in the more familiar language may be used as a procedure to prepare for training of reading in the less familiar language. This procedure would prove feasible if two language systems were enough alike to expect transfer of reading skills across languages. A perfect match of language structures across languages would not be necessary, nor could it be expected. Some of the cognitive component skills required in reading may be very general and not language specific. For example, learning how to guide visual movements in reading in one language may rely on skills that could be used in guiding reading in another language. Differences in languages and their printed format could, of course, affect the degree of transfer from reading in one language to reading in another language. Nonetheless, strategies such as the one mentioned may be flexible because they are in service of some of the higher level components of reading—such as searching for a completed idea in print. Certainly we would expect the latter sort of general component to transfer across languages.

The discussion of training of reading skills in a less familiar language is an exciting prospect. It is concrete in that we have an existing program, such as that of Frederiksen, that might be modified for use with bilinguals. Secondly, the kind of training application under consideraton is exciting theoretically in that it would advance our knowledge of cognitive and linguistic skills as they interact with bilingualism. Lastly, but not least important, the kind of training application cited has practical value, given the schooling problems faced in the United States by persons from bilingual backgrounds.

In closing this chapter, it is essential to mention a critical topic that cannot be thoroughly discussed here, but that merits attention elsewhere. This topic is the role of cultural modes of thought and language use that may be associated with the occurrence of bilingualism. This complex topic has not received very much attention from cognitive psychologists or from bilingualism researchers. Cross-cultural cognitive psychologists, however, such as Scribner (1979) and Scribner and Cole (1981) suggest that there are very intimate connections between the cultural organization of life and modes of thought and problem solving. One of the points emerging from research in this area is that formal schooling often seems to allow persons to develop skills in abstraction needed for problem solving in problem domains relying on literacy. At present, information-processing psychology by and large has yet to incorporate such research findings on connections between language and thought. There are some notable exceptions, such as the study of Tannen (1979) on cognitive schemata utilized by Greek and American women in formulating a narrative description of a filmed episode. Another exception is the research of Steffensen, Jogdeo, and Anderson (1978) on cultural influences on the recall of event narratives. Topics such as the foreging represent exciting areas for research on language and cognition that have just begun to be explored.

ACKNOWLEDGMENTS

Preparation of this chapter was supported in part by Grant NIE–G–80–0157 from the National Institute of Education. The contents of this chapter do not necessarily reflect the position, policy, or endorsement of the National Institute of Education.

REFERENCES

Angelis, P. (1982). *Language skills in academic study.* Princeton, NJ: Test of English as a Foreign Language Program, Educational Testing Service, unpublished manuscript.

Carpenter, P., & Just, M. (1975). Sentence comprehension: A psycholinguistic processing model of verification. *Psychological Review, 82,* 45–73.

Clark, H.H., & Chase, W.   (1972).   On the process of comparing sentences against pictures. *Cognitive Psychology, 3,* 472–517.

Duran, R. P. (1979.) *Logical reasoning skills of Puerto Rican bilinguals.* Final Report to the National Institute of Education. Princeton, NJ: Educational Testing Service.

Duran, R. P. (1983). *Hispanics' education and background: Predictors of college achievement.* New York: The College Board.

Duran, R.P. (1981). Reading comprehension and the verbal deductive reasoning of bilinguals. In R. P. Duran (Ed.), *Latino language and communicative behavior* (pp. 311–336). Norwood, NJ: Ablex.

Ekstrom, R. B., French, J. W., & Harman, H. H. (1976). *Manual for kit of factor-referenced cognitive tests.* Princeton, NJ: Educational Testing Service.

Feuerstein, R. (1980). *Instrumental enrichment: An intervention program for cognitive modifiability.* Baltimore, MD: University Park Press.

French, J. W., Ekstrom, R. B., & Price, L. A. (1963). *Manual for kit of reference tests for cognitive factors.* Princeton, NJ: Educational Testing Service.

Frederiksen, J., Warren, B., Gillote, H., & Weaver, P. (1982, May/June). The name of the game is literacy. *CCN, 23–27.*

Hakuta, K. (1982, June). *The second language learner in the context of the study of language acquisition.* Paper presented at the Society for Research in Child Development Conference on Bilingualism and Childhood Development, New York University.

Herrick, E.M. (1981, September). *Spanish-English orthographic issues in English composition.* Paper presented at the Conference on the Investigation of Form and Function in Mexican–American (Chicano) English, University of Texas at El Pasto.

Hines, T. M. (1978). *The independence of language in bilingual memory.* Unpublished doctoral dissertation, University of Oregon.

Hunt, E., & MacLeod, C. M. (1978). The sentence-vertification paradigm: A case study of two conflicting approaches to individual differences. *Intelligence, 2,* 129–144.

Kintsch, W. (1970). Recognition memory in bilingual subjects. *Journal of Verbal Learning and Verbal Behavior, 9,* 405–409.

Kintsch, W., & Kintsch, E. (1969). Interlingual interference and memory processes. *Journal of Verbal Learning and Verbal Behavior, 8,* 16–19.

Kintsch, W., & Vipond, D. (1979). Reading comprehension and readability in educational practice and psychological theory. In L. G. Nilsson (Ed.), *Perspectives on memory research.* Hillsdale, NJ: Lawrence Erlbaum Associates.

Kolers, P. Á. (1966a). Reading and talking bilingually. *American Journal of Psychology, 79,* 357–376.

Kolers, P. A. (1966b). Interlingual facilitation of short-term memory. *Journal of Verbal Learning and Verbal Behavior, 5,* 314–319.

Lambert, W. E. (1955). Measurement of the linguistic dominance of bilinguals. *Journal of Abnormal and Social Psychology, 50,* 197–200.

Lopez, M., & Young, R. K. (1974). The linguistic interdependence of bilinguals. *Journal of Experimental Psychology, 102,* 981–983.

Lopez, M. (1977). Bilingual memory research: Implications for bilingual education. In J. L. Martinez, Jr. (Ed.), *Chicano psychology* (pp. 127–140). New York: Academic Press.

MacLeod, C.M. (1976). Bilingual episodic memory: Acquisition and forgetting. *Journal of Verbal Learning and Verbal Behavior, 15,* 347-364.

MacLeod, C. M., Hunt, E. B., & Mathews, N.N. (1978). Individual differences in the verification of sentence–picture relationships. *Journal of Verbal Learning and Verbal Behavior, 17,* 493–507.

Macnamara, J. (1967). The effects of instruction in a weaker language. *Journal of Social Issues, 23*(2), 121–135.

Macnamara, J., & Kellaghan, T. D. (1967). Reading in a second language. Undated manuscript cited in Macnamara, J., The effects of instruction in a weaker language. *Journal of Social Issues, 23,* 121–135.

Marcos, L. R., & Trujillo, M. D. (1981). Culture, language and communicative behavior: The psychiatric examination of Spanish–Americans. In R. P. Duran (Ed.), *Latino language and communicative behavior* (pp. 187–194). Norwood, NJ: Ablex.

McCormack, P. D. (1977). Bilingual linguistic memory: The independence–interdependence issue revisited. In P. A. Hornby (Ed.), *Bilingualism: Psychological, social and educational implications* (pp. 57–66). New York: Academic Press.

Mestre, J. P., Gerace, W. J., & Lochhead, J. (1980). *The interdependence of language and translational math skills among Hispanic engineering students.* Unpublished manuscript, University of Massachusetts, Department of Physics and Astronomy.

Meyer, D. E., & Ruddy, M. G. (1974, April). *Bilingual word-recognition: Organization and retrieval of alternative lexical codes.* Paper delivered at the Eastern Psychological Association meeting.

Meyer, D. E., & Schvaneveldt, R. W. (1971). Facilitation in recognizing pairs of words: Evidence of a dependence between retrieval operations. *Journal of Experimental Psychology, 90,* 227–234.

NCES (National Center for Education Statistics). (1978a). *Geographic distribution, nativity, and age distribution of language minorities in the United States.* Spring 1976 (Report 78B–5). Washington, DC.

NCES (National Center for Education Statistics). (1978b). *The educational disadvantage of language-minority persons in the United States.* Spring 1976 (Report 78B–4). Washington, DC.

Newell, A., & Simon, H. A. (1972). *Human problem solving.* Englewood Cliffs, NJ: Prentice–Hall.

Oller, J. W. (1979). *Language tests at school.* London: Longman.

Palij, M. (1980, April). *Semantic facilitation on a bilingual lexical decision task.* Paper presented at the Eastern Psychological Association meeting.

Randle, J. W. (1981). *Analysis of English 7 and 8 Essays.* Unpublished manuscript, St. Edwards College, Austin.

Scribner, S. (1979). Modes of thinking and ways of speaking: Culture and logic reconsidered. In R. O. Freedle (Ed.), *New directions in discourse processing* (pp. 223–243). Norwood, NJ: Ablex.

Scribner, S., & Cole, M. (1981). *The psychology of literacy.* Cambridge, MA: Harvard University.

Steffensen, M. S., Jogdeo, C., & Anderson, R. C. (1978, July). *A cross-cultural perspective on reading comprehension* (Tech. Rep. 97). Champaign, IL: Center for the Study of Reading, University of Illinois.

Tannen, D. (1979). What's in a frame? Surface evidence for underlying expectations. In R. O. Freedle (Ed.), *New directions in discourse processing* (pp. 137–181). Norwood, NJ: Ablex.

Young, R. K., & Navar, M. I. (1968). Retroactive inhibition with bilinguals. *Journal of Experimental Psychology, 77,* 109–115.

Young, R. K., & Saegert, J. (1966). Transfer with bilinguals. *Psychonomic Science, 6,* 161–162.

Young, R. K., & Webber, A. (1967). Positive and negative transfer with bilinguals. *Journal of Verbal Learning and Verbal Behavior, 6,* 874–877.

9 Looking Across the River: Views from the Two Banks of Research and Development in Problem Solving

James G. Greeno
University of Pittsburgh

The researchers and program developers are like two groups of people who live on opposite sides of a river, and in the conference that led to these volumes each came to the banks to show what life is like on their side and what important products have resulted from their recent work.

My comments on the interchange regarding problem solving are in three sections. First, I mention some underlying attitudes that I believe both groups of investigators share. Second, I comment on some relationships between substantive issues that are emphasized in the training programs described in Volume 1 as well as the issues emphasized in current basic research on problem solving. Third, I point to three opportunities for new research directions that seem promising in light of conceptual and other resources made evident in the chapters of this volume.

Shared Attitudes

The domains of work and study represented in these volumes, and in the conference as a whole, have turned out to be surprisingly compatible. Many persons in society would not expect practitioners, developers, and basic scientists to communicate successfully. They would be surprised at the extent to which we have learned from one another through genuine exchange of information, concepts, and attitudes.

Successful communication requires some shared knowledge and belief, and, in our case, we share some very significant fundamental attitudes. I believe that all of us are in love with human intellect, but not in awe of it. Because of our love of intellect, we want to know it well and to understand it deeply. But we also want to find ways to strengthen and to improve intellectual capabilities. Because we are not awed by intellect, we believe that we can make genuine progress toward both of these ambitious goals. We believe that intellect can be understood, and that it can be made stronger.

There is also a powerful shared vision that inspires our efforts in research and in program development. We envision changes in the human condition that include more powerful intellectual skills and widespread understanding of the ways in which minds function. If this vision is fulfilled, there will be a great increase of intellectual resources for society; self-reliance in personal affairs, as well as an increase in analytical and critical abilities directed toward social organizations and leaders.

The vision that inspires our efforts differs drastically from one that many in society fearfully had in mind a few years ago concerning prospective influences of psychological science. The opinions that were developed so dramatically in Huxley's *Brave New World* represent a set of expectations widely held in the society. Perhaps these views are somewhat less dominant now than they were during the 1950s, when *Brave New World* was standard required reading in basic literature courses. The image of psychological science as a basis of thought control, however, is still present in society, and not without justification in some lines of experimental study. But a very different image is in our minds. We envision an enhancement of human intellectual power and independence resulting from our science and our technology.

Relationships Between Research and Development

The chapters on problem solving in these volumes have revealed an important difference in the substantive issues on which current research and developmental efforts have been focused. Empirical and theoretical analyses conducted in basic research have emphasized skills and knowledge that are tailored for specific domains of problems. Programs for training problem-solving skills (see Volume 1) have stressed general thinking skills and strategies and have encouraged positive attitudes about problems and the students' own problem-solving abilities.

I suspect that this difference in emphasis has emerged because of judgments by both groups of investigators concerning the likelihood of progress as well as the significance of alternative topics. Certainly, general skills and domain-specific knowledge are important components of successful problem-solving performance. Basic research investigators believe, given the concepts and methods that are available, that advances in understanding are more likely if we focus on relatively specific knowledge and skills rather than on general strategies and attitudes. Nevertheless, program developers have judged that they can bring about greater changes in children's cognitive abilities by emphasizing skills and motives at a general level.

Given this difference in the issues emphasized by the two groups of investigators, some may wonder about the substantive relationship between basic research and program development in this area. The connection appears to be much closer, however, if we consider basic research on problem solving conducted in the recent past. General cognitive and motivational factors in problem solving have been studied in considerable detail. Duncker (1945), Katona (1940), Maier (1930), Wertheimer (1945/1959), and others were concerned with factors that enable problem solvers to apprehend conceptual patterns in problem situations and to find productive formulations of problems. Gestalt psychologists, such as Duncker (1945) and Luchins (1942), as well as behavioristic investigators such as Maltzman (1960), stressed cognitive flexibility. Lewin, Dembo, Festinger, and Sears (1944) emphasized the importance of an individual's self-image and the level of aspiration. Atkinson (1957) and McClelland, Atkinson, Clark, and Lowell (1953) studied the general motivational factors regarding achievement and an individual's expectation of success. More recently, Newell and Simon (1972) worked out detailed analyses of general problem-solving strategies such as means–ends analysis.

I am not suggesting that the current training programs are simply applications of basic research findings. Whereas some developers such as Wickelgren (1974) have used available theories in a self-conscious way, others, such as de Bono (see Volume 1) have not explicitly identified sources of their ideas in basic research and theory. The relationship between basic science and application is complex even in highly developed domains of science and engineering. But it is even more complex in a field where concepts and methods are still being defined. Psychologists have not yet identified and formalized the basic theoretical concepts of their science, and, although giving specialized attention to systematic conceptualization and empirical evaluation, they are not the only source of significant concepts, phenomena, and principles that are relevant to the training of intellectual skills.

Consider the set of general concepts and principles available in the society as a kind of intellectual capital. (I first heard this metaphor used by William Estes.) Development of programs that improve the technological capabilities of the society draws on that intellectual capital. If we are to achieve further technological development, we must require a further increase in the supply of capital. Research investigators have invested their resources in an attempt to replenish intellecual capital in the domain of cognition, and substantial results have been obtained. Recent progress regarding problem-solving skills is described in Polson and Jeffries' analytical chapter (see Volume 1) as well as in the research chapters of this volume. We should expect to see the use of these recently developed concepts and principles in the next generation of programs for training problem-solving skills that will undoubtedly be constructed in the coming years.

Some Research Opportunities

Research problems usually emerge within a community of investigators working on a shared set of substantive questions. The opportunity for different groups of investigators to interact may be an occasion for new research problems to emerge, resulting in questions raised by one group's methods concerning the other group's ideas. Such an interaction can also show the feasibility of some new potential research directions by showing that resources are available for the study of questions not available in the context of one of the groups alone.

I mention three possible research directions that seem potentially promising to me in light of the interaction we had in the conference: First, program development could exploit results of current basic research; second, basic research could exploit the availability of current training programs; third,both research and development could extend current results by applying current methods to another topic.

Training Knowledge-Based Thinking Skills.   The emphasis in basic research on the role of domain-specific knowledge in problem solving suggests an interesting possibility for program development. In contrast, current training programs have emphasized general thinking skills and have given minimal attention to the content of the intellectual tasks in which the skills are applied.

Some interesting questions might arise if program developers were to address the relationships between general thinking skills and strategies, and knowledge structures that are acquired for specific substantive domains. Thinking skills rarely occur in a vacuum. In general training programs, tasks with familiar content are chosen so the requirements for knowledge are satisfied by virtually all the children without special instruction. If program developers considered the knowledge in a substantive domain and then tried to develop tasks requiring the application of general thinking skills along with knowledge in the domain, some important new approaches to intellectual training might emerge.

Analysis of General Skills.   A second potential direction for research involves the nature of general skills in problem solving. In current basic research, we are able to provide detailed analyses of the concepts and skills that are acquired in instruction. The methods used in these analyses could be applied to provide thorough analyses of the outcomes of general training programs. Studies of this kind would involve detailed observations of children performing the tasks involved in the instructional programs, with the goal of identifying the cognitive structures and processes that are utilized when these tasks are performed successfully. The results of such an analysis constitute a detailed hypothesis about the nature of skills acquired in the training program. The outcome would be interesting both as a theoretical contribution to our understanding of general intellectual skills and as a practical contribution that enables judgments concerning the value of the skills that actually are strengthened by the skills training programs.

Information Processing in Choices and Decisions.   The third potential research direction that I mention is suggested by Miles' (see Volume 1) emphasis on skill in making sound choices and decisions as a factor in practical life. The theoretical analysis of choice and decision processes has not yet made full use of the concepts and methods of information-processing psychology.

Detailed study of the processes and information structures used by successful decision makers would be a feasible undertaking using the successful methods used in recent studies of expert problem solvers. It also would be feasible to develop training programs that focus on skills required in making ordinary decisions, such as a systematic use of relevant information and evaluation of potential outcomes.

REFERENCES

Atkinson, J. W. (1957). Motivational determinants of risk-taking behavior. *Psychological Review, 64,* 359–372.

Duncker, K. (1945). On problem solving. *Psychological Monographs, 58* (Whole No. 270).

Katona, G. (1940). *Organizing and memorizing.* New York: Columbia University Press.

Lewin, K., Dembo, T., Festinger, L., & Sears, P. S. (1944). Level of aspiration. In J. McV. Hunt (Ed.), *Personality and the behavior disorders.* New York: Ronald Press.

Luchins, A. S. (1942). Mechanization in problem solving. *Psychological Monographs, 54* (Whole No. 248).

Maier, N. R. F. (1930). Reasoning in humans. I. On direction. *Journal of Comparative Psychology, 12,* 115–143.

Maltzman, I. (1960). On the training of originality. *Psychological Review, 67,* 229–242.

McClelland, D. C., Atkinson, J. W., Clark, R. W., & Lowell, E. L. (1953). *The achievement motive.* New York: Appleton–Century–Crofts.

Newell, A., & Simon, H. A. (1972). *Human problem solving.* Englewood Cliffs, NJ: Prentice–Hall.

Wertheimer, M. (1959). *Productive thinking.* New York: Harper & Row (Originally published, 1945).

Wickelgren, W. (1974). *How to solve problems.* San Francisco: Freeman.

Intelligence and Reasoning

10

Instrumental and Componential Approaches to the Nature and Training of Intelligence

Robert J. Sternberg
Yale University

Probably the most famous (or, perhaps, infamous) single statement ever made about attempts to remediate apparent deficiencies in mental abilities and scholastic achievements was Jensen's (1969) statement that "compensatory education has been tried and it apparently has failed" (p. 2). According to Jensen, the logic underlying many compensatory education programs has been that:

> since the IQ is known to predict scholastic performance better han any other single measurable attribute of the child, it is believed, whether rightly or wrongly, that if the child's IQ can be appreciably raised, academic achievement by and large will take care of itself, given normal motivation and standard instruction. Children with average or above-average IQs generally do well in school without much special attention. So the remedy deemed logical for children who would do poorly in school is to boost their IQs up to where they can perform like the majority—in short to make them all at least average children. (p. 5)

On the one hand, there are a number of respects in which people could take and have taken issue with all the points Jensen raised in these claims (see *Environment, heredity, and intelligence*, 1969). For example, there have been at least some successful programs of compensatory education (see Feuerstein, 1979, 1980), and probably very few people truly believe that merely raising IQ scores will in and by itself result in the disappearance of the woes that our educational system, our society, and even, in some cases, our genes have wrought. On the other hand, if one can see past Jensen's penchant for overstatement, there are some grains of truth in weaker versions of what he is saying. Many people would agree that compensatory education programs have not met initial hopes and expectations; that many of these programs have been based upon the hope that training the skills needed for improved performance on IQ tests would result in at least some gain in scholastic performance or potential; and that there is much room for improvement in our attempts to train the skills that are needed for enhanced performance on IQ tests, or that are central to intellectual functioning, whether or not these skills are measured by IQ tests.

This chapter presents and compares two alternative conceptions of intelligence and how to train it. The two conceptions are Reuven Feuerstein's (1979, 1980) and my own (Sternberg, 1977a, b, 1979, 1980b). In this chapter, I briefly review the antecedents of the two approaches, presenting and comparing Feuerstein's critique and my own, and discuss why the need for new approaches arose. Next, I describe the two theories of the nature of intelligence, compare them, and point out what I believe to be their strengths and weaknesses. Then, I outline the training programs based on the two theories, comparing them and again noting seeming strengths and weaknesses. Finally, I suggest future directions for research on the nature and training of intelligence.

HISTORICAL ANTECEDENTS: CRITIQUES OF THE PSYCHOMETRIC APPROACH

Historically, most attempts to train intelligent functioning have been based on a psychometric model of the nature of intelligence. In this model, intelligence is usually viewed as deriving from a set of underlying sources of individual differences called factors. One of the more popular theories of this type holds that intelligence draws on seven *primary mental abilities,* namely, verbal comprehension, verbal fluency, number, spatial visualization, reasoning, memory, and perceptual speed (Thurstone, 1938). In another such theory, intelligence is seen as hierarchical, with general intelligence *(g)* at the top of the hierarchy, verbal-educational ability and practical-mechanical ability at the next level, and successively finer abilities at succeedingly lower levels (Vernon, 1971). A similar theory has been proposed by Cattell (1971) and Horn (1968), whose crystallized and fluid abilities are similar to Vernon's verbal-educational and practical-mechanical ones. Still other theories postulate abilities of differing kinds and levels of generality. But all the theories postulate latent structures that in combinations generate differences in observable test performance. For example, observable differences in performances on a mathematical problem-solving test might be attributed to latent differences in number, reasoning, and verbal comprehension abilities, with each ability weighted according to its contribution to the observed differences in test scores.

I agree with Jensen (1969) and believe Feuerstein would agree as well, that the psychometric model of intelligence has not been particularly successful in generating successful programs for training intelligent functioning. This is not to say that this model has been an utter failure. Rather, its strengths may not be those most conducive to designing training programs for developing intelligent performance. I argue shortly that, even where the psychometric model appears to have been successful, it may have been for reasons other than those that derive directly from its essential features. Both Feuerstein and I have suggested reasons why the model might have been less than totally successful. Although our emphases have been different, there is much overlap in our views, and they are largely complementary.

Feuerstein's Assessment of Psychometric Models in Prediction, Diagnosis, and Training

Feuerstein (1979) devotes the first chapter of his *Dynamic Asessment* to the liberation of human potential via what he calls "the growing anti-test movement." He levels a number of criticisms at tests and their users, but his most important criticisms can be summarized in four major points relating to different aspects of intelligence tests and testing (see Feuerstein, 1979, p. 56).

1. The Structure of the Tests.   Psychometric test instruments are not constructed in a way that provides the examiner and the examinee with tasks that can be used in a teaching process and that can enable the examiner to evaluate the effect of the teaching process on the capacity of the individual to deal with new situations.

2. The Examination Situation.   Interaction between examiner and examinee in the conventional psychometric testing situation is forced, unnatural, and not conducive to learning as well as performance (showing what has already been learned) on the part of the examinee. Communication is essentially one-way from the examinee to the examiner: The examiner does not act in ways that might develop the potential that is latent in the examinee at the time of testing.

3. The Orientation of the Tests.   Psychometric tests emphasize the products of performance rather than the processes that give rise to these products. But learning and other forms of intellectual performance are dynamic in nature, and so a static approach to assessment emphasizing products rather than processes cannot do justice to the assessment or modification of human intelligence.

4. Interpretation of Results.   In the psychometric approach, the emphasis is upon aggregates of performance data, so that peaks and valleys in performance are averaged over. But the peaks in performance should be used as an indication of the cognitive potential of the examinee, rather than as error of measurement.

Sternberg's Assessment of Psychometric Models in Prediction, Diagnosis, and Training

On balance, my assessment of the psychometric model is probably more favorable than Feuerstein's (Sternberg, 1980a), although earlier it was less favorable than it is now (Sternberg, 1977b).

If one's goal is prediction of future success in some educational program or work setting, then, at present, at least, the psychometric model offered by factors is a very useful one. We are now able to obtain highly reliable measurements of general intelligence *(g)*, and these measurements have been shown to be predictively valid at a moderate level in a number of different settings, especially when the measurement is supplemented with information of other kinds. We have not had great success in obtaining discriminant validity for various kinds of narrower abilities (see Jensen, 1980; McNemar, 1964), although we can obtain reasonably reliable measurement of major group factors, such as fluid and crystallized abilities.

If one's goal is diagnosis of individual strengths and weaknesses, then again, factor analysis is of some use, although I believe of less use than for prediction. Factors such as those representing the primary mental abilities are useful in pointing out broad areas of strength and weakness. They might show a person's relative strength in areas such as verbal comprehension or word fluency, or a relative weakness in areas such as spatial visualization and reasoning. Factors can thus suggest the broad abilities in which training will be needed.

If one's goal is training intelligent performance, then I believe factors to be of minimal usefulness; they do not specify just what it is that should be trained. For example, labels such as *verbal comprehension, reasoning,* and *number* do not say what it is about verbal comprehension, reasoning, and number that leads to either high or low levels of performance. The information conveyed by factors is not specific enough for training, and when information is obtained about specific factors, that is, those specific to single tests, it is useless, because, by definition, training based upon such factors will not generalize to other tests or tasks. A seeming exception to these generalizations might seem to be Guilford's (1967) theory, in which factors specify particular operations, products, and contents that seem to be susceptible to training. But Guilford's theory is useful for training only because of its information-processing as opposed to its factor-analytic orientation. In fact, the psychometric evidence for the validity of Guilford's theory is quite weak (see Horn, 1967; Horn & Knapp, 1973; Undheim & Horn, 1977), and I believe the theory will be remembered more favorably as a precursor to full-blown information-processing theories than as the tail-end of factorial theories.

My approach has in common with Feuerstein's the emphasis upon information processing in the understanding and training of intelligent thinking and behavior. In order for a theory to be a useful basis for training, I believe it must specify, at minimum (1) the component processes used in performance of the tasks to which it applies, (2) the strategies into which these component processes combine, (3) the internal representations upon which these components and strategies act, (4) the executive processes that control the selection of component processes of performance, strategies, and internal representations, and (5) how all these elements combine to interact with different global patterns of ability to produce various levels of success in performance. The psychometric approach to intelligence does not provide these kinds of information.

Comparison between Feuerstein's and Sternberg's Critiques

The two critiques share the belief that the psychometric approach overemphasizes products of intellectual performance at the expense of underlying processes. Feuerstein and I agree that intelligence is a dynamic entity, and a static model such as the factorial one can capture only a part of it. I give that part greater weight than Feuerstein appears to.

There are several salient differences in the two critiques. First, Feuerstein's emphasis is more motivational. He believes that much of the failure of the psychometric approach can be attributed to the inadequate, or even damaging, motivational state it often induces. I view this difference as one in emphasis only and believe it derives in part from the difference in subject populations used in his and my research programs. Feuerstein's work has been largely with retarded individuals, with whom he and I both believe that motivational factors are of considerable importance to reduced performance. (See also Zigler, 1971, for a forceful and original statement of this view.) However, neither he nor I, nor Zigler for that matter, view motivational factors as the primary ones in mental retardation. After all, both our intervention programs are primarily cognitive in nature, though we agree that the motivational set created in examinees by traditional psychometric modes of testing can result in depression of test performance.

Second, Feuerstein is much more optimistic about our ability to measure latent learning potential, or what Vygotsky (1978) referred to as the "zone of potential development." The basic idea underlying its measurement is that by comparing a child's unaided performance to a performance aided by the skillfully graded interventions of an examiner, it is possible to determine latent learning potential. I am unaware of any empirical evidence to support this view, intriguing though it may be. Moreover, the range of interventions that are possible, and the inevitability of differences in the particular interventions that will be most successful with different people, make it difficult to conceive of how measurement of the zone of potential development could be soundly standardized. The assessed zone may reflect no more than compatibility between the type of intervention a given examiner can offer and the type of intervention that works well for a given examinee. The educational literature is replete with illustrations of how different styles of teaching work differentially for individuals, and it is unlikely that one person can teach in all the styles required for optimizing learning in various subjects. The construct of a zone of potential development is nonetheless quite attractive although in need of construct validation.

Third, Feuerstein is more optimistic than I about the use of extreme values in data (outliers) as diagnostic information about potential strengths and weaknesses. Psychometricians tend to suspect outliers as likely to be due, at least in part, to chance fluctuations in data. Like the psychometricians, I emphasize the need to replicate extreme patterns before drawing conclusions from them.

Fourth, I, like most psychometricians, would be more inclined than would Feuerstein to distinguish between assessment and training operations. Although I am quite impressed with the data, and especially the clinical data, that Feuerstein (1979) has presented to support the construct validity of his Learning Potential Assessment Device (which I discuss later in more detail), the controls that would distinguish more objective from subjective methods of assessment were lacking. Almost certainly, both methods have a place, and I am reluctant to replace objective ones with subjective ones. I instead wish, like Feuerstein, to see his more subjective methods supplement the standard objective ones.

Finally, I have probably been more inclined than has Feuerstein to view the limited success of the psychometric approach as due to a failure to specify precisely a formal model of cognition and the effects this model should lead one to expect to find in behavior (Sternberg, 1980b). Although formal modeling may seem burdensome at times, it can be useful in making clear one's theoretical claims, empirical predictions, and means of testing those claims and predictions.

CONCEPTIONS OF THE NATURE OF INTELLIGENCE

Feuerstein's (1980) instrumental enrichment program and my componential training program both derive from the investigators' theories of the nature of intelligence. Feuerstein does not explicitly present a theory of intelligence in his work, but most of the ingredients for such a theory appear in his books (Feuerstein, 1979, 1980). I have presented what I refer to as a componential subtheory of intelligence (Sternberg, 1980b; see also Sternberg, 1977b, 1979), which we have attempted to translate into a program for intervention as well as experimentation. Before describing each of these conceptions of intelligence, a few words about their structure might be helpful.

Feuerstein (1980) has presented a list of what he refers to as potentially deficient cognitive functions. These "deficient functions relate to and help identify the *prerequisites* of thinking. In this sense, they refer to deficiencies in those functions that underlie internalized, representational, operational thought" (p. 71). The deficient functions are of four kinds: impairments in cognition at the input phase, impairments in cognition at the elaborational phase, impairments in cognition at the output phase, and affective-motivational factors. Feuerstein makes several important points about his list of deficient functions. First, information regarding the identities and natures of the deficient functions stem from a large variety of stiuations in the lives of culturally deprived children and was gathered by means of a dynamic clinical assessment using Feuerstein's Learning Potential Assessment Device (LPAD) (see Feuerstein, 1979). Second, Feuerstein makes no claim that his list of deficient functions is either definitive or exhaustive. He acknowledges that overlap exists among the functions in his list. Third, not all these deficiencies exist in all retarded individuals. To the contrary, such individuals are distinguished among themselves by which deficiencies are present, and the extent to which the present deficiencies manifest themselves. Fourth, a deficiency is not the same as a total lack. A given deficiency might appear, in Flavell's (1970) terms, as the result of a production rather than a mediational deficit, whereby the function is available but not utilized. Finally, the attempt to distinguish the deficient functions on the basis of three phases of cognition—input, elaboration, and output—is admittedly somewhat artificial, because these phases cannot be viewed in isolation from each other. Nevertheless, Feuerstein's list is heuristically useful and provides a basis for producing the desired changes needed in behaviors.

I have presented a theory of intelligence that distinguishes among several different kinds of information-processing components, that speculates on the nature of interactions among them, that can be used both in the qualitative and quantitative analysis of information-processing behavior, and that seems to account for a fairly large number of findings (some of them more well-established than others) in the literature on intelligence. Like Feuerstein, I have emphasized the incompleteness of the theory, and the speculative nature of many of its aspects (Sternberg, 1980b).

With these introductory remarks completed, I turn to a description of the two conceptions of intelligence.

Feuerstein's Conception of the Nature of Intelligence[1]

The center of Feuerstein's (1980) theory is his listing of deficient functions. Two other parts must be considered as well—what he refers to as a *cognitive map* and his theory of intellectual development.

---

[1]The description of Feuerstein's (1980) theory is presented in Chapters 2–5 of his Instrumental Enrichment book, from which the following account is paraphrased. I have followed Feuerstein's language as closely as possible in order to convey as accurately as possible the precise sense of his remarks.

Potentially Deficient Cognitive Functions.   According to Feuerstein (1980), each of the four basic kinds of deficiencies in cognitive functions comprises a number of specific deficits. The first group of deficiencies includes impaired cognitive functions that affect the input phase of information processing. These impairments all concern the quality and quantity of data gathered by the individual as he or she begins to solve, or even to appreciate, the nature of a given problem. Some possible impairments include: blurred and sweeping perception; unplanned, impulsive, and unsystematic exploratory behavior; lack of, or impaired, receptive verbal tools and concepts that affect discrimination; lack of, or impaired, spatial orientation, including the lack of stable systems of reference that impair the organization of space; lack of, or impaired, temporal orientation; lack of or impaired, conservation of constancies (i.e., in size, shape, quantity, orientation) across variations in certain dimensions of the perceived object; lack of, or deficient need for, precision and accuracy in data gathering; and finally, lack of, or impaired, capacity for considering two sources of information at once, reflected in dealing with data in a piecemeal fashion rather than as a unit of organized facts. (For the reader who would like more detail, refer to Feuerstein's chapter in Volume 1 and his 1980 book.)

Feuerstein's second group of deficiencies in cognitive functions includes those affecting the elaboration phase of information processing. These curtail the individual's efficient gathering and use of the data available to him or her. In addition to impairments in data gathering and use, which may or may not have occurred at the input phase, there are deficiencies that obstruct the proper elaboration of those cues that do exist. Some possible impairments include: inadequacy in experiencing an actual problem and subsequently defining it; inability to select relevant, as opposed to irrelevant, cues in defining a problem; lack of spontaneous comparative behavior, or its limitations to a restricted field of needs; narrowness of the mental field; lack of, or impaired, need for summative behavior; difficulties in projecting virtual relationships; lack of a disposition to seek logical evidence as an interactional modality with one's objectal and social environments; lack of, or limited, interiorization of one's behavior; lack of, or restricted, inferential-hypothetical thinking; lack of, or impaired, strategies for hypothesis testing; lack of, or impaired, planning behavior; nonelaboration of certain cognitive categories, because the necessary labels are either not part of the individual's verbal inventory on the receptive level or are not mobilized at the expressive level; and finally, episodic grasp of reality.

The third group, impaired cognitive functions affecting the output phase of information-processing behavior, includes factors that lead to an adequate communication of the outcome of elaborative processes. Some possible impairments include: egocentric communicational modalities; blocking; trial-and-error responses; lack of, or impaired, verbal tools for communicating adequately elaborated responses; deficiency of visual transport; lack of, or impaired, need for precision and accuracy in communicating one's response; and finally, impulsive acting-out behavior, affecting the nature of the communication process.

The fourth and last group of deficiencies in cognitive functions that Feuerstein postulates includes affective-motivational factors. Feuerstein does not itemize these factors, as he does the others, but simply notes that they can combine negatively to influence the attitudes of the retarded. These attitudes may affect the general involvement of the individual with cognitive tasks, including academic studies, tests, and situations occurring in real life.

In addition to the potentially deficient cognitive functions, Feuerstein's conceptualization of intelligent behavior in task performance includes what he refers to as a "cognitive map," which I consider next.

The Cognitive Map.   Feuerstein's cognitive map involves seven parameters by which a mental act can be analyzed, categorized, and ordered. These parameters include the following:

1. *Content:*   Each mental act can be described according to subject matter and can be analyzed in terms of the content on which it is operating.

2. *Operations:*   An operation may be understood as an internalized, organized, coordinated set of actions in terms of which we elaborate upon information derived from external and internal sources.

3. *Modality:*   Modality refers to the fact that a mental act may be expressed in a variety of languages, including figurative, pictorial, numerical, symbolic, verbal, or a combination of these or others.

4. *Phase:*   There are three phases of cognition: input, elaboration, and output. These phases are interconnected and the role of each phase can only be considered in relation to the others.

5. *Level of complexity:*   Level of complexity may be understood as the quantity and quality of units of information necessary to produce a given mental act.

6. *Level of abstraction:*   Level of abstraction refers to the distance between the given mental act and the object or event on which it operates.

7. *Level of efficiency:*   Level of efficiency refers to the rapidity with which a problem can be solved for a specified level of precision. As a criterion of efficiency, one may use the "rapidity-precision complex" or the amount of effort objectively and subjectively exerted by the individual in his or her production of the particular act.

Feuerstein gives as an example of the use of a cognitive map the analysis of the problem

$$\text{given } A > B, B > C, C > D,$$

then A > D, B > D,

where the conclusions in the second line must be inferred via transitive inference. The content of this particular version of the problem is letters, although the problem could be presented with other kinds of content as well. The operations are those of transitive inference. The modality is symbolic, because no verbal, numerical, or figurative modes are used. Input is of the symbols and their relations; elaboration is of the transitive relations between nonadjacent pairs; output is of the two particular transitive relations linking A to D and B to D. The level of complexity is determined by the number of relations and their relative novelty. This particular problem has a relatively high level of abstraction, because it involves the generation of new information derived from the relationships obtaining between the objects or events rather than from the objects themselves. Level of efficiency will be reflected in the manner, rhythm, pace, precision, and degree of ease with which the problem is solved.

Theory of Intellectual Development.   Feuerstein's (1980) theory is largely based upon the concept of *mediated learning experience* (MLE). According to Feuerstein, the development of cognitive structure in an organism can be viewed as a product of two kinds of interaction between the organism and its environment: direct exposure to stimuli and mediated learning.

The first and most common kind is direct exposure to sources of stimulation impinging on an organism from the very earliest stage of its development. This exposure produces changes in the organism that affect its behavioral repertoire and its cognitive orientation; these changes in turn affect its interaction with the environment, even when the environment remains constant and stable. Direct exposure to stimuli continues throughout the organism's life-span.

The second kind, which is by far less common and is characteristic only of humans, is mediated learning experience, or MLE. This concept refers to the way in which stimuli emitted by the environment are transformed by a "mediating" agent, usually a parent, sibling, or other caregiver. This mediating agent, guided by his or her intentions, culture, and emotional investments, selects and organizes the world of stimuli for the child. The mediator selects stimuli that are most appropriate and then frames, filters, and schedules them; he or she acknowledges the appearance or disappearance of certain stimuli and ignores others. Through this process of mediation, the cognitive structure of the child is affected. The child acquires behavior patterns and learning sets, which in turn become important to the child's capacity to respond well to direct exposure to stimuli.

The relationship between MLE and direct exposure to stimuli can be set forth as follows: The more and the earlier an organism is subject to MLE, the greater will be his or her capacity to use efficiently and be affected by direct exposure to sources of stimuli. MLE, therefore, can be considered as the ingredient that determines differential cognitive development in otherwise similarly endowed individuals, even when they live under similar conditions of stimulation. Lack of MLE is a prime cause of cognitive deficits associated with mental retardation, and Feuerstein's training program consists in large part of the attempt to provide MLE to the retarded child.

Summary.   To summarize, Feuerstein's conception of the nature of intelligence has three basic parts: a list of potentially deficient cognitive functions organized around phases of input, elaboration, and output; a cognitive map that can be used to analyze tasks in seven dimensions; and a theory of development that stresses the role of mediated learning experience in the development of intelligence. These three parts of the theory motivate the training program to be described later.

Sternberg's Conception of the Nature of Intelligence[2]

My own theory of the nature of intelligence (Sternberg, 1980b), like Feuerstein's, can be understood as consisting of three major parts. The first is a listing of kinds of component information processes and specific instantiations of each. This list can be viewed as roughly analogous to Feuerstein's listing of deficient cognitive functions. The second part is a description of how these kinds of processes interrelate. The closest analogue in Feuerstein's theory is a diagram in Feuerstein (1980) showing bidirectional arrows interrelating each of the three phases of cognition—input, elaboration, and output—as well as the affective-motivational variables that affect them (see p. 75). The third part is a theory of intellectual development, which is roughly analogous to Feuerstein's, although it deals with phenomena of development that are almost nonoverlapping with those dealt with by Feuerstein's theory.

Components of Intelligence.   The basic construct in my own theory is the component. A component is an elementary information process that operates upon internal representations of objects or symbols. What is judged *elementary* is determined by theoretical context. *Elementary* processes in one theory, at one level of analysis, might be called "complex" in another theory, at another level of analysis. A component may translate a sensory input into a conceptual representation, transform one conceptual representation into another, or translate a conceptual representation into a motor output (Sternberg, 1977b; see also Newell & Simon, 1972). The basic idea is that components represent latent abilities of some kind that give rise to individual differences in measured intelligence and in real-world performance, and to individual differences in factor scores as well.

---

[2]This account of my theory is based on that in Sternberg (1980a).

Components can be classified on the basis of their functions into five different kinds: performance components, acquisition components, retention components, transfer components, and metacomponents, or higher level control processes. The functions of these kinds of components are illustrated in the context of their possible application to the solution of analogy problems of the sort found on many tests of intelligence. In recent years, I and several other researchers have given a great deal of attention to the anlaysis of the information processing required in these tasks.

Metacomponents are higher order control processes that are used for executive planning and decision making in problem solving. Metacomponents are used (1) to decide just what the problem is that needs to be solved (in an analogy problem, for example, one needs to decide just what kind of answer the problem requires— multiple-choice, fill-in, or whatever); (2) to select lower order components to effect solution of the problem (e.g., select the inductive operations that are needed to solve an analogy); (3) to select a strategy for combining lower order components (e.g., decide upon an order in which the inductive or other operations should be applied); (4) to select one or more representations or organizations of information upon which the lower order components and strategies can act (e.g., decide whether to represent information contained in the terms of the analogy using an attribute-value list, a multidimensional space, or whatever); (5) to decide upon a rate of problem solving that will permit the desired level of accuracy or solution quality (e.g., decide how much time can be allotted to a given analogy, given the constraints of other analogies or other kinds of tasks that may need to be completed in a given amount of time); and (6) to monitor progress toward a solution (e.g., monitor how well one is progressing toward finding the best of several possible analogy completions, possibly revising some or all earlier decisions if these decisions seem not to lead toward a solution).

Performance components are processes used in the execution of strategies for task performance. Performance components may be viewed as executing the plans and implementing the decisions laid down by the metacomponents. I have argued elsewhere that performance components in a variety of tasks tend to organize themselves into four stages of strategy execution (Sternberg, 1979, 1981). One or more components are usually needed to (1) encode the elements of a problem, such as the given terms of an analogy problem; (2) combine these elements in the execution of a working strategy, for instance, the strategy that is used for arriving at an ideal answer in a multiple-choice analogy problem; (3) compare the solution obtained to available answer options, for instance, the ideal answer to the given answer options; and (4) respond.

Acquisition components are processes involved in learning new information, retention components are processes involved in retrieving information that has been previously acquired, and transfer components are processes involved in carrying over retained information from one situational context to another. We isolate these components by trying to identify the variables that affect acquisition, retention, and transfer of information presented in real-world contexts. We have done this for vocabulary learning by presenting subjects with extremely low-frequency words embedded in natural contexts (such as articles from newspapers, passages from novels, and sections from textbooks), and asking subjects to define the words. The quality of definitions is then predicted on the basis of structural aspects of the reading passages. We have suggested that the variables that affect acquisition, retention, and transfer include (1) amount of experience with a given type of problem (as in analogies) or information (as in the vocabulary-from-context task); (2) variability of the contexts in which the problem or information has been encountered; (3) importance of the problem or information to the task context; (4) recency of occurrence of a given type of problem or piece of information; (5) helpfulness of context to understanding the problem or information; and (6) helpfulness of stored information to understanding the problem or new piece of information. Particular textual cues used to figure out meanings of unknown words include spatial, temporal, functional, descriptive, value, causal, class membership, and equivalence cues.

Interrelations Among Kinds of Components.   The various kinds of components are theorized to be interrelated in four different ways: First, one kind of component can directly activate another; second, one kind can indirectly activate another; third, one kind can provide direct feedback to another; and fourth, one kind can provide indirect feedback to another. Direct activation or feedback refers to the immediate passage of control or information from one kind of component to another kind. Indirect activation or feedback refers to the mediate passage of control or information from one kind of component to another via a third.

In the proposed system of interrelations, only metacomponents can directly activate and receive feedback from each other kind of component. Thus, control in the system passes directly from the metacomponents, and all information from the system passes directly to the metacomponents. The other kinds of components can activate each other only indirectly and receive information from each other only indirectly; in each case, mediation must be supplied by the metacomponents. For example, acquisition of information affects retention of information and various kinds of transformations (performances) upon that information, but only via the link of the three kinds of components to the metacomponents. Feedback from the acquisition components can be passed to any other kind of component, but only through the filter of the metacomponents.

The metacomponents are able to process only a limited amount of information at a given time. In a difficult task, the amount of information being fed back to the metacomponents may exceed their capacity to act upon this information. In this case, valuable information that cannot be processed will simply be lost. The total information-handling capacity of the metacomponents will thus be an important limiting aspect of the system.

Theory of Intellectual Development.   The system of interrelations just described contains a dynamic mechanism for cognitive growth.

First, the components of acquisition, retention, and transfer provide the mechanisms for a steadily developing knowledge base. Increments in the knowledge base, in turn, allow for more sophisticated forms of acquisition, retention, and transfer, and possibly for greater ease in execution of performance components. For example, some transfer components may act by relating new knowledge to old knowledge. As the base of old knowledge becomes deeper and broader, the possibilities for relating new knowledge to old knowledge, and thus for incorporating that new knowledge into the existing knowledge base, increase. There is thus the possibility of an unending feedback loop; the components lead to an increased knowledge base, which leads to more effective use of the components, which leads to further increases in the knowledge base, and so on.

Second, the self-monitoring metacomponents can, in effect, learn from their own mistakes. Early on, allocation of metacomponential resources to varying tasks or kinds of components may be less than optimal, with resulting loss of valuable feedback information. Self-monitoring should eventually result in improved allocations of metacomponential resources, in particular, to the self-monitoring of the metacomponents. Thus, self-monitoring by the metacomponents results in improved allocation of metacomponential resources to the self-monitoring, and so on. Here, too, exists the possibility of an unending feedback loop, one that is internal to the metacomponents themselves.

Finally, indirect feedback from kinds of components other than metacomponents to each other and direct feedback to the metacomponents should result in improved effectiveness of performance. Acquisition components, for example, can provide valuable information to performance components (via the metacomponents) concerning how to perform a task, and the performance components, in turn, can provide feedback to the acquisition components (via the metacomponents) concerning what else needs to be learned in order to perform the task optimally. Thus, other kinds of components, too, can generate unending feedback loops in which performance improves as a result of interactions between the kinds of components, or between multiple components of the same kind.

All the different kinds of components and instantiations of these kinds of components are potential sources of intellectual development. Components can become available or more accessible with increasing age, or they can become easier to execute as one grows older. There can be no doubt, however, that the major variable in the development of the intellect is the metacomponential one. All feedback is filtered through these metacomponential elements, and if they do not perform their function well, it will not matter very much what the other kinds of components can do. It is for this reason that the metacomponents are viewed as truly central in understanding the nature of human intelligence.

Summary.   To summarize, by my theory, intelligence is understood in terms of the operations of five kinds of components—metacomponents, performance components, acquisition components, retention components, and transfer components. Metacomponents are unique in being able directly to activate the other kinds of components as well as each other and also receive feedback directly from the other kinds of components and each other. The other kinds of components activate and receive feedback from each other via the mediation of the metacomponents. This dynamic system of interaction provides the basis for intellectual development throughout the life-span.

Comparison Between Feuerstein's and Sternberg's Theories

The two conceptions of intelligence have in common their information-processing orientations to understanding intelligence: Each can serve as a basis for task analysis over a broad range of tasks requiring intelligent performance. There are also a number of striking differences between the theories.

First, although both theories comprise components of various sorts, these components differ in kind. Feuerstein's represent a broad range of functions: cognitive styles (e.g., blurred and sweeping perception), knowledge base (e.g., lack of, or impaired, receptive verbal tools and concepts that affect discrimination), motivations (e.g., lack of, or deficient need for, precision and accuracy in data gathering), processes or metaprocesses (e.g., inability to select relevant, as opposed to irrelevant, cues in defining a problem), and processing capacity or space (e.g., narrowness of the mental field), among others. There is no attempt to classify these functions in terms of categories or to say just how such categories might fit together. My own components are all processes of various kinds, and an attempt is made to classify the processes according to the functions they serve. Thus, processes such as selection of a strategy or representation are referred to as metacomponents, processes such as encoding of stimuli or inference of a relation between two stimuli are referred to as performance components, and so on. In at least one sense, then, I perceive my own taxonomy as tighter than Feuerstein's.

Second, Feuerstein's theory is broader in scope, in large part because of the breadth that his functions encompass. Like Feuerstein, I believe in the importance of motivations, cognitive styles, dispositions, and the like in intellectual functioning. To speak of cognitive processing divorced from the motivations that drive the processing is willfully to limit one's possible ability to account for the outcomes of that processing. My own theoretical style is such that I would probably wait until I could impose an organization upon the motivational system that is comparable to that which I have imposed upon the cognitive system before incorporating it into my theory. But I am most sympathetic to Feuerstein's recognition of the need to introduce noncognitive elements and believe he has done so in an effective, if not tightly organized, way.

Third, the theories probably differ in their empirical disconfirmability. It is difficult for me to see how one could show that the functions that constitute

Feuerstein's list of potential deficiencies are wrong in any sense. One could show easily that they are highly overlapping, that important ones are probably missing, and that some are probably of less than major importance. But lists such as this one are probably not easily disconfirmable, and it would be difficult to say how one could go about choosing between alternative lists. The structure of the componential theory, too, is probably not disconfirmable. How could one decide, for example, whether a distinction is warranted between acquisition and transfer components, or between metacomponents and performance components? Such a classification, like Feuerstein's, is a matter of theoretical and practical convenience. But the particular instantiations of each kind of component can be and have been empirically tested. We have actually tested, for example, theories regarding performance components (Sternberg, 1977a, b; Sternberg & Nigro, 1980; Sternberg & Rifkin, 1979) and metacomponents (see Sternberg, 1980b) in analogical reasoning and other tasks. Quantification of information-processing models has enabled us to say, for example, that subjects do in fact do X but do not in fact do Y in the solution of various kinds of intellectual tasks. It is possible, of course, indirectly to test one's theory of intelligence by seeing whether it is trainable, using the results of a training program as indirect potential confirmation for one's theory. But training can succeed in the absence of a good theory or fail despite the presence of such a theory.

Fourth, the theories have rather different implications for training intellectual performance. My own theory would seem to imply the use of detailed process training, with emphasis upon transferability of the processes trained. For example, Sternberg and Gardner (1983) have shown that the processes used in analogical, serial, and classificational reasoning are very closely overlapping. Feuerstein's theory would imply a broader base for training, including training of affective and motivational elements. This difference reflects in part the data bases from which the theories were derived. Like Feuerstein, I believe that motivational and affective interventions are absolutely necessary if one is to obtain the results one desires in enhancing the performance of retarded individuals. Our own training efforts have been directed toward average and above-average subjects (and the theory derived from such subjects), and I believe that a greater emphasis upon cognitive processing with those groups will probably have higher payoff.

Fifth, the theories differ enormously in their descriptions of cognitive development. The two theories seem simply to address different issues. One could easily accept both accounts, which I in fact do, and find no conflict at all, because the ground covered by the theories is essentially nonoverlapping. I strongly applaud Feuerstein's emphasis upon mediated learning experience and, like him, believe it to be requisite to satisfactory intellectual development.

Finally, the theories differ in the extents to which they have been related to other theories. Such interrelations are important, I believe, if our goal is to understand psychological phenomena rather than psychologists. Often, different theories say the same or similar things in different language, and it is important to identify commonalities, because the generalizations that derive from a multiplicity of theories are the ones most likely to be powerful. Whereas I have gone to some lengths to point out relationships between my own theory and other psychometric and developmental ones (Sternberg, 1980a, b, 1982), I believe Feuerstein has been less explicit. For example, there are striking parallels between his theory and that of Vygotsky (1978); there are also resemblances to the theories of Piaget (1972), Zigler (1971), and Guilford (1967), among others. I think greater attention to these might help better clarify the unique contribution of Feuerstein's theory, as well as its partial confirmation of the work of others.

To summarize, there is a basic similarity in the information-processing orientation of the two theories. There are also some differences in the particular way in which this information-processing orientation is expressed. Because the theories differ in their styles and levels of analysis, there would be no point in trying to compare their relative validities. Rather, it would be a useful task to explore how the two theories might inform each other and be somehow combined into a more powerful unified theory. In particular, if it were possible to combine the greater breadth of Feuerstein's theory with the more explicit mechanisms in and means of testing the validity of my own theory, the product would almost certainly be better than either of its parts.

PROGRAMS FOR TRAINING INTELLECTUAL PERFORMANCE

Feuerstein's (1980) Instrumental Enrichment Program, as well as his Learning Potential Assessment Device (Feuerstein, 1979) have in common with our own componential training program their derivation from an information-processing theory of intellectual performance. In each case, the goal is to improve intellectual functioning by somehow training its underlying information-processing components. As we have seen, the components are rather different in the two theories, and as we see later, the approaches to and methods of training are rather different as well.

Feuerstein's Instrumental Enrichment Program and Learning Potential Assessment Device[3]

Although I concentrate in this section upon Feuerstein's Instrumental Enrichment Program (FIE), I mention the Learning Potential Assessment Device (LPAD) as well, because there are certain features of it I find particularly attractive and promising for future use.

---

[3]The descriptions of Feuerstein's FIE and LPAD are based upon Chapter 7 of Feuerstein (1980) and Chapter 3 of Feuerstein (1979), respectively. Paraphrase is used wherever possible to retain the original sense of the communication.

Goals of Instrumental Enrichment.   The major goal of FIE is to increase the capacity of the human organism to become modified through direct exposure to stimuli and experiences provided by encounters with life events and with formal and informal learning opportunities. In addition, there are six subgoals: (1) the correction of the deficient functions that characterize the cognitive structure of the deprived individual; (2) the acquisition of basic concepts, labels, vocabulary, operations, and relationships necessary for benefiting from FIE; (3) the production of intrinsic motivation through habit formation; (4) the production of reflective, insightful processes in the student as a result of his or her confrontation with both failure and success in the FIE tasks; (5) the creation of intrinsic task motivation; and (6) generating an attitude on the part of the retarded individuals whereby they perceive themselves as organisms able to generate information and function at a high level of competence.

Characteristics of FIE Materials.   The FIE material is structured as a series of units, or instruments, each of which emphasizes a particular cognitive function and its relationships to various cognitive deficiencies. Emphasis in analyzing FIE performance is on processes rather than products. A student's errors are viewed as a means to provide insights into how the student solves problems. Instrumental Enrichment does not attempt to teach either specific items of information or formal, operational abstract thinking by means of a well-defined, structured set of data. It is as content free as possible. The idea is to focus the individual's attention on his or her deficient functions, rather than on the content of one problem or another. However, instructors are encouraged to "bridge" between the abstract content and real-world situations.

Description of Materials.   The Instrumental Enrichment Program comprises the following tasks.

Organization of dots: The student is presented with an amorphous two-dimensional array of dots. The student's task is to identify and outline, within this array of dots, a set of such geometric figures as squares, triangles, diamonds, and stars.

Orientation in space: The student is shown two pictures, one at the left and one at the right of the page. The student is then presented with sentences containing blanks. The task is to fill in the blanks, thereby showing understanding of concepts such as *up, down, between, above, below,* and the like.

Comparisons: In one form of comparison exercise, the student is shown one picture at the left and two pictures at the right. The task is to indicate, for each picture, which of the attributes of direction, number, color, form, and size differs from its presentation in the other pictures.

Categorization: In one categorization task, the student is shown pictures of common objects and asked to name each one. After the student has done so, he or she is asked to list those objects that fit into each of a set of categories, such as means of transportation, clothing and footwear, objects that give light, tools, and furniture.

Analytic perception: In one such task, the student might see, at the top of the page, a large rectangle with a number of smaller rectangles embedded in it and the borders of the smaller rectangles clearly marked. The student might then be shown four alternative pictures, each containing a set of rectangles (or other figures) arranged in fashions differing from those in the large rectangle. The student's task is to indicate which figure contains smaller rectangles of the same sizes and shapes as those constituting the large rectangle in the first picture.

Family relations: In a family relations task, the student is asked questions such as "What are there more of in the world: sons or fathers? Why?"

Temporal relations: Problems of this kind require that various temporal inferences be made. For example, the student is told that Bill and John rode home from school on their bikes. They traveled at the same speed, yet Bill got home about half an hour later than John (without any problems or accidents en route). Explain.

Numerical progressions: These problems include geometric series continuations as well as numerical ones.

Instructions: These tasks require a student to understand and follow instructions.

Illustrations: In a typical exercise, the student is shown a series of four pictures illustrating an absurdity. The student must say why the sequence is absurd.

Representational stencil design: In these tasks, the student must construct, without aid of motor manipulation, a design that is identical to that in a colored standard.

Transitive relations: In transitive relations, the student must recognize relations between items that are nonadjacent in an underlying mental array, for example, if A is greater than B and B greater than C, the relation between A and C.

Syllogisms: Students are preented with various forms of verbal and pictorial syllogisms to solve.

These brief descriptions cannot do justice to the scope of each kind of task, or to how Feuerstein carefully relates the tasks to his subgoals for FIE. Nevertheless, they do convey, I hope, some sense of the training Feuerstein provides in his FIE program.

The Learning Potential Assessment Device. This assessment device also reveals various aspects of Feuerstein's theory. It contains problems designed to appraise the student's learning and reasoning abilities, in particular, (1) the capacity to grasp the principle underlying an initial problem and to solve that problem, (2) the amount and nature of instruction required to teach the examinee the given principle, (3) the extent to which the newly acquired principle is successfully applied in solving problems that increasingly vary from the initial task, (4) the examinee's preferences for one or more of the various modalities of presentation for a given problem, and (5) the differential effects of various training strategies offered to the examinee in the remediation of his functioning (Feuerstein, 1979). In using this device, the examiner establishes with the examinee a warm and trusting teacher/learner relationship. The examiner gives the examinee graded assistance with the problems and seeks to make the testing experience truly a learning experience as well. The LPAD can be administered either individually or in a group situation, although obviously the full power of the device requires individual administration. The problems used on the device are both verbal and figural and assess both of what I have referred to earlier as performance-componential and metacomponential functioning. The device not only differs from conventional tests in the humane atmosphere in which it is administered, but in its potential for eliciting student abilities that would be hidden in conventional tests and testng situations.

Sternberg's Componential Training Program

The componential program, which has been only partially implemented, seeks to train individuals in three basic kinds of skills—metacomponential skills, performance-componential skills, and skills involving components of knowledge acquisition, retention, and transfer (Sternberg, in press). The first planned full-scale implementation of the program was in the fall of 1984 at the Metropolitan University, Caracas, Venezuela. The description below is not of the full program, but only part of it.

Metacomponents. The training on metacomponents seeks to develop skills in seven areas (Sternberg, 1980b): (1) recognizing and defining problems, (2) selecting lower order components for solution of problems, (3) selecting a strategy for combining components, (4) selecting a representation upon which components and strategy act, (5) allocating processing resources, (6) monitoring progress in solution of problems, and (7) utilizing feedback from problem solving. Students are given real-world, practical examples of the use of each of these metacomponents to motivate the training, tips on how better to utilize each metacomponent, and exercises in implementing each type.

Consider, as an example, the first metacomponent—recognizing and defining problems. The training uses each of the steps indicated previously. The module opens with the example of a professor who misses a plane because he does not make it to a limousine terminal on time. As it turns out, the professor easily could have made the plane had he perceived the problem as one of making the plane rather than the limousine. Once he missed the limousine, he gave up hope, although he still could have made the plane by using alternative transportation. The second example given is of people who have trouble meeting expenses. Such people often see their problem as one of earning more money rather than cutting expenses. Yet, the latter perspective would be a more sure and faster way than the former to relieve the difficulty. The third example deals with the aftermath of the Watergate break-in. Because the President and his staff viewed the problem as one of covering up the break-in rather than of finding a way of presenting the facts in an honest but minimally damaging way, a chain of events was set off that ultimately led to Richard Nixon's resignation as President. The final real-world example is of U.S. interventions in other countries; this problem is often seen as one of containing Communism rather than of obtaining a satisfactory government, which would make a Communist, or other form of government seen as unacceptable, seem unnecessary to the people of the country.

Following the real-world example are training examples taken from psychological research. In the case of the metacomponent of recognizing and defining the nature of a problem, a research example is given from my own research on children's solution of analogies (Sternberg & Rifkin, 1979). Very young children often misinterpret analogies. For example, some young children in a Jewish parochial school tried to solve the problems reading from right to left, with the result that the problems made no sense. In other instances, children perceive verbal problems as ones of word association rather than reasoning (Sternberg & Nigro, 1980).

After the research examples, students are given some tips on improving their metacomponential skills. In the case of this particular metacomponent, the students are encouraged to (1) reread or reconsider the question being asked, (2) redefine their goals, as needed, and (3) ask themselves whether their goal is really the one they wish to reach.

Finally, the students receive exercises helping them stretch their ability to execute the metacomponent. For defining the nature of the problem, the first exercise is on the "nine-dot" problem. This problem, which requires people to connect all the nine dots arranged in a square without raising their pencils from their papers, requires that they go outside the borders of the nine dots in order to achieve a solution. Usually, they assume that they should not go outside this border, even though no such rule is stated in the problem. In other words, solution of the problem requires redefinition through questioning a common but incorrect assumption.

A second problem is the monk problem. If a monk starts up a mountain on one day and down at the same time on the next day, is there a point on the mountain path that the monk crosses at exactly the same time on the successive days? Realization that there must be such a point is easier to attain if one redefines the problem as though there were two monks, one going up and one going down the mountain simultaneously. In that case, the two monks would have to pass each other at a certain hour. This version of the problem is isomorphic to the original version and thus clarifies that there is a specific time on the successive days when the monk must cross in the same place.

Instruction for the other metacomponents is similar. Moreover, throughout the entire program, there are integrative reviews of the metacomponents, which reinforce the instruction given in the initial unit.

Performance Components.   Instruction on performance components involves those components involved in inductive and deductive reasoning. The inductive components include (1) encoding—recognition of stimuli and retrieval of relevant attributes from long-term memory; (2) inference—recognition of first-order relations between pairs of terms in the item stem; (3) mapping—recognition of second-order relations between relations in the item stem; (4) application—carrying over an inferred relation from the domain of the item and using it in the range of the item; (5) comparison—assessing how multiple answer options differ from each other; and (6) justification—comparing the preferred option to the ideal option and selecting it as best, although nonideal.

Training of the performance components, like that of the metacomponents, is at several levels. Consider, for example, the performance component of inference.

Initial training for inference focuses on relations that one might have to infer in various kinds of reasoning problems. For verbal reasoning, these include relations of (1) similarity, (2) contrast, (3) predication, (4) subordination, (5) coordination, (6) superordination, (7) completion, (8) part–whole, (9) whole–part, (10) equality, (11) word relations, and (12) nonsemantic relations (Sternberg, 1978). For figural reasoning, they include relations of (1) size change, (2) shape change, (3) shading change, (4) border change, (5) addition of parts, (6) deletion of parts, (7) transformation of parts, (8) permutation of parts, (9) rotation, reflection, and translation of parts, and (10) gestalt completion. Students receive a large number of verbal and figural analogies, series completions, classifications, and matrix problems that involve these particular inferential relations. Early items are worked out for the students, and later ones are left for them to do on their own.

A subsequent section provides training in inferential fallacies, namely: (1) representativeness—belief that the cause of some event must resemble that event; (2) irrelevant conclusions—drawing of a conclusion that is irrelevant to the line of reasoning; (3) division—assumption that what one assumes of the whole is necessarily true of each of its parts; (4) labeling—unjustifiable use of labels for people or objects; (5) hasty generalization—rapid generalization from unusual or extreme cases; (6) chance viewed as skill based—belief that chance events can be controlled; (7) personalization—viewing oneself as primarily responsible for an event outside one's control; (8) appeal to authority—claiming that support by an authority warrants a given view; (9) magnification/minimization—magnification of the importance of one's negative characteristics, or minimization of the importance of one's positive characteristics; (10) composition—reasoning that what is true of the parts must be true of the whole; (11) should statements—use of moral imperatives as the sole reason for one's behavior; (12) false cause—inferring a causal relation solely from temporal proximity; (13) invalid disjunction—believing that there are only two possible solutions to a problem that has many; (14) availability—accepting the first explanation that comes to mind; (15) argumentum ad populum—belief that anything agreed upon is right; (16) arguments from ignorance—arguing for something merely because it has not been proven to be false; (17) mental filter—picking out a minor aspect of a situation and focusing on it to the exclusion of others; (18) emotional reasoning—using one's emotions to validate a claim; and (19) argumentum ad hominem—attacking a person's character, lifestyle, etc., rather than the content of the person's arguments. The nature of these inferential fallacies may become more clear through a few examples.

> Betty had a date to go to dinner with an actor, after watching a performance of the play in which he had the lead role. However, Betty sent a note back to the actor after the play, saying, "You were so believable in your acting of that murder scene that I don't feel safe going out with you."

Betty assumes that the actor's behavior in the play was representative of his behavior, although she has no logical basis for doing so.

> After she finished college, Cleo went for her first interview for a job. The interviewer told her that her academic work looked quite good, but that her resume showed a lack of experience in the professional field, and that, therefore his company couldn't hire her. Cleo went home thinking, "If that company won't hire me without my having experience, no company will."

Cleo is rushing to a generalization because of a single experience. Such generalizations are typical of job seekers who have an initial unsuccessful interview. Often, hasty generalizations discourage these people, who then stop looking for a job prematurely.

> Nancy put quarters into a slot machine until she had spent a 10-dollar roll. She was considering whether or not to buy more quarters from the casino office. She thought to herself, "I am sure that if I can get enough practice with this darn machine, I'll eventually be able to start getting some money out of it."

In this instance, Nancy is assuming that a matter of luck can be altered through the development of a skill.

Students are given multiple examples of commissions of these fallacies and are then asked to spot them on their own.

Acquisition, Retention, and Transfer Components.   In this part of the training, students receive instruction in using context to infer the meanings of unknown words. The training consists of three parts:

1. Textual cues: Students receive instruction in locating cues to infer word meanings from textual context. The instruction centers on cues regarding the unknown word's duration or frequency, location, worth or desirability, properties, possible purposes, potential uses, as well as its possible causes or enabling conditions, and the groups or categories to which it belongs, and any synonyms or antonyms provided by the text.
2. Mediating variables: These variables, mentioned earlier in the chapter, include items such as discerning the location of cues, their helpfulness, importance, and so on.
3. Components: These include (1) selective encoding—deciding what information is relevant for decontextualization; (2) selective combination—combining relevant information in an integrated definition; and (3) selective comparison—relating new information about a word to that already stored in memory.

Students are presented with sentences and paragraphs containing unknown words and are shown how the textual cues, mediating variables, and components can be used to figure out meanings. For example, students might be given a sentence such as "At dawn, *sol* arose on the horizon and shone brightly." This sentence contains cues that could facilitate one's inferring that *sol* refers to the sun. "At dawn" provides a temporal cue, "arose" and "shone" provide functional cues. The student must decide which cues are relevant to decontextualization and also must find them. Some cues are more difficult to find than others. For example, cues that appear far from the unknown word in a passage, or that come after rather than before the word, are more difficult to use. (Alternative views of learning from context can be found in Ames, 1966; Collins & Smith, 1982; Cook, Heim, & Watts, 1963; Granger, 1977; Heim, 1970; Rankin & Overholzer, 1969; Werner, 1954; and Werner & Kaplan, 1950, 1952.)

To summarize, the training program provides instruction in (1) metacomponents, (2) performance components, and (3) acquisition, retention, and transfer components of intelligence. Each section of the training contains (1) theoretical material that relates the instruction to the overall theory of intelligence, (2) instruction in the particular processes of interest, (3) real-world examples of the use of the particular processes, (4) research examples of the use of the processes, (5) worked-out examples using the processes, and (6) multiple exercises requiring the students to use the processes on their own.

Comparison between Feuerstein's and Sternberg's Training Programs

The training programs represented by the FIE and LPAD of Feuerstein have much in common with the training programs we have devised. Some of these commonalities I believe to be wholly positive; others have negative aspects.

On the positive side, first, both sets of programs are theoretically based. I have long believed that the failure of at least some of the compensatory education programs reviewed by Jensen (1969) lay in their lack of a theoretical basis, and hence lack of contact between training, on the one hand, and knowledge about students' cognitive and motivational structures, on the other. If the present programs fail, it is not for lack of attempt to attain such contact.

Second, both programs are based on theories with an information-processing orientation, the orientation I believe most likely to underwrite sound training of intellectual performance. A sensible way to improve performance is to intervene in the processes that, in combination, constitute the performance. An information-processing orientation allows, indeed, demands, such intervention.

Third, the creators of both sets of programs show concern with durability and generalizability of training and act upon this concern by building the appropriate assessments into their evaluations.

I emphasize, moreover, the need for the great bulk of schooling to be heavily content based, and the need to teach children to utilize concepts in semantically rich domains. Programs like Feuerstein's and our own only supplement a regular curriculum, including reading, writing, mathematics, science, social studies, arts, physical education, and the like. At no point should such programs replace any aspect of a standard school curriculum, although they might hold within them some suggestions as to how the standard school curriculum might better be conveyed to the students. On the one hand, I do not think schools have done enough to train children how to think, and I believe programs such as Feuerstein's and our own provide a kind of instruction that has been missing. On the other hand, our schooling procedures will be not improved if one kind of excess is replaced with another. I suspect Feuerstein would agree with this point of view.

Our training program and that of Feuerstein differ in a number of respects. These differences reflect our particular theories, as well as the pretheoretical perspectives we bring to bear on the training problem.

First, Feuerstein's Instrumental Enrichment is a much larger scale program. His program shows the many years that went into it; ours does not represent that magnitude of effort. Feuerstein's program is broader in its greater motivational emphasis.

Second, the evaluation procedures of the two programs differ in the kinds of information they can extract. Feuerstein's evaluation is potentially capable of indicating how well the program as a whole has worked but does not seem to be geared toward evaluating the success of individual aspects of the program. For example, if one wanted to know the extent to which the program succeeded in remedying each of the individual potentially deficient cognitive functions, it is not clear how one could find this out on the basis of the evaluations that have been conducted. Yet, such information would probably be of greatest importance if one's goal were to improve the program by increasing its effectiveness in remedying each of the individual deficiencies. The componential assessment procedures in our own evaluation enable us to determine the extent to which each of the components specified in the theory has been affected by the intervention. Thus, specific strengths and weaknesses of the training program can be objectively evaluated.

Third, the programs differ in their relationships to their underlying theories of intelligence. The mainstay of my own theory of intelligence is a set of information-processing components of various kinds. These components are directly trained in the program. The mainstay of Feuerstein's theory is a set of potentially deficient cognitive operations. As far as I can tell, these operations are indirectly trained in the FIE program, which seems to emphasize tasks rather than components of tasks. In this respect, the emphasis seems to differ from that in Feuerstein's LPAD program, which is similar to our own training program in its greater emphasis upon training components of task performance rather than more global aspects of performance on tasks. In sum, the emphasis in LPAD training seems to be more componential, whereas the emphasis in FIE training seems to be more global.

Finally, the programs differ in just what they train. Although, in general, Feuerstein's motivational emphasis is greater than ours, his emphasis in the cognitive domain is almost exclusively on fluid and visual abilities. We ignore visual abilities (spatial visualization, form perception, and the like) but include crystallized abilities such as learning meanings of words from context. Our inclusion of such abilities probably reflects our belief in the need for at least some semantically rich content. We are not convinced that a content-free approach is ultimately the way to go and, indeed, we would see future efforts introducing even more, rather than less, content.

To summarize, there are some striking similarities between Feuerstein's programs and our own, and some equally striking differences. Both programs are theoretically based, both are based on information-processing theories, both show some concern with durability and transfer, both use relatively impoverished content bases, and both lose some degree of power in group implementation. The programs differ in their breadth, in the relationship between training and evaluation, in the nature of their evaluation procedures, in the ways the training is tied to the underlying theory of intelligence, and in the skills the programs train. I believe Feuerstein's program has been an exceptionally valuable contribution to the theory and practice of training intellectual skills and can only hope that our own program makes at least a modest further contribution.

KEY DIRECTIONS FOR FUTURE WORK

Programs such as the two discussed will prove valuable in subsequent research and development on the training of intelligent performance. But I think also that there are critical elements missing from both programs, and from the motivating theories as well, that will have to be incorporated into future programs. First, I think we need to know much more about how elementary processes of the kind I have studied operate in conceptually and semantically rich domains. Work such as that of Chi, Glaser, and Rees (1982) and of Larkin, McDermott, Simon, and Simon (1980) on the solution of physics problems by experts and novices seems promising, but it is only a start and cannot yet supply a detailed analysis of component processes and their relationships across physics (or other kinds of) tasks. Second, I think we will have to follow Feuerstein's lead in putting a greater emphasis upon motivation and its interaction with cognitive processes, particularly if our goal is to train retarded performers. Past efforts have shown how difficult it is to strike a balance between students' affective and cognitive needs, but the effort to attain this balance must continue, and neither kind of need can be disregarded, if a program is to be truly successful. Third, much more effort must be put into careful and thorough evaluation of new and existing programs. The weakness of previous evaluations makes it difficult not only to know what level of success we have achieved, but what kinds of changes we need to make in order to make this kind of training more successful. Fourth, programs are needed that can be implemented by ordinary classroom teachers and that require minimal specialized training for these teachers. (Both Feuerstein's and our program require some specialized training.) It will not be possible to send in special trainers or to give classroom teachers lengthy training courses, if the programs of the future are to be widely implemented. Finally, we need to develop better theories of intelligence and of instruction, and to base our future efforts on these better theories. The road to improved technology is through basic research! Our basic research efforts must be supported if our technological efforts are ultimately to succeed.

In conclusion, I believe that current efforts to train intellectual performance, such as those of Feuerstein and my own research team, represent promising starts toward intellectual training that will become both routine and successful. Barring the advent of a still bleaker funding situation for basic and applied research, such efforts will continue to yield greater and greater rates of success.

ACKNOWLEDGMENTS

Preparation of this chapter was supported by Contract N0001478C0025 from the Office of Naval Research to Robert J. Sternberg. I am grateful to Janet Powell for suggestions and comments for improving the chapter.

REFERENCES

Ames, W. S. (1966). The development of a classification scheme of contextual aids. *Reading Research Quarterly, 2,* 57–82.

Atkinson, R. C., & Shiffrin, R. M. (1968). Human memory: A proposed system and its control processes. In K. W. Spence & J. T. Spence (Eds.), *The psychology of learning and motivation: Advances in research and theory* (Vol. 2). New York: Academic Press.

Catell, R. B. (1971). *Abilities: Their structure, growth, and action.* Boston: Houghton–Mifflin.

Chi, M. T. H., Glaser, R., & Rees, E. (1982). Expertise in problem solving. In R. J. Sternberg (Ed.), *Advances in the psychology of human intelligence* (Vol. 1). Hillsdale, NJ: Lawrence Erlbaum Associates.

Collins, A., & Smith, E. (1982). Teaching the processes of reading comprehension. In D. K. Detterman & R. J. Sternberg (Eds.), *How and how much can intelligence be increased?* Norwood, NJ: Ablex.

Cook, J. M., Heim, A. W., & Watts, K. P. (1963). The word-in-context: A new type of verbal reasoning test. *British Journal of Psychology, 54,* 227–237.

Feuerstein, R. (1979). *The dynamic assessment of retarded performers: The learning potential assessment device, theory, instruments, and techniques.* Baltimore: University Park Press.

Feuerstein, R. (1980). *Instrumental enrichment: An intervention program for cognitive modifiability.* Baltimore: University Park Press.

Flavell, J. H. (1970). Developmental studies of mediated memory. In H. W. Reese & L. P. Lipsitt (Eds.), *Advances in child development and behavior* (Vol. 5). New York: Academic Press.

Granger, R. H. (1977). FOUL-UP: A program that figures out meanings of words from context. *Proceedings of the Fifth International Joint Conference on Artificial Intelligence.* Cambridge, MA.

Guilford, J. P. (1967). *The nature of human intelligence.* New York: McGraw–Hill.

Heim, A. (1970). *Intelligence and personality: Their assessment and relationship.* Middlesex, England: Penguin.

Horn, J. L. (1967). On subjectivity in factor analysis. *Educational and Psychological Measurement, 27,* 811–820.

Horn, J. L. (1968). Organization of abilities and the development of intelligence. *Psychological Review, 75,* 242–259.

Horn, J. L., & Knapp, J. R. (1973). On the subjective character of the empirical base of Guilford's structure-of-intellect model. *Psychological Bulletin, 80,* 33–43.

Jensen, A. R. (1969). How much can we boost IQ and scholastic achievement? In *Environment, heredity, and intelligence.* Cambridge, MA: Harvard University Press.

Jensen, A. R. (1980). *Bias in mental testing.* New York: Free Press.

Larkin, J., McDermott, J., Simon, D. P., & Simon, H. A. (1980). Expert and novice performance in solving physics problems. *Science, 208,* 1335–1342.

McNemar, Q. (1964). Lost: Our intelligence? Why? *American Psychologist, 19,* 871–882.

Newell, A., & Simon, H. (1972). *Human problem solving.* Englewood Cliffs, NJ: Prentice–Hall.

Piaget, J. (1972). *The psychology of intelligence.* Totowa, NJ: Littlefield, Adams.

Rankin, E. F., & Overholzer, B. M (1969). Reaction of intermediate grade children to contextual clues. *Journal of Reading Behavior, 1,* 50–73.

Sternberg, R. J. (1977a). Component processes in analogical reasoning. *Psychological Review, 84,* 353–378.

Sternberg, R. J. (1977b). *Intelligence, information processing, and analogical reasoning: The componential analysis of human abilities.* Hillsdale, NJ: Lawrence Erlbaum Associates.

Sternberg, R. J. (1978). *How to prepare for the Miller Analogies Test* (2nd ed.). Woodbury, NY: Barron's Educational Series.

Sternberg, R.J. (1979). The nature of mental abilities. *American Psychologist, 34,* 214–230.

Sternberg, R. J. (1980a). Factor theories of intelligence are all right almost. *Educational Researcher,* *9,* 6–13, 18.

Sternberg, R. J. (1980b). Sketch of a componential subtheory of human intelligence. *Behavioral and Brain Sciences, 3,* 573–584.

Sternberg, R. J. (1981). Toward a unified componential theory of human intelligence: I. Fluid abilities. In M. Friedman, J. Das, & N. O'Connor (Eds.), *Intelligence and learning.* New York: Plenum.

Sternberg, R. J. (1982). A componential approach to intellectual development. In R. J. Sternberg (Ed.), *Advances in the psychology of human intelligence* (Vol. 1). Hillsdale, NJ: Lawrence Erlbaum Associates.

Sternberg, R. J. (in press). *Understanding and increasing your intelligence.* San Diego: Harcourt, Brace, Jovanovich.

Sternberg, R. J., & Gardner, M. K. (1983). Unities in inductive reasoning. *Journal of Experimental Psychology: General, 112,* 80–116.

Sternberg, R. J., Ketron, J. L., & Powell, J. S. (1982). Componential approaches to the training of intelligent performance. In D. K. Detterman & R. J. Sternberg (Eds.), *How and how much can intelligence be increased?* Norwood, NJ: Ablex.

Sternberg, R. J., & Nigro, G. (1980). Developmental patterns in the solution of verbal analogies. *Child Development, 51,* 27–38.

Sternberg, R. J. & Rifkin, B. (1979). The development of analogical reasoning processes. *Journal of Experimental Child Psychology, 27,* 195–232.

Thurstone, L.L. (1938). *Primary mental abilities.* Chicago: University of Chicago Press.

Undheim, J. O., & Horn, J.L. (1977). Critical evaluation of Guilford's structure-of-intellect theory. *Intelligence, 1,* 65–81.

Vernon, P. E. (1971). *The structure of human abilities.* London: Methuen.

Vygotsky, L. (1978). *Mind in society.* Cambridge, MA: Harvard University Press.

Werner, H. (1954). Change of meaning: A study of semantic processes through the experimental method. *Journal of General Psychology, 50,* 181–208.

Werner, H., & Kaplan, E. (1950). Development of word meaning through verbal context: An experimental study. *Journal of Psychology, 29,* 251–257.

Werner, H., & Kaplan, E. (1952). The acquisition of word meanings: A developmental study. *Monographs of the Society for Research in Child Development,* No. 51.

Zigler, E. (1971). The retarded child as a whole person. In H. E. Adams & W. K. Boardman, III (Eds.), *Advances in experimental clinical psychology* (Vol. 1). New York: Pergamon.

11 The Language-Minority Child: A Psychological, Linguistic, and Social Analysis

Edward A. De Avila
Sharon Duncan
De Avila, Duncan and Associates, Inc.

The past decade has witnessed a renewed interest in the study of bilingualism. Federal involvement in the provision of compensatory services for the language-minority child has produced a plethora of programs that have been widely criticized and attacked. Unfortunately, however, there is a dearth of empirical research upon which to judge this quality, and one finds that the debate rages on about how the language-minority child should be characterized and treated. The purpose of this chapter is to review the highlights of a recent investigation in which nine diffcrent ethnolinguistic groups were examined on a number of dimensions thought to be important in understanding the character of the language-minority child in the schools. These dimensions were selected to represent the major previous approaches to understanding the performance of language minorities.

THE RESEARCH BACKGROUND

The study of language-minority students in the United States has varied greatly, depending on the perspective and purpose of the investigation. To a large extent, these differences in perspective can be seen as a function of a discipline (i.e., anthropological vs. psychological), method (observation vs. experimental), and unit of analysis (group vs. individual). Within the present context, and in order to facilitate discussion, however, it seems reasonable to characterize the study of the language-minority child as consisting of four basic approaches: (1) antecedent conditions, (2) individual differences, (3) intellectual development, and (4) social perceptions or adaptation. A fifth approach, the study of the effect of linguistic proficiency, has been relatively neglected. We briefly mention a number of points concerning each of these approaches to introduce the present state of research in this area.

Antecedent Conditions

In any study that proposes to understand or to investigate the sources of low achievement among language-minority students, much attention has been given to the study of personality and behavioral characteristics thought to result from different and/or limited environmental experiences.

Early studies of the academic achievement of Mexican–American and other Hispanic students were generally conducted in conjunction with studies on Black Americans, under the rubric of culturally disadvantaged (e.g., Deutsch, Katz, & Jensen, 1968; Horn 1970). These efforts, although well intentioned, were guided by the proposition that minority children in general are culturally deprived. The argument was that because minority children were subject to poor and unstimulating environments, they were likely to be slow in their linguistic, cognitive, and social development.

A more liberal—but nonetheless ultimately negative—view is one that describes the Hispanic background experiences as simply different from that of the mainstream American cultural experience (see Carter, 1970). In this view, the culturally different child is one who, coming from a language-minority background, does not possess the same values, attitudes, and motivation, has not developed the prerequisite academic skills, may be retarded in language and social development, and in general is considered deviant from the mainstream.

According to this view, the culturally deprived child is still one who is handicapped not by the school, but by his or her own culture and background. The school is thus the victim because it must take on the additional responsibility of dealing with the presumed reluctance to learn that these children bring to the classroom (Ogbu, 1974).

The culturally disadvantaged and culturally different views both posit that the low-achieving minority child has a limited social, cultural, and environmental background. In both approaches, much attention is given to those aspects of sociocultural and environmental background that correlate with academic achievement. Thus, for example, a significant number of studies are found in the literature that report correlations between family background characteristics and academic performance. Such variables as home language, family size, birth order, parental education and occupation, family composition (e.g., single parent, etc.), and other variables have been found to be significant predictors of school achievement.

Due to the emphasis on group comparisons, the relationship between background variables and achievement is based primarily in the observation that group differences occur concurrent to group differences in achievement. Hence, the tendency has been to infer a causal relationship between family-background variables per se and school achievement. This connection is perhaps not as direct as it may appear.

Individual Differences in Cognitive Style or Ability Patterns

The literature on individual differences with respect to language-minority students is fairly recent and has tended to focus on the demonstration of between-group differences as a means for identifying or explaining cultural differences, which are in turn linked to differences in academic performance. The following provides a brief review of several of the approaches that have been taken in the application of individual-difference constructs to the study of language-minority students. For more complete discussion, there are a number of excellent sources (Anastasi, 1958).

Perhaps the most important single study in the present context is Lesser's (Lesser, Fifer, & Clark, 1965) study in which significant ethnic differences were found among Chinese, Jewish, Black, and Puerto Rican children on tests of mental ability. Since then, there have been numerous similar studies that have identified differences in ability patterns. For example, Stewart, Dole, & Yuell (1967) found different patterns between given ethnic groups in Hawaii. Similarly, Werner, Simonian, and Smith (1968) found differences using four distinct groups. On the other hand, a significant number of researchers (Barnes, 1968; Sitkei, 1966; Stokes, 1970), have found that the attribution of these differences to culture and ethnicity were insufficient and that other factors such as socioeconomic status, socioeconomic class, etc. were equally important in explaining the apparent differences. Finally, more recent investigations (Flaugher & Rock 1972; Leifer 1972; Reiss, 1972), with black/white, with Chinese/black/Italian/Puerto Rican, and black/white/Mexican–American/Asian samples, found no evidence of consistent ethnic patterns on test performance.

Spurred by a recent court decision (Lau vs. Nichols[1]), other researchers have attempted to explain apparent ethnolinguistic differences in terms of cognitive-style constructs, alleged differences in modes of thinking and learning. As the term is used in the psychological literature, cognitive style refers to individual variations in modes of perceiving, remembering, transforming, and utilizing information (Kagan, 1971, as cited in Cazden and Leggett, 1976). Within the

---

[1]The Lau/Nichols case was a U.S. Supreme Court decision handed down in January of 1971. It involved approximately 1800 Chinese-speaking students in San Francisco, who, speaking no English, claimed they were denied "equal access to an educational opportunity." The court ruled in their favor, implying that an underlying cause for the underachievement of language-minority children was a lack of English-language proficiency.

sphere of interpersonal and social functioning, these preferred modes are believed to exist as traits that describe consistent behavioral predispositions across time and situations (see Messick, 1976). In the present context, it is important to bear in mind Messick's (1976) distinction between cognitive style and learning style. The former refers to what information has been learned, whereas the latter refers to how this information has been acquired.

The vast array of research on cognitive styles is best represented by the work of Witkin (Witkin & Berry, 1975; Witkin & Goodenough, 1976; Witkin & Goodenough, 1977; Witkin, Lewis, Hertzman, Machover, Meissner, & Wapner, 1954) and his colleagues on field dependence/independence, of Sigel (1965, 1967) on categorization styles, and of Kagan and his colleagues (Kagan, Moss, & Sigel, 1960, 1963) on conceptual tempo. These works, in addition to the research of Cole and Scribner (1974) and Guilford (1956) demonstrate significant variations in cognitive and sensory perceptions evidenced by children of different cultural and linguistic groups and have been addressed by a wide variety of researchers (see Berry & Dasen, 1971; Cohen, 1979; Cole & Bruner, 1971; Holtzman, Diaz–Guerrero, & Swartz, 1975; Witkin, Dyk, Paterson, Goodenough, & Karp, 1962; Witkin & Goodenough, 1976).

With respect to the present context, the application of Witkin's (1950) model to the education of language-minority children has been particularly significant. Ramírez, Castañeda, and Herold (1974) have argued that certain aspects of Witkin's theory, with modifications, may be particularly productive in designing responsive instructional programs. Specifically, Ramírez and his colleagues have observed that cognitive style varies with degree of assimilation to the Anglo cultural mainstream (Ramírez, Herold, & Castañeda, 1975; Ramírez & Price-Williams, 1974), and that children who can cope effectively with the demands of two cultures display bicognitivity—a concept somewhat akin to the sociolinguistic concept of code switching. Thus, as bilingual children switch codes in response to selected linguistic demands of a conversational situation, so the bicognitive child switches cognitive styles according to the different demands of different sociocultural settings.

Because Mexican–Americans in particular have been found to be considerably more field dependent that Anglo children (Buriel, 1975, Canavan, 1969; Kagan & Buriel, 1977; Kagan & Zahn, 1975; Ramírez & Price-Williams, 1974; Sanders, Scholz, & Kagan, 1976), field dependence has been used by some to explain academic differences as well as sociocultural differences in child rearing. This hypothetical explanation of the academic performance of Mexican–American children has broader implications that have only recently evoked interest in the United States. Few studies relate field dependence/independence directly to school achievement within multiple social groups, whereas factors such as ethnicity, language, socioeconomic status, and other variables are controlled. Most studies seem to focus on the issue of between-group differences rather than on the impact of cognitive styles on school performance across ethnolinguistic groups. More-over, the concepts used in describing field dependence have not escaped some questioning. One study examining the impact of field dependence on subject's performance (Kagan & Buriel, 1977) found, contrary to earlier findings, that differences in competitiveness or cooperation, as suggested by Ramírez, Cas-tañeda, & Herold (1974) were not predictive of school achievement. Kagan and Buriel (1977) concluded that differences in field dependence may relate more to the cognitive domain than to cooperation and affiliation, which relate more to school interaction style. Furthermore, there has been concern that the field-dependence hypothesis might be extended inappropriately to all language-minor-ity populations. Hsi and Lim (1977, p. 8) have cautioned: "though pedagogical approaches based on the field dependent cognitive style might be applicable to Mexican–American students, they should be examined with care when applied to Asian–American students."

A second important cognitive-style construct is cognitive tempo. Conceptual tempo as it was originally studied by Kagan, Rosman, Day, Albert, and Phillips (1964) refers to the tendency of children to respond to problem-solving tasks in either a reflective or an impulsive manner. Operationally, the construct has been defined by the length of time required to make a selection among several possible alternatives in a problem-solving task and by the accuracy of that selection. Impulsivity refers to the tendency to make fast decisions and many errors, whereas reflectivity refers to slow decision times with relative accuracy (Adams, 1972). The variables most commonly recorded in tests of impulsivity–reflectivity are latency to first response and number of incorrect choices.

This information-processing strategy seems to vary across children and with age. Reflectives seem to make more efficient use of strategy selection in test situations and to exhibit greater selective attention to relevant cues in problem-solving tasks. Kagan, Pearson, and Welch (1966) have found this response style predictive of a number of errors on inductive-reasoning tests. Ault (1973) and others have shown that reflective children seem to show more mature problem-solving strategies, whereas others (Kagan et al., 1966; Adams, 1972) have found that some children become increasingly reflective with age. An investigation by Adams (1972) of the possibility that conceptual tempo may be genotypically distinct at different ages concluded that although younger (6-year-old) impulsives showed immature problem-solving strategies, both older (8-year-old) impulsive and reflective subjects performed at equally mature problem-solving levels.

Some investigators (Campbell, 1973) have tied the conceptual tempo mode of behavior to child-rearing practices. Mothers of impulsive children have lower academic expectations for their children and do not intervene in or structure learning situations as much as mothers of either reflective or clinically diagnosed hyperactive children. Hyperactive children share some common characteristics with impulsive children, such as short attention spans, greater field dependency, and an inability to inhibit motor movement (Campbell, Douglas, & Morgenstern, 1971; Harrison & Nadelman, 1972; Hetherington & McIntyre, 1975).

In fact, it has also been suggested that cognitive impulsivity is one instance of a broader syndrome that includes high motoric activity and short attention span (Kagan et al., 1964; Ward, 1968). Baer and Wright (1974) also considered the possibility that failure on the part of impulsives to inhibit responses extends beyond the domain of cognition. In a study of motoric inhibition, Harrison and Nadelman (1972) found reflectives better able to inhibit motor movement than impulsives. However, Bucky, Banta, and Gross (1972) reported no such difference.

As recently as 1975, Hetherington and McIntyre referred to a conceptual overlap between field dependence and cognitive tempo. Field-independent, in contrast to field-dependent, children are less distracted by external cues in problem solving (Massari & Mansfield, 1973) and are more able to attend to relevant cues in conservation tasks (Fleck, 1972). They also attend relatively more to cues within the task rather than to social cues emitted by the experimenter, such as the experimenter looking at or leaning toward the correct stimuli in a discrimination learning task (Hetherington & McIntyre, 1975; Ruble & Nakamura, 1972).

A somewhat similar overlap was reported by Greer and Blank (1977) in a study that examined the relationships between cognitive style—the tendency to analyze a stimulus into its differentiated components—and conceptual tempo, with self-paced training to increase reflective and analytic strategies. They state:

> The pattern of response for the more impulsive would seem to be a quick succession of questions and solutions with very brief periods between each. The more reflective child asks as many questions and offers an equal number of solutions, but intersperses these verbalizations with silent periods, during which he is presumably 'reflecting.' (p. 312)

Thus, conceptual tempo, like field dependence/independence, has been used to explain individual performance differences in a number of cognitive problem-solving tasks. Unfortunately, the studies of conceptual tempo have been conducted with restricted subject populations and one finds very few studies directed toward language-minority populations that go beyond simple, between-group comparisons.

Intellectual Development

A frequently cited explanation for group differences is the concept of intelligence. This explanation draws its impetus from a belief that between-group differences across intellectually demanding tasks are best characterized by task-bound tests of IQ. Thus, differences in school achievement are presumed to be the results of differences in native intelligence. And, conversely, differences in IQ scores are presumed to be indicative of a lower overall potential for school achievement.

The use of the IQ test has been defended on the basis of its ability to predict achievement scores. Numerous authors have criticized this argument as being circular, because the contents of achievement and IQ tests are virtually indistinguishable. Because of this, the IQ test fails to distinguish background learning experiences (repertoire) from the child's ability to encode or transform information (capacity) within his or her repertoire. Because of this limitation and numerous others, many researchers have turned to less culturally specific assessments of intellectual status.

One such approach derives from the work of Piaget. Because Piaget's work is well known throughout the world, there seems to be little need to present the theory in any detail (Flavell, 1963; Furth, 1969) to review the vast cross-cultural literature that has supported the theory (Dasen, 1972). In a review of Piaget's work, Brown (1965) noted that the Piagetian approach, although not totally free from cultural impact, "on the whole . . . is nearer the culture-free pole." Brown cited the work of Wallach (1963), who summarized a large number of studies conducted in North America and Europe and found slight shifts in the age of acquisition—but the same sequential order of acquisition—of different conservation tasks. Brown also cited Goodenough (1963), who tested European and Chinese children in Hong Kong using conservation of space, weight, and volume and found no difference in acquisition regardless of level of schooling. "The most striking result is the very real and close similarity in performance among boys of different nationality and education" (Brown, 1965, p. 235). A similar finding was made by Merselstein (1969) with black children who were not attending school. It is exactly this similarity of sequence across cultural settings that makes the work of Piaget extremely relevant to the present research.

Another argument for the assessment of developmental stage is Sigel and Coop's (1974) admonition that the failure to consider developmental differences may produce spurious results in investigation of cognitive style; that is, apparent cognitive-style differences between groups may simply reflect different rates of development.

The application of Piagetian constructs to the study of bilingualism can be found in almost any review of the literature. Unfortunately, however, the results of these studies are equivocal for a variety of reasons. The primary flaw in previous studies, as we have suggested, has been the failure to control for the relative linguistic proficiency of the comparison groups. Although most conservation studies have focused on cross-cultural comparisons to determine the effects of schooling (see Gordon, 1923, cited in Al-Issa and Dennis, 1970; Heber, Garber, Harrington, Hoffman, & Falendar, 1972; Husén, 1951), more recent studies have been directly applied to the study of bilingualism within the United States.

For example, in an often cited study of the effects of early-childhood bilingualism, Feldman and Shen (1971) compared bilingual and monolingual subjects on Piagetian object-constancy tasks in which various transformations were made on different objects such as a cup, a paper plate, and a sponge. Two other types of tasks were used that asked children to recognize the arbitrary use of object names and to apply these names in simple sentences. Their results showed the bilingual group to be superior in performing all three tasks. Feldman and Shen argued that the ability to use arbitrary names in statements involves the ability to see language as an instrument or set of strategies that varies with linguistic and social context.

Unfortunately, the results of Feldman and Shen's study are flawed by the somewhat questionable criteria for the assignment to subject groups. For example, assignment to the bilingual group was made on the basis of the children's understanding of several simple Spanish questions and their ability to speak Spanish at home. No information was provided about the nature of these questions or about how the ability to speak Spanish at home was determined. Moreover, the comparison monolingual group was confounded by both linguistic and ethnic variables because it consisted of both Mexican–American and Black children residing in the same neighborhood. Thus, although the results of this study are generally supportive of the notion of cognitive advantage for the bilingual groups, they are nevertheless weakened by poor control over relevant variables.

The problem evidenced in the Feldman and Shen study is similarly evidenced in a study by Liedtke and Nelson (1968). In this study, where bilingual and monolingual subjects were compared on a number of Piagetian tasks, the criterion for assignment to the bilingual group was based on teacher observation. The group was defined as children who had used two languages before entering school and who were exposed to both languages at home. Unfortunately, no data were provided as to the actual level of proficiency for either the bilingual or monolingual groups. Similarly, the authors provided no information as to the comparability of the two groups across socioeconomic dimensions. As in the case of the Feldman and Shen study, it would thus appear that the results of this study, while generally supporting the hypothesis of a cognitive advantage for bilinguals, is weakened by the lack of appropriate linguistic controls.

Finally, similar criticism may be leveled against a more recent study (Dahl, 1976) that claimed to illustrate a superior performance by bilinguals on Piagetian tasks. In this study, "children identified as speakers of Spanish upon entry (to a bilingual preschool program in southern California) were assumed to acquire English because this was the language modeled" (p. 59). Unfortunately, no other data are provided as to the actual linguistic comparability of the two groups (bilingual and monolingual) studied.

The danger in a failure to control for linguistic variables is particularly evident in a number of other studies that use Piagetian constructs or tasks to support a negative view of bilingualism. The failure to control for level of linguistic proficiency can yield results opposite to those just cited. For example, in the recent study by Brown, Fournier, and Moyer (1977), Mexican–American children were tested with a battery of 10 Piagetian concepts, including various conservation tasks. The authors concluded from their study that the acquisition of a second language and, hence, bilingualism leads to a "developmental lag." This study, like those finding that bilingualism has a positive effect, employed no measure or control for language proficiency. In fact, not only was there no assessment of the linguistic proficiency of the two groups, but the tests were presented in written and oral form, thus making it more difficult for those with either poor reading skills (as is typical of language-minority children) or linguistic deficiencies in English.

Attitudes/Perceptions

The perceptions and attitudes of teachers toward language-minority students have been studied in a number of ways. In perhaps the largest study of teacher perceptions/attitudes (Jackson & Cosca, 1973), observers visited 494 fourth-, eighth-, tenth-, and twelfth-grade classrooms. Significant results showed that Anglo students were praised more often than Mexican–American students; teachers accepted and used more ideas presented by Anglo students; and, overall, they gave more positive feedback to Anglo students. In the present research, we were initially interested in the teacher's perception of the child and the extent to which perception matched similarly defined behaviors assessed through other means.

In a similar study, Laosa (1977) found that Mexican–American students receive more disapprovals (unless their dominant language was English) and fewer pieces of nonevaluative academic information. In the Jackson and Cosca study, it is noteworthy that teachers spent 23% more time talking to and interacting with Anglo students than with Mexican–American students. It would thus appear that the teachers' perceptions and attitudes may be related to certain linguistic variables in teacher behavior, which in turn may have an impact on academic performance.

Based on the theory of Status Characteristics and Expectation States (Berger, Cohen, & Zelditch, 1972), Cohen (1979) reported that the expectations of other nonminority students and teachers produce a self-fulfilling prophecy for minority students. Basically, she argued that the preconceived attitudes of students and teachers in the classroom do not foster equal-status relations in the school. As a consequence, minority students who tend to be the low achievers are directed by prior experience to fulfill this expectation.

If teachers tend to associate lack of oral English proficiency with a deficiency in other abilities (see Carter & Segura, 1979), it is easy to see the significance of Cohen's work. In fact, Cohen noted that one problem in the schools is that teachers and students tend to treat intelligence or ability as a unidimensional characteristic. They also associate reading ability (or achievement) as a valid indicator of this ability. Hence, the poor reading (and achievement) of many students is interpreted as a reflection of their ability in general.

In addition, she pointed out that even though teachers are able to identify the symptoms of the low-concept child, they fail to recognize that this is perhaps but a symptom of the students' reaction to the general expectations presented to her or him in the schools.

English Language Proficiency

The effects of oral English language proficiency on school achievement and cognitive development have not been empirically studied to any great extent. Measures of oral English language proficiency are noticeably absent from studies involving non-English language groups (see De Avila & Duncan, 1976, 1979b). In fact, the National Assessment of Educational Progress study of achievement for Hispanic Americans (Crane, 1977) noted that many of their questions probably measure English language proficiency, that there were not mechanisms to deal with this problem within the framework of the approach, and that the effect of language proficiency on achievement is not known. Crane (1977) concludes: "Until proficiency in English is carefully studied, we cannot be sure what English-speaking means. The category English-speaking might include any or all of the following groups: English monolingual, English dominant, bilingual, or Spanish dominant" (p.3).

When language is taken into account, children are usually classified on the basis of more global categories such as English dominance or in terms of whether their native language is English or not. Consequently, a common but meaningless result is that English-dominant minority children perform better on English achievement tests than non-English-dominant children. The resultant conclusion that the problem is thus language ability is often made but is not justifiable on the basis of such observations alone. In part, this intuitive claim is based on the fact that ethnolinguistically different children show such poor performance in the schools. It naturally follows that part of the problem must be related to English language skills.

Although this reasoning is in part true, much confusion abounds with respect to both the meaning and the measurement of English language proficiency (see De Avila & Duncan, 1976, 1979b). For example, oral English language proficiency is often confused with the concepts of language achievement and language dominance. As a result, so-called English-dominant minority children are often used as a criterion group with no measure of English language proficiency. Moreover determination of language dominance is often based solely on observations and other subjective rating scales (see Denker, 1977; Gordon, 1976; Michel, 1971; Rogers & Wright, 1969) that are of questionable validity.

English language achievement, on the other hand, is often not distinguished from English language proficiency. For example, language achievement refers to skills learned in a structured setting such as the classroom. To a major extent, the degree of achievement is directly related to the child's exposure to the specific content covered by the test. In contrast, language proficiency refers to the student's language skills in English that are learned in both school and natural settings. It is more generalizable in that it is not necessarily dependent on specific instruction or content. Moreover, language achievement is more likely to be dependent on proficiency than vice versa.

Because of the failure of previous research to clearly distinguish among different aspects of individual differences in language skills or to include language assessment at all, it is difficult to draw conclusions regarding the effects of oral English proficiency on achievement.

THE STUDY OF INFLUENCES UPON THE ACHIEVEMENT OF LANGUAGE-MINORITY CHILDREN

In an attempt to examine the interaction and relative importance of the variables we have described here, a 3-year cross-cultural study was taken at the Southwest Educational Development Laboratory. A particular concern of this study was to improve upon previous research, which simply computed the main values for groups, by examining the effects of variables such as cognitive development on achievement *within* ethnolinguistic groups.

Design: Predictor and Dependent Variables

In the following sections, each of the instruments we used is briefly described. As may be seen, an attempt was made to include several measures convergent to each construct. All tests were administered by locally trained administrators with ethnic backgrounds similar to those of the children.

Cultural Antecedents. A *Family Background Questionnaire* was designed that asked a number of questions regarding each student's family. The questions asked concerned such issues as: (1) educational background of parents, (2) language(s) used in the home, (3) family composition (i.e., number of people living in the home), (4) number of siblings and birth order, (5) place of birth, and (6) occupation. Questionnaires were filled out by school personnel, usually aides who were familiar with the families.

Cognitive Style. The *Children's Embedded Figures Test (CEFT)* was adapted by Karp and Konstadt (see Witkin, Oltman, Raskin, & Karp, 1971) as a measure of perceptual disembedding. The test requires the subject to locate a previously seen simple standard figure within a large complex figure. Score on the CEFT is determined by the number of correct choices made, and higher scores represent greater field independence. *The Draw A Person Test* (DAP) used in this study

TABLE 11.1
Summary of Variables/Measures.

Antecedents	Predictors	Moderators	Outcome variables
1. English in the home	1. Field dependence/ independence	1. Language	1. Achievement
2. Other language in the home	(a) CEFT	(a) Phonetic control	(a) Language arts
3. Number of persons in household	(b) DAP	(b) Vocabulary	(b) Reading
4. Father's educational level	2. Cognitive tempo	(c) Syntax comprehension	(c) Math
5. Mother's educational level	(a) MFFT	(d) Production } LAS	
6. Occupation of head of household	(b) RCT	2. Intellectual development	
7. Father absence	3. Categorization	(a) Identity	
	(a) SCST	(b) Length	
	(b) OST	(c) Number	
		(d) Substance	
		(e) Distance	
		(f) Horizontality	
		(g) Inclusion	
		(h) Egocentricity	
		(i) Probability	
		(j) Class inclusion } CCS	
		3. Teacher perception	
		(a) School Adjustment	
		(b) Dependence	
		(c) Social reserve } Teacher Observation Scale	

Presented by De Avila, Duncan and Associates, Inc., at the National Symposium on the Mexican–American Child—Language, Cognition and Social Development, Santa Barbara, California, December 14–16, 1979.

is a version based on Witkin et al.'s (1962) five-point sophistication-of-body-concept scale. It is used to measure subjects' level of primitiveness-sophistication of body concept. This version is considered to be a measure of cognitive style. *The Matching Familiar Figures Test (MFFT)* is another measure of cognitive style. It refers to the construct of conceptual tempo and is said to assess the dimension of reflectivity–impulsivity (Kagan, 1965; Kagan et al., 1964). The MFFT requires the individual to match a standard picture of a figure to one of six variants. The conceptual tempo classification is based on two scores: latency to first response and number of errors.

Language. The *Language Assessment Scales* (LAS) measures English oral language proficiency (De Avila & Duncan, 1977). The test presents a convergent language assessment procedure consisting of the following subtests: oral production (story retelling), phoneme discrimination (minimal pairs) and production, vocabulary, and oral comprehension. The combined subtests yield a composite score that represents levels of oral language proficiency that correspond to total fluent English, near fluent English, limited English, non-English with partial English language proficiency, or non-English with total English language deficiency. Each subtest score was used in the analysis.

Intellectual Development. The *Cartoon Conservation Scales* (CCS) is a neo-Piagetian paper–pencil measure of intellectual development (De Avila, 1977). There are two levels (K–3rd and 4th–7th grade), each consisting of six different Piagetian tasks. Two of the tasks, egocentricity and conservation of substance, overlap on the two levels. Thus, for the present study only these tasks were included in the analysis. Egocentricity-perspectivism requires that the subject be able to recognize other visual perspectives than the one visible from his or her vantage point. Conservation of substance represents the traditional Piagetian conservation task. It requires that the subject recognize the invariance of amount of substance when its form or shape is transformed. A more detailed description of the tests and their psychometric properties and validity are described elsewhere (De Avila, 1977; De Avila, Duncan, Fleming, Cervantes, & Laosa, 1978; De Avila, Havassy, & Pascual–Leone, 1976; De Avila & Pulos, 1978, p. 124–139; Ulibarri, 1974).

Perceptions. A *Teacher Questionnaire* (TQ) was developed for this study based in part on the work of Castañeda, Herold, and Ramírez (1974). It consists of a number of items generated from the Castañeda et al. (1974) discussion of field dependent/independent behaviors, and from their own teacher-observation rating forms. The TQ represents an attempt to provide an observationally based measure of three cognitive-style behaviors—school adjustment, dependence, and social reserve. A more complete description of the TQ and the rationale for its construction can be found in Fleming, De Avila, and Duncan (1979).

School Achievement.   The Standardized Achievement Tests were used in the various school districts where data were collected. They used different achievement tests, each having differing scales. Thus to perform our analyses, all test data were converted to standard scores based both on the test's published norms for each level and on the sample's standard deviation. This procedure resulted in a deviation score relative to the norms of the particular test.

Subjects

In all, a total of 903 children were tested. Roughly, the same number of children of each sex were selected from each ethnolinguistic group in the first, third, and fifth grades. For a more complete breakdown of subject parameters, the reader is referred to De Avila, Duncan, Ulibarri, & Fleming, 1979. Children were selected from nine communities for participation in the study as follows:

Urban Mexican–American.   Children in this group live in a northern California community just south of San Francisco The (K–6) school where the children were tested is located in a partially residential-commercial neighborhood.

Rural Mexican–American.   This group is located in southwest Texas, 10 miles from the United States–Mexico border. The community is basically agricultural, with some light manufacturing. The school is K-6 with about half the teachers being Mexican–American.

Puerto Rican.   Children in this ethnolinguistic group come from an inner-city K–3 school. The school is located in a highly urban city about 300 miles from New York City. The school is 77% Puerto Rican. Although it is an inner-city school, many of the children migrated from a rural area in Puerto Rico. About half the teachers are Puerto Rican.

Cuban–American.   The children in this community come from a lower middle to middle-class semiresidential suburb of Miami, Florida. The children were born in the community; however, most of the parents migrated from Cuba. The school is K–6 with about 45% Cuban–American enrollment. About 25% of the staff are native Spanish speakers.

Chinese–American.   This group comes from a northern California community near the San Francisco Bay Area. The school population is primarily Chinese–American; many of the teachers and all the aides are Chinese–American. However, not all the teachers speak Chinese (Cantonese).

Franco–American (Cajun).   The Franco–American children come from a rural-agricultural area in the backwaters of Louisiana. The (K-5) school is 95% French. Although most of the teachers are from the area and speak French, the primary language in the school is English.

Native American Navajo.   The Navajo children are from middle New Mexico just south of Santa Fe. All the children tested live on the Indian reservation and virtually all commute to school by truck. The rural school is approximately 60% native American. The aides are Navajo, but the teachers are Anglo and Chicano.

Anglo–American.   The children in this group are from a northern California community south of San Francisco. The community is industrial–commercial and is of low-middle to middle SES. The school is K–6 and is 90% Anglo.

Mexican.   The children from this site reside in the suburban middle-class section of a large metropolitan Mexican city. The children participating in the study were from lower-middle- to middle-class families. As such, they cannot be considered as middle class in the American sense but must be viewed as basically "mainstream" Mexican children receiving public instruction. All the students and faculty were Mexican and both groups spoke virtually no English.

SUMMARY OF RESULTS AND CONCLUSIONS

Because of space limitations and the extensiveness of the data, it is impossible to present any of the details regarding the analytic procedures (see De Avila & Duncan, 1980). Instead, we summarize only the most important findings and refer the reader to reports with more detailed discussions. In the discussion that follows, results are presented in four stages. In the first, we summarize the results of a series of factor analyses that were constructed on the entire data set to reduce the pool to a more manageable size and to test the construct validity of the measures. In the second series, analyses of variance (ANOVA) techniques were employed to test the extent to which the nine ethnolinguistic groups differed on those variables shown by the previous analyses to be valid and reliable. In a third series of analyses, multiple regression techniques were used to generate equations that were predictive of school achievement for each group. In the fourth series of analyses, the data were regrouped according to linguistic categories. Comparisons of test performance using analyses of variance (ANOVA) techniques were then employed to examine the extent to which relative linguistic proficiency was more predictive of test performance than ethnolinguistic group membership.

Factor Analysis of Variables

Teacher Perception/Observation.   In the first phase of the analyses, the 40 items of the teacher observation form were subjected to a factor analysis. The results of this initial analysis produced five interpretable factors. However, upon a subsequent analysis in which both the test–retest and interjudge reliability of the five factors were examined, only three were found to be sufficiently reliable to warrant discussion. A complete description of the procedures used to develop and analyze the teacher observation form may be found in Fleming et al. (1979).

The intercorrelations among the 40 items were analyzed by the method of principal components. Three factors were found to account for 50% of the original variance. The first factor (school adjustment) encompasses a number of socially desirable traits that reflect inquisitiveness, alertness, creativity, and the like, as well as some items thought to be related to field independence. The latter include independence, a preference for visual aids, and a trial-and-error approach to learning. Undoubtedly, this factor reflects a child's strong character and ability to please or impress the teacher. Because of the strong element of social desirability, we were reluctant to name this factor field independence.

The second factor was called dependence. The items appear to reflect personality characteristics associated with social dependence as well as with field dependence. Salient items include the inability to concentrate, dependence upon others, and anxiety over school work.

A child with a high score on the third factor, social reserve, would be labeled reserved, reflective, or perhaps just shy. This child is self-controlled in social situations. Such characteristics are sometimes associated with field dependence. However, no substantial (negative) correlation with independence was found.

Performance Variables.   The performance variables in this study involved five measures of language, two measures of cognitive development, and seven measures of cognitive style. However, because each measure also represented a different aspect or dimension of the constructs, they were grouped together on the basis of their similarities and differences through the procedure of cluster analysis (Tyron & Bailey, 1970). This allowed us to obtain a perspective on the nature of the constructs (because we know there is much overlap) and also to reduce the number of original, or a priori, variables. In addition, because the main objective of the study was to identify the best set of predictors, such a procedure was an appropriate preparation for the use of multiple regression for predictive purposes (Kerlinger & Pedhazur, 1973).

The results of the cluster analyses of the correlation matrix for the a priori variables indicate that the language measures, with the exception of minimal pairs (i.e., aural phoneme discrimination), loaded on the first cluster. The CEFT, DAP, and developmental measures loaded primarily on the second cluster, and the MFFT (latency and error) loaded on the third cluster. The Teacher Questionnaire tended to load equally and not very highly on all three clusters.

A clear pattern of the defining characteristics of each cluster is apparent. The first cluster is clearly language and the third, conceptual tempo. The second cluster, however, is loaded or defined by both cognitive-style and cognitive-development measures. This is not a surprising result and is, in fact, consistent with the relationship between Piagetian tasks and the field dependence/independence cognitive-style dimension (e.g., see Flavell, 1963; Pascual–Leone, 1970) and with the relationship of these two tasks to conceptual tempo (errors).

Performance on the MFFT is reported to show moderate correlations with field dependence/independence (about -.42) and developmental trends across age (Messer, 1976). The results found in this study concerning the relationship of the MFFT with CEFT errors and age are consistent with those reported by Messer (1976) and others (e.g., Hetherington & McIntyre, 1975). The results of the cluster analysis are also consistent with prior results. For a more complete discussion of both the empirical and theoretical details of this aspect of the study, see De Avila and Duncan (1979b).

Ethnolinguistic Group Comparisons

The results of the techniques described previously were used to generate a set of variables that was used to compare differences across ethnolinguistic groups. As is recalled, a factor analysis of cognitive-style, intellectual-development, and language variables produced three factors that were labeled style/development, language, and conceptual tempo. In addition, the results of the Teacher Questionnaire produced three reliable factors, labeled school adjustment, dependence, and impulsivity. In the following, a series of ethnolinguistic comparisons across these six superordinate variables is discussed.

The only substantial group differences occurred on the Social Reserve subtests. The means show that the Chinese–American pupils are the most reserved and the Mexican students are the least reserved. This finding may be of interest to some, but the Social Reserve subtest shows no relationship to any of the other measures of cognitive style. Thus, these differences do not appear meaningful in the present context. In sum, the ethnolinguistic group (ELG) differences for those subtests that most closely resemble the behavioral characteristics associated with cognitive style are quite small in magnitude and do not seem to justify the assumption that the ethnolinguistic groups can be distinguished on the basis of such characteristics.

With respect to the three performance factors, three separate three-way analyses of variance were conducted across ELG by Grade by Sex.

Language. Examination of means shows Anglo children (as would be expected) to be the most proficient in English, followed by Cuban- and French-background children. With respect to grade, it was found that age differences held for *some* groups and not others. Grade differences accounted for only 10%

of the total variance in language proficiency, whereas ethnolinguistic difference accounted for 39%.

Style/Development.   Examination of the ELG mean-score differences reveals few, if any, psychologically meaningful differences because ELG difference accounted for only .05% of the total variance. Regarding differences between the groups across the three grades, the data seem to show that, for the most part, all nine groups appear quite similar at the first grade. This similarity seems to break down at the third and fifth grades, as reflected in the Grade by ELG interaction ($p < .001$) found in the ANOVA. Thus, whereas the performance of the Chinese and Cuban children in the first grade is commensurate with the other groups, performance in the third grade is substantially higher. This higher level of performance is maintained by the Chinese group, but not by the Cuban group, whose performance in the fifth grade seems to drop off slightly.

In contrast to the Chinese and Cuban groups, the Navajo group seems to evidence lower overall performance relative to the other eight groups. A last comparison worthy of comment seems to suggest that, in contrast to previous research, the Anglo populations appears to perform at the lower end of the distribution relative to the other groups. However, it should be borne in mind that, because ethnolinguistic group differences accounted for only .05% of the total variance, these differences are not particularly meaningful in any real psychological sense.

Conceptual Tempo.   The three-way ANOVA conducted on the third factor, which had been labeled impulsivity, resulted in significant main effects for all three variables, ethnolinguistic group, grade, and sex, as well as in several significant interactions. The three variables, though statistically significant, accounted for only .07%, .11%, and .03% of the total variance, respectively. Examination of the cell means reveals, for example, that the Navajo children are the least impulsive in the first grade and the most impulsive in the fifth grade. On the other hand, the Cajun children seem to behave in a relatively more reflective mode throughout the grades. With respect to the other groups, it is difficult to locate a discernible pattern of differences. It is perhaps important to bear in mind that ethnolinguistic group accounted for only .07% of the variance in conceptual tempo.

In summary, it seems that the two most stable differences that occur between the ethnolinguistic groups in this study were related to language and age. Over and beyond these rather straightforward results, it would be difficult to infer any real or enduring difference between the ELGs based on these measures. This is particularly the case given the complex nature of the data set. In this regard, it seems necessary to bear in mind that in larger samples, such as the one used here, "psychological significance" is apt to be confused with statistical significance. In other words, the ANOVA procedures used herein were highly sensitive to even the slightest differences between groups. The problem of statistical power (Cohen, 1979) is one that plagues this type of research.

Regression Analyses of Academic Achievement

The basic approach taken in the following series was to analyze correlation data with stepwise multiple-regression techniques. In these analyses, each of the six superordinate variables just described were analyzed for each ethnolinguistic group separately as well as for the total. In the following, the emphasis is upon the combined group results. Academic performance in three areas was examined: reading, language arts, and math. For a more detailed presentation of the within-group/grade results, see De Avila et al. (1979).

The equation produced by regressing reading achievement on the six factors showed that oral language proficiency is the strongest predictor, accounting for approximately 10% of the total variance across seven of the eight ethnolinguistic groups (the Mexican sample was not included in this series of analyses). The second most important factor in the equation is school adjustment, as defined by the teacher questionnaire. This factor, however, accounted for a relatively small percentage of the total variance. The six factors accounted for only 18% of the total variance, suggesting that although oral language proficiency, school adjustment, and other factors are of importance, they do not form a complete picture because almost 80% of the variance remained unaccounted for.

The relationship between predictor and criterion variables is somewhat stronger in the second series of analyses where performance and observational factors were combined to examine language-arts achievement. The correlation was .71, accounting for 52% of the total variance. Clearly, in this equation, oral language proficiency is the strongest predictor, with school adjustment accounting only for 6%. The remaining four factors added only a total of 3% to the variance accounted for by the analyses.

With respect to math achievement, the predictive strength of the six factors was somewhat weaker than was the case for reading and language arts. The analysis reveals that only .09% of the total variance in math achievement scores was accounted for by the six factors. Simple correlations reveal that, although most of the six factors were significantly correlated with math achievement, the strength of this association is not strong. The three strongest variables were impulsivity, social reserve, and oral language proficiency. It is of some interest to note that oral language proficiency was negatively correlated with math achievement, suggesting that, as oral language proficiency is improved, it may be at the expense of math achievement. In this connection, it would be important to examine the relative proportion of time spent in the classroom on language as opposed to computational math drill exercise.

A similar series of analyses were conducted within each ethnolinguistic group. The results of this series of analyses produced a somewhat more complex picture.

For example, whereas oral language proficiency was the strongest predictor of reading achievement for Chinese, Rural Mexican–American, Puerto Rican, and Native American (Navajo) subjects, school adjustment was strongest for Anglo–American, Urban Mexican–American, and Franco–American (Cajun) students. For Cuban–American students, the first step in the equation was dependency. It seems obvious that this might be due to the language proficiency status of these groups.

Unfortunately, it is difficult to draw any firm conclusions from the attempt that was made to examine the within-group prediction of language arts achievement. This is because data existed only for four of the subgroups. Moreover, small and unequal subgroups made the interpretation of these data even more difficult. It is important, however, to note that the relative strengths of the predictors within the groups seems to match those obtained when groups were collapsed in order to increase the number of subjects per cell.

The analyses of the data within groups for math achievement reveal that there is a fair degree of variation between groups with respect to the relative strength of the predictors within groups. In other words, the patterns of relative importance between the predictors seem to be somewhat variable across the eight groups used in the analyses. It is perhaps of interest to note that the dependency factor was the most significant predictor in three of the eight separate analyses and second most important in two others. However, because previous analyses revealed this factor to have somewhat marginal reliability, it would be prudent to make much more of the finding.

Cognitive Style and Achievement.   With respect to the importance of the cognitive-style/development variable that was the primary focus of this investigation, it is also important to note that in only one case across all the analyses conducted is the cognitive-style/development factor the first step in the equation predicting to achievement.

In contrast, not only was the oral language factor included in virtually all the significant predictions, but the prediction equations tended to account for a meaningful amount of the variance in achievement. Thus, as defined by the present instrumentation, the importance of the cognitive-style dimension in academic achievement is not supported in the study. In particular, the field-dependence/independence dimension defined by the CEFT, DAP, and developmental variable was a better predictor than language in only 5 of the 32 analyses (or 5 of 24 that were significant). In contrast, language proficiency was a significant predictor in 19 of 32 analyses (or 19 of 24 that were significant).

A number of these analyses included only the three cluster scores (language, style/development, and conceptual tempo) because of the overlap between the Teacher Questionnaire variables and the measures of cognitive style.

When regression analyses were conducted that included the three Teacher Questionnaire (TQ) variables in addition to the three cluster scores, the results indicated that school adjustment, dependence, and social reserve were also better predictors of achievement than style/development. In some cases, these factors were even more efficient than language proficiency. In virtually every instance, regardless of achievement area or ethnolinguistic group, TQ variables tended to have the effect of removing style/development from the prediction altogether. The TQ variables were particularly efficient in the Urban Mexican–American group, where it removed style/development and showed significant prediction of achievement when none was found previously. In general, predictions that were not significant became so when TQ variables were entered into the prediction equations.

It should be noted that a criticism of these interpretations might be made of the small sample sizes relative to the number of predictors (i.e., Nihm's law, see Marascuilo & Levin, 1978). However, the preceding interpretations are based on the adjusted multiple R^2 per se. Thus, the statistics obtained should represent conservative and unbiased estimates.

Probably of most significance with regard to the previous finding is that, whereas many researchers report a significant relationship between degree of field dependence and achievement, they fail to take into account oral English language proficiency. The data reported here are significant in that they show that, when language proficiency is taken into account, field dependence/independence or cognitive style, at least as measured here, is of little significance in terms of its predictive validity. Additionally, when TQ variables were entered into prediction, style/development is no longer important for any of the groups. Children who have higher levels of English language proficiency tend to have higher levels of achievement. And children who have higher status according to teacher perceptions show higher achievement. This same statement cannot be made of either cognitive-style dimensions.

A second finding concerns the within-group analyses. Here the results are not as clear-cut because different patterns of predictions occur for different ethnolinguistic groups and for different areas of achievement. Nevertheless, the results indicate that a clear pattern of prediction regarding cognitive style does not emerge, so that any conclusion regarding the importance of this construct with respect to particular ethnolinguistic groups is not supported. With regard to the present set of predictors, style/development showed constancy as a predictor only, for the Anglo–American group. Again, however, when TQ was included, style/development was no longer important, even for the Anglo–American group.

In the two Mexican–American samples, cognitive style was significant only in the Urban Mexican–American sample. It was a significant predictor of achievement in language and reading, but not math. However, for reading it did not account for a meaningful amount of the variance, and for language achievement, language proficiency was virtually as good a predictor as cognitive style. Even more noteworthy is the fact that the relationship was reversed in this group for predicting language and reading. This is probably indicative of the instability of the cognitive-style construct. Nevertheless, when teacher perception of the student was entered into the analysis, style/development was not a meaningful predictor. These results support the position that the Mexican–American population is not a homogeneous one.

In addition, it should be noted that the pattern of prediction in the Urban Mexican–American sample is somewhat similar to that of the Anglo–Americans. Overall, this finding is interpreted to mean that cognitive style is more important (albeit not too important) in these groups than in Rural Mexican–American groups. This, together with the teacher-judgment data, suggests that cognitive style is probably important only with respect to teacher judgments and when language proficiency is no longer a factor, such as in the case of the Anglo–American children.

A general finding for all ethnolinguistic groups was that language was the most important predictor of achievement relative to the other factors in this study. There were, of course, some exceptions. For example, with Anglo–Americans and Cuban–Americans, English language proficiency did not figure into the predictions at all, which is entirely understandable given that both groups were totally English proficient. Cognitive style was the only significant and meaningful predictor of Anglo–American achievement, and although the style/development factor significantly predicted to Urban Mexican–American reading and language achievement, the correlations were reversed. This indicates, at least for this particular sample, that the standing toward the dependent end of the cognitive–style dimension does not preclude higher levels of achievement, an inference that is consistent with Saarni's (1973) finding for sex differences. Finally, when teacher perception of the student is included, even language, in some cases, becomes less important. It appears that langauge proficiency and teacher perceptions of school adjustment are the important variables in predicting achievement for the language–minority children examined in this study.

Relation of Relative Linguistic Proficiency to Cognitive Measures

Given the apparent relative importance of linguistic proficiency, a final series of analyses was conducted in which subjects were regrouped according to linguistic considerations.

In the first of the two substudies described later, the performance of bilingual and monolingual English and Spanish subjects was compared (De Avila & Duncan, 1979b). In the second study, linguistic subgroupings were expanded to include partial and limited bilinguals along with children who were late in developing either language (Duncan & De Avila, 1979b). The first study may be considered as a study on the effects of bilingualism in the traditional sense, whereas the second would be considered a more general examination of the concept of relative linguistic proficiency. In the analysis that follows, subjects were grouped according to scores on the Language Assessment Scales (LAS). Only those children who were the most proficient were selected. Thus, from the total of 152 Anglo children, a total of 119 scored as Level 5 in English and Level 1 in Spanish. This group was defined as monolingual English or 5/1. The Spanish monolingual group (1/5) was made up of children from the Mexican site who scored as Level 5 in Spanish and Level 1 in English. The bilingual or 5/5 group was made up of children from the four Hispanic sites, which included Urban and Rural Mexican–American, Puerto Rican and Cuban–American populations. In this sense, the subgroups could be considered as Monolingual–Anglo, Monolingual–Mexican, and Bilingual–Latino.

An attempt was made to control for possible age differences by analyzing the data by grade level. However, this could not be done for all three grades, and the first and third grades had to be combined due to the small number of bilinguals. Comparisons were made across CEFT, DAP, MFFT, CCS, and Teacher Questionnaire scores.

Results showed that bilingual (5/5) subjects received significantly higher scores than the two monolingual groups on both the CEFT and DAP, suggesting a relationship between cognitive style and bilingualism. On the MFFT, the bilingual group had only slightly fewer errors than either monolingual groups in the first and third grades. Mean errors for the fifth-grade groups were basically the same, with less than a point difference between the three groups. The latency scores showed the bilingual group to be intermediate to the two other groups in impulsivity.

The analyses of the CCS subtests data in the first- and third-grade groups showed that the bilingual group received higher mean scores on five of the six subtests as well as on total score. For the fifth grade, the results were somewhat mixed, with no discernible pattern of differences between the groups.

Finally, the bilingual group was seen as more school adjusted than either of the monolingual groups. No significant differences were found for either of the two other teacher factors.

In summary, it appears that there is some support for the contention that bilinguals, at least at the earlier grades, are advanced in the cognitive-style/developmental and school-adjustment dimensions. However, this difference that favors the bilinguals is either lost by the fifth grade or is not registered because of deficiencies in the current instruments, which are, possibly, sensitive to "ceiling effects." It may also be that the results of the fifth-grade groups were affected by the relatively few numbers of subjects, which may have distorted possible real differences.

In the second substudy, an attempt was made to expand the number of linguistic subgroupings and to include children who were less than fully proficient in either one or both of the two languages. The subjects in the second substudy were from the four groups whose home language was Spanish. These included Urban and Rural Mexican–Americans, Cuban–Americans and Puerto Rican children. Relative linguistic proficiency (RLP) was determined through the use of the LAS, and children were grouped as described on Fig. 11.1.

Given these groups, ANOVA procedures were then employed to test group differences. Posthoc comparisons were then made in order to determine the source of variations. Comparisons were made as in the aforementioned, across CEFT, DAP, CCS, and MFFT. Results of this substudy show for example, on the CCS, that the highest total score was by the proficient bilinguals. This group also produced the highest mean scores with five of the six CCS (Level 1) subscales. In order to test the relationship between RLP and intellectual development, an orthogonal contrast of mean scores was made. Results of this analysis reveal that the highest scores were obtained by the proficient bilinguals and the lowest by the late language learners. A similar pattern to this was obtained on the DAP and CEFT measures.

In addition to the preceding, there were a number of important findings about the intermediate RLP groups. Of particular significance was the fact that on the CEFT and DAP, the performance of the partial bilinguals, monolinguals, and limited bilinguals was basically the same and within one standard deviation of the published norm. The proficient bilinguals' score on the CEFT was slightly more than one standard deviation above the published norm, whereas the late language learners fell approximately one standard deviation below.

There are several important implications in the findings of the second study. The first important finding is that proficient bilingual children significantly outperformed all other monolingual and bilingual children on cognitive perspectivism tasks as well as on two cognitive perceptual components of field

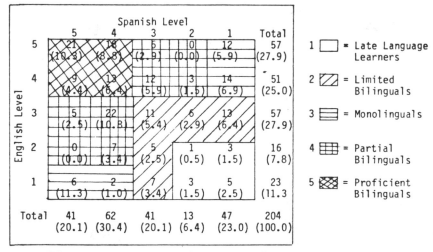

FIG. 11.1   Subject breakdown by Relative Linguistic Proficiency scores (percentages are shown in parentheses).

dependent/independent cognitive styles. The extent of the advantages revealed in this study are significant across a series of tasks. The nature of these differences or advantages can be described in terms of superior development of nonegocentricity, or ability to intellectually restructure or reorganize a three-dimensional display; in the relative ability to separate part of an organized field from the field as a whole; and in level of development of articulation of body concept.

In terms of the Witkins group's "differentiation hypothesis," the demonstrated advantages of the proficient bilingual children comprise one major indicator of greater differentiation, self/nonself segregation and autonomy of external referents. In other words, the proficient bilingual children are significantly more capable of "keeping things separate." In terms of metaset theory (De Avila & Duncan, 1979b), this "keeping things separate" would amount to the breaking of sets, which in turn leads to higher order restructuring of sets of functions.

The results of this study also reveal a positive, monotonic relationship between degree of relative linguistic proficiency and cognitive functioning. In other words, the more proficient the children were in each of their languages the better they performed on the dependent measures. However, contrary to commonly held views, the "deficiencies" of limited bilingual children appear to be linguistic rather than intellectual.

Lastly, the finding that there were significant differences in RLP, ranging from students with full native proficiency in two languages to those with total deficiencies in two languages, is important because it bears on recent educational policy regarding the treatment of language minority children. Clearly the "bilingual" population is not a homogeneous one as recent policy would presume. It will be the work of future research to elaborate the theoretical and practical implications of these findings. With respect to a theoretical explanation, De Avila & Duncan (1981) have used Harlow's (1949) notion of "learning sets" to describe the seemingly higher order processing of the proficient bilingual. Cummins (1978) has discussed "additive" and "subtractive" influence underlying performance differences within the bilingual population and has offered a "threshold hypothesis" to explain them. Finally, on a more practical level, De Avila, Cohen, and Intilli (1981) have examined treatment effects on different language types and found (under heterogeneous grouping) linguistic variability to have a positive influence on academic concept formation.

ACKNOWLEDGMENTS

The research summarized in this chapter is based in part on the results of a 3-year cross-cultural investigation of nine ethnolinguistic groups, supported by Contract #400-65-0051 between the National Institute of Education and the Southwest Education Development Laboratory. The opinions expressed are those of the authors and do not necessarily represent the position of the National Institute of Education.

REFERENCES

Adams, W. V. (1972). Strategy differences between reflective and impulsive children. *Child Development, 43,* 1076–1080.

Al–Issa, I., & Dennis, W. (1970). *Cross-cultural studies of behavior.* New York: Holt, Rinehart, & Winston.

Anastasi, A. (1958). *Differential psychology* (3rd ed.). New York: Macmillan.

Ault, R. L. (1973). Problem-solving strategies of reflective, impulsive, fast, accurate children. *Child Development, 44,* (2), 259–266.

Baer, D. M., & Wright, J. C. (1974). Developmental psychology. *Annual Review of Psychology, 25,* 1–82.

Berger, J. B., Cohen, B. P., & Zelditch, M., Jr. (1972). Status conceptions and social interaction. *American Sociological Review, 37*(3), 241–255.

Berry, J. W., & Dasen, P. R. (1971). Ecological and cultural factors in spatial skill development. *Canadian Journal of Behavioral Science, 3,* 324–336. (Reprinted in Berry & Dasen, 1973, 129–140).

Berry, J., & Dasen, P. R. (1973). *Culture and cognition: Readings in cross-cultural psychology.* Scranton, PA: Harper & Row.

Brown, R. B. (1965). *Social psychology.* New York: The Free Press.

Brown, R. L., Fournier, J. F., & Moyer, R. H. (1977). A cross-cultural study of Piagetian concrete reasoning and science concepts among rural 5th-grade Mexican– and Anglo–American students. *Journal of Research in Science Teaching, 14,*(4), 329–334.

Bucky, S. F., Banta, J. T., & Gross, R. B. (1972). Development of motor impulse control and reflectivity. *Perceptual Motion Skills, 34,* 813–814.

Buriel, R. (1975). Cognitive styles among three generations of Mexican–American children. *Journal of Cross-Cultural Psychology, 6,* 417–429.

Burnes, D. (1968). A study of relationship between measured intelligence and nonintellective factors for children of two socioeconomic groups and races (Doctoral dissertation, Washington University, 1968). *Dissertation Abstracts International, 29*(12B), 4839. (University Microfilms No. 69–898).

Campbell, S. B. (1973). Mother–child interaction in reflective, impulsive, and hyperactive children. *Developmental Psychology, 8,* 341–349.

Campbell, S. B., Douglas, V. I., & Morgenstern, G. (1971). Cognitive styles in hyperactive children and the effect of methylphenidate. *Journal of Child Psychology and Psychiatry, 12,* 55–57.

Canavan, D. (1969, August). *Field dependence in children as a function of grade, sex, and ethnic group membership.* Paper presented at the meeting of the American Psychological Association, Washington, DC.

Carter, T. P. (1970). *Mexican Americans in school: A history of educational neglect.* New York: College Entrance Examination Board.

Carter, T. P., & Segura, R. D. (1979). *Mexican Americans in school: A decade of change.* New York: College Entrance Examination Board.

Castañeda, A., Herold, P. L., & Ramírez, M. (1974). *New approaches to bilingual education.* Austin, TX: Dissemination and Assessment Center.

Cazden, C. B., & Leggett, E. L. (1976, June). *Culturally responsible education: A response to Lau Guidelines II.* Paper presented at the Conference on Research and Policy Implications of the U.S. Office of Civil Rights: Findings specifying remedies for eliminating past educational practices ruled unlawful under *Lau v. Nichols.* Southwest Educational Development Laboratory, Austin, Texas.

Cohen, E. G. (1979, April). *Status equalization in the desegregated school.* Paper presented at the meeting of the American Educational Research Association, San Francisco.

Cole, M., & Bruner, J. S. (1971). Cultural differences and inferences about psychological proc-essing. *American Psychologist, 26*, 867–876.

Cole, M., & Scribner, S. (1974). *Culture and thought.* New York: Wiley.

Crane, R. (1977, May). *Hispanic student achievement in five learning areas: 1971–1975* (National Assessment of Education Progress Report No. Br–2). Denver, CO: ERIC Document Reproduction Service No. ED138, 414.

Cummins, J. (1979). Linguistic interdependence and the educational development of bilingual chil-dren. *Review of Educational Research, 49*, 222-251.

Dahl, R. J. (1976). *The attainment of conservation of mass and verbal synthesis between Latin–American children who speak one or two languages.* Unpublished doctoral dissertation, University of Southern California.

Dasen, P. R. (1972). Cross-cultural Piagetian research: A summary. *Journal of Cross Cultural Psychology, 3*(1), 23–39.

De Avila, E. A. (1977). *Cartoon Conservation Scales (CCS), Level I and Level II.* San Rafael, CA: Linguametrics Group.

De Avila, E. A., Cohen, E. G., & Intili, J. K. (1981). *Multi-cultural improvement of cognitive abilities.* State of California, Department of Education, Contract No. 9372, August.

De Avila, E. A., & Duncan, S. E. (1976, June). *A few thoughts about language assessment: The Lau Decision reconsidered.* Paper presented at the NIE conference on Research and Policy Implications of the U.S. Office of Civil Rights: Findings specifying remedies for eliminating past educational practices ruled unlawful under *Lau v. Nichols.* Southwest Educational Devel-opment Laboratory, Austin, TX.

De Avila, E. A., & Duncan, S. E. (1977). *Language Assessment Scales, Level I* (2nd ed.). San Rafael, CA: Linguametrics Group.

De Avila, E. A., & Duncan, S. E. (1979a). Bilingualism and metaset. In R. Duran (Ed.), *Latino language and communicative behavior.* Norwood, NJ: Ablex.

De Avila, E. A., & Duncan, S. E. (1979b, October). *The construct validity of several measures of cognitive style for language–minority children.* (Study conducted as part of a 3-year cross-cultural investigation of cognitive styles of eight entholinguistic groups, supported by Contract #400–65–0051 between the National Institute of Education and the Southwest Educational Development Laboratory.) Austin, TX: Southwest Educational Development Laboratory.

De Avila, E. A., & Duncan, S. E. (1980, June). *The language-minority child: A social, linguistic, and psychological analysis.* (Final summary report to the Southwest Educational Development Laboratory.) Austin, TX: Southwest Educational Development Laboratory.

De Avila, E. A., Duncan, S. E., Fleming, J. S., Cervantes, R. A., & Laosa, L. (1978, March). *Cognitive styles of language-minority children: Some preliminary results.* Paper pre-sented at the meeting of the American Educational Research Association, Toronto, and at the National Association for Bilingual Education, Seventh Annual Bilingual/Bicultural Education Conference, San Juan, April. (Paper revised June 1978)

De Avila, E. A., Duncan, S. E., Ulibarri, D. M., & Fleming, J. S. (1979). *Predicting the academic success of language-minority students from developmental, cognitive style, linguistic, and teacher perception measures.* (Study conducted as part of a 3-year cross-cultural investigation of cognitive styles of eight ethnolinguistic groups, supported by Contract #400–65–0051 between the National Institute of Education and the Southwest Educational Development Laboratory.) Austin, TX: Southwest Educational Development Laboratory.

De Avila, E. A., Havassey, B. E., & Pascual–Leone, J. (1976). *Mexican–American school chil-dren: A neo-Piagetian analysis.* Washington, DC: Georgetown University Press.

De Avila, E. A., & Pulos, S. (1978). Developmental assessment by pictorially presented Piagetian material: The Cartoon Conservation Scale. In G. I. Lubin, M. K. Poulsen, J. F. Magary, & M. Solo–McAlister (Eds.), *Piagetian theory and its implications for the helping professions* (Pro-ceedings of the Seventh Interdisciplinary Conference, Vol. II). Los Angeles, CA: University of Southern California.

Denker, E. R. (1977). *Teaching numeric concepts to Spanish-speaking second graders: English or Spanish instruction?* Paper presented at the meeting of the American Educational Research Association, New York.

Deutsch, M., Katz, I., & Jensen, A. R. (1968). *Social class, race, and psychology development.* New York: Holt, Rinehart, & Winston.

Duncan, S. E., & De Avila, E. A. (1979, February). *Relative linguistic proficiency and field dependence/independence: Some findings on the linguistic heterogeneity and cognitive style of bilingual children.* Paper presented at the 13th Annual Convention of Teachers of English to Speakers of Other Languages, Boston.

Feldman, C., & Shen, M. (1971). Some language-related cognitive advantages of bilingual 5-year-olds. *The Journal of Genetic Psychology, 118,* 235–244.

Flaugher, R. L., & Rock, D. A. (1972). Patterns of ability factors among four ethnic groups. *Proceedings of the Annual Convention of the American Psychological Association, 7,* 27–28.

Flavell, J. H. (1963). *The developmental psychology of Jean Piaget.* Princeton, NJ: Van Nostrand.

Fleck, J. R. (1972). Cognitive styles in children and performance on Piagetian conservation tasks. *Perceptual Motion Skills, 35,* 747–756.

Fleming, J. S., De Avila, E. A., & Duncan, S. E. (1979). *Teacher assessment of cognitive styles among language-minority children.* (Study conducted as part of a 3-year cross-cultural investigation of cognitive styles of eight ethnolinguistic groups supported by Contract #400–65–0051 between the National Institute of Education and the Southwest Educational Development Laboratory.) Austin, TX: Southwest Educational Development Laboratory.

Furth, H. G. (1969). *Piaget and knowledge: Theoretical foundations.* Englewood Cliffs, NJ: Prentice–Hall.

Goodenough, J. J. (1963). *A test of milieu effects with some of Piaget's tasks.* (Air Force Contract AF49 638–682).

Gordon, J. S. (1976). Mixed dominant grouping and bilingual materials in mathematics and science class in two Puerto Rican Junior High Schools (Doctoral dissertation, University of Michigan at Ann Arbor). *Dissertation Abstracts International,* (University Microfilms No. 76-24,089)

Greer, R. N., & Blank, S. (1977). Cognitive style, conceptual tempo and problem solving: Modification through programmed instruction. *American Educational Research Journal, 14*(3), 295–315.

Guilford, J. P. (1956). The structure of intellect. *Psychological Bulletin, 53,* 267–293.

Harlow, H. F. (1949). The formation of learning sets. *Psychological Review, 56,* 51–65.

Harrison, A., & Nadelman, L. (1972). Conceptual tempo and inhibition of movement in black preschool children. *Child Development, 43,* 657–658.

Heber, R., Garber, H., Harrington, S., Hoffman, C., & Falendar, C. (1972). *Rehabilitation of families at risk for mental retardation.* Progress report. Madison: University of Wisconsin, Waisman Center.

Hetherington, E.M., & McIntyre, C. W. (1975). Developmental psychology. *Annual Review of Psychology, 26,* 97–136.

Holtzman, H. W., Diaz–Guerrero, R., & Swartz, S. D. (1975). *Personality development in two cultures.* Austin: University of Texas Press.

Horn, T. D. (Ed.). (1970). *Reading for the disadvantaged: Problems of linguistically different learners.* New York: Harcourt, Brace, & World.

Hsi, V., & Lim, V. (1977). *A summary of selected research studies on cognitive and perceptual variables.* (Research and Evaluation Working Papers, No. 1). Unpublished manuscript, Asian American Center, Berkeley, CA.

Husen, T. (1951). *Talent and environment.* Stockholm: Almqvist & Wiksell.

Jackson, E., & Cosca, C. (1973). *U.S. Commission on Civil Rights. Report V. Teachers and students.* Washington, DC: Superintendent of Public Documents.

Kagan, J. (1965). Reflection-impulsivity and reading ability in primary grade children. *Child Development, 36,* 609–628.

Kagan, J., Moss, H. A., & Sigel, I. E. (1960). Conceptual style and the use of affect labels. *Merrill–Palmer Quarterly, 6,* 261–278.

Kagan, J., Moss, H. A., & Sigel, I. E. (1963). The psychological significance of styles of conceptualization. *Monographs of the Society for Research in Child Development, 28*(4), 73–112.

Kagan, J., Pearson, L., & Welch, L. (1966). Modification of an impulsive tempo. *Journal of Educational Psychology, 57,* 359–365.

Kagan, J., Rosman, B. L., Day, D., Albert, J., & Phillips, W. (1964). Information processing in the child: Significance of analytic and reflective attitudes. *Psychological Monographs, 78*(1, Whole No. 578).

Kagan, S., & Buriel, R. (1977). Field dependence–independence and Mexican–American culture and education. In J. L. Martinez (Ed.), *Chicano psychology.* New York: Academic Press.

Kagan, S., & Zahn, G. L. (1975). Field dependence and the school achievement gap between Anglo–American and Mexican–American children. *Journal of Educational Psychology, 67,* 643–650.

Kerlinger, F. N., & Pedhazur, E. J. (1973). *Multiple regression in behavioral research.* New York: Holt, Rinehart, & Winston.

Laosa, L. M. (1977). Cognitive styles and learning strategies research: Some of the areas in which psychology can contribute to personalized instruction in multicultural education. *Journal of Teacher Education, 18,* 26–30.

Leifer, A. (1972). Ethnic patterns in cognitive tasks (Doctoral dissertation, Yeshiva University). *Dissertation Abstracts International, 72 23,* 1270–1271.

Lesser, G. S., Fifer, G., & Clark, B. H. (1965). *Mental abilities of children from different social-class and cultural groups.* Chicago: University of Chicago Press.

Liedtke, W. W., & Nelson, N. D. (1968). Concept formation and bilingualism. *Alberta Journal of Educational Research, 14*(4), 225-232.

Marascuilo, L. M., & Levin J. (1978). *Notes on multivariate techniques for behavioral research.* Unpublished manuscript, University of California, Berkeley.

Massari, D. J., & Mansfield, R. S. (1973). Field dependence and outer-directedness in the problem solving of retardates and normal children. *Child Development, 44,* 346–350.

Merselstein, E. (1969). *Genetic epistemology and the objectives of the center for Piagetian studies.* Los Angeles: American Educational Research Association.

Messer, S. B. (1976). Reflection-impulsivity: A review. *Psychological Bulletin, 83,* 1026–1052.

Messick, S. (1976). Personality consistencies in cognition and creativity. In S. Merrick (Ed.), *Individuality in learning.* San Francisco: Jossey–Bass.

Michel, J. (1971). *Teaching Spanish reading to the Spanish-dominant child.* (ERIC Document Reproduction Service No. ED 083 866).

Ogbu, J. U. (1974). *The next generation.* New York: Academic Press.

Pascual–Leone, J. (1970). A mathematical model for the transition rule in Piaget's developmental stages. *Acta Psychologica, 32,* 301–345.

Ramírez, M., & Castañeda, A. (1974). Cultural democracy, bicognitive development, and education. New York: Academic Press.

Ramírez, M., Castañeda, A., & Herold, P. L. (1974). The relationship of acculturation to cognitive style among Mexican Americans. *Journal of Cross-Cultural Psychology, 5,* 425–433.

Ramírez, M., Herold, P. L., & Castañeda, A. (1975). *Field sensitivity and field dependence in children, No. 4.* In New approaches to bilingual, bicultural education (Rev. ed.). Austin, TX: Dissemination and assessment center for Bilingual Education.

Ramírez, M., & Price–Williams, D. R. (1974). Cognitive styles of children of three ethnic groups in the United States. *Journal of Cross-Cultural Psychology, 5,* 212–219.

Reiss, E. W. (1972). The influence of race and social class upon the measurement of intelligence, cognitive style, and direct learning ability (Doctoral dissertation, Ohio State University). *Dissertation Abstracts International, 72 27,* 1770–1771.

Rogers, R. S., & Wright, E. N. (1969). *The school achievement of kindergarten pupils for whom English is a second language: A longitudinal study using data from the Study of Achievement.* Toronto Board of Education, Research Department. (ERIC Document Reproduction Service No. ED 066 220)

Ruble, D. N., & Nakamura, C. Y. (1972). Task orientation versus social orientation in young children and their attention to relevant social cues. *Child Development, 43,* 471–480.

Saarni, C. I. (1973). Piagetian operations and field independence as factors in children's problem-solving performance. *Child Development, 44,* 338–345.

Sanders, M., Scholz, J. P., & Kagan, S. (1976). Three social motives and field-independence–dependence in Anglo–American and Mexican–American children. *Journal of Cross-Cultural Psychology, 7*(4), 451–462.

Sigel, I. E. (1965, March). *Styles of categorization in elementary school children: The role of sex differences and anxiety level.* Paper presented at the meeting of the Society for Research in Child Development, Minneapolis.

Sigel, I. E. (1967). *Sigel Conceptual Styles Test.* Princeton, NJ: Educational Testing Service.

Sigel, I. E., & Coop, R. H. (1974). Cognitive style and classroom practice. In R. H. Coop & K. White (Eds.), *Psychological concepts in the classroom.* New York: Harper & Row.

Sitkei, E. G. (1966). *Comparative structure on intellect in middle- and lower class four-year-old children of two ethnic groups* (Doctoral dissertation, University of Southern California). (University Microfilms Order #67–5310)

Stewart, L. J., Dole, A. A., & Yeuell, Y. H. (1967). Cultural differences in abilities during high school. *American Education Research Journal, 4.*

Stokes, C. A. (1970). *Some effects of schooling, age, race, and socioeconomic status on the cognitive development of primary school boys* (Doctoral dissertation, University of Michigan). (University Microfilms Order #71-4742)

Tryon, R. C., & Bailey, D. E. (1970). *Cluster analysis.* New York: McGraw–Hill.

Ulibarri, D. M. (1974). Technical Manual: Multilingual Assessment Scale. Multilingual Assessment Project: Stockton Unified Schools, Stockton, CA.

Wallach, M. A. (1963). Research on children's thinking. In National Society for the Study of Education, 62nd yearbook, *Child psychology.* Chicago: University of Chicago Press.

Ward, W. C. (1968). Reflection-impulsivity in kindergarten children. *Child Development, 39,* 867–874.

Werner, E. E., Simonian, K., & Smith, R. S. (1968). Ethnic and socioeconomic status differences in abilities and achievement among preschool and school-age children in Hawaii. *Journal of Social Psychology, 75.*

Witkin, H. A. (1950). Individual differences in ease of perception of embedded figures. *Journal of Personality, 19,* 1-15.

Witkin, H. A., & Berry, J. W. (1975). Psychological differentiation in cross-cultural perspective. *Journal of Cross-Cultural Psychology, 6*(1), 4–87.

Witkin, H. A., Dyk, R., Paterson, H. F., Goodenough, D. R., & Karp, S. A. (1974). *Psychological differentiation.* Potomac, MD: Lawrence Erlbaum Associates. (Originally published, New York: Wiley, 1962)

Witkin, H. A., & Goodenough, D. R. (1976). Field independence and interpersonal behavior. *Psychological Bulletin, 84*(4), 661–689.

Witkin, H. A., & Goodenough, D. R. (1977, December). *Field dependence revisited* (Research Bulletin 71–16). Princeton, NJ: Educational Testing Service.

Witkin, H. A., Lewis, H. H., Hertzman, M., Machover, K., Meissner, P., & Wapner, S. (1954). *Personality through perception.* New York: Harper.

Witkin, H. A., Oltman, P. K., Raskin, E., & Karp, S. (1971). *A manual for the Embedded Figures Test.* Palo Alto, CA: Consulting Psychologists.

12 Comprehension Monitoring: Developmental and Educational Issues

Ellen M. Markman
Stanford University

All of us know the frustration that builds when we find nonsequiturs in material we need to learn, when we discover mutually incompatible assumptions in a theory we are trying to comprehend, or when we spot inconsistent premises in an argument we are struggling to follow. It becomes obvious that something is wrong, either with the material itself, or with our own comprehension of it. Detection of problems such as these reflects an essential component of critical academic reasoning. In this chapter, I consider what processes are involved in the detection of such inconsistencies or nonsequiturs, and what the developmental course of such abilities might be. I speculate about how educators can promote children's ability to monitor their comprehension in this way. The general framework I rely on has been reported more fully in Markman (1981). Also because several recent papers have provided extensive, up-to-date summaries of the literature in comprehension monitoring (Baker & Brown, 1980; Flavell, 1981), I do not attempt to review the empirical studies in detail, except when they bear on the particular issues addressed in this chapter.

Comprehension comes in many varieties. Understanding a word differs from understanding a movie, a graph, or a poem, which in turn differ from each other. There are many degrees as well as types of understanding. One can understand a novel well enough to read for pleasure but not nearly well enough to write a literary review. These endless variations in comprehension complicate the problem of deciding whether or not one has understood. Judgments about comprehension are complex, subtle, and open to error. What follows are some ideas about how to structure this problem and some hypotheses about what children must acquire to monitor their comprehension effectively. Though I focus on detection of inconsistencies, many of the issues apply to other types of comprehension problems as well (see Markman, 1981).

REQUIREMENTS FOR DETECTING INCONSISTENCIES

Constructive and Inferential Processing

Some types of comprehension failure can be discovered by processing small segments of material. An unfamiliar word can often be detected even in complete isolation from the remainder of a passage. One can also notice whether a single isolated sentence is confusing, ungrammatical, or false. In contrast, understanding an argument, a story, or expository prose requires more than understanding the individual words or sentences. To notice problems in comprehension thus depends on some difficulty discovered in integrating or relating one part of a passage to another. This requires inferential or constructive processing—the transforming, elaborating, expanding of incoming information. The difficulty of detecting an inconsistency should vary with the amount of processing required. This argument can, of course, be extended to cover a variety of comprehension problems, not just inconsistencies. Several studies with young children have demonstrated that, as information-processing demands decrease, children become better able to notice problems in their comprehension (Flavell, Speer, Green, & August, 1981; Markman, 1977; Patterson, O'Brien, Kister, Carter, & Kotsonis, 1981). To take one example, Patterson et al. had children participate as listeners in a referential communication situation. They listened as someone described a card that they were to select from a number of distractors. Patterson et al. varied the number of dimensions in which the cards could vary, reasoning that the processing demands would increase with the complexity of the stimulus array. In line with their predictions, they found that children were better able to judge the adequacy of the message for the simpler stimulus arrays.

In a series of studies (Markman, 1979), I investigated how inferential processing requirements affect children's awareness of their own comprehension failure when presented with inconsistent information. In these studies, children listened to essays that contained either explicit or implicit contradictions. Third-through sixth-grade children were enlisted as consultants to help the experimenter find problems in the essays and offer suggestions for how the essays could be improved. They then listened either to essays that contained explicit contradictions or to essays in which the contradictions were only implicit, requiring inferential processing to detect. Here is an example of the two versions of an essay about ants. The underlined portions varied with condition but the first half of the essay was identical in both conditions.

Ants: Explicit Condition.   There are some things that almost all ants have in common. For example, they are all amazingly strong and can carry objects many times their own weight. Sometimes they go very, very far from their nest to find food. They go so far away that they cannot remember how to go home. So to help them find their way home, ants have a special way of leaving an invisible trail. *Everywhere they go they put out a special chemical from their bodies. They cannot see this chemical but it has a special odor. An ant must have a nose in order to smell this chemical odor. Another thing about ants is they do not have a nose. Ants cannot smell this odor. Ants can always find their way home by smelling for this odor to follow the trail.*

Ants: Implicit condition.   Everywhere they go they put out an invisible chemical from their body. This chemical has a special odor. Another thing about ants is they do not have a nose. Ants never get lost.

After children listened to an essay (which was read to them twice), a series of probe questions was asked until the child indicated that he or she had noticed a problem. The first questions were very general: "That's it. That's the information about ants. What do you think? Do you have any questions?" After the general questions, the child's memory for the essay was tested and then, if the child still had not noticed the problem, he or she was asked about the very specific information needed to identify the inconsistencies.

The first study demonstrated that implicit contradictions were considerably more difficult for children to detect. In fact, 96% of the children failed to notice the problem until their memory for the essay was tested, and the majority of the children required very specific probing before showing any signs of awareness.

What was more surprising about the findings was that even the 12-year olds judged as comprehensible a sizable proportion of the essays with the obvious inconsistencies.

Several possible alternative explanations for these findings were ruled out by the data. One possibility was that children did not remember the information in the essays. Yet their probed recall of the essays was excellent. The vast majority (86%) of the essays were recalled without any errors or omissions.

Another possible explanation for the poor performance of the children in the implicit condition is that they lacked the logical capacity to draw the inferences. However, children's responses to the final questions revealed that they were, in fact, capable of drawing the inferences when each one was posed by the experimenter, though they were not spontaneously doing so. Here is a protocol from one third grader who, when probed, was able to draw the relevant inference about ants.

> *Child:* They don't have a nose. They never get lost. They go far from their nest.
> *Experimenter:* How do they get back?

Child: They leave an invisible path.
Experimenter: What kind of path?
Child: It has an odor.
Experimenter: Did everything make sense?
Child: Yes.
Experimenter: What do you need in order to smell.
Child: A nose.
Experimenter: Do ants have noses.
Child: No.
Experimenter: Can ants smell?
Child: Yes.
Experimenter: How do ants smell without a nose?
Child: That's a tough one.

A third possible explanation is that the children may have noticed the problem but made some sort of assumptions to resolve the contradiction. If so, then there should be some evidence of intrusion of these assumptions into the children's recall of the essay. However, almost no such evidence was found to support this hypothesis. Though I do not believe that this was happening in this particular study, it is an important issue to which I return shortly.

Finally, one last alternative explanation considered was that the demand characteristics of the task prevented children from admitting that they noticed a problem. Children were not generally reluctant however to criticize the essays or to ask questions. They did so quite often, even though they failed to mention the inconsistencies.

In the second study reported in Markman (1979), the essays were written so that the two incompatible propositions would be contiguous. In one condition, children were asked to repeat the two sentences together with the idea that this would establish the contiguity of the sentences in working memory and thus increase the chances that their incompatibility would be noticed. Because inferences are still required to notice implicit contradictions, the mere contiguity of the sentences was not expected to be very beneficial. In fact, it was not. Both third and sixth graders still failed to notice the implicit inconsistencies. The juxtaposition of the explicit contradictory information did seem to help the older children who now noticed the problems. However, the third graders repeated out loud the explicitly contradictory material and still failed to notice the problem. Although the sentences were activated in working memory, the children failed to compare them and notice their inconsistency. Flavell et al. (1981) also have found that when children repeated problematic instructions they did not notice any more of the problems.

The third study was designed to better define the limits of the children's spontaneous abilities. Without being taught any new skills or strategies, how capable are children of finding these problems? To find out, we warned children that there was a problem. When challenged to find a problem, children should be motivated to scrutinize the material. Under these circumstances sixth graders performed extremely well. They were just as able to find the implicit as the explicit problems, revealing that they are quite capable of carrying out the needed inferential processing. In contrast, third graders still failed to find many of the problems.

Taken together, these studies reveal that to notice inconsistencies, children must activate representations of both sentences in working memory. This becomes more difficult as other material intervenes. Establishing contiguity of the sentences in memory is not sufficient; the sentences must also be compared. To notice implicit contradictions, one must draw the relevant inferences as well.

If developmental or individual differences in comprehension monitoring are due to constructive processing, there should be evidence that the more successful children are relying on the context to generate expectations about subsequent material. A recent study provides some evidence for this hypothesis. Mosenthal (1979) presented third and sixth graders with stories that contained inconsistencies. He then examined children's recall to determine how they attempted to resolve the problems. Though he isolated several different strategies, there was one finding that is especially relevant here. He examined those parts of the information children tended to distort the most. Older children tended to distort new information to make it more consistent with prior information they had received. I believe that this suggests children were using prior context to generate expectations that guided their subsequent processing of the text. In contrast, younger children tended to misremember the old information as being consistent with the new. It makes sense that the most recent information would dominate children's thinking more if they are not being constrained as much by prior context.

STANDARDS FOR JUDGING COMPREHENSION

Skilled judgment of one's comprehension requires flexibility in processing. One must accommodate to the various types of materials and goals of understanding. Whether or not one has understood something, then, is not a clear-cut question but varies with the standard of evaluation. Children may have more difficulty selecting appropriate standards. In particular, they may not as readily consider consistency as a standard for evaluating their comprehension. Children may not find the logical or linguistic structure of a passage as salient as its truth or correspondence with empirical reality (Markman, 1976, 1978; Miller & Lips, 1973; Osherson & Markman, 1975). Some of the results from Study 3 of Markman (1979) suggest that, in monitoring their comprehension, young children tend to evaluate individual sentences rather than the consistency of a passage. In that study, children were warned that there was a problem in the passage, yet third graders still missed many of the contradictions. Warning these children did have an effect, however. Children who expected to find a problem questioned the truth of (nonproblematic) statements more often than children without such expectations. Perhaps they failed to find the two sentences that were incompatible because they were evaluating single sentences instead.

Poor readers may also tend to evaluate single sentences as opposed to the consistency of a passage (Garner, 1980,1981). In Garner (1980), junior high school children, all of whom were proficient decoders were classified as either good or poor comprehenders. The good comprehenders were more likely to notice the inconsistencies that had been built into the material. Fifth- and sixth-grade children attending a reading clinic participated in the second study (Garner, 1980). All children who participated scored at least at grade level for their ability to decode words but evidenced problems in reading comprehension. Passages could contain one or two types of problems: either an unfamiliar vocabulary word or two sentences that were inconsistent. These children with reading problems were quite sensitive to the difficulty of comprehending sentences with unfamiliar words and rated those passages as more difficult to understand. However, they rated inconsistent and consistent passages as equally comprehensible, suggesting that they were insensitive to the disruptive effects of the inconsistencies on their comprehension.

With L. Gorin, I investigated whether 8- and 10-year-old children are capable of adjusting their standards of evaluation (Markman & Gorin, 1981). We addressed this question by determining whether or not children could benefit from specific instructions about what type of problem to expect. In this study, children listened to essays, some of which contained either false statements or inconsistencies, and were asked to indicate which essays had problems. One group of children was told to expect problems in some of the essays, but was given no information about what the problems would be like. A second group was told that some of the essays contained statements that were not true and was given some examples of the type of problem to expect. A third group was told instead that some of the essays contained inconsistencies and was given examples to illustrate that type of problem.

As mentioned earlier, children in the Markman (1979) study tended to question the truth of nonproblematic statements while missing inconsistencies in the passage. Similarly, the children in the present study, but especially the 8-year-olds, questioned the truth of nonproblematic statements. This was particularly likely to occur when children were set to find falsehoods. Yet, children almost never spuriously questioned the consistency of an essay, even when set to find inconsistencies.

The main findings from Markman and Gorin (1981) were that the instructions did have an effect on children's ability to find the problems. Children found few of the problems when they were not given explicit information about what to expect. Specific information about the problems helped children detect more of them. Moreover, the relative order of finding falsehoods or inconsistencies shifted as a function of the type of problem children were set to find. They found relatively more inconsistencies than falsehoods when set to find inconsistencies, whereas this pattern reserved somewhat for children set to find falsehoods. When given examples of what types of problems to look for, children are capable of adjusting their standard of evaluation.

Measures of Metacomprehension

Most of the studies reported previously used some type of self-report of a problem as a measure of problem detection. In studies of referential communication (Bearison & Levy, 1977; Ironsmith & Whitehurst, 1978; Patterson, Cosgrove, & O'Brien, 1980) or of following instructions (Flavell et al., 1981) there is evidence that, although children report that they see nothing wrong with a message, this is belied by their nonverbal behavior. In terms of hesitations, puzzled facial expressions, eye contact, or some other nonverbal indication, children seem to have noticed the problem; yet in terms of self report, they judge the message to be adequate or their comprehension to be complete. The least interesting interpretation of this discrepancy in measures is that measures of self-report are vulnerable to demand characteristics of the situation. Children hesitate to question or criticize or admit ignorance. This is, of course, a serious methodological concern and cannot be dismissed lightly. Yet, I believe there is enough evidence to suggest that it is by no means the entire explanation. As I mentioned earlier, children are far more willing to criticize and question than their failure to find the relevant problems would indicate (Markman, 1979). Flavell et al. (who had a child deliver the messages) report a similar finding. Moreover, in several studies, self-report took the form of button pressing (Markman & Gorin, 1981), replaying a tape recorder (Flavell et al., 1981), or filling out a rating scale (Garner, 1981), and not just announcing to an adult that their message was flawed. Before I consider some of the interesting possible explanations for this discrepancy in measures, let me report a recent study designed to determine whether such discrepancies are found for older children's judgments of inconsistencies.

Building on a procedure used by Harris, Kruithof, Terwogt, and Visser (1981), C. Capelli and I had third and sixth graders read a set of stories, some of which contained anomalous sentences (Capelli & Markman, 1982). Each story had two alternative titles. With one title, all the sentences would make sense. With the other title, one of the sentences became anomalous. Here is an example of one of the stories. The underlined sentences fit well with the first but not with the second title.

Title 1: Playing the Piano
Title 2: Playing a Record

Janet decides to play some music.

She looks through all the songs and picks her favorite.

It is a song called "As Time Goes By."

"I haven't played this one in a long time," she says to herself.

"She plays it quietly so that she won't disturb her family.

<u>She is out of practice, so it sounds funny sometimes.</u>

Janet likes to sing along with the music.

She knows some of the words and she hums the rest.

The last verse of the song is the part she likes best.

After that song is finished, she plays another.

Children read the stories under one of two conditions. In the first condition, children were timed as they read each sentence and were told that when they completed the story they would be asked if there were any sentences that did not make any sense and if so which ones. In the second condition, children were timed as they read each sentence but were told to report immediately any sentence that did not make any sense.

The purpose of the two conditions was to test for one possible explanation for the discrepancies in explicit judgments versus nonverbal measures. Most of the time, verbal reports or other explicit judgments were requested at the completion of an entire passage or message, whereas the nonverbal measures were taken as children processed the material. Perhaps, children initially have some fleeting sense of a problem, but, by the time they are questioned, they have forgotten its existence. However, the results from this study lend only a little support to that hypothesis. There was a slight trend of the younger children to report more problems when they had to judge each sentence, but it was only marginally significant.

As in previous studies, children, especially the third graders, often failed to report that they did not comprehend the anomalous stories. Yet, they took significantly longer to read anomalous sentences than appropriate ones, even when they claimed not to have noticed a problem. It was of particular interest that the rate of reading interacted with age. Older children showed a much more dramatic drop in their reading rate than did the younger children.

One possible explanation for these findings is that younger children are less sensitive to whatever internal signs of incomprehension are being generated (Flavell, 1981; Harris et al., 1981). Perhaps older children interpret pauses or rate changes in their reading as an indication of some breakdown in processing and thus become alerted to a problem, whereas younger children are less sensitive to such cues. Once alerted to a problem, older children spend more time rereading, puzzling over it, or somehow trying to make sense of the material.

Another related possibility is that younger children may set a higher criterion for attending to possible failures to comprehend. Young children who are in general less knowledgeable, less skilled than others, may as a consequence be more often confused. To avoid having to question interminably, they may have a higher threshold for reporting a problem.

Finally, it is possible that though younger children noticed the problem, they may have somehow thought they resolved it and no longer judged anything problematic with the passage.

Note that these latter hypotheses suggest a second source for children's less-effective comprehension monitoring. It is not only necessary that children execute the appropriate mental processing to notice a problem, as was argued earlier, but once a problem is detected at some level, children must cope with it in some appropriate way. This leads to another set of developmental issues: how children learn what counts as legitimate solutions to detected problems.

Deciding When a Problem Warrants Attention. At first, it might seem that whenever it is necessary to draw an inference to make sense of material, we would have some warning of a potential problem in comprehension. However, most routine comprehension requires continual inferences to bridge gaps, concretize vague information, find references for expressions of definite reference, etc. At one extreme, the context is so compelling that we barely recognize an inference has been made; it is a barely perceptible inferencial step from "Three turtles rested on a floating log and a fish swam beneath them" to "Three turtles rested on a floating log and a fish swam beneath it" (Bransford, Barclay, & Franks, 1972). The spatial context is so compelling and constrains our interpretations so tightly that we quite readily understand that "it" refers to the log. Another simple imperceptible inference occurs in definite reference. For example, if someone asks "Please pass the salt," usually the context is so compelling and the purpose of the utterance so clear that we do not have to figure out which salt or where to pass it. Given that these inferences are so highly constrained, occur in nearly all comprehension, and are most likely so automatic that we are hardly aware of making them, it is not often that their existence would signal a problem in comprehension. It is possible, however, that, at least occasionally, we might momentarily suspect a problem but suspend concern as soon as the inference resolves it.

At the other extreme, the context provides so little information that we have no arbitrary way of settling on an interpretation. In such cases, we would have to guess wildly if we tried to solve the problem without asking for clarification.

Many cases lie somewhere in between these two extremes. There are undoubtedly continua here in terms of whether or not we notice any ambiguity, inconsistency, or obscurity, and if noticed, whether we judge it severe enough to warrant concern about our comprehension. In these cases, we must implicitly judge how well the context constrains the interpretation and how legitimate the inferences are. Because there is no clear boundary for an appropriate inference, there are likely to be many developmental and individual differences in these judgments, and they are likely to depend on one's interest and motivation, the type of problem, the importance of complete understanding, what degree of error can be allowed, and so on.

What to Do Once a Problem I Detected.   Given that a problem is noticed, what should one do? One possibility is to search for an immediate clarification or solution. This is probably an inefficient option in many ongoing conversations. Using it too often could become tedious and disruptive. Most likely, it would be efficient only in relatively severe problems that would otherwise block further attempts at comprehension.

One could wait hoping that subsequent information would resolve the problem. This is an option that I am sure we often use. For example, if someone tells you, "I believe the director missed an opportunity in the film I saw last night," rather than immediately asking "which director?," "which film?,""what opportunity?," you might wait and listen assuming the speaker would provide that information. This strategy requires that the listener maintain the problem in mind, for if it is not eventually clarified, the listener will then need to ask for more information.

One could also tentatively offer a resolution to the problem, marking the resolution as tentative and leaving open the possibility of revision. Again this must be a common strategy and it also entails a memory load of recalling the tentative hypothesis. If a subsequent context is inconsistent with the tentative solution and one has forgotten which information was only assumed and which was given, it will make it more difficult to revise the hypothesis in accord with the later information.

Judgments About Inferences

One way then that we make decisions about whether our inferences or assumptions are correct is to see how useful an inference turns out to be in light of subsequent information. We make assumptions to solve problems, hoping that later information will either support or refute them. To use this strategy, one must notice the problem, draw the relevant inference, mark it as tentative, hold it in working store, check it against incoming information, and revise it as needed. For children in particular, this procedure could be cognitively taxing and prone to a number of sources of error.

This process requires that judgments be made about the inferences or assumptions. These are judgments about whether or not the context sufficiently constrains the inference or whether the assumptions are unwarranted or ad hoc. This is analogous to judgments of elegance and parsimony in science. These are not simple dichotomous decisions about an inference but entail instead a whole range of possible variations in the effectiveness, appropriateness, and ingenuity of the inference.

Sensitivity to such nuances is likely to have a protracted development. At present, however, there are very few developmental studies of these issues. Young children have been found to be less tolerant than older children of "lack of closure," that is, they are more likely to draw premature unwarranted inferences, especially for difficult material (Wollman, Eylon, & Lawson, 1979). Of somewhat more direct interest, Geoffrey (1979) found children to be poor judges of the quality of explanations. In this study, fifth- and seventh-grade children listened to short passages containing problems that can be viewed as violations of scripts. For example, one was a short story about a child going into a store to buy a pair of shoes. The child enters the store, sits down, and is waited on by a saleswoman. After selecting a pair of shoes, the child took them to a dressing room, closed the curtain, and tried them on. The violation here is that people ordinarily do not try on shoes behind closed curtains in a dressing room. Problems such as these were pointed out to the children, if they had not already noticed them on their own. Then several ways of explaining the violations were posed for the children who were to rate them for how well they solved the problems. There were four types of explanation as follows:

1. Adequate explanations that provided a possible causal explanation for the violations. In the case of the story about shoes, children were told that the child wanted shoes to go with the dress she had, and only the dressing room had a full-length mirror in which she could see them together.

2. Repetitions that simply paraphrased the violations without adding any new information.

3. Pseudoexplanations that mentioned some aspect of the violation and added new information but did not explain why the violation had occurred. In the case of the passage about shoes, the pseudoexplanation was that "you have to be able to tell if things are too big or too small. It is important to try things on to see if they fit."

4. Irrelevant explanations that contained new information but bore no relation to the violation. For example, "Some people have trouble picking out something to buy when they are shopping. Either they don't like anything they see, or they can't decide which thing to buy."

Which explanations were judged best interreacted with age. At fifth grade, children judged the repetition explanation as being significantly worse than the three other types of explanations. However, they made no differentiation between adequate, pseudo, or irrelevant explanations. Apparently, if any new information was provided, children judged the explanations as equally good regardless of how well the information addressed the problem. In contrast, seventh graders judged the adequate explanations as superior to the other three that were judged equally inadequate. These findings suggest that developmental changes in the ability to judge the quality of explanations might play an important role in children's comprehension judgments.

INDIVIDUAL DIFFERENCES

Though most of this chapter has been framed in terms of developmental differences, I believe very similar points can be made about individual differences. Some people are more likely than others to draw appropriate inferences, engage in constructive processing, appreciate the quality of potential explanations, etc. There is some evidence for individual differences in inference types in a recent paper by Mosenthal and Na (1980). Mosenthal and Na interpret their findings in terms of an analysis of children's perception of social situations. Because I interpret their findings rather differently, one should check their paper for an alternative explanation. The basic findings were that there are consistent differences in the way children process information, whether this occurs while they are answering questions from teachers who are conducting lessons in reading groups or when they are answering written questions on the texts they have read. Mosenthal and Na first classified children according to the types of answers they gave in response to oral questions by the teachers and then found that children gave rather similar responses in answering written questions.

The classification based on oral responses was as follows: Some children tended to be largely imitative. They often answered questions by repeating or paraphrasing what the teacher or text said, rather than elaborating or drawing inferences from the text. Older children were classified as noncontingent responders. They provided new information but it did not make reference to the old information from the teacher's utterance. An example given was that in response to a question about what the dog wanted most in this story, a child responsed, "I have to go to the bathroom." Another example given was that in response to "Can anyone tell me who the most important person in the book (about George Washington) was?," a child answered, "President Lincoln was more important than George Washington." I interpret these responses as suggesting the child was distracted, failed to pay attention, or misunderstood the questions. It is important to note that in order to be classified as a noncontingent responder (or any other category), children had to give a minimum of 47% such responses over a 10-week period. Thus, it can be a fairly consistent response style. Contingent responders were children who provided information relevant to the teacher's question, but rather than limiting themselves to imitations or paraphrases, they elaborated or expanded on the information, sometimes introducing another related topic for discussion.

Apparently, at least in classroom situations, children adopt fairly consistent styles of processing information. Some appear to be inattentive, finding it difficult to follow material. Others attend to the material but in a rigid way, sticking closely to the superficial form of the information. Others seem to process more completely, drawing inferences and elaborating the information presented. In light of the arguments presented in this chapter it is hard to imagine that the inattentive or rigid processors are monitoring their comprehension or comprehending the material nearly as well as the other children. If consistent response styles can be reliably diagnosed, then perhaps remedial training could be applied.

I have already mentioned the work of Garner who found that poor readers are less likely to spot inconsistencies than good readers, apparently because of their tendency to process material in a more piecemeal fashion. Though more empirical work on this question is needed, I am confident that metacomprehension must be an essential part of what makes a good reader. However, poor readers are not a homogeneous group, and I would be hesitant about advocating the same type of remediation for all children with reading difficulties. To take some more obvious cases, consider the problem faced by good decoders with poor comprehension monitoring abilities. Here, one would suggest a variety of techniques to promote cognitive monitoring abilities, a point to which I return shortly. But consider the poor decoders who have good comprehension monitoring abilities. First, their ability to monitor their comprehension will most likely be obscured when they read. It would only be with some type of oral comprehension test that we could discover that these children are sensitive to nonsequiturs, that they notice inconsistencies, etc. If the children are struggling to decode words and as a consequence reading at a very slow pace, it may be impossible for them to extract the meaning from a passage, let alone check their comprehension in any but the most crude way (see Markman, 1981). What the poor decoders lack, in part, is some coherent represenation of the meaning of the passage. Instead, they have a choppy segmented version. These children might need to be encouraged to repeat and reread a passage until they achieve a fluent rendition. To suggest that they self-check, paraphrase, summarize, or whatever, while they are struggling with the prose, might slow them down and actually interfere with their ability to decode the passage. Perhaps, for these children, comprehension monitoring should be trained using oral not written prose. These may not always be comparable as Schallert and Kleiman (1979) have pointed out, but for some children, there may be little alternative until their ability to decode improves. Empirical work is needed on this issue before we can recommend what types of training will be more beneficial for individual children.

HOW TO PROMOTE COMPREHENSION MONITORING

1. One of the arguments that ran throughout this chapter was that deliberate attempts to monitor one's comprehension may not always be a necessary or even an effective way to achieve that goal. Instead information about one's comprehension may often come as a by-product of active attempts to comprehend. Therefore, practice at drawing inferences and formulating expectations should

benefit comprehension monitoring. When we find that we are too rigidly bound to the superficial form of a passage and find ourselves unable to paraphrase or move beyond the material, then we have important information about the limits of our comprehension. Further, it is the failure to relate to two parts of a passage or the violations of expectations we have formulated that inform us that we have failed to comprehend.

Educators should provide children with a variety of well-organized, tightly structured material. Even quite young children can understand simple logical, causal and temporal relations (Gelman, 1978). Yet, in a casual examination of textbooks written for young children, I found a scarcity of clearly structured material. Most of the paragraphs had no inherent structure and consisted, instead, of descriptive sentences. The sentences could have been randomly reordered without disrupting comprehension. Children's material may have been deliberately written in this way under the assumption that children could not understand more complex material. However, oversimplification may work to children's disadvantage.

Children could be asked to predict what will happen next in a story or how a sentence will be completed. They could be asked to infer the order of events in a causal sequence, or to guess a cause given an effect. They could be asked to predict the actions of a character or to infer his motives. This type of practice can involve a wide variety of inferences and hypotheses that can be calibrated to the appropriate level. Collins and Smith (in press) suggest that when children are encouraged to formulate such hypotheses teachers should take great care to reward their attempts, perhaps by pointing out all the evidence that is consistent with their hypotheses.

2. Children could be provided with a set of general questions to ask themselves to enable them to monitor other comprehension. They could be trained to ask "Do I understand?," "What is the main point?," "What else do I know that is related?" This is the suggestion made by Baker and Brown (1980). Using such a self-testing method of training, Brown, Campione, and Barclay (1979) have had remarkable success with educable retarded children. Yet there are aspects of this procedure that warrant further investigation. We do not yet know the locus of the effect of the training, exactly how it works, nor how effective it will be with normal children. Second, it may be that practice in more specific questions, as those I suggested earlier, could be more beneficial than very general questions. Children may need more guidance as to how to answer these general questions. Third, I do not believe that I am in any literal sense asking myself "Do I understand?" as I read or listen to material. I believe instead that I am forced to notice my comprehension failure, when I become tense or frustrated, when a feeling of anticipation is thwarted, when I sense either lack of closure or mild surprise due to an unexpected violation of an expectation. Correspondingly, I feel pleased or satisfied by a correct prediction or verification of hypotheses I have. My guess is that it is by the type of inferential constructive processing

I described earlier that much information about comprehension is obtained, rather than by more explicit self-questioning about one's own comprehension. See Markman (1981) for a fuller account of this argument. Of course, even if my intuitions about myself and other adults are correct, that does not necessarily bear on what an appropriate training method would be. For example, adults often skim material and rarely sound out a new word; yet I certainly would not recommend that this is how we teach beginning readers to read. Again, empirical work is needed to address these issues.

3. Children should be given practice at making judgments about and evaluations of inferences and explanation. They could be provided with several explanations and asked to judge which is best. Or they could be asked to explain why an inference follows, why some solutions are ingenious and others far-fetched.

4. Comprehension monitoring should be enhanced by challenging children to find problems in text. Children would find this task enjoyable and it should promote the requisite skills.

5. Collins and Smith suggest that teachers should model some of the comprehension monitoring skills, that they should formulate both correct and incorrect hypotheses and demonstrate how the evidence helps them decide whether they are right or wrong. A study by Sonnenschein and Whitehurst (1980) suggests that, though modeling may be effective, children's attributions about the model may have important consequences on how they interpret errors that the model makes. Sonnenschein and Whitehurst had both adults and children model appropriate messages in a referential communication situation. They found that children observers tended to imitate both models and as a consequence produced more adequate messages than controls. They also had adults and peers model poor messages. The rationale for this was that, as a child listens to a poor message, he or she would sense his or her own confusion, realize what was inadequate about the message, and thus counterimitate it. In fact, this prediction was born out for the peer model. But it backfired for the adult model. Children hearing poor messages from adults produced more inadequate messages than controls. A possible interpretation of this finding is that, though children attribute their poor understanding of the message to problems with the message when the speaker is a child, they attribute it to their own deficiencies when the speaker is an adult. To extrapolate these results to Smith and Collins' suggestion, one should think carefully before having adults deliberately formulate erroneous hypotheses. If such modeling is done, children must be made to understand the source of the error, otherwise they may tend to formulate careless, unconstrained hypotheses themselves.

In conclusion, children, even preadolescents, can be surprisingly oblivious to their own comprehension failures. Though children often are capable of all the component processes necessary for comprehension monitoring, they may not have yet learned how to orchestrate them. Though some children have the ability to monitor their comprehension, they often do not spontaneously think to do so. Because of these findings, we can be optimistic that this fundamental academic skill can be taught. Based on the existing empirical work and theoretical analyses, we can make some educated guesses about what some of the remedial procedures should be. Yet there remain critical questions about which method is most effective for which children, and about which methods are easiest to train, generalize to the most material, remain in the childs repetoire of skills, etc. Empirical work is needed to determine how we can best tailor the educational procedure to the needs of the individual students.

REFERENCES

Baker, L., & Brown, A. L. (1980). Metacognitive skills of reading. In D. Pearson (Ed.), *Handbook of reading research*. New York: Plenum.

Bearison, D. J., & Levy, L. M. (1977). Children's comprehension of referential communication: Decoding ambiguous messages. *Child Development, 48,* 716–720.

Bransford, J. D., Barclay, J. R., & Franks, J. J. (1972). Sentence memory: A constructive versus interpretive approach. *Cognitive Psychology, 3,* 193–209.

Brown, A. L., Campione, J. C., & Barclay, C.R. (1979). Training self-checking routines for estimating test readiness: Generalization from list learning to prose recall. *Child Development, 50,* 501–512.

Capelli, C. A., & Markman, E. M. (1982). *Children's sensitivity to incomprehensible material in written text.* Manuscript in preparation.

Collins, A., & Smith, E. E. (in press). Teaching the process of reading comprehension. *Intelligence.*

Flavell, J. H. (1981). Cognitive monitoring. In W. P. Dickson (Ed.), *Children's oral communication skills.* New York: Academic Press.

Flavell, J. H., Speer, J. R., Green, F. L., & August, D. L. (1981). The development of comprehension monitoring and knowledge about communication. *Monographs of the Society for Research in Child Development, 46* (5, Serial No. 192).

Garner, R. (1980). Monitoring of understanding: An investigation of good and poor readers' awareness of induced miscomprehension of text. *Journal of Reading Behavior, 12,* 55–64.

Garner, R. (1981). Monitoring of passage inconsistency among poor comprehenders: A preliminary test of the "piecemeal processing" explanation. *Journal of Educational Research, 74,* 159-165.

Gelman, R. (1978). Cognitive development. *Annual Review of Psychology, 29,* 297-332.

Geoffrey, A. (1979). *Familiarity and the development of comprehension monitoring.* Unpublished manuscript, Stanford University.

Harris, P. L., Kruithof, A., Terwogt, M. M., & Visser, T. (1981). Children's detection and awareness of textual anomaly. *Journal of Experimental Child Psychology, 31,* 212-230.

Ironsmith, M., & Whitehurst, G. J. (1978). The development of listener abilities in communication: How children deal with ambiguous information. *Child Development, 49,* 348-352.

Markman, E. M. (1976). Children's difficulty with word-referent differentiation. *Child Development, 47,* 742-749.

Markman, E. M. (1977). Realizing that you don't understand: A preliminary investigation. *Child Development, 48,* 986-992.

Markman, E. M. (1978). Empirical versus logical solutions to part–whole comparison problems concerning classes and collections. *Child Development, 49,* 168-177.

Markman, E. M. (1979). Realizing that you don't understand: Elementary school children's awareness of inconsistencies. *Child Development, 50,* 643–655.

Markman, E. M. (1981). Comprehension monitoring. In W. P. Dickson (Ed.), *Children's oral communication skills.* New York: Academic Press.

Markman, E. M., & Gorin, L. (1981). Children's ability to adjust their standards for evaluating comprehension. *Journal of Educational Psychology, 73,* 320–325.

Miller, S., & Lips, L. (1973). Extinction of conservation and transivity of weight. *Journal of Experimental Child Psychology, 16,* 388-402.

Mosenthal, P. (1979). Children's strategy preferences for resolving contradictory story information under two social conditions. *Journal of Experimental Child Psychology, 28,* 323–343.

Mosenthal, P., & Na, T. J. (1980). Quality of text recall as a function of classroom competence. *Journal of Experimental Child Psychology, 30,* 1-21.

Osherson, D., & Markman, E. M. (1975). Language and the ability to evaluate contradictions and tautologies. *Cognition, 3,* 213-226.

Patterson, C. J., Cosgrove, J. M. & O'Brien, R. G. (1980). Nonverbal indicants of comprehension and noncomprehension in children. *Developmental Psychology, 16,* 38-48.

Patterson, C. J., O'Brien, C., Kister, M. C., Carter, D. B., & Kotsonis, M. E. (1981). Development of comprehension monitoring as a function of context. *Developmental Psychology, 17,* 379-389.

Schallert, D. L., & Kleiman, G. M. (1979). *Some reasons why teachers are easier to understand than textbooks* (Tech. Rep. No. 9) Champaign: University of Illinois, Center for the Study of Reading.

Sonnenschein, S., & Whitehurst, G. J. (1980). The development of communication: When a bad model makes a good teacher. *Journal of Experimental Psychology, 3,* 371-390.

Wollman, W., Eylon, B., & Lawson, A. E. (1979). Acceptance of lack of closure: Is it an index of advanced reasoning? *Child Development, 59,* 656-665.

13 Logical Thinking: Does it Occur in Daily Life? Can it Be Taught?

P. N. Johnson-Laird
MRC Applied Psychology Unit

Overview

There is an important distinction between two sorts of inference that occur in daily life. On the one hand, *implicit* inferences are rapid, effortless, and usually outside conscious awareness; they play a crucial role in the comprehension of discourse. This chapter reports some experimental results showing that children are often poor at making such inferences, and that one difference between good readers and bad readers is precisely the ability to make such inferences. On the other hand, *explicit* inferences are made in answering questions and solving problems. They can be genuinely deductive, unlike implicit inferences that tend to be plausible conjectures that may subsequently be discounted.

Psychologists committed to the view that conscious thought is rational have argued that there is a mental logic underlying deduction. This chapter reviews some alternative systems of logic, including programs based on the "resolution" principle, the PLANNER programming language, and the so-called method of "natural deduction." However, it goes on to argue, from a consideration of how children might acquire logic, that valid inferences can be made without the use of any rules of inference.

A summary of some experimental studies suggests that there are at least two levels at which discourse is normally represented: a relatively superficial representation close to the linguistic form of sentences, and a more profound representation that takes the form of a *mental model* of the state of affairs described by the discourse. This concept is used to explain how valid deductions are made without logic. Human reasoners follow the fundamental semantic principle governing all deduction: An inference is valid if there is no way of interpreting the premises that is consistent with the denial of the conclusion. Implicit inferences may well occur in the construction of mental models. What distinguishes explicit deductions, however, is an attempt to construct and to evaluate alternative mental models of the same premises. A number of experimental findings are reported that support this hypothesis. Fallacious inferences occur as a consequence of failures to carry out the search for counterexamples in a systematic and comprehensive way. These failures seem to be the result of inherent limitations in the capacity of working memory, because the main differences in logical ability from one individual to another concern those deductions that demand the construction of more than one mental model. Some pedagogical implications of the theory are briefly sketched.

INTRODUCTION

At the end of a lecture on ethics, Epictetus, the Stoic philosopher, recommended the study of logic to his audience because it was useful. One of his listeners was unconvinced and asked: "Sir, would you *demonstrate* the usefulness of the study of logic?" Epictetus smiled and replied: "That is my point. How could you, without the study of logic, test whether my demonstration would be valid or not?"

The late Yehoshua Bar-Hillel, who recounts this story, comments that if the audience had signed up to take the course in logic that Epictetus announced, then they must surely have been very disappointed. Epictetus had shown merely that there was a need for a theory that would make it possible to test the validity of arguments in ordinary language, not that he possessed such a theory. Indeed, as Bar-Hillel (1970) emphasizes, logic until very recently was insufficiently powerful to cope with natural language.

To a psychologist, the story of Epictetus suggests a different moral. No matter how much we understand the logic of an inference, we are not thereby vouchsafed any insight into its underlying mental processes. In particular, logic does not determine which inference should be drawn from a given set of premises; there are always a potentially infinite number of valid conclusions that follow from any premises. Likewise, the fact that an inference is valid does not guarantee that the process of thought that yielded it invariably delivers valid conclusions. The impotence of logical knowledge in the face of psychological phenomena is increased still further by the fact that many inferences that people make are invalid. But, what exactly is an inference?

The answer to this question ought to take the form of a theory, but it is nevertheless useful to draw a rough line around the domain to which the theory is intended to apply. This delineation is provided by a working definition. An *inference* is a mental process by which new information is obtained from old, either by transforming the old information or by combining two separate pieces of old information. This broad specification encompasses much, but it has the advantage of excluding nothing that might reasonably be taken as an inference. There are many sorts of inference, but I argue that the major distinction to be recognized by any psychological theory is between what I call *explicit* and *implicit* inferences.

Suppose you were to read in the paper: "There was a fault in the signaling circuit. The crash led to the deaths of 10 passengers." You are likely to infer that the passengers were killed in the crash. The text does not make this assertion, and it might even continue: "They were arrested when the airplane crashed and subsequently shot as spies." Plainly, you have jumped to a conclusion based partly on the content of the passage and partly on your general knowledge. You make such inferences automatically, rapidly, almost involuntarily, and often without being consciously aware of what you are doing. Because a valid inference is one for which, if the premises are true, the conclusion must be true, the most important feature of the inference that you drew, to a logician, is its invalidity. To a psychologist, however, the striking feature of your inference is the tacit and automatic way in which it was drawn. It is an example of an *implicit* inference.

Suppose, on the other hand, you read the following two assertions.

Arthur is not related to Bill

Bill is not related to Charles

and then you are asked: Is Arthur related to Charles? You are now faced with a task that requires a moment's thought before you can respond correctly. You need to figure out that Arthur could be related to Charles but need not be. Perhaps surprisingly, not everyone is able to do so: When Bruno Bara and I tested some university students in an experiment that included this inference, one or two of them concluded that Arthur was not related to Charles. Happily, the majority of subjects gave the correct answer. Once again, however, the important psychological feature of this deduction is perhaps not its validity, but the fact that it requires a conscious and cold-blooded effort. You must make a voluntary decision to try to answer the question, and you are aware of trying to make a deduction. It is an example of an *explicit* inference. Let us examine each sort of inference in more detail.

Implicit Inference

Ever since Helmholtz, there have been psychologists who argue that there are unconscious inferences underlying perception, and other psychologists who vehemently deny this claim. It is not my intention to enter into this controversy, but what seems certain is that implicit inferences, which are unconscious, occur ubiquitously in understanding discourse. Indeed, without an ability to make such inferences written and spoken discourse would not function in its customary way. In order to understand the following discourse it is necessary to make a variety of inferences:

> The pilot put the plane into a spin just before landing on the strip. He just got it out of it in time. Wasn't he lucky?

Every word in the first sentence is ambiguous, and the appropriate meanings can only be recovered by making inferences from linguistic context and general knowledge. To make sense of the second sentence, a number of inferences have to be made in order to determine the referents of the pronouns: The first "it" refers to the plane, and the second "it" refers to the spin. The third sentence is not to be taken as a question, though it is interrogatory in form. An inference from the context establishes that it has the force of an assertion. At the point at which most of these inferences are made, they can seldom be securely established. They are plausible conjectures rather than valid deductions. Many psychologists are accordingly tempted to suppose that a probabilistic inferential mechanism underlies them. However, there is no need to suppose that individuals compute probabilities in determining, say, that a pronoun refers to one entity rather than to another. The mechanism is much more like one that yields a conclusion by default—the conclusion is justified provided that there is no (subsequent) evidence to overrule it: It lacks the guarantee, the mental imprimatur, associated with all explicit deduction.

If the present thesis about the role of implicit inferences is correct, then children must acquire the ability to make such inferences in order to understand discourse. This hypothesis has been borne out by a number of experimental studies. Til Wykes, a former student of mine, showed that young children (about 4½ years old) have considerable difficulty in correctly acting out with glove puppets such pairs of sentences as:

> Jane needed Susan's pencil.
> She gave it to her.

The task is much easier for them if gender can be used as a cue:

> Susan needed John's pencil.
> He gave it to her.

In general, the greater the number of pronouns in a sentence, the harder it is for young children to understand it properly. They appear to adopt a syntactically based procedure for assigning referents to pronouns rather than an inferential one. They assume that a pronoun refers to the subject of the previous clause (see Wykes, 1978). In a further study, we discovered that children are poor at making commonsense inferences to work out the meaning of such sentences as:

"The Smiths saw the Rocky Mountains flying to California" (Wykes & Johnson–Laird, 1977). Similarly, children presented with such sentences as, "The man stirred his cup of tea," tend not to infer spontaneously that the man used a *spoon* to stir his tea. In all these cases, it was clear from control studies that the children are able to make relevant inferences. The point is that they do not usually do so as a normal part of understanding discourse.

The ability to make implicit inferences is equally important, of course, for reading. Jane Oakhill, a former student of mine, has shown that an important distinction between good readers and average ones lies precisely in their inferential ability. In one study, Oakhill gave a sample of 168 children (aged 7 to 8 years) a variety of vocabulary and reading tests. She was then able to select two groups matched on vocabulary and phonic skills, but differing considerably in their general reading ability. The two groups of children took part in an experiment that investigated the extent to which they made inferences when *listening* to very simple stories. Each story consisted of three sentences:

The car crashed into the bus.
The bus was near the crossroads.
The car skidded on the ice.

After the children had heard eight such stories, their memory for them was tested. A child who has built up an integrated mental representation of the events in the story might well assume that the sentence, "The car was near the crossroads," had originally occurred in the story. Given the nature of the original events, this inference is extremely plausible. A sentence such as, "The bus skidded on the ice," is much less plausibly inferred, because there is no reason to make this inference in building a representation of the events in the story. The results of the memory test using such sentences showed, as expected, that good readers tended to make more errors based on plausible inferences than did average readers. Good readers, however, performed better than average ones in recognizing the original sentences from the stories and in rejecting implausible inferences. It seems that a really good reader is likely to make implicit inferences in order to build up an integrated representation of a story, whereas an average reader is less likely to do so. Obviously, this study tells us nothing about causal direction. Good readers may be good because they spontaneously make inferences, or they may make such inferences because they are good readers as a result of other factors. But, in a series of additional experiments, Oakhill has so far failed to find any other major distinction in the abilities of her two groups of readers. Their memory spans for digits, words and short sentences, and the size of their vocabularies do not differ significantly.

One addendum to this work is worth noting. The procedure is based on one devised by Paris and his colleagues (e.g., Paris & Carter, 1973), though these investigators were not concerned with differences in reading ability. These studies have been criticized on the grounds that the sentences used in the memory tests allowed children to detect the new sentences, which had not occurred in the original stories, solely because they contained words not in the original stories. The materials used by Oakhill, as the preceding example shows, were carefully selected so as to obviate this criticism.

If understanding discourse depends on the ability to make implicit inferences, then an important pedagogical task is to inculcate this ability in those who lack it. Unfortunately, we do not know whether the difference in reading ability reflects an inability to make inferences, or merely—as with the children in Wykes's studies—the failure to mobilize them spontaneously. What we do know is that implicit inferences are so automatic that most people are unaware of making them. Like many skills, children must somehow pick up the ability in a wholly tacit way. This characteristic suggests that we must be especially careful that we do not unwittingly interfere with the normal acquisition of this skill if we try to enhance it. The educational task is more akin to trying to promote the development of a child's native tongue than to giving explicit instruction in reading.

Explicit Inference

Logical thinking in daily life is most likely to occur in those explicit inferences that are consciously made in trying to answer questions or to solve problems. The following dialogue illustrates such rational sequences of thought:

1. Does this train go to Ickenham?

   Yes—it's going to Uxbridge, and all trains that go to Uxbridge go to Ickenham.

2. Play a let.

   Why?

   You served out of turn, and the rules of badminton state that any point on which a player serves out of turn is a let.

3. Could the suspect have committed the murder?

   No. The victim was stabbed to death in a cinema during the afternoon showing of *Bambi*. The suspect was traveling to Edinburgh on a train throughout that afternoon.

The last example is certainly a valid inference, because there is no way in which the premises could be true and the conclusion false. Yet there is no existing logic that directly establishes its validity, which depends, of course, on many obvious but unstated premises, such as:

For one person to stab another it is necessary for them to be at the same place at the same time.

There are no cinemas on trains traveling to Edinburgh.

Trains to Edinburgh do not pass through cinemas on the way there.

The inference also depends on the meaning of the terms *during* and *throughout*. It is crucial that the suspect was on the train throughout the afternoon—if he was able to leave it, he might have done the murder. How then does the legal mind—or what the rest of us have to serve the same function—make this particular deduction?

The majority of psychologists have argued that there must be a mental logic that underlies the ability to make valid deductions. The attraction of this hypothesis is that it explains how it is possible for logic to have been invented in the first place. It also leads naturally to a quest for the correct specification of mental logic. The fact that people often perpetrate fallacies is mildly embarrassing to the doctrine, but it is easy—all too easy—to explain invalid inferences away: "I have never found errors which could be unambiguously attributed to faulty reasoning," Mary Henle (1978) remarks characteristically. The trouble is that there appear to be no independent "ground rules" for deciding whether a mistaken inference is the result of a logical error or some other deficiency. Nevertheless, the doctrine of mental logic has led to much research into reasoning, and, not surprisingly, to attempts to enhance children's logical ability by teaching them patterns of valid inference (see Falmagne, 1980). Before one can readily assess the pedagogical implications of such studies, it is important to try to establish the nature of mental logic and whether or not it really exists.

SYSTEMS OF LOGIC AND RULES OF INFERENCE

If there is a mental logic, then its most essential component must consist of a set of rules of inference, or some such schemata enabling conclusions to be drawn from premises. In an orthodox formulation of a logic, a rule of inference is essentially syntactic in nature. It governs uninterpreted expressions, specifying what can be derived from them wholly in terms of their form, not their meaning. The semantic content of the deduction is irrelevant. Indeed, its irrelevance is the essential foundation on which all formal logic rests: The principle of validity can be captured in a wholly general way.

One group of workers in artificial intelligence has capitalized on the content independent aspect of logic and developed programs that operate proof procedures for the predicate calculus. One of the major developments in formal logic during this century is Church's proof that there can be no mechanical decision procedure for this calculus: There can be procedures that will determine sooner or later that an inference is valid, but there can be no procedure that is guaranteed to discover that an inference is invalid. Hence, the quest in mechanical theorem proving is to cut down the time it takes to discover that an inference is valid (if indeed it is), because as the program grinds away there is no way of knowing whether it will ultimately reveal that the inference is valid or go on computing forever. Programs have been devised that use just a single rule of inference, the so-called "resolution" rule (see e.g., Robinson, 1965):

$$\frac{\begin{array}{c} \text{A or B} \\ \text{not } -\text{A or C} \end{array}}{\therefore \text{B or C}}$$

Thus, whenever an assertion and its negation occur in disjunctive premises, they can be deleted to have a disjunction of whatever is left. The uniform proof procedure has the overall pattern of a *reductio ad absurdum*, but in order to apply the resolution rule it is necessary to translate the premises into a special notation in which the quantifiers are eliminated and all the connectives are transformed into disjunctions.

Only if a deduction is valid will the uniform proof procedure ultimately yield a proof. It is accordingly important to cut down the time to prove valid arguments, and the problem is to find the best way of eliminating assertions and their negations; a variety of heuristic procedures have been devised to help to speed up the search (see Robinson, 1979). A uniform theorem prover is undoubtedly intelligent, but it is highly artificial. Indeed, its critics within artificial intelligence have pointed out that it is both inflexible and remote from ordinary reasoning (see e.g., Winograd, 1972). One might add that, because there are doubts about whether natural language can be accommodated within the orthodox predicate calculus, there must also be doubts about such a formalization.

A very different approach to rules of inference is represented by the development of PLANNER and its cognate languages (Hewitt, 1972). Programs written in PLANNER-like languages have a data base that consists of a set of assertions, specified in a predicate-argument format, such as:

(SCIENTIST   FRED)

(DRIVER   BILL)

The assertion, "Fred is a scientist," is accordingly true with respect to this data base, and PLANNER enables the programmer to implement procedures (1) that will evaluate a sentence with respect to the assertions in the data base and return its truth value, and (2) that will take a sentence and add the corresponding assertion to the data base. However, if the assertion is of the form, "All scientists are drivers," then rather than tamper with the data base—going through it and adding an assertion about each individual who is a scientist to the effect that he or she is a driver, PLANNER allows a form of representation in which such a data base is merely *described* rather than actually established. For example, a procedure known as a consequent theorem can be set up:

(CONSEQUENT(×)(DRIVER x)
   GOAL(SCIENTIST x))

and in effect added to the data base. What this procedure says is that *x is a driver* is true for any x provided that the goal of showing that *x is a scientist* is achieved—the consequent is true provided that the goal is satisfied. It is just one of the ways in which any general assertion can be represented by a procedure in a PLANNER system.

If the program's goal is to show that *Fred is a driver*, then the preceding procedure can be called if there is no simple assertion to that effect in the data base. If the consequent theorem satisfies its goal, i.e., discovers that there *is* an assertion that *Fred is a scientist*, the desired conclusion follows at once. By representing general assertions in the form of rules of inference, PLANNER allows the programmer to take into account information specific to their content, for example, hints or heuristics about how to achieve a particular inferential goal. Hence, PLANNER-like systems seem more plausible psychologically than uniform theorem provers. However, people do possess certain general inferential abilities, and no studies in artificial intelligence have yet illuminated them.

If human beings possess a mental logic, it is likely to have more than one rule of inference unlike a "resolution" system, and rather fewer rules of inference than a PLANNER system. This consideration renders a system based on the so-called method of "natural deduction" quite plausible, and a number of psychologists have proposed such a theory (see Braine, 1978; Johnson–Laird, 1975; Osherson, 1975). A natural deduction system puts no premium on parsimony and contains inference schemata for each operator and connective in the logic, e.g.:

A and B

∴A

A or B, not (A)

∴B

There are a number of technical difficulties with any psychological theory based on natural deduction, but they are not insuperable. The major problem, however, is to explain how children could acquire such a system of inferential schemata.

THE ACQUISITION OF MENTAL LOGIC

Any version of the doctrine of mental logic needs to explain how logic gets into the individual human mind. Prior to its acquisition, that mind will not be capable of valid reasoning, and so obviously the event is momentous. In fact, however, it runs the risk of paradox, for how could logic be acquired by someone who was not already able to reason soundly? Three main answers have been given to this question, but none of them will do.

First, it is said that logic is acquired according to the ordinary processes of learning as delineated by conventional theory. Children are positively reinforced for making valid deductions and not reinforced (or even perhaps punished) for making invalid deductions. Unfortunately, even casual observation shows that there can be few children who are brought up under such a regimen; training in logic is the prerogative of philosophers, not parents. Moreover, the hypothesis begs the question in assuming that parents have themselves somehow acquired the distinction between valid and invalid inferences. A related question begging conjecture is that children are able to infer rules of inference by abstraction from the valid inferences that they encounter in daily life. Hence, children are obliged to be already able to discriminate between validity and invalidity as a precursor to the learning process. But, if they already have the ability to make this distinction, why should they need to learn rules of inference? The trouble with both proposals is that they assume the prior existence of logic in order to account for the acquisition of logic.

Second, it is said that mental logic is inborn. It is part of our innate intellectual equipment, just as there are supposedly genetically endowed constraints on the possible forms of human grammar (see Chomsky, 1965). Although this supposition may well be correct, a disinterested psychologist might suspect that it is a rather convenient way of passing on the problem to biology.

Third, Piagetians argue that logic is neither learned nor innate but constructed. It is the result of actions on the world, the internalization of those actions, and reflection on their organization, in a hierarchical sequence of stages that gradually liberates the individual from direct dependence on the evidence of the senses. Unfortunately, neither Piaget nor his colleagues have ever spelled out the nature of the mechanism guiding this developmental sequence in a sufficiently clear and explicit way to allow it to be either modeled or effectively evaluated. Accounts of the theory use vagueness to mask its potential inadequacies from its proponents (and others).

Perhaps, however, there is no logic in the mind, and perhaps humanity is intrinsically and irredeemably irrational. The follies and horrors of the human condition certainly lend credence to this view. Yet human beings cannot be wholly irrational. Logic could not have been invented by a species incapable of logical thought. Indeed, it was originally invented to help people to think more precisely. What could be more rational than the desire to make valid inferences, an appreciation that the unaided mind was not invariably able to do so, and the invention of a technology for reasoning? Psychology has in the past too often assumed that there is a dichotomy: People either have a mental logic and are rational or else they lack such a logic and are irrational. What has hitherto been unquestioned is that these two alternatives are exhaustive. In fact, there is a third possibility. Human beings do not possess a mental logic, but they are capable of rational thought. Before I spell out the case for this point of view, I want to introduce the notion of a *mental model*.

Mental Models

Let us suppose that you are reading the famous story, *Charles Augustus Milverton*, by Conan Doyle (1905). In this story, Sherlock Holmes and Dr. Watson set out to burgle the house of the eponymous Milverton, a blackmailer and "the wickedest man in London." The following sequence of events then occurs:

> We stole up to the silent, gloomy house. A sort of tiled veranda extended along one side of it, lined by several windows and two doors.
>
> "That's his bedroom," Holmes whispered. "This door opens straight into the study. It would suit us best, but it is bolted as well as locked. Come round here. There's a greenhouse which opens into the drawing room."
>
> The place was locked, but Holmes removed a circle of glass and turned the key from the inside. An instant afterwards he had closed the door behind us. The thick warm air of the conservatory took us by the throat. He seized my hand in the darkness and led me swiftly past banks of shrubs which brushed against our faces. Holmes had remarkable powers, carefully cultivated, of seeing in the dark. [!] He opened a door, and we entered a large room in which a cigar had been smoked not long before. He felt his way among the furniture, opened another door, and closed it behind us. Putting out my hand I felt several coats hanging from the wall, and I understood that I was in a passage. We passed along it, and Holmes very gently opened a door upon the right-hand side. Something rushed out at us, and my heart sprang into my mouth, but I could have laughed when I realized that it was the cat. A fire was burning in this new room, and again the air was heavy with tobacco smoke. Holmes entered on tip-toe, and waited for me to follow. We were in Milverton's study, and a doorway at the farther side showed the entrance to his bedroom.
>
> It was a good fire and the room was illuminated by it. At one side of the fireplace was a heavy curtain, which covered the bay window we had seen from outside. On the other side was the door which communicated with the veranda. A desk stood in the centre, with a turning chair of shining red leather. In the corner between a bookcase and the wall, there stood a tall green safe, the firelight flashing back from the polished brass knobs upon its face.

Doubtless, in reading this passage, you were more than usually aware of the role of implicit inferences in comprehension—the windows and door referred to in the second sentence were those of the house, for example, though this fact is not stated explicitly. You probably also noticed that Holmes does *not* make one of his celebrated deductions. In fact, that omission is deliberate on my part because I want you to try to make a deduction. Here is a simple plan of the house with the veranda running down one side of it:

Which way did Holmes and Watson make their way along it—from left to right or from right to left?

In my experience, about one in 100 people can spontaneously give the right answer for the right reason. However, if you read the passage again with the aim of solving this riddle, it is relatively simple. (The solution, for those who are still perplexed, can be found at the end of this chapter.)

In order to make this inference you must build a mental model of the spatial layout. The fact that you are unlikely to be able to draw the correct conclusion unless you are forewarned suggests that there are at least two sorts of representation for discourse: a relatively superficial representation close to the linguistic form of the discourse and a mental model that is much closer to being a representation of a state of affairs—in this case the plan of a house—than to a set of sentences.

My colleagues and I have investigated this hypothesis about levels of representation in a series of experiments (see Johnson-Laird, 1983). Kannan Mani and I took the idea that readers can construct a mental model of a spatial layout, and examined it in a properly controlled study (Mani & Johnson-Laird, 1982). The subjects heard a series of spatial descriptions such as the following one:

> The spoon is to the left of the knife.
> The plate is to the right of the knife.
> The fork is in front of the spoon.
> The cup is in front of the knife.

They then judged whether a diagram such as:

> spoon   knife   plate
> fork   cup

was consistent or inconsistent with the description. If you think of the diagram as depicting the arrangement of the objects on a table top, then obviously it is consistent with the description. Half the descriptions were determinate as in the example, but the other half were grossly indeterminate. The indeterminacy was introduced merely by changing the last word in the second sentence:

The spoon is to the left of the knife.
The plate is to the right of the spoon.
The fork is in front of the spoon.
The cup is in front of the knife.

This description is indeterminate in that it is consistent with at least the two radically different arrangements shown here:

| spoon | knife | plate | | spoon | plate | knife |
| fork | cup | | | fork | | cup |

After the subjects had evaluated a whole series of pairs of descriptions and diagrams, which were presented in a random order and each with a different lexical content, they were given an unexpected test of their memory for the descriptions. On each trial they had to rank four alternative descriptions in terms of their resemblance to the actual description that they had been given. The alternatives consisted of the original description, a description that was inferrable from a model of the original description, and two confusion items that described completely different arrangements. The inferrable description for the previous example included the sentence:

The fork is to the left of the cup.

which could be inferred from the layout corresponding to the description (either the determinate or the indeterminate one).

The subjects remembered the gist of the determinate descriptions very much better than that of the indeterminate descriptions. The percentage of trials on which they ranked the original and the inferrable description as closer to the original than the confusion items was 88% for the determinate descriptions, but it was only 58% for the indeterminate descriptions. All 20 subjects conformed to this trend, and there was no effect of whether or not a diagram had been consistent with a description. However, the percentage of trials on which the original description was ranked higher than the inferrable description was 68% for the determinate descriptions, but it was 88% for the indeterminate descriptions. This difference was also highly reliable.

A plausible explanation for the pattern of results is that subjects construct a mental model for the determinate descriptions but abandon such a representation in favor of a superficial linguistic one as soon as they encounter an indeterminacy. Mental models are relatively easy to remember but encode little or nothing of the original sentences on which they are based, and subjects accordingly confuse inferrable descriptions with them. Linguistic representations are relatively hard to remember, but they do encode the linguistic form of the sentences in a description.

Working Memory and Inference

A crucial factor in the construction of a mental model, or indeed of any sort of integrated representation, is the capacity of working memory. The representation must be held there while at the same time the relevant information from the current sentence is extracted and added to it. This problem is not obviated by merely allowing subjects to have the written premises in front of them throughout the task; the integration of premises has to occur in working memory, unless the subjects are allowed to use paper and pencil as an external substitute for it.

Kate Ehrlich and I have demonstrated the importance of working memory in another series of experiments on spatial reasoning (Ehrlich & Johnson-Laird, 1982). In one such experiment, the subjects listened to a verbal description of a spatial layout, and then they attempted to draw a diagram of the corresponding arrangement. The main variable that we manipulated was the continuity of the descriptions. Each description occurred in three different versions (though with different lexical contents for an individual subject). A continuous description such as:

> The sugar is on the left of the fork.
>
> The mug is in front of the fork.
>
> The ashtray is on the right of the mug.

allows a mental model of the layout to be built up in a continuous sequence. The first premise corresponds to the arrangement:

    1. sugar   fork

The second premise allows the mug to be added:

    2. sugar   fork
               mug

The third premise allows the ashtray to be added so as to complete the layout:

    3. sugar   fork
               mug   ashtray

and the subject can proceed to translate this mental model into an actual diagram.

A discontinuous version of the same description is created by reordering the premises:

> The ashtray is on the right of the mug.
>
> The sugar is on the left of the fork.
>
> The mug is in front of the fork.

The first premise yields the arrangement:

    1. mug   ashtray

But the second premise makes no reference to either of these objects and a subject is obliged to create a separate representation of it:

2a. mug   ashtray   2b. sugar   fork

It may even be that subjects at this point abandon the attempt to construct a mental model and rely instead on a superficial linguistic representation. Only when the third premise is presented can the representations of the first two premises be integrated:

3. sugar   fork
   mug   ashtray

As we expected, the task was very much harder with the discontinuous descriptions. The continuous descriptions yielded 69% correct diagrams, whereas the discontinuous descriptions yielded only 42% correct diagrams. The effect is not simply a consequence of there being two consecutive sentences that have no referent in common. In a third "semicontinuous" condition, the sentences were presented in the order:

The mug is in front of the fork.

The ashtray is on the right of the mug.

The sugar is on the left of the fork.

Here the third sentence makes no reference to any item in the second sentence, but the task is not reliably harder (60% correct diagrams) than in the continuous case—presumably because the third sentence does refer to an entity already present in the model of the previous premises.

The limitations of working memory play a crucial part in the form of the conclusions that reasoners draw in their own words. This effect was originally apparent in a study of syllogistic reasoning (see Johnson–Laird & Steedman, 1978). For example, with such premises as:

Some of the parents are drivers.

All of the drivers are scientists.

there is an overwhelming bias to draw the conclusion:

Some of the parents are scientists

rather than its equally valid converse:

Some of the scientists are parents.

In general, any syllogism in which the terms are arranged:

A – B
B – C

creates a bias toward subjects drawing a conclusion:

A — C

and any syllogisms in which the terms are arranged:

B — A

C — B

creates a bias toward subjects drawing a conclusion:

C — A

This so-called "figural" effect applies both to valid and invalid conclusions and is singularly reliable. Whenever I have lectured on it, I have invariably illustrated the phenomenon, and audiences at universities as far afield as Milano, Padova, Nijmegen, Amsterdam, Edinburgh, Cambridge, Chicago, San Diego, and New York have universally conformed to it.

For several years I took the view that the figural effect was the result of the way in which syllogistic premises were mentally represented—a matter that is taken up again later—but it now seems much more likely to be a consequence of how information is put together in working memory.

Bruno Bara and I have recently discovered that there is a figural effect in very simple three-term series problems, such as:

Ann is taller than Beryl.

Beryl is shorter than Carol.

Who is tallest?

Studies of such problems have invariably either asked a specific question, as in the example, or else presented a specific conclusion for evaluation. Bara and I, however, presented the premises to subjects and asked them to draw conclusions in their own words (Johnson-Laird & Bara, 1984). Likewise, in order to obviate any differences as a result of the linguistic contrast between such pairs of antonyms as "taller" and "shorter," we chose to use only a single relational term. We found that with premises of the form:

Ann is related to Beryl.

Beryl is related to Carol.

nine of ten subjects drew a conclusion of the form:

Ann is related to Carol.

With premises of the form:

Beryl is related to Ann.

Carol is related to Beryl.

there was no reliable bias either way. In the case of symmetrical problems such as:

Ann is related to Beryl

Carol is related to Beryl

or:

Beryl is related to Ann.

Beryl is related to Carol.

there is a slight bias toward drawing a conclusion in which the end individual in the first premise (Ann) is the subject.

The results of this experiment suggest that when reasoners combine the information presented in premises, they try to form a mental model of the first premise to which they add the information in the second premise. Thus, the premise, "Ann is related to Beryl," yields the following sort of model:

a → b

They then interpret the second premise and substitute the relation to Carol in place of the middle term.

a → c

On the plausible assumption that working memory operates according to a "first-in first-out" principle, the resulting model is then translated into the conclusion:

Ann is related to Carol.

The same procedure with a problem of the form:

Beryl is related to Ann.

Carol is related to Beryl.

yields a conclusion of the appropriate bias. The fact that the phenomenon is considerably reduced in this case suggests that the "figure" of the premises is less conducive to such a substitution. The first premise yields a model of the form:

b → a

where the middle term is first into working memory. The second premise introduces the middle term last. There may be accordingly be a tendency to scan the first model in the opposite direction, and then to make the required substitution.

Constructing a superficial linguistic representation is effortless and automatic for a native speaker of the language. Constructing a mental model requires effort and places a load on working memory. A mental model has a structure that corresponds to a state of affairs rather than to a set of sentences, and this structure has to be constructed by the reasoner. Mental models may take the form of images in certain cases, but that is not essential: There are grounds for supposing that everyone can construct such models, but many people claim to be bereft of imagery.

How to Reason Validly Without the Use of Logic

If you are told as a matter of fact:

Consultant surgeons in Brighton earn £20,000 per annum

and you subsequently learn that:

Arthur is a consultant surgeon in Brighton,

then you will have little difficulty in inferring that

Arthur earns £20,000 per annum.

The inference is so simple that its underlying mechanism eludes introspection. It may depend on a rule of inference as adherents of mental logic suppose, and I have described a number of systems that have been implemented as computer programs that are also capable of the inference. What I want to outline now is a very different way of making the same inference that relies, not on any rules of inference or inferential schemata, but on mental models.

Let us first consider an overt, though somewhat impractical, way of making the inference. Suppose you were able to gather together in one room all the consultants in Brighton. The first premise asserts that all the *surgeons* among them earn £20,000, and so you hand out to each of them a placard, which they are to carry, bearing the legend, "I earn £20,000 per annum." The second premise asserts that Arthur is a consultant surgeon in Brighton. You now search through the room until you come upon Arthur: He will be carrying a placard that says he earns £20,000 per annum. Thus, you may readily draw the appropriate conclusion. All that is necessary to convert this outlandish procedure into a psychological theory is to suppose that you carry out the entire procedure in your mind. You construct a *mental model* that satisfies the premises and derive the conclusion from an inspection of its contents.

At first sight, this way of making inference may seem too simple to be true. You may feel that a sort of deception has occurred. In order to dispel this feeling, let us consider another example and deal with it in a more abstract way. We suppose that the premises are of the form:

All the A are B.
All the B are C.

Instead of employing a roomful of people, we suppose that the reasoner merely imagines arbitrary numbers of individuals or entities of the appropriate sorts. A mental model of the first premise accordingly contains some arbitrary number of members of the class, A, which we designate thus:

a

a

a

Because the premise asserts that all of them are also members of the class, B, each *a* must be identical to a member of that class:

a = b

a = b

a = b

The premise is entirely consistent with the possibility that there are *b*'s that are not *a*'s—there may be, or there may not be—and this possibility must also be represented in the mental model. We use the notational convention that anything within parentheses denotes a possible individual. Hence, a complete mental model for the premise, "All the A are B," has the form:

a = b

a = b

a = b

   (b)

In order to draw an inference, your task is to form an integrated representation of both premises. Such an integration is only possible of course because the same set of individuals is referred to in both of them. A representation of the second premise, "All the B are C," could, by itself, take the form:

b = c

b = c

b = c

   (c)

But, obviously, because B refers to the same class in both premises, it should be represented by the same number of individuals, and hence the representations of the two premises can be combined as follows:

$$a = b = c$$
$$a = b = c$$
$$a = b = c$$
$$(b) = c$$
$$(c)$$

A more plausible maneuver, however, is to operate directly on the model of the first premise and to substitute c's for each b within it, and add an optional c, as sanctioned by the second premise:

$$a = c$$
$$a = c$$
$$a = c$$
$$(c)$$

Alternatively, a's can be substituted for b's in the model of the second premise, yielding the same ultimate result. In any case, the integrated model yields the conclusion "All A are C."

When an inference is made in this way, the reasoner imagines a state of affairs that satisfies the description provided by the premises and then draws a conclusion that is consistent with that state of affairs omitting any reference to those entities referred to in both premises, i.e., the so-called "middle-term" that makes the inference possible.

The example, of course, was chosen with benevolence aforethought. Here is a case where there is more than one way of combining the information in the premises. Suppose they are of the form:

Some A are B

No B are C

The first premise is satisfied by the state of affairs:

$$a = b$$
$$(a)   (b)$$

Likewise, the second premise is satisfied by:

$$b \neq c$$
$$b \neq c$$

though strictly speaking, this notation is a slight oversimplification because there should be a nonidentity between every b and c. In seeking to form an integrated model that satisfies both premises, a prudent reasoner ought to consider all the different possibilities. It is easier to discern them from a composite representation formed by sticking the two models directly together rather than by substituting the information in one into the representation of the other. Such a model would have the following form:

a = b ≠ c

(a)   (b)≠ c

Because there is no specified relation between (*a*) and (*b*), it can obviously be either an identity or a nonidentity. Hence there are two possible integrations:

$$a \neq c \qquad a \neq c$$

(a) ≠ c   (a) = (c)

These two models are consistent with the conclusion:

Some A are not C.

And they are also consistent with its converse:

Some C are not A.

However, the number of possible *a*'s that are not *b*'s is arbitrary, and accordingly the following integrated model is also possible:

a ≠ c
  //
(a)

(a) = c

This model plainly refutes the putative conclusion, "Some C are not A," because all the *c*'s are *a*'s. But there is no way in which to make all the *a*'s identical to *c*'s, and it is therefore valid to conclude:

Some A are not C.

This more complicated deduction was drawn entirely without relying on any mental logic, rules of inference, or inferential schemata. There is one fundamental principle that guides it: An inference is valid if there are no counterexamples to it. What reasoners must do in order to be rational is to ensure that there is no way of interpreting the premises that is consistent with a denial of the conclusion. They must try to consider all the different ways in which the information in the premises can be combined in an integrated model, and this task is obviously one in which the meanings of the premises must not be violated. Logic, and particularly the method of natural deduction, can be conceived of as a device for making this search systematically; human beings, however, very often fail to examine all the possibilities—they have no logic to help them. Moreover, logic alone can never guide the reasoner to a particular conclusion—it always permits an infinite number of alternative valid conclusions from any premises whatsoever. The overwhelming majority of such conclusions are entirely trivial, consisting of such assertions as the mere conjunction or disjunction of the premises, and so human reasoners must obviously be guided by principles entirely outside logic to the particular conclusions that they draw. The heuristic principle that people appear to follow is to build a model that establishes a connection between those items that are referred to only in separate premises.

There are many other different sorts of valid deduction, and I cannot deal with all of them here. What should be reasonably evident, however, is that the same general principle of constructing mental models with a view to finding counterexamples can apply to any sort of deduction. The reader who wishes to see the application of this thesis to other forms of inference is referred to Johnson–Laird (1978, 1980a, 1980b). The present account of reasoning without logic has taken its truth very much for granted. The first example of an inference presented earlier was one in which the premises yield only a single integrated model; the second example was one in which the premises yield three different models. In general, valid conclusions deriving from these sorts of premises require one, two, or three different mental models. We can predict that the greater the number of models to be constructed, the harder the task will be. The results of many experiments overwhelmingly confirm this prediction (see Johnson–Laird, 1983).

Individual Differences in Reasoning Ability

The inferences in the previous section are known to logicians as "syllogisms." People differ considerably in their ability to make such inferences, which have long been used in tests of intelligence. The present theory of inference, which is described in full in Johnson–Laird and Bara (1984), throws considerable light on the source of these individual differences. The first component of importance is whether or not a person is prepared to play the game of making inferences in a laboratory setting. Sylvia Scribner (1977) and her colleagues have shown that people in nonliterate cultures are often not prepared to play this game. The following dialogue illustrates the performance of such a nonparticipant. The subject was given the following problem:

All Kpelle men are rice farmers.

Mr. Smith is not a rice farmer.

Is he a Kpelle man?

The following dialogue then ensued:

S: I don't know the man in person. I have not laid eyes on the man himself.
E: Just think about the statement.
S: If I knew him in person, I can answer that question, but since I do not know him in person, I cannot answer that question.
E: Try and answer from your Kpelle sense.
S: If you know a person, if a question comes up about him you are able to answer. But if you do not know the person, if a question comes up about him it's hard for you to answer.

This dialogue illustrates that the Kpelle subject is not prepared to make inferences about people that he does not know. Yet, at the same time, it also shows that he is quite capable of just such inferences. The claim that underlies his behavior can be put in the following form:

If I do not know an individual, then I cannot draw any conclusions about that individual.

I do not know Mr. Smith.

Therefore I cannot draw any conclusions about Mr. Smith.

Luria (1977) reports very similar findings in a study with nonliterate Uzbekistanian women. As Scribner argues, it seems likely that literacy or schooling, rather than other cultural differences, is the critical variable. In our experiments, we have encountered only one adult subject—a student in an Italian university—who was not prepared to play the game of deductive inference.

In order to form an integrated mental model of premises, a subject must clearly be able to understand them and to know what would count as a state of affairs that would satisfy them. The subject must be able to hold a representation of both premises in working memory so as to combine the information that they contain. This problem is not merely one of remembering the premises, because it is not obviated by having the premises in front of the subject throughout the whole task. It is necessary that both should be mentally encoded simultaneously, or at least that sufficient information from both should be present in working memory to permit the integrated model to be formed. However, these accomplishments are merely the normal ability to understand one's native language, and to form a mental model of discourse. Although people do differ in their verbal competence, particularly in the speed with which they can understand or produce complicated discourse, this source of variation tends to be smaller than other components of deductive inference; there is very little difference in subjects' skill with those syllogisms that require only a single model to be constructed.

Where more than one model is required, then the subjects must appreciate the need to construct them, carry out this process without error, and be able to remember all of them so as to determine what, if anything, they have in common. With those premises that yield a valid conclusion interrelating the items in the separate premises, the single biggest source of individual differences is a subject's capacity to cope with two or three alternative models. With premises that do not permit a valid inference to be drawn interrelating the end terms, the situation is more complicated. There are some individuals who are prone to responding "No valid conclusion," whenever the going gets tough, i.e., whenever it is possible to form more than one model. They are right for the wrong reasons with these problems; they are wrong, of course, with premises that yield valid conclusions.

Conclusions

I have argued that there is an important psychological distinction between implicit and explicit inferences. Implicit inferences occur as an automatic part of the comprehension of discourse, whereas explicit inferences are consciously made in attempts to answer questions or solve problems. Implicit inferences tend to occur as an aid to constructing a representation of discourse, and their conclusions are plausible rather than valid. Explicit inferences include those deductions that are intended to be valid. Contrary to the tradition that they depend on a mental logic, the theory presented here argues that they depend on two basic skills: (1) the ability to construct mental models of situations described in sentences, which is a process that occurs in much of the ordinary comprehension of discourse; and (2) the ability to construct and to evaluate alternative mental models of the same premises in order to determine whether or not there are any counterexamples to a putative conclusion. A major cause of difficulty in deduction is indeed the need to consider alternative models within working memory.

Logical thinking does occur in daily life, but the errors that occur in the laboratory suggest that ordinary individuals do not possess a mental logic. If my thesis that errors arise largely as a consequence of the limitations of working memory, then there is perhaps little that can be done pedagogically to enhance logical skill. Yet one should not be too pessimistic. The simple experience of inferential tasks without feedback on the correctness or incorrectness of performance can lead to a significant improvement in performance (see Johnson-Laird & Steedman, 1978). The teaching of logic may likewise effect an improvement in performance or at least suggest the use of overt techniques to relieve the load on working memory. In general, however, the techniques of logic are too complicated to have an immediate practical application, and the standard logical calculi are remote from ordinary language. There is one as yet untested device that may prove to be effective. It would be a simple matter to train people to use paper and pencil in building overt models of premises and to teach them to try to search more exhaustively for counterexamples to putative conclusions. Sherlock Holmes, you may recall, asserted that: "When you have eliminated the impossible, whatever remains, however improbable, must be the truth." My aim has been to argue that logic is a consequence, not a cause, of our unsystematic but happy ability to search for counterexamples. The more overt we can make this task, the more likely we are to succeed in it.

The Solution to the Sherlock Holmes Riddle

The solution to the Sherlock Holmes riddle is that Watson and he must have gone along the veranda from right to left, as it is shown in the plan. Having entered the house from near one end of the veranda and passed from room to room, they turned *right* from the passageway into Milverton's study with its door that opened directly onto the veranda.

ACKNOWLEDGMENTS

Many individuals helped in this research, and I am particularly indebted to Bruno Bara, Kate Ehrlich, Alan Garnham, Dave Haw, Jane Oakhill, Patrizia Tabossi, for some fruitful collaborations, and to Steve Isard, Christopher Longuet–Higgins, and Stuart Sutherland, for much encouragement and advice.

REFERENCES

Bar-Hillel, Y. (1970). Argumentation in pragmatic languages. In Y. Bar-Hillel, *Aspects of language*. Amsterdam: North–Holland.

Braine, M. D. S. (1978). On the relation between the natural logic of reasoning and standard logic. *Psychological Review, 85*, 1–21.

Chomsky, N. (1965). *Aspects of the theory of syntax*. Cambridge, MA: MIT Press.

Conan Doyle, Sir Arthur. (1905). *The return of Sherlock Holmes*. London: Murray.

Ehrlich, K., & Johnson-Laird, P. N. (1982). Spatial descriptions and referential continuity. *Journal of Verbal Learning and Verbal Behavior, 21*, 296–306.

Falmagne, R. J. (1980). The development of logical competence: A psycholinguistic perspective. In R. H. Kluwe & M. Spada (Eds.), *Developmental models of thinking*. New York: Academic Press.

Henle, M. (1978). Foreword for R. Revlin & R. E. Mayer (Eds.), *Human reasoning*. Washington, DC: Winston.

Hewitt, C. (1972). *Description and theoretical analysis of PLANNER* (MIT AI Laboratory Rep. MIT-AI-258). Cambridge, MA: MIT, Artificial Intelligence Laboratory.

Johnson-Laird, P. N. (1975). Models of deduction. In R. J. Falmagne (Ed.), *Reasoning: Representation and process in children and adults*. Hillsdale, NJ: Lawrence Erlbaum Associates.

Johnson-Laird, P. N. (1978). The meaning of modality. *Cognitive Science, 2*, 17–26.

Johnson-Laird, P. N. (1980a). Mental models in cognitive science. *Cognitive Science, 4*, 71–115.

Johnson–Laird, P. N. (1980b, June). *Propositional representation. Procedural semantics → mental model*. Paper presented at the Royaumont Conference on Cognitive Psychology, Paris. Reprinted in J. Mehler, E. C. T. Walker, & M. Garrett (Eds.), *Perspectives on mental representation*. Hillsdale, NJ: Lawrence Erlbaum Associates, 1982.

Johnson-Laird, P. N. (1983). *Mental models: Towards a cognitive science of language, inference, and consciousness.* Cambridge, MA: Harvard University Press.

Johnson–Laird, P.N., & Bara, B. (1984). Syllogistic inference. *Cognition, 16,* 1–61.

Johnson-Laird, P. N., & Steedman, M. J. (1978). The psychology of syllogisms. *Cognitive Psychology, 10,* 64–99.

Luria, A. R. (1977). *The social history of cognition.* Cambridge, MA: Harvard University Press.

Mani, K., & Johnson-Laird, P. N. (1982). The mental representation of spatial descriptions. *Memory & Cognition, 10,* 181–187.

Osherson, D. (1975). Logic and models of logical thinking. In R. J. Falmagne (Ed.), *Reasoning: Representation and process in children and adults.* Hillsdale, NJ: Lawrence Erlbaum Associates.

Paris, S. G., & Carter, A. Y. (1973). Semantics and constructive aspects of sentence memory in children. *Developmental Psychology, 9,* 109–113.

Robinson, J. A. (1965). A machine-oriented logic based on the resolution principle. *Journal of the Association for Computing Machinery, 12,* 23–41.

Robinson, J. A. (1979). *Logic, form and function: Mechanization of deductive reasoning.* Edinburgh: Edinburgh University Press.

Scribner, S. (1977). Modes of thinking and ways of speaking: Culture and logic reconsidered. In P. N. Johnson–Laird & P. C. Wason, *Thinking: Readings in cognitive science.* Cambridge: Cambridge University Press.

Winograd, T. (1972). *Understanding natural language.* New York: Academic Press.

Wykes, T. (1978). *Inference and children's comprehension of prose.* Unpublished doctoral thesis, University of Sussex.

Wykes, T., & Johnson–Laird, P. N. (1977). How do children learn the meanings of verbs? *Nature, 268,* 326–327.

14 Mental Orthopedics, the Training of Cognitive Skills: An Interview with Alfred Binet

Ann L. Brown
University of Illinois

Glaser, in his discussion of the entire volume, looks toward the future in preparing his time capsule for generations of psychologists and educators yet to come. His aim is to describe and justify current theory and practices in cognitive skills training to our successors. In this chapter, I look in the other direction and interview Alfred Binet, a pioneer in the theoretical description, measurement, and training of intelligence.

A similar literary conceit was used by Greeno (1978) in his discussion of the papers on the development of problem solving at the Carnegie–Mellon Symposium on Children's Thinking. Greeno imagined a discussion among Siegler, Trabasso, Klahr, and Gelman, the presenters, and Binet, Dewey, Thorndike, Piaget, and Wertheimer, the historical discussants. I limit myself to just one historical discussant, Binet, because he seems to have addressed most of the controversies active today.

Unlike Greeno, who sought to capture the spirit of the writers' theories, I was fortunate in that Binet directly discussed the central theme of this volume in his popular book for parents and teachers, *Les idées modernes sur l'enfant* (1909). Therefore, with some poetic license to preserve the illusion of dialogue, Binet's following comments are direct quotations.[1]

---

[1] Special thanks are due to Chantal Gensse for her help with translation. Liberties in style are all attributable to the author. Copies of the translated Chapter 5 of *Les idées modernes sur l'enfant*, from which the majority of the Binet quotes were abstracted, can be obtained from the author.

ALFRED BINET ON LEARNING AND THINKING SKILLS

Interviewer: Dr. Binet, this conference on thinking skills and how one might train them must be particularly interesting for you, given your life-long interest in the topic. Perhaps we can begin by discussing what you think are the essential components of intelligence?

Binet: Well, knowledge, of course. A child is less experienced than an adult; he doesn't know as much, has fewer ideas, doesn't know as many words, and, furthermore, he doesn't have the same goals, interests, and preoccupations.

Interviewer: A great many of the chapters in this volume have shown the importance of organized coherent knowledge within a domain, and no one can seriously doubt this fact; but the authors of this group of chapters seem to be concentrating on something other than content knowledge, i.e., the processes one uses to operate on that knowledge.

Binet: But, of course, we must distinguish between an ignorant person, one who has little knowledge, and an imbecile, one who cannot think. And, let us not say that a child's intelligence differs from ours only by degrees; instead, let us look with as much precision as possible for essential differences.

Interviewer: Which are?

Binet: Intelligence is first of all knowledge directed toward the outside world. Such knowledge is a synthesis, continually adding to itself by means of automatic perception and conscious research. Numerous faculties are involved: comprehension, memory, imagination, judgment, and, overall, language; but the essential process of thinking is invention. We just have to add two more points and the schema will be complete. Such work (thinking) cannot be done randomly, without knowing what is going on, without following a certain line. There must be direction. Also thinking cannot be performed without having ideas judged as they show up and rejected if they don't correspond to the goal. There must be self-criticism. *Comprehension, invention, goal-direction* and *autocriticism* are the four words that describe intelligence.

Interviewer: So intelligence involves thinking skills and knowledge. In your book *Les idées modernes sur l'enfant,* you talked about *passive knowledge.* This sounds to me very like the *inert knowledge* that Bereiter and Scardamalia (this volume)[2] mention and very similar to Simon's (1979) statement that "bare facts

---

[2]The volume number for chapters in this two-volume series shown only where they are cited first.

in memory do not solve problems." One has to judge and criticize the information one has in intelligent ways. This clearly is the implication from the Bransford, Stein, Arbitman-Smith, and Vye chapter (Volume 1). These general thinking skills have been a central issue in these volumes. Bransford et al. , Hutchinson, and Lochhead (Volume 1), Markman, and Sternberg (this volume) all talked about such general skills, and they were also central issues of the Baron, Bereiter and Scardamalia (this volume), Campione and Armbruster (Volume 1), and Meichenbaum (this volume) chapters. There seems to be considerable agreement that some form of general thinking skills, though perhaps poorly understood, is central to intelligence.

Binet: This is not surprising; anyone who has worked with children, particularly slow-learning children, as I have, is repeatedly struck by the lack of these skills in children in the face of school tasks. The child's power of self-criticism is very weak. He is not well aware of the appropriateness of what he says or does. He is awkward with his mind as well as with his hands. He is known for using words without realizing that he does not understand them.

It is easy to test this lack of adequate self-criticism; it appears as a problem on tests in general, but we have an excellent exercise intended to demonstrate failures of autocriticism, i.e., sentences to critique. We tell the child that we are going to read a sentence in which something is wrong, and he will have to say what it is. These are some examples: (1) An unfortunate cyclist fractured his skull and died at once; he has been taken to the hospital and we are afraid that he won't be able to recover; (2) yesterday there was a train crash, but nothing serious; only 48 people died; (3) I have three brothers, Pierre, Ernest, and me; (4) yesterday we found a woman's body sliced in 18 pieces; we believe she killed herself. You would be surprised at how many of the "thoughtless young" are quite happy with this nonsense.

Interviewer: Yes, Markman's chapter shows that problems of monitoring one's own comprehension do seem to beset the young reader. And Bransford, Feuerstein, Hutchinson, Lochhead, and Sternberg all mention autocriticism in some guise or another. You have suggested that perhaps schools encourage such uncritical acceptance of information?

Binet: Yes, we were struck by transfer students to our program who came from schools where they received a bad education, i.e., were taught with a defective method. We would say of such a child: "He has been badly started." When he reads, one can see the bad habits that he has already acquired; he sings or mumbles, or he has a neat, fluid reading, but he regularly distorts—without scruples—all the difficult words that he encounters, or even skips them. What is observed for reading is seen as well with other subjects, particularly arithmetic. Some students can perform the four operations perfectly but are unable to use them in a problem; they use multiplication when division is required; they find, for instance, that a salesman has more merchandise after the sale than before, and other fantastic results. They have been taught to calculate, not to reason. Everyone knows schools where the instruction becomes nothing but a routine. The teacher develops their memory but doesn't do anything to develop their judgment, their spontaneity, in other words, their intelligence. Everything is taught by question and answer, just like catechism, but if someone uses an unexpected sentence, the student remains silent. To answer, he waits for the exact question "A," which is in the book, and immediately knows the corresponding answer "B."

William James tells an amusing story on this topic: "One of our friends, visiting a school, was invited to ask a few questions about geography. Taking a glance at the textbook, she asks: 'Suppose that you dig a hole of several hundred meters. Will it be warmer, or cooler, at the bottom or at the top of this well?' Nobody answered, so the teacher said: 'I think they know the answer, but I believe that you are not asking the right way.' And taking the book, she asked: 'What is the state of the center of the globe?' Half the students immediately answered: 'The inside of the globe is in the state of igneous fusion.'" This is an example of automatic teaching. There is worse!

Interviewer: But surely these are primarily the problems of the slow child, not the normal.

Binet: That is a fundamental mistake. We all know adults who are full of inert, useless knowledge. Also, I know of many cases where students don't benefit from school because they are too smart. Work does not challenge them. I have argued that we need "abnormal" classes for them too. These classes would be very useful, for it is because of the elite, and not because of the effort of the average, that humanity invents and progresses. Therefore, it is in society's interest to have this elite receiving the culture it needs. A child with a superior intelligence is a strength not to lose. I believe that after studying the exercises first created for mentally deficient children, we will see that the method from which they were derived is not only for "dummies" but is appropriate for all normal children. I will be more ambitious, I think our method is a unique method of teaching. But it is appropriate to all children, it makes them think for themselves. One of the best teachers of the special classes (for mentally deficient children) was telling me with a sparkle in his eyes: "What wouldn't I have gotten from my intelligent students if I had treated them like this!"

Interviewer: Yes, many of the chapters we have seen in this volume point out that even the college student can benefit from direct training in thinking skills. For example, Hayes (Volume 2) has talked about the 100 or so skills that may be needed, and Perkins (Volume 2) talks about the need to educate the gifted as well as the slow learner. So we seem to be in agreement that there are general thinking skills and that they need to be taught to everyone. But how can they be taught?

Binet: I have always believed that intelligence can, to some extent, be taught, can be improved in every child, and I deplore the pessimism that this question often evokes. In my day there was a frequent prejudice against the educability of intelligence. The familiar proverb that says "When we are stupid, it is for a long time" seemed to be taken for granted by unthinking teachers. They are indifferent to children lacking intelligence; they don't have any sympathy for them, or even respect, for their intemperancy of language is such that they would say "This is a child who will never do anything . . . he is not gifted, not intelligent at all." I have too often heard such uncautious language.

I remember that during my Baccelaureate exam, one examiner, horrified by one of my answers, declared that I would never have the mind for philosophy, never! What a big word! Some contemporary philosophers seem to have given their moral support to such lamentable verdicts, asserting that intelligence is a fixed quantity, a quantity that cannot be increased. We must protest and react against this brutal pessimism and show that it doesn't have any foundation.

If it were not possible to change intelligence, why measure it in the first place? *"Après le mal, le remède."* Diagnosis is crucial but it must lead to remedy. Suppose that we discover that one of the children presents a distressing inability to understand what is said in class. The child cannot understand, judge, imagine. He is definitely behind. What can we do with him, for him? If we don't do something, if we don't act, he is going to keep wasting his time, and, witnessing the futility of his efforts, he will end up being discouraged. Remediation is crucial for him, and because this is not an exceptional case, children with faulty comprehension are numerous, the matter is of great importance for all of us, for society; the child who in class loses his interest for work is not likely to find it after school.

Interviewer: There is considerable agreement in this book that thinking skills can be trained, at least to some extent.

Binet: Well, of course, there are limits. Practice leads to progress, and this progress, large at the beginning, slowly diminishes later. It may even end up by becoming insignificant, and despite our effort, become equal to zero. At that point, we have reached our limit, for there is a limit, this is uncontestable. It varies according to the student, and for each according to his function.

Interviewer: How do you help people reach their limit? Would you describe the program of Mental Orthopedics that you and your colleagues have developed?

Binet: Well, the basic idea is that intelligence can be developed, with exercise and training. We can improve our attention, our memory, our capacity of judgment, and literally become more intelligent than before, and so on until we reach our limit.

I would add that essential for intelligent behavior is not so much the strength of our faculties, but the way we use them, that is the art of intelligence, and this art must necessarily refine itself with exercise, with practice.

Interviewer: But practice of a special kind?

Binet: Yes, for there have been objections to our work, critics say "What you are increasing here and what you measure with such a precise method is the degree of the students' knowledge, not their intelligence. You demonstrate fairly well the possibility of rapidly teaching illiterates, but you don't show that their intelligence has improved." This is a good point. What we try to train are some habits of work, attention, effort. We believe that these children's intelligence has been increased. We improve what composes a child's intelligence, his ability to learn, and assimilate.

Interviewer: So the aim of your program is to increase the child's ability to learn independently, learning to learn is the name of the game. Bransford et al. pinpoint this as the essential feature of Feuerstein's programs, and this tried and true notion is receiving renewed popularity today. Can you be more specific about your methods?

Binet: What I am going to tell you will seem so simple, so down to earth, that it might require some time and thought to grasp its importance.

The first concern for the teachers has been *to bring the material to the child's level*. That must always be understood. If many of the mentally retarded didn't profit from their former classes, it is because of a lack of attention because the material was well above their heads. It was too complex for them, too abstract. It required too much preliminary knowledge that they didn't have.

By maintaining children at too high a level, one disregards the most important role of pedagogy: *one has to proceed from the simple to the complex*. Every day, I observe students who are confronted by too difficult assignments; but the teacher easily comforts himself by making this facile supposition: "At least that will make them work." Recently I saw a young girl who, as a beginner in sculpturing, had to reproduce a figure with complex movement. "You will have some difficulties" said the teacher, "but you will learn a lot." Why not send an illiterate to learn differential equations? A little difficulty is good and stimulating, but too much discourages, disgusts, is a loss of precious time, but worse, it teaches bad habits. The learner makes mistakes, which are difficult to correct, because he is unable to judge, he gives up trying to understand and works blindly, that is badly.

The result is a confused mind whereas the goal is to organize it. I have seen zealous parents indignant by their child's fear of difficult work, trying to correct this fault. They did wrong. The true method is to go from the easy to the difficult. The child will then have to deal first with the simple fears, which he will be able to dominate, and that's the point, one has to learn to control one's self. And then, as this power of control increases, he will be able to deal with experiences that get more troublesome, but gradually, and with circumspection: This way, success is almost always guaranteed at the end of the apprenticeship. But if we want to act suddenly, brutally, without adaptation to the child's strength, we harm him more than anything else. If we confront him with a terrible fear that he is unable to dominate, then we teach him the habit of mental perturbation or unbalance. We teach him not to control but to be fearful.

Interviewer: I think that it is an interesting phenomenon that the closer the participants in this volume have actually been to (1) children and (2) classrooms, the more they are likely to emphasize such motivational factors in learning. I agree with Bransford and Sternberg's call for the need to incorporate emotional components into our theories and to avoid what they call cold cognition. Sternberg assumes that retarded performers have particular problems with motivation, and although this may be true, I would hate to see this relieve us of the responsibility of considering such factors if our students are putatively normal. It may be that retarded adolescents have enormous motivational problems, as Feuerstein (Volume 1) has amply documented. But even normal adolescents placed in repeated failure situations are also dominated by fear of failure.

You have demonstrated how willing and eager are young retarded children, who, provided you give them a judicious mixture of success and failure, are extremely motivated to please and will work long and hard on difficult problems. I don't think it is an inherent characteristic of retarded populations that they are reluctant to learn in De Avila's (this volume) phrase; it is just that they are exposed to more than their fair share of failure in academic settings. By adolescence, they have been quite convinced of their general academic inadequacies. They have a generalized failure set.

As Meichenbaum points out, however, average and bright children can also be divided into those who are success oriented and those who are failure oriented. Bright, failure oriented children show many of the *deficient strategies* that Feuerstein describes for his retarded population. Note also the prevalence of math anxiety. It would seem necessary to take cognizance of motivational determinants in our cognitive training attempts regardless of the level of cognitive achievement of the student.

Binet: I quite agree.

Interviewer: You also seem to agree with the claims of the developmentalists in this volume, notably Case, Chi, Scardamalia and Bereiter, and Siegler, that one should tune instruction to the students' existing knowledge and capacities.

Binet: Yes, but not just knowledge; don't forget the motivational factor. Our lessons are unpretentious, corresponding to the child's ability, all involving training his will; his control. To give a lesson in will, to teach effort, and *the pleasure of self-confidence* is well worth a lesson of history or arithmetic.

Interviewer: Hutchinson and Lochhead suggest that we should increase a student's *courage spans* (Wertime, 1979), the level of difficulty he can stand before giving up. And Feuerstein has repeatedly stressed the importance of success experience in helping students cope with academic experiences. But not just success; the student must also deal with failure. As Lochhead and Bransford et al. point out, the student must learn to treat an error, not as an indictment of his stupidity, but as an opportunity to learn.

Aiming instruction at the child's level is also a common theme of psychologists interested in interactive learning situations, the "zone of potential development" (Vygotsky, 1978) or "region of sensitivity to instruction" (Wood & Middleton, 1975), within which the child and teacher can operate most effectively.

Binet: This is an essential feature of our classroom for slow learners. The teacher, with only a few students to work with, is able to know each of them. The teacher looks after them, making sure that the students understand. If not, he starts over, instead of keeping going. He asks each student for a little effort, always proportional to his ability, and makes sure that it is accomplished. He teaches them only a few things, but they are well learned, well understood, and well assimilated. *To ask a child only what he is really able to do*—what is more right, more simple?

But I digress; it remains for me to define the method used. About this, too, these classes (for slow learners) taught us a great deal. Having to deal with children who don't know how to listen, how to watch or stay quiet, we guessed that our first goal wouldn't be to teach them content that we thought would be useful for them, but first to teach them how to learn. Thus, we created, with Mr. Belot and all our other collaborators' help, what we called *exercises of mental orthopedics*. The words are expressive and have become famous. One can guess the meaning. As physical orthopedics give remedy to a bent spine, mental orthopedics cultivate and reinforce attention, memory, perception, judgment, will. We don't try to teach the child content nor memory; we shape his mental faculties by exercise and practice in attention, perception, and self-control. For example, we train them to answer questions about what they saw in the street, in the class, then on the board, in their books, etc. But it is important that the child be active, be the participant, be the leader. The teacher encourages and guides.

Interviewer: Ah, yes! In many of the chapters, notably those of Lochhead, Hutchinson, Bransford, Feuerstein, Collins (this volume), etc., there is a strong emphasis on interactive learning situations with the *teacher as coach,* i.e. buddy systems with peers as coaches (Bloom & Broder, 1950), etc. By working in a social situation, the learners will see their (and others') errors, see the correct solution, observe their own mental operations, and learn critical self-analysis.

Binet: Precisely. What I object to in traditional classes is that it is the teacher who produces, and the student who passively listens. Such a lesson has two faults: It does not impress the student other than by its verbal function, it gives him words instead of making him deal with actual objects, and it appeals only to his memory, reducing him to a passive state. He doesn't judge, doesn't think, doesn't invent, and doesn't produce. He needs only to retain. His aim is to repeat without mistake, make his memory work, know what is in the lecture, in the textbook, and to reproduce it. The results of such practices are deplorable: e.g., a lack of curiosity for what is not in the book or lecture; a tendency to look for the truth only in the book, the belief that one is doing some original research by going through a book, it results in too much respect for the writer's opinion, a lack of interest in the world and the lessons it gives, a naive belief in the power of simple formulas, a difficulty in adapting oneself to contemporary life, and above all, a static regimentation unwelcome at a period when social evolution is so fast.

What kind of reform do we need then, and how can we fight teacher-directed rote learning? Surely, we won't reach the point at which we ask the teacher to give up speaking. But the lecture shouldn't constitute the entire substance of the lesson. *It should be only a guide, or a help.* The student should deal directly with the problems, and the teacher's main role should be to comment. Above all, the student must be active. The teaching is poor if it leaves the student inactive, inert. It must be exciting, pushing the student to act. Entering a classroom, if all you see are immobile students listening to a restless teacher vociferating from the front, or if you see these children copying, writing down the lesson that the teacher is dictating, you can be sure the instruction is bad. I rather like a class where the students are less quiet, but busy, no matter how modest is the activity, as long as it is a personal effort; it is their own, it requires some reflection, judgment, and critical evaluation.

There is no doubt that these methods are excellent for practicing at home, or even in class, for the training of the child's mind. Instead of explaining some ideas to the child, it is better to have him discover them himself. Instead of giving him orders, it is better to let him be spontaneous and just control him when necessary. It is excellent to have him develop the habit of judging for himself, the content of a book, a conversation, the event that everybody is talking about; excellent that he learns how to speak, how to explain, to relate what he has seen; to defend his own opinions clearly, logically, methodically.

All this, one might argue, is excellent for everyday life, provided of course that the reduced role of teaching remains efficient enough to correct mistakes. But can such a method, with the teacher being passive and the students being active, be applied to general education? All the material (content) described in the curriculum remains to be taught. The student will still have to assimilate grammar, arithmetic, geometry, and so on. Isn't it necessary, in order to teach this, to appeal to memory. And isn't it true that if we end up with this necessity, it makes memory the foundation of teaching?

I don't believe this at all; those who understood the deeper meaning of the exercises of mental orthopedics will easily guess that similar exercises can be used to assimilate any kind of knowledge. It is possible to learn through acting— learning by doing according to the favorite formula of Americans. To know grammar doesn't mean to be able to repeat it rote, but to be able to express a thought with correct sentences, clear and logical; to know multiplication doesn't mean to be able to repeat the definition of this operation, but to be able to combine any multiplicator and multiplicand, and to get the right result. Thus, it is always possible to replace formulas with exercises, or rather, to start with the exercise and wait until it produces a habit, before introducing the formula, the definition, the generalization. Instead of appearing as obstacles before, the formula will only occur after, thus making conscious rules already known by their use.

Teach arithmetic by giving problems to solve; geometry by construction; the metric system by taking measurements; physics by building simple apparatus; aesthetics by showing and comparing reproductions of masterpieces and mediocre works, and guessing, explaining, and testing the differences; drawing by allowing for a free expression and only later explaining all the laws of perspective; and languages by imposing the habit of speaking them, and facilitating that of understanding them.

By following this, we achieve tremendous benefit; instead of starting with a general idea that is not understood, that is empty for those who don't yet know its content, we always start with an actual experience, with a particular fact, for an exercise is always particular. We follow then the easiest way, the most natural, the one that goes from *the particular to the general*. Furthermore, by having a child be active, we lead him to become interested in his work, we give him the precious stimulation of the warm sensations that accompany action and reward the success of effort. And more so if we keep track of his natural activities, and of his special capacities. All, or almost all, children, before they are taught, exhibit some aptitude for signing, drawing, narrating, inventing, handling objects, moving them, using them in some construction; by grafting education and instruction on to these natural activities, we profit from the push already given by nature. The child provides the initial activity, curiosity, etc.; the teacher directs it.

Interviewer: To sum up, Dr. Binet, you would be in essential agreement with the approach taken by today's psychologists and educators who advocate: (1) training in general thinking skills of self-criticism as well as task-specific skills; (2) interactive learning situations where the teacher acts as a coach; (3) instruction aimed at increasing the students' self-confidence; (4) instruction aimed at the child's existing level of knowledge; (5) proceeding from the simple to the complex; and (6) proceeding from the concrete specific experience to the general principle, all at the child's own rate. And you would advocate that such a program is applicable for both the gifted and the slow as well as normal children?

Binet. Yes, in a nutshell that's it—and it works!

AUTHOR'S NOTES ON CONTEMPORARY WORK

Although Binet sounds amazingly contemporary in his opinions about what cognitive skills are and how they can be trained, I do not want to give the impression that no progress has been made since the early 1900s. Even though pioneers such as Binet described the essential features of effective cognitive skills training programs, these ideas were by no means assimilated into the general educational practices of American schools. And, dominated by the psychological learning theories of the 1940s and 50s, educators turned away from the early emphasis on discovery, discussion, self-criticism, and judgment. Even today, when these ideas are again fashionable, concrete details concerning how to go about teaching general skills (and domain-specific ones for that matter) are by no means readily available. Binet and some of his contemporaries spelled out the philosophy, but it is today's cognitive scientists who are developing the practical technology of cognitive engineering (Norman, 1979). The chapters presented in this volume attest to the enormous amount of work that has been done in situating Binet's suggestion in concrete training programs. This point is well illustrated by the three sets of program analyzers, Bransford et al., Campione and Armbruster, and Polson and Jeffries (Volume 1). Similarly, take any of the points raised in the preceding interview, for example, the importance of knowledge, readiness, autocriticism, etc., and we can find chapters in these volumes that illustrate how detailed our knowledge has become concerning what for years have been merely educational truisms. Particularly noteworthy are the advances made in mapping what it means to say that an expert knows more than a novice (see Chi, Larkin, Siegler, etc., these volumes). But we are also making progress in terms of understanding and training general cognitive and motivational determinants of effective learning (Bransford et al., Volume 1).

Discussants as a breed usually manage to include reference to their own interests and work. To avoid breaking with this tradition entirely, I end with a consideration of two central points that Binet emphasized and with which we have been working: (1) general autocritical, or metacognitive, skills and (2) interactive learning situations.

One theme that was a central issue at this conference was the specific versus general skills controversy. A session was devoted to this issue and the three sets of program analyzers, Bransford et al., Campione and Armbruster, and Polson and Jeffries, all pinpointed this as a main theme. The issue was prominent in other chapters as well, for example, those of Baron, Bereiter and Scardamalia, Hutchinson, Lochhead, Markman, and Sternberg. As Allan Newell (1979) pointed out, it was also the central theme of the 1978 Carnegie-Mellon Conference on Problem Solving and Education.

An obvious problem facing those who would engage in cognitive skills training is deciding what level of help the student needs. Discussions of this point have also centered around the issue of specific and general skills. To illustrate this problem, Newell (1979) introduced the metaphor of an inverted cone of skills. At the bottom of the cone, the broad base, he conceived of a large set of specific powerful routines that are applicable to a limited number of domains; they are powerful in that once they are accessed, problem solution should follow (assuming only that they are executed properly). It is important to note that as we move up the cone, there is a tradeoff between generality and power. At the tip of the cone, there are a few highly general but weak routines—general in that they are applicable to almost any problem-solving situation, but weak in that they alone will not lead to problem solution. Examples here include exhortations to stay on task or to monitor progress. They are weak in that, for example, merely noticing that progress is not being made or that learning is not occurring cannot rectify the situation unless the student brings to bear more powerful routines that can result in better learning.

Should one teach the general skills from the tip of the cone or the specific skills at the base? The answer would be either or both depending on the specific *diagnosis* of a particular student's learning problem in a domain. If there are students who do possess most of the specific procedures needed for mastery, instruction aimed primarily at general self-regulatory skills would be indicated. In contrast, there may be students who have had considerable experience with many of the general self-regulatory routines in a variety of other domains and who are likely to employ them to guide learning in a novel area. What they may lack in a new problem space are the powerful and specific procedures unique to that domain. The relative emphasis on general and specific skills in a particular case will vary as a function of both the ability of the learner and the complexity of the procedures being taught.

A great deal of the existing training research has concentrated on very specific and/or very general skills (Brown, Bransford, Ferrara, & Campione, 1983; Brown

& Campione, 1981; Brown, Campione, & Day, 1981; Brown & Palincsar, 1982). This general-specific dimension is related to ease of transfer of the acquired skill. Specific skills are powerful enough to enable problem solution *if* they are accessed; but the problem of access or transfer remains a major one. The executive, self-regulatory skills that are weak to some extent evade the transfer problem because they are appropriate in almost any situation; no subtle evaluation of task demands is necessary. The result of including both types of skills in training programs is clear; use of the instructed activity is more effective on the original training task, and there is evidence for increased transfer (Brown et al., 1983). Note, however, that most experimental work has involved single strategies and their use, not larger sets of specific skills—and it is the latter case that is more typical of educational settings (Campione & Armbruster, Volume 1). The task of accessing, coordinating, and sequencing subordinate skills is a formidable one.

Rather than teaching a large number of specific routines and some extremely general supervisory ones, an alternative approach would be to identify and teach intermediate level skills, or packages of skills (Campione & Armbruster, Volume 1). These would be more general than the extremely specific routines investigated in much of the literature, but at the same time more powerful than the weak self-regulatory metacognitive skills that have attracted so much recent interest (Brown, 1982). An excellent example of such a development comes from work inspired by cognitive behavior modification (Meichenbaum, Volume 2). Initial work in this area could be characterized as concentrating on the weak general methods. The main interest was in *impulse control*. And the research entailed little instruction in task strategies. Rather the student is trained in general coping skills such as "slow down," "look carefully at all your choices," "check your work." The results suggest that students will emulate reflective behavior and increase time on task following fairly brief training sessions in self-instruction. However, increased response latency has not always been accompanied by a concomitant increase in accuracy with the target task, and the findings from research that have investigated maintenance and generalization are equivocal (Meichenbaum, Volume 2). In general, however, these programs produce excellent short-term results with children who have at their disposal the necessary task-specific skills and whose learning problems reside primarily in controlling and overseeing the use of those skills. Hyperactive, impulsive children respond very well to such regimes.

These impulse-control programs are, however, insufficient for the problem learners who do not already know how to perform the task-specific elements of the problem. To deal with this eventuality, cognitive behavior modifiers have added to the general coping litany direct instruction in task-specific elements, referred to as response guidance. I have argued elsewhere that such combined packages, containing both specific and general skill training, are very successful (Brown et al., 1983).

The second main point I pick up from Binet is the teacher-as-coach argument. Collins' call for teachers to *model* and *guide* comprehension-monitoring activities is a recurrent theme in the educational literature. For example, many prescriptions for teaching reading comprehension suggest that teachers should function as models of comprehension-fostering and monitoring activities largely by activating relevant knowledge and questioning basic assumptions. These are essential features of the teaching style referred to variously as Socratic, case, or inquiry methods. Collins and his colleagues (Collins, Volume 2, and Collins & Stevens, 1982) have examined a variety of such teachers and developed a taxonomy of tactics that are commonly used, such as *entrapment ploys* of counterexamples and invidious generalizations, *extension ploys* that force students to apply their new-found knowledge broadly, and *debugging ploys* that force students to examine their misconceptions (cf. Collins & Stevens, 1982).

Collins and Stevens point out that a main goal of such dialogue is not to convey the content of a particular domain; if this were the aim, such dialogues would be most inefficient due to the low information-transfer rate. If the method is successful, it is because it teaches students to think scientifically, to make predictions, to question and evaluate, and to verbalize and defend their rules or theories—all themes dear to Binet's heart.

In order for these activities of questioning, predicting, hypothesis generation, testing, and revision to be of service to the child, it is necessary that they be transferred from the teacher to the child in such a way that they form part of the child's battery of comprehension-fostering skills. A common problem with all these approaches is that they presuppose that the child, witnessing these activities, will come to employ them on his or her own. This is the problem of *internalization,* how the child comes to use personally activities that were originally social.

In order for children to become effective readers, they must somehow come to employ regulatory functions such as predicting, hypothesis testing, questioning, etc. on their own; they must develop a battery of what Binet (1909) called *autocritical* skills, and what are now called *self-regulatory* mechanisms (Brown, 1982; Brown et al., 1983).

Social settings, where the child interacts with experts in a problem-solving domain, are settings where a great deal of learning occurs. Indeed, some would argue that the majority of learning is shaped by social processes (Laboratory for Comparative Human Cognition, in press; Vygotsky, 1978). A great deal of this learning involves the transfer of the critic's role, the censor in Binet's terms, from the expert to the child. Children first experience active problem-solving activities in the presence of others, then gradually come to perform these functions for themselves. This process of *internalization* is gradual; first the adult (parent, teacher, etc.) controls and guides the child's activity, but gradually the adult and the child come to share the problem-solving functions, with the child taking initiative and the adult correcting and guiding when he or she falters. Finally, the adult cedes control to the child and functions primarily as a supportive and sympathetic audience (Brown & Ferrara, in press; Laboratory for Comparative Human Cognition, in press; Vygotsky, 1978).

I end with a description of a recent series of training studies from my laboratory that incorporated both of Binet's main themes: combined general and specific skills training and interactive learning situations.

Palincsar and Brown developed a training procedure based on this theory of the internalization of comprehension-fostering skills first experienced in social contexts (Brown & Palincsar, 1982). The basic situation was an interactive tutoring dyad, where seventh graders were receiving instruction aimed at improving their reading comprehension skills. The children were referred by their teachers because, although they were able to decode at grade level, they had severe comprehension problems (three grades behind). Over many sessions, the tutor and the child engaged in an interactive learning game that involved taking turns in leading a dialogue concerning each segment of text. Both the tutor and the child would read a text segment silently and then the dialogue leader would paraphrase the main idea, question any ambiguities, predict the possible questions that might be asked about that segment, and hypothesize about the content of the remaining passage segments. The dialogue leader would then ask the other a question on the segment. In the next segment, the roles were reversed.

Initially, the tutor modeled these activities, and the child had great difficulty in assuming the role of dialogue leader when his or her turn came. The tutor was forced to resort to constructing paraphrases and questions for the tutee to mimic. In this initial phase, the tutor was modeling effective comprehension-fostering strategies, but the child was a relatively passive observer.

In the intermediate phase, the tutee became much more capable of playing his or her role as dialogue leader and, by the end of 10 sessions, was providing paraphrases and questions of some sophistication. For example, in the initial sessions, 55% of questions produced by the tutees were judged to be nonquestions or questions needing clarification, but by the end of the sessions, only 4% of responses were so judged. And, at the beginning of the sessions, only 11% of the questions were aimed at main ideas. But by the end of the sessions, 64% of all questions probed comprehension of salient gist. Similar progress was made in producing paraphrases of the main ideas of the text segment. At the beginning of the sessions, only 11% of summary statements captured main ideas; at the end, 60% of statements were so classified. The comprehension-fostering activities of the tutees certainly improved, becoming more and more like those modeled by the tutor. With repeated interactive experiences, with the tutor and child mutually constructing a cohesive representation of the text, the tutees became able to employ these question functions for themselves, i.e., they developed autocriticism.

This improvement was revealed not just in the interactive sessions, but also on privately read passages that required the students to answer comprehension questions on their own. In the laboratory, such tests of comprehension were given each day after the interactive sessions. On these independent tests, performance improved from 10 to 85% correct, and the effect was maintained for at least 6 months. And in the classroom, the students moved from the 7th to the 50th percentile compared with all other seventh graders in the school. Not only did the students learn to perform comprehension-fostering activities in interaction with their tutor, but they were also able to *internalize* these procedures as part of their own cognitive processes for reading.

In a second study (Palincsar, 1982; Palincsar & Brown, 1984), these main features were replicated when the tutoring was conducted in triads, i.e., one teacher and two tutees. Improvement on the daily passages was found (from 20–90%), and this effect was maintained for at least 2 months, when the last test was administered. Generalization to the classroom was also found; students began below the 20th percentile and finished at between the 40th and 70th percentile rank. In addition, in this second study, transfer to other laboratory tasks was achieved. Students improved in their ability to (1) *predict questions* that teachers might ask about texts, (2) *summarize* expository passages, and (3) *detect incongruities* presented in textual materials.

Finally, in a third study (Palincsar, 1982; Palincsar & Brown, 1984), the intervention was repeated by regular classroom teachers interacting with slow-reading groups in the classroom setting. Group size ranged from four to seven students. All the major effects of the individual tutoring programs were replicated in the reading group setting.

This series of studies featured the explicit instruction of both specific and general skills in interactive learning situations. But what do we mean by *explicit* instruction? We mean that the student is fully informed about his or her (1) *diagnosis,* (2) the *purpose* of the *activity,* (3) *how* and *when* to summarize, to question, etc., (4) his or her *progress,* etc. As we have argued in the previous section, ideal cognitive skills training programs should include practice in the specific task-appropriate strategies (skills training), direct instruction in the orchestration, overseeing, and monitoring of these skills (self-regulation training), and information concerning the significance of those activities and their range of utility (awareness training). In short, such programs should train not only the component skills but the executive orchestration of those skills and sensitivity to appropriate occasions of use.

The interactive learning situation, where children and adults swap roles, is also an essential feature of the Palincsar and Brown studies. Via the intervention of a supportive and knowledgeable other, the child is led to the limits of his or her own understanding. The teacher does *not,* however, simply tell the child what to do—a procedure deplored by Binet; she enters into an interaction where the child and the teacher are mutually responsible for getting the task done. As the child adopts more of the essential skills initially undertaken by the adult, the adult relinquishes control. Transference of power is gradually and mutually agreed upon.

Although the supportive other in the laboratory is usually an experimenter, these interactive learning experiences are intended to mimic real-life learning. Mothers, teachers, and mastercraftsmen all function as the coach, the guide, the supportive other, the agent of change responsible for structuring the child's environment in such a way that he or she will experience a judicious mix of compatible and conflicting experiences. The interrogative, regulatory, critic's role is transferred from adult to child so that the child becomes able to fulfill some of these functions for him or herself via self-regulation and self-interrogation, which are Binet's autocritical skills.

Mature thinkers are those who provide conflicting experiences for themselves, practice thought experiments, question their own basic assumptions, provide counterexamples to their own rules, become their own Socratic coach, etc. And, although a great deal of thinking and learning may remain a social activity (Laboratory for Comparative Human Cognition, in press), mature reasoners become capable of providing the supportive-other role for themselves. Under these systems of tutelage, children learn not only how to get a particular task done independently; they also learn how to set about learning new problems. In other words, the child learns how to learn—the desired result of cognitive training according to Binet.

Note that in the Palincsar and Brown studies, the students were continually reminded of why the modeled activities were useful, given feedback concerning their effectiveness, and told that they should engage in such self-questioning any time they studied. And self-questioning skills are quite general, being applicable to a wide variety of texts. In this way, the transfer problem is in some sense finessed, as the occasions for use of the instructed activities are quite clear.

We now have considerable evidence that intervention aimed at improving both the specific skills needed to perform the task and the students' self control is successful. Ideal cognitive skills training programs include practice in the specific task-appropriate strategies, direct instruction in the orchestration, over-seeing and monitoring of these skills, and information concerning the significance of those activities. The level of intervention needed depends critically on the preexisting knowledge and experience of the learner and the complexity of the procedures being taught. Successful cognitive training packages that have included these elements, such as those by Bird (1980), Brown, Campione, and Barclay (1979), Day (1980), Palincsar and Brown (1984), Palincsar (1982) and Paris, Newman, and McVey (1982), all suggest that combined packages that include such metacognitive supplements to strategy training result in satisfactory maintenance and transfer of the trained skill. Concentration on self-questioning, comprehension-inducing strategies that are of general use in a variety of settings is one way of finessing the transfer problem. The success of these training programs suggests that such combined packages may have broad educational utility; but as Binet pointed out, they may be particularly appropriate for children with diagnosed learning problems and a concomitant sense of helplessness in academic milieus.

ACKNOWLEDGMENTS

Preparation of this chapter was supported by grants HD–06864 and HD–05951 from the National Institute of Child Health and Human Development and Contract No. US-NIE-C-400-76-0116 from the National Institute of Education.

REFERENCES

Binet, A. (1909). *Les idées modernes sur les infants*. Paris: Ernest Flammarion.

Bird, M. (1980). *Reading comprehension strategies: A direct teaching approach*. Unpublished doctoral thesis. University of Toronto.

Bloom, B. S., & Broder, L. J. (1950). *Problem-solving processes of college students*. Chicago: University of Chicago Press.

Brown, A. L. (1982). Metacognition, executive control, self-regulation and other even more mysterious mechanisms. In F. E. Weinert & R. H. Kluwe (Eds.), *Learning by thinking*. West Germany: Kuhlhammer.

Brown, A. L., Bransford, J. D., Ferrara, R. A., & Campione, J. C. (1983). Learning, remembering, and understanding. In J. H. Flavell & E. M. Markman (Eds.), *Carmichael's manual of child psychology* (Vol. 1). New York: Wiley.

Brown, A. L., & Campione, J. C. (1981). Inducing flexible thinking: A problem of access. In M. Friedman, J. P. Das, & N. O'Connor (Eds.), *Intelligence and learning*. New York: Plenum Press.

Brown, A. L., Campione, J. C., & Barclay, C. R. (1979). Training self-checking routines for estimating test readiness: Generalization from list learning to prose recall. *Child Development, 50*, 501–512.

Brown, A. L., Campione, J. C., & Day, J. D. (1981). Learning to learn: On training students to learn from texts. *Educational Researcher, 10*, 14–21.

Brown, A. L., & Ferrara, R. A. (in press). Diagnosing zones of proximal development. In J. Wertsch (Ed.), *Culture, communication and cognition: Vygotskian perspectives*. New York: Cambridge University Press.

Brown, A. L., & Palincsar, A. S. (1982). Inducing strategic learning from texts by means of informed, self-control training. *Topics in Learning and Learning Disabilities, 2*(1), 1–17.

Collins, A., & Stevens, A. (1982). Goals and strategies of inquiry teachers. In R. Glaser (Ed.), *Advances in instructional psychology* (Vol. 2). Hillsdale, NJ: Lawrence Erlbaum Associates.

Day, J. D. (1980). *Training summarization skills: A comparison of teaching methods*. Unpublished doctoral dissertation, University of Illinois.

Greeno, J. G. (1978). A discussion of the chapters by Siegler, Trabasso, Klahr, & Gelman. In R. S. Siegler (Ed.), *Children's thinking: What develops?* Hillsdale, NJ: Lawrence Erlbaum Associates.

Laboratory for Comparative Human Cognition. (in press). The zone of proximal development: Where culture and cognition create one another. In J. Wertsch (Ed.), *Culture, communication, and cognition: Vygotskian perspectives*. New York: Cambridge University Press.

Newell, A. (1979). One final word. In D. T. Tuma & F. Reif (Eds.), *Problem solving and education: Issues in teaching and research.* Hillsdale, NJ: Lawrence Erlbaum Associates.

Norman, D. A. (1979). Cognitive engineering and education. In D. T. Tuma & F. Reif (Eds.), *Problem solving and education: Issues in teaching and research.* Hillsdale, NJ: Lawrence Erlbaum Associates.

Palincsar, A. S. (1982). *Improving the reading comprehension of junior high students through the reciprocal teaching of comprehension-monitoring strategies.* Unpublished doctoral dissertation, University of Illinois.

Palincsar, A. S., & Brown, A. L. (1984). Reciprocal teaching of comprehension-fostering and comprehension-monitoring activities. *Cognition and Instruction, 1,* 117–175.

Paris, S. G., Newman, R. S., & McVey, K. A. (1982). From tricks to strategies: Learning the functional significance of mnemonic actions. *Journal of Experimental Child Psychology, 34*(3), 450–509.

Simon, H. A. (1979). Problem solving and education. In D. T. Tuma & F. Reif (Eds.), *Problem solving and education: Issues in teaching and research.* Hillsdale, NJ: Lawrence Erlbaum Associates.

Vygotsky, L. S. (1978). *Mind in society. The development of higher psychological processes* (M. Cole, V. John-Steiner, S. Scribner, & E. Souberman, Eds. and Trans.). Cambridge, MA: Harvard University Press.

Wertime, R. (1979). Students, problems, and courage spans. In J. Lochhead & J. Clement (Eds.), *Cognitive process instruction: Research on teaching thinking skills.* Philadelphia: Franklin Press.

Wood, D., & Middleton, D. (1975). A study of assisted problem solving. *British Journal of Psychology, 66,* 181–191.

The Generality and
Specificity of Cognitive Skills

15 General Cognitive Skills: Why Not?

D. N. Perkins
Harvard University

Of "why?" and "why not?," the latter asks the more provocative question because it seems to exemplify what it seeks to deny. "Why not?" requests reasons for why there are not general cognitive skills, or at least not in the sense or to the degree currently conceived. Yet the habit of asking the question "why not" is itself a prime example of what a general cognitive skill might be. "Why not?" seeks disconfirmation. It challenges the proposition at hand. It strives to avoid a well-documented error in human reasoning—the tendency to focus on confirming instances of a proposition while neglecting to search out, diligently or at all, potentially disconfirming instances (Nisbett & Ross, 1980; Wason & Johnson–Laird, 1972). Accordingly, and somewhat paradoxically, asking that very question about the existence of general cognitive skills hints that there cannot be a wholly negative answer. To ask "why not?" is almost to say, "Of course there are general cognitive skills—and here's one of them."

Although this argument is not airtight, there is some truth both in it and its conclusion. There are indeed entities that could reasonably be called general cognitive skills, as the following pages urge. At the same time, what such skills are like and what they might do for people's thinking abilities are matters subject to considerable oversimplification and easy optimism these days. This article attempts a critique of the general cognitive-skills notion, and, getting more constructive in the closing sections, explores some ways to cope with the many difficulties and to advance the aim of education for better thinking and learning.

339

GENERAL COGNITIVE SKILLS: WHY NOT?

The why and the why not of general cognitive skills depends on what "general cognitive skills" is taken to mean. It is important to recognize that the term does more than label a subclass of human skills. Currently, such skills usually are taken to constitute a revisionary theory of intellectual competence and its training. An idealized version of this theory might go as follows: *Intellectual competence consists largely of a few cognitive-control strategies that can be taught by informing learners of them and providing some practice.* This summary characterization can be unpacked into four hypotheses.

The Strategies Hypothesis. This hypothesis holds that having certain cognitive-control strategies is one important way a person can have general cognitive skills. *Having a strategy* here means understanding and being habitually ready to try to apply the strategy. Cognitive-control strategies can be defined as those that direct the deployment of cognitive resources. For example, the heuristics discussed by Polya (1957) or Wickelgren (1974) for mathematical problem solving take for granted a knowledge of basic mathematical concepts and operations. The heuristics concern how to direct that knowledge to solve problems. Such strategies are metacognitive, in Flavell's (1976) sense. Speaking of cognitive-control strategies gives a particular interpretation to the phrase "cognitive skills." As is seen later, there are other psychological constructs besides cognitive-control strategies that might be considered cognitive skills, but a strategies interpretation surely is the most common one, and hence the one adopted in this characterization of the paradigm.

Built into the notion that having certain cognitive-control strategies endows a person with intellectual skill are three subordinate hypotheses. First, knowing and being ready to try to use a strategy suffices for effective use. Second, skill derives from an elaborative approach to mental processing, wherein basic mental operations are governed by an increasingly sophisticated tactical repertoire. Finally, the particular strategies put forth by various instructional programs are in fact effective.

The Comprehensiveness Hypothesis. This hypothesis states that cognitive-control strategies in combination with specific knowledge account for intellectual competence. Differences in intellectual competence correspond to differences in a person's repertoire of cognitive-control strategies *and* differences in the knowledge base upon which those strategies operate (Baron, 1978). Denied here is the power model of intelligence suggested by the IQ tradition, which sees intellectual competence as a matter of general mental effectiveness as measured by g.

The Economy Hypothesis. This hypothesis holds that a *few* cognitive-control strategies account for considerable or even all intellectual competence because of their high generality. My choice of the vague quantifier "a few" is deliberate. Different instructional efforts have espoused varying numbers of strategies and have generally avoided claiming that a certain set of strategies exhausts all relevant considerations. Nonetheless, the tone of many such efforts is clear: Whether the general strategies fit into a tidy list of 5, 10, or perhaps 20, mastery of a relatively short list will yield considerable intellectual leverage.

The Teachability Hypothesis. According to this hypothesis, being able to assimilate cognitive-control strategies is a matter of being informed of them and their benefits, and of practicing them in limited contexts. With this hypothesis, there is no particular problem about acquiring cognitive-control strategies. Like any recipe, they can be mastered with a little persistence.

I stated at the outset that my characterization of the general cognitive-skills paradigm would be an idealization, and certainly the four hypotheses spelled out previously make that apparent. The foregoing account combines all the assumptions about general cognitive skills that would be appropriate if this were Candide's best of all possible worlds. However, it would be a great mistake to suppose that the four hypotheses have no relation to contemporary theorizing and practice. True, no one, so far as I am aware, has explicitly advanced all four. However, many a popular book promising to teach skills of thinking, reasoning, or inventing would seem implicitly to subscribe to them. The approach in such books is to present a few strategic principles backed by a barrage of anecdotes; such books are exemplars of the cognitive-skills approach in its most naive form. Moreover, more scholarly efforts to design instruction in intellectual skills do not entirely avoid the foregoing hypotheses. Every one of the four hypotheses seems to be an implicit, perhaps unrecognized, assumption of one or another such text or course aimed at inculcating intellectual competence.

These points should make it plain that, far from erecting a straw man, my purpose in this section has been to abstract from practice a prototypical version of the general cognitive-skills perspective. The aim of the following four sections is to subject that version to critical scrutiny. In this, I have the help of many other thinkers, because those interested in such matters have not been blind to the presumptive character of a cognitive-skills approach. I review some of their reservations, and some of my own, about the breadth and power of general cognitive skills. Following this is a more constructive exercise: speculations about some better ways to enhance intellectual competence.

CRITIQUE OF THE STRATEGIES HYPOTHESIS

The strategies hypothesis and several of its subordinate hypotheses were just described. In the present section, I want to argue that those hypotheses not only are questionable—they are just plain false.

Particular Strategies Thought by Many to be Sound are Not

There is reason to believe that some strategies often considered effective are not in fact effective. Of course there could still be other, better strategies for the same purpose. Nonetheless, to find that certain strategies commonly thought to be potent are not would offer an important warning. Because most strategies have not been sufficiently tested, adequate testing might reveal that general cognitive skills are far fewer and weaker than the lists of plausible strategies in various sources would suggest.

Let us consider two examples. First of all, a stock strategy for inventive thinking is the long search. The thinker is urged to generate many alternatives, thereby avoiding premature closure and an impoverished selection. Such advice has the support of commonsense and figures in many programs of instruction, for example, those described by Covington, Crutchfield, Davies, and Olton (1974), de Bono (1970, 1973), Feldhusen, Speedie, and Treffinger (1971), Noller, Parnes, and Biondi (1976), and Wheeler and Dember (1979). (See also, de Bono's and Covington's chapters, Volume 1.) However, contemporary research has challenged its validity. Johnson (1972) reviewed a series of experiments examining a long search and other strategic approaches to solving simple problems requiring some invention. Among the problems studied were the titling of summarized stories and the captioning of cartoons. In brief, these studies disclosed two problems with long searches. Individual ideas were, on the average, lower in quality—to carry out the long search, the subjects lowered the standards guiding their idea generating. Second, although the longer lists of ideas contained some higher quality items, subjects did not reliably select these. The net result was that subjects instructed to try to think of the best one or two ideas in the first place did at least as well with much more efficiency.

Other research challenges the notion that highly skilled people achieve their good results by means of deferred closure and long searches. Studies of chess players have disclosed that experts search no more elaborately than merely competent players for a sound move (de Groot, 1965; Newell & Simon, 1972; Simon & Chase, 1973). Rather, chess mastery apparently requires a sizable repertoire of internalized schemata accessed by efficient pattern-recognition processes. Thus sound moves, tactical problems, and so on suggest themselves without extensive search. Perkins & Gardner (1978), conducting process-tracing studies of poetry writing with amateur and professional poets, discovered that the better poets (so judged by an expert panel) explored no more alternatives in selecting words than those poets judged less effective. Again, as with chess, mastery apparently resided in internalized productive and critical capacities rather than in extended search processes.

It would be going too far to suggest that such findings show that long searches are a bad idea. Certainly there are occasions when a long search may be the ideal approach. (For instance, see the later remarks on problem finding.) However, they do suggest that, in general, long searches neither explain much of expertise nor improve performance greatly.

Besides strategies for inventive thinking and problem solving, mnemonic strategies have attracted the attention of researchers and educators. Here, too, the usefulness of certain supposedly effective strategies can be questioned. A case in point is the familiar pegword strategy, where the user memorizes a list of mnemonic hooks—one is a bun, two is a shoe, and so on. Then the user can remember lists of items by forming visual associations between an object on the list and the thing to be remembered. Research has demonstrated decisively that this tactic yields results far superior to those of unmediated efforts to remember (e.g., Bower, 1972; Bugelski, 1970; Hunter, 1964; Wood, 1967). Furthermore, this research indicates the sorts of imagistic associations that are more effective; for example, imagined interaction between the objects to be associated leads to better memory than simple juxtaposition (Bower, 1970; Morris & Stevens, 1974; Neisser & Kerr, 1973). However, despite common belief, bizarreness of the combination appears not to be important (Collyer, Jonides, & Bevan, 1972; Wollen, Weber, & Lowry, 1972; Wood, 1967).

So far, the pegword strategy seems sound. However, Baddeley (1976) has offered a wry appraisal of such maneuvers:

> With one or two exceptions . . ., mnemonic systems are typically not particularly helpful in remembering the sort of information which one requires in everyday life. They are, of course, excellent for learning the strings of unrelated words which are so close to the hearts of experimental psychologists, but I must confess that if I need to remember a shopping list, I do not imagine strings of sausages festooned from my chandeliers and bunches of bananas sprouting from my wardrobe. I simply write it down. (p.369)

Baddeley thereby suggests that such strategies poorly match most of our memory needs and seem roundabout compared with writing. Let me add, from personal experience, a reliability problem. Despite the high recall rate with the pegword method, even a 10% loss cannot be tolerated when important items are on that list.

Therefore, in historical fact, strategies of dubious worth have been and still are being taught as though they were relatively powerful. However, of more general interest are the reasons for this popularity. Two reasons seem obvious. First, the plausibility of certain strategies makes them appear effective—an unreliable appearance. Second, laboratory studies affirming their effectiveness may overestimate their power in everyday circumstances, where other quite different approaches may be available and where the specific problem addressed by a strategy may not even be too important. The point is that strategies need to be evaluated for their contributions to thinking and learning in *natural* situations, despite the methodological inconveniences of doing so.

Having a Strategy Does not Necessarily Provide its Benefits

As described earlier, having a strategy means understanding it and being ready to apply it. Schoenfeld's (1978, 1979) writings on heuristics in mathematical problem solving have emphasized the limitations of merely having a strategy. The most familiar limitation concerns difficulties of application. A person may understand perfectly well what it means to divide a problem into subproblems but fail to see how to do so. Although simple lack of familiarity with the subject matter can lead to such an impasse, the real difficulty is deeper than this. A person can, in some sense, have the prerequisite knowledge and yet fail in an attempt to apply a heuristic. Commonplace in efforts to teach heuristics of mathematical problem solving, the difficulty is hardly limited to that domain. To note an example I recently encountered, Scardamalia and Bereiter (1978) mention a study in which fourth and sixth graders readily differentiated among prose passages that had the same content and either more or less integration and continuity; these children could also explain the linguistic devices that accomplished this. However, asked to produce prose either more or less coordinated than their normal prose, the children failed. They could not translate their understanding into action.

A second and somewhat less familiar problem is when to apply strategies. Most typically, strategies are taught as beneficial with little advice on when to use them. Schoenfeld (1978, 1979) and Larkin (1979) emphasize that selection of an appropriate strategy is as critical as skillful application. (See also Bereiter & Scardamalia's and Larkin's chapters, this volume.) In an experiment on teaching integration, Schoenfeld (1978) provided materials that not only reviewed standard methods such as integration by parts but also taught a strategy for deciding when to apply each method. A group studying for an exam with these materials outperformed a control group, and they had spent less time preparing for the exam.

As with the critiques of research on long searches and the pegword method, such reservations have an import beyond the contexts of integration or effective prose. General conceptual weaknesses in the strategies hypothesis are implicated. In particular, simply having a strategy will accomplish little unless the person knows how and when to apply it. These two additional types of knowledge should not be taken for granted, though many instructional efforts have done so.

Tactical Elaboration is not Necessarily Productive

Deliberate application of a new heuristic often carries considerable cognitive overhead. Compounding the problem is the fact that, in many instructional situations, a number of strategies are to be learned. The effort to remember, consider, select, and apply can become unwieldy and distracting and might occasionally lead learners to bypass the techniques they have been taught. This could explain results obtained in a study by Rigney, Munro, and Crook (1979), in which students were asked to employ a complex procedure for selective reading. The results indicated that the students did not in fact use the tactics they were supposed to. One suspects that they could not, or did not care to, cope with the complexity.

The implication is not that expertise does not involve elaborated tactics at all. Indeed, Schoenfeld (1979) mentions that mathematicians, on examining their thought processes, generally have acknowledged the contribution of the sorts of heuristics Polya (1957) identified. Larkin (1979) emphasizes that experts in solving physics problems evolve an approach to a problem at a rough qualitative level, whereas novices do not. Rather, the point is that expertise does not appear to involve extremely elaborate *conscious* management of the course of thought. The expert does not tolerate a high tactical overhead. General strategies have been automatized and function rather spontaneously. The expert often notices opportunities and problems rather than having to seek them out. In keeping with this, the rapidity with which experts grasp problems has been noted in several domains—chess play (de Groot, 1965; Newell & Simon, 1972; Simon & Chase, 1973) and the solving of problems in mathematics (Heller & Greeno, 1979; Perkins, 1975), for example.

CRITIQUE OF THE COMPREHENSIVENESS HYPOTHESIS

The comprehensiveness hypothesis avers that general cognitive-control strategies account for differences in intellectual competence. This notion has provided a useful and provocative challenge to the view of intellectual competence as a wholistic and largely unalterable capacity. However, as with the strategies hypothesis, the comprehensiveness hypothesis suffers from several limits sometimes recognized but often ignored.

Neglected Strategies

There are two ways to interpret the comprehensiveness hypothesis—as proposing that general cognitive-control strategies of some sort explain intellectual competence or as proposing that general cognitive control strategies of the sorts predominant in the contemporary literature do so. The latter, bolder suggestion holds that we already have well in mind the relevant set of strategies. On the contrary, I want to argue with examples that whole domains of strategies have been largely ignored.

Problem Finding as Well as Solving.   For some years, Getzels and his col-
league Mihaly Csikszentmihalyi have been advocating the importance of problem
finding. Getzels and Csikszentmihalyi (1976) presented evidence that creativity
in student artists, as measured by panels of judges and by later professional
success, depends partially on what might be called a problem-finding syndrome.
Artists who are problem finders tend to explore more alternatives early, before
settling on a definite approach to a work, to remain open to changes in direction
as the work proceeds, and to think of a work as never entirely finished even if
it has been nominally finished. The investigators identified several other characteristics as well and suggested that such traits characterize the inventive individual in any discipline. A problem-finding pattern of behavior has even been
proposed as another stage of cognitive development beyond Piaget's formal
operations (Arlin, 1975).

The payoffs of instruction in problem finding (a matter Getzels and Csikszentmihalyi did not address) might well be greater than those from instruction in
problem solving. The thoughtful selection of what problem to address is a very
powerful operation, a fundamental decision about how a person will allocate his
or her resources. Given a moderately competent problem solver, what problems
the person addresses may well have more to do with his or her ultimate well-
being and satisfaction than whether the person addresses them a little more or
a little less effectively. Despite this opportunity, no instructional effort known
to me gives much attention to problem finding.

Procedure Learning as Well as Content Learning.   A number of books offer
practical advice to the student (for example, Higbee, 1977; Langan, 1978; Marshak, 1979; Robinson, 1970), whereas, at the same time, recent years have seen
a number of formal investigations concerning the teaching of learning strategies
and their effectiveness (for example, see the collections edited by O'Neil, 1978,
and O'Neil & Spielberger, 1979). However, for the most part, such sources
emphasize the learning of content—meaning what a text says, what foreign words
go with what English words, and so on. There is little attention to strategies for
learning and automatizing procedures. In fact, this might seem appropriate,
because superficially the societal demands for learning difficult content seem
much greater than the demands for learning difficult procedures. However, that
impression does not stand up to scrutiny for several reasons. First of all, the
contemporary constructivist view of thinking and learning would argue that
understanding of a difficult content area is a highly procedural matter. Also, in
many school situations, and certainly outside of school situations, relatively
straightforward retrieval from a large knowledge base is likely to be less to the
point, and complex coping procedures more to the point. Furthermore, in the
teaching of intellectual competence, there is an advantage of bootstrapping to
be gained in teaching techniques of procedure learning, because all the other

general cognitive-control strategies one might like to convey are, in effect, procedures.

Projects as Well as Problems. Instruction in cognitive-control strategies tends to be organized around problem-solving tasks. However, the isolated problem is a creature largely of the classroom. The nonstudent, whether operating in scholarly or more everyday contexts, is likely to find himself or herself involved in what might be called *projects*—which could mean anything from writing a novel, to designing a shoe, to starting a business. Complex, ongoing, often indefinite in their requirements, and open to diverse approaches, projects confront those involved in them with difficulties not represented in the microcosm of the isolated problem. At the same time, they offer certain advantages; for example, greater chance of meaningfulness and personal involvement and the opportunity to resolve problems by redefining needs. To my knowledge, only one effort to enhance cognitive functioning is organized specifically around projects—the LOGO project developed by Seymour Papert and colleagues at M.I.T., in which youngsters undertake computer programming projects, using an especially designed language called LOGO, and perhaps learn general skills and concepts of thinking through their experiences (Papert, 1971a,b; Papert, Abelson, Bamberger, diSessa, Weir, Watt, Hein, & Dunning, 1978).

Indirect as Well as Direct Strategies. Most efforts to instruct students in general cognitive-control strategies aim to convey direct strategies, those that prescribe a procedure straightforwardly designed to effect some cognitive goal. In contrast, indirect strategies might depend on metaphoric instructions that can not be followed literally; for example, the instructions call for attending to one thing when the real concern seems to be something else, and so on. Such strategies are familiar in developing performance skills. Vernon Howard (1982) considers a variety in an examination of skill in the production of art. For instance, an instructor may direct a singer to make the tone "brighter" or "darker" because such manifestly impossible advice prompts the desired vocal adjustment. Indirect strategies may also mean not teaching the ultimately desired method. Resnick (1976), concerned with the difficulties of teaching a complex procedure for an arithmetic task, got good results by presenting a less efficient but conceptually simpler procedure, which the children themselves revised for efficiency as they became versed in it. McCabe (1965) reported success with a related approach to writing, where students at first followed a model paragraph but, rather than becoming stuck on the stereotype, spontaneously branched out in worthwhile ways. In developing athletic skills, some writers have worried about the risks of trying directly to accomplish an objective. For example, Gallwey (1976), author of *Inner Tennis,* urged that accuracy in placing the ball be improved, not by trying for better aim, but simply by attending to where the ball lands. Supposedly, once one has developed heightened awareness of this, adjustments of stroke to attain greater accuracy will happen spontaneously. I do not know whether this is so, but it might be. The real point is that the potential power of indirect strategies appears to be largely unexplored in the area of instruction in general cognitive skills.

Can the Smart Get Smarter?—a Weakness in the Available Evidence

The comprehensive hypothesis predicts that teaching general cognitive-control strategies ought to produce gains in intellectual competence. Does this in fact happen? There have been a number of instructional efforts that, to some degree, test this prediction. Many of these efforts have been directed at below-normal performers. Despite frequent failure, there are several encouraging instances where definite and sometimes surprising gains have been reported (see, for example, those considered in Feuerstein, 1980, see also Volume 1, Frankenstein, 1979, Meichenbaum, 1977, Whimbey, 1975). On the other hand, other instructional efforts try to enhance the general intellectual competence of persons of normal or better ability. Here, decisive evidence of success seems harder to come by. For example, the well-known Productive Thinking Program of Covington, et al., (1974, Volume 1) and other programs designed to teach inventive thinking have failed to demonstrate their effectiveness unambiguously according to a recent review by Mansfield, Busse, and Krepelka (1978). The CoRT program of Edward de Bono (1973) includes some evaluational data, but this only suggests that students may become more flexible thinkers, entertain more possibilities; it leaves open whether they will become more precise and penetrating thinkers. The Practicum in Thinking at the University of Cincinnati (Wheeler & Dember, 1979) produced no objective gains. It is easy to extend this list of negatives and "don't knows," but I have no very firm positives to add.

There are many possible reasons for this situation. One is that much time and many other resources have been invested in helping weak intellectual performers than in helping normal or above-normal performers. Quite possibly the latter groups have not been given the several really good tries required to demonstrate success. On the other hand, there is a reason why making the smart smarter might be more difficult. As performance in a domain improves, quite likely it becomes more and more attuned to the specific requirements of the domain; that is, the higher the level of competence concerned, the fewer *general* cognitive-control strategies there are. Making the smart smarter may require instruction in several specific subject matters where they will exercise their intelligence, rather than in overarching cognitive skills. The successful, domain-specific education for the mathematically gifted done by Stanley (1977) encourages such a view.

Alternative Models of Competence

Perhaps the most obvious reason to question the comprehensiveness of a general cognitive-control strategies approach is that alternative models of intellectual competence have some merit. The paragraphs following describe four (and there are others). Some comments on choosing among them or synthesizing follow.

Faculties. Although faculty psychology by name has vanished, it has returned in other guises, a point Mann (1979) emphasizes in his recent history of instruction in mental processes. A faculties perspective proposes that intellectual competence resides in the abilities to conduct various mental operations effectively. The obvious contemporary example of such an analysis is the structure of intellect theory (Guilford & Hoepfner, 1971). Furthermore, instructional efforts have been designed after the structure of intellect model. Meeker (1969 a,b 1979) has developed a system of remedial instruction where the strengths and weaknesses of students according to the structure of intellect are gauged and training is offered to bolster the students' weaknesses. The author claims considerable success for this approach.

Domain-Specific Knowledge and Know-How. This perspective on competency denies that there are general cognitive skills in any powerful sense. Instead, the domain specificity of intellectual skill is emphasized and it is suggested that whatever general cognitive skills there may be will be of secondary importance. For instance, Simon and Chase (1973) found that chess expertise depends on a large repertoire of chess-specific schemata, not on general mnemonic and problem-solving abilities. The finds of Elstein, Shulman, and Sprafka (1978) underscore the importance of medical knowledge in medical diagnosis, rather than general hypothetico-deductive skills, and Goldstein, Papert, and Minsky (1976) argue, in general, for the importance of field-specific schemata rather than general problem-solving processes. Although not addressing specifically the existence of general cognitive skills, Larkin (1979, also this volume) and Heller and Greeno (1979) underscore the importance of a repertoire of methods in problem solving in mathematics and physics. Cole and Scribner (1974) note that, in certain cross-cultural studies of reasoning, subjects proved able to perform logical tasks with familiar but not with unfamiliar materials and that subjects who fail the experimenter's formal tests must of necessity employ logical operations of the sort tested simply to get along in life. Even Piaget (1972) acknowledges that the use of formal operations may be limited to a person's special aptitudes, enthusiasms, and professional involvements.

Cognitive Style. It has often been suggested that intellectual competence depends on an individual's cognitive style, meaning various slow-changing characteristics that pervade a person's manner of thought and perception, characteristics such as field dependence/independence (Witkin, 1976), or impulsivity/reflectivity (Kagan & Kogan, 1970). Such characteristics differ from strategies, as the term is used here, in that strategies are specific actions to be taken at specific points in a problem solving or other process. For example, trying to divide a problem into subproblems or trying to review what one has just read are activities that occur at certain places in the overall course of problem solving or reading to remember, respectively. In contrast, characteristics like reflectivity supposedly figure almost continuously in a person's behavior. Various instructional programs have emphasized cognitive-stylistic characteristics along with strategies, for example, the one described by Feuerstein (1980) and several by Meichenbaum (1977). Indeed, the distinction between strategies and cognitive style is not always made. Baron (1978), for example, subsumes both under the label strategies. However, I want to urge that the distinction is worth making. Because strategies occur at particular points within an ongoing process, whereas cognitive-stylistic characteristics pervade the process, the dynamics of learning one or the other might be quite different. Also, which one or what synthesis best accounts for intellectual competence is an important question.

Understanding of Fundamental Principles.   Yet another view of intellectual competence suggests that the individual's understanding-in-practice of fundamental principles lies behind intelligent behavior. The obvious example of this view is the developmental psychology of Piaget, with its stages of concrete and formal operations. Whether intellectual development actually occurs in specific unified stages is much debated today (see, for example, Brainerd, 1974, 1978). Furthermore, Deanna Kuhn (1979) has argued that the vagueness of Piaget's theories makes it difficult to judge just what the curricular implications are or whether efforts supposedly based on Piaget's theories actually exemplify them. Nonetheless, the approach exists and serious instructional efforts have adopted its language, for instance the work in science education by Karplus and colleagues (Karplus, 1980; Karplus, Karplus, Formisano, & Paulsen, 1979; Karplus, Lawson, Wollman, Appel, Bernhoff, Howe, Busch, & Sullivan, 1977) and the work in enhancing general cognitive abilities in young schoolchildren by Furth and Wachs (1974). Whatever the true relation to Piaget's theories, it is hard to gainsay that students of science ought to have some understanding of control of variables, correlational reasoning, and like patterns of reasoning emphasized by Karplus.

Furthermore—and this may be the most important point—there are many senses other than the Piagetian one in which cognitive efficacy might depend on understanding fundamental principles or structures. It could be argued, for example, that in the vexed area of probabilistic reasoning (Slovic, Fischhoff, & Lichtenstein, 1977; Tversky & Kahneman, 1971, 1973, 1974) instruction must convey not just an appropriate set of do's and don'ts, but also some basic understanding of the underlying principles.

Comparing Alternative Models of Competency.   The preceding examples illustrate the crowded quarters of competency models, although others could be listed as well. What can be said about the situation? First, with the exception of the domain-specific knowledge and know-how model, all the aforementioned have room for general intellectual competence in some sense—but only the strategies model posits general cognitive control strategies. Second, each of the aforementioned has the support of its own methods of analysis and range of phenomena. Whatever model one might prefer, the others present challenges that have to be, in the Piagetian phrase, assimilated or accommodated. Third, it is by no means clear that a strategies model can readily assimilate the phenomena emphasized by the others. Perhaps it can, but a compelling case remains to be made.

CRITIQUE OF THE ECONOMY HYPOTHESIS

The economy hypothesis hopes for great leverage from general cognitive-control strategies: Possessing only a few such strategies—say 10—ought to provide considerable intellectual power. One reason to doubt the hypothesis rests on the evidence that skills tend to be rather context bound. This point was reviewed in the previous section. Another point already made concerns the possibility that context boundedness may be a particular problem at higher performance levels. The most pessimistic interpretation of such indications is that there are no general cognitive skills worth worrying about. A more positive reading is that general cognitive skills are not all that general, and that, therefore, quite a number are required to impart intellectual competence.

Pondering a particular area of cognitive functioning with general import encourages such a conclusion. For example, Nisbett and Ross (1980) review a number of disparate difficulties people have with everyday reasoning and grounds for belief. The varied principles people use and misuse in making inferences suggest that a variety of strategies would be needed to correct and empower everyday reasoning. There is no obvious way that a prescription resting on two or three powerful rules can be offered. Much the same conclusion seems to hold for many other skill domains, as a cluster of skills associated with a kind of cognitive performance might be called. Furthermore, several such domains invite serious attention. Here is a brief list: reasoning (the one already mentioned), in the sense of developing grounds for belief; problem solving, as is traditionally examined in game and mathematical problem-solving contexts; inventing, as in the psychological literature on ideational fluency, problem finding, and creativity; learning, as in investigations and instruction concerning study skills; planning and decision making, as in studies of decision making under uncertainty, consumer decision making, game theoretic models, and as in modeling and management techniques like PERT; communicating, as in the literature on developing writing skills; understanding, as in the literature on internal representations, models of speech comprehension, models of reading, and efforts to instruct students in skills of comprehension.

For a low estimate, let us assume there would be at least 10 important general strategies *per domain,* rather than in all. Then the preceding list of skill domains implies that a comprehensive effort to instruct students in general cognitive-control strategies would mean inculcating some 70 strategies. This actually is not a very large number, considering the 50,000 chess-specific schemata that Simon and Chase (1973) estimate the master chess player must have acquired. Certainly students could be expected to master 70 strategies, even when problems discussed earlier are kept in mind, problems of automatization, of knowing when to apply strategies, as well as how to go about it, and so on. However, just as certainly, imparting such a set of strategies in a useful way poses a serious problem of educational method and management and requires classroom time much greater than that usually committed to direct instruction in cognitive strategies.

CRITIQUE OF THE TEACHABILITY HYPOTHESIS

This hypothesis held that assimilating cognitive-control strategies was a matter of being informed of them and their benefits and then practicing the strategies in limited contexts. The uncertain track record of efforts to teach such strategies and produce measurable improvements in intellectual competence, especially among normal or above-normal students, has already been mentioned. This in itself gives reason to doubt the teachability hypothesis. Several other points already made also show that simply being informed of a strategy is not nearly enough. Three of the critical points follow:

1. How to Apply: It is not enough to try to apply a strategy. One must have the necessary background knowledge and specific means of putting the strategy to work, and the latter especially has often been neglected.

2. When to Apply: Choosing the right strategy for the occasion is just as critical as being able to apply it.

3. Automatization: There are too many pertinent strategies for the learner to handle deliberately. The strategies need to become automatized.

Some related problems have to do with the dynamics of acquisition—how learners view strategies they might acquire and what using the strategies is like. These points reflect not formal research but both my personal experiences in trying to master certain strategies and the reports of students who, in seminars I have taught, tried several strategies as part of the course work.

Forgetting. Not infrequently, a strategy will be practiced for a few days, considered helpful, and then simply forgotten. Reminded of a strategy later, sometimes people express regret and puzzlement as to how this could have happened.

Cognitive Load. As indicated earlier, many strategies substantially increase the cognitive load of the activity concerned, at least until some automatization occurs. Presumably, with the greater effort comes more effective performance. Nonetheless, it is hard to be persuasive about beneficial net effects when a student complains about the very vividly awkward experience of, let us say, trying to apply the well-known SQ3R reading strategy (Morgan & Deese, 1969; Robinson, 1970). Although the increased cognitive load, which eventually will lessen in any case, may be a price worth paying, in practice it often appears to lead people to give up strategies simply because they are unpleasant.

Plausibility. The willingness of a person to give a strategy a serious try depends on whether the person thinks the strategy might help. The problem is that people differ considerably in their concepts of mental functioning and their ideas about what makes sense and what does not. Here too, people find reasons for rejecting strategies.

Perceived Need. Another relevant consideration is a person's own perception of his or her needs. Often, I have heard individuals report, "My reading is good enough," or, "I'm a pretty effective problem solver already." The person may be right, of course, but just as often the person may not appreciate what improvements are possible. Another somewhat different response is, "Oh, yes that's a good strategy. I already do that." Frequently, of course, the person does not behave as he or she imagines. It has been pointed out by Meichenbaum (1977), Argyris and Schon (1978), and others that very often people's avowed strategies do not match their behavior, quite unbeknown to them. Piaget (1976) reports numerous instances of this sort in an examination of children's ability to describe their own behavior.

Personalization. A person learning a strategy often will personalize the strategy, altering it in various ways to suit himself or herself. Quite possibly, this works in favor of the learner. It is not clear that this is always the case, however.

Drift. In a few personal efforts to learn various strategies, I have sometimes kept written records of a strategy as I construed it at various points. It seems that a kind of drift occurs: One will think one is using just the same strategy that had been adopted several days before but, on examining the notes, discover that the behavior had shifted substantially. This drift very often appears to have reduced the effectiveness of the strategy.

The import of all this is hardly mysterious. Teaching a number of general cognitive-control strategies so that they work *and* stick poses complicated instructional problems not recognized by the teachability hypothesis.

ARE THERE GENERAL COGNITIVE SKILLS?

This chapter has criticized the notion that intellectual competence derives from general teachable cognitive-control strategies. As explained earlier, psychologists and educators often seem to have that in mind when they speak of general cognitive skills. Now we should ask what is left. Despite the reservations, are there general cognitive-control strategies, and in what sense?

Many of the reservations here concerned the state of the art rather than fundamental flaws in the notion. Psychological theory and pedagogical practice could do better simply by accommodating several complications. For example, bad strategies could be winnowed out by testing for effectiveness and ecological validity. Neglected kinds of strategies, such as strategies of problem finding, could be added. The affective dimensions of strategy learning and the crucial role of automatization could receive more attention.

However, besides such tractable troubles, at least two fundamental difficulties have emerged. The first is that many strategies are context-bound. The best evidence suggests that skillful intellectual performance tends to be rather context specific. The second is the presence and persuasiveness of rival models of intellectual competence. Such models also have their limits, but it is difficult to bet solely on a general cognitive-control strategies model of intellectual competence when models based on cognitive style, understanding, and other constructs can each find some support.

Does all this mean that general cognitive-control strategies do not exist? By no means. In fact, let me affirm their existence by listing a few. There was the strategy of asking "why not?," an intellectual habit that has much to recommend it. The pattern of behavior Getzels and Csiksentmihalyi labeled problem finding provides another good example. Still another is the tactic of evaluating and revising one's products. Although simple to state and taken for granted by adults, this practice does not appear, for instance, in the early writing or drawing of children.

The problem is not so much whether anything exists that could reasonably be called a general cognitive-control strategy as it is a matter of what such strategies can deliver. On the positive side, general cognitive-control strategies certainly are important to effectiveness. If they were magically stripped away from an expert, the expert's performance would suffer. Novices often do not deploy these strategies, and sometimes novices have enough resources of knowledge and skills that such strategies can help them to use those resources more effectively.

On the negative side, however, often novices do not have the resources in a particular domain to gain much from a very general strategy. Often, the expert, deprived of such strategies, would still greatly outperform the best that a novice could muster. For example, the conclusions cited earlier concerning master chess play in part reflected the observation that master level players often discern what will become their final move within a few seconds in a reflexive perceptual manner. Furthermore, a "look-ahead" strategy of reasonable depth is as characteristic of the experienced amateur as of the chess master. Perhaps there are points to teach the rank beginner concerning an adequate search, but, beyond that, having an elaborate look-ahead strategy is not what makes the difference.

In summary, general cognitive skills, in the sense of general cognitive-control strategies, do exist and may sometimes be worth teaching. However, they provide only limited power for complex intellectual tasks. And what about general cognitive skills in other, looser senses? Some rival models of intellectual competence such as the cognitive style or the understanding model also provide for general cognitive abilities, although the term skills does not fit so well. However, the problem of context boundedness remains.

All this could be taken as a negative appraisal of the potential of teaching thinking and learning skills, especially to those already reasonably able. Not so. I intend it as a realistic appraisal, not a pessimistic one. There are approaches to teaching intellectual competence that might accommodate reasonably well the fundamental difficulties with the general cognitive skills notion. The remainder of this chapter is committed to a speculative exploration of one such approach.

CONTEXT BOUNDEDNESS AND PRODUCT TYPES

Most often, efforts to enhance intellectual competence are organized around a broad area of performance like problem solving and strategies that supposedly help. The sorts of tasks the learners practice their skills upon are treated as less central. The philosophy seems to be that, for example, problem solving is problem solving, and general skills of problem solving can be equally honed by puzzling over the dilemmas of cities, solving riddles, proving theorems, or inventing a business.

The evidence concerning the context boundedness of skill urges that we ought to be less sanguine about this. However, if the notion of general intellectual competence is to make any sense at all, *field* boundedness has to be avoided. One has to be identifying and teaching something with more range than competence in mathematics specifically, or medical diagnosis, or urban design.

One approach to achieving this would organize instruction about what might be called *product types*. Product types are kinds of molar products calculatedly chosen for their ecological validity across fields. Generality lies not directly in the scope of the strategies taught, but in the wide applicability of the product type. For example, one target ability might be skill in inductive argument, meaning skill in supporting propositions from both hard data and personal experience. A product-types approach to teaching inductive argument would involve extensive writing and criticism of such arguments. Likewise, inventive thinking might be fostered by teaching students to produce designs for a range of things, from an innovative shoe to an innovative classroom schedule. Reading for understanding might be fostered by teaching students to write good summaries of what they read. Written arguments, written and drawn designs, and written summaries are themselves useful intellectual products of wide applicability. Furthermore, although arguments, designs, and summaries need not always be expressed overtly, practice in doing so ought to sharpen the learner's covert thinking processes, a point pursued further later.

A product-types approach can be contrasted with approaches that assume that the task on which learners practice supposedly general skills need only be reasonably complex and engaging. For example, the Productive Thinking Program of Covington et al. (1974) demonstrates thinking strategies mostly in the context of solving whodunits, with exercises ranging somewhat more widely to encompass what Wardrop, Olton, Goodwin, Covington, Klausmeier, Crutchfield, and Ronda (1969) characterize as complex extended problems. These are problems, however, that call for relatively short answers arrived at relatively quickly, at least as the problems are presented in the course, and it is not clear how typical of intellectual activities such problems are. A product-types approach also can be contrasted with instruction specific to a subject matter, such as Wickelgren's (1974) book on mathematical problem solving. Finally, a product-types approach can be contrasted with instruction oriented to relatively short tests or puzzle-like tasks, such as Whimbey and Lochhead (1980). Such instruction may very likely inculcate worthwhile cognitive style traits and expertise with certain sorts of test problems, but it offers little practice with more molar project-like activities and their difficulties.

A natural question arises. If a product types approach is taken, what happens to process instruction and, in particular, general cognitive-control strategies? The answer is that cognitive-control strategies would still be taught, but in the context of specific product types chosen for ecological validity. When a cognitive-control strategy has generality beyond a particular product type, instruction would highlight this, pointing out the parallels as one and then another product type became the focus. The principal difference between a product types and cognitive-control strategies approach would be one of organizational priority. Lessons would be organized around product types with cognitive-control strategies worked in, rather than the reverse.

Another natural question concerns the emphasis on concrete products such as written arguments. Thinking often occurs without any such concrete vehicle, so why should instruction stress concreteness? The worth of concrete products is suggested by Vygotsky's (1962, 1978) notion of thought as, in part, internalized speech. Through working with concrete intellectual products, the learner has the chance to deal overtly, under conditions minimizing memory load and maximizing opportunities for revision, with matters that later can sometimes be dealt with covertly. Moreover, there will always be difficult occasions where intellectual products demand explicit overt treatment. Indeed, Olson (1976) has argued that writing has made systematic analytical thought possible, by providing the kinds of stable overt representations necessary to sustain such thought.

In summary, a product types approach bets that general molar product types are specific enough so that the strategic lore concerning producing the products can be fairly rich. At the same time, the product-types approach bets that the product types can be chosen to be general enough to impart intellectual capability that cuts across subject areas. To foster this, instruction organized around product types would draw examples from many subject areas and would explicitly encourage learners to assimilate problems to a familiar product type.

ALTERNATIVE COMPETENCY MODELS AND THE TEXTURE OF PROBLEM SPACES

Whereas the previous section discussed an approach to the problem of context boundedness, the present section explores one way of accommodating the different models of intellectual competence. It is handiest to begin with a particular area of skill. Consider, for instance, inductive argument, understood as a process of mustering evidence from experience and experiment in defense of a proposition. Inductive argument in this sense was mentioned as a possible product type. But just how are we to understand the nature of skill in producing inductive arguments?

The literature documents a variety of lapses in the use of inductive evidence, for example, basing generalizations on a scanty or biased sample; crediting vivid evidence much more than statistical evidence, which really has more import; and even allowing a mix of confirming and disconfirming evidence to enhance one's confidence in a belief (Nisbett & Ross, 1980). Perhaps what makes a good reasoner, in fact, is exactly a greater alertness to such mishaps than others enjoy. Conceivably, instruction concerning these and similar pitfalls would help the novice reasoner.

Plausible though this is, it seems to me to leave out something. Perhaps the best way to make the point is to consider the reasoning skills of well-educated individuals. The research literature has emphasized that those with professional motivation to avoid errors of inference are far from immune to error (e.g.,

Tversky & Kahneman, 1971, 1974). Even so, such people have something that youngsters or less educated people do not. They can write and discourse in a seemingly rational and, for the most part, actually rational way, although mishaps sometimes occur. They know the reasoning game in a general sense, even if they occasionally fall prey to problems of biased samples, elevating correlations to causation, and so on. But what is it exactly that they know?

A partial answer might be this. Such people can be thought of as knowing the "texture" of the relevant problem space. Let me explain this terminology. The notion of a problem space is borrowed from Newell and Simon (1972), who have argued that problem solving can be conceptualized as an activity occurring within a space of alternative paths through which the problem solver must somehow navigate to a solution state. The term texture aims to suggest that certain classes of problems have certain constant features of the problem spaces natural to them, features concerning the sorts of local steps one can take to get around in the space. Familiarity with the texture allows the problem solver to cope to some extent, even when the kind of problem in a more specific sense is somewhat unfamiliar. Traveling about in a city makes a good metaphor for this. There is no substitute for really knowing a city if one wants to get from A to B. However, even in an unfamiliar city, one can know certain trends concerning street layouts that help considerably; for example, that cities tend to be laid out in rectangular blocks, so that one can travel in any direction by appropriate zigzagging. One knows that one can make a hard or illegal left turn by going straight through an intersection and rightward entirely around the block. And so on. Quite different from intimate knowledge of a particular terrain, such textural knowledge puts one in a position to cope somewhat with problems of a very general type.

With this metaphor in mind, what would the texture of some kinds of problem spaces be like? First, consider problems of deduction where, given certain premises, one must try to infer some target proposition. The basic local feature of this space might be described as an entailment relationship between one or more propositions and an implication. The crucial understanding of this texture seems to be that one has to solve problems by chaining together entailments to make a bridge from the given to the target proposition. If one knows specifically what the target proposition is, one can chain backward from it as well as forward toward it. If, as in a typical algebra word problem, the target proposition (the solution) is not given at the outset, one can only chain towards it. In a way, this sort of textural understanding is very primitive. Certainly, it is no substitute for understanding particular tactics suited for particular sorts of problems. Nonetheless, in facing new problems, such basic resources are often all that one has, and we cannot assume that such basic resources can be taken for granted. In experiments addressing a related issue, Scandura (1977) has shown that children will not always chain operations together to reach an objective.

The concept of texture would not be so interesting if all useful problem spaces had pretty much the same texture. However, this is not the case. Consider

inductive argument. Here, the relationship between propositions and their implications is not as strong as strict entailment. Where there is no counterargument
to a strict deduction, counterarguments behind every bush seem to be a principal
textural characteristic of the inductive reasoning problem space. Even where
there are no problems of a statistical character, such as too small a sample size,
there are always potential problems of whether the evidence is properly described,
whether alternative causes or other models might also account for events, and
so on.

Accordingly, good performance in contexts of formal and informal inductive
argument would seem to require constant vigilance for why nots. The strategy
of asking why not might be seen not just as one more strategy in a good strategic
armamentarium for inductive reasoning, but as truly central to the whole enterprise.

In fact, at this juncture, a strategies model of competence and an understanding
model intersect somewhat. Behaving with an appreciation of the texture of a
problem space amounts to having one sort of core understanding that backs an
understanding model of intellectual competence.

Furthermore, the term strategy seems somewhat inappropriate. The skilled
reasoner would not remember the ask-why-not strategy time after time. Rather,
the skilled reasoner would benefit from a fairly permanent why not set, an abiding
state of alertness to potential counterarguments. Such an alertness is a far cry
from cognitive-control strategies in the sense of mental moves applied on select
occasions within an ongoing thinking process. In fact, such an alertness would
have the pervasive character of a cognitive style. So a cognitive style model of
intellectual competence is also implicated.

WHY NOT "WHY NOT?"

The point of this chapter's opening paragraphs was that simply inquiring "why
not?" of general cognitive skills seemed to demonstrate such a skill. So it does,
but to stop there would be to miss the considerably more subtle circumstances
just sketched. The real power of the why not principle is both greater and less
neatly characterized. The why not principle informs the thinking of a skilled
reasoner in a much more central and pervasive manner than calling it a strategy
would suggest. Theorizing and instruction concerning intellectual competence
needs to treat it that way.

Much the same would hold in any domain where the texture notion makes
sense. As far as instruction is concerned, the texture of problem spaces may
merit some explicit attention. As far as theory is concerned, this point demonstrates the perversity of some theories of competence that we would like to keep
separate and decide among: Rather than remaining disjoint, or even collapsing
into one, they appear intricately entangled. It is with such conceptual dilemmas
that better theories about teaching intellectual competence will have to cope.

ACKNOWLEDGMENTS

This chapter was prepared with support from The Spencer Foundation for a research project entitled "Difficulties in Everyday Reasoning and Their Change with Education." Some of the ideas were developed with the help of Ed Smith, José Buscaglia, Ray Nickerson, and others in the context of Project Intelligence at Harvard University and Bolt, Beranek, and Newman, sponsored by the Venezuelan Ministry for the Development of Human Intelligence, the Ministry of Education, and Petroleos de Venezuela. The author gratefully acknowledges these sources, adding the disclaimer that the opinions expressed here do not necessarily reflect the positions or policies of those that have contributed their ideas, the projects mentioned, or the sponsoring agencies.

REFERENCES

Argyris, C., & Schon, D. A. (1978). *Theory in practice.* San Francisco: Jossey–Bass.
Arlin, P. K. (1975). Cognitive development in adulthood: A fifth stage? *Developmental Psychology, 11,* 602–606.
Baddeley, A. D. (1976). *The psychology of memory.* New York: Harper & Row.
Baron, J. (1978). Intelligence and general strategies. In G. Underwood (Ed.), *Strategies of information processing.* New York: Academic Press.
Bower, G. H. (1970). Imagery as a relational organizer in association learning. *Journal of Verbal Learning and Verbal Behavior, 9,* 529–533.
Bower, G. H. (1972). Mental imagery and associative learning. In L. W. Gregg (Ed.), *Cognition in learning and memory.* New York: Wiley.
Brainerd, C. J. (1974). Neo-Piagetian training experiments revisited: Is there any support for the cognitive-developmental stage hypothesis? *Cognition, 2* (3), 349–370.
Brainerd, C. J. (1978). The stage question in cognitive-developmental theory. *The Behavioral and Brain Sciences, 2,* 173–182.
Bugelski, B. R. (1970). Words and things and images. *American Psychologist, 25,* 1002–1012.
Cole, M., & Scribner, S. (1974). *Culture and thought: A psychological introduction.* New York: Wiley.
Collyer, S. C., Jonides, J., & Bevan, W. (1972). Images as memory aids: Is bizarreness helpful? *American Journal of Psychology, 85,* 31–38.
Covington, M. V., Crutchfield, R. S., Davies, L., & Olton, R. M. (1974). *The productive thinking program: A course in learning to think.* Columbus, OH: Merrill.
de Bono, E. (1970). *Lateral thinking: Creativity step by step.* New York: Harper & Row.
de Bono, E. (1973). *CoRT Thinking.* Blandford, Dorset, England: Direct Education Services Limited.
de Groot, A. D. (1965). *Thought and choice in chess.* The Hague: Mouton.
Elstein, A. S., Shulman, L. S., & Sprafka, S. A. (1978). *Medical problem solving: An analysis of clinical reasoning.* Cambridge, MA: Harvard University Press.
Feldhusen, J. F., Speedie, S. M., & Treffinger, D. J. (1971). The Purdue creative thinking program: Research and evaluation. *NSPI Journal, 10*(3), 5–9.
Feuerstein, R. (1980). *Instrumental enrichment: An intervention program for cognitive modifiability.* Baltimore: University Park Press.
Flavell, J. H. (1976). Metacognitive aspects of problem solving. In L. B. Resnick (Ed.), *The nature of intelligence.* Hillsdale, NJ: Lawrence Erlbaum Associates.
Frankenstein, C. (1979). *They think again: Restoring cognitive abilities through teaching.* New York: Van Nostrand Reinhold.

Furth, H. G., & Wachs, H. (1974). *Thinking goes to school: Piaget's theory in practice.* New York: Oxford University Press.

Gallwey, W. T. (1976). *Inner tennis—playing the game.* New York: Random House.

Getzels, J., & Csikszentmihalyi, M. (1976). *The creative vision: A longitudinal study of problem finding in art.* New York: Wiley.

Goldstein, I., Papert, S., & Minsky, M. (1976). Artificial intelligence, language, and the study of knowledge. In *Artificial intelligence and language comprehension.* Washington, DC: National Institute of Education.

Guilford, J. P., & Hoepfner, R. (1971). *The analysis of intelligence.* New York: McGraw–Hill.

Heller, J. I., & Greeno, J. G. (1979). Information-processing analyses of mathematical problem solving. In S. H. White & R. W. Tyler (Eds.), *Testing, teaching and learning.* Washington, DC: National Institute of Education.

Higbee, K. L. (1977). *Your memory: How it works and how to improve it.* Englewood Cliffs, NJ: Prentice–Hall.

Howard, V. A. (1982). *Artistry: The work of artists.* Indianapolis: Hackett.

Hunter, I. M. L. (1964). *Memory* (rev. ed.). Middlesex, England: Penguin Books.

Johnson, D. M. (1972). *A systematic introduction to the psychology of thinking.* New York: Harper & Row.

Kagan, J., & Kogan, N. (1970). Individuality and cognitive performance. In P. Mussen (Ed.), *Carmichael's manual of child psychology* (Vol. I). New York: Wiley.

Karplus, R. (1980). Teaching for the development of reasoning. In A. E. Lawson (Ed.), *The psychology of teaching for thinking and creativity.* Columbus, OH: ERIC–SMEAC.

Karplus, R., Lawson, A., Wollman, W., Appel, M., Bernhoff, R., Howe, A., Rusch, J., & Sullivan, F. (1977). *Science teaching and the development of reasoning.* Berkeley, CA: University of California.

Karplus, R., Karplus, E., Formisano, M., & Paulsen, A. C. (1979). Proportional reasoning and control of variables in seven countries. In J. Lochhead & J. Clement (Eds.), *Cognitive process instruction.* Philadelphia: Franklin Institute Press.

Kuhn, D. (1979). The application of Piaget's theory of cognitive development to education. *Harvard Educational Review, 49*(3), 340–360.

Langan, J. (1978). *Reading and study skills.* New York: McGraw–Hill.

Larkin, J. H. (1979). Information processing models and science instruction. In J. Lochhead & J. Clement (Eds.), *Cognitive process instruction.* Philadelphia: Franklin Institute Press.

McCabe, B. J. (1965). A program for teaching composition to pupils of limited academic ability. In M. F. Shugrue & G. Hillocks (Eds.), *Classroom practices in teaching English.* Washington, DC: National Council of Teachers of English.

Mann, L. (1979). *On the trail of process—a historical perspective on cognitive processes and their training.* New York: Grune & Stratton.

Mansfield, R. S., Busse, T. V., & Krepelka, E. J. (1978). The effectiveness of creativity training. *Review of Educational Research, 48*(4), 517–536.

Marshak, D. (1979). *Hm study skills program level II.* Reston, VA: The National Association of Secondary School Principals.

Meeker, M. (1969a). An evaluation of the educationally handicapped program: The measurables and the unmeasurables after two years. *Educational Therapy, 2,* 481–495. (Special Child Publications, Seattle.)

Meeker, M. N. (1969b). *The structure of intellect: Its interpretation and uses.* Columbus, OH: Merrill.

Meeker, M. (1979). The relevance of arithmetic testing to teaching arithmetic skills. *The Gifted Child Quarterly, 23*(2), 297–303.

Meichenbaum, D. (1977). *Cognitive-behavior modification.* New York: Plenum.

Morgan, C. T., & Deese, J. (1969). *How to study* (2nd ed.). New York: McGraw–Hill.

Morris, P. E., & Stevens, R. (1974). Linking images and free recall. *Journal of Verbal Learning and Verbal Behavior, 13,* 310–315.

Neisser, V., & Kerr, N. (1973). Spatial and mnemonic properties of visual images. *Cognitive Psychology, 5,* 138–150.

Newell, A., & Simon, H. (1972). *Human problem solving.* Englewood Cliffs, NJ: Prentice–Hall.

Nisbett, R., & Ross, L. (1980). *Human inference: Strategies and shortcomings of social judgment.* Englewood Cliffs, NJ: Prentice-Hall.

Noller, R. B., Parnes, S. J., & Biondi, A. M. (1976). *Creative actionbook.* New York: Scribner.

Olson, D. R. (1976). Culture, technology, and intellect. In L. B. Resnick (Ed.), *The nature of intelligence.* Hillsdale, NJ: Lawrence Erlbaum Associates.

O'Neil, H. F. (Ed.) (1978). *Learning strategies.* New York: Academic Press.

Papert, S. (1971a). *Teaching children thinking* (LOGO Memo No. 2). Cambridge: Massachusetts Institute of Technology Artificial Intelligence Laboratory.

Papert, S. (1971b). *Teaching children to be mathematicians vs. teaching about mathematics* (LOGO Memo No. 4). Cambridge: Massachusetts Institute of Technology Artificial Intelligence Laboratory.

Papert, S., Abelson, H., Bamberger, J., diSessa, A., Weir, S., Watt, D., Hein, G., & Dunning, S. (1978). *Interim report of the LOGO project in the Brookline public schools.* (LOGO Memo No. 49). Cambridge: Massachusetts Institute of Technology Artificial Intelligence Laboratory.

Perkins, D. N. (1975). Noticing: An aspect of skill. In *Conference on basic mathematical skills and learning (Vol. I): Contributed position papers.* Washington, DC: National Institute of Education.

Perkins, D., & Gardner, H. (1978). *Analysis and training of processes and component skills in the arts* (Final report of NIE Project Number 3–1190). Cambridge, MA: Project Zero, Harvard Graduate School of Education.

Piaget, J. (1972). Intellectual evolution from adolescence to adulthood. *Human Development, 15,* 1–12.

Piaget, J. (1976). *The grasp of consciousness.* Cambridge, MA: Harvard University Press.

Polya, G. (1957). *How to solve it: A new aspect of mathematical method* (2nd ed.). Garden City, NY: Doubleday.

Resnick, L. B. (1976). Task analogies in instructional design: Some cases from mathematics. In David Klahr (Ed.), *Cognition and instruction.* Hillsdale, NJ: Lawrence Erlbaum Associates.

Rigney, J. W., Munro, A., & Crook, D. E. (1979). Teaching task oriented selective reading: A learning strategy. In H. F. O'Neill, Jr. & C. D. Spielberger (Eds.), *Cognitive and affective learning strategies.* New York: Academic Press.

Robinson, F. P. (1970). *Effective study.* New York: Harper & Row.

Scandura, J. M. (1977). *Problem-solving. A structural/process approach with instructional implications.* New York: Academic Press.

Scardamalia, M., & Bereiter, C. (1978). (Review of *The philosophy of composition* by E. D. Hirsch, Jr.). *Harvard Educational Review, 49,* 116–119.

Schoenfeld, A. H. (1978). Presenting a strategy for indefinite integration. *American Mathematical Monthly, 85*(8), 673–678.

Schoenfeld, A. H. (1979). Can heuristics be taught? In J. Lochhead & J. Clement (Eds.), *Cognitive process instruction.* Philadelphia: Franklin Institute.

Simon, H., & Chase, W. (1973). Skill in chess. *American Scientist, 61,* 394–403.

Slovic, P., Fischhoff, B., & Lichtenstein, S. (1977). Behavioral decision theory. *Annual Review of Psychology, 28,* 1–39.

Stanley, J. C. (1977). Rationale of the study of mathematically precocious youth (SMPY) during its first five years of promoting educational acceleration. In J. C. Stanley, W. C. George, & C. H. Solano (Eds.), *The gifted and the creative: A 50-year perspective.* Baltimore: Johns Hopkins University Press.

Tversky, A., & Kahneman, D. (1971). The belief in the "law of small numbers." *Psychology Bulletin, 76,* 105–110.

Tversky, A., & Kahneman, D. (1973). Availability: A heuristic for judging frequency and probability. *Cognitive Psychology, 5,* 207–232.

Tversky, A., & Kahneman, D. (1974). Judgment under uncertainty: Heuristics and biases. *Science, 185,* 1124–1131.

Vygotsky, L. S. (1978). *Thought and language.* Cambridge, MA: MIT Press.

Vygotsky, L. S. (1978). *Mind in society: The development of higher psychological processes.* Cambridge, MA: Harvard University Press.

Wardrop, J. L., Olton, R. M., Goodwin, W. L., Covington, M. V., Klausmeier, H. J., Crutchfield, R. S., & Ronda, T. (1969). The development of productive thinking skills in fifth-grade children. *Journal of Experimental Education, 37,* 67–77.

Wason, P. C., & Johnson–Laird, P. N. (1972). *Psychology of reasoning: Structure and content.* Cambridge: Harvard University Press.

Wheeler, D. C., & Dember, W. N. (Eds.) (1979). *A practicum in thinking.* Cincinnati: University of Cincinnati.

Whimbey, A. (1975). *Intelligence can be taught.* New York: Dutton.

Whimbey, A., & Lochhead, J. (1978). *Problem solving and comprehension: A short course in analytical reasoning.* Philadelphia: The Franklin Institute Press.

Wickelgren, W. A. (1974). *How to solve problems: Elements of a theory of problems and problem solving.* San Francisco: W. H. Freeman.

Witkin, H. A. (1976). Cognitive style in academic performance and in teacher–student relations. In S. Messick & Associates (Eds.), *Individuality in learning.* San Francisco: Jossey–Bass.

Wollen, K. A., Weber, A., & Lowry, D. H. (1972). Bizarreness versus interaction of mental images as determinants of learning. *Cognitive Psychology, 3,* 518–523.

Wood, G. (1967). Mnemonic systems in recall. *Journal of Educational Psychology, 58,* 1–27.

16

What Kinds of Intelligence Components are Fundamental?

Jonathan Baron
University of Pennsylvania

The chapters in these volumes attest to a belief among many researchers that psychology is about to make significant advances in finding out how to make people more intelligent. This optimism is the result of a new set of shared assumptions about the nature of intelligence. It is assumed that intelligence consists of components, which can be described in terms of human information processing as studied by modern cognitive psychology. The modern theory of information processing seeks to characterize mental processes in terms of rules for cause and effect relations between mental states. It thus promises to remedy the deficiencies of the psychometric approach to the structure of intelligence (summarized by Gould, 1981, Chapter 6; Sternberg, 1977).

According to the shared assumptions, intelligence can be characterized in terms of certain kinds of processes or properties of processes. Intelligent people are thought to use these processes more often or more efficiently than less intelligent people. Some of these components are thought to be affected by learning and are thus potentially modifiable by environmental manipulations such as education. There may be other components that are manipulable only through medical interventions. This chapter, however, concerns only the components that may be affected by learning.

The question that inspired this chapter was, "Which components of intelligence might qualify as being fundamental under this process view?" A fundamental component is highly general, that is, useful in a wide variety of tasks, and it is also useful in promoting the acquisition of other components of intelligence. I argue here that this question cannot now be answered. However, it is possible to answer a different question: "What *kinds* of components might be fundamental?" The literature (e.g., Hunt, 1978; Meichenbaum, this volume;

Nickerson, Perkins, & Smith, 1980; Sternberg, 1979) suggests a division of components into three types: processing components, strategies, and styles. Processing components are parameters that represent limits on: (1) the use of pathways by which one mental code activates another (in Posner, 1978) or (2) the maintenance, storage, and retrieval of such codes. Examples are speed of retrieval from long-term memory, speed or accuracy of inducing a relation, or capacity of working memory. Individual differences in such parameters (as discussed by Hunt, 1978; Sternberg, 1977) are measured in tasks in which all subjects attempt to do the same task in the same way. Strategies are plans for achieving limited goals in mental tasks, such as solving a problem or committing some material to memory. Examples are self-monitoring in memorizing or working backward in problem solving. Individuals are said to differ in strategies when they tend to do the same task in different ways. Styles are general behavioral dispositions that characterize performance in mental tasks; they are intellectual personality traits. Examples are reflection–impulsivity and sensitivity to evidence against one's favored beliefs. Unlike strategies, styles are described in general terms, rather than in terms of particular goals. Styles and strategies, but not processing components, are to some extent under voluntary control.

I argue here that styles are the most fundamental components, the ones that ought to be of greatest concern to educators who seek to increase intelligence. The evidence suggests that processing components cannot be trained in general. Strategies, as usually conceived, are too limited in generality to count as fundamental. However, there is some evidence that styles can be trained and that they are quite important in thinking and learning.

Components of "intelligence," as distinct from those of "knowledge and skill," are general by definition; that is, these components must be defined without reference to particular contents of knowledge or sets of learning experiences. They should thus be measurable in a variety of situations characterized by different content. Such abilities as "perfect pitch," no matter how precisely defined in information-processing terms, could not count as general components. By definition, perfect pitch is an ability useful only in the situation in which pitches of tones are to be identified. I do not mean to say that specific components, such as perfect pitch, are useless. I mean only that it is convenient to restrict our definition of "intelligence" so that it does not include every mental ability or component. Of course, generality is likely to be a matter of degree. The search for the components of intelligence is thus the search for the most general components we can find.

The search for such general components is dictated by a practical concern about education as well as a theoretical concern about the nature of intelligence. General components are those we would want a person to have if we have little idea what environment that person will have to adapt to, what problems he will be called upon to solve, or what skills he will have to learn. I assume that it is increasingly true of the children we educate that we do not know these things.

It is harder now than it used to be, in more stable periods of human history, to know what a person will need to know in the future. I think this uncertainty holds as much for traditional cultures as for complex technological societies.

Another reason for seeking general components is to develop a theory of intelligence and its training that is cross culturally valid. General components should thus be definable without regard to the specific skills considered useful in certain cultures. Cultures may differ in the importance they assign to different components, but a truly general component should be of some value in any culture. (I thus assume that it may be impossible to develop an intelligence test that is cross culturally valid, because the weight assigned to different components of the test in computing the total score will vary across cultures. However, it may be possible to specify a short list of components that any intelligence test should include.) This goal may be the most difficult one to achieve, but an effort to achieve it may lead to a more powerful theory of intelligence.

If teachable general components are found, there is nothing in their definition that will restrict instruction to certain situations, such as Piagetian tasks or geometry problems. It may turn out that the components are most easily taught in certain contexts, but this will be an empirical fact and not a consequence of the way a component is defined. It may turn out that they can be effectively taught in many different contexts; if so, it would be natural to try to teach them along with whatever specific knowledge and skill is considered important.

In this chapter, I first discuss the three different kinds of components, processing components, strategies, and styles. I present evidence that processing components are either not teachable or not general, but strategies and styles are teachable. Strategies and styles differ mainly in generality; styles are more general. Thus, if there are any teachable general components of intelligence, they are best described as styles. In this sense, styles include the components that are most fundamental. These claims, if true, have implications for educational efforts designed to increase intelligence, and I try to make these implications explicit. I also illustrate this discussion with examples of some research on strategies and styles that I and my collaborators have been doing. Finally, I conclude with some recommendations for further research.

PROCESSING COMPONENTS

The idea of processing components rests on the analogy between information processing in the human and in the computer (e.g., Snow, 1980). For a computer, performance components would consist of the speed and capacity (in bits) of its basic operations such as depositing an item in memory, as well as such general properties as its memory capacity. For a human, performance components might consist of the speed and accuracy of such processes as encoding of a multidimentional stimulus (Sternberg, 1977) or retrieval from memory (Hunt, 1978).

Individuals appear to differ in the efficiency of these processes. For example, subjects who differ in aptitude-test scores differ in speed of searching memory for a given item (Hunt, 1978). Subjects also differ in the speed of processes used in solving analogy problems, such as finding the relation between the first two terms (Sternberg, 1977).

It would be reasonable to try to increase intelligence by providing practice at such basic processes as these. The processes involved in analogical reasoning might be an example. By some theories of how analogy problems are solved (e.g., Mulholland, Pellegrino, & Glaser, 1980; Sternberg, 1977), we can break the solving of these problems into steps, such as finding the relation between the first pair of terms, finding the relation between the second pair of terms (or one possible second pair), and comparing the two relations. We might think that practice at solving these problems will transfer to any situations in which relations must be found or compared. This would be true if the speed or efficiency of each process were a general processing component in the sense I mean, and if such processing components could improve with practice. Because practically all problems can be described as involving discovery or comparison of relations, such practice might be thought to improve the ability to solve any problem, and thus to increase intelligence in this sense. The primary question is whether practice at finding a relation in one task transfers to finding a relation in another.

The designers of programs to increase intelligence (such as those discussed in these volumes) may sometimes assume that their programs are effective because of such general practice effects in processing components. Practice is assumed to operate in much the way that exercise strengthens a muscle or improves blood circulation. In particular, general practice effects are assumed to occur without any changes in strategy, that is, in the steps students take to perform a task, and without any changes in what the student tries to do, that is, in any parameters under voluntary control. If the practice were effective for either of these other reasons, it might be possible to circumvent it by instructing the student in the steps he is to take (e.g., "Test yourself after you study the list") or in the ways he should modify his goals (e.g., "Try harder to be accurate even at the expense of speed"). Changes in the way a task is done are properly conceived as changes in strategy. Changes in general kinds of goals or in other general parameters under voluntary control are, I argue later, best conceived as styles. The assumption that a program is effective because of general practice effects in performance components is not explicit in any program description I have seen, but it is often hard (for me) to think of any other justification for some of the exercises that some programs contain.

I know of no well-controlled research in educational settings on whether there is transfer of training on processing components. However, there is some literature from the experimental psychology laboratory that bears on this question. In almost every case, the answer is that there is no transfer of practice for processing components, that is, no transfer unless there are changes in the way a task is done or in the goals the subject tries to achieve. In making this claim,

I assume, of course, that a distinction may be made between improvement that is due to such changes and "pure" improvement, which is not. Although such an assumption may be questioned, evidence in support of my claim is also evidence for the assumption; that is, the distinction between pure practice effects and those that result from changes in what the subject does or tries to do may be supported best by the study of transfer of practice.

Early experiments on transfer of practice (e.g., Thorndike & Woodworth, 1901) grew out of the idea of formal discipline, the idea that the study of Latin and Greek, for example, conditions the mind in the way we think that jogging conditions the body. These experiments were unanimous in showing no transfer of practice unless there were common stimulus elements or unless it appeared that subjects were learning new ways of doing a task (Woodworth & Schlosberg, 1954, Chapter 24). For example, Woodrow (1927) found no transfer of practice at memorizing across different material (poems, Turkish vocabulary, etc.) unless students were instructed in "proper methods of memorizing"—i.e., new ways of doing the task.

Recent studies agree with the earlier ones in finding no general transfer that could be ascribed to processing components. In one (Chase & Simon, 1973), chess masters, when shown a position from a chess game for 5 seconds and asked to reproduce it from memory, performed several times better than beginning chess players. Yet, when the masters were asked to reproduce a random arrangement of pieces instead of a real position, they performed as badly as beginners. They had apparently received considerable practice at holding sensible chess positions in memory, and this skill probably involves several different processing components by anyone's account, but the practice did not seem to transfer to another memory task, which would seem to involve many of the same components.

Ericsson, Chase, and Faloon (1980) taught a heroic subject to improve his memory span for digits, from 7 to 79, with more than 230 hours of practice. When tested on sequences of consonants, however, his span was approximately six. He had, it was convincingly argued, learned and perfected certain strategies for memorizing strings of digits. These strategies could not be applied to strings of letters. But more importantly for our purposes, all that practice at digit memorizing did not seem to affect his ability to memorize letters, even though the tasks presumably share many common components.

Other studies measure reaction time to determine the effect of practice on general processing components. The most exensively studied task involves search for a digit in a short memorized string of digits (Sternberg, 1966). A subject is presented with a set of up to six digits before each trial. A different set is used for each trial. The subject is then presented with a single digit, and he must indicate as quickly as possible whether that test digit is in the set. Usually, the response is made by pressing one of two keys. The time to make the response increases linearly with the number of digits in the positive set (Sternberg, 1966). Each additional digit in the set adds about 40 msec to the reaction time. The effect of set size on reaction time, in msec per digit, is taken to measure the speed of searching working memory. This procedure allows us to look at the effect of practice on just the speed of search, a processing component if anything is. Sternberg (1966) and Kristofferson (1972a) found that the speed of search does not change with practice in adults. In effect, there is no transfer of practice across different sets of digits. However, the mean reaction time does improve with practice in this task. The improvement in mean reaction time may be due to the subject's experience with aspects of the task that remain constant, such as the display and the response keys. This experience may affect the speed of other processing components aside from memory search. However, because these components remain constant from the practice task (certain sets of digits) to the transfer task (other sets), no generality of the practice effect can be inferred.

These results are obtained only with the use of a different set of digits on every trial. The subject gets no special practice at associating a particular digit with a particular response, because each digit is associated with both positive and negative responses. In other studies (Kristofferson 1972b; Shiffrin & Schneider, 1977), each stimulus is always associated with the same response, and the effect of set size decreases over trials. Logan (1978) used fixed sets and varied sets under otherwise identical conditions and found an effect of practice on search rate only with fixed sets. With a fixed assignment of stimuli to responses, a subject can, and apparently does, learn an association between the digit and the response and circumvent the search of working memory that would otherwise be required. (The learning of associations seems to occur for both positive and negative responses, provided that sufficient practice is provided, Prinz, 1977. This fact may explain the one apparent exception to the rule that general processing components do not improve with practice, namely, Kristofferson's 1977 finding of complete transfer of practice to an entirely new positive set. In Kristofferson's experiment, the negative set consisted of eight items, and these items were the same before and after the change in the positive set.)

It is fortunate for my argument that digits and letters were used as stimuli for these experiments. These stimuli are highly familiar, and there are therefore no practice effects due to experience with the stimuli themselves. When unfamiliar stimuli are used (Marcel, 1970), or when subjects are children who are less familiar with digits and letters than adults, effects of practice on memory search are to be expected, even with a different positive set on each trial. Search speed could be expected to improve with practice because the time required to compare each item in memory to the test item would improve. Again, such transfer effects must be interpreted as specific effects, not general ones. The best way to avoid such specific transfer effects from experience with the stimuli is to use entirely different stimuli in the test of specific transfer.

In sum, the rate of memory search does not appear to change unless the subject can learn to do the task some other way than by searching memory on each trial, or unless the subject is initially unfamiliar with the stimuli used.

Logan (1979) used another task in which subjects had to press a different key for each stimulus. He found, as have others, that reaction time increases with the number of alternatives. The increased time presumably reflects the increased burden on a decision process. We can ask whether practice affects this process, regardless of its effects on other processing components. When constant stimulus–response pairings are used over several sessions, the effect of number of pairings decreases. However, when Logan changed the pairings after six sessions, the effect returned to its original strength. Again, no transfer of practice to a new stimulus set was found.

Reisberg, Baron, and Kemler (1980) examined the effect of practice on a distraction task analogous to a Stroop task. Subjects were given rows of up to four items and were asked to say how many items were in each row. When the items were digits (e.g., "3 3 3 3," to be responded to as "four"), reaction time was slowed. When the same digits were used for a few hundred trials, this slowing due to distraction decreased. However, when the subject changed to new digits, the distraction effect returned to its original strength. Subjects apparently learned not to be distracted by particular digits, but they did not learn not to be distracted by digits in general. Somehow, the association between the distractor digit and the response to it was weakened with practice, and this effect was specific to the associations used. In this study, there was transfer of practice from digits to names of digits (ONE, THREE). When transfer stimuli are coded by the subject in the same way as practice stimuli, transfer is to be expected.

In sum, there are several cases in which there appears to be no general transfer of practice. These cases are easily described as ones in which general performance components are held constant between practice and transfer tasks, but other components either are changed, do not enter the measurement of transfer, or are not subject to practice effects. All practice effects appear to be specific to the stimuli used. So far as I can determine, all the practice effects in simple tasks can be ascribed to practice on particular stimulus–response associations. This is essentially what Thorndike and Woodworth (1901) claimed, and there is as yet no reason to modify their view.

It might be argued that the amounts of practice given are too small to show general effects. Although this is possible, practice effects are usually most easily noticed at the beginning of practice and would thus be apparent fairly early. Also, many of these experiments involved 30 hours, or so, of practice in as many days. Finally, all the procedures I have discussed have also been shown to be highly sensitive to specific practice effects. It is thus unlikely that general practice effects have been missed.

A more subtle objection to my argument holds that practice effects are not found in laboratory experiments because practice is being continually provided by events outside the laboratory. The general components are thus up to as high a level of practice as they can reach, and they do not show effects of additional practice. This objection requires a more careful statement of my argument than I have yet made. The reason we are interested in practice effects is that we want to know whether educational intervention should focus on general processing components. We may take the laboratory experiments as models of the kinds of interventions that might be made (albeit with different components). These experiments allow us to distinguish specific practice effects—which may be attributed to practice at certain stimulus–response pairings—from general practice effects in a processing component. The former will show up as improvement in the task in which practice is provided; the latter, as transfer of this improvement to a new task of the same form but with different stimuli and responses. The experiments I have discussed show no such transfer. Thus, these experiments show that *extra* practice has no effect on general components, where *extra* means "practice not provided by daily life." Although practice might be shown to have some general effect—if we could ever do the experiment to find out—extra practice appears not to have any effect, and the educational implications are the same as if practice itself had no effect.

The results I have described, and the claims I have made, are limited to certain kinds of tasks. These tasks are ones that the subject already knows how to do, once the experimenter's instructions are understood. There is nothing further the subjects can be told about how to do the task more proficiently, except "practice makes perfect." This situation contrasts with many other situations involving skilled processing, such as playing the violin. Here, instructions such as "listen to what you are playing" might lead to immediate improvements and might even transfer to playing the bassoon, where the stimuli and responses are quite different.

Early researchers, when faced with evidence against the existence of general transfer of practice, tended to conclude that the effects of education were specific to the material taught. Likewise, modern research in cognitive psychology tends to focus heavily on the analysis of performance of particular tasks, such as use of maps, solution of algebra problems, or memorization of stories, rather than on potentially general properties of intelligent behavior. Perhaps modern researchers have in mind a similar justification for their choice of topic; specifically, they might concude that studies of specific knowledge and skill are more likely to pay off in application. This conclusion might be supported by the same kinds of negative evidence for general transfer that I have just reviewed. However, the conclusion is unwarranted. Lack of transfer is specific to the kinds of processing components I have described. Other kinds of components do show general transfer. Educational efforts to improve intelligence must be directed toward the kinds of components that show general transfer, and away from those processing components that do not.

STRATEGIES

There has been considerable discussion of the idea that "strategies" are crucial in intelligent behavior (e.g., Baron, 1978; Brown, 1975; Flavell, 1970). The concept of strategy is usually explained by example rather than by definition, so a brief discussion of the historical roots of the term may help us to understand its present use. One important root is Miller, Galanter, and Pribram's (1960) concept of a plan. A plan is analogous to the program of a computer, not only in its structure, but also in the fact that most plans are thought to be acquired. A plan may be thought of as having a structure defined in terms of goals and subgoals. When a plan is put into effect, a certain goal is chosen, for example, "learn this list of items." Subgoals are chosen on the basis of the main goal and the conditions present. For example, there might be a rule that specifies that items are to be rehearsed when they are in a list that must be learned in order. Thus, rehearsal, or rote repetition, becomes a subgoal. In turn, this goal requires that each item be named. A plan yields a certain sequence of actions, but the plan is identified by its goal, not the actions themselves. If certain subplans have not been learned, or if the world is ornery, it may be impossible to carry out a plan. Yet, as long as behavior is governed by the goal structure of the plan, by the search for useful subgoals, etc., the plan can be said to be in effect.

A second source of the concept of a strategy is the concept of control processes in memory (Atkinson & Shiffrin, 1968). These are the processes by which a person controls the flow of information among different memory-storage systems. They include rehearsal, other mnemonics, and plans for retrieval (e.g., "I know her first name begins with M. Perhaps I can think of it by listing girls' names beginning with M.").

The claim has been that intelligence may consist in large part of a tendency to use certain strategies for learning, understanding, or problem solving. The import of this claim does not hinge on any notion of what strategies are, or of which strategies are the important ones. Rather, it is that the limits on performance are *not* unmodifiable capacities. So far, most investigations have concerned the development of the ability to memorize arbitrary material, such as sequences of pictures. The deficiencies of young children in memorization can be attributed largely to their failure to use certain strategies, such as rehearsal and self-testing. When young children are taught to rehearse, for example, their ability to learn a sequence of pictures improves. Retardates, like young children, show deficiencies in the use of strategies for learning. The deficits of retardates in memorization can be at least partially overcome through instruction in certain strategies, such as rehearsal (e.g., Belmont & Butterfield, 1971; Brown, 1974). If the ability to memorize arbitrary material is part of intelligence, these results show that intelligence can be raised by training in strategies, especially if it is found that the strategy trained is general.

Recently, it has been suggested that strategies are crucial to mature performance in other kinds of tasks. Strategies may be involved in comprehension of meaningful material as well as memorization of arbitrary material (Adams & Collins, 1977). One strategy of interest in reading comprehension is: "Form a hypothesis about the text and look for evidence to test it." There have been speculations that use of similar strategies distinguishes effective and ineffective problem solving (Baron, 1978; Flavell, 1977). Here too, it has been proposed that deficits in problem solving can be overcome through instruction in relevant strategies. Some strategies considered have been: "Solve the problem one part at a time"; "think of consequences of what is given" (Polya, 1957; Wickelgren, 1974). Only a little research (e.g., Brown, Campione, & Barclay, 1979; Brown, this volume) has so far been directed at instruction in general strategies for these more significant kinds of tasks.

Strategies in Rule Statement

With the intent of filling this gap, I began a program of research on a set of strategies that might be used to formulate and criticize general statements and arguments, or, put loosely, to think critically. One such strategy is thinking of a counterargument, a reason for a conclusion opposite to the one stated. Another strategy is thinking of counterexamples when a general rule is stated. The general form of many critical thinking strategies is: propose a statement, think of a criticism of the statement, and modify the statement so that the criticism no longer applies. In this form, critical thinking strategies are crucial to most kinds of productive scholarship. Acquisition of these strategies may be promoted by higher education, as their use is the bread and butter of academic discourse. But these strategies are important outside the academy as well, for example, in political debate (Perkins, Allen, & Hafner, 1980).

I describe some studies of the use of counterexamples to refine the statement of general principles. These studies were conceived as studies of strategies, as just noted. Later, I reinterpret them as having more to do with style. They thus serve as an example of the distinction between strategies and styles, and the value of this distinction.

In these studies, subjects are asked to discover rules on the basis of knowledge the subjects already have. The type of rule we have studied is the type that relates speech sounds to English spellings. For example, we asked our subjects when the letter C at the beginning of a word is pronounced as if it were S. To arrive at this rule, one might begin with a provisional rule based on a single example, such as CENT. One might propose that the rule is "C followed by a vowel is pronounced S." Then one might think of a counterexamples, such as CANT. One would then modify the rule. A new rule statement that took into account both the example and the counterexample would be "C followed by E . . . ." This rule is also wrong, as one would soon discover by the same method.

In an initial experiment (Baron, Freyd, & Stewart, 1980), the subjects were graduate students and age-matched controls from a part-time employment service. The subjects were asked to figure out simple spelling-sound rules of the sort indicated. They were told to talk aloud while they were thinking so that we could obtain a record of their thoughts. Of interest was the finding that the students were more likely to improve their own rules through use of counterexamples they themselves provided. Control subjects were less likely to try to think of counterexamples once they had proposed a rule, and they were less likely to modify their rule once they had thought of a counterexample.

In a second study, Elise Sutter and I tried to teach a group of college students to use the counterexample strategy. This time, we used a microcomputer as a tutor and an examiner. We asked subjects about fairly restricted rules, e.g., "When is C, at the beginning of a four-letter word, pronounced S?" By restricting the task to four letter words beginning or ending with a certain letter, we could load the entire vocabulary of such words into the (8K) memory of the computer, coded for pronunciation. The computer could thus determine whether the subject's rules were correct, in the sense of accounting for all examples. It could also provide the subject with counterexamples if the subject was unable to think of his own.

To make the test easier for the computer—although harder for the subject I fear—the rule had to be stated in a certain format. The subject had to specify the letters required for the given pronunciation of the critical letter. A dash indicated that any letter would do in a given position, a star indicated that a consonant was required, and a plus indicated a vowel was. (Subsequently, I have found that that task appears to be easier if uppercase C and V are used.) Exceptions were indicated with parentheses following the dash, star, or plus. Disjunct conditions were indicated by listing them separately. For example, the C as S rule could be stated as follows:

    c + (aou) − −.

This means "C is pronounced as S when followed by any vowel except A, O, or U. Alternatively, the rule could be stated disjunctively as:

    ce − −
    ci − −
    cy − −

This means that C is pronounced as S when followed by E, by I, or by Y. These two statements of the rule are equivalent because they both account correctly for all the examples. The first illustrates the notation for exceptions, and the second illustrates the notation for disjunct conditions.

Table 16.1 shows the record of a subject's interaction with the computer on the first and on the last rule he worked on. When the subject gave a false rule, the tutor told him so and asked whether he could think of a counterexample. If the subject said he could, the computer told him to go ahead and try, and then, if the subject was successful, to state a new rule. (If the subject's counterexample was not a counterexample, the computer told him so and asked him again if he could think of one.) If the subject said he could not think of a counterexample, the computer gave him one and went directly to the point of asking the subject

TABLE 16.1

Example of First and Last Dialogues in the Experiment on Use of
Counterexamples. (Explanations Are in Parentheses.)

First Rule

Computer: What is the rule for pronouncing A at the beginning of three-letter words? Can you state the rule?

Subject: A*E (A followed by a consonant and then E, as in APE.)

C: Your rule is incorrect. Can you think of an example that shows that your rule is wrong?

S: ARE

C: Very good. Can you state the rule?

S: A*(RWX)E (This specifies that the consonants R, W, and X are exceptions to the previously given rule.)

C: Your rule is not correct. Can you think of an example that shows that your rule is wrong?

S: Yes.

C: What is your example?

S: AIM.

C: Very good. Can you state the rule?

S: A*(RWX)E

AI – (A disjunction of two conditions, one the last rule, the other A followed by I and any other letter.

C: Correct!

Last Rule

C: What is the rule for pronouncing the plural S added to a three-letter word as Z? Can you state the rule?

S: – – – (CKPT) (Any word except those ending with these four letters.)

C: Your rule is not correct. Can you think of an example that shows that your rule is wrong?

S: No.

C: What about OAFS? Can you state the rule?

S: – – – (CFKPT)

C: Correct!

---

for a new rule. In sum, the computer walked the subject through the strategy it was trying to teach. When the subject could not think of his own counterexamples, the computer helped by using its own memory.

The subject in Table 16.1 illustrates the result obtained for 12 undergraduates who were run through four different rules in a balanced order. (This took about two hours total for each subject.) It took subjects an average of 8.4 statements of the rule to arrive at a correct statement of the first rule and an average of 4.2 for the last rule ($t[11] = 2.00$ for the improvement, $p < .05$). They were also more likely to think of their own counterexamples and more likely to modify the rule so as to take a counterexample into account. In essence, the training succeeded in teaching them the strategy of interest, at least within the task situation. Although these results are what we hoped for, they fall far short of being of interest from the point of view of a theory of intelligence. We have not shown transfer of the strategy to a new kind of rule. In this respect, our results are like most other results in the study of strategies.

Possible Fundamental Strategies

There are two approaches to research on strategies and intelligence that can be taken. One is to try to enumerate and study useful strategies for a variety of tasks of the sort taken to manifest intelligence. There might be a relatively small set of, say a hundred or so, strategies that might give at least the appearance of intelligence in specific content areas. Such strategies might include those involved in critical thinking: use of alternative explanations in the discovery of truth through science, use of counterarguments in the formulation of adequate principles, and use of counterexamples in the formulation of general statements. Other strategies might include those designed to overcome effects of natural biases on our reasoning (Nisbett & Ross, 1980; Slovic, 1976), in particular, the use of simple probabilistic models and calculations in terms of expected value.

The second approach is to look for a small set of strategies that are in some sense fundamental. There would be a much smaller number of these. In Baron (1978), I proposed three such strategies: relatedness search, stimulus analysis, and checking. I also proposed some other strategies that might be used in critical thinking of the sort just described; these were thought to be not quite so fundamental as the first three, but still fundamental enough to be of interest. (Others, e.g., Campione & Brown, 1977; Sternberg, 1979, have provided similar lists of possible central strategies, often in the context of a discussion of "metacognition" or "metacomponents.") I now review what has become of my proposals. To anticipate, I see these proposals as too much of a mixed bag to be of more than transient usefulness. In Baron (1978), I explicitly argued that the distinction between strategies and styles was useless. In retrospect, some of the proposed strategies might be better thought of as styles. More seriously, the proposals were fundamentally arbitrary; there was no motivation for the choice of these strategies rather than others as the ones to study.

Relatedness search was the strategy of searching memory, before giving up, for information related to the problem at hand. For example, if the problem was one of memorization, the related material could later help in retrieval. For any problem, relatedness search might yield memories of similar problems that had already been solved. Relatedness search would thus promote the transfer of strategies among situations. People would think of related situations as a way of deciding what to do in a new situation: They would discover a strategy used in a similar situation and use that strategy as a basis to construct a new strategy. In this way, a strategy taught in one situation could become even more general than anticipated by the teacher. (A similar idea was proposed by Campione & Brown, 1977.) I know of no research addressed to the question of whether individual differences or developmental differences in relatedness search can be found.

Stimulus analysis was the tendency to discover identical attributes of stimuli that were otherwise different. The importance of the use of identical attributes resides in the fact that many of the regularities in our environment (e.g., rules about what attributes are affected by what transformations) are best stated in terms of attributes of objects rather than in terms of objects as wholes or unique identities. The proposal for this strategy was based on the work of Smith and Kemler (1977), and others, showing developmental trends in the tendency to classify stimuli according to dimensional identity rather than overall similarity. This work suggested stimulus analysis was a strategy or style rather than a processing component, because the task used to measure stimulus analysis was one in which the subject was free to use either mode of classification, and most subjects showed themselves to be capable of using either mode; the age differences seemed to be a matter of preference. Processing components are assumed not to be under such voluntary control.

However, Kemler (in press) has found more recently that retardates have great difficulty learning to classify stimuli on the basis of common attributes. This suggests that their tendency to make similarity classifications is not a matter of choice, but lack of ability to do otherwise. A similar, but less drastic, difficulty may account in part for children's preferences for similarity classifications. Smith and Baron (1981) have obtained additional evidence that relevant individual differences in stimulus analysis are not a matter of choice. Dimensional free-classification of the sort studied by Smith and Kemler (1977) did not correlate with intelligence in adults. Ability to ignore variation on an irrelevant dimension, however, did correlate. Although both tasks require attention to identity on a single dimension, despite irrelevant variation on another dimension, only in the first task can the subject control his performance. In sum, the view that stimulus analysis is a strategy related to intelligence has not stood up to its initial tests. The relation to intelligence does seem to exist, but the type of stimulus analysis involved does not seem to be under voluntary control. It is better characterized as a processing component. (Note that my earlier argument implies that general transfer of the ability to ignore irrelevant variation will not occur; this has not to my knowledge been tested.)

The third proposed strategy was checking. The problem with this proposal is that there are several different kinds of checking. One is doing a problem over again the same way, as when one checks an arithmetic calculation. Another, of more interest, is doing a problem over again a different way (or using a different method to get an approximate answer instead of an exact one). When two methods agree on the solution, the solution is more likely to be correct. A third type of checking is monitoring of performance. For example, in learning a list of items, one may monitor by self-testing. In many motor tasks, such as driving, one may monitor by observing the effects of one's actions and comparing them to some desired effect, such as staying on the road. A fourth type of checking is continuing to search for an answer to a problem or question even after a provisional answer is found. It may involve relatedness search, which is search of memory for related information. It may also involve search of an external space. Do these kinds of checking have anything in common? If they do, what are the other major classifications of strategies or styles? It was questions like these that led to the proposed framework described in the next section.

The idea of relatedness search has similar problems. When one searches memory for information relevant to an idea one has, this can be called either checking or relatedness search; thus, these two strategies or styles overlap. It would be desirable to avoid such overlap. A second problem is that, as defined, relatedness search seems arbitrarily limited. For example, why shouldn't it include search of the external world as well as search of memory, or any search at all, as opposed to search for related information?

The list of strategies I proposed in 1978 is thus inadequate in several ways. First, one strategy, stimulus analysis, does not seem after all to be under voluntary control insofar as it matters for intelligence. Second, at least one of the strategies, checking, seems to consist of several different strategies lumped together only because of the applicability of the same rubric. Third, there is no system for choosing strategies, no periodic table, as it were. Fourth, the strategies could be described in ways that make them sound more like styles in the usual use of that term, for example, the tendency to analyse stimuli, the tendency to check, or the tendency to search before responding. Each of these flaws might be tolerable if the path to remediation were clear or if there were no alternative perspective to take. But neither of these conditions applies. In the next section, I describe what I think is a more useful perspective.

STYLES

The traditional idea of cognitive styles makes them unlikely candidates for fundamental components of intelligence, but I believe that a sympathetic redefinition of them will considerably improve their suitability. The traditional idea is that styles are stable dispositions to behave in a certain way in mental tasks. The best studied styles (in this traditional sense) are: field-independence, the ability to ignore irrelevant aspects of a perceptual field; impulsivity, the tendency to make errors as a result of going too quickly in tasks involving uncertainty; and breadth of categorization, the tendency to assume, in the absence of relevant information, that a category of objects has wide boundaries. Kogan (1976) and Baron (1982a) review the history of cognitive styles and the relevant evidence about them.

According to the traditional view, cognitive styles ought to be general. By ought I mean that evidence against the generality of a style is taken to make the style less interesting. So far, this makes them good candidates for fundamental components. Second, most styles are thought to be subject to some voluntary control. This is why the subject is not usually told how his performance is being scored. If he were told, in most style measures, he could influence his score at will. This property stands in contrast to measures of intelligence or achievement, where the criterion good performance is usually clear to the subject. (The reason for keeping the subject in the dark might be an assumption that styles are *not* under control ordinarily, but the subject may distort their measurement through extraordinary effort. To my knowledge, such an assumption is never made explicitly, and the host of studies of environmental influences on styles attest to a general assumption that styles are modifiable over the long term as well as controllable in the short term.) This property of cognitive styles makes them appropriate for a theory of modifiable general components of intelligence. A third traditional property of styles is that their optimum is not usually at the end of the continuum. Thus, it is possible to be too field-independent, too reflective, or too broad in categorization, even though most people may tend to err in the opposite direction in most situations. This property appears to make cognitive styles less than ideal as components of intelligence, but I argue that it is really an advantage. In particular, a dimension of behavior is more likely to be modifiable toward the optimum when the optimum is not at one end of the dimension. When the optimum is at one end, it is more likely that everyone will try to perform at that end, and that little can be done to bring them closer to it. When the optimum is not at one end, many factors may cause a person to be nonoptimal, and some of these factors may be easily influenced.

Styles, like other traits (Baron, 1982a; Bem & Allen, 1974; Mischel, 1973), may be somewhat situation specific. Although each person has a modal style of walking, he will walk faster when in a hurry, swing his arms more when he is in a carefree mood, and walk a more irregular path when inebriated. Different people will react differently to changed circumstances; some can walk a straight line until they pass out. Likewise, a person may be impulsive only when doing math problems. The class of situations in which a person exhibits a certain style may vary from person to person. The individual differences in the generality of styles exist because of the many factors that affect the development of styles. We should, however, expect some correlation across individuals between style in one situation and style in another, regardless of how discrepant the situations are. Of course, more discrepant situations will generally yield lower correlations. If correlations are very low for moderately discrepant situations, we may question the usefulness of a particular dimension of style. However, the important property of styles, for a theory of the teachable components of intelligence, is that they may be taught in general, even if they do not exist as completely general traits.

I propose to redefine styles in a way that would exclude some particular style dimensions that have been studied, yet keep the spirit of the enterprise. By my definition, styles are parameters (quantifiable properties) of thinking. They are to some extent under voluntary control. They have optimum points for each situation, and in most situations the subject can voluntarily set his style on either side of the optimum. Over the long term, a person can be taught in general to set a particular style at a point closer to the optimum, regardless of the situation. It may be that no styles exist by my definition, but if they do, they would seem to be good candidates for components of teachable intelligence. Teaching a person to set the parameters closer to the optimum point would make him more effective in any situation that required thinking. Although I have left "intelligence" undefined, relying on the intuitive concept, it would seem that a person who thought better in all situations would, other things equal, be considered more intelligent by any definition. (Styles might still be interesting if we drop the requirement that they be teachable in full generality, for it may be of value to teach a style within a more limited domain, such as mathematics, or school. In such a case, we might say we were teaching intelligence in that domain.)

A Framework for the Study of Styles

A critical problem with the styles studied so far is that their choice is arbitrary, like the choice of strategies (as I argued earlier). Although I can see no way to systematize the study of strategies, I have proposed a framework for the study of styles (Baron, in press; earlier versions were described in Baron, 1981, 1982).

According to this framework, all thinking tasks can be analyzed into phases or functions. In particular, thinking begins with a problem, a situation in which a person is in doubt about a judgment or decision. Usually, this problem arises in the course of trying to achieve some goal. One phase is a *search for possibilities* to achieve the goal in question. A possibility is something that might achieve the goal. When the goal is to find the answer to a question, a possibility may be called a hypothesis. Each possibility may be assigned a strength, which represents how well it satisfies the goal, given the thinker's beliefs, etc. When the goal is to discover the truth, the strength may correspond to a subjective probability. Possibilities may be sought actively, as when a person tries to think of possible moves in a chess game, or passively, as when a person "mulls over" a decision for weeks, remaininng open to any suggestion or any thought that might enter his mind.

Much of the rest of thinking consists of the evaluation of possibilities. To evaluate a possibility, the thinker conducts a *search for evidence*. Evidence is anything (including another possibility) that can be used to strengthen or weaken a possibility. For example, in science, an experiment is a search for evidence, and the result of the experiment is the evidence itself. Evidence may come from the outside world or from the thinker's own memory, and it may be sought actively or passively. Eech piece of evidence can be said to have a weight with respect to a given possibility and goal; the weight determines whether the evidence ought to strengthen or weaken the possibility in question. For example, in evaluating students for a fellowship, a high grade-point-average, relative to other students, will weigh in a student's favor.

Evidence must be used as well as collected; hence, there must be a phase of *use of evidence*. In the extreme, possibilities might be totally rejected on the basis of evidence, or a decision among them might be made. This completes the evaluation of a possibility.

In addition to search for possibilities and their evaluation, I have argued (Baron, in press) that thinking may also involve a *search for goals*. Especially in creative tasks such as art, science, and design, the initial goal might be only a general one, such as "write a poem about the rain." Part of the task itself— indeed, in many cases, the most crucial part—is "discovering" what one "really wants to do," and this amounts to searching for new, more explicit, goals and subgoals. Even ordinary problem solving frequently involves a search for subgoals, or clearer versions of the original goal.

Each of the three search processes—search for possibilities, evidence, and goals—may be carried out to a greater or lesser extent. When search is active, a person may spend more or less time on it. When search is passive, a person may be more or less responsive to suggestions that cross his mind. A good thinker, according to the theory I have proposed (Baron, in press) is one who searches neither too much nor too little, according to the values the thinker would have on reflection. (There need not be a single optimum amount of search; rather, there may be a range of acceptable amounts.) Thus, one way of defining style of thinking is in terms of the amount of search, relative to the optimum range. People who search too little might be called impulsive. Impulsiveness might be separately measurable for each of the three search processes, and in each of several different content areas. It might turn out that impulsiveness as a trait is general across types of search, or across content areas—or it might not. This is not crucial for the theory.

Another type of style dimension concerns whether a person is fair to possibilities in the search for evidence and the use of evidence. In the use of evidence, a person might be biased toward (or against) possibilities that are already strong, especially when only a single possibility is being considered. Such a bias in favor of possibilities already strong would lead to premature conclusions in favor of the first possibilities to be considered. Biases are also possible in the search for evidence. When evidence is sought from the thinker's own memory, it is possible to look for evidence that favors a possibility that is already strong. If I am leaning toward buying a Toyota, I try to think of reasons why I ought to do so, and when I find these reasons, I might allow them to increase the strength of my tentative decision more than is warranted. Again, styles may be defined as deviations from an optimum (or an optimum range). In the case of search for evidence and use of evidence, the optimum is one of fairness to possibilities that are strong and weak. A thinker who is fair in this way will not be unduly influenced by chance factors in the order of evidence. A thinker who is biased toward strong possibilities, on the other hand, would tend to be overinfluenced by early evidence in favor of one possibility, whose strength would then be resistant to (what would otherwise be) equally good evidence in favor of other possibilities.

All of these style dimensions are presumably under the thinker's control (although they may also be affected by factors beyond his control). Thus, they are subject to influence by instruction, and a thinker may be taught to change them either temporarily or in a more lasting way.

People may differ in the direction and magnitude of their biases. Some people (in some situations) will be impulsive and un-self-critical; others will be overly cautious and overly self-critical. Although biases can go both ways, there are reasons to think that—in the absence of corrective education—they will go predominantly one way, that is, in the direction of impulsiveness and too little self-criticism. One reason is that the costs of search—in time, effort, and lost opportunities—are usually immediate, while the benefits of extra search are usually far in the future. For example, a student who does her homework carefully, giving even the most difficult problems her best effort while missing her favorite TV show, will reap the rewards of this diligence only on the final exam and beyond. When it comes to thinking about moral matters, the only reward will be a clear conscience for having thought a matter through. The asymmetry in the costs and benefits of thinking will thus in general cause impulsiveness, if people are overly influenced by the immediate as opposed to the distant. The asymmetry will also cause unfairness in favor of strong possibilities, because (as noted earlier) such a bias will lead to less need for further thinking.

A second reason for the biases being one-way is that the opportunity for learning about one's biases is asymmetrical. People who think too much have a chance to learn that the extra thinking is not doing them any good, for they are no more sure of their conclusions than they would have been much earlier. People who think too little have no chance to experience what more thinking would have accomplished. The same mechanism also favors biased search for evidence and biased use of evidence, in part because these biases are consistent with impulsiveness.

In sum, the styles I have mentioned here seem fundamental in that they are derived from an analysis of what thinking is and what factors are likely to cause biases. This view of styles also provides a standard, or a prescriptive model, for the definition of good thinking, and it leads to a view of the teaching of good thinking as the changing of styles toward the optimum range on each style dimension.

Reflection–Impulsivity

There is little evidence that bears on the styles generated by this framework. However, the idea that there are individual differences in impulsive*ness* as I have defined it is consistent with the research on individual differences in reflection–impulsi*vity* (Kagan, Rosman, Day, Albert, & Phillips, 1964; Messer, 1976—

I use different endings to distinguish their concept from mine). This dimension is defined as the tendency to be accurate at the expense of speed in tasks in which there is subjective uncertainty about which response to make.

In studies of children, reflectivity has usually been measured with a matching test in which the child must say which of six figures matches a standard. The six figures and the standard are presented simultaneously, and the figures differ only in small details, such as the length of the leg of a pictured chair. Reflective children are those who take a long time but make few errors relative to other children. Impulsives take little time but make many errors. Those who respond accurately and quickly, or inaccurately and slowly, are assigned to the middle of the dimension. Direct measures of accuracy and speed are used, and there is no attempt to take into account possible individual differences in what the optimum speed-accuracy tradeoff would be. However, impulsivity as measured ought to be correlated with impulsiveness as I have discussed it, because the optimum amount of search should be somewhat independent of the amount of search actually done. Thus, the literature on reflection-impulsivity might provide at least some indication of the usefulness of this particular style dimension.

The results are encouraging for my argument. Impulsivity appears to decrease with increasing age and IQ, and impulsives do less well in school even with IQ held constant (Messer, 1976). Impulsivity can be reduced through training, and when this is done, it appears that transfer to schoolwork is possible. Egeland (1974) taught an experimental group to decrease their impulsivity in the matching task. Several months later, the experimental group showed higher reading-comprehension scores than the control group (although other measures of school performance were unaffected). Meichenbaum (1977) reports similar findings.

More recently, Irene Gaskins and I (Baron, Badgio, and Gaskins, in press) designed a more comprehensive training program with the goal of improving the cognitive style of children in the Benchmark school, a private school for children with reading disability. We tested the children at the beginning and the end of the school year with a set of tasks designed in part to measure impulsivity. There was a test of logic, a test of mental arithmetic (consisting mostly of word problems), and a test of figural matching similar to the test I described earlier. The training went on throughout the year. The children who received the traininig slowed down on the three tasks, taking approximately 80% more time; the control group took only 16% more time. Some members of the experimental group also became more accurate, particularly those who had been rated by their teachers as highly impulsive to begin with. Some experimental and control subjects graduated from Benchmark and went to other schools. At the end of the next year, those in the experimental group were rated more highly by their teachers than those in the control group, in terms of quality of academic work. This study provides additional evidence that cognitive style is improvable and that improvement in cognitive style can improve academic performance.

We also found, as have others, that impulsivity correlates with IQ (as measured by the WAIS). In particular, children who took more time in our tasks had higher

IQ scores, despite the fact that some parts of the IQ test are timed. Thus, success at IQ tests, as well as academic work, may be partly a function of impulsivity and, by implication, a function of cognitive styles such as impulsiveness.

A Reinterpretation of the Strategy Literature in Terms of Styles

Cognitive styles, particularly impulsiveness, can account for many of the results from the literature on strategies. It has been found, for example, that young children and retardates are deficient in the use of memory strategies; when training in the strategies is provided, memory performance improves as a result (e.g., Belmont & Butterfield, 1971; Brown, 1974, 1975). In almost every case, use of the strategy in question takes more time (and, of course, results in fewer errors) than failure to use the strategy. This tradeoff between time and accuracy is explicit in some studies (e.g., Belmont & Butterfield, 1971; Brown et al., 1979). In other studies, time is not measured, or a fixed time interval is used, which permits the subjet to lapse into other activity if he is not using the strategy of interest. Even here, however, the strategy involves doing something that takes more time for the sake of an increase in accuracy. Such a training effect could result if the training affected only impulsiveness. For example, extra rehearsal can be seen searching for additional evidence on whether one has learned a list well enough to recall it. (A full analysis of learning in terms of the previous phases is beyond the scope of this chapter.) Thus, most comparative studies can be interpreted as showing that young children or retardates are more impulsive in the sense of searching less thoroughly.

Other studies show that strategies, such as monitoring memory, can apparently be trained so that they transfer to other tasks (e.g., Brown et al., 1979). Transfer of training between tasks might also be ascribed to transfer reduction in impulsiveness. This is expecially true when it is hard to specify exactly what "strategy" is transferred (e.g., Brown, et al., 1979).

The styles I have indicated also encompass many of the other strategies I discussed earlier in this chapter. Search for counterexamples can be part of a more general style involving an appropriate balance between search for confirming evidence and search for disconfirming evidence. Relatedness search would occur in all three search phases. Some of the types of checking would occur in the phase of searching for evidence, particularly the search for other reasons why an answer is correct (or reasons why it might be incorrect). Part of monitoring also involves gathering evidence about the quality of possible beliefs or actions, and part involves using that evidence to decide whether to continue thinking.

In sum, the framework I have outlined can accommodate my previous speculations about useful strategies. This framework focuses attention on certain parameters of the thought process in all its manifestations. I should note that the value of this framework is primarily for education and measurement of its effectiveness, although it may have other uses in accounting for individual differences

(Baron, 1982). However, there is no reason to claim that the style parameters I have listed will appear as factors in a factor analysis or as particularly salient and general sources of individual differences, although they should be sufficiently general to provide some hope that they could be trained in general.

A final comment is in order about the nature of styles as behavioral dispositions. As discussed by Baron (in press), a person's position on each parameter of thinking may be affected by values, expectations, and habits. For example, a person may have a lax criterion for evaluation because he places too much value on answering quickly; he may falsely expect that further thinking will not pay off; or he may simply be in the habit of answering impulsively. By habit, I mean either that he does so automatically or that he is following a self-made rule about how to behave. Values, expectations, and habits may be affected by emotions and beliefs about one's self (such as one's self-esteem). The inculcation and modification of styles may need to take all these factors into account. If styles also affect a person's use of strategies, as I have argued, then the use of strategies may be affected by values, beliefs, etc., as much as by knowing what strategy is appropriate. When a person fails to use a strategy, this need not imply that he could not use it (or figure it out) if he cared to do so.

SUGGESTIONS FOR FURTHER RESEARCH

In the letter inviting me to write this chapter, I was asked "to speculate as to what further research is necessary to determine whether central cognitive skills exist and to identify these skills." This question needs to be modified slightly. The argument I have made suggests that the word skill, although traditional, is inappropriate. This word would naturally encompass the kinds of processing components I discussed earlier, and it would seem to exclude the kinds of styles I think are important. However, I proceed.

One question is whether people tend to show biases, that is, nonoptimal settings of the parameters of thinking. By comparing behavior to that prescribed by a normative model of the sort I have sketched, we can ask whether people show biases in a particular direction. We can also ask whether people differ in the direction and magnitude of such biases. For example, people might in general be too impulsive, just as we may in general be too rigid in our sensitivity to evidence (Nisbett & Ross, 1980, Chapter 8). Peter Badgio and I are at present investigating impulsiveness from this point of view. We are using a matching task of the sort used by Baron, Badgio, and Gaskins (in preparation), but with two modifications. First, we have made the payoffs for correct and incorrect answers, and the cost of the time spent looking at the display, explicit. Second, we ask the subject to state the probability that he knows the correct answer both at 4-second intervals throughout each trial and at the end to the trial, and the probability that he will find a difference in the next interval if he has not found one yet. Both the explicit values and the probability estimates allow us to compare the subject's performance to an explicit normative model (Baron, in press). This sort of experiment could be done with each of the parameters I have outlined, as a way of discovering both prevalent biases in a population and individual differences in these biases.

A second question concerns how styles should be taught. Gaskins and I used whatever methods we could think of, attempting to match the teaching method to the problems and needs of each child, but more systematic evidence might be useful. We might begin by finding out how styles are learned now. Further correlational and observational studies can suggest methods for experimental tests. However, in the domain of style, experimental tests are not so easily done as in the domain of strategies. Because of the potential generality of styles, teaching them may involve affecting an entire personality. The amount of effort required to make a person more reflective in a lasting way, for example, ought to be comparable to the amount required to make a person more honest or more outgoing. Interventions of the magnitude of those now done only in psychotherapy are needed. Education has much to learn, I think, from recent theoretical and empirical work on psychotherapy (e.g., Semmer & Frese, 1981).

Finally, there is room for work on development of new techniques, analogous to new therapies. This is partly a problem of invention rather than empirical science. I would like to see teaching develop into the kind of craft that can be studied in the intense way that is now reserved for certain kinds of psychotherapy (e.g., psychoanalytic therapy and family therapy). The most encouraging developments I have seen here are Marion Blank's (1973) work in the tutorial method for preschool children, Alan Collins's (1977) work on Socratic dialogue with older students, and the work of Lipman (reported in Volume 1 of this set). What is important about these approaches is the presence of a theory about what kinds of thinking are being taught, coupled with precise rules that a teacher can learn. Blank's teachers, for example, went through the kind of rigorous training usually reserved for psychotherapists. Teachers trained in this way will probably have to be good thinkers themselves; even the best tutors have to resort to modeling when they cannot analyse what they are doing.

CONCLUSION

I have asked what kinds of teachable components of intelligence are the most general and the most fundamental. I have argued that processing components of skills are probably not teachable as general components. When practice is given at such components, and when the stimuli are clearly changed, there is usually no transfer of practice at all. Some have argued that the teaching of strategies of thinking and learning can effectively increase a person's intelligence. Indeed, there is considerable evidence that the deficiencies of young children and retardates are the result of failure to use certain strategies, which can be taught with some generality, rather than to lack of ability (processing components). However, strategies as usually conceived are not sufficiently general to count as fundamental components of intelligence. There are too many possible strategies, and the choice of which ones to teach is unnecessarily arbitrary. Styles, however, may account for observed group differences in use of strategies of learning and thinking, and they may account for transfer effects in studies of strategy training. If styles are fundamental, both research and education should focus on the inculcation of styles, as well as the teaching of specific strategies.

There is another reason for looking more closely at the idea of teaching styles rather than strategies. When we teach styles, we try to change personality, to mold a person's habits and even motives in situations that require thinking. When we teach strategies, we usually simply try to make sure that the students are able to use a strategy if they want to. Strategy instruction alone could produce students who can use all sorts of thinking strategies but who do not use them after school. Such instruction is like teaching a child to play the violin without at the same time imparting either a love of music or the habit of playing it.

ACKNOWLEDGMENTS

I thank Judy Baron, Susan Chipman, Doug Davis, Jay Schulkin, and especially Henry Gleitman for comments on earlier drafts.

REFERENCES

Adams, M. J., & Collins, A. M. (1977). A schema-theoretic view of reading. In R. O. Freedle (Ed.), *Discourse processing: Multidisciplinary perspectives.* Norwood, NJ: Ablex.

Atkinson, R. C., & Shiffrin, R. M. (1968). Human memory: A proposed system and its control processes. In K. W. Spence & J. T. Spence (Eds.), *The psychology of learning and motivation: Advances in research and theory* (Vol. 2). New York: Academic Press.

Baron, J. (1978). Intelligence and general strategies. In G. Underwood (Ed.), *Strategies in information processing.* London: Academic Press.

Baron, J. (1981). Reflective thinking as a goal of education. *Intelligence, 5,* 291–309.

Baron, J. (1982). Personality and intelligence. In R. J. Sternberg (Ed.), *Handbook of human intelligence.* New York: Cambridge University Press.

Baron, J. (in press). *Rationality and intelligence.* New York: Cambridge University Press.

Baron, J., Badgio, P., & Gaskins, I. W. (in press). Cognitive style and its improvement: A normative approach. In R. J. Sternberg (Ed.), *Advances in the psychology of human intelligence* (Vol. 3). Hillsdale, NJ: Lawrence Erlbaum Associates.

Baron, J., Freyd, J., & Stewart, J. (1980). Individual differences in general abilities useful in solving problems. In R. Nickerson (Ed.), *Attention and performance* (VIII). Hillsdale, NJ: Lawrence Erlbaum Associates.

Belmont, J. M., & Butterfield, E. C. (1971). Learning strategies as determinants of memory deficiencies. *Cognitive Psychology, 2,* 411-420.

Bem, D. J. & Allen, A. (1974). On protecting some of the people some of the time: The search for cross-situational consistencies in behavior. *Psychological Review, 81,* 506-520.

Blank, M. (1973). *Teaching learning in the preschool.* Columbus, OH: Merrill.

Brown, A. L. (1974). The role of strategic behavior in retardate memory. In N. R. Ellis (Ed.), *International review of research in mental retardation* (Vol. 7). New York: Academic Press.

Brown, A. L. (1975). The development of memory: Knowing, knowing about knowing, and knowing how to know. In H. W. Reese (Ed.), *Advances in child development and behavior* (Vol. 10). New York: Academic Press.

Brown, A. L., Campione, J. C., & Barclay, C. R. (1979). Training self-checking routines for estimating test readiness: Generalization from list learning to prose recall. *Child Development, 50,* 501–512.

Campione, J. C., & Brown, A. L. (1977). Memory and metamemory development in educable retarded children. In R. V. Kail & J. W. Hagen (Eds.), *Perspectives on the development of memory and cognition.* Hillsdale, NJ: Lawrence Erlbaum Associates.

Chase, W. G., & Simon, H. A. (1973). Perception in chess. *Cognitive Psychology, 4,* 55–81.

Collins, A. (1977). Processes in acquiring and using knowledge. In R. C. Anderson, R. J. Spiro, & W. E. Montague (Eds.), *Schooling and the acquisition of knowledge.* Hillsdale, NJ: Lawrence Erlbaum Associates.

Dewey, J. (1933). *How we think: A restatement of the relation of reflective thinking to the educative process.* Boston: Heath.

Egeland, J. (1974). Training impulsive children in the use of more efficient scanning techniques. *Child Development, 45,* 165–171.

Ericsson, K. A., Chase, W. G., & Faloon, S. (1980). Acquisition of a memory skill. *Science, 208,* 1181–1182.

Flavell, J. H. (1970), Developmental studies of mediated memory. In H. W. Reese & L. P. Lipsett (Eds.), *Advances in child development and behavior* (Vol. 5). New York: Academic Press.

Flavell, J. H. (1977), *Cognitive development.* Englewood Cliffs, NJ: Prentice Hall.

Gould, S. J. (1981). *The mismeasure of man.* New York: Norton.

Hunt, E. (1978). The mechanics of verbal ability. *Psychological Review, 85,* 109–130.

Kagan, J. (1965). Reflection–impulsivity and reading ability in primary grade children. *Child Development, 36,* 609-628.

Kagan, J., Rosman, B. L., Day, D., Albert, J., & Phillips, W. (1964). Information processing in the child: Significance of analytic and reflective attitudes. *Psychological Monographs, 78* (Whole No. 578).

Kemler, D. G. (in press). The ability for dimensional analysis in preschool and retarded children: Evidence from comparison, conservation, and prediction tasks. *Journal of Experimental Child Psychology.*

Kogan, N. (1976). *Cognitive styles in infancy and early childhood.* Hillsdale, NJ: Lawrence Erlbaum Associates.

Kristofferson, M. W. (1972a). Effects of practice on character-classification performance. *Canadian Journal of Psychology, 26,* 54–60.

Kristofferson, M. W. (1972b). When item recognition and visual search functions are similar. *Perception and Psychophysics, 12,* 379–384.

Kristofferson, M. W. (1977). The effects of practice with one positive set in a memory scanning task can be completely transferred to a different positive set. *Memory and Cognition, 5,* 177–186.

Logan, G. D. (1978). Attention to character-classification tasks: Evidence for the automaticity of component stages. *Journal of Experimental Psychology: General, 107,* 32–63.

Logan, G. D. (1979). On the use of a concurrent memory load to measure attention and automaticity. *Journal of Experimental Psychology: Human Perception and Performance, 5,* 189-207.

Marcel, A.J. (1970). Some constraints on sequential and parallel processing, and the limits of attention. In A. F. Sanders (Ed.), *Attention and performance III.* Amsterdam: North Holland.

Meichenbaum, D. (1977). *Cognitive-behavior and modification: An integrative approach.* New York: Plenum.

Messer, S. B. (1976). Reflection–impulsivity: A review. *Psychological Bulletin, 83,* 1026–1052.

Miller, G. A., Galanter, E., & Pribram, K. H. (1960). *Plans and the structure of behavior.* New York: Holt.

Mischel, W. (1973). Towards a cognitive social learning reconceptualization of personality. *Psychological Review, 80*, 252–283.

Mulholland, T. M., Pellegrino, J. W., & Glaser, R. (1980). Components of geometric analogy solution. *Cognitive Psychology, 12*, 252–284.

Newell, A. (1980). Reasoning, problem solving, and decision processes: The problem space as a fundamental category. In R. Nickerson (Ed.), *Attention and performance VIII*. Hillsdale, NJ: Lawrence Erlbaum Associates.

Nickerson, R. S., Perkins, D. N. & Smith, E. E. (1980, June). *Teaching thinking*. Bolt, Bernaek, & Newman.

Nisbett, R., & Ross, L. (1980). *Human inference: Strategies and shortcomings of social judgment*. Englewood Cliffs, NJ: Prentice Hall.

Perkins, D. N., Allen, R. E., & Hafner, J. M. (1980). *A procedure for the investigation of everyday reasoning*. Project Zero, Harvard Graduate School of Education.

Polya, G. (1957). *How to solve it*. Garden City, NY: Doubleday.

Posner, M.I. (1978). *Chronometric explorations of mind*. Hillsdale, NJ: Lawrence Erlbaum Associates.

Prinz, W. (1977). Memory control of visual search. In S. Dornic (Ed.), *Attention and performance VI*. Hillsdale, NJ: Lawrence Erlbaum Associates.

Reisberg, D., Baron, J., & Kemler, D. G. (1980). Overcoming Stroop interference: Effects of practice on distractor potency. *Journal of Experimental Psychology: Human Perception and Performance, 6*, 140–150.

Semmer, N., & Frese, M. (1981). Implications of the theory of action for cognitive therapy. In N. Hoffman (Ed.), *Foundations of cognitive therapy*. New York: Plenum.

Shiffrin, R. M. & Schneider, W. (1977). Toward a unitary model for selective attention, memory scanning, and visual search. In S. Dornic (Ed.), *Attention and performance VI*. Hillsdale, NJ: Lawrence Erlbaum Associates.

Slovic, P. (1976). Toward understanding and improving decisions. In E. I. Salkovitz (Ed.), *Science, technology, and the modern navy: Thirtieth anniversary, 1946–1976*. Arlington, VA: Office of Naval Research.

Smith, J. D., & Baron, J. (1981). Individual differences in classification of stimuli by dimensions. *Journal of Experimental Psychology: Human Perception and Performance, 7*, 1132–1145.

Smith, L. B., & Kemler, D. G. (1977). Developmental trends in free classification: Evidence for a new conceptualization of perceptual development. *Journal of Experimental Child Psychology, 24*, 279-298.

Snow, R. E. (1980). Aptitude processes. In R. E. Snow, P. Federico, & W. E. Montague (Eds.), *Aptitude, learning, and instruction*, (Vol. 1): *Cognitive process analysis of aptitude*. Hillsdale, NJ: Lawrence Erlbaum Associates.

Sternberg, R. J. (1977). *Intelligence, information processing, and analogical reasoning: The componential analysis of human abilities*. Hilsldale, NJ: Lawrence Erlbaum Associates.

Sternberg, R. J. (1979). The nature of mental abilities. *American Psychologist, 34*, 214–230.

Sternberg, S. (1966). High-speed scanning in human memory. *Science, 153*, 652–654.

Thorndike, E. L., & Woodworth, R. S. (1901). The influence of improvement in one mental function upon the efficiency of other functions. *Psychological Review, 8*, 247–261.

Wickelgren, W. A. (1974). *How to solve problems: Elements of a theory of problems and problem solving*. San Francisco: Freeman.

Woodrow, H. (1927). The effect of type of training on transference. *Journal of Educational Psychology, 18*, 159–172.

Woodworth, R. S. & Schlosberg, H. (1954). *Experimental psychology* (rev. ed.). New York: Holt.

17 Three Problems in Teaching General Skills

John R. Hayes
Carnegie-Mellon University

A major premise of these volumes is that we need educational practices that will help people to adapt to a rapidly changing environment. We want students to acquire general skills—skills likely to transfer to the new situations that will face them. I, and the other authors in this section, were asked to consider whether there are any general skills to be taught. I believe that there are, and I also believe that it will not be as easy as we would like to teach them.

In this chapter, I discuss three problems that anyone who wants to teach general skills must face. The first is that proficiency in some general skills may require vast bodies of knowledge—knowledge that could take years to acquire. A second problem is that the task of teaching learning and thinking skills may be complicated by their number. If there were just three or five candidate strategies, it would be a relatively straightforward matter to set about evaluating them and teaching the useful ones. However, I argue that there are actually several hundred plausible strategies we might teach. Finally, the third problem with teaching general skills is that even after we identify a useful strategy and teach it successfully in one application, students may and frequently do fail to transfer that strategy to other applicationns.

THE REQUIREMENTS FOR KNOWLEDGE

The work of DeGroot (1965), Simon and Chase (1973), and Simon and Gilmartin (1973) has demonstrated clearly that skillful chess players employ an enormous amount of knowledge of chess patterns. To acquire this knowledge, the chess player must spend thousands of hours of preparation—playing chess, reading chess magazines, and studying chess positions. Simon and Chase (1973) note that it is very rare for a person to reach the grandmaster level of skill with less than 10 years of intensive study.

I do not want to argue that chess is an important general skill. It may well be that chess knowledge equips people to do little beyond playing chess. However, I do want to argue that there are valuable skills—specifically musical composition, painting, and perhaps other skills—that like chess depend on acquiring large bodies of knowledge. To explore this question in the area of music, I examined the lives of famous composers.

I started my investigation with the incredibly precocious Mozart because he is the composer who seems least likely to have required a long period of preparation. He began to study music at four and wrote his first symphony at the age of eight.

I have graphed the number of works that Mozart produced in each year of his career in Figure 17.1. The figure shows that Mozart's productivity increased steadily for the first 10 or 12 years of his career, as reported by Groves (1954) and Koechel (1965). It also shows that Mozart did produce works in the very early part of his career when he had had only a year or two of preparation. If these are works of very high quality, then we could conclude, for Mozart at least, that long preparation is not a necessary condition for the production of outstanding musical works. However, these early works may not be of very high quality. Perhaps they have been preserved for their historical rather than for their musical value.

To obtain some measure of the quality of Mozart's work, I turned to Schwann's Record and Tape Guide. I reasoned that an excellent work is likely to be recorded more often than a poor one. The decision to record a work presumably reflects both musical judgment and popular taste—that is, it reflects the musical judgment by a conductor that the work is worthwhile and the belief of the record companies that the record will sell.

Figure 17.2 shows the number of recordings listed in Schwann's guide (August, 1979) of works written in each year of Mozart's career. Although about 12% of Mozart's works were written in the first 10 years of his career, only 4.8% of the recordings came from this early period. Further, many of the recordings of early works are included in collections with labels such as, "The Complete Symphonies of Mozart." Perhaps the early works were included for reasons of completeness rather than excellence. When recordings included in complete collections are omitted from the calculations, the percentage of recordings in this early period drops to 2.4. These observations suggest that Mozart's early works are not of the same high quality as his later ones. The music critic, Harold Schonberg (1970), is of the same opinion. He says:

> It is strange to say of a composer who started writing at six, and lived only thirty-six years, that he developed late, but that is the truth. Few of Mozart's early works,

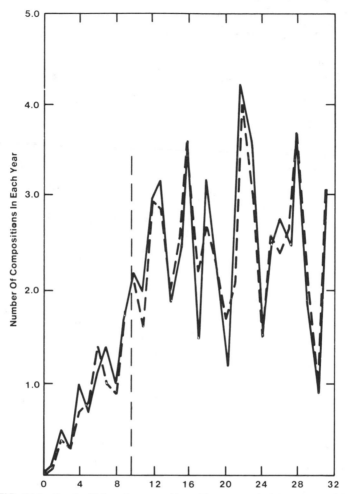

FIG. 17.1   Graph of Mozart's compositions. The year marked 0 on the graph is 1760, the year when Mozart was 4 and began intensive musical training. The solid line in the figure is based on information from *Grove's Dictionary of Music* (1954). The dashed line is based on Koechel's listings (1965) as revised by modern musicologists. These two sources are in reasonable agreement about what works were produced when.

elegant as they are, have the personality, concentration, and richness that entered his music after 1781. (pp. 82–84)

In 1782, Mozart was in the 21st year of his career.

Some works are recorded two or three times in different complete collections. Therefore, to weed out works recorded for reasons other than musical quality, I defined a masterwork (for the purposes of this study) as one for which five

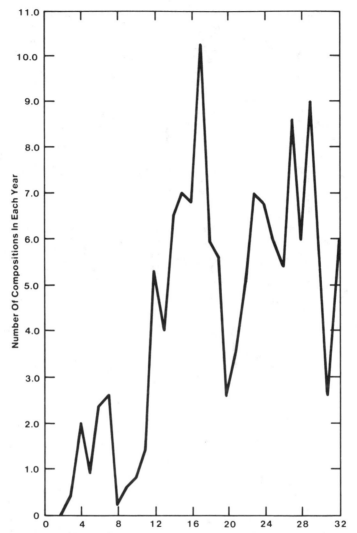

FIG. 17.2 Number of recordings listed in *Schwann's Guide* (August, 1979) of works written in each year of Mozart's career.

different recordings are currently listed in Schwann's guide. By this definition, Mozart's first masterwork was written in the 12th year of his career.

To explore the question about creativity and preparation more generally, I searched for biographical material about all the composers discussed in Schonberg's *The Lives of the Great Composers* (1970). For 76 of these composers, I was able to determine when they started intensive study of music. Incidentally, all these composers had at least one work listed in Schwann's guide, and 64 had one or more works available on five different records.

In Fig. 17.3 all of the careers of the composers are shown on the same scale, that is, the 10th year of Handel's career is graphed in the same place as the 10th year of Brahms' career. The figure shows that very few composers produced masterworks with less than 10 years of preparation. There are just three exceptions: Satie's "Trois Gynopédies," written in year 8; Shostakovich's Symphony #1, and Paganini's Caprices, both written in year 9. Between year 10 and year 25, there is a rapid and essentially linear increase in productivity from almost zero to slightly more than half a work per composer per year.

I have not continued Fig. 17.3 beyond year 25 because to do so would have given a misleading impression of changes in productivity with age. All the composers in our sample had careers of 25 years or more. However, some composers died quite young. Schubert, for example, died in the 25th year of his career and Mozart died in the 31st year of his. Famous composers who die young tend to be unusually productive. This observation does not imply that especially creative musicians compose themselves to death. Rather, we believe that it is a statistical artifact captured by Hayes' maxim, "Late bloomers who want to be famous shouldn't die young."

If Handel and Verdi had died as young as Schubert, they would probably not be considered major composers. All their major works were written after they

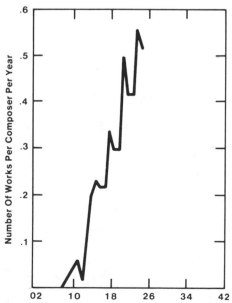

FIG. 17.3   A graph of the careers of all the composers in Hayes' study.

had been in music for 25 years. Averaging together short and long careers would make it appear that composers get less productive after 25 or 30. Actually, this is not so. This distortion is avoided in Fig. 17.4 by including only composers who have had careers of 40 years or more, and in Fig. 17.5 by including only composers who had careers of 55 and 60 years or more.

Figure 17.4 shows that composers maintain their productivity at least through the 40th year of their careers. Figure 17.5 indicates that a decline in productivity begins at about 50 years into the composers' careers. These figures, of course, do not take the composer's health into account. If we were to consider only composers in good physical and mental health, the decline in productivity might be much less marked. Clearly, productivity can continue far beyond the 50th year of the composer's musical career. For example, Albeniz's first masterwork was written in the 72nd year of his career!

It is reasonable to ask whether the important factor in the composers' productivity is really preparation or if perhaps the important factor is simply age.

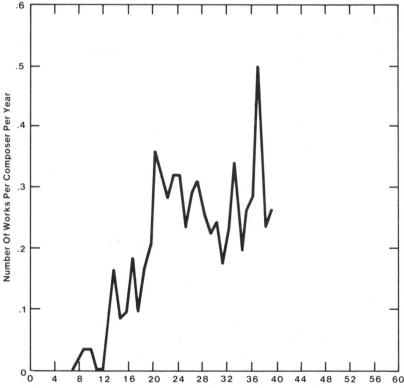

FIG. 17.4   Graph showing that composers maintain their productivity through the 40th year of their career.

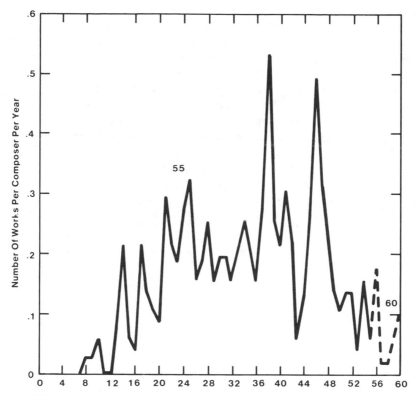

FIG. 17.5 Graph indicating a decline in productivity for composers, beginning at about the 50th year of their careers.

It is conceivable, for example, that composers have to be, say, 16 or 22, before they can write good music. Perhaps it is experience in life rather than experience in music that is critical. To test this possibility, I divided the composers into three groups. The first consisted of 14 composers who had begun their careers between the ages of 3 and 5. The second consisted of 30 composers who began their careers between 6 and 9 years of age. The third groups consisted of 20 composers who began their careers at 10 or later.

I reasoned that if age were the critical factor, those who started their careers early would have to wait longer to produce good work than those composers who started late. In fact, this was not the case. The median number of years to first notable composition was 16.5 for the first group, 22 for the second group, and 21.5 for the third group.

It appears then that what composers need to write good music is not maturing but rather musical preparation. The results make it dramatically clear that no one composes outstanding music without first having about 10 years of intensive musical preparation.

These results *do not* means that there is no such thing as genius. They *do not* mean that just anyone with 10 to 25 years of experience can write great music. They *do* mean that even a person endowed with the genius of Mozart or Beethoven will still need 10 years or more of intense preparation to realize his or her potential.

Do painters also require years of intense preparation to be productive? Sandra Bond, Carol Janik, Felicia Pratto, and I have conducted a parallel study of painters designed to answer this question. For the purpose of the study, we defined an outstanding painting as one reproduced in any of 11 standard histories of art. We defined the beginning of the artist's career as the point at which he or she began intensive study of art. For many, this point was marked by the beginning of an apprenticeship or by entry into an art academy.

Figure 17.6 shows how productivity (the number of outstanding works produced per year per painter) varies with the painters' years of experience in the profession. The 16-year curve presents data for 132 painters who had careers of at least 16 years. The 40-year curve presents data for 102 painters who had careers of at least 40 years.

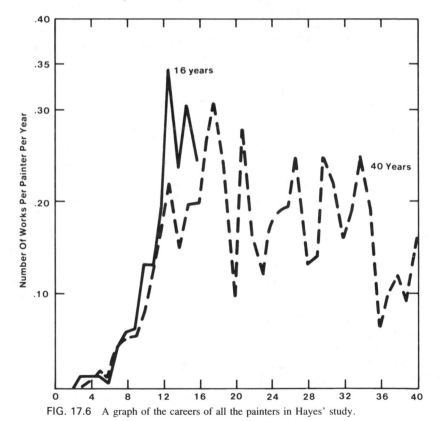

FIG. 17.6   A graph of the careers of all the painters in Hayes' study.

The results for painters are generally similar to those for composers. The productivity curve for painters has an initial period of very low productivity followed by a period in which productivity increases very rapidly. Then there is a long period of stable productivity followed by a gradual decline. The period of rapid increase in productivity occurs between 6 and 12 years for painters rather than between years 10 and 24 as was observed for composers. This difference may reflect differences in the nature of the skills involved in the fields or differences in our criteria for identifying outstanding works in the two fields. In part, we believe it reflects a difference in the sensitivity of our biographical measures to experience in music and art. We believe that parents are more likely to notice and record musical activity, perhaps because it makes a noise, than drawing. For many of the painters, there was evidence of early but undated drawing activity. Because it was unquantifiable, this early experience could not be included in our study as part of the painter's preparation.

If skill in chess, musical composition, and painting depend on large amounts of knowledge, it is easy to believe that there are other skills that do so as well, for example, skills in writing poetry, fiction, or expository prose, and skill in science, history, and athletics as well as many others. Strategies may help in acquiring or executing such skills. However, it is unlikely that the use of strategies can circumvent the need to spend large amounts of time acquiring a knowledge base for such skills.

THE LARGE NUMBER OF REASONABLE STRATEGIES

People differ in their proficiency in learning, in reasoning, and in problem solving, and in the strategies they employ to do these things. It seems reasonable to teach the strategies used by good learners and thinkers to those who are less proficient. I teach a course at Carnegie-Mellon University intended to do just this. It is a freshman course that assumes little sophistication on the part of the student. Its structure is reflected in my text, *The Complete Problem Solver* (1981). In the course, I teach basic strategies in problem finding, representation, solution search, decision making, memory, and learning. In examining the course materials, I was surprised to find that I present at least 50 different strategies during the semester. The strategies, listed in Table 17.1 include such diverse procedures as searching for counterexamples, working backward, perspective drawing, brainstorming, fractionation, satisficing, the keyword method, and time management skills.

When I say that the strategies are diverse, I mean that they are quite distinct. They are not simple variants of a few general strategies. They have different purposes and different contexts and must be taught separately. I am not suggesting that the strategies taught in my course are exactly the right ones. Of course, each of them seems plausible to me, but most of them have not been evaluated. I am suggesting, though, that the number of plausible strategies is large.

TABLE 7.1
Strategies Taught in Problem-Solving Course

Problem Finding
  Bug lists for identifying needed innovations
  Search for counter-examples
  Search for alternative interpretations

Representation
  When in difficulty, examine problem statement to see if information has been properly extracted
  When in difficulty, search for a new problem representation
    Change point of view
    Choose new sensory code, e.g., imagery
    Work backwards
    Try hypothetical reasoning
    Try proof by contradiction
  Be active in defining ill-defined problems by
    Making gap filling decisons
    Trying to solve the problem as a method for understanding it
  Use external representations where possible
    Use perspective drawing
    Use matrices for keeping track of information
    Use drawing to find implicit relations in the problem

Search
  Brainstorm
  Use heuristic search where possible
    Planning
    Means-End analysis
    Auxiliary problems
    Fractionation
    Analogies

Decision Making
  Explicit decision methods help
    Satisficing
    Dominance
    Additive weighting
    Expected value
    Signal detection model
    Bayes' Theorem
    Minimax
    Minimize maximum regret
  Cost benefit analysis
    Bargaining strategies
    Schelling's task

TABLE 17.1 (*continued*)

Memory and Learning
  Use external memory aids
  Mnemonics
    Method of loci
    Keyword method
  Learning strategies
    Elaborative rehearsal
    Notice hierarchical structure
    Use overlearning
    Monitor own learning
    Generate examples
    Use information in word roots

Evaluation
  Check results
  Get external criticism

General
  Consolidate
  Examine own process
  Time management skills

Another person teaching a course with the same orientation as mine might choose to teach many of the same strategies. However, there are many different ways to orient a basic strategies course. For example, a course could be focused on human relations problems or on math, on writing or on spoken communication, on learning through reading or on the analysis of arguments. Further, courses could be aimed at college students, or high school or grammar school students. Each focus and each age level would require a very different selection of strategies. Polya's *How To Solve It* (1973), which focuses on mathematics, includes some 60 strategies. Relatively few of these, perhaps 15, overlap with those in Table 17.1. Taken together, these courses might easily include several hundred different plausible strategies—perhaps as many as a thousand.

The large number of plausible strategies poses a problem for us. Evaluating hundreds of strategies is a major research task—one that will not soon be completed. Fortunately, some excellent strategy evaluation work is already under way. However, until much more is done, choosing which strategies to teach will involve guesses and potentially faulty judgment.

Being mistaken about strategies can have serious consequences. For example, a student in my course had written an essay that had omitted an important qualification of its major point. The student's teaching assistant pointed out this flaw and precipitated the following dialogue:

Student: "I know, but I already have three paragraphs."
  TA: "What?"

Student: "I've already proposed three ideas, so I've used up my three paragraphs."

TA: "What?"

Student: "An essay has just three paragraphs."

TA: "What?"

Student: "Beginning, middle, and end. So you see, I just couldn't add an extra idea."

Clearly, this student has learned some rather odd strategies for writing that put serious constraints on what he was able to do with language.

College English teachers report that they frequently observe equally bizarre strategies. One teacher, for example, reported that a student had asked her, "Aren't you going to give me extra credit because I didn't use any pronouns in my paper?"

FAILURE TO GENERALIZE STRATEGIES

Sometimes a strategy that ought to generalize does not. Herb Simon and I have worked a good deal with problem isomorphs (1976)—that is, with sets of problems that have the same underlying structure, but different cover stories. For example, we have developed and studied a set of problems, all of which are identical in form to the famous Tower of Hanoi puzzle. Four of these problems, which involve the actions of an imaginary set of "monsters," are shown in Table 17.2. In the first puzzle, the monsters pass globes of various sizes back and forth; in the second, they move themselves from globe to globe; in the third, they change the sizes of the globe; and in the fourth, they change their own sizes.

Ideally, because these problems are formally identical, people who have solved one of them should behave as if they had solved them all. In fact, this is not the case. There is a lot of transfer between problems that involve moving either monsters or globes, and there is a lot of transfer between problems that involve changing the sizes of either monsters or globes. But there is relatively little transfer between move and change problems.

Failure of transfer is a frustrating reality in our classrooms. A statistics teacher at CMU who had taught the Poisson distribution to this class through a distance example was surprised that the next day his students could not apply the distribution to an example involving time.

POSSIBLE RESPONSES TO THESE PROBLEMS

The possibility that mastery of a field may take many years is an important item of metacognitive knowledge that we ought to teach to our students. Some students may be inappropriately discouraged by early setbacks because they believe that

TABLE 17.2
Four Monster Problems

---

1. Monster Problem (Transfer Form 1)

Three five-handed extraterrestrial monsters were holding three crystal globes. Because of the quantum-mechanical peculiarities of their neighborhood, both monsters and globes come in exactly three sizes with no others permitted: small, medium, and large. The medium-sized monster was holding the small globe; the small monster was holding the large glove; and the large monster was holding the medium-sized globe. Because this situation offended their keenly developed sense of symmetry, they proceeded to transfer globes from one monster to another so that each monster would have a globe proportionate to its own size.

Monster etiquette complicated the solution of the problem because it requires that:

1. only one globe may be transferred at a time;
2. if a monster is holding two globes, only the larger of the two may be transferred;
3. a globe may not be transferred to a monster who is holding a larger globe.

By what sequence of transfers could the monsters have solved this problem?

2. Monster Problem (Transfer Form 2)

Three five-handed extraterrestrial monsters were standing on three crystal globes. Because of the quantum-mechanical peculiarities of their neighborhood, both monsters and globes come in exactly three sizes with no others permitted: small, medium, and large. The medium-sized monster was standing on the small globe; the small monster was standing on the large globe; and the large monster was standing on the medium-sized globe. Because this situation offended their keenly developed sense of symmetry, they proceeded to transfer themselves from one globe to another so that each monster would have a globe proportionate to its own size.

Monster etiquette complicated the solution of the problem because it requires that:

1. only one monster may be transferred at a time;
2. if two monsters are standing on the same globe, only the larger of the two may be transferred;
3. a monster may not be transferred to a globe on which a larger monster is standing.

By what sequence of transfers could the monsters have solved this problem?

3. Monster Problem (Change Form 1)

Three five-handed extraterrestrial monsters were holding three crystal globes. Because of the quantum-mechanical peculiarities of their neighborhood, both monsters and globes come in exactly three sizes with no others permitted: small, medium, and large. The medium-sized monster was holding the small globe; the small monster was holding the large globe; and the large monster was holding the medium-sized globe. Because this situation offended their keenly developed sense of symmetry, they proceeded to shrink and expand globes so that each monster would have a globe proportionate to its own size.

Monster etiquette complicated the solution of the problem because it requires that:

1. only one globe may be changed at a time;
2. if two globes have the same size, only the globe held by the larger monster may be changed;
3. a globe may not be changed to the same size as the globe of a larger monster.

By what sequence of changes could the monsters have solved this problem?

TABLE 17.2 (*continued*)

---

4. Monster Problem (Change Form 2)

Three five-handed extraterrestrial monsters were holding three crystal globes. Because of the quantum-mechanical peculiarities of their neighborhood, both monsters and globes come in exactly three sizes with no others permitted: small, medium, and large. The medium-sized monster was holding the small globe; the small monster was holding the large globe; and the large monster was holding the medium-sized globe. Because this situation offended their keenly developed sense of symmetry, they proceeded to shrink and expand themselves so that each monster would have a globe proportion to its own size.

Monster etiquette complicated the solution of the problem because it requires that:

1. only one monster may be changed at a time;
2. if two monsters have the same size, only the monster holding the large globe may be changed;
3. a monster may not be changed to the same size as a monster holding a larger globe.

By what sequence of changes could the monsters have solved this problem?

Note: From Hayes, J. R., & Simon, H. A. (1976). Psychological differences among problem isomorphs. In N. Castellan, Jr., D. Pisoni, & G. Potts (Eds.), *Cognitive theory* (Vol. II, pp. 23–24). Potomac, MD: Lawrence Erlbaum Associates.

failure indicates lack of talent rather than lack of knowledge. Others, perhaps too well endowed with self-confidence, may believe that they are destined to perform great acts of creativity with little or no effort on their part. Some may even defend themselves against knowledge on the grounds that it may spoil the purity of their individual spark. Students of either type could profit by learning that large quantities of knowledge may be essential for skilled performance in their fields.

The possibility that there are several hundred plausible learning and thinking strategies may be an important piece of metacognitive knowledge for teachers and educational researchers. As teachers, this knowledge should lead us to question whether we can expect very much general benefit from teaching any single strategy and to consider instead designing courses that allow students to choose among large numbers of strategies. As educational researchers, the knowledge may lead us to try to simplify the evaluation task by searching for categories of strategies that may be evaluated together.

What can we do to reduce the difficulty that people experience in transferring skills? I offer the following speculation based distantly on observations made by Simon and me: People employ certain fundamental categories when they construct representations. I suggest that the most fundamental ones are object, event, action, location, time, and attribute. When the elements of one problem isomorph fall in the same categories as the corresponding elements of another isomorph, then transfer between the two will be easy. For example, it should be easy to transfer from a problem isomorph in which people are moved among apartments to one in which checkers are moved among board positions, because people and checkers are both objects and apartments and board positions are both locations. However, transfer should be difficult to a third isomorph in which events are shuffled in time, because the categories of the elements of the first two problems are different from those in the third problem.

If this speculation is correct, it would suggest that we should not expect students to transfer knowledge across category boundaries without help. Rather, when full understanding of a principle requires students to generalize across category boundaries, we should be prepared to provide the student with examples that illustrate the application of the principle in each major category.

REFERENCES

DeGroot, A. D. (1965). *Thought and choice in chess*. The Hague: Mouton.

Grove's dictionary of music and musicians. (1954). J. A. F. Maitland (Ed.). Philadelphia: T. Presser.

Hayes, J. R., & Simon, H. A. (1976). Psychological differences among problem isomorphs. In N. Castellan, Jr., D. Pisoni, & G. Potts (Eds.), *Cognitive theory* (Vol. II). Potomac, MD: Lawrence Erlbaum Associates.

Hayes, J. R. (1981). *The complete problem solver*. Philadelphia: The Franklin Institute Press.

Koechel ABC. (1965). H. Von Hase (Ed.). New York: C. F. Peters Corporation.

Polya, G. (1973). *How to solve it*. (2nd ed.). Princeton, NJ: Princeton University Press.

Schonberg, H. C. (1970). *The lives of the great composers*. New York: Norton.

Schwann-1 Record & Tape Guide. (1979, August). Boston: ABC Schwann.

Simon, H.A., & Chase, W. G. (1973). Skill in chess. American Scientist, 61, 394–403.

Simon, H. A., & Gilmartin, K. (1975). A simulation of memory for chess positions. *Cognitive Psychology, 5*, 29–46.

Simon, H. A., & Hayes, J. R. (1976). The understanding process: Problem isomorphs. *Cognitive Psychology, 8*, 165–190.

18 Teaching Thinking: A Cognitive-Behavioral Perspective

Donald Meichenbaum
University of Waterloo

Recently, Lester Mann (1979) has traced the history of the work on cognitive processes and their training. This engaging historical account provides an interesting backdrop for the present conference. Mann indicates that the preoccupation in training processes is time honored. As he notes, Socrates and Plato espoused it and Itard, Seguin, Montessori, and Binet reiterated it. Each in his or her own way were preoccupied with the question: Can one *train the mind*, or in modern terms, can one teach thinking?

Because my penchant is to put things into historical perspective, I think it is useful to trace my involvement with this question.

Some Beginnings

Let me set the stage for my interest in this issue by characterizing the zeitgeist in the late 1960s and early 1970s. A variety of different influences contributed to the development of a cognitive-behavioral training approach with children. One prominent research area evolved from social learning theory and it gave impetus to a variety of laboratory-based investigations of children's self-mediated cognitive strategies. The work of Mischel, Kanfer, and others indicated the important role of children's cognitive strategies in enhancing self-control on such tasks as delay of gratification and resistance to temptation. A related influence was the work on verbal mediation, in which learning to use task-appropriate mediators was viewed as involving the separate phases of comprehension (Bem, 1971), production (Flavell, Beach, & Chinsky, 1966), and mediation (Reese, 1962). This verbal-mediational deficiency literature suggested that a training program designed to improve task performance and engender self-control should provide explicit training in the comprehension of the task, the spontaneous production of mediators, and the use of such mediators to control nonverbal behavior.

The research in the early 1970s (see Meichenbaum, 1977) on children who have self-control problems suggested that such mediational deficits play a central role in their disturbance. Children with self-control problems were viewed not as intrinsically impulsive but rather as impulsive, because they did not know how or did not desire to deal effectively with task demands. Their disruptiveness was seen as secondary to deficits in cognitive strategies. As Virginia Douglas (1972) concluded, such impulsive children fail to stop, look, and listen. More recent research as reviewed by Douglas and Peters (1979) further supports the role of a mediational (or in current terminology, a metacognitive deficit) in such impulsive children. In fact, investigators of other child populations have suggested that defective metaprocesses or deficits in executive cognitive skills contribute to poor performance in learning-disability children (McLeskey, Reith, & Polsgrove, 1980; Torgesen, 1977), retarded children (Borkowski & Cavanaugh, 1978; Brown, Campione, & Murphy, 1977), and children who have problems in academic performance such as in reading comprehension (Meyers & Paris, 1978; Ryan, 1981).

Another development of a related influence on the cognitive-behavior modification approach with children was the work of the Soviet psychologists Luria (1961) and Vygotsky (1962). On the basis of his work with children, Luria (1959) proposed three stages by which voluntary motor behaviors come under verbal control. During the first stage, the speech of others, usually adults, controls and directs a child's behavior. During the second stage, the child's overt speech becomes an effective mediator or regulator of his behavior. Finally, the child's covert or inner speech comes to assume a self-governing role. From this hypothetical developmental sequence, we developed a treatment paradigm to train impulsive children to talk to themselves as a means of developing self-control (Meichenbaum & Goodman, 1971).

Thus, the stage was set for us to bring together the clinical observations of those investigators who had studied impulsive children with the theoretical frameworks of social learning theory and Soviet psychology. Added to this amalgam was the increasing concern about the *inability* of behavior management procedures, such as operant conditioning programs, to foster changes that were generalizable and durable. Problems with generalization and maintenance have plagued attempts to use operant procedures to reduce children's disruptive behavior or to increase academic behavior (see Coates & Thoresen, 1982; Conway & Bucher, 1976; Emery & Margolin, 1977; Keeley, Shemberg, & Carbonell, 1976; Wahler, Eerland, & Coe., 1979 for review and discussion). The hope when we began our cognitive-behavioral training program was that by supplementing behavior procedures with cognitive interventions, such as self-instructional training or social problem solving, we could enhance the efficacy, generalization, and maintenance of our interventions. This hope was predicated on the assumption that if you changed the child by training self-regulatory cognitive skills, the intervention would have greater impact than a procedure that influenced the child only indirectly by controlling environmental contingencies. The goal was to train the child to regulate his or her behavior to act more effectively on the environment across situations.

Thus a strange set of bedfellows were brought together in order to give rise to a training approach.

COGNITIVE-BEHAVIORAL TRAINING

The training regimen we designed taught children to spontaneously generate and employ cognitive strategies and self-instructions. By self-instructions, we meant verbal statements and images to oneself that prompt, direct, or maintain behavior. More specifically, the training regimen was designed to teach the child to engage in mediating responses that exemplify a general strategy for controlling behavior under various circumstances. The following procedural steps were included: (1) An adult model performed a task while talking to himself out loud (cognitive modeling); (2) the child performed the same task under the direction of the model's instructions (overt, external guidance); (3) the child performed the task while instructing himself aloud (overt self-guidance); (4) the child whispered the instructions to himself as he went through the task (faded, overt, self-guidance); and finally, (5) the child performed the task while guiding his performance via inaudible or private speech or nonverbal self-direction (covert self-instruction).

Over a number of training sessions, the package of self-statements modeled by the experimenter and rehearsed by the child (initially aloud and then covertly) was enlarged by means of response chaining and successive approximation procedures. For example, in a task that required the copying of line patterns, the examiner performed the task while cognitively modeling as follows (Meichenbaum & Goodman, 1971).

> Okay, what is it I have to do? I have to copy the picture with the different lines. I have to go slowly and carefully. Okay, draw the line down, down, good; and then to the right, that's it; now down some more and to the left. Good, I'm doing fine so far. Remember, go slowly. Now back up again. No, I was supposed to go down. That's okay. Just erase the line carefully . . . Good. Even if I make an error I can go on slowly and carefully. I have to go down now. Finished. I did it! (p. 117)

In this thinking-out-loud phase, the model displayed several performance-relevant skills: problem definition ("What is it I have to do?"), focusing attention and response guidance ("Carefully . . . Draw the line down"), self-reinforcement

("Good, I'm doing fine"), and self-evaluative coping skills and error-correcting options ("That's okay . . . Even if I make an error I can go on slowly").

Thus, the child was taught to generate questions about the goals of the task, answers to these questions, self-instructions that guide the execution of the task, coping thoughts and images in case of failure, and self-praise for having tried. Training evolved toward this complete set of self-instructions through successive approximations. Training was arranged so that the child received adequate practice in the use of a strategy. The focus of the training was *not* to teach the child what to think, but rather how to think.

A variety of tasks were employed to train the child to use self-instructions to control nonverbal behavior. The tasks varied from simple sensorimotor abilities to more complex problem-solving abilities. The sensorimotor tasks (such as copying line patterns and coloring figures within boundaries) provided first the model, then the child, with the opportunity to produce a narrative description of the behavior, both preceding and accompanying performance. Over the course of a training session, the child's overt self-statement about a particular task were faded to the covert level. The difficulty of the training tasks was increased over the training sessions, using more cognitively demanding activities. Hence, there was a progression from tasks such as reproducing designs and following sequential instructions to completing such pictorial series as those in the Primary Mental Abilities test, to solving conceptual tasks such as Raven's Matrices. The experimenter modeled appropriate self-verbalizations for each of these tasks and then had the child follow the fading procedure.

In the initial Meichenbaum and Goodman (1971) study, the the self-instructional training procedure, relative to placebo and assessment control groups, resulted in significantly improved performance on Porteus Mazes and improved IQ on the WISC, as well as showing increased cognitive reflectivity on the Matching Familiar Figures Test (MFF). The improved performance was evident in a 1-month follow-up. Moreover, it was observed that 60% of the self-instructionally trained impulsive children were talking to themselves spontaneously in the post-test and follow-up sessions.

The cognitive-behavioral paradigm has now been used successfully to establish inner speech control over the disruptive behavior of hyperactive children (Douglas, Parry, Marton, & Garson, 1976), aggressive children (Camp, Blom, Hebert, & Van Doorninck, 1977), disruptive preschoolers (Bornstein & Quevillon, 1976), cheating behavior of kindergarten and first graders (Monahan & O'Leary, 1971), Porteus Maze performance of hyperactive boys (Palkes, Stewart, & Freedman, 1972; Palkes, Stewart, & Kahana, 1968), and the conceptual tempo of emotionally disturbed boys (Finch, Wilkinson, Nelson, & Montgomery, 1975) as well as that of normal children (Bender, 1976; Meichenbaum & Goodman, 1971). Although these early findings have been promising, results do *not* give rise to a sense of complacency. It is becoming apparent that we are becoming more sophisticated in our understanding of cognitive-behavior modification procedures in that we are starting to understand the limitations of our procedures. Hopefully, increased understanding of the conditions under which cognitive-behavior modification procedures fail will lead us to take steps to ensure that requisite conditions for success are met before and during our training interventions.

What are some of the necessary training conditions to ensure durable generalizable results? The Douglas et al. (1976) study nicely illustrates the general treatment approach. The hyperactive children treated were initially exposed to a model who verbalized cognitive strategies, which the children could in turn rehearse, initially aloud and then silently. These strategies included stopping to define a problem and the various steps within it, considering and evaluating several possible solutions before acting on any one, checking one's work throughout and calmly correcting any errors, sticking with a problem until everything possible has been tried to solve it correctly, and giving oneself a pat on the back for work well done. Verbalizations modeled by the trainer to illustrate these strategies, stated by Douglas et al. (1976), included:

> "I must stop and think before I begin." "What plans can I try?" "How would it work out if I did that?" "What shall I try next?" "Have I got it right so far?" "See, I made a mistake there—I'll just erase it." "Now let's see, have I tried everything I can think of?" "I've done a pretty good job!" (p. 408)

The cognitive-behavioral training was applied across tasks in order to ensure that the child did *not* just develop task-specific response sets but instead developed generalizable cognitive representations. This latter point needs to be underscored. The process by which socialized (or external) speech develops into egocentric (or internal) speech and then into inner speech requires much consideration. As Vygotsky (1962) noted in *Thought and Language*, this process of internalization and abbreviation should *not* be viewed merely as a process of faded speech; instead the transformation from interpersonal speech to thought represents qualitative differences. How interpersonal instructions modeled by a therapist, teacher, or parent change into the child's own private speech and thought is a major theoretical and practical question. The answer to this question will have major implications for the potential of cognitive-behavioral training with children (see Meichenbaum, 1977, and Toulmin, 1978, for a discussion of these issues).

Elsewhere (Meichenbaum, 1977), I have described a host of clinical suggestions for conducting cognitive-behavioral self-instructional training with children. These include: (1) using the child's own medium of play to initiate and model self-talk; (2) using tasks that have a high pull for the use of sequential cognitive strategies; (3) using peer teaching by having children cognitively model while performing for another child; (4) moving through the program at the child's own rate, and building up the package of self-statements to include self-talk of a problem-solving variety as well as coping and self-reinforcing elements; (5) guarding against the child's use of self-statements in a mechanical noninvolved fashion; (6) including a trainer who is animated and responsive to the child; (7) learning to use the self-instructional training with low-intensity responses; (8) supplementing the training with imagery practice; (9) supplementing the self-instructional training with correspondence training (Rogers–Warren & Baer, 1976); and; (10) supplementing the self-instructional training with operant procedures such as a response cost system (Kendall & Finch, 1976; Nelson & Eirkimer, 1978; Robertson & Keeley, 1974). A host of treatment manuals for cognitive-behavior modification in children are now available (e.g., Camp & Bash, 1981; Hinshaw, Alkus, Whalen, & Henker, 1979; Kendall, 1979; and Wilson, Hall & Watson, 1978). It is important to recognize that these manuals are experimental in nature and that further critical evaluation is now under way. A number of major review papers on cognitive behavior modification with children have been written recently (Craighead, Craighead–Wilcoxon, & Meyers, 1978; Hobbs, Moguin, Tyroler, & Lahey, 1980; Karoly, 1977; Kendall, 1977; Mash & Dalby, 1978; Meichenbaum & Asarnow, 1979; O'Leary & Dubey, 1979; and Rosenthal, 1979, as well as an entire recent issue of *Exceptional Education Quarterly* May, 1980 that was devoted to the teaching of cognitive strategies).

In general, these review articles of the cognitive-behavioral modification studies highlight the importance of instructing children in the self-management skills of goal setting, strategy planning, and self-monitoring. They indicate that, the more information a child has about his or her cognitive functioning and the ways they can be combined, the more functional will be the child's approach to new situations.

A Parallel Development: Metacognition

Although the work on cognitive-behavior modification arose from the efforts of clinicians to help children develop self-control by means of learning to use cognitive strategies, a parallel development was evident in the area of developmental psychology under the rubric of metacognition.

Cognition refers to the actual ongoing processes and strategies that a person uses. For example, when a child remembers something, memory processes, per se, are involved. Metacognition refers to what a person *knows* about his or her cognitions (i.e., consciously aware of the processes and being able to relate them in some way) and to the *ability to control* these cognitions (e.g., planning cognitive activities, choosing among alternatives, monitoring and changing activities). For example, Flavell (1976) uses the construct *metamemory* to refer to what a person knows about memory processes and what he or she is able to do about them.

Brown's (1978) summary of these metacognitive processes includes analyzing and characterizing the problem at hand, reflecting upon what one knows or does not know that may be necessary for a solution, devising a plan for attacking the problem, and checking or monitoring progress.

Metacognition is concerned with the nature of the *intensive intellectual commerce* of Flavell (1976), the *executive processes* of Belmont and Butterfield (1977), or what Gagné and Briggs (1974) call *cognitive strategies:* "the internally organized skill(s) that select and guide the internal processes involved in defining and solving novel problems. In other words, it is a skill by means of which the learner manages his own thinking behavior" (p. 29). These notions of metacognition are reminiscent of Skinner's (1968) *self-management behaviors* and Miller, Galanter, and Pribram's (1960) *plans*, Neisser's (1967) *executive routines*, and Atkinson and Shiffrin's (1968) *control processes* that organize and control the operations of what may be thought of as the more basic on-line learning and memory processes.

Attempts at assessing metacognition began in the area of memory (Kreutzer, Leonard, & Flavell, 1975); recent work has studied metacognition in relation to attentional processes (Miller & Bigi, 1979), reading comprehension (Meyers & Paris, 1978; Ryan, 1981), self-control (Mischel, Mischel, & Hood, 1978), and communication (Markman, 1977). See Meichenbaum, Burland, Gruson, and Cameron (in press) for a discussion of the issues in assessing metacognition.

The importance of such executive processes in the area of instruction is indicated in the literature review by Belmont and Butterfield (1977). Belmont and Butterfield reviewed 114 studies on the use of cognitive instruction, none of which involved superordinate processes, *nor did any of them report generalized results.* The children who received cognitive instruction often improved on the trained tasks and exhibited improved performance immediately following training, but this improvement did *not* generalize to other tasks or across time. In contrast, Belmont, Butterfield, and Ferretti (in press) reviewed six recent studies that have produced substantial transfer, each of which focused on teaching executive cognitive skills. To quote:

> The experiments that have produced substantial transfer not only delivered specific instruction in subordinate skills, but also led the children to perform, or to see the wisdom of performing activities such as defining goals, designing appropriate plans, and monitoring the implementations and outcomes of those plans. (p. 6)

The children in these studies were taught to know when they were confronted with a problem and were encouraged to try to solve problems when they encountered them.

Both the literatures on cognitive-behavior modification and the training of metacognitive skills offer suggestions for how one can teach thinking.

GENERAL GUIDELINES FOR TEACHING THINKING

Because the evidence that one can teach thinking is only encouraging and in no way conclusive, one can identify from both the research on cognitive-behavior modification and metacognition general guidelines that should be considered. No study has included all the guidelines to be enumerated. A brief consideration of these guidelines provide a useful framework for the development of a curriculum to teach thinking.

The first suggestion is that the instructor (be it a teacher or researcher) should adopt a metacognitive perspective. The teacher needs to employ executive cognitive skills in setting up such a training program. In particular, a variety of coping-skills self-statements will be required, because inevitable failures will be encountered. Such failures should be the occassion *not* to catastrophize and conclude that the business of teaching thinking is fruitless and insurmountable, but rather such failures should be anticipated, and when they occur, should be viewed as problems to be solved. This cognitive style should permeate the entire training program, from the designers to the pupils.

A corollary of this first point is that the instructor should not only be conscious of his or her own superordinate problem-solving skills, but also of the attributions he or she is likely to emit when encountering failure. Attribution theory suggests that when the investigator or teacher encounters failure, he or she may be more disposed to attribute blame to something out there (such as the characteristics of the subjects, than to oneself or more aptly to one's training program). For example, Belmont and Butterfield (1977) argue that the poor transfer performance of subjects in the Keeney, Cannizzo, and Flavell (1976) memory training study led to the proposition that the children had a deficit (*production deficiency*). Instead, we could suggest that the experimenter suffers from a deficit. It could be argued that the experimenter has shown an instructional deficit in nurturing the processes required to ensure generalization. The results of a related training study by Asarnow and Meichenbaum (1979) indicated that altering the nature of the training can lead to success in areas where training had previously failed. These results underscore Belmont and Butterfield's point. Turnure, Buium, and Thurlow (1976) have offered a similar argument for an *instructional deficiency* (i.e., the trainer failed to provide the child with efficient learning cues) in contrast to attributing a production deficiency to the child.

The concern with the features of training highlight the need for the trainer to conduct a careful task analysis of the skills to be taught, which is the third guideline for teaching thinking. There is a need to carefully specify the component processes required on respective tasks. As Brown (1974) recommends, the trainer should analyze the desired target behavior into its component strategy and capacity requirements. The implication is that strategy training may have to be preceded by or accompanied by skill training, if deficits in requisite skills are discovered. Put in other words, Wood, Bruner, and Ross (1976) indicate that training, or to use their term, tutoring, requires that the tutor must have at least two theoretical models: a theory of the task or problem and how it may be completed, and a theory of the performance characteristics of the tutee. Such aspects as the cognitive capacity of the pupil will obviously influence the form, content, and rate of training. Thus, it is necessary to test for the spontaneous use of task strategies to assess the pupil's capacity. In this way, the trainer can encourage pupils to use whatever skills they possess.

To teach thinking, a fourth guideline suggests that the trainer must recognize that generalization of the learned skills will not just occur and that one must develop the implicit technology to ensure such generalization. The literature indicates that pupils become welded to the specific training material and regimens. Researchers (Borkowski & Cavanaugh, 1978; Meichenbaum & Asarnow, 1979; Stokes & Baer, 1977) from quite divergent frameworks have offered a host of suggestions as to how such generalization can be achieved. Let us consider these suggestions, and then in a later section, we can consider some of the pedogogical implications.

1. It is important to appreciate that the training of cognitive skills or the teaching of thinking will not happen quickly. Training often needs to be prolonged, in depth, and involve feedback. The pupil requires the interplay between the adoption of a cognitive strategy and the opportunity and experience to employ that strategy. The feedback that the pupil receives should convey not only the strategy to be used, but also the purpose and usefulness of such strategies. The trainer should determine that the child can transfer or adapt the strategy to a variety of tasks before discontinuing training. In addition, the trainer should provide explicit feedback about the effectiveness with which the pupil implemented the strategy.

2. From the outset one needs the pupil to be a collaborator in the generation of the cognitive strategies. It is important to insure that the purpose and rationale for the training is explained to the pupil as fully as possible.

3. The cognitive strategies to be taught should be general in nature and applicable across situations. But at the same time, the cognitive training should be individualized (not predetermined) in order to ensure that the private speech trained is compatible with the style of the individual child. As Kendall and Wilcox (1980) and Schleser, Meyers, and Cohen (1981) found the use of conceptual (i.e., general) *versus* concrete (i.e., task specific) strategies maximized generalization and durability. It is important that the pupil not adopt these strategies as a blind rule. In order to help achieve this, practice with the cognitive strategy should be employed across tasks and settings. A number of general problem-solving strategies have been successfully taught including self-interrogation, self-checking, analyzing tasks and breaking the problems into

manageable steps and then proceeding sequentially, scanning one's strategic repertoire to match task demands, and so forth. The pupil must not only have such strategies in his or her repertoire but must learn when and how to use such strategies and have a sense of efficacy of being able to employ them. The pupil is taught to become more aware of internal cognitive processes, to deautomatize the learning process, and to then employ the problem-solving strategies. This training approach is cognizant of the process by which a skill is acquired as described by Shiffrin and Schneider (1977). The acquisition of a skill involves a progressive shift from controlled conscious processing to automatic processing; a sequence that allows attention to be redirected from the specific required response to the more general demands of the situation. With the development of proficiency, the explicit use of cognitive strategies is faded.

4. The use of a coping model, one who shares feelings and thoughts about performances, enhances the training regimen. The next section on the role of the affect further underscores the importance of training regimen that anticipates and subsumes the pupil's thoughts and feelings that may interfere with perform-ance. As Friedling and S. G. O'Leary (1979) indicate, it is important in cognitive training to identify and alter existing maladaptive and idiosyncratic self-statements rather than merely training new, and presumably, adaptive private speech. (See Meichenbaum, 1975), for an example of this approach in teaching problem-solving skills to a college population.

In the same way that cognitive-behavior modification researchers have focused on relapse prevention with adults (e.g., Marlatt & Gordon, 1980), it is possible that one can use a coping model approach with children to teach thinking. One could discuss with the pupils the conditions and factors that may interfere with their use of cognitive strategies and metacognitive skills. As we develop a technology of behavior change, these principles can be applied to the area of teaching thinking.

5. The timing of when cognitive strategies are taught and employed is impor-tant. The research suggests that it is important that component skills and expe-rience with the task are in the pupil's repertoire before training with a cognitive strategy is undertaken.Recent reports (Higa, 1975; Robin, Armel, & O'Leary, 1975; Wein & Nelson, 1975) have suggested that cognitive training may be most appropriate for children who have elemental performance skills in their repertoire, but who fail to self-regulate their behavior appropriately. It is quite likely that training self-regulatory skills will not promote improved performance unless the subskills requisite for successful execution of the target behaviors are in the child's repertoire. Meichenbaum (1977) has emphasized the importance of con-ducting a detailed analysis of task-related subskills before embarking on self-regulatory treatment and has provided suggestions for conducting such subskill assessments. Both Kendall (1977) and Lloyd (1980) have also commented on the importance of ensuring that performance-related subskills are in the child's

repertoire before initiating cognitive training. The importance of experience in the use of cognitive training is also illustrated in the following example. Consider the novice skier who reads an instructor's manual prior to the initial attempt to ski. "Bend the knees" the manual instructs. But only after the actual experience on the slope does the instruction take on its true meaning and impact. The actual experience provides the basis for translating the instruction into a self-guiding self-instruction—"Oh, bend the knees!"[1] It is necessary for the pupil to spend a certain amount of time engaged in training activities before he or she can develop correspondence between verbalizations and the behaviors that are to be controlled by them.

6. The training tasks should be chosen to ensure a sequential gradation of difficulty. In this way, the pupil can be taught to transfer recently learned skills to situations other than the one in which initial learning was accomplished. The pupil must recognize the new situation as one requiring transfer, must want to solve it, and must manage his or her efforts to solve it appropriately. Tasks should be chosen that have a high "pull" for the strategy that is the target of training. As Borkowski and Cavanaugh (1978) note, the instructional package should be chosen so that common elements between training and generalization contexts are evident and distractors are minimal. For example, in order to teach impulsive children to systematically scan alternatives in matching tasks, Zelniker and Oppenheimer (1976) used a Difference Familiar Figures test that required the impulsive children to search all alternatives in order to find one alternative that matched a standard stimulus. This task pulled for systematic scanning, which in turn generalized to other matching tasks. Judicious selections of tasks can be supplemented by the cognitive modeling and overt and covert rehearsal as described earlier.

7. The training tasks that are chosen should actively involve the child and require mental transformation of the strategies that are taught. The trainer must be careful not to call for rote repitition, but to require the pupil to mentally transform and extend the strategy across academic and interpersonal domains. Such active involvement and mental transformation increases the likelihood of deeper processing and the development of new cognitive structures. One can teach pupils to extend the principles underlying domain specific knowledge across areas.

8. Such active pupil involvement may be achieved as the instructor fades, prompts, and supports. In fading such supports, it is necessary to maintain the child's interest and attention and foster a positive relationship with the trainer. For example, one investigator (Weinreich, 1975) who was trying to use cognitive

---

[1] The author is grateful to Marvin Goldfried for this example.

training with impulsive children reported that treatment efficacy was vitiated by problems with incentives (scheduling problems and absence of contingent reinforcers).

9. Training should be conducted in multiple settings. This may involve training other agents (i.e., parents) to prompt or model cognitive strategies in natural settings. Friedling and O'Leary (1979) note that "teaching children why and when to use self-instruction, and ensuring that they do, may be as important as teaching them how to self-instruct" (p. 218). Cognitive training would be more successful if it included explicit coaching and practice in the appropriate use of the skills being trained. The trainer should explicitly encourage the child to generalize the strategy to certain types of tasks or situations. This coaching might be supplemented by having children enumerate situations where the strategy could be used and having them imagine themselves using the strategy in a variety of situations.

For example, in the teaching of a constraint-seeking strategy (as employed in a game of Twenty Questions), not only should the pupil learn this approach on academic material, but he or she should be encouraged and taught to seek use of this strategy is everyday situations (e.g., a car mechanic or a doctor making a diagnosis). The child who is learning to self-interrogate by asking "What is the problem?," "How do I know it is problem?," and so forth can do this not only on a variety of academic tasks, but also with regard to social situations as depicted in videotapes of social interactions. If we train in isolation, we will fail to achieve generalization. The pupil should be given the opportunity to use and encouraged to become inventive in using the newly learned cognitive skills in a variety of situations.

10. The use and compliance with such cognitive strategies should be reinforced, and a sense of self-satisfaction should be nurtured in the pupil. The naturally occurring environmental contingencies should be arranged to reinforce the use of cognitive strategies and metacognitive skills.

Surely the way in which these guidelines are implemented will vary depending upon the age and capacity of the pupil, but the intent of the program is as applicable in kindergarten as it is in graduate school. In order to appreciate that such a tutorial program should not be cold or dispassionate, the next section on the role of affect provides an important caveat.

The Role of Affect

The clinical perspective of cognitive-behavior modification offers an important caveat in conducting any tutorial program for the teaching of thinking. Any training program must consider the child's feelings about both the training program and his or her own performance (e.g., sense of efficacy, helplessness, and so forth). As Piaget (1962) noted "We must agree that at no level, at no stage, even in the adult, can we find a behavior or a state which is purely cognitive without affect nor a purely affective state without a cognitive element involved. There is no such thing as a purely cognitive state" (p. 130).

In light of the intimate connections between cognition and emotion, it is surprising that the literature on cognitive psychology and cognitive training, in general, has been silent on the role of affect. As Zajonc (1980) has commented, " contemporary cognitive psychology simply ignores affect" (p. 151). The words *affect, attitude, emotion, feeling, and sentiment do not appear in the indices of any major works on cognition,* with the exception of very few works cited by Zajonc (viz., Mandler, 1975; Miller & Johnson–Laird, 1976). It should be noted that Zajonc examined 10 major works on cognition and noted that in the six volumes of the *Handbook of Learning and Cognitive Processes* (Estes, 1975–1978) there is only one entry for affect and only one for attitude, both of which, parenthetically, were by a social psychologist.

Miller and Johnson–Laird (1976) state: "The information-processing system that emerges is fearfully cognitive and dispassionate. It can collect information, remember it, and work toward objectives, but it would have no emotional reaction to what is collected, remembered or achieved" (p. 111).

But people have feelings as well as perceptions, memories, and intentions. These feelings have important implications for the teaching of thinking. Several examples could be offered of the role of affect on cognitive processes (see Meichenbaum & Butler, 1980). One such example has been offered by Diener and Dweck (1978, 1980). They found that so-called helpless children as identified by the Intellectual Achievement Responsibility (IAR) Scale (Crandall, Katkovky, & Crandall, 1965), as compared to mastery-oriented children, differed in the time and occurrence of attributions when exposed to failure. The helpless children made the expected attributions for failure to lack of ability, whereas mastery-oriented children made surprisingly few attributions but instead engaged in self-monitoring and self-instructions. The helpless children focused on the cause of failure, whereas the mastery-oriented children focused on remedies of failures. The helpless children tend to attribute failures to the lack of ability and view them as insurmountable. Mastery-oriented children, in contrast, tend to emphasize motivational factors and to view failure as surmountable.

This pattern of results found in school-age children is also evident in college students who perform problem-solving tasks (Bloom & Broder, 1950; Goor & Sommerfield, 1975; Henshaw, 1978). Each of these studies used a think-aloud procedure to assess the flow of the subject's ideation while trying to solve some problems. Illustrative of the results is the work by Henshaw from our laboratory. Henshaw studied the think-aloud protocols of high- and low-creative college students while they engaged in various problem-solving tasks. He classified each unit of the subject's think-aloud protocols into one of six categories (reviewing given information, strategy units, solution units, facilitative idea-tion, negative inhibitive ideation, and silence). He was then able to conduct a sequential Markovian probability analysis of the sequence of verbalized thoughts.

The highly creative, good problem-solving subjects differed from the less creative or poor problem-solving subjects not only in the frequency of certain categories of thought, but also in the patterning or sequence of their thoughts. Following every major category of verbal behavior, highly creative subjects were significantly more likely than less creative subjects to emit facilitative cognitive ideation and expressions of positive affect ("What else can I do?" "Just try to think of possibilities." "Hey, I'm pretty good at this."), and less likely to become silent. In contrast, the less creative individuals produced significantly more inhi-bitive ideation, reflecting a negative feeling about their own personality or abil-ities, their task strategy or solution, the task itself, or the experiment as a whole. Expressions of negative affect were manifested in terms of negative self-referent self-statements reflecting frustration, anger and/or boredom, for example, "I don't think I ever could do this." "How would Mary do this? She is always better than me. I'm not a very good problem solver." "I'm dumb!"

Interestingly, facilitative positive ideation functioned similarly in both the high- and low-scoring creative groups, especially during the first 5 minutes of a 10-minute problem-solving task, whereas inhibitive negative ideation func-tioned differently over time in the two groups. Both the high- and low-scoring creative individuals came up with good responses at the outset of the task, but over the course of the task, both affect and cognitions changed in a negative direction for the less creative individuals. It is as if one's cognitions became self-fulfilling prophecies that merely reconfirm one's negative beliefs; thus the cycle is self-perpetuating. One can well imagine how poor performance could lead to affective disturbance and negative self-statements and, in turn, to further poor performance as the cycle continues.

Such an affectively tied internal dialogue tends: (a) to be self-oriented rather than task oriented, which serves to deflect attention from the task at hand; (b) to have a basic orientation that is negative (often catastrophizing) rather than positive and coping, which serves to deflate motivation; and (c) to have an automatic, stereotyped, run-on character, which has the effect of escalating rather than controlling anxiety. Meichenbaum, Henshaw, and Himel (1982) have suggested that a common pattern of ideation contributes to poor performance in diverse achievement or stressful situations. The *absence* of a problem-solving set (i.e., viewing a task, social situation or stressor as a problem to-be-solved) leads to inadequate performance.

Any training program that is designed to teach thinking must take into con-sideration the important role of the child's feelings and the accompanying images, self-statements, attributions, appraisals, and expectations.

Pedagogical Implications

For the last several months, we have been conducting observations in grade school classrooms in order to identify the opportunities that are available to teach cognitive strategies and metacognitive skills. Because any specific training program competes for time with other instructional content and usually results in teacher and administrative resistance, our approach has been to consider how cognitive training could become part of the entire curriculum. Could one imbue the entire school curriculum and environment with the possibility of nurturing metacognitive skills? Our hope (or delusion) is to eventually develop a program to teach cognitive and metacognitive skills from kindergarten to graduate school. We see our approach as supplementing the already existing school curriculum, which we would use as the basis for training cognitive and metacognitive skills.

Because those who have delusions often like to enlist others (i.e., a kind of folie a deux or trois) into their delusional system, let me challenge you to imagine what a curriculum would look like that was designed to teach mental processes, to teach thinking? How can you incorporate the guidelines we have just reviewed into the daily curriculum? Could one affect the metacognitive style of teachers? Could one make cognitive coping modeling films to teach both children and teachers to use cognitive strategies? How could one use peer teaching?

Some attempts along these lines have recently begun by cognitive-behavior modification investigators who are employing problem-solving techniques in the classrooms (see Meichenbaum, 1978 for a review of this literature). The focus of the problem-solving approach has been on teaching children to become sensitive to both academic and interpersonal problems, to develop the ability to generate alternative solutions, to understand means–end relationships, and the effect of one's social acts on others. Children are taught the distinction between facts, choices, and solutions. A variety of teaching aids such as verbal and behavioral videotapes, cartoon-workbooks, poster-pictorial cards, and activities are used to teach children to identify problems, generate alternatives, collect information, recognize personal values, make a decision, and then review that decision at a later time. Modeling procedures, behavioral rehearsal, role playing, and other procedures seem to provide useful ways of teaching such metaprocesses.

We can conceive of academic tasks where the teacher provided the children with a set of tasks, both academic and interpersonal, and the child's job was to identify across the variety of tasks what the problem is, how he or she will go about solving the task, where the likely pitfalls are, etc. In short, we would suggest that training should be focused on the production and evaluation of metacognitive skills. Children could be presented with a variety of tasks that require the production of plans to produce plans. Teachers could give assignments and ask children to describe in detail how they are going to go about performing the assignment. Discussion could center on the process, not only the product, of the assignment. In short, the entire study-skill process could become the focus of education.

No less of a challenge was put forth by Plato and Socrates, Itard, and Seguin. If you are going to have a delusion, you should be in good company.

ACKNOWLEDGMENTS

This chapter was written while the author was on sabbatical leave supported by a grant from the Social Science Research Council of Canada.

REFERENCES

Asarnow, J., & Meichenbaum, D. (1979). Verbal rehearsal and serial recall: The mediational training of kindergarten children. *Child Development, 50*, 1173–1177.

Atkinson, R., & Shiffrin, R. (1968). Human memory: A proposed system and its control processes. In K. Spence & J. Spence (Eds.), *The psychology of learning and motivation* (Vol. 2). New York: Academic Press.

Belmont, J., & Butterfield, E. (1977). The instructional approval to developmental cognitive research. In R. Keil & J. Hagan (Eds.), *Perspectives on the development of memory and cognition.* Hillsdale, NJ: Lawrence Erlbaum Associates.

Belmont, J., Butterfield, E., & Ferretti, R. (in press). To secure transfer of training, instruct self-management skills. *Intelligence.*

Bem, S. (1971). The role of comprehension in children's problem solving. *Developmental Psychology, 2*, 351–354.

Bender, N. (1976). Self-verbalization versus tutor verbalization in modifying impulsivity. *Journal of Educational Psychology, 68*, 347–354.

Bloom, B., & Broder, L. (1950). *The problem-solving processes of college students.* Chicago: University of Chicago Press.

Borkowski, J., & Cavanaugh, J. (1978). Maintenance and generalization of skills and strategies by the retarded. In N. Ellis (Ed.), *Handbook of mental deficiency: Psychological theory and research* (2nd ed.) Hillsdale, NJ: Lawrence Erlbaum Associates.

Bornstein, P., & Quevillon, R. (1976). The effects of a self-instructional package on overactive preschool boys. *Journal of Applied Behavior Analysis, 9*, 176–188.

Brown, J. (1974). The role of strategic behavior in retardate memory. In N. Ellis (Ed.), *International review of research in mental retardation.* (Vol. 7). New York: Academic Press.

Brown, A. (1978). Knowing when, where, and how to remember: A problem of metacognition. In R. Glaser (Ed.), *Advances in instructional psychology.* Hillsdale, NJ: Lawrence Erlbaum Associates.

Brown, A., Campione, J., & Murphy, M. (1977). Maintenance and generalization of trained meta-mnemonic awareness of educable retarded children. *Journal of Experimental Child Psychology, 24*, 191–211.

Camp, E., & Bash, M. (1981). *Think aloud.* Champaign, Ill. Research Press.

Camp, E., Blom, G., Herbert, P., & Van Doorninck, W. (1977). "Think aloud": A program for developing self-control in young aggressive boys. *Journal of Abnormal Child Psychology, 8,* 157–169.

Coates, T., & Thoresen, C. (1982). Self-control and educational practice or do we really need self-control? In D. Berlinger (Ed.), *Review of research in education.* Ithaca, Ill.: Praeger.

Conway, J., & Bucher, E. (1976). Transfer and maintenance of behavior changes in children: A review and suggestions. In E. Mash & C. Handy (Eds.), *Behavior modification and families.* New York: Brunner/Nazel.

Craighead, E., Craighead–Wilcoxon, L., & Meyers, A. (1978). New directions in behavior modification with children. In M. Hersen, R. Eiseler, & P. Miller (Eds.), *Progress in behavior modification* (Vol. 6). New York: Academic Press.

Crandall, V., Katkovky, W., & Crandall, U. (1965). Children's relief in their own control of reinforcements in intellectual academic achievement situations. *Child Development, 36,* 91–109.

Diener, C., & Dweck, C. (1978). Analysis of learned helplessness: Continuous changes in performance, strategy, and achievement cognitions following failure. *Journal of Personality and Social Psychology, 36,* 461–482.

Diener, C., & Dweck, C. (1980). An analysis of learned helplessness, II. The processing of success. *Journal of Personality and Social Psychology, 39,* 940–952.

Douglas, V. (1972). Stop, look and listen! The problem of sustained attention and impulse control in hyperactive and normal children. *Canadian Journal of Behavioral Science, 4,* 259–276.

Douglas, V., Parry, P., Martin, P., & Garson, C. (1976). Assessment of a cognitive training program for hyperactive children. *Journal of Abnormal Child Psychology, 4,* 389–410.

Douglas, V., & Peters, K. (1979). Toward a clearer definition of the attentional deficit of hyperactive children. In C. Hale & M. Lewis (Eds.), *Attention and the development of cognitive skills.* New York: Plenum Press.

Emery, R., & Margolin, D. (1977). An applied behavior analysis of delinquency: The irrelevancy of relevant behavior. *American Psychologist, 32,* 860–873.

Estes, W. (Ed.) (1975–1978). *Handbook of learning and cognitive processes.* (Vols. 1–6). Hillsdale, NJ: Lawrence Erlbaum Associates.

Finch, A., Wilkinson, M., Nelson, W., & Montgomery, L. (1975). Modification of an impulsive cognitive tempo in emotionally disturbed boys. *Journal of Abnormal Child Psychology, 3,* 49–52.

Flavell, J. (1976). Metacognitive aspects of problem solving. In L. Resnick (Ed.), *The nature of intelligence.* Hillsdale, NJ: Lawerence Erlbaum Associates.

Flavell, J., Beach, D., & Chinsky, J. (1966). Spontaneous verbal rehearsal in a memory task as a function of age. *Child Development, 37,* 283–299.

Friedling, C., & O'Leary, S. (1979). Effects of self-instructional training on second- and third-grade hyperactive children: A failure to replicate. *Journal of Applied Behavior Analysis, 12,* 211–219.

Gagne, R., & Briggs, L. (1974). *Principles of instructional design.* New York: Holt, Rinehart, & Winston.

Goor, A., & Sommerfeld, R. (1975). A comparison of problem-solving processes of creative students and noncreative students. *Journal of Educational Psychology, 67,* 495–505.

Henshaw, D. (1978). *A cognitive analysis of creative problem solving.* Unpublished doctoral dissertation, University of Waterloo, Ontario.

Higa, W. (1975). *Self-instructional versus direct training in modifying children's impulsive behavior.* Unpublished doctoral dissertation, University of Hawaii.

Hinsaw, S., Alkus, S., Whalen, C., & Henker, B. (1979). *STAR training program.* (A cognitive behavior modification training manual). Unpublished manuscript, University of California at Los Angeles.

Hobbs, S., Moguin, L., Tyroler, M., & Lahey, B. (1980). Cognitive behavior therapy with children: Has clinical utility been demonstrated? *Psychological Bulletin, 87*, 147–165.

Karoly, P. (1977). Behavioral self-management in children: Concepts, methods, issues and directions. In M. Hersen, R. Eisler, & P. Miller (Eds.), *Progress in behavior modification* (Vol. 5). New York: Academic Press.

Keeley, S., Shenberg, K., & Carbonell, J. (1976). Operant clinical intervention: Behavior management or beyond? Where are the data? *Behavior Therapy, 7*, 292–305.

Keeney, T., Cannizzo, S., & Flavell, J. (1976). Spontaneous and induced verbal rehearsal in a recall task. *Child Development, 38*, 953–966.

Kendall, P. (1977). On the efficacious use of verbal self-instructional procedures with children. *Cognitive Therapy and Research, 1*, 331–341.

Kendall, P. (1979). *Developing self-control in children: A manual of cognitive-behavioral strategies.* Unpublished manuscript, University of Minnesota.

Kendall, P., & Finch, A. (1976). A cognitive-behavioral treatment for impulsivity: A group comparison study. *Journal of Consulting and Clinical Psychology, 46*, 110–118.

Kendall, P., & Wilcox, I. (1980). Cognitive-behavioral treatment for impulsivity: Concrete versus conceptual training in nonself-controlled problem children. *Journal of Consulting and Clinical Behavior, 48*, 80–91.

Kreutzer, M., Leonard, C., & Flavell, J. (1975). An interview study of children's knowledge about memory. *Monographs of the Society for Research in Child Development, 40*(1, Serial No. 159).

Lloyd, J. (1980). Academic instruction and cognitive techniques: The need for attack strategy training. *Exceptional Education, 1*, 53–64.

Lurie, A. (1959). The directive function of speech in development. *Word, 15*, 341–352.

Lurie, A. (1961). *The role of speech in the regulation of normal and abnormal behaviors.* New York: Liveright.

Mandler, G. (1975). *Mind and emotion.* New York: Wiley.

Mann, L. (1979). *On the trail of progress: A historical perspective on cognitive processes and task training.* New York: Grune & Stratton.

Markman, E. (1977). Realizing that you don't understand: A preliminary investigation. *Child Development, 43*, 986–992.

Marlatt, A., & Gordon, J. (1980). Determinants of relapse: Implications for the maintenance of behavior change. In P. Davidson (Ed.), *Behavioral medicine: Changing health lifestyles.* New York: Brunner Mazel.

Mash, E., & Dalby, J. (1978). Behavioral interventions for hyperactivity. In R. Trites (Ed.), *Hyperactivity in children: Etiology, measurement and treatment implications.* Baltimore, MD: University Park Press.

McLeskey, J., Reith, H., & Polsgrove, L. (1980). The implications of response generalization for improving the effectiveness of programs for learning disabled children. *Journal of Learning Disabilities, 13*, 59–62.

Meichenbaum, D. (1975). Enhancing creativity by modifying what subjects say to themselves. *American Educational Research Journal, 12*, 129–145.

Meichenbaum, D. (1977). *Cognitive-behavior modification: An integrative approach.* Teaching children self-control. In B. Lahey & A. Kazdin (Eds.), *Advances in child clinical psychology* (Vol. 2). New York: Plenum Press.

Meichenbaum, D. (1978). Teaching children self-control. In B. Lahey & A. Kazdin (Eds.), *Advances in child clinical psychology* (Vol. 2). New York: Plenum Press.

Meichenbaum, D., & Asarnow, J. (1979). Cognitive-behavior modification and metacognitive development: Implications for the classroom. In P. Kendall & S. Hollon (Eds.), *Cognitive behavioral interventions: Theory research and procedures.* New York: Academic Press.

Meichenbaum, D., Durland, S., Gruson, L., & Cameron, R. (in press). Metacognitive assessment. In S. Yussen (Ed.), *Growth of insight.* New York: Academic Press.

Meichenbaum, D., & Butler, L. (1980). Cognitive ethology: Assessing the streams of cognition and emotion. In K. Blankstein, P. Pliner, & J. Polivy (Eds.), *Advances in the study of communication and affect: Assessment and modification of emotional behavior* (Vol. 6). New York: Plenum Press.

Meichenbaum, D., & Goodman, J. (1971). Training impulsive children to talk to themselves: A means of developing self-control. *Journal of Abnormal Psychology, 77*, 115–126.

Meichenbaum, D., Henshaw, D., & Himel, N. (1982). Coping with stress as a problem-solving process. In W. Krohne & L. Daux (Eds.), *Achievement, stress and anxiety*. Washington, DC: Hemisphere.

Meyers, M., & Paris, S. (1978). Children's metacognitive knowledge about reading. *Journal of Educational Psychology, 70*, 680–690.

Miller, P., & Bigi, L. (1979). The development of children's understanding of attention. *Merill–Palmer Quarterly, 25*, 235–250.

Miller, G., Galanter, E., & Pribram, K. (1960). *Plans and structure of behavior*. New York: Holt, Reinhart, & Winston.

Miller, G., & Johnson–Laird, P. (1976). *Language and perception*. Cambridge, MA: The Harvard University Press.

Mischel, W., Mischel, H., & Hood, S. (1978). *The development of effective ideation to delay gratification*. Unpublished manuscript, Stanford University.

Monahan, J., & O'Leary, D. (1971). Effects of self-instruction on rule-breaking behavior. *Psychological Reports, 29*, 1059–1066.

Neisser, U. (1967). *Cognitive psychology*. Englewood, NJ: Prentice-Hall.

Nelson, W., & Eirkimer, J. (1978). Role of self-instruction and self-reinforcement in the modification of impulsivity. *Journal of Consulting and Clinical Psychology, 46*, 183.

O'Leary, S., & Dubey, D. (1979). Applications of self-control procedures by children: A review. *Journal of Applied Behavior Analysis, 12*, 449–465.

Palkes, H., Stewart, M., & Freedman, J. (1972). Improvement in maze performance on hyperactive boys as a function of verbal training procedures. *Journal of Special Education, 5*, 237–242.

Palkes, H., Stewart, M., & Kahana, B. (1968). Porteus maze performance after training in self-directed verbal commands. *Child Development, 39*, 817–826.

Piaget, J. (1962). The relation of affectivity to intelligence in the mental development of the child. *Bulletin of Menninger Clinic, 26*, 129–137.

Reese, H. (1962). Verbal mediation as a function of age. *Psychological Bulletin, 59*, 502–509.

Robertson, D., & Keeley, S. (1974, August). Evaluation of a mediational training program for impulsive children by a multiple case study design. Paper presented at the meeting of the American Psychological Association, New Orleans.

Robin, A., Arnel, S., & O'Leary, D. (1975). The effects of self-instruction on writing deficiency. *Behavior Therapy, 6*, 178–187.

Rogers–Warren, A., & Baer, D. (1976). Correspondence between saying and doing: Teaching children to share and praise. *Journal of Applied Behavior Analysis, 9*, 335–354.

Rosenthal, T. (1979). Applying a cognitive behavioral view to clinical and social problems. In G. Whitehurst & B. Zimmerman (Eds.), *The functions of languages and cognition*. New York: Academic Press.

Ryan, E. (1981). Identifying and remediating factors in reading comprehension: Toward an instructional approach for poor comprehenders. In E. Mackinnon & T. Waller (Eds.), *Advances in reading research*, (Vol. 3). New York: Academic Press.

Shiffrin, R., & Schneider, W. (1977). Controlled and automatic human information processing, II: Perceptual, learning, automatic attending and a general theory. *Psychological Review, 84*, 127–190.

Schleser, R., Meyers, A., & Cohen, R. (1981). Generalization of self-instructions: Effects of general versus specific content, active rehearsal and cognitive level. *Child Development, 52*, 335–340.

Skinner, B. F. (1968). *The technology of teaching*. New York: Appleton–Century–Crofts.

Stokes, T., & Baer, D. (1977). An implicit technology of generalization. *Journal of Applied Behavior Analysis, 10*, 349–367.

Torgesen, J. (1977). The role of nonspecific factors in the task performance of learning disabled children: A theoretical assessment. *Journal of Learning Disabilities, 10*, 27–34.

Toulmin, S. (1978). The Mozart of psychology. *New York Review of Books, 25*, 50–56.

Turnure, J., Buium, N., & Thurlow, M. (1976). The effectiveness of interrogatives for prompting verbal elaboration productivity in young children. *Child Development, 47*, 851–855.

Vygotsky, L. (1962). *Thought and language*. New York: Wiley.

Wahler, R., Eerland, R., & Coe, T. (1979). Generalization processes in child behavior change. In B. Lahey & A. Kazdin (Eds.), *Advances in clinical child psychology* (Vol. 2). New York: Plenum.

Wein, K., & Nelson, R. (1975). *The effect of self-instructional training in arithmetic problem-solving skills*. Unpublished manuscript, University of North Carolina.

Weinreich, R. (1975). *Inducing reflective thinking in impulsive, emotionally disturbed children*. Unpublished thesis, Virginia Commonwealth University.

Wilson, C., Hall, D., & Watson, D. (1978). *Teaching educationally handicapped children self-control: Three teacher's manuals grades 1 to 9*. Unpublished manuscripts, San Diego County School Board.

Wood, D., Bruner, J., & Ross, G. (1976). The role of tutoring in problem-solving. *Journal of Child Psychology and Psychiatry, 17*, 89–100.

Zajonc, E. (1980). Feeling and thinking: Preferences need no inferences. *American Psychologist, 35*, 151–175.

Zelniker, T., & Oppenheimer, I. (1976). Effect of different training methods on perceptual learning in impulsive children. *Child Development, 47*, 492–497.

Learning and Development in the Acquisition of Cognitive Skills

19

The Development of Science Explanations in Children and Adolescents: A Structural Approach

Michael P. Krupa
Robert L. Selman
Daniel S. Jaquette
Harvard Graduate School of Education

Two scientists-in-the-making were overheard heatedly discussing the nature of atoms while being driven to the science museum. The 9-year-old agonized over how he could walk through atoms without seeing or feeling them. His 6-year-old brother countered that atoms were only "in things that you can see" such as tables and chairs, and that they were really just "little pieces of sand glued together."

Although differing in method from the research presented here, the naturalistic observations just reported raise interesting questions for educators and psychologists concerned with the development of scientific understanding. We might consider, for example, whether the boys' explanations of atoms differ in significant ways and whether this difference could be apparent in their explanations of other phenomena. The origin of each boy's understanding of atoms would also be of interest. Perhaps their teachers presented the concept of atoms differently and this difference is manifest in their explanations. Alternatively, their explanations may be more a function of world views that reflect their maturational levels than any specific educational experiences. Finally, their discussing atoms at all places the conversation in the 20th century (as does the automobile), thus suggesting questions about the influence of cultural factors. The research presented in this chapter suggests some ways to study these questions.

This chapter reports the results of two studies of science explanations given by children and adolescents in response to demonstrations of and questions about electromagnetism and gravity. Using a structural-developmental framework (Kohlberg, 1969; Piaget, 1970; Pinard & Laurendeau, 1969) and the clinical method (Piaget 1960), subjects' explanations were analyzed to identify common themes. The work presented thus represents a step toward constructing and validating a developmental account of explanations in two content areas. The research also presents methods of potential value to psychologists and educators in assessing explanations so that curriculum demands can be matched to children's developing conceptual abilities.

Piaget was one of the first to conduct extensive investigations into the development of science concepts among young children. Two books, *The Child's Concept of The World* (1967) and *The Child's Conception of Physical Causality* (1960), outlined this research and highlighted 17 different principles invoked in children's explanations of phenomena, ranging from the origins of the sun, wind, or dreams to explanations of mechanical devices. Explanations using animism, magical thinking, artificialism, intellectualism, and others were examined in this work. These two books also gave numerous examples of the clinical interview as an assessment technique for eliciting children's explanations of various phenomena.

Piaget's early interest in specific developmental advances is exemplified in his work on children's explanations of steam engines (1960). In this research, a model steam engine whose inner workings were almost entirely visible was presented to subjects, and explanations were elicited on the nature of its operation. Piaget suggested that subjects' responses could be classified into three developmental levels. In a first stage (common in children from ages 4 to 6 years), subjects said that the fire or heat directly produced the movement of the wheel. In a second stage (at 6 to 8 years), intermediaries such as the water in the boiler and a pipe connected to the wheel were said to be necessary. A final stage (at 8 or 9 years) was characterized by the discovery that the fire and water combined to make steam, which directly drove the wheel.

In each stage, the general form of subjects' responses was "This made that happen." Thus at each stage, some connection was made between two or more events. Specific developmental advances were inferred from the number and kinds of events that were posited.

Subjects' explanations were said to develop when they introduced mediating events in the causal chain. Younger subjects tended to introduce fire as the sole causal agent, whereas older subjects construed the phenomena in terms of serially ordered, multiple events. That this is a developmental advance is confirmed both by the observation that older children introduced more (but related) events in the causal chain and by an analysis showing the sophistication or greater utility of those responses containing a greater number of events.

As later Piagetian research concentrated more on underlying logical-mathematical operations, there was less concern with the applied knowledge that was invoked in science understanding. Correspondingly, the tasks presented to children began to employ less educationally relevant information. Piaget's own research moved away from the study of specific abilities in understanding the concepts of the physical world to a theory of the more general, structural aspects of logical-mathematical reasoning.

A closer examination of a cognitive task in physical causality—one directed at logical-mathematical thought—may help illustrate this shift. In a study of explanations of the mechanism of bicycles, Piaget (1960) asked children to draw this machine and explain how it worked. These explanations were then examined in a manner similar to those elicited by the steam engine example presented earlier.

An example of Piaget's later research on logical-mathematical thought is his investigations of class inclusion (Inhelder & Piaget, 1969). In this work, he probed children's understanding of subsets by presenting several white and black buttons and asking them if there were more black buttons or more buttons altogether. He also asked subjects to divide the buttons into a pile of white buttons and one of all the buttons. Subjects' responses were then analyzed to determine the degree to which they reflected a knowledge of sets and subsets.

In the earlier assessments of conceptions of physical phenomena, cognitive processes are linked to information about the mechanics of the bicycle, the child's experience with bicycles, and what he has been taught. In the latter example, however, the child requires little or no outside information about buttons per se and must only be able to differentiate their color. Thus specific experience with the content of the class inclusion problem has little effect on the child's capacity to perform the mental operations it is designed to test. In contrast, familiarity with the characteristics of bicycles is critical to successful performance.

The tasks Piaget selected for his later research thus reflected his growing interest in more universal, abstract qualities of knowledge acquisition. However, the emerging descriptions of formal, or concrete operational, thought were not too specific about how children and adolescents understood the basic educational tasks challenging them on a daily basis. When educators wished to use Piagetian theory to know precisely what kinds of scientific concepts children could assimilate at a given level of development, they used a deductive approach (Cantu & Herron, 1978; Good, 1977; Lawson & Renner, 1974). Concepts were characterized as either formal operational, dealing with a postulatory-deductive or hypothetical system, or concrete operational, "dealing with first-hand experience with objects" (Lawson & Renner, 1975, p. 9). These classifications of concepts break down when one observes how facile young children can be in dealing with "hypothetical" constructs such as "atoms."

Some researchers, however, have adopted earlier Piagetian aims and methods while incorporating greater scientific rigor. Standardized clinical interviews have been used, for example, to assess children's developing conceptions of complex natural phenomena (Albert, 1978; Inbody, 1963; Za'rour, 1976). Nussbaum's analysis of children's conceptions of the earth and gravity (Nussbaum, 1979) provides an elaborate example of developmental work on science understanding in a particular content area. In this research, both standardized clinical interviews and multiple-choice instruments were used to assess children's concepts about the earth. The five *notions* he described can serve as a developmental typology in that the higher-numbered notions are decreasingly egocentric.

Notion 1: The earth is flat and continues indefinitely.
Notion 2: The earth is round, but people can only live on the "top."
Notion 3: People can live only on the top of the round earth, but sky surrounds the earth.
Notion 4: "Down" always points to the ground, yet inside the earth down is toward the "bottom."
Notion 5: Down directions are related to the earth's center as the focal point.

Cross-age results indicate some developmental trends, and cross-cultural research suggests these concepts are present in American, Israeli, and Nepali children (Mali & Howe, 1979; Nussbaum, 1979). Mali and Howe (1979) also report a correlational relationship between these concepts and logical reasoning. One benefit of this kind of study is the use of standardized in-depth, clinical interviews and the attempt to isolate conceptual structures that explain a variety of specific responses.

Present Orientation

The theoretical approach taken in the present work is to conceptualize the influence of three factors on science understanding and consequently, on the form of science explanations. First the possible influence of a developmental structuring of thought, as proposed by Piaget, is considered. For example, Piaget designed problems with very familiar, undemanding content in order to reveal fundamental changes in the logic of children's thought. When a subject states that a clay ball's weight and mass remain constant throughout a series of perceptual transformations (as when the ball is rolled into an elongated shape), he is giving evidence of the presence of concrete operational structuration underlying the manifest content of his responses. This logical structure is presumed to determine, to varying extents, the subject's view of science phenomena.

A second factor is composed of the specific content presenting itself to the subject in each encounter with the environment. Piaget (1974) refers to this second factor as the *responses of the object:*

> Examining a physical phenomena must presume the use of operations because the search for causality always ends in going beyond the observable . . . But, in addition, there are the responses of the object . . . (which) can resist as well as yield to the subject's operational treatment. (p. ix)

This second factor is thus composed of the specific properties of the phenomena before the subject; properties that can *resist as well as yield* to the subject's efforts to understand the phenomena.

A third factor is composed of the learning paradigms that are provided by the subject's cultural milieu particular to the content at hand. The opening, naturalistic example showed a discussion of atoms—20 years from now, the discussion may be about quarks and neutrinos. The culture makes scientific advances that are passed on to its young and influence the way they experience the world. The classroom, books, television, and other sources all contribute to the development of scientific understanding, under the rubric of this third factor.

Whereas our theoretical stance is that these three factors contribute to the development of scientific thinking, our methodological approach has been to first identify the form of children's explanations and work backward to consider the relative influence of each of the factors. In the opening discussion of atoms, for example, we consider first the underlying form of each of the explanations and, second, the possible contributions of maturation, education, and the concept of atom itself. The goal of the present analysis has been to identify common, underlying features of subjects' explanations of science phenomena, hence the "structural approach" cited in the subtitle of this work. In this way, we have adopted Piaget's method of examining within- and between-subject variations and similarities of response to identify common structures of thought. We have also borrowed from subsequent research into conceptions of natural phenomena by using more standardized interviews than were used in Piaget's early research.

The present work examines explanations of phenomena in the domains of electromagnetism and gravity. The phenomena were selected because their overt effects, the movement of a compass needle while close to a magnet or the fall of an object, for example, cannot be adequately explained by events that are discernible to unaided human senses. We are not especially aware, for example, of "feeling" gravity; nor do we experience it through other senses. Similarly, electromagnetism is perceived only in terms of its effects on objects. Of interest were the ways subjects explained these phenomena and the extent to which their explanations could be characterized by a developmental progression through levels in an internally consistent logic. After we describe one possible developmental pattern of science explanations of these phenomena we pose two more functional questions: (1) What is the distribution of subjects' response types (levels) on each of the interviews and how do these distributions compare within and between subjects, and (2) what is the empirical relationship between levels of science explanations and the subject's level of logical-mathematical reasoning as described by Inhelder and Piaget (1958)? These questions are of interest because they address the degree to which subjects' responses are structured and the relation between this structure and the content to which it is applied. Great variety in the level of responses with no apparent relation to age would suggest that explanations are not related by virtue of some underlying structure. Similarly, if a one-to-one correspondence is identified between subjects' level of science explanations and their level of operational development, we might conclude that science explanations are simply a particular manifestation of logical structures; that the particular content of the phenomena examined does not "resist or yield" in any different way than does the content of the tasks used to reveal Piagetian operational thought.

In Study 1, a cross section of children and adolescents from first, third, fifth, seventh, ninth, and eleventh grades were administered clinical interviews incorporating demonstrations of electromagnetic and gravitational phenomena. As interviews were transcribed, Piagetian notions of preoperational, concrete operational, and formal thought were used as analytic tools to organize responses into developmental patterns of science explanations.

In Study 2, the relationship between patterns of science explanations and logical-mathematical thought as defined by Piaget was assessed through correlational and contingency table analyses. Of particular interest was the parallel between young children's developing concrete operational skills and their understanding of unseen, inanimate forces as displayed in their explanations of gravity and electromagnetism phenomena. Also of interest was the distribution of these explanations within and between subjects in the sample.

Each of these studies provides unique information concerning the development of science explanations; several assumptions alluded to earlier are common to both. First, we characterize science explanations as involving the interplay between underlying cognitive-developmental variables (structure) and experientially induced information (education, for example) and phenomena (content). This interplay makes it difficult for us to know what children understand in a particular domain when we only know their general intellectual development. Domain-specific structures must therefore be more directly assessed.

Second, our approach assumes that there is utility in drawing a parallel between the child's developmental profile in the area of (Piagetian) logical development and that of science explanations as here defined. Although specific areas of logical-mathematical development or science explanations may move ahead, it is hypothesized that, from the perspective of progress across the life-span, the overall developmental 'front' is relatively homogeneous.

Third, our developmental account of science explanations posits that change in certain aspects of science understanding are orderly and sequential in the direction of the developmentally more advanced structure. The form of science explanations develops in an orderly direction imposed by the concepts the child is able to assimilate at any given point in time.

Fourth, we assume that new information or experiences alter science explanations by providing the child with conceptual tools that free thinking from more primitive explanations. Science understanding, even among very young children, improves not only through direct, untutored experience, but through the introduction of new facts and concepts that promote change. Contrary to the assumptions of some Piagetian-based science curricula, where the teacher is viewed merely as a facilitator of the child's internal restructuring (Espejo, Good, & Westmeyer, 1975; Good, 1977; Lawson & Renner, 1975), we hypothesize that the teacher *induces* developmental change by challenging children's theories with experiences and concepts that conflict with their incomplete theories. New thought patterns are thus believed to result from children's efforts to assimilate new, potentially conflicting information into their theories.

STUDY 1 (PILOT STUDY)

The goals of the pilot work were to construct standardized interviews and demonstrations of gravity and electromagnetic phenomena and to obtain samples of science explanations from a cross section of subjects at different ages. These explanations were then analyzed to identify common, underlying features. A developmental system for characterizing science explanations in two content areas was thus constructed.

Method

A suburban community of Boston served as the research site.[1] The area is divided between Caucasion working-class and middle-class families. Teachers selected five boys and five girls each from the first, third, fifth, seventh, ninth, and eleventh grades to participate in the study under the instruction that these students should represent a range from average to above average in science-related activities.

Measures and Procedures.   The first task of our research was to assess the status of certain science explanations at different points along an age-experience continuum emphasizing the range from preoperational to emerging formal operational thought.

Separate interview/demonstrations were developed that provided subjects with an experiential context for rendering science explanations. Each problem allowed for direct manipulation of materials and posed at least one experiment whose observable outcome was likely to conflict with the child's predictions. The resulting cognitive conflict increased the ease with which we could observe the child's knowledge as he tried to explain the phenomena. Portions of the gravity and electromagnetism interviews are provided here:

The Gravity Problem

Materials: 1-, 2-, 3-, and 4-ounce fishing weights, one additional 2-ounce weight,

[1]The cooperation of the Watertown Public Schools in Watertown, Massachusetts, particularly the Lowell Elementary School, is greatly appreciated.

two pieces of paper (8½ × 11 inches), and an illustration of the earth with characters on one side.

We are going to do some experiments to see how fast things drop and what makes them drop faster or slower. What do you think makes things fall? What do you think would make them fall faster or slower?

Here are two lead weights that are the same. I am going to drop them at the same time from here. Do you think they will hit at the same time or will one hit before the other? Why? (Demonstrate) Why did they hit at the same time?

Here are two weights, one weighs 1 ounce and the other weighs 2 ounces. Now, if I drop these weights from the same height at the same time, will one hit before the other or will they both hit at the same time? Why? Let's try it. What happened? Why do you think that happened? Why did both weights hit at the same time?

Does gravity have an effect on how fast things fall? Why is that? What is gravity? (If S DOES NOT KNOW, SAY: Gravity is the pull that the earth has on things so that they fall to earth rather than going up into the sky. All things, like planets or the sun or the moon have gravity that pulls things toward them. The bigger the object, the more gravity it has.)

I am going to take these two pieces of paper and hold one like this (edge-down) and one like this (flat). If I drop them at the same time, do you think one will hit before the other, or will they both hit at the same time? Why? Try it. What happened? Why did the edge-down one hit before the flat one? What makes things fall? How is that? What makes things fall faster or slower?

Electromagnetism Problem

Materials: two nails, one 6-volt dry cell, one 1½ volt battery, two 3-foot pieces of fine strand insulated copper wire, one magnetic compass, assorted weights to be used in judging increase in magnetic effect.

What do you know about magnets? Today we are going to make an electromagnet. What do you think that would be? (IF S DOES NOT KNOW SAY: An electromagnet is made by wrapping a piece of metal, like a nail, with insulated wire and putting electricity through it, which makes the metal into a magnet.)

(E constructs electromagnet). Now tell me, what do you think is happening to make that nail into a magnet?

Does an electromagnet use electricity? (Probe) What is electricity? Now put the compass near the wire, but away from the nail. What happens to the needle? Does it move? Why do you think it moves even when it is away from the nail?

Do you think there is any way to make a stronger electromagnet so we could pick up all this weight? How? Why would that work?

If we used two batteries or a bigger battery, would that make a stronger electromagnet? Why?

What do you think would happen if we wrapped the nail with twice as many wraps of wire? Do you think that would make the electromagnet weaker, stronger, or would it stay the same? Try it. What happened? Why?

What makes an electromagnet work?

By conducting interviews in this manner, subjects were given maximum opportunity to explain the phenomena being investigated. This method was meant to at least partially control for the effects of prior experience and exposure to explanations of the phenomena by providing the child with at least some exposure to the phenomena and related concepts.[2] By following up ambiguous responses with flexible probe questions aimed at the specific explanation, the method was able to reduce the possibility of making mistaken assumptions about the child's developing science theories. For example, consider the first response of David upon completing the electromagnet:

WHAT MAKES THE ELECTROMAGNET WORK?

You wrapped the wire around the nail and when you touched both wires to the battery the nail picked up the washers.

Without probing, this response reflects a description of the perceptual qualities of the magnet. The interviewer probes further, however:

WHAT IS IT ABOUT WRAPPING THE NAIL AND TOUCHING THE WIRES TO THE BATTERY THAT MAKES THE NAIL PICK UP THE WASHERS?

Well, the electricity in the battery can go through the wires and when they are wrapped around the nail it is turned into a magnet that can pick up things. It is the power of the electricity in the wires.

In this follow-up statement, the subject suggests that his notions of electromagnetism are not bound simply to the perceptual qualities of the apparatus in front of him. The introduction of probe questions inspired this clarification.

Another example comes from the gravity interview:

WHY DO THINGS FALL TO THE GROUND?

There is nothing holding them up or someone knocks them off the table.

---

[2]Although the interviews were designed to elicit subjects' theories of gravity and electromagnetism rather than their knowledge of facts, it can be argued that subjects in higher grades, by virtue of having received more science courses, react to the interview differently than younger subjects. Thus not only may their conceptions be more sophisticated but so too their ability to respond to interviews in general. Although we acknowledge this difficulty, further research is needed to determine such spurious effects.

WHY DOES THAT MAKE THEM FALL?

When nothing is holding them up, the force of the ground pulls them down.

An example of the inability of probe questions to "dislodge" explanations based on perceptual qualities follows:

WHAT MAKES THINGS FALL TO THE GROUND?

When you let them go.

WHAT IS IT ABOUT LETTING THEM GO THAT MAKES THEM FALL TO THE GROUND?

When you let them go they hit the ground. Sometimes the loud noise does it. The wind blows things to the ground too.

WHY DO THEY FALL INSTEAD OF GOING UP?

Because they can't float.

Including a number of contexts within an interview and providing probe questions yielded protocols rich in subjects' explanations.

Interviews with subjects were about ½ hour in length (1 hour for both) and were conducted during the regular school day.

Results

Transcribed protocols of the interviews were examined to identify the types of explanations used. These explanations were then analyzed to discern common features having the same developmental level of sophistication. Piaget's stages of logical-mathematical development were used as guides in this process: lower levels of science explanations were based on overt properties of the phenomena, whereas higher levels included references to covert properties. Piaget's stages were also used as rough indications of the general conceptual abilities to be expected of subjects given their age.

Global analysis of the cross-sectional data for both science problems resulted in the cataloging of four hierarchical types or levels of science explanations (see Table 19.1). Level 1 explanations were based on overt, correlated events. Children of ages 3–7 generally based their scientific explanations on descriptions of overt cause and effect relations (e.g., "The wire makes the electromagnet work."). They provided accurate explanations of the tangible actions and objects associated with the phenomenon but did not posit unseen, inanimate causes that might reside behind the perceptually linked events. Although the child was able to imagine unseen entities causing an overt effect, he really projected an overt cause and effect relationship (e.g., "God made the compass needle move by touching it.").

Level 2 explanations, given by children of ages 5–9, were based on unilateral unseen forces that are covert and inanimate (e.g., "The power from the battery

TABLE 19.1
Developmental Levels of Science Explanations

Level	Conceptual Description	Age Range
1	Perceptual Linkage Explanations	3 to 7
2	Simplified Unseen Force Explanations	5 to 9
3	Coordinated Unseen Force Explanations	7 to 15
4	Balanced Systems Explanations	12 to 18

makes the compass needle move."). The child at this level also used generalized and internalized dimensions such as weight or velocity. Despite the use of unseen-force explanations, these responses suggested an inability to consider more than one such influence in any given situation. The child was unable to consider the interplay of two gravitational forces on a single object.

Children giving explanations based on multiple or interactive unseen forces were assigned to Level 3. These 7–15 year-olds were able to consider that multiple covert processes can influence a situation. For example, the child was able to consider competing gravitation pulls (e.g., "One planet is pulling it this way and the other is pulling it that way.") and was able to consider causes based on interactive relationships. Despite being able to consider multiple covert processes, however, the child was unable to view them as a system of potential transformations. For example, the transformation of electrical energy to magnetic energy was understood only through its effects (e.g., "The electricity supplies power to make the magnet.").

Children from ages 12 to 18 gave Level-4 explanations, which were based on balanced or transformational systems. At this level, scientific thinking was governed by a system of balanced relationships between various unseen processes (e.g., "The force of gravity is stronger the closer you get to earth."). The subject at this level was able to perform a number of transformations between these forces. For example, electrical energy was seen to be transformed into magnetic energy, which in turn produces the tangible effect. Understanding of a system of equilibrium relations was utilized to explain scientific phenomena where the effect demonstrates formal relationships.

Although individual children may perform at slightly higher levels on different tasks, these four levels appear to represent a developmental scheme for science explanations that cuts across both problems. These levels are described in greater detail in the interview scoring manual (Jaquette, Krupa, & Selman, 1979).

Cross-sectional analysis also provided rough age norms for the presence of the four developmental levels. Although both task difficulty and individual differences may result in variation (see Table 19.1), the norms provide useful information regarding the general ways children explain particular phenomena at different ages.

Discussion

The significance of Study 1 lies in the evolution of the clinical interview/demonstration method for eliciting science explanations and in the construction of a system for characterizing those explanations. The approach taken in the research was that of a structural analysis. This analysis was conducted by examining a number of science explanations from subjects varying in age for the purpose of isolating common, underlying features. This structural similarity between explanations that vary in their manifest content allows the investigator to make inferences about the underlying unity of subjects' responses. Such an analysis coupled with an examination of the qualities of the particular phenomena also aids in predicting the explanations of new phenomena. If a first-grade subject, for example, tends to present Level 1 explanations to the two science phenomena examined in this study, we might predict that his explanations of the workings of an automobile would be of the same form. "It works because you turned it on," "because it is making noise," etc. would be likely responses. The specific, educational implications of this work is discussed in subsequent sections.

The pilot study also highlighted the growing intricacy of children's notions of causality. Moving from a level of confused cause and effect sequences and/or single, perceptually based causal relationships, older subjects explicated systems of relationships, drawing on events that are not necessarily seen. This finding suggests that although subjects may develop by considering more mediating events, as was the case in Piaget's early work with steam engines, they also appear to make developmental advances in the ability to infer unseen, covert events as causal agents.

The four-leveled, developmental typology that emerged from this cross-sectional data is only one of many possible category systems. The usefulness of the descriptive system can be measured, however, by its utility in predicting how children explain a wide variety of science phenomena, and, in turn, the general patterns observed can be validated by further research.

STUDY 2

The developmental account of science explanations yielded by Study 1 has roots in Piaget's system of operational development and yet contains several differences. The greatest similarity lies in its structural properties. As is the case in Piaget's work, we have attempted to isolate common, conceptual structures that underly the surface manifestations of subjects' responses. This hypothesized structure allows the educator or psychologist to see the similarity in logic between a subject's statement that, "Things fall to the ground because you let them go," and her statement that, "It can pick up things because you touch the wire to the battery."

The levels of science explanations also bear a relation to Piaget's theory of intellectual development in terms of their actual logic. In the example of science explanations just presented, the subject relied on perceptual variables to explain the phenomena; in the period of preoperational development subjects also rely on perceptual qualities. In the example on the conservation of matter and weight (clay balls) presented earlier, subjects who failed to conserve relied on perceptual transformations of objects in making judgments about their mass and weight. When rolled out into a hot dog, the clay looked bigger and was judged to be bigger. The subject's reasoning has not yet moved to the point of considering underlying factors.

This second study was conducted to examine more closely two features of the developmental system constructed in the pilot work. Of interest was the distribution of levels of subjects' responses and the relationship between the form of these responses and logical-mathematical reasoning as defined by Piaget.

Little empirical work has been conducted to test the developmental relationship between logical reasoning and science explanations. Primarily deductive approaches (Blasi & Hoeffel, 1974; Dale, 1975; Good, 1977) have sought to link curriculum demand characteristics to features of formal and concrete operational thought. Attempts to operationalize formal and concrete science concepts (Cantu & Herron, 1978; Lawson & Renner, 1975) have found modest correlations between science performance and logical reasoning. However, because this work has relied on multiple-choice approaches for assessing science ability, it is difficult to know exactly how logic skills are related to specific science skills.

In addition to these methodological difficulties, there has been wide diversity of opinion concerning the theoretical relationship between logical thought and science concepts. One viewpoint (Mali & Howe, 1979) has been that the logical reasoning skills represent necessary but not sufficient conditions for the development of logically parallel levels of science understanding. A second viewpoint holds that the relationship between logical reasoning and science conceptions is based on general maturation or task difficulty and not on any structural isomorphism between the two domains (Novak, 1977a, b).

Our perspective represents a modification of both viewpoints. We hypothesize that a general structural parallel exists between logical reasoning and science explanations (see Table 19.2) making for moderate correlations. However, neither expressed science explanations nor logical reasoning is an absolute prerequisite for development in the other domain. Rather, we suggest specific task difficulties and informational complexity make for an uneven developmental progression. Some areas of logical reasoning will precede some structurally parallel areas of science understanding, which will precede other areas of logical reasoning. Analysis of the specific task and information requirements is necessary to make further and more precise predictions.

One primary criterion of cognitive-developmental stages has been the quality of structured wholeness—the degree to which a child's mode of response is

TABLE 19.2
Theoretically Parallel Developmental Structures in Logical Reasoning
and Science Explanations

Logical Reasoning	Science Explanations
Preoperational Thinking. Intuitive operations that are not reversible. Objects are classified, but classes are not grouped. Thinking is based on the perceptual cues.	*Perceptual Linkage Explanations.* Explanations are based on tangible cause and effect relationships and overt properties. No use of inanimate, unseen processes.
Early Concrete Operations. Basic operative groupings including class inclusion, seriation are available. Operations are reversible however, child cannot consider two relations as they covary.	*Unseen Force Explanations.* Explanations are based on the use of inanimate, unseen forces and the use of generalized concepts. Only one unseen process can be considered as operating in a given phenomenon.
Consolidated Concrete Operations. Full mastery of logical groupings for concrete operations including those requiring simultaneous consideration of two covarying relations. However, child is unable to step outside concrete relations to overview overall system.	*Coordinated Unseen Force Explanations.* Child is able to consider multiple unseen processes at work in a given phenomenon; however, he/she is unable to view the transformation of one process into another nor the balanced system of relations between the multiple processes.
Formal Operational Thought (Early and Consolidated). The subject develops a system for combinatorial logic making possible the coordination of groupings into a conceptual whole. Observed events are placed in a framework of logical possibility. The subject is able to hold all variables constant while systematically varying one property of the system.	*Balanced Systems.* Science explanations are governed by formal principles of relations between unseen processes, by which a dynamic equilibrium is maintained.

generally consistent across a variety of tasks. This notion has come under increasing skepticism in recent years because of the number of findings illustrating variation along task-specific dimensions. Although some task fluctuation may be due to poor measurement procedures for assessing formal and concrete operations, a serious challenge to the structured wholeness notion is posed by an increasing number of studies showing heterogeneous responses. The more carefully conducted studies report that, although task fluctuations do not appear between widely discrepant developmental levels (e.g., formal operational to preoperational), there is significant fluctuation between two adjacent stages.

We take this to mean that the developing child or adolescent moves ahead in some cognitive areas whereas moving more slowly in others. At some time, a given developmental milestone is consolidated across all areas, so that, for example, most adolescents are at least concrete operational in all assessed areas, although each may maintain an uneven performance at his/her developmental "front." However, children who are relatively high in one area will be relatively high in other areas compared to children who are advancing more slowly.

Because logical reasoning is often assessed without significant reference to the content of reasoning, there is reason to believe there would be less structural synchrony across measures of science explanations than there would be across measures of logical reasoning. Each measure of science understanding requires a different set of concepts and different phenomena. Whereas logical problems may employ different variables, contents are not as essential in the logical or mathematical operation. Understanding of the concept of gravity, for example, would seem to be highly contingent on whether the child has been exposed to this specific concept. By assessing correlations among scientific understanding and logical ability, one could begin to sort out the actual degree to which performance across domains is uniform.

Method

Subjects.   Subjects were 105 children in the age range of 5–9, at which ages unseen force explanations were first seen in the pilot study. Sixty first-grade students and 30 kindergarteners, equally divided between boys and girls, and 15 preschool children (10 boys and 5 girls) were selected to take part in the study. Subjects were referred to the study by teachers who had been asked to provide subjects representing a range of general abilities.

Measures and Procedures.   Scientific explanation was assessed through performance during the electromagnetism and gravity interview/demonstrations. The interview procedure had been designed during the field tests to provide ample opportunities to exhibit explanations based on unseen forces (see excerpts previously presented).

Two tests of logical reasoning appropriate for this age group were also given: (1) a measure of class inclusion (Inhelder & Piaget, 1969), and (2) a measure of substance and weight conservation (Inhelder & Piaget, 1958). In the measure of class inclusion, children were required to distinguish between subclasses and superordinate classes. In the conservation task, the subjects were asked to differentiate between changes in the appearance of clay objects and their conservation of amount and weight, tasks that are commonly defined as part of the general development of concrete operations (Inhelder & Piaget, 1958).

Scoring.   Scoring used the descriptions of Level 1 and Level 2 explanations constructed from the pilot data (Jaquette, Krupa, & Selman, 1979). The scoring procedure called first for an examination of the entire protocol and designation of scorable responses. Unscorable responses were those that did not express the reasoning behind a response or took the form of one-word utterances. The designated responses were then assigned a score of "1" or "2" according to whether or not they were indicative of reasoning based either on perceptually given cause and effect relations or on unseen forces. In Level 1 responses, the child appeared to rely solely on the observable properties of the demonstrations in positing causal events or to introduce notions of magical thinking. In those responses designated Level 2, mediating, unseen forces were introduced as causal events. To compare this to Piaget's earlier work with steam engines, we would say that not only are more transformations introduced in the causal chain, but that the nature of these transformations moves away from the plane of perceptually given events toward the conceptualization of events that are not seen. Typical representations of these explanatory types are given in Table 19.3.

After assigning levels to each of the responses, an overall score based on the percentage usage of Level 2 responses was computed for each interview. For example, an interview containing 10 responses (which was typical of both interviews) of which nine were designed Level 2 was given an overall score of 90% Level 2.

Because the same variance was observed in subjects' logical reasoning, a percentage scoring approach was again employed. The class inclusion and

TABLE 19.3
Typical Level 1 and Level 2 Responses to Gravity and
Electromagnetism Interview/Demonstrations

Question	Level 1 Response	Level 2 Response
	Gravity Interview/Demonstration	
What makes things fall to the ground?	You let them go. They hit the ground. They were too close to the edge.	The weight of them. (Probe.) The heaviness pulls them down. The earth pulls them.
If we drop these (unequal weights), will they hit at the same time? (Why or why not?)	Yes, because you drop them. No, because one is bigger. (Probe.) Because it will hit first.	The weight must not make a difference in how fast it falls. The pull must be the same.
	Electromagnetism Interview/Demonstration	
(Construct electromagnet.) What makes this work?	The battery and the wire. (Probe.) The wire picks up the metal.	The electricity going through the wire makes the nail into a magnet.
What is electricity?	It is the wire. It is the lights.	It is something in the battery that can go through the wire. It makes the lights work.
What is a magnet? What makes it work?	It is metal. It works by putting things close to it.	It is a metal that can pull on things—just other kinds of metal. It works by pulling on things in the metal.

conservation tasks were divided into six components that were scored individually. These scores (1 for preoperational and 2 for concrete operational) were computed to yield an overall percentage usage of concrete operational thought.

All subjects were assessed during the regular school day. All interviews were audiotape-recorded. The two logical measures, class inclusion and conservation, were scored from this audiotape. The two science understanding problems, electromagnetism and gravity, were transcribed. Because both logical measures were scored from the same tape, blind scoring of class inclusion and conservation was not feasible. The electromagnetism and gravity interviews, however, were scored separately, so that the scorer had no knowledge of either the subjects' score on the other science measure or of his/her functioning on measures of logical reasoning.

Six science understanding and logical reasoning scores (mean level of conceptions) were derived from the children's interview data and were expressed as the percentage of Level 2 science concepts and of concrete operational responses, respectively: (1) gravity, (2) electromagnetism, (3) overall science understanding (mean of (1) and (2) above), (4) class inclusion, (5) conservation, and (6) overall logical reasoning (mean of (4) and (5) above). In addition to these cognitive variables, each child's grade, age, and sex were recorded for demographic analyses.

Interrater reliabilities were obtained for the electromagnetism, gravity, class inclusion, and conservation (weight and mass) measures. Ten subjects' logical reasoning scores were coded by two raters. Interrater reliabilities were checked by computing Pearson correlation coefficients for the two sets of mean scores.[3] Interrater reliability for the class inclusion task yielded a .89 correlation coefficient. The interrater correlation coefficient for the conservation task (mass and weight) was computed to be .94. The interrater reliability for science explanations was based on percentage usage for gravity and for electromagnetism. The interrater reliability for 15 randomly selected electromagnetism protocols was reflected in a .93 Pearson correlation coefficient. The interrater reliability for 15 gravity protocols was reflected by a .83 correlation coefficient. The relatively high correlation coefficients, despite the narrow age spectrum, represents strong evidence that the clinical interview technique and structural coding procedure yielded reliable assessments of level of scientific explanations.

Results

Data analysis for the present study focused on four main issues. The first issue was that of the distribution of Level 1 and Level 2 explanations within each interview. Of interest was whether subjects tend to give all Level 1 or all Level 2

---

[3]In hindsight we realize that a percentage concordance analysis would be more appropriate than a correlation coefficient.

responses, or, conversely, a mixture of response types. A second issue was the degree of concordance between each subjects' use of Level 1 and Level 2 explanations on each of the interviews. Variation in the use of science explanations at a particular level was again of interest. A third issue was the relation between age and the distribution of Level 1 and Level 2 explanations. Finally, the relationship between the use of Level 2 science explanations and the use of concrete operational thought was examined. (A more in-depth examination of the relationships between science explanations and level of logical reasoning is given in Selman, Krupa, Jacquetee, and Stone, [1982].)

Analysis of the distribution of Level 2 explanations within each interview (electromagnetism and gravity) could yield two findings of interest within the age range sampled in this study. Subjects could exhibit all Level 1 or all Level 2 explanations, thus suggesting the presence of some rather strong underlying organizing structure responsible for the form of explanations. Conversely, subjects could use a mixture of these explanatory types, suggesting that either the phenomena under investigation is not stage like in nature or that development is not a lock-step phenomena. To examine this issue, subjects with between 15 and 85% Level 2 explanations within each domain were classified as having a mixture of reasoning types. We examined the use of Level 2 explanations rather than both Level 1 and Level 2 explanations because the two explanation types are mutually exclusive; that is, subjects who gave 15% Level 2 explanations gave 85% Level 1 explanations. Subjects with either less than 15% Level 2 explanations or more than 85% Level 2 explanations were designated as *pure* types. This 15% criterion was adopted to guard against the inclusion of subjects in the mixture group, who had so few Level 2 statements (generally one or fewer statements out of 10) that some measurement error could have been responsible for their score.[4]

Table 19.4 shows that 49 of 105 subjects were classified as using all Level 1 or all Level 2 explanations on the electromagnetic interview. On the gravity interview, 60 of 105 subjects used all Level 1 or all Level 2 explanations. Thus, 47 and 62% of subjects used explanations reflective of one level only within the electromagnetic and gravity interviews, respectively. The remaining subjects used mixed responses. Investigation of this first issue thus suggests that subjects in this age range are about as likely to use a mixture of Level 1 and Level 2 explanations as they are to use primarily one of these two levels within an interview.

The second issue of interest regarding the pervasiveness of each explanatory type was whether Level 2 explanations were used in one interview or both. One

---

[4]Although other criteria could be adopted, 15% of a level is within the bounds used by other researchers making stage or level arguments based on percentage usage of some construct. See, for example, Kohlberg (1969) and Selman (1980), who use 25% of a stage as the criterion for operating at that stage.

TABLE 19.4
Number of Subjects Giving One Type of Explanation (Level 1 or
Level 2) Versus Those Using a Mixture of Level 1 and Level 2
Explanations on the Electromagnetism and Gravity Interviews

	Electromagnetism	*Gravity*
Level 1 or Level 2	49	60
Mixture of Level 1 and Level 2	56	45

TABLE 19.5
Contingency Table Analysis of Some ($\geq$ 15%) Use of Level 2
Explanations on the Gravity Interview and Electromagnetic Interview

		Electromagnetism	
		$\geq$15%	$<$15%
Gravity	$\geq$15%	38	7
	$<$15%	25	35

Note: $x^2 = 19.6$, $p < .005$

measure of this relationship may be found in the correlation between the percentage of use of Level 2 explanations in each of the interviews. A Pearson correlation coefficient between the use of Level 2 explanations on the gravity and electromagnetism interviews was computed to be .53. Although this is significant ($p < .005$), it is possible that scaling effects not reflected in the correlation existed between performance on the interviews rather than concordance. For this reason, an analysis of whether using some Level 2 explanations on one interview corresponded with using some Level 2 explanations on the second interview was conducted. Of interest was the question of whether the use of Level 2 explanations, even if relatively infrequently, was predictive of the use of similar explanation types on the second interview.

To examine this relationship, the use of at least 15% Level 2 explanations was again used as the criterion for using Level 2 explanations. Table 19.5 shows that a highly significant relationship exists between the use of some unseen force explanations in one domain and the presence of some of these explanation types in the other domain. About 73% of subjects used either some Level 2 explanations in both interviews or no Level 2 explanations in either interview. An interesting trend emerges in those cases that are split. Those subjects exhibiting some Level 2 explanations in just one of the interviews were much more likely to do so in the electromagnetism interview.

Analysis of this relationship within each grade shows a similar trend. Table 19.6 shows the relationship between the use of some Level 2 explanations within each of the domains for each grade. Again, subjects are more likely to exhibit some Level 2 explanations in both domains or no Level 2 explanations in either domain and are again more likely to exhibit Level 2 explanations in the electromagnetism interview than the gravity interview when performance in the two domains was split.

Grade trends may also be examined with respect to the mean proportion of Level 2 explanations given in each interview by each subject. This analysis is of interest because grade-related trends may exist not only in the introduction

TABLE 19.6
Contingency Table Analysis of the Number of Subjects in Each
Grade Exhibiting ≥ 15% Level 2 Explanations on the
Electromagnetism and Gravity Interviews

19.6a

Electromagnetism

		≥15%	<15%
Gravity	≥15%	2	0
	<15%	1	12

Preschool
(Ages 3:5–5:5)

19.6b

Electromagnetism

		≥15%	<15%
Gravity	≥15%	9	3
	<15%	10	8

Kindergarten
(Ages 5:3–6:11)

19.6c

Electromagnetism

		≥15%	<15%
Gravity	≥15%	27	4
	<15%	14	15

First Grade
(Ages 6:5–7:10)

of some Level 2 explanations, but older subjects may also use Level 2 explanations more frequently, thus resulting in a greater proportion of such statements in each protocol.

Table 19.7 shows the mean number of Level 2 statements used by subjects in each grade. These data suggest that not only is the *onset* of Level 2 explanations grade-related but the pervasiveness of this explanatory type also increases in higher grades.

The third issue, that of the age relatedness of using Level 2 explanations, is addressed in the analysis presented in Table 19.8. Table 19.8 presents the proportion of subjects of each age who displayed more than 15% Level 2 explanations to each interview. These data indicate that the trend in number of subjects who display at least some Level 2 explanations is similar to that indicated by the grade distributions presented earlier. The youngest group contained no subjects displaying greater than 15% Level 2 explanations to either interview, whereas both of the older age groups contained subjects whose protocols contained 15% or more Level 2 explanations.

The analyses presented in Tables 19.6, 7, and 8 portray rather radical shifts in both the onset and the proportion of Level 2 statements given by subjects with respect to age and grade. This shift parallels findings in other mental abilities reported by researchers studying the 5 to 7 age shift (cf., White, 1970).

The fourth issue, that of the relationship between levels of logical reasoning and science explanations, was addressed through correlational and contingency table analyses. Table 19.9 displays correlations among the logical-mathematical

TABLE 19.7
Average Percentage of Level 2 Explanations Used by Subjects as a
Function of Grade

Grade	n	Electromagnetism	Gravity
Preschool	15	5.8%	5.4%
Kindergarten	30	37.7%	15.3%
First Grade	60	38.5%	21.2%

TABLE 19.8
Percentage of Subjects Within Each Age Range Exhibiting 15% or
More Level 2 Explanations in the Electromagnetism and Gravity
Interviews

Age	n	Electromagnetism	Gravity
3:6 − 5:0	11	0	0%
5:1 − 6:6	45	71%	47%
6:7 − 8:0	49	62%	48%
	105	60%	43%

TABLE 19.9

Pearson Correlation Coefficients[a] Between Measures of Science Explanations and
Measures of Logical Reasoning

	Gravity	Electromagnetism	Logic Mean	Class Inclusion	Conservation
Science mean	—	—	.64	.51	.60
Gravity	—	.53	.66	.44	.65
Electromagnetism	—	—	.51	.46	.45
Logic mean	—	—	—	—	—
Class inclusion	—	—	—	—	.52
Conservation	—	—	—	—	—

[a] $p < .005$ for all correlations.

and science domains, the two science areas, and the two logical-mathematical areas. The scores were positively and significantly related. Reasoning on the gravity interview was slightly more congruous with logical reasoning than was reasoning on the electromagnetism interview, and the conservation task more closely corresponded to assessments of gravity than to electromagnetism explanations.

Computation of a partial correlation coefficient controlling for the effect of age yielded a correlation of .59 between overall logical reasoning and overall science reasoning. Thus the uncontrolled correlation of .64 between these two measures does not appear to be substantially amplified by the effects of age.

Correlations indicate a consistent correspondence among the reasoning measures, but they do not describe the nature of that correspondence. Do children who reason at the level of concrete operations in logical problems also use Level 2 explanations in science problems? Do any children reason at a higher level in science than in logical problems? This more differentiated analysis is presented in contingency tables (Tables 19.10 a, b, and c). In this analysis percentages of concrete operational logic and Level 2 science concepts was divided into low (0–49%) and high (50–100%) level usage. Table 19.10 displays the relationship between mean science understanding and mean logical reasoning. It shows that subjects were much more likely to score high on the measures of logical reasoning if they scored high on the measures of science understanding; conversely high logical reasoning did not necessarily predict high science reasoning. Taken in isolation, these data suggest that general logical-mathematical reasoning skills emerged prior to structurally parallel Level 2 science concepts. This relationship also held when comparing mean logical reasoning to performance on the gravity interview (Table 19.10b). No subjects who scored low on the measures of logical reasoning scored high on the gravity interview. Table 19.10c, however, shows that 16 subjects who scored low on the meausres of logical reasoning scored high on the electromagnetism interview. This suggests that the use of Level 2 electromagnetism concepts may emerge prior to the use of concrete operational skills as measured by traditional tasks of logical-mathematical reasoning.

Discussion

Study 2 was undertaken as a first step toward validating the developmental system of science explanations constructed during pilot work. The investigation focused on subjects in the age range during which unseen force (Level 2) explanations were found to be emergent. The results of this study suggest that the developmental system constructed during pilot work can be used to reliably code science explanations elicited by the gravity and electromagnetic interviews within this age range. The results also provide knowledge about the distribution of Level 1 and Level 2 explanations within the sampled population and the relationship

TABLE 19.10
Relationship Between Science Explanations and Logical Reasoning[a]

		19.10a Mean Logic Reasoning	
		Low	High
Mean Science Understanding	Low	62/59%	26/25%
	High	2/2%	15/14%

$$x^2 = 18.22 \qquad df = 1 \qquad p < .001$$

		19.10b Mean Logic Reasoning	
		Low	High
Gravity	Low	64/61%	33/31%
	High	0/0%	8/8%

$$x^2 = 10.88 \qquad df = 1 \qquad p = .001$$

		19.10c Mean Logic Reasoning	
		Low	High
Electromagnetism	Low	48/46%	19/18%
	High	16/15%	22/21%

$$x^2 = 7.69 \qquad df = 1 \qquad p = .006$$

[a]Top number within cell is cell frequency; bottom number is percent subjects of total ($n = 105$)

between these explanatory types and operational development as defined by Piaget.

Results of this study suggest that explanations utilizing unseen forces as causal events began to appear with regularity in kindergarten subjects, and that by first grade these explanatory types represent a significant proportion of subjects' explanations. The findings also suggest that the use of Level 1 and Level 2 explanations do not necessarily occur in response to some phenomena (i.e., electromagnetism or gravity) and then transfer in parallel to other areas within this (transitional) age range. Rather, our data suggest that with increasing age, subjects are more likely to exhibit Level 2 explanations in greater proportion than Level 1 explanations.

Several hypotheses may be entertained to account for the greater proportion of Level 2 statements generated in response to the electromagnetism interview compared to the gravity interview. First, the gravity interview may present phenomena that are less familiar to subjects than those presented in the electromagnetism interview. Although children are exposed to the *effects* of gravity and to phenomena such as falling objects that are the products of gravity, its presence is not novel in the same way that electromagnetic phenomena are. Children's substantial exposure to advanced technology may result in a greater wealth of experiences with the properties and explanations of electromagnetism, electricity, etc. than to gravity phenomena. Thus subjects may simply have more first-hand experience with these phenomena and explanations of them and thus have a greater chance to hypothesize about causality in this area than in gravity. Second, it may be that the gravity interview somehow contains fewer cues that elicit Level 2 explanations than the electromagnetic interview. In this latter interview, batteries, wires, etc. may be greater aids to the production of Level 2 explanations than the falling objects and other demonstrations presented in the gravity interivew. Finally, in addition to nonschool-related experiences, children may gain more exposure in school to electromagnetic phenomena than to gravity phenomena, thus increasing the probability that explanations based on unseen forces will be produced.

Results of this study also indicate a correlation between science explanations based on unseen forces and concrete operational thought as manifested in logical-mathematical tasks. Contingency table analyses also support the notion of a structural parallelism between the two domains. Although the general contingency table analysis suggests that logical reasoning is a temporally prior skill, breakdown by specific tasks indicates that children may be higher on specific measures of science explanations than on particular measures of logical reasoning. This suggests that although the less content-laden logical reasoning skills detected in the class inclusion and conservation tasks are generally achieved earlier than various science concepts, some science content areas, especially electricity and magnetism, may be so motivating and culturally pervasive that a child's scientific knowledge of these phenomena could be more advanced than his overall logical reasoning ability. The possibility that advances in one domain are necessarily dependent on skills in another domain is not supported by these results. Rather, there appears to be a variety of strands in the child's cognitive development, including scientific understanding and logical-mathematical reasoning. Although all strands are influenced by general developmental trends, development of one individual strand (content area) does not necessarily depend directly on development in another.

Further study is required to determine the significance of these findings. Although advances of the kind described—the use of unseen forces as causal events—seem on the surface to represent an important developmental principle for children's understanding of a range of science phenomena, it is not clear how pervasive this construct is or how important it is to children's thinking in other areas.

Summary and Educational Implications

This chapter has reported the results of two studies investigating the structure of explanations given by children and adolescents in response to interview/ demonstrations of gravity and electromagnetic phenomena. The goal of the research has been to provide methodological and descriptive knowledge for psychologists and educators interested in the development of science explanations in children.

The approach used in the present research was structural. By using this approach, common, underlying characteristics of subjects' explanations were identified for the purpose of describing the logic of science explanations. The work has drawn on both Piaget's theory of intellectual development and on his early studies of notions of causality. Somewhat greater scientific rigor was incorporated by using standardized interview procedures with probe questions.

Like Piaget's early studies, and his later writings about the development of notions of causality, the present research assumed that science explanations are determined by the interaction of logical-mathematical structure, the responses of the object, and educational efforts that provide subjects with key concepts and experiences. Science explanations are in turn hypothesized to have a unifying structure beneath their manifest content. Contrary to operational development, however, science explanations are hypothesized to have greater variability resulting from the responses of the object and differential educational experiences. Further research controlling for these sources of variation will be necessary to investigate these hypotheses.

In the validation phase of the research (Study 2), the data suggested that subjects begin to regularly give explanations of science phenomena based on unseen forces in kindergarten and first grade. It was hypothesized that both maturational factors and educational experiences may have been responsible for this finding. This study also suggested that subjects do not explain all science phenomena using the construct of unseen forces once this construct is at all present; rather, greater proportions of these statements occur as subjects mature. That this is the case may be due either to the transition period sampled or to other factors. These developmental hypotheses are also tentative because of the cross-sectional methods used; further, longitudinal studies are necessary to test these hypotheses.

The present work has two educational implications of note beyond the normative and descriptive aspects of the findings. The first is that subjects' theory building may be enhanced by the provision of key concepts to students. The naturalistic observation reported in the introduction to this chapter showed two boys conversing about the nature of atoms. Such a conversation could only take place because each boy had been introduced to the concept of atoms in some way. In the present study, prevalence of Level 2 explanations of electromagnetic phenomena was hypothesized to have been determined in part by subjects' greater experience with these phenomena. In both cases, it is suggested that subjects' construction of these concepts was aided by educational experiences.

The example of probe questioning presented in Study 1 implies that subjects' initial explanations may be seen, upon probing, to be more sophisticated than they first appear. This finding suggests that through such probing not only may teachers be clearer about what students mean when they explain a phenomena, but students may become clearer about the nature of the phenomenon. The provision of demonstrations within the interview also forced subjects to integrate discrepant observations into their reasoning about the phenomena presented here. Although further research is again indicated, it is suggested that such efforts to integrate discrepant information forces students to reformulate their theories to account for a greater number and kinds of phenomena.

The structural analysis and resulting developmental system of science explanations also provides educators with a knowledge of the direction and end points of science explanations. In this way, curriculum developers are given indices as to the appropriate level of materials for students. The present research suggests that some younger children tend to conceptualize science phenomena only in terms of their overt characteristics. Although further research is needed to determine the extent to which these explanations are amenable to change, this finding would indicate that materials should take this structuration as the starting point for educational interventions. Materials that contain Level 3 conceptions are not likely to be assimilated by young children. Conversely, materials designed for first-grade children and older that present only concepts related to overt characteristics of phenomena may fail to make use of children's conceptual abilities.[5]

This structural analysis also provides indices of development that are not normally present in standard science materials for children. Typically they are asked to memorize the "facts" of the science world. Although important, this method does not encourage students to develop theories about such processes as gravity and electromagnetism. The present approach suggests that students do construct such theories, that these theories are better thought of as incomplete than wrong and that these theories may change in a systematic sequence as the child develops.

ACKNOWLEDGMENTS

The research reported in this chapter was supported by NIE–NSF Grant # SED–78–22191. Additional support was provided by the National Institute of Mental Health through a Career Development Award, K02–MH00157-04, to the second author.

---

[5]During the third phase of the project a science curriculum was constructed for elementary-aged school children. This curriculum is presently available through the second author.

REFERENCES

Albert, E. (1978). Development of the concept of heat in children. *Science Education, 62* (3), 389–399.

Blasi, A., & Hoeffel, E. C. (1974). Adolescence and formal operations. *Human Development, 17,* 344–363.

Cantu, L. L., & Herron, J. D. (1978). Concrete and formal Piagetian stages and science concept attainment. *Journal of Research in Science Teaching, 15* (2), 135–143.

Dale, L. G. (1975). Some implications from the work of Jean Piaget. In P. L. Gardner (Ed.), *The structure of science education.* Hong Kong: Longman.

Espejo, M., Good, R., & Westmeyer, P. (1975). Evaluation of a child-structured science curriculum using the intellectual models of Piaget and Guilford. *Journal of Research in Science Teaching, 12*(2), 147–155.

Good, R. G. (1977). *How children learn science.* New York: Macmillan.

Inbody, D. (1963). Children's understanding of natural phenomena. *Science Education, 47,* 270–279.

Inhelder, B., & Piaget, J. (1958). *The growth of logical thinking from childhood to adolescence.* New York: Basic Books.

Inhelder, B., & Piaget, J. (1969). *The early growth of logic in the child.* New York: Norton.

Jaquette, D., Krupa, M. P., & Selman, R. L. (1979). *Developmental levels of science reasoning: A descriptive manual of four levels of science reasoning in four content areas.* Manual available through Dr. Robert L. Selman, Graduate School of Education, Harvard University, Cambridge, MA, 02138.

Kohlberg, L. (1969). Stage and sequence: The cognitive-developmental approach to socialization. In D. Goslin (Ed.), *Handbook of socialization theory and research.* New York: Rand McNally.

Lawson, A. E., & Renner, J. W. (1974). A quantitative analysis of responses of Piagetian tasks and its implications for curriculum. *Science Education, 58* (4), 454–459.

Lawson, A. E., & Renner, J. W. (1975). Relationships of science subject matter and developmental levels of learning. *Journal of Research in Science Teaching, 10* (3), 001–012.

Mali, G. B., & Howe, A. (1979). The development of earth and gravity concepts among Nepali children. *Science Education, 63* (5), 658–691.

Novak, J. D. (1977a). An alternative to Piagetian psychology for science and mathematics education. *Science Education, 61* (4), 453–477.

Novak, J. D. (1977b). Epicycles and the homocentric earth: Or what is wrong with stages of cognitive development. *Science Education, 61* (3), 393–395.

Nussbaum, J. (1979). Children's conceptions of the earth as a cosmic body. A cross-age study. *Science Education, 61* (1), 83–93.

Piaget, J. (1960). *The child's conception of physical causality.* Totowa, NJ: Littlefield, Adams.

Piaget, J. (1967). *The child's conception of the world.* Totowa, NJ: Littlefield, Adams.

Piaget, J. (1970). Piaget's theory. In P. H. Mussen (Ed.), *Carmichael's manual of child psychology* (Vol. I). New York: Wiley.

Piaget, J. (1974). *Understanding causality.* New York: Norton.

Pinard, A., & Laurendeau, M. (1969). "Stage" in Piaget's cognitive-developmental theory: Exegesis of a concept. In D. Elkind & J. H. Flavell (Eds.), *Studies in cognitive growth: Essays in honor of Jean Piaget.* New York: Oxford University Press.

Selman, R. (1980). *The growth of interpersonal understanding: Developmental and clinical analyses.* New York: Academic Press.

Selman, R. L., Krupa, M. P., Jaquette, D. S., & Stone, C. R. (1982). Concrete operational thought and the emergence of the concept of unseen force in children's theories of electromagnetism and gravity. To appear in *Science Education, 66*(2), 181–194.

White, S. H. (1970). Some general outlines of the matrix of developmental changes between five and seven years. *Bulletin of the Orton Society, 20*, 41–57.

Za'rour, G. I. (1976). Interpretation of natural phenomena by Lebanese school children. *Science Education, 60*(2), 277–287.

20

Interactive Roles of Knowledge and Strategies in the Development of Organized Sorting and Recall

Michelene T. H. Chi
University of Pittsburgh

This chapter addresses the issue of how existing knowledge in semantic memory affects children's use of cognitive strategies. Briefly, I propose that strategy usage is not a simple matter of whether a given cognitive strategy is or is not available to and usable by the child depending on his stage of maturation. Instead, the use of a given cognitive strategy, it appears, has a complex interaction with the amount and structure of the content knowledge to which the strategy is to be applied. Such a view brings up questions concerning the role of maturation per se in the acquisition of strategies. It suggests the possibility that maturation is correlated, but not causally related, to the rate at which more knowledge is acquired and also implies that the acquisition of this knowledge facilitates the acquisition and use of strategies. Empirical data that begin to demonstrate such an interaction is presented.

The fact that both knowledge and strategies (and their interaction) are discussed here implies that they are two separate components. Whether or not this is actually true is probably an academic question, and the debate concerning distinction between knowledge and strategies is unresolved at present (see Winograd, 1975, for a discussion). Nevertheless, in order to make some sense of the current developmental literature, it seems reasonable to assume, at least as a working hypothesis, that (domain) knowledge and strategies are separable and distinct.

I begin by describing a very robust developmental finding, the absence of organization in the young child's recall output. Typically, in the past, this has been attributed mainly to a strategic deficiency. It is hypothesized that the child fails to organize the inputs for proper storage, so that retrieval often fails to show any systematicity in the recall outputs.

457

ABSENCE OF ORGANIZATION

In a typical free recall task, a list of items is presented, and the subject is asked to recall them in any order. The sequence of recall may reveal the organization that the subject imposes on the stimulus items. Because the order of the output sequence does not match the order of the input sequence, some rearrangement of the input has been made by the subject so that the stimuli may be more compatible with an existing internal organization.

The presence of organization in the output is assessed by several measures, such as category clustering or subjective organization. For simplicity, this chapter focuses mainly on category clustering. The adult data show in general that, when items belonging to different categories (such as *Clothing, Furniture, Vehicles*) are randomly presented to an adult subject, the recall sequence will manifest clustering of items belonging to the same category (Mandler, 1967; Tulving, 1962). Young children, on the other hand, are not as likely to show strong category clustering (Bousfield, 1953; Cole, Frankel, & Sharp, 1971; Laurence, 1966; Nelson, 1969; Shapiro & Moely, 1971); and this tendency to cluster increases with age (Mandler & Stephens, 1967; Vaughan, 1968). Furthermore, this increase in clustering correlates with the general increases in the amount recalled, as well as with increasing age (Bousfield, Esterson, & Whitmarsh, 1958; Cole et al., 1971; Horowitz, 1969; Lange, 1978; Lange & Jackson, 1974; Liberty & Ornstein, 1973; Moely, Olson, Halwes, & Flavell, 1969; Neimark, Slotnick, & Ulrich, 1971; Rossi, 1964; Shultz, Charness, & Berman, 1973; Vaughan, 1968).

Although there is a general correlation between the amount of recall and the amount of clustering in both adults and children, it is not clear that the correlations denote the same kind of relationships for children and adults. First, the number of categories present in a stimulus list does not affect recall developmentally in children, but does so in adults (Mandler & Stephens, 1967). That is, for adults an increasing (up to 7) number of categories into which the stimulus set can be divided produces an increasing number of items recalled (Mandler, 1967), whereas this has not been a consistent finding in children (Mandler & Stephens, 1967; Worden, 1975). Second, first graders can recall unrelated items even when the subjective organization scores are low (Rosner, 1974). Finally, it has been possible to obtain clustering with even the youngest children, ages 2–3 (Rossi & Rossi, 1965). Hence, the relevance of the relation between amount of clustering and amount of recall is tenuous at best. Therefore, it is simply not clear that young children's low amount of recall is related to an inefficient organizational strategy, as might be the case in adults.

Nevertheless, there is a real absence of category clustering per se in young children's recall output, which can be further confirmed by their failure to form taxonomic categories in sorting tasks. Taxonomic categories generally refer to a category hierarchy, whereby basic objects such as chairs and tables can be grouped into the superordinate category, "Furniture" (Rosch, Mervis, Gray, Johnson, & Boyes–Braem, 1976). This level of organization is most commonly probed in the experimental paradigm, but the hierarchy can also include a lower level in which subordinate objects, such as rocking chair and captain's chair, can be grouped into the basic level category, *Chair.*

When asked to form groups of basic objects, young children typically do not do so taxonomically—they do not group together basic objects from the same superordinate category. Instead, children tend to group things for a variety of other reasons, such as on the basis of perceptual similarity (Melkman, Tversky, & Baratz, 1981; Tomikawa & Dodd, 1981), concrete situations (Goldman & Levine, 1963; Olver & Hornsby, 1966), association, and so on.

Children's sorting categories are also smaller and more fragmented; they often are constructed with different items, different sorting criteria, and presumably different conceptual properties than those of adults and older children (Goldman & Levine, 1963; Lange & Hultsch, 1970; Liberty & Ornstein, 1973; Saltz & Sigel, 1967; Saltz, Soller, & Sigel, 1972). Furthermore, even if children do form taxonomic categories, they are not often exhaustive; that is, they do not include all the items on the list in a given category (Annett, 1959; Flavell, 1970). Thus, children divide a set into more categories with a smaller number of items in each category (Lange & Jackson, 1974; Worden, 1974). Also, the younger children tend to take a longer time to reach a consistent sort than do the older children, suggesting that the bases of their organization are less stable.

Although it is not at all clear that there is a simple relation between categorization of the stimuli during sorting and clustering in recall, the two measures have been attributed to the same underlying deficiency—namely, that children lack abstract classification principles. In fact, there actually may be a very tenuous relation betweem the two measures, as is seen in Study Three.

AVAILABILITY OF KNOWLEDGE AND THE STRUCTURE OF CATEGORIES

In attempting to understand the absence of strong category clustering and the deficiency in taxonomic sorting in children, the natural questions to raise are whether categorical knowledge is available to children in the first place, and if the structures of children's categories are adequately developed to allow for the presence of categorical organization in the recall and sorting outputs.

The general consensus among investigators in this research area is that categorical knowledge is available to young children for the tested stimulus material. This conclusion is based on a variety of techniques used to assess categorical knowledge. In the majority of the cases, assessment of categorical knowledge is conducted by using supplementary tasks in conjunction with the primary task of sorting or free recall. Liberty and Ornstein (1973), in a postquestioning task, asked fourth graders to group "things that go together." Although these children did not initially cluster their recall outputs, they were able to "put things that go together." This is taken as evidence that they do have knowledge of the semantic relations among the items, but only the older children used this knowledge to organize their recall. Thus, the interpretation was one of production deficiency. Kobasigawa and Middleton (1972) also indicated that young children have explicit knowledge of taxonomic categories by asking subjects in the posttest interview to identify the six pictures (out of 24) that belonged to each of four categories. None of the children, including those in kindergarten, had any difficulty doing this even though their clustering and recall scores were significantly worse than the fifth graders. This is again taken as evidence for the availability of the knowledge that is not used for the purpose of recall or clustering.

In other cases, the research goal was to assess directly the structure and content of children's categorical knowledge. The evidence accumulated so far indicates that the structure of children's categories is fundamentally the same as adults, except that the children's categories may be more restricted, but both children and adults basically have the same categories and the same set of "core" or "typical" items. What may differ is the extent and size of the categories; the boundaries of young children's categories may be more restricted and less well defined than adults. Several studies support this conclusion. Using a recognition procedure, Saltz, Soller, and Sigel (1972) asked children to select exemplars of categories from a large set of pictures. Exemplars that were picked by 75% of the children were considered to be the "core" members, which are the "typical" members of a category. The basic finding was that the younger children's core members are a subset of older children's core members.

Using a sentence verification procedure to examine children's category structure, Rosch (cited in Mervis, 1980) asked subjects to indicate the truth of sentences such as "A dog is an animal." Both children and adults responded more quickly to such sentences if the instance was a typical exemplar of the category than if it was not. Furthermore, children made a greater number of errors in verifying atypical instances, suggesting that children have already learned the good, but not the poor, exemplars. Similarly, using a production task, Nelson (1974) asked children to generate instances of a superordinate category such as "Animals." Again, 5- and 8-year-olds generated predominantly the same set of core items, except that the younger children produced (1) fewer exemplars for each category, (2) inappropriate instances of a category, and (3) a more limited set of core items than adults (Rosner & Hayes, 1977).

In sum, it seems fairly safe to conclude that young children have knowledge of categories and their members, but their category members are limited in number, the core items are more restricted, and the boundaries are less well defined.

DISCREPANCY BETWEEN THE AVAILABILITY OF KNOWLEDGE AND THE ABSENCE OF ORGANIZATION

How does one resolve the discrepancy between the apparent availability of categorical knowledge in young children, the apparent similarity in the categorical structures of children and adults, and children's failure to use this knowledge in their clustering ouptuts? This discrepancy can be interpreted in two ways. First, in studies that assess knowledge directly (such as in a postquestioning task), the instruction is usually so explicit that the subject taps a specific set of links between two concepts and not necessarily the entire hierarchical or categorical structure. For example, to be able to answer correctly the question "Is a robin a bird?" one needs only to activate the link *Robin* and *Bird;* this does not necessarily imply that *Robin* is hierarchically embedded in the *Bird* category. This distinction is pointed out more explicitly in Study One (also see Chi, 1983). It is also suggested here that assessing the presence of links between things that go together is not a legitimate way to determine knowledge of semantic relations (see Study Four). Thus, this first interpretation denies the conclusion that the necessary categorical knowledge is always present on the basis of the way it has been assessed.

A second way to resolve the apparent discrepancy is to accept the assumption that young children do have categorical structures much like those in older children and adults, as is shown in the studies cited previously, except that young children's categories have fewer members than the older children's and adults'. If this premise is true, we should be able to find evidence of elevated sorting and clustering scores in young children when the material used in the recall tasks is the central members of the category.

Four kinds of experimental paradigm can provide this type of evidence. First, studies prior to the work on Rosch's notion of typical members manipulated the stimulus materials in terms of high and low associates, or good and poor exemplars, rather than typicality. If one assumes that high associates are, more or less, the central members of a category, the evidence shows that clustering occurs even in very young children (Corsale, 1978; Haynes & Kulhavy, 1976; Rossi & Rossi, 1965; Rossi & Wittrock, 1971; Vaughan, 1968). Likewise, children are also more capable of answering class-inclusion questions for good versus poor exemplars (Carson & Abrahamson, 1976). A second type of paradigm uses subject-generated members of categories. Again, if one makes a similar assumption that subject-generated members are the subject's more central members, then presumably recall, as well as clustering, should be better. This tendency occurs developmentally (Nelson, 1969; Worden, 1976). Third, if one directly manipulates the typicality of the members, then one should find that "core" members of a category should be easier to recall than the peripheral members. Bjorklund and Ornstein (1976) found that the clustering scores for the typical members were higher than for the less typical members. The results of Moely and Jeffrey (1974), using lists constructed to contain highly cohesive versus uncohesive members of the same category, may be interpreted in the same way. Six-year-olds had better recall and greater organization for the cohesive members. (Study Three may be interpreted in the same way.) Likewise, Northrop (1974) found that a list containing easy-to-sort items was recalled and organized better than a list containing items that were difficult to sort into categories. Both the cohesive members and the easy-to-sort members closely correspond to Nelson's (1974) "core" category exemplars. Finally, in a fourth kind of manipulation, children sort subordinate category members (rocking chair and captain's chair) into the "basic" level category, *Chair*. Again, young children can do this quite successfully for both natural (Rosch et al., 1976) and artificial categories (Horton & Markman, 1980).

In sum, the evidence seems fairly persuasive that there is no discrepancy between the availability of categorical knowledge and clustering if we consider recall and clustering for "core" members separately from the wider range of stimulus items, including the noncentral members, which young children do not yet have in their categorical structures. (The results of Study Four, to be reported later, can also be interpeted in the same way.) Thus, the tentative conclusion suggested here is that children's recall is elevated, and they do cluster their outputs, if the knowledge of the category members is in their knowledge structure in a form that is comparable to adults'. Hence, the issue is not one of availability/ accessibility; rather, the suggestion is that children's knowledge is not usually in the form that we have assumed it to be.

ACQUISITION OF SPECIFIC RULES VERSUS KNOWLEDGE REORGANIZATION

The foregoing discussion has basically attributed children's deficiency in organization and recall to a deficiency in their knowledge base and, in particular, the representation of that knowledge. In contrast, the interpretation in the literature puts more emphasis on a deficiency in the organizational strategy at input and/or output. Thus, the interpretation centers on the children's failure to impose an organization on the incoming stimuli so that retrieval can be facilitated. Because such interpretation is based on strategic deficiency, the literature on categorized recall has not recognized that a discrepancy exists between the availability of categorical knowledge and the absence of organization in recall. The basic assumption has been that the needed knowledge of categories is present, and absence of clustering during recall is a function of the deficient organizational strategy.

The focus on an interpretation based on strategic deficiency (rather than an inability to perceive organization due to a lack of structure in semantic memory) is evident in the emergence of abundant training studies that teach children to actively use an organizational strategy. In recall clustering tasks, most of the training studies induce children to notice the categories, for example, by blocking the stimulus presentation (Moely & Shapiro, 1971) or by providing names or labels for the categories (Nelson, 1969). These indirect training procedures have produced disappointing results. Providing labels or blocking the stimulus presentation often does not lead to greater conceptual organization in younger children.

In direct training procedures, children were taught to (1) sort the items into taxonomic categories, (2) label the categories, (3) count the members of each category, and (4) further organize recall by remembering each category. The amount of clustering was increased but only when the same stimuli were used for both training and subsequent recall tasks (Moely et al., 1969; Worden, 1975). Once again, such improvements were not dramatic when a different set of stimuli was used for the recall task (Moely & Jeffrey, 1974). There are two interpretations to these results. First, the training could have produced context- or domain-specific rules that are not generalizable to other contexts. Second, the training could have reorganized the representation of the stimuli used in training so that the categorical structure of these stimuli would be apparent during subsequent presentations. But again, such training would not be generalizable because stimuli in other domains have not undergone a representational reorganization.

Knowledge Reorganization

To elucidate the difference between the two foregoing interpretations—acquisition of specific rules and reorganization of the representation—it is instructive to see how modern cognitive theories of knowledge representation can help us understand these phenomena. Knowledge is often separated into two types, facts and rules. Factual knowledge is knowledge that we know and can talk about, such as the fact that "a robin is an animal." Rule knowledge concerns how something is done. For example, doing long division requires a set of rules, which, if followed properly, can produce the answer to a problem.

Differences between facts and rules can be captured by the formalism used to represent them. Factual knowledge is typically represented by an interrelated network of nodes and links. The nodes can be conceived of as concepts, and the links denote the relations among the nodes. A variety of node-link network structures has been proposed, beginning with Collins and Quillian's (1969) hierarchical network model. In this model, knowledge such as "a robin is an animal" is stored as two separate propositions. There are direct (isa) links between *robin* and *bird* and *bird* and *animal,* but no direct link between *robin* and *animal.* Hence, in order to verify the truth or falsity of the statement "a robin is an animal," an inference must be made. Concepts are assumed to be organized hierarchically with nonredundant storage of properties. General properties of robins that are common to all birds are stored at the most general (*Bird*) node, whereas properties specific to robins are stored directly with *Robin*. Hence, a robin is inferred to fly, sing, lay eggs, and so on (because these are properties true of all birds), but no inference needs to be made to retrieve the proposition that "a robin has red breast" (because red breast is a specific property attached to robins).

Hence, one could postulate that a canonical (and perhaps adult-like) representation is one in which the general concept (*Bird*) subsumes more specific concepts (such as *Robin* and *Sparrow*). The clustering of all types of birds into the *Bird* category necessitates a hierarchical representation in memory in which specific birds (*Robin* and *Sparrow* and so on) are subsumed under the *Bird* concept node. Thus, the reorganization interpretation provided earlier specifies that a child's original representation of conceptual knowledge may not conform to the canonical one. Training, however, could induce a new representation, thereby producing results that are consistent with adult performances because the representaion is now more adult-like. On the other hand, training fails to generalize to other domains because the representations of the other domains have not undergone any reorganization. The first study in this chapter points out that children's initial representation of factual knowledge need not conform to one an adult expects. Nevertheless, their performance variability can be understood in terms of its correspondence to the representations that exist.

Domain-Specific Rules

Knowledge of rules, on the other hand, can be represented by using the formalism of a production system. A production system is simply a set of rules, each rule having both a condition and an action side. The condition side of the rule specifies the conditions that must be satisfied before the actions can take place. The conditions must match the contents of working memory. For example, an organizational strategy can be represented as a rule that looks for similarities within a set of inputs. If the conditions are met, then the action is to group them together for storage. Thus, subsequent recall simply would retrieve the stimuli (in clusters) that have been stored in a group.

Suppose the strategic deficiency interpretation assumes that a rule that seeks categorical relations among inputs is lacking in the child. This may take the following form:

Rule 1:

IF the two successively presented words come from the same category,

THEN tag them as similar, store them together, and retrieve them together.

The problem with this rule, however, is that in order for it to take effect the condition side of the rule must be satisifed by matching the incoming information with patterns in semantic memory. In order to decide whether *Robin* and *Sparrow* (the two successively presented words) come from the same category, one must out of necessity have *Robin* and *Sparrow* in the semantic network and associated in such a way that their categorical structure becomes apparent. Thus, the success of applying such a general rule rests on the existence of an appropriate semantic representation; one that has the concepts organized according to salient dimensions (as in the canonical form).

The reason we postulate that training succeeds in producing clustering is that training sometimes induces specific rules rather than general ones. The nature of specific rules is such that the condition side of the rules spells out the specific similarities that are being sought. When these are presented in the stimulus context of the experiment, the child recognizes them. In more general contexts, however, the child fails to use the learned rule, not because the child fails to apply it (a production deficiency interpretation), but because in a different context the conditions of the specific rule no longer match the new context.

To illustrate, suppose the child is told (or trained) to find and group all the birds. The child can select all the birds (such as, robin, sparrow, parrot, canary) out of a list of pictures containing other items (such as sofa, chair, bed, coat, gloves, etc.). There are two reasons why a child can easily do this task. First, as was already stated, the ability to recognize that robin, sparrow, parrot, and canary is a bird does not imply that they are represented in the canonical form. (Study One provides the evidence.) Second, young children, without any knowledge of birds, can pick out all the birds on the basis of perceptual similarity. (Evidence will be provided in Study Four.) Hence, once children have been taught to group the birds together, they may form a specific rule such as:

Rule II:

IF sparrow, robin, canary, and parrot are presented,

THEN tag them as similar, store them together, and retrieve them together.

Of course the acquisition of such a rule would not be generalizable and may also be transitory for at least two reasons. First, the rule itself may not have been learned well enough to be maintained over time. Second, the action of the rule, "storing them together," also implies that a temporary representation may be created that involves the storage of these birds in a cluster. Again, new or temporary representaions may not last and can be rather unstable. Both of these interpretations are consistent with the findings in the literature about children's failure to maintain trained strategies. Notice that if a child already has in memory a canonical representation of birds, then the actions of Rule II would be redundant. Hence, older children's learning of such a rule would be less susceptible to decay and more amenable to generalization (that is, the acquisition of Rule I), assuming that older children would more likely have the canonical representation.

Study One, following, illustrates several things. The first is that a child need not have the canonical representation that adults often think is the best. But that does not mean that children do not have a robust representation of some kind that they can and do work with. The second point is that a canonical representation is not needed in order to recognize that certain concepts are of a specific type. Nevertheless, this knowledge need not imply that certain concepts are then subsumed under their type in a hierarchical manner.

Study One: Exploring a Child's Knowledge of Friends

The goal of this study was to explore a child's representation of a specific overlearned domain and then to examine the relationship between the child's representation and how it affected classification. In order to elicit a child's knowledge of a domain (classsmates), a 5-year-old girl (M.C.) was asked to generate all her classmate's names. The results of four separate trials are shown in Table 20.1. A majority of the 23 names was generated on every trial, and the retrieved order shows a fair amount of regularity. Groups of two, three, and even four children appear across trials and tend to appear in the same location on each list. One measure of the stability of organization of these lists, at the level of pairs, is Nelson's (1969) Repeated Pairs Index (RPI). The value of the RPI for the present data of one subject is .44. By contrast, 5-year-olds in Nelson's (1969) study of free recall of lists achieved average RPIs in the range of about .2 to .25. Although we are comparing two different studies, Bjorklund and Zeman (1982) have gathered data that permit a direct comparison to corroborate this point. They found first graders' clustering scores with classmates to be around .51, whereas the same children's clustering scores on a standard tax-onomic list of items was in the range of .10.

The reason for such a stable organization became apparent when M.C. was asked to sort 23 cards with the name of one classmate on each card. She completed the task in about 3 minutes and made four groups. Postquestioning revealed that her reason for this grouping was that it corresponded to the seating arrangement in class. Consultation with the teacher confirmed that this was true and the actual plan is shown in Figure 20.1. (It has since been shown by Bjorklund and Zeman, 1982, that this is a very popular way for children to represent their classmates.) The partitions of the lists in Table 20.1 correspond to these groups. Clearly, M.C. generated the lists section by section. Over four trials, only one instance occurred in which a boundary was crossed before the entire section was generated (Trial 1), and in that instance she corrected herself later and inserted the two missing names. (Notice that this finding contrasts sharply with that in the literature showing that young children are often not exhaustive in their inclusion of all the items on the list into a given category. One may now interpret that finding by assuming that children's categories are smaller; hence, they appear to be nonex-haustive by the adults' standards.)

Another way to test the reality of these sections is to look at the interitem pause times. On the average, over the four trials, the times were 6.5 seconds

TABLE 20.1
Four Trials of Generation of Classmates' Names

Trial 1	Trial 2	Trial 3	Trial 4
Michelle	Mallory	Laura	Mallory
Mallory	Michelle	Michelle	Michelle
Not Sasha	Eric	Josh	Josh
Laura	Josh	Mallory	Laura
Josh	Laura	Eric	Eric
Eric			
	Paul	Eva	Kimani
Eva	Eva	Kimani	Eva
Kimani	Leah	Oliver	Oliver
Oliver	Brian	Brian	Brian
Brian	Oliver	Tamara	Tamara
	Kimani	Leah	Leah
Terry			
Stephanie	Terry	Terry	Terry
Andrei	Stephanie	Stephanie	Stephanie
Paul	Andrei	Andrei	Andrei
Not Paul	Matthew	Nicki	Nicki
Matthew	Nicki	Matthew	Matthew
Nicki	Dana	Dana	Dana
Dana			
	Paul	Paul	Paul
Paul	Michael	Emma	Sasha
Leah	Emma	Sasha	Emma
Tamara	Sasha	Lisa	Becky
Paul	Becky	Michael	Michael
Michael		Becky	
Lisa			
Sasha			
Emma			
Becky			

between sections, whereas within-section times were 3.1 seconds. M.C. was asked to recall after she had sorted the names, because recall, as opposed to generation, is the standard procedure used to tap output organization. The set of 23 classmates' names was presented in random order and then M.C. was asked to recall them. The retrieval (which was perfect) produced the same kind of ordering, with more uniform pause times. Between-section times were 2.7 seconds, and within-section times averaged 2.4 seconds.

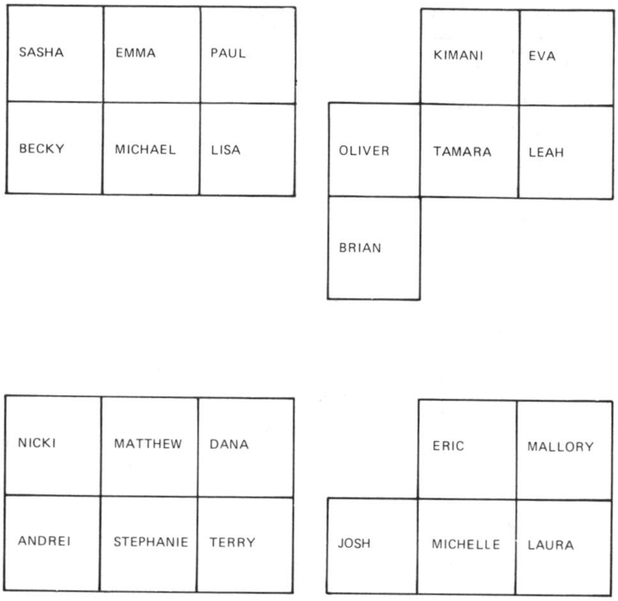

FIG. 20.1   Seating arrangement of classmates.

Although M. C. did not use the kind of taxonomic categories to organize classmates that seem salient to an adult, such as age, grade (this was a mixed classroom containing first and second graders), gender, and race, it seemed highly unlikely that she did not know these attributes for each individual classmate. To test how this knowledge might be organized, two further tasks were conducted. The first was to generate the names of classmates with certain attributes, such as second-grade boys or all the girls. Over eight trials, utilizing different subgroups of classmates, M.C.'s section-by-section organization remained stable. All members of a section satisfying the subgroup constraint were named before she moved on to the next section.

The second task was to confirm whether a given child was of the stated gender, e.g., "Andrei is a girl." The latencies for this task were measured from audio tapes, and there were no systematic differences among the times it took to verify that a child was of a given gender or not. Although measuring response latencies from aural tapes may not be very sensitive, the data are systematic in that a positive confirmation (correct gender) was faster (913 msec) than a negation (942 msec). This is consistent with data in the literature on confirmation and negation (Wason, 1959).

To summarize, the three specific results were: (1) The classmates' names were generated by seating sections, (2) specific subgroups were also generated in this way, and (3) it took equivalent amounts of time to verify the gender of any given child. The first two results show that M.C.'s grouping by section was quite stable over time and robust under different task demands; indeed, these results were obtained over four trials of free generation, one sorting trial, two free recall trials, plus various other tasks spread over six sessions. Consistent with the hypothesis proposed here, one could conclude that a possible representation for M.C.'s classmates starts with *Classmates* as the top level, followed by *Sections* as superordinate nodes, *Names* as basic levels nodes, and *Attributes* at the lowest level linked to each basic node (see Fig. 20.2). The third result confirms this picture in the following way. If the representation took an alternative form, one in which all the girls were grouped under a *Girl* node, Rosch's (1978) results would predict that a category verification task should produce time differentials because there were 13 girls in the class and not all of them could be central members of the *Girl* category. However, the absence of time differentials in verification suggests that the task required the activation of nodes to the same depth in a hierarchy as the network (depicted in Fig. 20.2) indicates. To confirm that a named child was or was not a girl required the activation of the child node and his/her gender.

In sum, this study illustrates that the preferred mode of representation for a child is not taxonomic in the adult sense; that is, it need not conform to an adult experimenter's conception of the ideal canonical representation that may organize

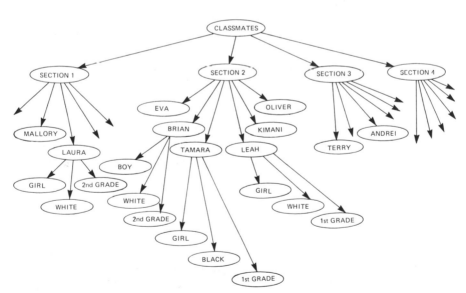

FIG. 20.2.   A possible hierarchical representation for the child's knowledge of classmates.

a classroom of children according to grade, gender, or race. Nevertheless, the child's representation, consisting of children with their seating locations, constitutes a valid representation that permits an orderly and high level of recall—a finding that is also supported by Bjorklund and Zeman's (1982) data.

The second point of this study was to show that certain attributes of a concept (such as the gender of a child) may be known, and yet this does not imply that the concept is organized around that attribute as the dominant or salient dimension. This point has been made several times earlier in this chapter. Thus, assessing that a child knows that "Mallory is a girl" (or "A robin is a bird") cannot lead to the conclusion that the child possesses a canonical representation with the more inclusive category at the higher level node. It can only suggest that the specific link between the two concepts is present. Therefore, one must assess the larger integrated knowledge structure, rather than the piecemeal links, in order to ascertain that children know something.

Study Two: The Application of an Alphabetization Strategy to the Retrieval of Friends

In Study One, it was shown that M.C. had a very stable representation of her classmates, and that she retrieved those names by using a representation based on seating arrangement. The representation was postulated to be very robust because it was manifested in every opportunity to retrieve those names. The conclusion, therefore, was that the child retrieved the names in that particular order because that is how they were stored and represented in memory. The purpose of this study was to see if the child could be taught to use a strategy of retrieval that is not compatible with the way the names were represented, that is, in an alphabetical order.

This study was motivated by the theoretical analyses presented earlier concerning the two possible conditions under which the teaching of a strategy succeeds in producing the desired performance. In the one case, we postulated that in order for a strategy to take effect (Rule I), the necessary factual knowledge must already be represented in a certain way. In this study, suppose the rule of recalling by alphabetic order takes the form:

IF two names start with the same letter,

THEN store them together, and retrieve them together.

If the child already has the names stored in alphabetical order (supposing a representation such as Fig. 20.3, then alphabetic retrieval is fairly automatic. The condition of the rule will always be satisfied. On the other hand, if the names are not already stored in alphabetic order, in order for the child to manifest alphabetical recall, the child is required to form a new representation (that is, store the names in memory) so that those names with the same initial letter are

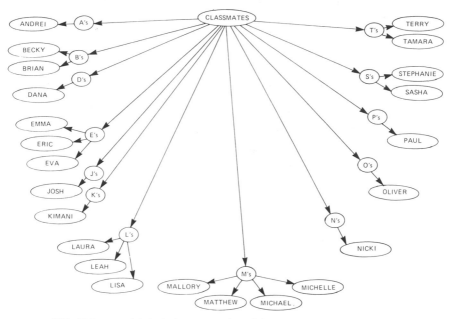

FIG. 20.3.   An alphabetical representation of classmates.

stored together. Here, the specific assumption of recall is that the order of retrieval reflects the way the stimuli are organized and stored in memory after they have been encoded. One could, of course, also assume that organization occurs during retrieval, but due to the way the present study was designed, that did not happen, as is shown shortly.

Training consisted of teaching the child how to alphabetize. She was asked to alphabetize the 23 names on cards. She was able to learn the rule in one trial, although she took a while to complete the trial. After that, she was asked to recall the names in alphabetical order. Surprisingly, she did so perfectly, although she often had to stop and ask what the next letter was in the alphabet.

There was one interesting difference between the retrieval protocols of names in alphabetical order versus the retrieval according to the seating arrangement. In the latter case, retrieval occurred in quick succession, with 1- to 2-second intervals between names, and 5- to 6-second pauses between sections. In the former case, retrieval time of names within a given letter was around 2 to 3 seconds, but between letters ranged anywhere from 10 to 30 seconds. For example, it took 26 seconds to generate the name Emma after generating Dana, but only 2 seconds to then generate Eva and 3 seconds to generate Eric. In fact, because it took her so long to generate the next letter, she often would ask the experimenter what the next letter was, so that the experimenter began to prompt her with the next letter when she paused. (This is not because she did not know the alphabet sequence.) What does this timing data suggest? It suggests that a new, and perhaps temporary, representation much like that schematized in Fig. 20.4 was created (or the existing representation was reorganized) while the subject was asked to sort the names according to the alphabet.

With just one training trial, she only had time to create a representation with names grouped together by individual letters, but not in any specific (alphabetical) order. Therefore, the alphabet list was used as a pointer to retrieve the "next" cluster, and it was difficult for her to keep track of her place on the alphabet list. Once a cluster of names beginning with the same letter was entered, however, retrieval was fast. Because this representation was not ordered in a specific (alphabetic) way, it took time to jump back and forth between retrieving the content of a cluster and finding the next location on the alphabet list.

The pattern of interitem pause times is not consistent with the alternative interpretation, that is, names are searched *during* recall in alphabetical order according to the seating sections. Hence she did not search for all the A names in Sections 1, 2, 3, 4, then search for the B names in Sections 1, 2, 3, 4, and so on. To do so would mean that she did not create a new representation but used the existing one and organized her recall during retrieval. One might expect recall to be achieved by this on-line method had the child not already been asked to alphabetize the whole deck of 23 names. This initial training experience probably biased the whole organization to occur at input. The pattern of pause times suggests that recall was not on-line and supports the interpretation that one way a strategy can be taught and used is to provide an occasion when the child can create a new representation of her already familiar factual knowledge.

How successfully can a strategy be applied if a new representation cannot be easily formed? In order to test this hypothesis, the child was asked to memorize a list of names that had no immediate semantic references for her (at least not in a cohort group), even though she was familiar with each individual name. This is a matched set of 23 names with the same number of syllables and the same number of names beginning with the same letter. For example, instead of having Andrei the new list had Anna. After three sort–recall trials, including one where the child was explicitly told to alphabetize the names, the child's recall was still poor, about 11 out of 23 names, compared to the perfectly alphabetized recall of familiar names.

This study demonstrates that when the stimuli tested conform to a knowledge base that is very familiar and has a clear existing representation, a child seems to have no difficulty creating a new representation so that the new pattern of retrieval is consistent with the new representation. By this interpretation, the mechanism of retrieval operates by changing the knowledge base first (either creating a new one or rearranging the old one). This is more likely to be true in M.C.'s case because retrieval followed sorting, probably providing the opportunity to create a new representation that was more or less consistent with the alphabetization strategy. (A perfect representation would have been one where

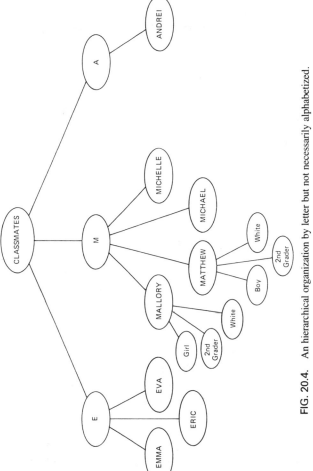

FIG. 20.4.   An hierarchical organization by letter but not necessarily alphabetized.

the clusters were sequenced alphabetically.) If she had been asked to recall in alphabetical order without prior sorting, she might have had to retrieve the names in the alternative on-line mode, that is, searching for names with a given initial letter, section by section. Nevertheless, the finding that the child could readily recall her classmates in a different pattern suggests that the use of a strategy greatly interacts with the knowledge base. When the conceptual knowledge is well organized initially, a 5-year-old child can easily benefit from instruction on the use of a new strategy. Otherwise, the utility of a new strategy is more limited, as in the case of alphabetical recall of familiar names that did not correspond to an existing organized representation.

Such data give a plausible interpretation for why training studies in the use of strategies are not often maintained over time. This study suggests that the new representation may be temporary; these data also had implications for interpreting why older children seem to benefit more from training. One possibility is that older children may already have data bases analogous to M.C.'s representation of classmate names—that are organized. Younger children, however, may have data bases corresponding to this child's knowledge of a random list of familiar names that are not organized, leading to an inefficient use of strategies. In that case, the utility of a strategy was less apparent (this is what has been called a mediation deficiency).

Study Three: Classification of Dinosaurs

Study One attempted to explain why a young child did not retrieve a set of concepts in a taxonomically organized way. Instead, the organization reflected one that was learned after 1 year's experience. The presence of strong organization and the impressive number of classmates retrieved, as opposed to the frequent lack of any organization and poor retrieval in young children, may be attributed to the highly familiar nature of the stimuli. Delfosse and Smith (1979) also found preschoolers to be extremely accurate at recalling one of many companions they had played with on the previous day and week; Bjorklund and Zeman (1982) found superior recall of classmates by first, third, and fifth graders as compared to recall of the standard taxonomic categories, such as *Animals, Furniture,* and so on.

The goal of the present study was more ambitious; to show that a child is capable of taxonomic classification if the stimuli are highly familiar and are represented in memory so that they conform to a taxonomic organization that might be expected by adults. Again, it is hypothesized that such a representation is achieved through learning, which could have reorganized the earlier (more immature) representation so that the relevant attributes become the salient dimensions.

A 4½-year-old child (M.K.) was studied intensively. This child could be considered an expert in the knowledge domain of dinosaurs, because his parents had read dinosaur books to him for about 1½ years. We proceeded to explore the knowledge he had of dinosaurs, how that knowledge was represented, and how that representation affected his classification of dinosaurs. (For details see Chi & Koeske, 1983).

In order to determine which dinosaurs the child knew and what he knew about each, we began by eliciting dinosaur names from him in a production task, with the child freely generating the names of the dinosaurs he knew. Across six sessions, he generated a total of 46 dinosaurs. From this, a set of 40 was selected for further testing. When one dinosaur name elicited another, we assumed there was a link between them in memory. To determine what the child knew of the 40 dinosaurs, a clue game was played in which the "chooser" generated a list of properties and the "guesser" identified the dinosaur to which these properties belonged. By alternating roles between the experimenter and the child, the game provided information about the child's recognition and spontaneous generation of dinosaur-property links or relations.

The dinosaur–dinosaur linkages gathered in the production protocols and the dinosaur–property linkages derived from the clue game were used to map a network representation of the total set of 40 dinosaurs. In order to simplify the network, we artificially segregated the 40 dinosaurs into two groups of 20 each— one set is referred to as the better known dinosaurs and the other as the lesser known. The division was based on two external criteria: the frequency of inclusion in the child's nine dinosaur texts and the mother's independent judgment of the child's best and least known dinosaurs. Seven dinosaurs from each set of 20, henceforth referred to as the targets, were selected for detailed analyses of their structure. The targets were chosen on the amount of information (number of properties) mentioned about each dinosaur. The focus on a subset from each set of 20 was necessitated by both a theoretical reason and a methodological one. Had the structure of the entire set of 20 been analyzed, the better known set would have overwhelmed the lesser known set in terms of the sheer number of properties known about each dinosaur. Theoretically, our interest was not in the quantity of information, but in the structure of information if quantity could be held constant. The methodological reason was that the better known dinosaurs were probed with greater frequency in the clue game, thus resulting in a sampling bias.

The two sets of 20 dinosaurs were then divided into seven categories each, corresponding more or less to the way these dinosaurs were introduced in the books. As it turned out, the better known target dinosaurs fell into two of the seven categories: armored and large plant eaters. The lesser known target dinosaurs belonged to five of the seven categories: armored, small bird or egg eaters, water dwellers, duckbills, and early meat eaters.

Basically, the better known targets were better structured and formed more cohesive groups in memory than the lesser known targets, even though the same amount of information (five properties) was known about each target. This can be illustrated from the data in the following ways. First, better known target dinosaurs showed multiple links to target dinosaurs within the same category but only showed single links to target dinosaurs of other categories. Second, target dinosaurs in the better known portion of the network shared properties with target dinosaurs in the same category more often than with target dinosaurs from the other categories. Such a contrasting pattern of greater within- and lesser between-category linkages did not appear for the lesser known dinosaurs. The connections for the lesser known target dinosaurs were much more uniformly distributed among the categories. Third, when we subsequently measured M.K.'s recall of the two sets of dinosaurs, his recall outputs manifested greater clustering according to these predefined categories in the better known rather than in the lesser known set.

Would the child's classification of the 20 better known dinosaurs reflect the existence of these predefined categories? When M.K. was asked to sort the dinosaurs, he did so very quickly, without hesitation or pauses into two groups: meat eaters and plant eaters. This sorting pattern was consistent across two separate trials. The child's sorting pattern did not correspond entirely to the presumed categories in his knowledge structure. As we stated earlier, sorting and clustering should perhaps not be attributed to the same underlying processes even though their deficiencies are often correlated in young children.

Because we have argued that cohesive groups corresponding to categories existed (at least for the better known dinosaurs), this child's grouping data could be interpreted as evidence showing that he chose to use a higher level (or superordinate) relation to sort the dinosaurs; that is, one can assume that the representation can be schematized as in Fig. 20.5, with every dinosaur fitting into one of the categories that we have postulated. Furthermore, the categories can be collapsed into higher level superordinate nodes, such as *meat eaters* and *plant eaters*. *Meat eater* and *plant eater* were precisely the two abstract categories Storm (1978) had used to divide the *Animals* category. In her study, she found that third graders (about 9 years old) had difficulty sorting according to these abstract dimensions even after training. Our data would support the notion that a child can classify taxonomically if there is sufficient knowledge about the interconnections (or contingencies) to allow such groupings. Furthermore, his sorting performance is very adult-like in the sense of being fast, exhaustive, and stable across trials.

Consistent with our interpretation that the grouping of the lesser known dino-saurs are less cohesive, M.K.'s sorting performance on the lesser known dino-saurs was more variable. He could not reach a stable sort in three trials. His first sort was meat versus plant eaters; his second sort was land meat eaters, plant eaters, and water swimming; that is, he introduced two additional dimen-sions: habitat and locomotion. In his third sort, he changed it again into land plant eater, water meat eater, and water plant eater. His sorting performance matches those typically exhibited by young children—slow, nonexhaustive, and

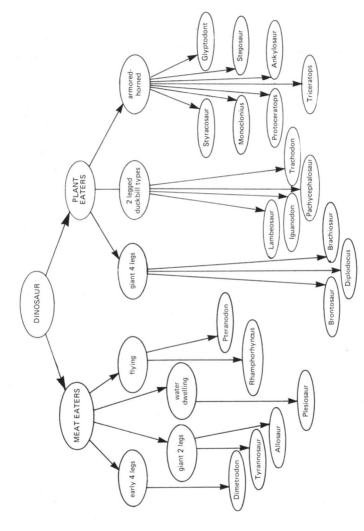

FIG. 20.5. A possible representation for dinosaur knowledge.

477

inconsistent. An explanation for his inconsistencies is that the lesser known dinosaurs are not as well structured and cohesive as the better known dinosaurs in terms of our criteria for patterns of interlinkages within and between groups.

To summarize, this study illustrates that a very young child is capable of sorting at a superordinate level (food habits), one that has been found by zoologists to be basic to classifications of mammals. The ability to classify at this level is not often found in the literature even for 9-year-olds (Storm, 1978). This impressive sorting performance can be attributed to the well-organized and highly enriched representation that M.K. had of dinosaurs. The enriched, well-integrated, and coherent representation, at least for the better known dinosaurs, was shown by the presence of multiple and interrelated links in a specific configuration. We hypothesize that such a well-formed representation came about from frequent exposures to dinosaurs, so that the relevant conceptual dimensions (food habits) became salient. This is why the lesser known dinosaurs were not as well represented, and sorting performance was more variable (see Chi, 1983).

Study Four: Classification of Dinosaurs by Expert and Novice Children

Study Three indicates that when a child is knowledgeable, he or she is capable of exhibiting taxonomic classification at an earlier age than has been traditionally found. Another way to examine the interaction of domain knowledge with the use of a particular classification principle is to compare and contrast expert and novice children's classification performance. The idea here is that if expert children classify in a different but more sophisticated way than do novice children, one could conclude that it is not the appearance of a classification principle (like a strategy) in the children's repertoire that makes the difference, but rather the classification outcome consists of the interaction of a particular mode of retrieval with the representation of the domain knowledge.

A set of 20 dinosaurs that could be categorized into five groups was selected. Most of the categories were determined from books about dinosaurs, and they tended to have perceptual attributes that define their similarities. For example, a common category is the duckbill dinosaurs because they all have a mouth that looks like a duck's bill. Children who knew a lot about dinosaurs, as well as children who had very little knowledge of dinosaurs, participated. They were each asked to do two tasks: (1) to tell everything they knew about a dinosaur, when a picture of it was presented, and (2) to classify the 20 dinosaurs and give explanations for their categories. Only the results of the second task are discussed here.

The data from two expert and two novice children, with a mean age of 7.2 years, are presented. Expertise was determined by a posthoc criterion: the number of dinosaurs out of 20 that a child could correctly identify by name. The two expert children each named 12 out of 20 correctly, whereas both the novices could not identify any correctly.

The sorting data are interesting in a variety of ways. First, novices could group the dinosaurs fairly accurately according to the a priori category specification. For example, novice M.C. basically grouped the dinosaurs in the way specified, perhaps with one "error." Novice A.R. had three groups. From scanning the data collected on other novices, it is fairly clear that children, without any explicit knowledge of the stimuli, can classify them based on their visual resemblance and visual similarities. This finding is consistent with both Rosch et al.'s (1976) results and Horton and Markman's (1980) results, in which they found that children can classify and easily acquire objects that are at the basic level, because at that level instances of the concept are relatively similar to each other. Hence, one could postulate that each dinosaur (see Fig. 20.5) is an exemplar of the "basic" categories such as the duckbills. Thus, based on Rosch et al.'s findings, it is not surprising that the novice children could sort the dinosaurs into their respective categories.

We can further substantiate the basis of their classification by examining children's explanations. In almost every case, the reasons provided were perceptual in nature. For example, one of the novice's reasons for grouping the duckbills together was because their heads looked alike; they had small hands, rough skin, and so on.

Note that investigators in the past have attributed semantic knowledge to children when they could sort or group things taxonomically. The present data contradict that assumption directly for natural categories where perceptual similarity and taxonomic category are correlated.

How are the sorting patterns of the experts different? We expected the categories to be salient (not only on a perceptual basis, but also because books tend to introduce them as a group), and that all the experts group them the same way. Surprisingly, the two experts grouped them pretty much the way the 4½-year-old expert (M.K.) did from the previous study: plant eaters and meat eaters. One of the experts (A.P.) had an additional group based on aggressiveness. There are two things to note about the experts' data. First, they tended to group the dinosaurs according to more abstract than perceptual features. For example, they were grouped on the basis of the diet and/or whether they were mean or not. In Rosch et al.'s (1976) taxonomy, this would correspond to sorting at the superordinate level. Secondly, we further know that the groupings were based on a more superordinate node because when both experts were asked to further subdivide the large groups (meat versus plant eaters), they created subgroupings that looked very much like the novices' initial groups (such as duckbills) and were based also on perceptual features. Hence, the adult-like sorting according to superordinate level categories was observed in 7-year-old children who were experts in a knowledge domain. This suggests that the development of classification skill interacts strongly with knowledge about the stimulus domain.

SUMMARY

This chapter began by summarizing the developmental research of the last two decades that has shown the absence of organization in young children, particularly as exhibited in the recall output. This absence of clustering is in direct contrast to the apparent capabilities of young children to sort or categorize items into their taxonomic categories when explicitly requested. This discrepancy has not been seen in this way in the literature because the interpretation has centered on a strategic (or production) deficiency explanation. It has been postulated that children have the requisite knowledge to organize the stimuli but are simply not doing so. One of the points made in this chapter is that knowledge of the stimuli is not needed at all in order to sort them properly. This can be done on the basis of perceptual similarities, as shown in Study Four. Furthermore, one could also properly sort stimuli into their respective requested categories, not because the knowledge is necessarily organized in a taxonomic way in memory, but because the task explicitly demands the assessment of specific links and not the integrated knowledge structure, as shown in Study One.

Another way to explain the occasional success of young children in sorting and clustering is by postulating that young children do have categorical knowledge much like adults', but their categories are smaller with a more restricted set of core or central members. Consequently, when an experiment uses a restricted set of central members as the stimuli, recall and clustering will be much improved. This is also shown in Studies One and Four.

Finally, this chapter makes the important point that in some cases when young children do manifest a performance that conforms to the use of a strategy, it may be a reflection of how the content knowledge was stored and represented in memory. When the memory representation takes a certain format as in Studies Two, Three, and Four, children will appear to be able to use a sophisticated strategy. When the content knowledge is not represented in a certain way, as when the child is asked to retrieve a set of names that did not belong to a cohort group (Study Two), or when a novice is asked to sort dinosaurs (Study Four), recall is more difficult and does not manifest the use of a general strategy. Hence, the relationship between strategies and knowledge is necessarily an interdependent one.

ACKNOWLEDGMENTS

This research was supported by the Learning Research and Development Center, funded in part as a research and development center by the National Institute of Education, United States Department of Education. The opinions expressed do not necessarily reflect the position or policy of NIE and no official endorsement should be inferred. The author is also grateful for funds provided by the Spencer Foundation in support of this research.

Susan Chipman's comments improved this chapter immeasurably. Comments and editing by Mary Beth Curtis and Ernest Rees are also greatly appreciated.

REFERENCES

Annett, M. (1959). The classification of instances of four common class concepts by children and adults. *British Journal of Educational Psychology, 29*, 223–236.

Bjorklund, D. F., & Ornstein, P.A. (1976). *The development of taxonomic concepts: The effects of list saliency on recall.* Unpublished manuscript, University of North Carolina at Chapel Hill.

Bjorklund, D. F., & Zeman, B. R. (1982). Children's organization and metamemory awareness in their recall of familiar information. *Child Development, 53*, 799–810.

Bousfield, W. A. (1953). The occurrences of clustering in the recall of randomly arranged associates. *Journal of General Psychology, 49*, 229–240.

Bousfield, W. A., Esterson, J., & Whitmarsh, G. A. (1958). A study of developmental changes in conceptual and perceptual associative clustering. *The Journal of Genetic Psychology, 92*, 95–102.

Carson, M. T., & Abrahamson, A. (1976). Some members are more equal than others: The effect of semantic typicality on class-inclusion performance. *Child Development, 47*, 1186–1190.

Chi, M. T. H. (1983). Knowledge-derived categorization in young children. In D. R. Rogers & J. A. Sloboda (Eds.), *Acquisition of symbolic skills.* New York: Plenum Press.

Chi, M. T. H., & Koeske, R. D. (1983). Network representation of a child's dinosaur knowledge. *Developmental Psychology, 19*, 29–39.

Cole, M., Frankel, F., & Sharp, D. (1971). Development of free recall learning in children. *Developmental Psychology, 4*, 109–123.

Collins, A. M., & Quillian, M. R. (1969). Retrieval time from semantic memory. *Journal of Verbal Learning and Verbal Behavior, 8*, 240–247.

Corsale, K. (1978). *Factors affecting children's use of organization in recall.* Unpublished doctoral dissertation, University of North Carolina at Chapel Hill.

Delfosse, P., & Smith, P. K. (1979). Memory for companions in preschool children. *Journal of Experimental Child Psychology, 27*, 459–466.

Flavell, J. H. (1970). Developmental studies of mediated memory. In H. W. Reese & L. P Lipsitt (Eds.), *Advances in child development and behavior* (Vol. 5). New York: Academic Press.

Goldman, A. E., & Levine, M. (1963). A developmental study of object sorting. *Child Development, 34*, 649–666.

Haynes, C. R., & Kulhavy, R. M. (1976). Conservation level and category clustering. *Developmental Psychology, 12*, 179–184.

Horowitz, A. B. (1969). Effect of stimulus presentation modes on children's recall and clustering. *Psychonomic Society, 14*, 297–298.

Horton, M. S., & Markman, E. M. (1980). Developmental differences in the acquisition of basic and superordinate categories. *Child Development, 51*, 708–719.

Kobasigawa, A., & Middleton, D. B. (1972). Free recall of categorized items by children at three grade levels. *Child Development, 43*, 1067–1072.

Lange, G. (1978). Organization-related processes in children's recall. In P. A. Ornstein (Ed.), *Memory development in children.* Hillsdale, NJ: Lawrence Erlbaum Associates.

Lange, G., & Jackson, P. (1974). Personal organization in children's free recall. *Child Development, 45*, 1060–1067.

Lange, G. W., & Hultsch, D. F. (1970). The development of free classification and free recall in children. *Developmental Psychology, 3*, 408.

Laurence, M. W. (1966). Age differences in performance and subjective organization in the free recall learning of pictorial material. *Canadian Journal of Psychology, 20,* 388–399.

Liberty, C., & Ornstein, P. A. (1973). Age differences in organization and recall: The effects of training in categorization. *Journal of Experimental Child Psychology, 15,* 169–186.

Mandler, G. (1967). Organization and memory. In K. W. Spence & J. T. Spence (Eds.), *The psychology of learning and motivation* (Vol. 1). New York: Academic Press.

Mandler, G., & Stephens, D. (1967). The development of free and constrained conceptualization and subsequent verbal memory. *Journal of Experimental Child Psychology, 5,* 86–93.

Melkman, R., Tversky, B., & Baratz, D. (1981). Developmental trends in the use of perceptual and conceptual attributes in grouping, clustering, and retrieval. *Journal of Experimental Child Psychology, 31,* 470–486.

Mervis, C. B. (1980). Category structure and the development of categorization. In B. C. Spiro, B. C. Bruce, & W. F. Brewer (Eds.), *Theoretical issues in reading comprehension: Perspectives from cognitive psychology, linguistics, artificial intelligence, and education.* Hillsdale, NJ: Lawrence Erlbaum Associates.

Moely, B. E., & Jeffrey, W. E. (1974). The effects of organization training on children's free recall of category items. *Child Development, 45,* 135–143.

Moely, B. E., Olson, F. A., Halwes, T. G., & Flavell, J. H. (1969). Production deficiency in young children's clustered recall. *Developmental Psychology, 1,* 26–34.

Moely, B. E., & Shapiro, S. I. (1971). Free recall and clustering at four age levels: Effects of learning to learn and presentation method. *Developmental Psychology, 4,* 490.

Nelson, K. J. (1969). The organization of free recall by young children. *Journal of Experimental Child Psychology, 8,* 284–295.

Nelson, K. J. (1974). Variations in children's concepts by age and category. *Child Development, 45,* 577–584.

Niemark, E., Slotnick, N. S., & Ulrich, T. (1971). Development of memorization strategies. *Developmental Psychology, 5,* 427–432.

Northrop, S. K. (1974). *The effects of organization training and list difficulty on children's free recall over varying delay intervals.* Unpublished master's thesis, Tulane University.

Olver, R. R., & Hornsby, J. R. (1966). On equivalence. In J. S. Bruner, R. R. Olver, & P. M. Greenfield (Eds.) *Studies in cognitive growth.* New York: Wiley.

Rosch, E. (1978). Principles of categorization. In E. Rosch & B. Lloyd (Eds.), *Cognition and categorization.* Hillsdale, NJ: Lawrence Erlbaum Associates.

Rosch, E., Mervis, C. B., Gray, W. D., Johnson, D. M., & Boyes–Braem, P. (1976). Basic objects in natural categories. *Cognitive Psychology, 8,* 382–439.

Rosner, S. R. (1974). Effective list length and part–whole transfer in first graders' multitrial free recall. *Journal of Experimental Child Psychology, 17,* 422–435.

Rosner, S. R., & Hayes, D. S. (1977). A developmental study of category item production. *Child Development, 48,* 1062–1065.

Rossi, E. (1964). Development of classificatory behavior. *Child Development, 35,* 137–142.

Rossi, E. L., & Rossi, S. I. (1965). Concept utilization, serial order and recall in nursery school children. *Child Development, 36* 771–778.

Rossi, S. I., & Wittrock, M. C. (1971). Developmental shifts in verbal recall between mental ages 2 and 5. *Child Development, 42,* 333–338.

Saltz, E., & Sigel, I. E. (1967). Concept overdiscrimination in children. *Journal of Experimental Psychology, 73,* 1–8.

Saltz, E., Soller, E., & Sigel, I. (1972). Development of natural language concepts. *Child Development, 43,* 1191–1202.

Shapiro, S. I., & Moely, B. E. (1971). Free recall, subjective organization, and learning-to-learn at three age levels. *Psychonomic Science, 23,* 189–191.

Shultz, T. R., Charness, M., & Berman, S. (1973). Effect of age, social class, and suggestion to cluster on free recall. *Developmental Psychology, 8,* 57–61.

Storm, C. (1978). Acquiring principles of semantic organization. *Journal of Experimental Child Psychology, 25,* 208–223.

Tomikawa, S. A., & Dodd, D. H. (1981). Early word meanings: Perceptually or functionally based? *Child Development, 51,* 1103–1109.

Tulving, E. (1962). Subjective organization for recall of "unrelated" words. *Psychological Reports, 69,* 334–354.

Vaughan, M. E. (1968). Clustering, age and incidental learning. *Journal of Experimental Child Psychology, 6,* 323–334.

Wason, P. C. (1959). The processing of positive and negative information. *Quarterly Journal of Experimental Psychology, 11,* 92–107.

Winograd, T. (1975). Frames and the procedural-declarative controversy. In D. G. Bobrow & A. M. Collins (Eds.), *Representation and understanding: Studies in cognitive science.* New York: Academic Press.

Worden, P. (1974). Development of the category-recall function under three retrieval conditions. *Child Development, 45,* 1054–1059.

Worden, P. (1975). Effects of sorting on subsequent recall of unrelated items: A developmental study. *Child Development, 46,* 687–695.

Worden, P. (1976). The effects of classification structure on organized free recall in children. *Journal of Experimental Psychology, 22,* 519–529.

21

Are Children Fundamentally Different Kinds of Thinkers and Learners Than Adults?

Susan Carey
Massachusetts Institute of Technology

The task set for me was to debate, with special attention to Piaget's position, the following propositions: (1) that children are fundamentally different kinds of thinkers and learners from adults, and (2) that children differ from adults only in accumulation of knowledge.

Quite obviously, this issue cannot be joined until we have agreed what is meant by *fundamentally different kinds of thinkers and learners*. There are five quite different interpretations of the first proposition, and textual evidence from Piaget's writings (that are not presented here) for all five can be provided. I argue that it is important to keep these interpretations clear and separate, for under some interpretations the claim is clearly true and under others it is clearly false. Also, the educational implications vary with each interpretation of the claim.

Table 21.1 shows the five interpretations that are considered here The most radical is the first: that children differ from adults in the kinds of concepts they can represent mentally, and/or in the logical operations that can be computed using their mental representations. I call either type of difference one of *representational format;* in the developmental literature such changes are often called structural.[1] Several current metaphors provide the flavor of a developmental difference in representational format: One computer metaphor, for example,

---

[1]Whereas putative developmental changes in representational format (e.g., the shift from pre-operational to concrete operational thought) clearly involve structural change, so do important classes of conceptual change that do not involve any changes in representational format. Theory change, for example, is structural in that it involves simultaneous adjustments of many different concepts and the relations among them, but one is not tempted to think of later scientists (e.g., Einstein) as possessed of different mental machinery than earlier scientists (e.g., Newton), except with regard to physics itself.

TABLE 21.1
Five Interpretations of "Fundamentally Different Kinds of Thinkers
and Learners"

---

1. Representational format: The data structures for the representation of information and/or processes that manipulate these structures differ between children and adults.

2. Metaconceptual knowledge: Unlike adults, children cannot think *about* their mental representations and inferential processes.

3. Foundational concepts: Children differ from adults in certain concepts fundamental to many domains of knowledge, such as causality.

4. Tools of wide application: Children lack specific tools that apply broadly, such as mathematical tools.

5. Domain-specific knowledge: Children's theories of the world differ from adults'.

---

might say that young children do not have some higher order compiled language (such as LISP) that older children and adults do have. Or, in the language-of-thought metaphor, differences in the power of the syntax or semantics of *mentalese* would also constitute a difference in representational format (see Fodor, 1975). Developmental changes in representational format would be the most fundamental differences in thinking or learning possible.

Piaget's work on operational thinking has often been seen as an attempt to formalize developmental changes in the logic of the child's conceptual system. Inhelder and Piaget (1964) claimed that children before age 6 or 7 are not capable of carrying out certain deductive inferences (those dependent on class inclusion relations or those dependent on the transitivity of relations such as *shorter than*). Inhelder and Piaget (1958) also claimed that before ages 13 to 15, young children neither entertain hypotheses nor have available the logic of confirmation that is part of learning in science. The putative differences in representational format between children and adults extend beyond limitations in the operations the young child can perform over mental representations; Piaget (Inhelder & Piaget, 1964) and others (Bruner, Olver, & Greenfield, 1966; Vygotsky, 1962) also claim that preschool children cannot represent true concepts, being limited to *complexes* instead. That the complex/concept shift was thought to occur at the level of representational format was most explicit in the case of Vygotsky. Vygotsky argued that if it is assumed that word meanings are concepts, and if there are limitations on the types of concepts children can represent, then it follows that children's word meanings are fundamentally different in kind from adults.'

Many would argue that in his work on operational development, Piaget did not intend the claim that children differ from adults at the level of representational format. With respect to classes, for example, Inhelder and Piaget sometimes emphasize the child's developing ability to become conscious of the basis of their categorization. And certainly much of the work on formal operations was intended to be about metaconceptual development; e.g., although the young child clearly represents propositions, only in adolescence does the child become able to consciously scrutinize the proposition. In Piaget's writings, the distinction between metaconceptual change and format level change is not clearly drawn. Format level changes are considered at length in this chapter for three reasons. First, even if Piaget did not intend this interpretation of operational change, he himself slipped into it occasionally, and others have certainly interpreted *fundanmentally different kinds of thinkers and learners* in this way. Second, this is the only interpretation of the first proposition that I consider that actually contrasts with the second (children differ from adults only in the accumulation of knowledge). Third, the implications for education of the existence of format level changes in development are gloomy, because such changes would not be amenable to instructional manipulation. Given a hypothesis-testing model of learning, the child cannot possibly learn something he cannot represent. Therefore, he cannot be taught to represent something that he cannot at that time represent (see Fodor, 1972).

As important as the distinction between thinking differently or merely knowing more is the distinction between two kinds of knowledge—domain-specific and domain-independent knowledge. By domain here I mean what Dudley Shapere, a philosoper of science, meant. He characterized a domain as encompassing a certain set of real-world phenomena, a set of concepts used to represent those phenomena, and the laws and other explanatory mechanisms that constitute an understanding of the domain. Domain here is roughly synonymous with theory (in the philosophy of science, however the word theory is often reserved for a slightly narrower usage). One cannot know a priori what phenomena constitute the subject of a domain—the first step in the development of any new theory is the recognition of a new domain.

Some domain-independent knowledge, some skills, some stances toward learning might be so basic and have such far-reaching consequences that developmental differences in these might qualify as fundamental differences in thinking or learning. Any candidate who seeks such a qualification should satisfy two criteria: (1) The developmental change must affect knowledge acquisition and understanding in all conceptual domains—or at least in a very wide variety of different domains; that is, it should *be* domain independent; (2) the developmental change must somehow involve reasoning or problem-solving skills. I mean to rule out, for the purposes of the present chapter, such overwhelmingly important developmental changes as learning to talk and learning to read, although these changes certainly meet the first criterion.[2]

---

[2]Learning to talk and learning to read each opens the child to vast new sources of information. This alone must have a large effect on the child's learning. Each development might well have other influences on learning and thinking—e.g., learning to read both requires and fosters metalinguistic skills. Although I do not argue the point here, I believe that all effects of learning to read (or talk) can be classified in one of the categories in Table 21.1.

Developmental differences in metaconceptual skills concerning memory, problem solving, learning, reasoning, the doing of science, and so on would meet these criteria. Piaget has pointed out that some of what distinguished Aristotelian mechanics, on the one hand, and post-Galilean mechanics, on the other, involves some of the same metaconceptual developments that characterize the shift to formal operational thought. It is certainly true that Aristotelian physics was not experimental in the ways that science was to become in the 16th century and thereafter. Thus, a second interpretation of the fundamental-differences proposition to be considered here is that children acquire metaconceptual skills that affect learning and thinking in a very wide variety of domains.

The third class of possible differences between children's and adults' thinking to be considered here is closely related to the second. In his early work, Piaget (e.g., 1972) concentrated on domain-independent developmental changes that were not changes in metaconceptual skills involved in conscious hypothesis formation and testing. Rather, in this early work, he concerned himself with such changes as the shift away from egocentricity, the growing appreciation of the distinction between appearance and reality, changes in content of such basic concepts as causality, and so forth. In Piaget's treatment of such changes, they were certainly domain independent—becoming less egocentric was reflected in such diverse domains as language acquisition (Piaget, 1926), moral reasoning (Piaget, 1932), and spatial representaions (Piaget & Inhelder, 1967); similarly, the young child's putative failure to distinguish intentional, purposeful causality from mechanical, physical causality is at the root of the child's animistic reasoning about many different aspects of the physical world. I call this third class of putative differences *foundational* because almost every particular scientific advance involves interalia some distinction between relatively surface appearance and some deeper reality and some changes in the causal mechanisms believed to apply in the world. The failure to grasp the distinction between appearance and reality or that between animate and purposeful causality as opposed to mechanical causality would certainly affect learning in a wide variety of domains.

There are some tools that affect science very broadly. For example, calculus proved invaluable not only for its original applications in mechanics, but also for most of physical science. Unlike the concept of causality, or the distinction between appearance and reality, a tool like calculus is not a foundational concept necessary to all theories, and its moment of invention can at least roughly be pinpointed. There may be analogous developments during childhood such that children who have some tool can be said to be fundamentally different learners than younger children who lack that tool. This is the fourth interpretation of the fundamental-differences proposition that I consider.

Notice that interpretations 2, 3, and 4 of this proposition do not contrast with the second proposition which states that children differ from adults merely in the accumulation of knowledge. On these three interpretations, the child thinks or learns differently because he or she has acquired some knowledge whose domain cross-cuts other domains. For example, metaconceptual knowledge has mental phenomena as its domain and its acquisition does not differ in kind from knowledge whose domain encompasses, say, biological phenomena or mechanical phenomena. However, having explicit views about problem solving and hypothesis formation and testing could affect learning and thinking in many diverse domains.

Historians of science (e.g., Hanson, 1961; Kuhn, 1962) often used the locution think differently to refer to scientists working within two theoretical frameworks. By this they mean adherents of competing theories accept different explanatory constructs and different characterizations of basic reality. This is the fifth interpretation of the first proposition that I consider. On this final interpretation, the distinction between the first and second propositions *totally* collapses. Theory change is a paradigm example of knowledge acquisition; indeed, it is the most challenging case. Also, a little reflection dictates that on this fifth interpretation, it is a truism that children are fundamentally different thinkers and learners from adults. Children are novices in a multitude of domains where adults are experts.

The question for us in this chapter, then, is whether the fundamental-differences proposition is true on any of the other four interpretations. To limit the discussion, I consider the developmental period from roughly age 3 to adulthood. I present my argument in terms of particular proposals that have been made for developmental changes of each type—in each case I evaluate the evidence that has been offered in support of that proposal. My conclusions are necessarily limited—there can be no general argument, for example, that there *cannot* be developmental changes in representational format. Rather, all one can do is submit actual proposed developmental changes in thinking or learning to close scrutiny.

THE FORMAT-LEVEL INTERPRETATION

In his work on logical development, Piaget described two major shifts—that between preoperational and concrete operational thinking (occurring around age 6) and that between concrete operational and formal operational thinking (occurring in early adolescence). He attempted to formalize the logical structures that become available to the child with each transition (the groupings of concrete operational thought and the 16 binary operations, plus the INRC group, of formal operations; see Flavell, 1963, for a clear exposition of these formal systems; see Osherson, 1974, and Parsons, 1960, for criticisms of Piaget's formal work). I have chosen two cases for brief exposition—one from each of these two putative developmental stages.

Case 1: Classes and Class Inclusion

As mentioned earlier, many developmental psychologists once held that pre-school children cannot represent true concepts. According to Inhelder and Piaget (1964), this limitation took form in preoperational children's inability to represent classes, a limitation overcome with the development of concrete operations in the early elementary years. Similarly, Bruner et al. (1966) and Vygotsky (1962) saw the limitation in the context of broad changes in these years, when children switch from Bruner et al.'s iconic to symbolic thinking, and from Vygotsky's intuitive to scientific thought. All three research teams agreed on the characterization of adult concepts. All held a version of the classical empiricist view, in which a concept's intension is a Boolean function[3] over some primitive base. The extension of a concept is the class of real-world objects (or events, or actions, or whatever one's ontology allows) to which the concept applies. The properties represented in the concept's intension provide necessary and sufficient conditions for category membership; intensions determine extensions. All three research teams also agreed that complexes (young children's concepts) differed from true concepts in that intensions do not contain properties common to all the extensional members. Rather, the criteria for category membership shift from member to member, with some overlap among different subgroups of the set (see Bruner et al., 1966, for a discussion of complexes with different kinds of structures).

Evidence for the complex/concept shift is of three sorts: the wild overgeneralizations in production found in very early speech, the results from the Vygotsky block concept attainment tasks, and the results from studies of free classification. Let us consider these three types of evidence.

Vygotsky was aware of the striking examples from diary studies of apparent complexes in early speech (e.g., "dog" being used to refer to dogs, fur pieces, hour glasses, thermometers, mantel clocks . . .). But diary studies certainly do not demonstrate a stage in the acquisition of the lexicon where all words are mapped onto complexes rather than adult-type concepts. Such striking complexes are found only in earliest speech production, and even then they do not characterize all the child's lexicon. Many children never produce them at all. Further, some writers have recently questioned the assumption that in such utterances the child is trying to refer to the particular object; rather, the child might be trying to indicate that the fur piece, for example, is like a dog in some respects (e.g., Winner, 1976). In sum, the diary data will not do the work Vygotsky wanted it to.

---

[3] The combinatorial syntax of Boolean functions is limited to the operators "and," "or," and "not." Thus, typical concepts on this view would be "animal or plant" (equals living thing); "not green," "tables and chairs," "not red or green," and so on.

That there is systematic developmental change on the Vygotsky block problems, in contrast, is not in doubt. Vygotsky set up for children typical concept-attainment problems in which the child has to discover that a new word refers to something like *large, red or blue, block*. He found developmental differences revealed by the children's guesses about which blocks the new word referred to. Young preschool children kept changing their bases of categorization in a complex-like manner (Vygotsky, 1962). However, for such changes to support a complex/concept shift in development, these tasks must in fact model concept attainment. For this, the classical view of adult concepts as Boolean functions of attributes must be correct. As is well known, the empiricist view is under heavy attack. There are three major lines of criticism—Rosch's, Fodor's, and Kripke's (see Carey, 1982, for a brief review of all three). Although all three critics have different views of the nature of concepts, all three agree that adult concepts, for the most part, are nothing like *round, red or blue, block*. Even modern adherents to the classical view (e.g., Katz, 1972) agree this is so, because the syntax of combinations of primitive concepts into complex concepts must be more powerful than Boolean functions. If adult concepts do not resemble those aspired to in the Vygotsky block problems, then developmental changes on these problems cannot support claims for a format level change in the very kinds of concepts that can be represented (see Fodor, 1972). Indeed, if Rosch's line of attack on classical concepts is correct, then adult concepts as well as children's are complexes (see E. E. Smith & Medin, 1981, for a review of psychological research that undermines the classical view).

Parallel results are found when the child is merely asked to group objects according to similarity—a free classification task. After the earliest stage of *graphic collections,* where the child makes pictures out of materials, there is a period where complex-like collections are produced, in which the bases of similarity among members of the collections keep shifting. Adult taxonomic grouping is not achieved until age 7 (Inhelder & Piaget, 1964). As in the Vygotsky block case, the relevance of these data to the claim of a change in the nature of concepts is doubtful. But another point can be made with regard to the free classification results. If the task is simplified (e.g., fewer items to sort) and if basic level categories (e.g., "dog," "cat," rather than "animal," see Rosch, Mervis, Gray, Johnson, & Boyes–Braem, 1976) are used, young preschoolers perform in an adult manner. Data from the habituation paradigm indicate that even 12, 18, and 24 month-olds categorize different kinds of food, different animals, and different kinds of furniture together (Ross, 1980).

Why children do not group objects according to taxonomic categories in the Piagetian free classification task is an interesting developmental question (see Markman & Callanan, 1983, for an excellent review). However, as long as there is positive evidence that children represent the very concepts in question, their failure to group taxonomically cannot be the result of format limitations on the very nature of concepts that are represented by young children.

The Piagetian claims for changes at around age 6 in representation of classes go far beyond the complex/concept shift. Piaget also claimed that preoperational children could not represent the relation of class inclusion and therefore could make no deductive inferences that depend on inclusion. In contrast to the paucity of evidence for the putative complex/concept shift, evidence for the young child's problems with class inclusion is forthcoming from many different sources.

Most problems emerge when the child must make use of the asymmetry of the inclusion relation. For example, Inhelder and Piaget (1964) presented preschool children with arrays such as that in Fig. 21.1 and asked questions like, "Are all the dotted ones square?" A common error was the answer, "No, some squares are striped." A question about the inclusion of dotted ones in the class of square ones seems to have been interpreted as a question of equivalence. Similarly, C. Smith (1979) found poor performance by 4- to 6-year-olds when asked questions about natural language hierarchies, such as, "Are all animals lions?" and "Are all lions animals?" Children often said yes to both questions, suggesting a failure to appreciate the asymmetry of the relation. Another reflection of difficulty with inclusion is found on what is often referred to as Inhelder's and Piaget's class-inclusion task. The child must evaluate arrays such as that in Fig. 21.2 to answer such questions as "Are there more animals or squirrels?" The child answers, "more squirrels," comparing squirrels and cats rather than squirrels and all the animals. Markman (1978) recently extended this work in an ingenious way. She showed that many 6- to 11-year-old children, who *could* pass the Piaget class-inclusion task, did not appreciate the necessity of there being more animals than squirrels. For example, they did not know whether or not by adding more squirrels to the array one could make it so there were more squirrels than animals! A third class of results concerns inferences, where appreciation of the asymmetry of the relation again comes to the fore. Harris (1975) taught 4- to 6-year-old children that all birds had some new property and found that the children correctly inferred that all robins have the property. But, when

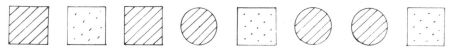

FIG. 21.1   Stimuli from Piagetian classification task.

FIG. 21.2   Stimuli from Piagetian class-inclusion task.

taught that all robins have some property, children of this age are also likely to conclude that all birds do! C. Smith (1979) pointed out that the second question has no determinate answer; from what the child had been told, it is *possible* that all birds might have the property. She changed Harris' procedure by adding the words "have to" to the question: "All birds have X, do all robins have to have X?" "All robins have X; do all birds have to have X?" The 4- to 6-year-old children continued to perform badly on the task. Finally, Markman, Horton, and McLanahan (1980) have added still one more phenomenon to the battery that indicates problems with class inclusion. They presented 6- to 11-year-old children with arrays such as Fig. 21.3 and told them that the As were zugs, the Bs were laks, and the Cs (indicating all the animals) were bivs. The children were then interrogated to see if they had constructed an inclusion hierarchy, specifically if they realized that an individual A was both a zug and a biv. To a remarkable extent the children resisted this interpretation. They preferred to think of biv as referring to the entire collection of C's, as if it were a word like forest rather than a word like tree.

These results leave no doubt that the young child differs from the adult in ability to impose inclusion hierarchies on new materials and in ability to make various deductive inferences that depend on inclusion. One explanation for these difficulties may be that the representational-format interpretation of the funda-mental-differences proposition is correct: the child simply is unable to mentally represent the inclusion relation or is unable to make inferences over it . However, other explanations are hinted by at the data briefly summarized previously. First of all, there are particular problems afforded by each task that could result in failure despite no format differences. For example, the syntax of quantification may pose difficulties independent from the representation of inclusion relations, the question, "Are there more flowers than daisies?" may violate certain con-versation maxims, knowledge of the particular hierarchies used in these tasks may sometimes be limited, and so on. (See Gelman & Baillargeon, 1983, for a review.) Secondly, the child very probably lacks metaconceptual awareness of the inclusion relation (see later section). Representing the inclusion relations

A   B

C

FIG. 21.3   Stimuli from Markman's class-inclusion collection task.

among concepts is quite a different matter from being aware of that relation. For example, it is quite possible that a child might know that all robins are birds and that not all birds are robins, but that same child might not be able to learn to classify pairs of concepts according to whether the inclusion relation holds, to state formal properties such as transitivity, or to classify various relations according to their formal logical properties. It is possible that lack of metaconceptual awareness of the inclusion relation precludes the child's appreciation of the necessity of various consequences of inclusion (as Markman, 1978, and C. Smith, 1979, both demonstrated). It is also possible that metaconceptual awareness of the inclusion relation would help the child in others of the task that are failed at this age. This possibility is returned to later.

Any unequivocal evidence that the child does represent inclusion relations and can make deductive inferences over them militates against the representational-format interpretation of these results. C. Smith (1979) provides such evidence. She devised an inference problem that was determinate and also did not require an appreciation of the necessity of the inference (no modal like "have to" was needed). She also probed the child's knowledge of the vocabulary in the problems beforehand, constructing inference problems with three level hierarchies each child knew. She contrasted two inference types: "A pug is a kind of animal, but not a dog. Is a pug a poodle?" (No) and "A pug is a kind of animal, but not a poodle. Is a pug a poodle?" (Yes). Answering both types correctly required deductive inferences and an appreciation of the asymmetry of inclusion. Children as young as 4 had no trouble, justifying their answers with such statements as "You said it wasn't a dog, and poodles are dogs" or, "You said it was a dog and all dogs are animals." Smith also showed that young children's problems with strings of questions such as "Are all dogs animals?" and "Are all animals dogs?" are due to surface strategies in the face of repeated questioning. In a test with just eight questions (four yes and four no), every 4-year-old showed the adult pattern, again reflecting the representation of the inclusion relations and an appreciation of a quantificational consequence of the asymmetry of inclusion. Smith presented a third analysis with the same lesson: Three tasks on which 4- to 6-year-olds do badly were given to each of several children in this age range. If lack of success was due to failure to represent inclusion relations, then the children who fail should fail at all three tasks, because each task depends on this relation. If, however, lack of success in each case was due to reasons idiosyncratic to the task, one might expect children succeeding on one or two of the tasks. The latter pattern was observed. An adult pattern of responses on only one of the tasks is all that is required to demonstrate that the child's representational formal is capable of representing inclusion, and this is what was found, even among the 4-year-olds. Finally, Markman et al. (1980) included a condition in which children were told, after being taught about laks, zugs, and bivs as described earlier, that "Zugs and laks are kinds of bivs." With the addition of this sentence, children then imposed an inclusion hierarchy on the materials. Note that in the task Smith found solved correctly by 4-year-olds, inclusion was flagged by "kind of" as well. This locution may be necessary for children and not for adults, but the results such as Markman's and Smith's show that the failure to impose inclusion hierarchies in so many situations cannot be due to a format limitation that *precludes* such an organization among concepts.

In sum, there is no compelling evidence that the child's basic representational format differs from the adult's in type of concepts, capacity to represent class-inclusion hierarchies, or abiity to recognize at least some quantitative and deductive consequences of inclusion. Nonetheless, in many different situations the child fails to deal with classes and class-inclusion hierarchies as would an adult. Although the child is able to represent class-inclusion hierarchies, this organizational principle is less salient than others and therefore not always invoked. A very important question for developmental psychologists is why this is so. One important factor in the problems children have with inclusion is lack of knowledge of particular hierarchies. A series of my own studies shows the role played by acquisition of biological knowledge in the construction of the hierarchy of plants and animals, on one level, and living things, on the next (Carey, in press). Another important factor, as already suggested, is the young child's lack of metaconceptual awareness of the relation of inclusion. It is likely, then, that acquisition of two kinds of knowledge—metaconceptual knowledge and domain-specific knowledge—underlies much of the developmental change in handling class inclusion.

Markman (1981) has supplied another piece of the puzzle—an account of why the class-inclusion relation is so hard for the child to handle, compared to a very similar relation, the part–whole inclusion relation. She has systematically compared class-inclusion hierarchies (e.g., oak, tree) with part whole hierarchies (e.g., oak, forest). In many different tasks, from Piaget's class-inclusion problems, to number conservation, to her own studies of the child's appreciation of the necessity for more members in the superordinate than the subordinate category, she has found that children solve the problem much earlier in the case of part-whole hierarchies than in inclusion hierarchies. Her interpretation is that the superordinate concepts in part–whole hierarchies have an internal structure lacking in the case of class-inclusion hierarchies. This internal structure helps the child with two problems—keeping the levels of the hierarchy separate and keeping the relations between subordinate and superordinate straight. To understand Markman's hypothesis, consider the relation of oak to forest. For forest to be superordinate to oak, the oaks in the forest must be in a certain relation to each other (in this case spatial). Similarly, for family to be superordinate to child, the people in the family must have a particular structure (in this case social). Such differences between the two levels of the hierarchy are not present in the case of inclusion relations—there are no relations among people necessary for children to be people. Markman's hypothesis is that this difference between class-inclusion hierarchies and part-whole hierarchies makes the latter more salient and more accessible to metaconceptual awareness.

In Case 1, I have reviewed the literature on two claims concerning format-level differences between preschool children and early elementary-age children. With respect to both, important differences between the two age groups are found, but I have argued that these differences do not support the claims for limitations of the young child's basic representational capacities. In my next section, Case 2 develops parallel argument for an aspect of formal operational thought.

Case 2: Hypothesis Formation and Testing

Inhelder and Piaget (1958) claim that before ages 13 to 15, young children do not entertain hypotheses nor do they have available to them the logic of confirmation that characterizes scientific learning. If these claims are true, then children certainly are fundamentally different kinds of learners than adults.

Representational theories of mind presuppose hypothesis-testing theories of learning. In explaining the acquisition of any body of knowledge, one must specify the class of hypotheses the organism entertains, the evidence that is taken as relevant to decisions among the hypotheses, and evaluation metrics for that evidence (see Fodor, 1967, and Pinker, 1979, on hypothesis-testing theories of syntax acquisition). If the child is not a hypothesis generator, then representational theories of mind are false, and cognitive psychology is in trouble. My argument here, of the this-is-the-only-theory-you've-got variety, is that given basic assumptions shared by all cognitive psychology there could not be developmental differences at the format level, such that inductive theories of learning do not describe the young child's acquisition of knowledge as well as the adult's.

In their rich book, *The Growth of Logical Thinking from Childhood to Adolescence* (1958), Inhelder and Piaget present 15 experiments, each of which illustrates an aspect of the development of formal operational thought; that is, each chapter focuses on one particular skill supposedly acquired with formal operations. Each chapter also is used to illustrate the acquisition of hypothetical reasoning in general. One skill they examined was the capacity to separate variables in establishing causal relations. A general claim they made was that the child does not reason hypothetically (a better word might be theoretically), considering cases he or she has not yet encountered, and therefore cannot plan observations to confirm or disconfirm hypotheses. The bending rods experiment (Inhelder & Piaget, 1958, Chapter 3) presented evidence for developmental changes of both kinds. The child was shown rods varying along four dimensions (material, length, thickness, cross-sectional form) and was asked to find out which variables affect whether or not the rods will bend enough to touch the water when they are weighted at one end. A fifth variable was the size of the weights. In fact, all these variables are relevant, and Inhelder and Piaget were interested in the child's ability to systematically show this. Whereas they grant that children in the concrete operations stage are capable of registering the raw data and drawing the correct conclusions, Inhelder and Piaget claim that children at this stage are unable to verify the effect of one factor by leaving all the other known factors constant. Also typical of preformal operational children is an incomplete solution of the problem—only two or three of the relevant factors will be discovered. Piaget and Inhelder argue that this results from the lack of a consciously systematic approach to the task.

These are fascinating and important results. However, Inhelder and Piaget's descriptions themselves belie a representational format interpretation of these changes. The ability to separate variables and entertain hypotheses underlies the successes 7- and 8-year-old children *do* have on this task. Without these abilities, children could not register the relevant data and draw correct conclusions. In another book, Inhelder and Piaget (1964) also show children of 7 or 8 who succeed in separating variables. In this task, one of three variables (size, weight, and color) is relevant to making a ball appear when boxes varying in these three dimensions are placed on a pan on top of an apparatus. Not only are 7- and 8-year-olds able to isolate weight as the relevant variable, they understand that to prove that size and color are not relevant they must show a large box that does not make the ball appear, and a red (or blue) box that does not as well. They also understand that to show that weight does matter, they must hold other variables constant!

Case (1974) gave 6- and 8-year-olds about 1 hour of teaching on the control-of-variables scheme, using materials unrelated to the bending rods apparatus. Field independent 8-year-olds (as assessed by performance on the WISC blocks test) were able to do the bending rods test (able to produce proofs for the effects of each variable and to indicate and explain when the experimenter produced an inadequate demonstration). If the experimenter picked a long aluminum rod and a short brass rod, showed that the long rod bent more, and argued that this proved that longer rods bend more, these children maintained that the proof was flawed because it could be the material that makes the difference! Over half of a control group of field independent 8-year-olds who received no prior training also showed considerable facility with the task. Thus, at least some 8-year-olds are able to do Inhelder and Piaget's bending rods task well before they could be "formal-operational."

Clearly, the 8-year-old child can separate variables and does understand that other variables must be controlled in order to demonstrate the effect of any one. What accounts for the lack of success until age 15 on the Inhelder and Piaget bending rods test? In Inhelder and Piaget's version, the child is not credited with success unless he or she systematically discovers for himself or herself the effect of all the variables, whereas in Case's version the experimenter structured the task so the child considered only one variable at a time. No doubt there are metaconceptual changes of great importance concerning such notions as hypothesis and proof. Although the child's inductive practices, like anybody's, require that he or she disentangle variables, the child need not be fully aware of doing so. Note that the performances of the 8-year-olds in Inhelder and Piaget (1964) and Case (1974) show *some* metaconceptual command of these notions, for the children are able to explain what they are doing. Systematic, self-conscious planning may require further metaconceptual development. Indeed, Inhelder and PIaget's (1958) work on formal operational thought is often interpreted as being *about* metaconceptual change. My argument is that the format interpretation (i.e., claims about the logic of confirmation available to the child) and the metaconceptual interpretation (i.e., claims about the child's beliefs about learning and knowledge) are not clearly distinguished in the literature, and that the data do not support Piaget's claims if interpreted as pertaining to representational format.

In the studies just cited (Case, 1974; Inhelder & Piaget, 1958, 1964), the behavior of children younger than 7 or 8 appeared incoherent and self-contradictory in their unsuccessful attempts at finding and justifying the relevant variables. Perhaps the changes Inhelder and Piaget documented after these ages are mainly metaconceptual, but changes at the representational format level in the ability to formulate and evaluate hypotheses occur before these ages. We are now in the same position we have been in twice before. We must decide whether the failures, which we do not doubt, provide evidence that younger children cannot entertain and evaluate hypotheses. I believe that they do not, for the simple reasons that these experiments confound knowledge of particular scientific concepts with scientific reasoning more generally. It is well documented, by Piaget and others (Piaget & Inhelder, 1974; Smith, 1981) that before ages 10 or 11 or so the child has not fully differentiated weight, size, and density and does not have a clear conception of what individuates different kinds of metals (density being an important variable). If these concepts are not completely clear in the child's mind, due to incomplete scientific knowledge, then the child will of course be unable to separate them from each other in hypothesis testing and evaluation. Coming to distinguish two related concepts, such as weight and size, both different kinds of bigness, reflects theory change on the part of the child, just as coming to distinguish heat and temperature reflected theory change among self-conscious, formal operational, adult scientists in the 17th and 18th centuries (McKie & Heathcote, 1935). The Inhelder and Piaget (1958) book on formal operational reasoning repeats this fundamental confounding in every chapter; every study involves scientific concepts not available to the younger of the children tested, and so in each case, general scientific reasoning is not separable from knowledge of particular scientific domains. Similarly, Case's study concerned variables such as weight and kind of material, even in the training procedure. Little wonder that 6-year-olds who were nonconservers of weight and substance failed to benefit from the training procedure.

Of course, in order to rule out developmental changes at the format level in ability to formulate and evaluate hypotheses, positive demonstrations of this ability among still younger children are needed. I return to the this-is-the-only-theory-you've-got argument. How does the child learn the meanings of words such as red and big from uses in contexts except by formulating hypotheses that require the separation of the variables of size and color for their evaluation? More empirically, it is possible to show that many of the phenomena that typify doing science by adults also typify the behavior of young children with respect to their hypotheses. This point is elaborated in detail in Carey and Block (1976) and is merely touched on here.

Kuhn (1962), Hanson (1961), Toulmin (1953), Feyerabend (1962), and others have sketched a view of the activity of science according to which hypotheses are generated and evaluated relative to conceptual systems (called "paradigms" by Kuhn). Paradigms determine what questions are asked, what hypotheses entertained, what data are relevant, indeed, even what data are seen. Although contemporary philosophy of science has rejected an extreme interpretation of these claims, according to which paradigms render themselves immune from refutation and cannot contradict each other because they are incommensurable, a less extreme version is widely accepted (see Shapere, 1966 and Suppe, 1974, for summaries of the issues). In support of the core of truth to this position, many historical examples are cited of scientists not seeing phenomena counter to their hypotheses and seeing confirmation of their hypotheses when it is not actually there. For example, Chinese atronomers observed many comets, new stars, and other stellar phenomena that went unnoticed by contemporary pre-Copernican western astronomers committed to the Aristotelian doctrine of the immutability of the heavens. And Galileo claimed to observe that his prediction that the period of a pendulum is independent of its amplitude was born out of his experiments, even though air resistance makes this prediction far from true. Another manifestation of the core of truth to the Kuhnian position is tolerance of anomaly. Here counterevidence to a hypothesis is seen and recognized as counterevidence, but the hypothesis is not abandoned. For example, according to Newtonian mechanics, the difficulty in predicting the perihelion of Mercury was a pesky puzzle of little consequence; according to relativity theory, it was one of the crucial facts that show that Newtonian mechanics were false and relativity theory was true.

This characterization of how adult science makes sense of the world also characterizes the activity of children making sense of their world. Karmiloff–Smith and Inhelder's (1975) classic paper on children's coming to understand some aspects of the determination of balance points provides many examples. An early hypothesis formulated by children is that blocks balance in their spatial middle. Presented with a stimulus such as that in Fig. 21.4, children with this hypothesis repeatedly tried to balance it in the middle, failed, announced that it could not be done, but remained unshaken in the belief that blocks balance in

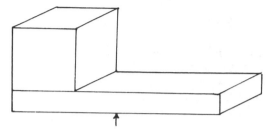

FIG. 21.4   Stimulus from Karmiloff–Smith and Inhelder's balance task.

the spatial middle. This massive counterevidence was treated merely as a pesky anomaly. Going even further, children at this point were asked to find the balance point with their eyes closed and could solve the problem by feel, but they rejected the solution when they opened their eyes. The same experience on the part of children who had begun to formulate the concept of a center of gravity led them to reject their hypothesis. Like adult scientists, they rejected a well-confirmed hypothesis in the light of counterevidence only when the glimmerings of an alternative had been appreciated. Carey (1972) provides many examples of this sort involving children as young as 2.

Two developments during childhood in formulating and evaluating hypotheses are certain. First, the child elaborates conceptual systems that allow more and more sophisticated hypotheses and encompass wider and wider classes of phenomena as evidence of the evaluation of these hypotheses. This is acquisition of particular domains of knowledge. Second, the child can engage in hypotheses formation and evaluation more consciously. This is acquisition of metaconceptual knowledge. But although these developmental processes are important and far from understood, neither constitutes a change at the level of representational format.

It is of course possible that other changes than those discussed so far (Cases 1 and 2) do occur at the level of representational format. A full discussion of this issue would require consideration of every proposal ever made, clearly beyond the scope of this chapter. In all the cases I have examined, the same problems as those that appeared here also arise. Basically, other interpretations of the phenomena offered in support of developmental changes in representational format seem preferable. The reinterpretation commonly involves distinguishing a format change from a metaconceptual change, or else it involves specification of particular real-world knowledge the child does not command.

METACONCEPTUAL DEVELOPMENT

I have appealed to metaconceptual development several times already in this chapter and do so more in later discussions. I granted that the child does not appreciate class inclusion nor the logic of confirmation metaconceptually, but I argued that nonetheless he or she represents the inclusion relations among natural language concepts and uses inductive reasoning in learning about the world. That there is metaconceptual development during childhood (and adulthood, for that matter) is beyond doubt. The child's conception of thought, language, memory, and learning change with age. These domains of knowledge certainly cross-cut other domains, so it is possible that we should accept the fundamental-differences proposition on the second interpretaton. It remains to be demonstrated, however, just *how* metaconceptual change affects learning in other domains. For example, how does having the concepts *hypothesis, experiment, confirmation* consciously available actually affect inductive reasoning? There are only two ways to answer this question. One is to compare cases of conceptual change among self-consciously experimenting adults and metaconceptually unaware children. Of course there will be differences—the adult will set up experiments and discuss the logic of confirmation. But at the level of theory change itself—the representations of the domains, the use of evidence, the concepts that articulate both the phenomena and explanatory mechanisms, the kinds of explanatory mechanisms—will the two cases differ? I am currently involved (with M. Wiser and C. Smith) in such a comparison—the adult case is the development of the concepts of heat and temperature in the 17th and 18th centuries and the childhood case is the development of the concepts of weight and density. A second way to answer the question is to teach the metaconceptual skills to subjects who lack them and then compare knowledge acquisition in a new domain by subjects so taught and controls subjects. Although such studies have been attempted, the results are by no means in (as many of the chapters in this volume attest).

Case 3 concerns a tiny aspect of metalinguistic development. I argue that there is metalinguistic change against a background of constancy at the level of representational format. I also argue that the metalinguistic change involves nothing more than domain-specific knowledge acquisition; the domain here is language. Finally, I argue that metalinguistic development of this sort *does* have implications for other domains of learning, although the evidence so far concerns only very closely related domains.

Case 3: The Mental Lexicon

Any theory of the mental representation of language must specify a lexical component. Represented here are the words of the language, including how they are pronounced, what syntactic categories and subcategories they belong to, and their meaning. The young child is a word-learning wizard. Miller (1977) estimated that between the ages of 6 and 8 children learn over 20 new words a day, and following him I estimated that between the ages of 18 months and 6 years, children learn approximately 9 new words a day (Carey, 1978). By age 3 (and probably earlier) there is every reason to believe that the child's lexicon is represented as is the adult's. Although the child will not have worked out the exact adult meaning for many of the words in this lexicon, there is no evidence that his or her meanings differ in kind from the adult (see Case 1 and Carey, 1982, for a review). Young children also certainly represent the syntactic categorization and subcategorizations of words, for they use both the open class (nouns, verbs, adjectives, and adverbs) and closed class (prepositions, articles, conjunctions, demonstratives, and so on) productively and syntactically correctly, although again, they have not worked out much of the syntactically complex rules of this language, nor the morphological rules for irregular verbs and nouns. Thus, at the level of representational format, words are not represented differently by 3-year-olds and adults.

However, it is abundantly clear that the 3-year-old, or even the average 5-year-old, does not have the concept of a *word*. Piaget (1929) introduced the phenomenon of nominal realism to psychology, showing that preschool children cannot answer questions such as "Is the word 'needle' sharp?" correctly; they say yes. Another example, "Which word is longer, 'snake' or 'caterpillar?'" Answer: "the word 'snake.'" Apparently, the child has difficulty focusing on the word itself, rather than on what is represented by the word. Nominal realism errors are also revealed when the child is asked to say what is and what is not a word. Preschool children deny that "ghost" is a word, because there are no ghosts (Papandropoulou & Sinclair, 1974) and claim that if all the giraffes in the world were destroyed there would no longer be the word "giraffe" (Osherson & Markman, 1975). Problems other than nominal realism are also revealed in this paradigm. When asked to distinguish words from nonwords (e.g., "tiv"), the young child denies that closed class items (e.g., "very," "of," "more.", "this," "and," and "he" are words). This is not a simple matter of concreteness of reference, for abstract content words (e.g., "idea," "go") are granted word status (Egido, 1983). When asked to tap once for each word of a spoken sentence, the child either taps only for content words or taps for every syllable. Thus, there seem to be several aspects of the concept *word* that the 5-year-old does not yet command—the notion of word as representation and several purely linguistic distinctions such as word/syllable or word/bound morpheme.

Acquiring these concepts is garden-variety domain-specific learning, where the domain in this case is language. The child must be a linguist examining his or her own language (as a representational system) to formulate these notions. I do not mean to say that characterizing the acquisition of metalinguistic knowledge is easy. Rather, I am arguing that it is the same difficult problem as characterizing the acquisition of any domain of knowledge (see the last section of this chapter on domain-specific knowledge).

Not having the metalinguistic concept word has clear implications for learning in some other domains—most notably, learning to read. If one does not know what a word is, it will obviously be difficult to learn what the convention of spaces in text represents. And indeed, these metalinguistic tasks are part of the reading readiness batteries, and training in concepts such as word and syllable help poor readers learn to read (Liberman, Schankweiler, Fischer, & Carter, 1974). Of course, the converse is also true: Learning to read is one occasion for becoming a little linguist working out the concepts. Osherson and Markman (1975) show that metalinguistic awareness of the type discussed here is a pre-requisite for the notion of logical necessity, although there the distinction the child must master is validity/truth rather than word/referent. In sum, learning such basic linguistic notions as word does have implications for other domains of knowledge, albeit ones that also intimately concern linguistic representations—reading and logic.

Other domains of metaconceptual development that do not concern language and logic so directly have also been studied. Most notable is metamemorial development (cf. Flavell, 1977, for a review). The story is familiar: That there is metamemorial development is not in doubt, nor is there doubt that such development contributes to the developmental changes in the capacity for mem-orizing, especially in the case of relatively unstructured materials. What is yet to be shown is whether, or how, metamemorial development contributes to the most important problem concerning memory—the changes in knowledge struc-tures that constitute our vast store of knowledge (called in the literature our long-term memory).

THE FOUNDATIONAL CONCEPTS INTERPRETATION

Piaget's parallels between childhood and the history of science extended beyond common metaconceptual developments concerning the nature of science. Other putative parallels concern changes in the content of foundational concepts such as *cause*. According to Piaget, the only causal concept available to the young child is intentional causality, in which an object seen as agent is the purposeful initiator of an event that results in an effect. Development consists, among other things, in the differentiation of human, physical causality and physical mechan-ical causality. As evidence for this claim, Piaget (1929) offered such phenomena as childhood animism and artificialism. Children below age 10 claim that inan-imate causal agents such as the sun, the wind, and clouds are alive, do what they do on purpose, and so on (animism). Children of this age also claim that all things that exist were made by people or God (artificialism).

Clearly, a developmental change of this sort would have wide-ranging ram-ifications for the acquisition of knowledge in all domains where mechanistic causality is at issue and would therefore qualify as a fundamental change in learning.

Piaget claimed that there has been a similar domain-independent change his-torically in the notion of causality. Kuhn (1977a) disagrees decisively with Piaget's historical claim. I present his argument and suggest that it applies equally to claims concerning development of causal notions in childhood.

Case 4: Causal and explanatory notions

Kuhn (1977a) distinguishes concepts like space, time, motion, and atom, which are the object of scientific inquiry, from concepts like cause, which are not. The former concepts figure in laws, are subject to measurement, and are objects of study; theories get built around them. The latter concept, cause, in contrast, functions entirely differently in scientific theories. All theories provide causes and explanations.

Kuhn (1977a) argues that every theory has its own explanatory concepts, but that at the level of the structure of explanation, there is no historical change. "Studied by themselves, ideas of explanation and cause provide no obvious evidence of that progress of the intellect that is so clearly displayed by the science from which they derive" (p.30).

He describes the phenomena that led Piaget to claim that the concept of cause itself has changed during the history of physics. Kuhn agrees that four stages in the evolution of causal notions in physics can be distinguished. According to Aristotelian thought, which dominated Western science until Galileo, every change, including coming into being, has four causes: material, efficient, formal, and final. The Aristotelian example most often cited in illustrating these is the causal explanation of a new statue:

material cause—the marble
efficient cause—the artist's chiseling and shaping the marble
formal cause—the idealized form that was the sculptor's intention
final cause—the increase in the total number of beautiful objects

Aristotle's efficient cause is the narrow notion of causality; the other three types are aspects of the broader notion of explanation. In Aristotelian physics proper, only formal causes were considered adequate as explanation. Violent motions, such as thrown balls, had efficient causes but were not in the domain of physics. For example, the explanation of why smoke rises and most objects fall is the respective innate levity or gravity of each object; an object's form can only be completely realized in its natural position, and it seeks that position if unimpeded. In the 17th century, explanations of this sort were seen as defective and subject to derision, as in Moliere's doctor who explained that opium put people to sleep because it had dormitive power. This parody is fair, but not because of the form of the doctor's explanation—this form of explanation becomes a problem only if there begin to be as many powers, or formal causes, as there are things to be explained. Physics in the 17th and 18th centuries stressed mechanical explanation—all change was to be understood as the result of the physical impact of one group of particles on another. This is a species of Aristotle's efficient cause. But in the 19th and 20th centuries, formal explanation again became dominant, as in the case of the orbit of Mars discussed earlier. As types of causes, innate levity and Newton's gravity do not differ. They differ, of course, but only because of the power and precison of the physical theory in which each is embedded. There have been further revolutions in the 20th century, whereby fields replace particles and positions as the basic forms of matter, and whereby individual events such as alpha-particle emission are uncaused, due to Heisenberg's uncertainty principle and the emergence of probabilistic explanation. But although the explanatory principles have changed, the structure of explanation has not.

In sum, Kuhn does not deny that explanatory concepts in physics have changed through history. He does deny that the foundational notions, cause and explanation, have themselves changed. Causal explanation has the same form it did in Aristotle's day. Explanatory concepts are parasitic on the theories from which they derive, so the root of increased explanatory power is theory change. But theory change is domain-specific knowledge acquisition.

Although Kuhn's arguments are directed toward the cause of conceptual change in history, I believe they apply equally to conceptual change in children. It is just as important for developmental psychologists as for historians of science to distinguish between concepts that are the object of scientific enquiry from foundational concepts that are not. In Piaget's study of the former type of concepts—e.g., time, velocity, space, weight, density, he often explicitly considered the theory change in which the conceptual change is embedded. This is perhaps clearest in *The Child's Construction of Quantities* (Piaget & Inhelder, 1974) in which the development of the concepts of size, weight, and density was discussed in terms of the child's construction of a naive atomistic theory of matter. For children, as in the history of science, these concepts become elaborated in the course of knowledge acquisition and the accompanying theory change. Piaget claims that in addition to limitations in domain-specific knowledge, limitations in the young child's causal reasoning constrain his or her achievements in any particular domain. It is possible, of course, that Kuhn is correct in believing that there have been no changes in the structure of causal explanation since Aristotle, that there have been only changes in theories. It is possible too that Piaget is correct that in child development both kinds of changes occur.

Unfortunately, Piaget's experimental demonstrations of immature causal reasoning on the part of the child all involve phenomena in domains where the child does not yet command the relevant domain-specific concepts or principles. For example, in *The Child's Conception of Physical Causality,* Piaget (1972) considered the nature of air, wind, heavenly bodies, the floating of boats, and shadows. Dickenson (1982) has shown that the child under 12 has shaky notions of material kind and cannot sharply distinguish differences in kind (plastic, glass) from differences in phase (ice, water, steam). These confusions are related to the child's problems with the concept of matter—children under 6 are unclear how shadows differ from, say tables—that in turn are related to the child's problems with weight and density. Such profound differences in domain-specific knowledge between children and adults may account for the child's inability to provide adequate causal accounts of phenomena from these domains (e.g., Archimedes' law). Thus, in his work on causal reasoning, just as in his work on formal operational thought, Piaget utterly confounded an aspect of domain-independent reasoning with theory change.

There is by now much evidence that when physical mechanisms the child knows about are at issue, the child's causal reasoning (at least from age 4 on) does not differ from the adult's. The young child knows that causes typically precede their effects, and the young child reasons as does an adult about physical mechanisms that consist of chains of simple contact forces acting on successive objects (see Bullock, Gelman & Baillargeon, 1982, for a review). Similarly, Shultz (1982) has shown that children as young as 4 appreciate causal relations among objects that act on each other at a distance (e.g., a fan blowing out a candle, a flashlight shining on a wall) and that they conceive of these events in terms of transmission of some causal power (to call it energy would be misleading, because 4-year-olds do not have anything like the physical concept energy). The main evidence for Shultz's assertion is that properties of the path between the cause and effect dominate the child's causal attribution and explanation.

Bullock et al. point out that although the child's causal attributions and predictions indicate that they appreciate the same principles of causal explanation as does the adult, the 3- and 4-year-old is markedly deficient, compared to children 5 and older, at articulating explanations and justifications that embody those principles. Although the young preschooler's reasoning embodies the same explanatory principles as does the adult's, there is metaconceptual change concerning the concepts of cause and explanation. Also, there is acquisition of knowledge of causes and explanations, this knowledge being domain specific.

The preceding remarks concern the child's reasoning in domains of physical science. Research of my own suggests that acquisition of knowledge specific to a different domain—biology—also plays a role in the phenomena Piaget offered in support of his claims for development changes in causal reasoning. Remember, Piaget (1929) claimed that the child does not distinguish mechanical efficient causes from animate efficient causes. The result is that the child sees as alive those inanimate objects that are active and capable of motion, especially autonomous motion (Piaget, 1929). In this way Piaget explained the overattribution of life to inanimate objects, as when the child says that the sun or fire is alive, in terms of limitations in causal reasoning.

My studies show a major reorganization of biological knowledge between the ages of 4 and 10. For young children (4- to 7-year-olds), biological properties such as eating, breathing, sleeping, and having internal organs such as hearts are primarily properties of people and only secondarily properties of animals. This is shown from the analysis of how children generate answers to questions such as "Does a shark breathe?"—namely, by comparing the animal in question to people. The more similar the animal is seen to be to people, the more likely the child is to judge that the animal breathes, sleeps, eats, has a heart, and so on. One consequence of this organization is that properties that are in fact true of all animals, such as the fact that they eat, have the same pattern of attribution as properties of people that are not true of all animals, such as having bones; that is, 4- to 7-year-old children are just as likely to say that worms have bones (about 30–40% of the time) as that they eat. And a new property, taught as a property of people, e.g., that people have spleens, is attributed to other animals according to the same similarity metric. Strikingly, the same property taught as a property of dogs is not attributed to any other animals. By age 10 this has all changed. Fundamental biological properties such as eating and breathing are attributed to all animals and differentiated from other properties of people such as having bones. More important, people are now just a mammal among many, so the pattern of attribution of a property taught for dogs is the same as that taught for people. I interpret these changes as reflecting reorganization of knowledge abut animal peoperties; for 4- to 7-year-olds these properties are primarily organized in terms of the children's knowledge of human activities. By age 10 they are organized in terms of biological function. Presumably, the main impetus for this reorganization is the acquisition of biological knowledge in school.

What does all this have to do with childhood animism? *Alive* is a theoretical term in biology. If the child knows so little biology that he or she does not even know that all animals must eat, how on earth is he or she to understand what animals and plants have in common? But children do know that both animals and plants are alive; this they have been taught. I am suggesting that the over-attribution of life to inanimate objects results from the child's inability to justify the inclusion of animals and plants into a single category, and that this, in turn, results from the child's lack of biological knowledge. A child who does not know enough biology to understand that all animals must eat and breathe is unlikely to be able to understand why animals and plants are alike. This proposal has been put to a simple test: The patterns of generalization when children were taught that people and bees have golgi were compared to the patterns of generalization when children were taught that people and flowers have golgi. In the second case there was substantial attribution of golgi to inanimate objects and virtually none in the former case. In this respect, the pattern of judgments for having golgi, about which children knew nothing more than that people and flowers have golgi scattered through them, was remarkably similar to the pattern of judgments for being alive that characterize childhood animism (Carey, in press).

This research places the phenomenon of childhood animism squarely in the court of knowledge acquisition, and acquisition of domain-specific scientific knowledge, at that. It is difficult to state precisely what structural reorganization of knowledge about biological properties occurs during these years and it is also difficult to understand exactly what occasions it. As Piagetians and historians of science stress, knowledge acquisition is not the mere accretion of facts.

Nonetheless, the lesson of this case is clear. A phenomenon taken to reflect developmental changes in the concept of causality, childhood animism, is seen to actually reflect the acquisition of domain-specific knowledge.

Case 5: The Appearance/Reality Distinction

Piaget and others (Braine & Shanks, 1965a,b) claim that before concrete operations the young child cannot distinguish between appearance and reality. This failure is putatively one reason behind nonconservation; the young child is seduced by the perceptually salient changes in length (number conservation) or height (quantity conservation) and cannot distinguish between looking like more and being more. Braine and Shanks attempted to show that distinguishing appearance and reality is a far-reaching conceptual achievement of children around age 5 or 6. They studied various illusions, such as that illustrated in Fig. 21.5. The shaded shape was actually larger than the unshaded shape, could be seen when the figures were superimposed (Fig. 21.5a). Children were shown the shapes in Fig. 21.5a and asked which was bigger, to which they replied the darker. The two shapes were then rearranged as in Fig. 21.5b, where the illusion made the

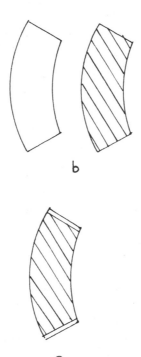

b

a

FIG. 21.5   Stimuli from Braine and Shanks' appearance/reality task.

unshaded one appear larger. If the child now answered that the lighter was bigger, he or she was asked, "Is it really bigger, or does it just look bigger?" Children under 5 were happy to maintain that the darker was really bigger in Fig. 21.5a and the lighter was really bigger in Fig. 21.5b.[4]

The distinction between appearance and reality is an example of what I am calling a foundational distinction. Discovering reality, like finding causal mechanisms, is the goal of all scientific enterprise; it is not the object of domain specific enquiry. Almost every particular scientific advance involves inter alia some distinction between relatively surface appearance and some deeper reality. Each succeeding theory has its own commitments to the nature of reality—e.g., Copernicus demonstrated that the powerful appearance of the sun revolving around the world was misleading and the underlying reality was that the earth turns on its axis while revolving around the sun. Thus, coming to distinguish appearance and reality is not a very promising candidate for an across the board developmental change, for the same reasons as Kuhn outlined in the case of causality.

What then of Braine and Shank's results? Their task requires knowledge and concepts the child under 5 very probably does not have. For adult performance on this task, one must know that appearance when the objects are superimposed is a better measure of relative size than appearance when the objects are side by side. But the concepts of size and measurement are shaky, to say the least, in 5-year-olds, as Piaget has taught us. Also, the child must know that mere spatial rearrangement does not change size, and we all know what a literature there is on that! These are aspects of domain-specific knowledge. Again, we are seeing the confusion of particular scientific advances with general ways of thinking.

Of course, to make this argument convincing, one needs a demonstration of very much younger children succeeding at an appearance/reality distinction with the same structure of Braine and Shanks' task. Flavell, Flavell, and Green (1983) provide an elegant review of studies that show children failing to distinguish appearance and reality and provide three experiments of their own that show that 3-year-olds command the distinction. The success of the 3-year-olds requires a pretraining period, where the locutions "really, really," and "just looks like" were rehearsed. The success also depend on the child's command of the domain-specific concepts in question and of the transformation that caused the mismatch between appearance and reality. Two problems solved almost perfectly by 3-year-olds involved disguising a clown doll so it looks like a ghost and changing the color of something from white to pink by using a red filter. The concepts of objects and disguises, of colors and color filters, are available to children of

---

[4]Similar results were found for size illusions produced by a magnifying lens and for shape illusions produced by immersing rods in water (Braine & Shanks, 1965a, b).

this age.[5] De Vries (1969) also showed good command of the appearance/reality distinction with materials involving a disguise (she fitted a cat with a life-like mask of a dog), at least from age 4 up.

Although 3-year-olds are able to distinguish appearance from reality, there is definitely marked improvement in the years between 3 to 5. Flavell et al. suggest there is metaconceptual development concerning this distinction—the child becomes increasingly *aware* that things are not always as they appear, and this awareness helps in these tasks. The other source of improvement on these tasks is likely to be acquisition of domain-specific knowledge that allows the child to tell, in every particular case, the difference. Thus, the concusions we draw in the case of putative development of the appearance/reality distinction thus exactly parallel those drawn in the case of putative developmental changes in the notion of causality. The evidence suggests that the young child's learning and thinking about the world is not constrained by different causal and explanatory notions from the adult's, nor by the failure to distinguish appearance from reality.

My argument in cases 4 and 5 closely parallels that in cases 1 and 2, which concerned putative changes at the level of representational format. Here, too, there can be no a priori argument that other candidate foundational notions will never be found where young children differ radically from adults. Those other candidates that have come under the same kind of scrutiny as those in Cases 3 and 4 have suffered a comparable fate.[6]

In summary, I have argued that the first proposition, that there are fundamental developmental differences in thinking or learning, should be rejected on two of the three interpretations so far discussed—1 and 3 in Fig. 21.1. Let us turn now to the fourth interpretation.

TOOLS OF WIDE APPLICATION

Causal explanation plays a role in all theories and it is unlikely that one particular moment saw its invention, either historically or ontogenetically. Not so for certain mathematical systems, such as calculus in the 17th century or arithmetic in the

---

[5]Flavell et al.'s paper goes far beyond the use to which I am putting it here. Three- to 5-year-olds still make errors. Flavell et al. attempt to distinguish the conditions under which children make realism errors from the conditions under which children make phenomalism errors.

[6]For example, Piaget claimed that there is a domain general shift from egocentric to nonegocentric thinking during the years of 5 to 7. It is a nontrivial finding that when point of view is at issue the immature response is usually to neglect the other fellow's. However, point of view is at issue in many different domains (e.g., moral reasoning, use of deixis in language, astronomy) and the egocentric errors are overcome at 18 months in some cases and not until adulthood in others (cf. Flavell, 1977, for a review).

elementary grades. These achievements are datable and it is likely that the acquisition of such powerful tools affects knowledge acquisition in a diversity of domains.

Case 6: The Concepts of Number and Measurement

It is certainly true that the child does not acquire an abstract concept of number until age 5 or 6. The best known phenomenon that shows this is nonconservation—children who agree that two bunches of pebbles each contain the same number will say that they no longer have the same number when one is spatially rearranged. Piaget (1965) argued that the absence of concrete operations prevented younger children from representing the concept of number; that is, he argued that format limitations were responsible for nonconservation of number by children under 5 or 6. Gelman and Gallistel (1978) argue that the 2-year-old's competence with counting requires all the operations Piaget formalized as concrete operations, and indeed, they showed that children as young as 3 conserve number, so long as they know what number it is (i.e., it is within their counting competence). Gelman and Gallistel see the achievement of age 5 or 6 as the abstraction of the concept *number* from particular numbers.

It is also certainly true that facility with measurement develops in the early elementary grades. This achievement, too, has been tied to the development of concrete operations. For example, the use of a measuring device to tell whether two quantities are the same along some dimension requires a transitive inference, putatively beyond preoperational children. The claim that children younger than 6 or 7 cannot make transitive inferences has already been refuted (see Case 1). Bryant (1974) discusses these issues as they relate to measurement.

Although I am denying the account of the acquisition of the abstract concepts of number and of measurement in terms of concrete operation, I am not denying that these tools become available to the child for the first time in the years from 6 to 9 or 10. And it is certainly plausible that the acquisition of such tools affects learning and thinking quite broadly, at least in all domains where quantitative measurement is an issue. But before we simply accept the fundamental-differences proposition on this fourth interpretation, two caveats are in order. First, nobody has yet shown the impact of acquiring these tools on the learning of any particular domain-specific knowledge. As of yet, the argument for developmental changes in learning or thinking on this fourth interpretation is merely one of plausibility. Second, in the history of science it is quite clear that the important aspect of most breakthroughs in measurement have concerned qualitative reasoning rather than the quantitative techniques involved in each breakthrough. Even when new instruments are invented, such as the thermometer, hundreds of years have sometimes intervened before scientists have discovered what they measured (Kuhn, 1977b; see Wiser & Carey, 1983, for a discussion of the earliest systematic work using the thermometer). The bottleneck has not been the concept of measurement but rather the conceptualization of the quantities to be measured. The bottleneck has been domain-specific knowledge. There is every reason to expect this to be so in the case of individual child development as well. Strauss' work on the child's concept of temperature illustrates the same point. Well after the achievements of the abstract concept of number, arithmetic, and the notion of measurement, the child reasons as follows: If you have two cups of water at 200 and you mix them together, you get water at 400 (Strauss, Stavy & Orpaz, 1981). Sorting this out requires realizing that temperature is an intensive quantity, and this in turn requires a minimal differentiation of the concepts of heat and temperature. We should not be surprised that the 10-year-old has not worked this out; it took over 100 years in the history of science!

In conclusion, although I do not doubt that the child is a fundamentally different kind of learner from the adult on this fourth interpretation, it is likely that in most cases what distinguishes the child from the adult in the use of quantitative reasoning in any given domain is domain-specific knowledge, not the quantitative reasoning skills themselves. An important task for development psychology is to show the limits of my pessimistic generalization, to show the ways in which lack of some tool that cuts across different domains actually does constrain knowledge acquisition in any particular domain.

ACQUISITION AND REORGANIZATION OF DOMAIN-SPECIFIC KNOWLEDGE

Nobody doubts that the 3-year-old knows less than the adult. Indeed, if the lesson drawn in cases 1 and 2 about putative format-level developmental changes (i.e., there are none) is correct, then all the ways in which 3-year-olds differ from adults reduce to their knowing less. Even granting that some domains of knowledge cross-cut others (e.g., metaconceptual knowledge, mathematical knowledge), the acquisition and reorganization of strictly domain-specific knowledge (e.g., of the physical, biological, and social worlds) probably accounts for most of the cognitive differences between 3-year-olds and adults. I have argued that in many cases developmental changes that have been taken to support format-level changes, or changes due to the acquisition of some tool that cross-cut domains, in fact are due to acquisition of domain-specific knowledge. This point was often a comment on methodological artifacts—e.g., one cannot study the schema for controlling variables by using variables the child cannot conceptualize given the nature of his or her naive physics! In other cases the point was more conceptual. I argued (following Kuhn) that putative changes in concepts that cross-cut different domains (e.g., in causality, or the appearance/reality distinction) are actually entirely parasitic on theory change, i.e., change in domain-specific knowledge.

Let us explicitly dispense with the implicit *mere* in the second proposition, that children differ from adults merely in the accumulation of knowledge. There are hosts of unsolved problems concerning the acquisition of knowledge, and these are where developmental psychologists may fruitfully concentrate their attention to advance explanations of developmental change. One such outstanding problem can serve as illustration: What kinds of reorganization of knowledge occur during development?

I know of two bodies of literature specifically concerned with the acquisition of domain-specific knowledge. Cognitive scientists studying the so-called "novice/expert shift" (cf. Chi, Glaser, & Rees, 1982, for an excellent review) and historians and philosophers of science studying theory change (cf. Suppe, 1974, for a review) both agree that the acquisition of domain-specific knowledge cannot be thought of as the mere accumulation of facts. Both groups emphasize the reorganization that is a crucial part of the process. Chi et al. review two well-studied examples of the novice/expert shift—from novice to expert chess players, and from novice to expert physics (mechanics) problem solvers. Two kinds of restructuring seem to be involved. Most important is the emergence of higher order concepts (e.g., weak pawn position in chess, or problems solvable by application of the principle of conservation of energy in mechanics that organize the expert's view and that are unavailable to the novice). As Chi et al. put it, what is basic level for the novice is subordinate for the expert. Also important is the enrichment of connections (on a semantic network metaphor) among the concepts that articulate the domain, giving the domain stability and inferential power. Notice, on these two views of the restructuring there is nothing *incompatible* between the expert's conceptual system and the novice's; rather, the novice's is merely incomplete in some very crucial ways. The view of restructuring that emerges in the literature on theory change is more radical. There is a degree of incompatibility between successive theories; the concepts that articulate successive theories carve the world at different joints that are not merely hierarchically related to each other. Wiser and Carey (1983) provide an example from the historical development of the physics of heat. The earliest practitioners of this science, students of Galileo, worked in Florence during the 17th century. Although they had the thermometer, they did not know what it measured; indeed, they had not distinguished heat and temperature. Their source-recipient model of thermal phenomena allowed them certain successes—the description of the thermal expansion of solids, the description of the contraction and expansion of water during freezing—but it also fundamentally inhibited progress. On their view, heat and cold were necessarily different concepts. Heat (or cold) was emitted from hot (or cold) sources such as fire or the sun (or ice). Passive recipients were affected by the heat (or cold) entering them. The effects the Florentine scientists were interested in were mechanical—the rate and force of expansion and contraction. Wiser and Carey (1983) argue that their source-recipient model was quite incompatible with the modern equilibrium theory of heat exchange in which heat is exchanged between two bodies as a function of temperature differences. In modern theory, the effects of source and recipient are mutual. This incompatibility between the two theoretical frameworks played a role, we argue, in the Florentine experimenters' failure to differentiate heat and temperature. Indeed, this differentiation was not achieved until 100 years later, by Black, who finally lay the foundations for modern theories of thermal phenomena.

Clearly, stating precisely what kinds of restructuring characterize theory change and finding ways for representing them is a major challenge for cognitive scientists. Equally important is to establish whether restructuring in this stronger sense also occurs in at least some cases of the novice/expert shift; that is, do some novice/expert shifts involve theory change, rather than merely the transition from no theory to first theory? Recent work on the physics misconceptions of novice physicists (Caramazza, McCloskey, & Green, 1981; Clement, 1982) and of the differences between novice and expert representations of problems (Larkin, 1983) suggest that the stronger sense of reorganization will be needed in the description of the novice/expert shift. Most important for us here is to carry this question one step further—does knowledge acquisition in the case of the child exhibit the properties of theory change, as I suggested earlier? Much analytic work is required before that question may be answered either yes or no.

CONCLUSIONS

If one is free to use the locution think differently however one pleases, then whether the young child thinks differently from the adult or not is partly a semantic matter. But only partly. I have argued that on two interpretations of think differently (1 and 3 on Table 21.1), considered judgment dictates that young children and sophisticated adults think alike.

Developmental psychologists wish to account for the variance in behavior among populations of different ages. I have argued that by far the most important source of variance is in domain-specific knowledge. Children know less than adults. Children are novices in almost every domain in which adults are experts. Perhaps, too, children hold theories in some domains actually at variance with the adults'.

If my diagnosis of the problem that developmental psychologists face is correct, then at least we know what we are up against—the fundamental problems of induction, epistemology, and philosophy of science. We ignore the work in these fields at our peril.

ACKNOWLEDGMENTS

This chapter was prepared while I was a Sloan Fellow at the University of California, Berkeley's, Center for Cognitive Science. My research was supported by NIE-NSF grant number SED 791 3278 (1979-1982).

REFERENCES

Braine, M., & Shanks, B. (1965a). The conservation of shape property and a proposal about the origin of the conservations. *Canadian Journal of Psychology, 19,* 197–207.

Braine, M., & Shanks, B. (1965b). The development of conservation of size, *Journal of Verbal Learning and Verbal Behavior, 4,* 227–242.

Bruner, J. S., Olver, R., & Greenfield, P. M. (1966). *Studies in cognitive growth.* New York: Wiley.

Bryant, P. (1974). Perception and understanding in young children. New York: Basic Books.

Bullock, M., Gelman, R., & Baillargeon, R. (1982). The development of causal reasoning. In W. Friedman (Ed.), *The developmental psychology of time* (pp. 209–253). New York: Academic Press.

Caramazza, A., McCloskey, M., & Green, B. (1981). Naive beliefs in "sophisticated" subjects: Misconceptions about trajectories of objects. *Cognition, 9,* 117–123.

Carey, S. (1972). *Are children little scientists with false theories of the world?* Unpublished doctoral dissertation, Harvard University.

Carey, S. (1978). The child as word learner. In J. Bresnan, G. Miller, & M. Halle (Eds.), *Linguistic theory and psychological reality.* Cambridge, MA: MIT Press.

Carey, S. (1982). Semantic development, state of the art. In L. Gleitman & E. Wanner (Eds.), *Language acquisition, state of the art.* Cambridge, England: Cambridge University Press.

Carey, S. (in press). *Conceptual change in childhood.* Cambridge, MA: Bradford Books, MIT Press.

Carey, S., & Block, N. (1976, June). *Conceptual change in children and scientists.* Paper presented to the Piaget Society, Philadelphia.

Case, R. (1974). Structures and strictures: Some functional limitations on the course of cognitive growth. *Cognitive Psychology, 6,* 544–573.

Chi, M., Glaser, R., & Rees, E. (1982). Expertise in problem solving. In R. Sternberg (Ed.), *Advances in the psychology of human intelligence* (Vol. 1, pp. 7–75). Hillsdale, NJ: Lawrence Erlbaum Associates.

Clement, J. (1982). Students' preconceptions in introductory mechanics. *American Journal of Physics,* (pp. 66–71), 50(1).

De Vries, R. (1969). Constancy of generic identity in the years three to six. *Monographs of the Society for Research in Child Development, 34*(3, Serial No. 127).

Dickenson, D. (1982). *The development of children's understanding of materials: A study of theory construction and conceptual development.* Unpublished doctoral dissertation, Harvard University.

di Sessa, A. (in press.) Unlearning Aristotelian physics: A study of knowledge-based learning. *Cognitive Science.*

Egido, C. (1983). The functional role of closed class vocabulary in children's language processing. Unpublished doctoral thesis, Massachusetts Institute of Technology.

Feyerabend, P. (1962). Explanation, reduction and empiricism. In H. Feigl & G. Maxwell (Eds.), *Minnesota studies in philosophy of science* (Vol. III). Minneapolis: University of Minnesota Press.

Flavell, J.H. (1963). *The developmental psychology of Jean Piaget.* Princeton, NJ: Van Nostrand.

Flavell, J. (1977). *Cognitive development.* Englewood Cliffs, NJ: Prentice–Hall, Inc.

Flavell, J., Flavell, E., & Green, F. (1983). Development of the appearance–reality distinction. *Cognitive Psychology, 15*(1), 95–120.

Fodor, J. (1967). How to learn to talk, some simple ways. In F. Smith & G. Miller (Eds.), *The genesis of language.* Cambridge, MA: MIT Press.

Fodor, J. (1972). Some reflections on L. S. Vygotsky's *Thought and language. Cognition, 1,* 83–95.

Fodor, J. (1975). *The language of thought.* New York: Thomas Y. Crowell.

Gelman, R., & Baillargeon, R. (1983). A review of some Piagetian concepts. In J. H. Flavell & F. M. Markman (Eds.), *Cognitive development* (Vol. II) of P. H. Musson (Gen. Ed.), *Handbook of child psychology*. New York: Wiley.

Gelman, R., & Gallistel, C. (1978). *The child's understanding of number*. Cambridge, MA: Harvard University Press.

Hanson, N. R. (1961). *Patterns of discovery: An inquiry into the conceptual foundations of science*. Cambridge, England: Cambridge University Press.

Harris, P. (1975). Inferences and semantic development. *Journal of Child Language, 2*, 143–152.

Inhelder, B., & Piaget, J. (1958). *The growth of logical thinking from childhood to adolescence*. New York: Basic Books.

Inhelder, B., & Piaget, J. (1964). *The early growth of logic in the child*. New York: Norton.

Karmiloff–Smith, A., & Inhelder, B. (1975). If you want to get ahead, get a theory. *Cognition, 3*(3), 195–212.

Katz, J. (1972). *Semantic theory*. New York: Harper & Row.

Kuhn, T. S. (1962). *The structure of scientific revolutions*. Chicago: University of Chicago Press.

Kuhn, T. S. (1977a). Concepts of cause. In *The essential tension*. Chicago: University of Chicago Press.

Kuhn, T. S. (1977b). The function of measurement in modern physical science. In *The essential tension*. Chicago: University of Chicago Press.

Larkin, J. H. (1983). The role of problem representation in physics. In D. Gentner & A. Stevens (Eds.), *Mental models*. Hillsdale, NJ: Lawrence Erlbaum Associates.

Liberman, I., Shankweiler, D., Fischer, F., & Carter, B. (1974). Explicit syllable and phoneme segmentation in the young child. *Journal of Experimental Child Psychology, 5*, 201–212.

Markman, E. M. (1970). Empirical versus logical solutions to part–whole comparison problems concerning classes and collections. *Child Development, 49*, 168–177.

Markman, E. M. (1981). Two different principles of conceptual organization. In M. E. Lamb & A. L. Brown (Eds.), *Advances in developmentl psychology* (Vol. 1). Hillsdale, NJ: Lawrence Erlbaum Associates.

Markman, E., & Callanan, M. (1983). An analysis of hierarchical classification. In R. Sternberg (Ed.), *Advances in the psychology of human intelligence* (Vol. 2). Hillsdale, NJ: Lawrence Erlbaum Associates.

Markman, E. M., Horton, M S., & McLanahan, A. G. (1980). Classes and collections: Principles or organization in the learning of hierarchical relations. *Cognition, 8*, 227–241.

McKie, D., & Heathcote, N. (1935). *The discovery of specific and latent heats*. London: Edward Arnold.

Miller, G. (1977). *Spontaneous apprentices: Children and language*. New York: Seabury Press.

Osherson, D. N. (1974). *Organiztion of length and class concepts: Empirical consequences of a Piagetian formalism*. Potomac, MD: Lawrence Erlbaum Associates.

Osherson, D., & Markman, E. (1975). Language and the ability to evaluate contradictions and tautologies. *Cognition, 3*(3), 213–226.

Papandropoulou, I., & Sinclair, H. (1974). What is a word? *Human Development, 17*, 241–258.

Parsons, C. (1960). Inhelder and Piaget's *The growth of logical thinking: A logician's viewpoint*. *British Journal of Psychology, 51*, 75–84.

Piaget, J. (1926). *The language and the thought of the child*. New York: Harcourt, Brace, & World.

Piaget, J. (1929). *The child's conception of the world*. Totowa, NJ: Littlefield, Adams.

Piaget, J. (1932). *The moral judgment of the child*. New York: Harcourt, Brace & World.

Piaget, J. (1965). *The child's conception of number*. New York: Norton.

Piaget, J. (1972). *The child's conception of physical causality*. Totowa, NJ: Littlefield, Adams.

Piaget, J., & Inhelder, B. (1967). *The child's conception of space*. New York: Norton.

Piaget, J., & Inhelder, B. (1974). *The child's construction of quantities*. London: Routledge & Kegan Paul.

Pinker, S. (1979). Formal models of language learning. *Cognition, 7*(3), 217–283.

Rosch, E., Mervis, C., Gray, W., Johnson, D., & Boyes–Braem, P. (1976). Basic objects in natural categories. *Cognitive Psychology, 3*, 382–439.

Ross, G. (1980). Categorization in 1- to 2-year-olds. *Developmental Psychology, 16*, 391–396.

Shapere, D. (1966). Meaning and scientific change. In R. Colodny (Ed), *Mind and cosmos*. Pittsburgh: University of Pittsburgh Press.

Shultz, T. R. (in press). Rules of causal attribution. *Monographs of the Society for Research in Child Development*.

Smith, C. (1979). Children's understanding of natural language hierarchies. *Journal of Experimental Child Psychology, 27*, 437–458.

Smith, C. (1981). *A study of the differentiation of the concepts of size and weight*. Paper presented to the Society for Research in Child Development, Boston.

Smith, E. E., & Medin, D. (1981). *Concepts and categories*. Cambridge, MA: Harvard University Press.

Strauss, S., Stavey, R., & Orpaz, N. (1981). *The child's development of the concept of temperature*. Unpublished manuscript, Tel–Aviv University.

Suppe, F. (1974). *The structure of scientific theories*. Urbana, IL: University of Illinois Press.

Toulmin, S. (1953). *The philosophy of science: An introduction*. London: Hutchinson.

Vygotsky, L. (1962). *Thought and language*. Cambridge, MA: MIT Press.

Winner, E. (1976). New names for old things: The emergence of metaphoric language. *Journal of Child Language, 6*, 469–491.

Wiser, M., & Carey, S. (1983). When heat and temperature were one. In D. Gentner & A. Stevens (Eds.), *Mental models*. Hillsdale, NJ: Lawrence Erlbaum Associates.

22 Social Class and Ethnic Differences in Cognition: A Cultural Practice Perspective

Warren Simmons
Center for Children and Technology

As part of an extensive review and critique of cross-cultural cognitive research, members of the Laboratory of Comparative Human Cognition (cf. LCHC, 1982; LCHC, in press) outline a theoretical framework, which maintains that behaviors giving rise to judgments of intelligence, behaviors that have traditionally been treated as general mental abilities, are, instead, best thought of as performances that are specific to particular contexts.

The term context is often used without being defined adequately. In LCHC's theory, a context refers to interactions between individuals, and between individuals and objects, that are delimited by a unique arrangement of goals, behaviors, expectations, demands, and rules constructed by the participants. As Green & Smith (1982) observe, contexts are not determined by the physical setting; the physical environment may constrain the types of interactions that occur, but it does not determine their nature entirely.

For example, a baseball game is far more than a bat, a ball, people, and a field with bases. As a context, baseball occurs when people interact with each other, objects, and the environment in accordance with a set of agreed upon rules, expectations, and goals that may change over time. If too much change in any one or group of factors comprising a context occurs, a context may come to be defined differently. Presently, baseball aficionados are debating whether American Leaguers are actually playing baseball because of the existence of the designated hitter rule in that league.

Returning to the subject of intellectual skills, the Laboratory of Comparative Human Cognition maintains that cognitive abilities are organized and constrained by the contexts in which they are used, and that culture influences the presence and arrangements of certain contexts. LCHC's cultural practice theory views cognitive abilities as skills that are adapted to the unique arrangement of factors that constitute a particular context. Aside from biological factors, the appearance or absence of a certain type of cognitive ability is seen to be a function of the intellectual demands that contexts place on individuals and of individuals' awareness of how to apply their skills.

It was mentioned earlier that LCHC maintains that culture influences the presence and arrangements of certain contexts. Because cognitive skills are organized and constrained by contexts, a basic tenet of the theory is that the cognitive abilities that constitute intelligence are culturally organized practices. To put it differently, the intellectual repertoire of a biologically sound person is largely shaped by the nature and availability of opportunities for exercising the range of behaviors that represent cognitive skills.

With its emphasis on intellectual skills as behaviors within a given context, another feature of LCHC's cultural practice theory is that cognitive activity is viewed as behavior that gets accomplished through interactions between individuals. Cognition, therefore, does not reside solely in the external world, nor in a person's head, but as an intersubjective process, a process that is socially constructed and organized and is context specific.

One major line of evidence supporting this view of intelligence comes from research showing performance differences between Western and non-Western, and schooled and unschooled groups that can be clearly linked to differences in knowledge, cultural practices, stimulus familiarity, and/or task familiarity. Research spanning quite a variety of cognitive skills (cf. Cole & Scribner, 1974) has found that the relative performance levels of cultural groups can be reversed by changes in these aspects of tasks. For example, Fjellman (1971) used a variety of tasks to gauge the classification ability of Kamba children in Kenya. Children were tested using sorting tasks with animal pictures and tools. Comparisons were drawn between Kamba children from rural and urban settings, and between those with and those without schooling. Fjellman's results demonstrated that although schooling was associated with use of form as a basis for categorization on the figures task, urban children's responses on the animal task were less "abstract" than those given by rural children. Because Fjellman had previously determined that all the children were equally familiar with the stimuli, as measured by their ability to name the items, the findings could not be related to group differences in familiarity as ordinarily assessed. It was argued, instead, that the performance differences reflected the greater knowledge of animals possessed by rural children and the fact that, through schooling, urban children know more about geometric figures. Differences in stimulus familiarity as "knowledge" derived from experience, then, was used to explain the findings.

Evidence of cross-over effects have also been found in cross-cultural contrasts in perceptual ability. Serpell's (1979) research exemplifies the methods used to produce such findings. Four tasks were used to measure the representational ability of English and Zambian children. As reported by the Laboratory of

Comparative Human Cognition (1982), one task "involved copying the positions of the experimenter's hands (mimicry), the second involved copying two dimensional figures with pen and paper (drawing), the third involved constructing copies of two-dimensional wire objects (molding), and the fourth involved making copies of three-dimensional objects from clay (molding)." As LCHC reports, the findings showed that the "English children did better in the drawing task and the Zambian children did better in the wire molding task" (p.126).

The fact that cross-over effects were exhibited in the previous two studies is not accidental. These effects are typically found when investigators make an effort to become familiar with the knowledge and practices of the groups being studied. This knowledge is often, then, used to guide the selection of tasks and analysis of data in ways that represent local cultural practices as well as Western ones. Serpell's choice of tasks and his prediction that Zambian children would do better on the wire molding task than English children was guided by his awareness of the cognitive implications of Zambian versus English children's activities. Similarly, Fjellman's ethnographic descriptions of life among the Kamba fueled her selection of stimulus materials and aided in the analysis and interpretation of the data.

The concept of individual or group differences in general ability is clearly inadequate to account for such a pattern of results. Unlike a general ability framework, the cultural practice approach points to these findings as evidence that culture-specific knowledge and activities constitute contexts that organize the development and deployment of a repertoire of task-specific cognitive skills. This position holds that the generality of cognitive skills depends on the extent to which contexts have common features that come to be perceived as such by an individual, thus enabling a transfer of skills.

In elaborating the context-specific hypothesis, LCHC does not minimize the need for a theory to account for consistencies in performance across situations. Cultural practice theory accounts for these generalities by identifying the similarities in the distribution and organization of activities across contexts.

Though a major portion of the discussion and the development of the cultural practice theory is grounded in cross-cultural research, much of the theory is informed by recent developments in cognitive research within the United States. Recent research in this field departs from the Ebbinghaus tradition of studying intellectual processes without consideration of the effects of prior knowledge. Experiments conducted during the past decade have demonstrated that many performances, once exclusively thought to be related to differences in developmental levels or individual capacity, are a function of database or knowledge discrepancies. Chi's (in press) research, for instance, shows that, when compared to adult novices, 10-year-old chess experts do better at memorizing the arrangement of pieces on a chessboard. Chi argues that the children's superior knowledge of chess, in comparison to the adult novices', fostered the selection of strategies that led to greater recall. If we assume that the general knowledge of adults in this study was greater than the childrens, one is left to conclude that the adults' advantage was not sufficient to overcome the children's possession of more chess-related information.

In the previous experiment, differences in the knowledge bases of experts and novices were linked to variations in memory performance. Age differences in knowledge have also been associated with developmental differences in children's classification behavior. Markman's (1973; Markman & Siebert, 1976) work on collections and classes suggests that young children's difficulty with class-inclusion problems may stem from the salience of collections over classes for young children. According to Markman, collections differ from classes in four ways: (1) the criteria for membership, (2) their internal structure, (3) part-whole relations, and (4) in the nature of the higher units that are constructed. For example, in comparison to classes, membership in collections is determined by an item's relationship to other members of the collection. In addition, whereas the part equals the whole in the case of members of a class, the same is not true for objects in a collection. Although Markman's data suggest that there is a developmental trend in the criteria used for classification (i.e., collections vs. classes), her results also indicate that this trend depends on age-related differences in knowledge that contribute to the salience of collections over classes in young children.

Differences in knowledge have also been related to differences in performance among adults and older children. In this area, knowledge discrepancies have been related to individual differences in recall performance (e.g., Bransford & McCarrell, 1974), diagram recognition (Brown, Collins, & Harris, 1978), and text comprehension (e.g., Brown, 1977).

SCHEMATA AND METACOGNITIVE SKILLS

The results of these investigations reveal that prior knowledge influences intellectual outcomes in quite specific and predictable ways. This has left researchers with the task of specifying the mechanism(s) by which prior knowledge influences cognitive activity. The cultural practice theory and researchers who adopt ability framework treat this issue somewhat differently. General ability theorists use the concept of schemata to account for the effect of prior knowledge on cognition. Schemata have been described as sets of knowledge stored in long-term memory that outline the information in a set, its significance and rules of use (cf. Adams & Collins, 1978; Rumelhart & Norman, 1978). Rumelhart even suggests that schemata are internal representations of situations used to guide subsequent processing once an appropriate match is made between input and existing schemata. Evidence of the hypothesized relation between schemata and subsequent processing comes, in part, from the story comprehension research in which individuals asked to recall stories add information not present in the original story (cf. Bransford & Johnson, 1973). This evidence indicates that the story recall and comprehension is partially dependent on a close fit between the information related in a story and that stored in the form of an individual's schemata.

Culture practice theory handles this problem in a different way. Instead of emphasizing the representation of situations internally, this framework maintains that schemes for guiding behavior do not exist solely "in" the individual but are constructed in the interaction between individuals or between an individual and "the task" in a particular context. The distinction between the two approaches vis-a-vis the role of prior knowledge should become clearer in the following paragraphs.

If schemata are construed as internal representations of situations or knowledge sets, and if processing difficulties occur when schemata are inappropriately matched with input, then, one also must provide for a mechanism by which the appropriateness of matches is evaluated and schemata are learned, revised, and replaced. Rumelhart and Norman's (1978) classification of learning in terms of accretion, tuning, and restructuring establishes a theory of the latter process. Generally speaking, accretion, tuning, and restructuring represent three modes of learning that have different implications for the status of schemata. Accretion refers to expansions of data bases through the accumulation of new knowledge. Tuning occurs when existing schemata are modified in response to either new information, or new or greater demands. Finally, restructuring represents the development of additional schemata to interpret new information or meet new demands.

Rumelhart and Norman's theory provides a good description of the hypothetical process of schema growth and development, but the controlling, evaluation, and change mechanisms remain underspecified. These uncertainties about the source of change arise because of the framework's tendency to place these kinds of functions in the head and treat them as general abilities. Cultural practice theory, on the other hand, emphasizes the fact that these functions are a part of ongoing social interactions that are an important source of feedback related to monitoring, checking, and evaluating in specific task domains. "Thinking" in the traditional sense of the term is treated as truncated interaction in which the individual supplies both sides of the interaction. Thus, where general ability theorists see a sharp distinction between schemata and cognitive processes, cultural practice theory views them as being intertwined and separable only for purposes of very specific analyses.

The distinction between the two approaches to cognition, then, arises from the fact that one treats cognition as a socially mediated activity, whereas the other represents intellectual behavior internally. However, both cultural practice theory and recent developments in cognitive psychology have important implications for understanding the factors underlying majority–minority culture differences in cognitive performance within the United States. Unfortunately, cognitive psychologists as a group have not devoted much attention to group or cultural differences in cognitive behavior, being more concerned with identifying common general processes, more or less of which are said to characterize one group vis-a-vis another (cf. Ginsberg, 1980). The context-specific hypothesis was developed in response to trends observed in cross-cultural studies comparing Western and non-Western groups. A viewpoint that says that contexts or schemata guide cognitive activity also has implications for how research contrasting the mental abilities of different cultural groups within the United States is interpreted.

The criticisms that LCHC (1982) direct toward cross-cultural research done in foreign settings with respect to the use of an ecocultural model, sampling problems, and task specificity also have their counterpart in the domestic equivalent of this research.

THE ECOCULTURAL MODEL IN DOMESTIC RESEARCH

Almost all the research on minority–majority culture differences in cognition has been carried out within the domestic equivalent of the ecocultural approach used in cross-cultural research done abroad (cf. LCHC, in press). Briefly, this model relates cultural differences in cognitive capacity to varying ecological, social, and economic circumstances (e.g., Berry, 1974). Applications of this model to subcultural group differences within the United States present a variety of problems in addition to those discussed in cross-cultural research.

The range of ecocultural variables explored in the United States is truncated in comparison to the variables studied in the cross-cultural literature. Ecological variability drops out, and the activities people engage in as a means of support are represented, if at all, by such social indicators as socioeconomic status, race, or ethnicity. Family, social organization, and child-rearing practices are the dominant cultural domains studied, with few exceptions (see Bronfenbrenner, 1979).

In short, when researchers apply the ecocultural model to study subcultural group differences within the United States, they generally sample a restricted range of variables within the model. This problem is compounded by a widespread use of social indicators as representatives of ecocultural variables. These indicators are themselves collections of variables at different levels in the model (e.g., education is component of SES scales, or covariation between social class and race). The amount of covariation that exists between the ecological variables studied within the United States makes it extremely difficult to isolate the unique effects of independent variables on cognitive capacity or performance.

Various Types of Sampling Problems

Sampling and Social Indicators.   The widespread use of social indicators as independent variables leaves unexamined the extent to which the variables in question have equivalent meaning across subcultural groups, and the extent to which an indicator adequately represents the domain sampled. These issues are more than hypothetical.

Trotman's (1977) research investigated the equivalence and effects of social class indicators across racial groups. In comparing the features of the home environments of middle-class black and white families, Trotman found that the homes of whites were characterized by the availability of more educational resources and the presence of a learning orientation more consistent with that found in school than was true in black homes of "equivalent" SES. Trotman also found other interesting differences between the homes of blacks and whites whose SES status was assumed to be equivalent. For instance, the findings showed that more black mothers worked full or part time; the number of prior generations achieving middle-class status were fewer for black families than for white ones; and that black children in the sample experienced greater academic pressure concomitant with more household responsibilities than their white counterparts.

These differences in "cultural ecology" were associated with different levels of cognitive outcomes as measured by IQ tests and school achievement. Number of generations in the middle class was related positively to children's IQ; increasing mother's employment was associated negatively with children's IQ and school performance. In addition, Trotman created an index of home environment variables (HE ratings) and found that the relationship between HE and IQ was greater among blacks than whites. The different indices of class also related differently to alternative cognitive dependent variables; for example, HE was a better predictor of school achievement for blacks than whites.

These data speak strongly to the need for research that identifies the subcomponents of independent variables said to produce change in dependent variables while simultaneously documenting the process that accomplishes this change. If domestic subcultural research continues to rely on "indices" of both independent (most egregiously, socioeconomic indicators) and dependent variables, the enterprise will constantly be plagued by "third variable" explanations that point to some untested subcomponent of group differences as an "underlying" cause.

Sampling and Cognitive Performance.   The problems engendered by the use of global indices on the independent variable side are paralleled and exacerbated on the dependent variable side by the use of cognitive "indices" within a general processor framework. Here the issue of sampling is again central. An approach to culture and cognition that uses culturally organized indigenous practices as its starting point urges us to reexamine the literature on group variation for information about the range and nature of contexts that members of the contrasting groups routinely encounter. We seek descriptions that would allow us to identify seemingly similar situations encountered by both groups as well as contexts unique to each. We would then seek experimental work that samples behavior from the set of contexts that organize people's lives for detailed explication of what people are doing.

When we survey the existing literature, we find enormous imbalances in the availability of relevant information in many domains that play a central role in a cultural practice approach. Relatively few studies sample cognitive skills in a variety of contexts. Even when this occurs, the sampling usually gets done within the general ability framework (e.g., rating scales are summarized as indices of maternal teaching styles that are related to IQ as in Trotman's work and Hess and Shipman's, 1968, research). The school setting has been sampled most widely, either through the pragmatically derived procedures of IQ testing, cognitive-psychological research of an experimental variety, or more macro, sociological descriptions. Schools are exceedingly important contexts in American society, but they are probably not equally significant across subcultures.

Several recent lines of research show that problems arise when information gathered in school settings is used to make inferences about what goes on in the home or community. A classic demonstration of this point was Labov's (1972) study of how the complexity of black children's language increased dramatically when interviews were made in informal rather than formal situations. A more elaborate view of situational variability in children's talk is illustrated by Cole, Dore, Hall, and Dowley's (1978) comparisons of black children's speech in a supermarket and a Head Start classroom. A preliminary examination of the data revealed that children's talk in the supermarket was grammatically more complex and lexically more diversified than in the classroom. However, detailed analysis of adult—child conversational acts across settings demonstrated that the frequency and complexity of specific conversational acts are what vary according to the unique task constraints of each setting, not grammatical or lexical complexity "in general." When roughly comparable constraints were identified *within* each setting, language behavior was strikingly similar. The settings could not be uniquely indexed by a global-dependent variable such as mean length of utterance, or by a global-independent variable such as "school" or supermarket. Such indexing only obscured the real variables at work.

This kind of evidence undergirds our point that the results of experiments conducted in one context warrant claims that are limited to the original context in the absence of data-linking contexts. Regrettably, generalizations about group differences in basic competence (i.e., cross-situational capacity) have primarily been grounded in the uses of central capacity sampled in school or laboratory settings. For instance, in Sigel's research on social class differences in classification ability (e.g., Sigel & McBane, 1967; Sigel & Olmstead, 1970), lowerclass children have shown a preference for relational sorting strategies. Middleclass children, in contrast, produce more descriptive and categorical grouping responses. These methods of categorizing pictures or objects are hypothesized indices of pervasive cognitive styles that are said to organize a great deal of these children's intellectual lives (cf. Kagan, Moss, & Sigel, 1963). However, by varying the subcultural salience of test materials, Simmons (1979) showed that the use of categorical and descriptive responses depended on the particular pictures involved. Typical social class differences in performance were either absent or reversed in some cases; it was even possible to produce within-subject differences in "cognitive style."

Yando, Seitz, and Zigler's (1979) recent work uses multiple tasks to make a similar point. They investigated SES and ethnic differences in five areas of cognitive functioning presumably related to intellectual ability: creativity, self-confidence, curiosity, frustration threshold, and autonomy. With two exceptions, behaviors representing each of the constructs were sampled using at least three different tasks. The measures of behavior within each domain were made as game like as possible.

This study investigated several issues related to SES, ethnicity, and cognition, but the following points are central to this discussion. Within a particular ability domain, the pattern of SES differences varied depending on the criterion for "good" performance. Low SES children, for instance, outperformed middle-class children on creativity tasks in which the quantity of responses was the criterion for good performance. Middle-class children did better on creativity tasks that used the quality of responses as the performance criterion. SES differences in performance also varied with the "academic" quality of a task. The performance of lower class children was significantly better on game-like tasks than on tasks that resembled school activities. The reverse was true for the middle-class children. This finding was obtained even when the low and middle SES groups were matched for tested IQ.

These studies demonstrate how individual and group use of particular skills may vary across contexts and within contexts, depending on the structure of the activity and the particular stimulus characteristics. The results show that there is a need for a more sophisticated theory about the specific performance or ability (the dependent variable) being studied, because without it we are not going to find any adequate explanations of interactions such as those we have just mentioned.

The within-subject variations in performance obtained in the prevous studies is not compatible with a general ability approach to intelligence. More sense can be made of such findings when behavior is viewed as being differentially organized in different contexts. It should be apparent, then, that we need more research that samples behavior to illustrate how a particular skill is used across a variety of contexts and studies that use different tasks to measure the "same" ability.

Theoretical Explanations of Task Performance

A second theoretical problem concerns explanations of the relation between independent and dependent variables. Having weak "indices" of both the independent and dependent variables, researchers face too many choices in explaining away weak correlational effects. It is this dilemma that led Mischel and Bem (cited in Shweder, 1979) to comment that: "nothing is glued together until proved otherwise . . . The heuristic advantage of this strategy is not guaranteed, of course. But the difference in morale if + .30 correlations continue to come in is itself worth considering" (p.255).

This problem is seen very clearly in the mother–child interaction work. Presumably, this work fits into the ecocultural model by relating SES to family socialization practices and family socialization practices to cognition. However, there is little explanatory power in much of this work because the research does not attempt to specify the mechanisms by which the independent variable has its effects.

This is related to the problems inherent in Kirk's (1977) work that, although carried out in Africa, embodies precisely the logic of domestic research; in one instance Kirk found that a mother's use of a relational teaching style on a construction task was related positively to the age at which her child achieved conservation of quantity. But on a second task (Piaget's Three Mountain Problem) also said to be dependent on relational thinking, mothers' teaching styles did not predict children's performance. Exposure to photographs was cited as a reason for this latter negative finding.

In this example, Kirk is forced to resort to a "third variable" explanation for want of an adequate model of the relation between teaching strategies adopted by mothers' and children's behavior on tasks in which relational thinking is thought to be a prerequisite for performance. Kirk's interpretative difficulties are further complicated by a lack of evidence in support of her assertion that both tasks require relational thinking. Even if this point was proved correct, there is the possibiity outlined by Estes (1974) that the two task environments might lead children to assemble the constituents of each task differently.

Without an adequate theory of the constituents of task performance, researchers must generally resort to tenuous post hoc explanations of how the independent variable causes its effect. This is a recurrent problem in research seeking to increase children's competence through program enrichment or by changing patterns of cognitive socialization. For instance, Slaughter (1979) studied the effect of mothers' participation in one of two programs or a control group on, among other things, the cognitive development of their children. One of the experimental conditions was modeled after Levenstein's Toy Demonstration program (Levenstein, 1977); the other was an informal discussion group. The Toy Demonstration condition was specifically aimed at getting mothers to adopt cognitively more favorable methods of interacting with their children.

The discussion program focused exclusively on discussing strategies for alleviating the mothers' general problems; children were not directly involved in this group. It was hypothesized that children of program participants would achieve greater cognitive development than the children of control-group mothers. It was also expected that the cognitive development of children with mothers in the Toy Demonstration group would be slightly better than children of mothers in the discussion group, because the latter mothers did not receive any direct instruction in how to facilitate their children's cognitive development.

As it turned out, where significant differences between program- and control-group children were obtained, the scores of children with discussion-group mothers were higher than those whose mothers were in the Toy Demonstration group across a variety of measures directly and indirectly related to intellectual development. Correlations, unfortunately, were generally in the range lamented by Mischel and Bem.

Slaughter did not do any normative observations of the program mothers' interaction with their children; hence she was unable to document specific changes in the program mothers' behavior that may have heightened the skills of their children. But even if Slaughter had been able to identify modifications in the program mothers' approach to their children, the absence of a good theory of the relation between particular aspects of mother–child interaction and children's development makes it difficult to ascribe increases in children's intellectual abilities to change in the way mothers relate to their children.

Slaughter's research is certainly not alone in having this problem. Few studies have been able to specifically demonstrate the process by which parents mediate their children's acquisition of cognitive skills. Werstch and Stone (1978) advocate microgenesis as a method for this kind of investigation. Microgenesis refers to examining "the development of a skill, concept, or strategy within a single observational or experimental session" (p.8.). Such an analysis requires the identification of the component processes underlying task performance.

This criterion returns us to our concern about the analytical deficiencies inherent in many of the intervention studies. Slaughter's research, for example, would have provided an excellent opportunity to observe the changes over time in the program mothers' guidance of the intellectual behavior of their children in tasks that were related strongly to the cognitive tasks that were administered. Such a strategy would allow mother–child interaction researchers to make stronger claims about how intervention affects other behavior that facilitates children's competence. Moreover, one would be able to ascribe the increased benefits of one program over another to specific types of interaction. Presently, this kind of research program is hindered by a dearth of tasks for which we have both strong models of behavior and that assess cognitive abilities of widespread significance. Resorting to IQ tests because of their correlation with schooling does not solve this problem.

EDUCATIONAL APPLICATIONS

Evidence that some intervention programs are able to influence positively the cognitive performance of minority culture children in relatively short periods of time (e.g., Sigel & Olmstead, 1980; Slaughter, 1979) indicates that, rather than changing basic capacities, these programs narrowly affect children's understanding of how to go about solving the experimenter's or school's tasks. Brown (in press) suggests that the academic deficiencies of low-SES children may largely be due to problems they have generating strategies that guide the processes they use in academic problem solving. These strategies or metacognitive skills are generally defined as processes that control, direct, and regulate other cognitive processes (cf. Brown, 1980; Flavell, 1978).

An individual's ability to complete successfully an academic task requires that s/he understand the goal and be able to regulate and select the processes that will lead to the successful solution of the problem (Wertsch & Stone, 1978). Following Vygotsky's line of reasoning, Wertsch claims that the capacity for self-regulation grows out of social interaction. A potentially important topic for future research dealing with subcultural differences in cognitive aspects of social-ization, then, is exploration of the contexts in which the self-regulatory capacities of minority culture children develop. Another important issue is the focus of these capacities and its relation to academic tasks.

Moll, Estrada, Diaz, and Lopes' (1980) recently completed study represents a step in this direction. They videotaped the *same* third-grade native Spanish-speaking children as they participated in reading lessons in separate classrooms—one teaching in Spanish, and one in English. Only those children judged by their teachers as sufficiently fluent in English to take part actively in lessons partic-ipated in this dual arrangement. The analysis focused on the communication systems that the teachers set up in order to implement the bilingual reading lessons. Moll et al. observed that in all the lessons the teacher acts as a mediator between the curricular materials and goals and the children; that is, the teacher regulates the level of difficulty of the lessons by modifying, changing, and adjusting task demands and characteristics on the basis of the behavior of the different groups and individual children. This regulation of difficulty is usually accomplished by varying the requirements for communication and independent work. For example, in the first language classroom (Spanish), the role of the teacher was observed to change in systematic ways as she interacted with the different groups. These role changes ranged from adjusting the extent to which the teacher actively directs and, in fact, does much of the task for the student (in the low group) to subtle "distancing" as she deals with children more expe-rienced with the problem and able to take over more of the task themselves (the middle group), to having the children apply all the skills found in the previous contexts independent of the teacher's help and direction (the high group).

Variations in the systematic organization of these mediating strategies became very significant as the *second-language* lessons were examined. The second-language environments were organized to focus primarily on lower level "mechanical" tasks such as decoding skills, phonics, and simple language devel-opment activities. Practically absent from the middle and high groups in English were the types of directing activities or mediating strategies that characterized these groups in the more advanced first-language classroom. For instance, chil-dren in the high-ability group in English were involved in tasks that corresponded to the lower and sometimes the middle group in the Spanish-speaking classroom. Moll and his colleagues further noted that these adjustments are influenced clearly by the children's characteristics, in particular, the children's ability to communicate in the form appropriate and relevant to the given lesson context. Moll et al. argued that the differential social organizations of reading lessons in great part determine the nature of the intellectual experiences for the children and the benefits they may receive from formal instruction. Similarly, McDermott (1977) recognized that one of the consequences of the different social organization of reading lessons for low- and high-ability students was fewer opportunities for learning in the low group as compared to the high group. This circumstance compounds the difficulties of students who are already deficient in academic skills.

The research discussed earlier points to the need to understand how the culture of the child and that of the school interact to produce contexts that either facilitate or impede academic achievement. Educational equity is linked directly to our abilities to organize learning environments that include activities that use a child's prior experience to extend his/her existing skills.

The Kamehameha Early Education Program (KEEP) provides a good example of the academic gains that can be achieved when an approach of this kind is adopted. The Kamehameha project was initiated in the early 1970s by a group of researchers and practitioners who were interested in improving the historically poor school achievement of disadvantaged Hawaiians, a group that includes, among others, Samoan and Filipino children (see Tharp, 1980, for an excellent overview of KEEP). KEEP adopted the much used "mismatch hypothesis" as an explanatory framework, suggesting that cultural discontinuities between the school and the communities of disadvantaged Hawaiian children were a major cause of school failure. The KEEP staff, however, went one step further than most social scientists who invoke the mismatch hypothesis. They conducted a descriptive study of the families and communities of disadvantaged Hawaiian children in an attempt to identify both beliefs and practices that might conflict with school achievement and ones that could be modeled in school to improve learning.

The results of this study showed that the child-rearing practices in these communities fostered a strong peer orientation among young children. It was also noted that young children ordinarily interacted in small groups without much adult supervision. Older siblings were largely responsible for the care and teaching of younger children. Furthermore, KEEP researchers observed that children tended to learn by doing or through observation, rather than by direct instruction from adults. When viewed against the requirements of school, many of these characteristics were seen as sources of conflict between the culture of the school and that of the community. Members of the Kamehameha project believed, however, that some of the local culture's practices could be accommodated in school settings to increase learning. For example, the social organization of the classroom was changed to allow children to work in small groups that were heterogenous with respect to reading level. According to Calfee et al. (1981), this was done to make the classroom environment "more consistent with the character of sibling work groups outside of school" (p. 47). The Kamehameha staff, it should be noted however, did not take a culturally relativistic position and assume that the school should mirror every facet of the local culture that it serves.

The findings from the ethnographic study were integrated with cognitive and linguistic data on disadvantaged Hawaiian children to develop a direct instruction reading curriculum with a comprehension, rather than code orientation. The latter decision was influenced partly by cognitive research showing that the decoding of written symbols is an active process in which the individual constructs meaning by relating old information to new data (cf. Tharp, 1980). The direct instruction format used a consistent lesson structure involving what were referred to as Experience-Text-Relations (E-T-R) sequences. Reading lessons were begun by teachers introducing "content drawn from the child's experience (E), followed by text (T) material, followed by establishing relationships (R) between the two" (p. 15). As part of this routine, teachers asked questions that were hierarchically organized according to their cognitive difficulty.

In summary, the KEEP program started by identifying the features of situations where learning took place in the local culture and incorporated certain aspects of these contexts in developing a reading curriculum that also reflected recent advances in cognitive research on reading comprehension. Comparisons of the Gates–MacGinitie Reading Test scores between children in the KEEP program and those receiving other types of instruction show that the scores of KEEP children are significantly higher than those of children in comparison groups.

Implications for Educational Policy

Demonstrations such as those provided by the Kamehameha reading project represent positive examples of the research promoted by cultural practice theory: By identifying the content and social organization of analogous intellectual activities in two cultural settings, Tharp and his colleagues were able to develop an approach to instruction that maximized the reading achievement of disadvantaged Hawaiian children.

However, a little thinking about how to construct other curricular activities along the lines of the Kamehameha project reveals a fundamental restriction of the straightforward application of a cultural practice framework to improve academic skills. Because studies like the Kamehameha project are extremely useful for demonstrating the presence of intellectually valued skills in populations where they might have been assumed to be absent, they may be of limited utility in our schools as presently structured. The fact remains that in order for our school system to succeed in educating all our children, children's activity must be organized to give them the requisite kinds of practice both inside and outside of school. This is the basic idea behind all compensatory education programs, no matter the rationale that brings them to organize extra practice. It is correctly assumed that success within a restricted activity domain (e.g., reading) is dependent on the amount of practice one gets in that domain; but a theory of how such practice can be organized and generalized to occur in environments where its occurrence is low (e.g., after school time) is lacking. Compensatory education programs generally proceed by changing aspects of either the school or the family environment, changes that often produce short-term gains in achievement. Few of these programs, however, have considered the complementary changes necessary in both educational institutions and communities to support the continued success of students once they leave a program.

Educators and parents alike generally recognize that the success of compensatory and regular educational programs depends on community–school collaboration; yet, there is little agreement about the precise form such collaboration should take and the functions it should serve. Part of this uncertainty is due to a lack of understanding of how schools and communities interact to produce academic successes and failures. Ogbu's (1974) descriptive analysis of education in a low-income community is one of the few that documents both the community's and the school's role in the academic failure of certain students. Ogbu identifies school policies, parent and teacher attitudes, and economic constraints affecting the school and the community that produce failure in children from specific minority groups.

Similarly, McDermott et al.'s (as part of a final report in preparation) study of homework in working-class families shows how homework can extend academic failure when used, or perceived to be used, for reasons other than practice. Ideally, homework is used by both teachers and parents to diagnose problems and to give students an opportunity to practice old skills and develop new ones without being concerned about grades. Parents', teachers', and students' responses to homework, however, vary when it is used (or perceived to be used) for reasons such as the school's accountability to the community or parents' commitment to their children's education. When schools use homework as a window into the child's family, many parents respond by exerting tremendous pressure on children to do it correctly. McDermott et al. describe how one family's concern with doing it "right" undermined the function of homework in the ideal sense. The family managed to recreate "school" in the home, an experience, which for this particular child, was filled with failure.

Although Ogbu and McDermott's studies underscore the need for undertanding and improving community–schools relations, more research is needed before general prescriptions for collaboration are handed down. We must know more about the ways some of the contexts encountered by minority culture people produce school failure. Unfortunately, most of the ethnographic work done on minority groups (e.g., Liebow, 1967; Stack, 1974) restricts the analyses to ways the local culture gallantly perpetuates failure. The majority group's role in failure among minority groups is less clearly analyzed.

CONCLUSION

From the perspective of cultural practice theory, the fact that some social groups outperform others in valued social contexts like the school needs to be explained with the same rigor that we demand of our cross-cultural work. We clearly recognize differential performance; it is when seeking causes that our strategy for research and our guesses about social policy differ. We seek to explain cultural differences in performance by examining differences in the experiences people have in a given context, recognizing, of course that differences in experience often amount to differences in practice. To bring about change, we seek changes in the contexts that are available to a given group both within and outside the local culture.

Thus, cultural practice theory acknowledges the existence of domain-dependent cultural differences that can, in some circumstances, be called "cultural deficits." However, as Cole and Bruner (1971) pointed out several years ago: "Cultural deprivation represents a special case of cultural difference that arises when an individual is faced with demands to perform in a manner inconsistent with his past (cultural) experience" (p. 874).

We believe this statement to be true. What has occurred in the intervening decade is increased sophistication in carrying out the research program that such an assertion promises. In this chapter we have offered for the first time a comprehensive statement of what sort of theory seems to best serve such a program and our recommendations for future research.

ACKNOWLEDGMENTS

This chapter was written while the author was a research fellow at the Laboratory for Comparative Human Cognition, University of California, San Diego. Special thanks to Michael Cole, Luis Moll, Hugh Mehan, Denise Borders Simmons, and the members of the Laboratory for Comparative Human Cognition for their support, comments, and criticisms.

REFERENCES

Adams, J. J., & Collins, A. (1978). A schema-theoretic view of reading. In R. Freedle (Ed.), *Discourse processing: A multidisciplinary perspective*. Norwood, NJ: Ablex.
Berry, J. W., & Dasen, P. R. (1974). *Culture and cognition: Readings in cross-cultural psychology*. London: Metheun.

Bransford, J. D., & Johnson, M. K. (1973). Consideration of some problems of comprehension. In W. Chase (Ed.), *Visual information processing.* New York: Academic Press.

Bransford, J. D., & McCarrell, N. D. (1974). A sketch of a cognitive approach to comprehension. In W. B. Weiner & D. S. Palermo (Eds.), *Cognition and the symbolic processes.* Hillsdale, NJ: Lawrence Erlbaum Associates.

Bronfenbrenner, U. (1979). *The ecology of human development.* Cambridge: Harvard University Press.

Brown, A. L. (1977). Development, schooling and the acquisition of knowledge about knowledge. In R. C. Anderson, R. J. Spiro, & W. E. Montague (Eds.), *Schooling and the acquisition of knowledge.* Hillsdale, NJ: Lawrence Erlbaum Associates.

Brown, A. L. (1980). Metacognitive development and reading. In R. Spiro, B. Bruce, & W. F. Breuer (Eds.), *Theoretical issues in reading comprehension.* Hillsdale, NJ: Lawrence Erlbaum Associates.

Brown, A. L., Campione, J. C., & Day, J. (in press). Learning to learn: On training students to learn from texts. *Educational Researcher.*

Brown, J. S., Collins, A., & Harris, G. (1978). Artificial intelligence and learning strategies. In H. F. O'Neil (Ed.), *Learning strategies.* New York: Academic Press.

Calree, R. C., Cazden, D. B., Duran, R. P, Griffin, M. P., Martus, M., & Willis, H. D. (1982). *Designing reading instruction for cultural minorities: The case for the Kamehameha Early Education Program.* Unpublished manuscript, Harvard University Graduate School of Education.

Chi, M. T. H. (in press) Knowledge development and memory performance. In M. Friedman, J. P. Das, & N. O'Connor (Eds.), *Intelligence and learning.* New York: Plenum Press.

Cole, M., & Bruner, J. S. (1971). Cultural differences and inferences about psychological processes. *American Psychologist, 26,* 867–876.

Cole, M. Dore, J., Hall, W. S., & Dowley, G. (1978). Situation and task in young children's talk. *Discourse Processes, 1*(2), 119–176.

Cole, M., & Scribner, S. (1974). *Culture and thought.* New York: Wiley.

Estes, W. K. (1974). Learning theory and intelligence. *American Psychologist, 20*(10), 740–749.

Fjellman, J. A. (1971). *The myth of primitive mentality: A study of semantic acquisition and modes of categorization in Akamba children of South Central Kenya.* Unpublished doctoral dissertation, Stanford University.

Flavell, J. H. (1978, October). *Cognitive monitoring.* Paper presented at the Conference on Children's Oral Communication Skills, University of Wisconsin.

Ginsberg, H. (1980). *Adult learning: Cognitive psychology.* Unpublished manuscript, University of Maryland.

Green, J. L., & Smith, D. C. (1982). *Teaching and learning: A linguistic perspective.* Unpublished manuscript, University of Delaware.

Hess, R. D., & Shipman, V. (1968). Maternal influences upon early learning: The cognitive environments of urban preschool children. In R. D. Hess & R. M. Bears (Eds.), *Early education.* Chicago: Aldine.

Kagan, J., Moss, H. A., & Sigel, I. E. (1963). The psychological significance of styles of conceptualization. In J. C. Wright & J. Kagan (Eds.), Basic cognitive processes in children. *Monographs of the Society for Research in Child Development, 28*(Serial No. 86).

Kirk, L. (1977). Maternal and subcultural correlates of cognitive growth rate: The Ga pattern. In P. R. Dasen (Ed.), *Piagetian psychology.* New York: Gardner Press.

Laboratory of Comparative Human Cognition. (1982). Culture and cognitive development. In W. Kessen (Ed.), *Mussen's handbook on child development* (Vol. 1). New York: Wiley.

Laboratory of Comparative Human Cognition. (in press). Culture and intelligence. In R. Sternberg (Ed.), *Handbook of human intelligence.* Cambridge, MA: Cambridge University Press.

Labov, W. (1972). *Language in the inner city.* Philadelphia, University of Pennsylvania Press.

Levenstein, P. (1977). The mother–child home programs. In M. Day & R. Parker (Eds.), The preschool in action. Boston: Allyn & Bacon.

Liebow, E. (1967). *Tally's corner.* Boston: Little, Brown.

Markman, E. M. (1973). Facilitation of part–whole comparisons by the use of the collective noun "family." *Child Development, 44,* 837–840.

Markman, E. M., & Siebert, J. (1976). Classes and collections: Internal organization and resulting holistic properties. *Cognitive Psychology, 8,* 561–577.

McDermott, R. P. (1977). Social contexts for ethnic borders and school failure. In A. Wolfgang (Ed.), *Nonverbal behavior.* New York: Academic Press.

McDermott, R., Varenne, H., & Leichter, H. (1982). The family's role in the acquisition of literacy for learning. Final report for NIE contract #400–79–0046. Washington, DC: National Institute of Education.

Moll, L. M., Estrada, E., Diaz, S., & Lopes, L. (1980, July). The organization of bilingual lessons: Implications for schooling. *The Quarterly Newsletter of the Laboratory of Comparative Human Cognition, 2*(3), 53–58.

Ogbu, J. U. (1974). *The next generation: An ethnography of education in an urban neighborhood.* New York: Academic Press.

Rumelhart, D. E., & Norman, D. A. (1978). Accretion, tuning and restructuring: Three modes of learning. In J. W. Cotton & R. L. Klatzky (Eds.), *Semantic factors in cognition.* Hillsdale, NJ: Lawrence Erlbaum Associates.

Serpell, R. (1979). How specific are perceptual skills? A cross-cultural study of pattern reproduction. *British Journal of Psychology, 70,* 365–380.

Shweder, R. A. (1979). Rethinking culture and personality theory, Part I: A critical examination of two classical postulates. *Ethos, 7*(3), 255–278.

Sigel, I. E., & McBane, B. (1967). Cognitive competence and level of symbolization among 5-year-old children. In J. Helmuth (Ed.), *The disadvantaged child* (Vol. 1). Seattle, WA: Special Child Publications.

Sigel, I. E., & Olmstead, P. (1970). Modification of classificatory competence and level representation among lower class Negro kindergarten children. In A. H. Passow (Ed.), *Reaching the disadvantaged learner.* New York: Teachers College Press.

Simmons, W. (1979, July). The effects of the cultural salience of test materials on social class and ethnic differences in cognitive performance. *The Quarterly Newsletter of the Laboratory of Comparative Human Cognition, 1*(3), 43–47.

Slaughter, D. (1979). *Early intervention, maternal development and teaching and children's verbal expressions.* Unpublished manuscript, Northwestern University, School of Education.

Stack, C. B. (1974). *All our kin: Strategies for survival in a black community.* New York: Harper.

Tharp, R. G. (1980, April). *The direct instruction of comprehension: Description and results of the Kamehameha Early Education Program.* Paper presented at the meeting of the American Educational Research Association, Boston.

Trotman, F. K. (1977). Race, IQ, and the middle class. *Journal of Educational Psychology, 69*(3), 266–273.

Werstch, J. V., & Stone, C. A. (1978, September). Microgenesis as a tool for developmental analysis. *The Quarterly Newsletter of the Laboratory of Comparative Human Cognition, 1*(1), 8–10.

Yando, R., Seitz, V., & Zigler, E. (1979). *Intellectual and personality characteristics of children.* Hillsdale, NJ: Lawrence Erlbaum Associates.

23

The Developmental Perspective on the Problem of Knowledge Acquisition: A Discussion

Rochel Gelman
University of Pennsylvania

In the past, developmentalists have urged those who study learning to pay heed to a particularly compelling claim. The claim, made on firm ground, held that cognitive structures develop through qualitatively different stages. Taking a strong cue from Piaget, many asserted that young children lack concrete operations; they fail in tests of their ability to conserve, seriate, and classify. Additionally, it was claimed that preschoolers are precausal and apparently willing to allow causes to follow their effects (e.g., Piaget, 1930), egocentric, perception-bound, and so on. If it is indeed true that the young have qualitatively different structures, there will be things they cannot learn. Likewise, they will often interpret stimuli in a fundamentally different way than do older children and adults. However, evidence from recent research on the nature of cognitive development in preschoolers calls into question the idea that they have structures that differ fundamentally from those of older children, or that they lack pieces of mental structures that older children have. Although understanding how and why the young are different remains an important question for research, appeals to an absence or difference in basic structure does not seem to provide the answer. Does it then follow that developmentalists can be ignored by those who study learning? I submit not. For I believe that recent findings on the cognitive capacities of young children shed new light on critical issues in the study of thinking and learning skills. To show why I need to first outline some of these new findings.

Two of the chapters presented in these volumes lend support to an ever growing body of evidence undercutting the view that the young child has a fundamentally different set of mental structures guiding his or her acquisition of knowledge.

Chi's elegant studies (this volume) on the role of knowledge in memory development speak directly to the claim that preschoolers lack certain mental structures. I draw attention to the fact that her 4½-year-old dinosaur expert was able to organize his knowledge within a class-inclusion structure. This should not be possible according to a theory that holds that a preschooler lacks concrete operations and therefore cannot deal with such a structure. Carey's chapter (this volume) provides further evidence that there are classification structures available to young children and that these are used under some circumstances.

Bullock, Gelman, and Baillargeon (1982) show that there are, likewise, cases where preschoolers use the same principles as do adults when reasoning about physical cause and effect relations. They report preschoolers use a priority of order principle much as do adults. Consider Bullock and Gelman's (1979) demonstration. They had young children watch the exact same event—a ball rolling down a runway and disappearing into a box—before and after a puppet jumped up from the box. When asked to choose the ball that made the puppet jump, 3- to 5-year-old children systematically chose the ball that was dropped first. They did this even when the order information conflicted with a cue of spatial contiguity, i.e., when the before event was in a runway that was separated from the box, but the after event was not. These findings favor the view that preschoolers can sometimes honor a principle of priority when reasoning about physical cause and effect relations. Bullock et al. summarize the evidence that preschoolers also make implicit use of the principles that effects have causes and that mechanisms relate cause and effect sequences.

Recent research on number concepts reveals the availability to young children of some arithmetic reasoning principles used by older children and adults. (See Gelman & Baillargeon, 1983, for a review.) Research on concepts of order undercuts the presumption that young children are insensitive to ordering relations (e.g., Trabasso, 1975). Carey provides still other examples of early cognitive competence. And for those who might still resist the idea that preschoolers do make implicit use of the kinds of structures that we once were sure they lacked, there are further examples in Flavell and Markman (1983).

Findings of the foregoing kind highlight the fact that young children's competences are more like older children's than once assumed. They cast serious doubt on the hypothesis that age differences in performance reflect fundamental differences in structural (or, in Carey's terms, format) characteristics. Indeed, as Simmons (this volume) points out, comparable findings in the cross-cultural literature rule out such a hypothesis regarding different levels of performance across cultures and subgroups within cultures. Is it that the differences observed are trivial and can be ignored? I think not. Indeed, I believe that an explanation of the differences provides answers to some of the questions raised in these volumes, or at least helps to better focus the questions.

I want to highlight a general characteristic of the work with young children. To demonstrate competence, it was necessary to design tasks especially suited for them (Donaldson, 1978; Gelman, 1978). A variety of intuitions led people to develop tasks that cut through or sidestepped variables judged to be irrelevant to the basic question "Is the competence there?" The search for competence has often been a search for appropriate tasks, special settings, "just right" stimuli, and instructions. These stripped-down versions of the original task succeeded; we managed to devise (or stumble upon) assessments that got to the core of the piece of cognition we wanted to demonstrate.

There is another way of looking at the fact that it took the design of tasks especially suited to young children to demonstrate competence. Where the young might reveal a given capacity on one carefully crafted task, the older child will reveal it on many tasks. The implication is that there are major differences in the range of situations to which young children can apply their competence. Put differently, the competence of the younger child is fragile; that of the older child is fluid and generalizable. The young child needs to be tested with a particular set of stimuli in a particular setting with a particular task. The older child can transfer his or her knowledge across a variety of domains. From such facts it follows that part of the tale of cognitive development is a tale of how a restricted piece of competence is generalized and transferred. This alone should be enough reason for those who study learning to look carefully at early cognitive development. For, unlike the situation in many studies of human learning, this is a clear case where transfer and generalization eventually do come about. It would seem that efforts to study this naturally occurring success story could yield insight into the question of what produces transfer and generalized use of a core capacity.

I have stated that part of cognitive development involves a trend from a restricted use of an ability to a more generalized use of it (cf. Fodor, 1972, 1975). This cannot be the whole story, and a consideration of what else occurs yields yet further examples of success stories that could be studied to answer questions raised by various speakers at this meeting.

Carey provides two further candidate accounts of cognitive development. One is that cognitive capacities themselves become the objects of thought; this in turn yields advances in the child's abilities. She suggests, for example, that the development of metacognitive abilities makes it possible for the child to apply classification abilities to the task of organizing newly acquired knowledge. Whether this is correct needs to be studied. But, it is clear that metacognitions come as a function of development (at least in this culture), and they do not seem to be available to very young children. Again, here is a success waiting to be explained. Having read much in this volume about the need to understand how to teach executive-function skills, should we be able to explain this developmental success story, we might better be able to teach these skills to students.

Carey also suggested that part of the story of cognitive development is about theory change. I agree (a fact that should be obvious from her review of the work I and my collaborators have done on the development of causal reasoning). Carey notes that, in some cases, a theory change can be so profound as to yield qualitatively new insights into the nature of a scientific phenomenon. Indeed, I think that this is the kind of development reflected in Krupa, Selman, and Jaquette's (this volume) findings on the acquisition of scientific concepts. A corollary of my interpretation of the Krupa et al. work is that the observations they report probably do not reflect a shift from concrete to formal operational thought. Let me expand a bit.

There are two components to Piaget's account of the development of scientific reasoning. The first is that young children simply lack the relevant formal operations. The second is that they lack the ability to make causal inferences about physical (including chemical) cause and effect sequences. Both Carey and I have gone over the reasons for rejecting the latter view. As regards the former, Gelman and Baillargeon's (1983) review of the correlational studies that sought to validate Piaget's account and description of concrete operations highlights how unsuccessful this line of research has been. Simply put, the predicted high interitem correlations are not observed. Given this, it is difficult to interpret demonstrated correlations between performances on one of Piaget's tests for the presence of concrete operations and performances on other tasks presumed to depend on the presence or absence of these operational structures. Were it the case that performance on any concrete operational task could be taken as evidence of an underlying homogeneous ability, there would be no problem concluding that the ability of interest, e.g., metamemorial capacities or the understanding of scientific concepts A, B, and C, depend on the acquisition of something akin to concrete operations. But it is not the case. The same logic applies to arguments about the role of formal operations, in which the correlational evidence is even more problematic (Neimark, 1981). Parenthetically, it is hard to interpret the Krupa et al. findings without an analysis that partials out the effect of age.

I do not mean to claim that the Krupa et al. results are uninteresting. But, to the extent that they reveal qualitative developmental changes, I believe they reveal qualitative theory changes and not the acquisition of qualitatively new and more powerful cognitive structures. (See Gelman & Baillargeon, 1983, for further discussion on this point). As Krupa et al. point out, some kinds of theory change come with relative ease. There are, however, other kinds that do not. Green, McCloskey, and Caramazza (this volume) make it clear that many college students' physical intuitions reflect a commitment to a Medieval theory of physics, one that is very resistant to instruction (Champagne, Klopfer, & Gunstone, 1981). I venture the guess that we could line up different theory changes on a continuum of ease and derive some strong clues as to how to proceed to account for them. Again, because some theory changes come with relative ease (consider Carey's work on the development of the concept of animal) in the normal course of development, it would do well to keep developmental matters in mind.

There are yet further candidate accounts of cognitive developmental differences. Although I and my collaborators grant principles of counting and causal reasoning to the very young child, we do not assume that knowledge of these is explicit; quite the contrary. In that young children respond systematically as opposed to randomly, we postulate an underlying set of principles that guide these responses. Following Greeno and Riley (1984), when I distinguish between implicit and explicit knowledge of the counting principles, I mean to distinguish between the ability to verbalize or state the counting principles and the ability to demonstrate that one's behavior is systematically governed by the principles; that is, we invoke the principles as accounts of why performance is systematic, be it error free or error prone. We do not, at the same time, assume that 2- and 3-year-olds know the counting principles in an explicit way, as do adults who can say that there is no largest number, in part, because there is no limit to the continued application of the counting principles.

One might ask why add a shift from implicit to explicit knowledge to the list of candidate developmental functions. Is it not the same as acquiring metacognition? The answer must be both yes and no. Yes for the reasons that lead one to pose this question. No because one could have explicit knowledge without having metacognitive awareness of that knowledge. For example, one could know that everytime one rehearses a text, recall for that text will improve. Still, one might not know that it is a property of memory that is at work here. In the latter case, one looks down on the way memory works; in the former case, one simply makes an empirical generalization. To be sure, we need to be more precise about the differences between the two phenomena before accepting the view that they are different. But the same can be said about metacognition itself. We might know a case of it when we see it, but I am not convinced that we have articulated what it is that we see.

There is another kind of development to which I think we have paid too little attention. Rozin (1976) argues that cognitive development, both phylogenetically and ontogenetically, involves an increase in accessing capacity. Early in development, pieces of cognitive structure(s) serve special, and therefore restricted, purposes. With the development of accessing abilities, these pieces, which are initially used in a restricted way, can be accessed and put together in the service of a new task.

The example offered in Rozin's presentation was the ability to read. He notes that it is likely that there is a genetic program in the service of speech production; yet, it is unlikely that there is one that works in the service of reading. (I know of no one who maintains that we are genetically programmed to learn to read, per se). Nevertheless, many can learn to read. According to Rozin we can because of our ability (with development) to access the machinery that is used to produce and comprehend speech. The ability to do so makes it possible to access components of the speech stream and treat them as sounds to be coded into a visual mode.

Again, there is the question of whether an accessing hypothesis differs from a metacognitive hypothesis about the course of cognitive development. And again, I believe there is a difference. Rozin's notion of accessing provides the outline of an account of how innate mental structures can be used in the service of acquiring new knowledge and new capacities. Pieces of special purpose abilities are pulled out of that core ability and combined with pieces of other core structures, the result being a new ability that brings with it new mental power—witness the case of reading. Metacognition concerns already existing structures and capacities and not the combinations or recombination of these structures.

I want to switch from a focus on matters of structure to matters of function. In particular, I want to highlight a fact about development that deserves careful attention from those who study learning processes. Historically, developmentalists in the comparative tradition have assumed that learning is guided by innate structural constraints that help the young pick relevant inputs from the environment (see Seligman & Haeger, 1972 for many examples). Put differently, the motive for learning is taken to be part and parcel of the capacity to do X, Y, or Z. Those familiar with Piaget's theory will recognize a similar argument. Structures are said to assimilate and accommodate or to seek out that environment that will support the use of a given structure as well as the eventual development of that structure. An example helps illustrate what is meant here.

I have argued that the counting principles guide the young child's acquisition of skill at counting (e.g., Gelman, 1982). Consider the stable-order principle. As a constraint, the principle requires that children find an ordered list with which to tag items as they count. In our culture, there are two conspicuous candidates, the number words and the letters of the alphabet. By 2½ years of age children usually have fixed on the number list and use it when counting. The compelling case for the argument that the child seeks out the list comes from those instances where the child uses the alphabet to count. Greek and Hebrew allow this but English does not. There is no way to account for the young child who does use the alphabet without allowing for the availability of a structure that guides a search of the environment. Parenthetically, since I first reported that some beginning counters use their own lists, people have been sending me the lists their child first used. A favorite of mine is "1–2–3–4–5–6–7–h–i–j–k" (The switch in lists is most likely due to an acoustic confusion error between 8 and h).

The case of counting is but one example of the view that constraints do not dictate simply that a child respond to a particular environment; there are other compelling cases of how they carry with them a competence motivation that leads them to work very hard at the task of early learning. Recall Weir's (1962) observations about busy toddlers lying in their cribs at night going over what they have learned to say that day. Similarly, it appears that young children need not be told to count the number of steps in their house, or the cows in a field, or the cracks in the sidewalk. They do so spontaneously. A similar tendency to self-rehearse holds for a new-found motor skill. Indeed, it looks like much of early learning is motivated from within.

If we grant that there are constraints guiding acquisition, we provide a source of monitoring for errors and the tendency to self-correct. We find that young children are not only motivated to count on their own; they often self-correct. We have transcripts of some children doing so for 5 minutes in a row, e.g., "Let me see, that's 1–2–3–5–10–9–11. No, try 'dat again. 1–2–3–6–9–10," and so on.

Some may be surprised with the finding that young children monitor their own learning and rehearse spontaneously; for, we have heard from some quarters that these are late-developing strategies. They might very well be in the cases where learning is not guided by constraints. But in the case of natural acquisitions, they are part and parcel of early learning. So once again, development offers a case of where something is done and thus another source of clues regarding the nature of knowledge acquisition.

I hope I have convinced you that the study of development is still an important task for those who are interested in the acquisition of learning skills. It provides natural instances of cognitive changes. We should get down to the business of finding out how these work. I could be wrong; it could be that what is acquired naturally in the course of development is too different from what is acquired later on in school. I do not think so; still, I end with a cautionary note.

Research over the last decade has revealed some remarkable abilities in young children. This research has led to questions about implications for curriculum development. But I am not yet sure what they are. The kinds of learning I have focused on here are, I think, natural. Yes, they do require an environmental support system, but they probably do not require an explicit lesson plan. There are tutors in the natural environment (see Simmons, this volume), but they catch the child on the run. At the very least, school places a new set of conditions on the nature of learning. We need to consider whether the learning that takes place in a natural environment is like learning in the structured environment provided by schools. Then, we might better be able to consider the role of early cognitive abiities vis-a-vis school curricula.

ACKNOWLEDGMENTS

Preparation of this chapter was supported by NSF grants BNS–8004885 and BNS–8140573 and a grant from the Sloan Foundation to the program in Cognitive Science.

REFERENCES

Bullock, M., & Gelman, R. (1979). Preschool children's assumptions about cause and effect: Temporal ordering. *Child Development, 50*, 89–96.

Bullock, M., Gelman, R., & Baillargeon, R. (1982). The development of causal reasoning. In W. J. Friedman (Ed.), *The developmental psychology of time*. New York: Academic Press.

Champagne, A. B., Klopfer, L. E., & Gunstone, R. F. (1981). Students beliefs about gravity and motion. *Problem Solving, 3*, 12–14.

Donaldson, M. (1978). *Children's minds.* New York: W. W. Norton.

Flavell, J. H., & Markman, E. M. (Eds.). (1983). *Cognitive development.* In P. Mussen (Ed.), *Carmichael's manual of child psychology* (Vol. 3). Wiley.

Fodor, J. A. (1972). Some reflections on L. S. Vygotsky's thought and language. *Cognition, 1*, 83–95.

Fodor, J. A. (1975). *The language of thought.* New York: Thomas Y. Crowell.

Gelman, R. (1978). Cognitive development. *Annual review of psychology* (Vol. 29). Palo Alto, CA: Annual Reviews.

Gelman, R. (1982). Basic numerical abilities. In R. J. Sternberg (Ed.), *Advances in the psychology of intelligence* (Vol. 1). Hillsdale, NJ: Lawrence Erlbaum Associates.

Gelman, R., & Baillargeon, R. (1983). A review of some Piagetian concepts. In J. H. Flavell & E. M. Markman (Eds.), *Cognitive development.* In P. Mussen (Ed.), *Carmichael's manual of child psychology* (Vol. 3). New York: Wiley.

Greeno, J. G., & Riley, M. S. (1984). Process and development of understanding. In F. E. Weinert & R. Kluwe (Eds.), *Learning by thinking.* West Germany: Kuhlhammer.

Neimark, E. (1981). Explanation for the apparent nonuniversal incidence of formal operations. In I. E. Sigel, D. M. Brodzinsky, & R. M. Golinkoff (Eds.), *New directions in Piagetian theory and practice.* Hillsdale, NJ: Lawrence Erlbaum Associates.

Piaget, J. (1930). *The child's conception of physical causality.* London: Routledge & Kegan Paul.

Rozin, P. (1976). The evolution of intelligence and access to the cognitive unconscious. In J. M. Sprague & A. D. Epstein (Eds.), *Progress in psychobiology and physiological psychology* (Vol. 6). New York: Academic Press.

Seligman, M. E. P., & Haeger, J. (Eds.). (1972). *Biological boundaries of learning.* New York: Appleton–Century.

Trabasso, T. R. (1975). Representation, memory and reasoning: How do we make transitive inferences. In A. D. Pick (Ed.), *Minnesota Symposium on Child Psychology* (Vol. 9). Minneapolis: University of Minnesota Press.

Weir, R. (1962). *Language in the crib.* The Hague: Mouton.

Approaches to the Teaching of Cognitive Skills

24

A Developmentally Based Approach to the Problem of Instructional Design

Robbie Case
University of Toronto

The present chapter is divided into four sections. In the first, I present an analysis of chidren's intellectual development. In the second, I suggest a method of instruction that derives from this analysis. In the third, I present an illustration of how this method can be applied to the teaching of conventional classroom content. In the fourth, I suggest a number of conditions that must be met if children's response to this method is to be optimized.

CHILDREN'S INTELLECTUAL DEVELOPMENT: A NEO-PIAGETIAN ANALYSIS

The changes in reasoning that children exhibit on Piaget's Balance Beam Task are typical of those observed during the elementary school period and may be used to illustrate the nature of the underlying developmental process. At the age of 3 or 4, when asked which side of a balance beam will go down, children make a very global evaluation of each side, often based on salient perceptual characteristics that the weights exhibit. At the age of 4½ to 6, they carefully quantify the number of weights on each side and pick the side with the greater number. At the age of 7 or 8, they also quantify the number of weights on each side. However, if the number of weights on each side is equal, they predict that the weight at the greater distance from the fulcrum will go down. Finally, at the age of 9 or 10, they succeed in effecting a primitive compensation between the weight and distance. Either they make their decision on the basis of the dimension of greater difference, or else they form some mental sum of the total weight and distance on each side. These latter strategies do not always yield the correct answer, of course, because they are not yet based on proportional reasoning. Nevertheless, the strategies do work in the majority of cases and represent the pinnacle of what Piaget has labeled "concrete operational reasoning" (Inhelder & Piaget, 1958; Siegler, 1976).

If the sort of progression that is observed on Piaget's Balance Beam problem were unique to that problem, it would be of interest primarily to developmental psychologists, or perhaps to educators who are interested in the origins of scientific reasoning. As mentioned at the outset, however, this is not the case. Precisely the same progression is observed on a wide variety of other problems. The only thing that varies is the specific dimensions of relevance (Case, 1978b). Even the rate of progression appears to be very similar across task domains, at least in the age range from 3 to 8 (Siegler, 1981; Case, 1985). It is worthwhile, therefore, to analyze the underlying process.

What sort of changes in children's cognitive structures might be responsible for producing the changes that are observed on the Balance task? The type of structural analysis I present is drawn from the information-processing tradition. In this tradition, an *executive control structure* is defined as a procedure for getting from an unsatisfactory initial situation to a more satisfactory terminal situation, via a set of intermediate mental operations that are executed in a regular sequence. As such, any executive control structure may be analyzed in terms of three components: (1) a representation of the problem situation, (2) a representation of the objective to be achieved, and (3) a representation of the step or set of steps for achieving this objective. In the case of the child's earliest thinking about the balance beam, these components might be as follows.

Problem Situation
A mental plan or blue print (scheme) representing the fact that a balance beam with weights has been placed in front of the child.

Objective
A scheme representing the goal to be achieved, namely to predict which side of the balance will go down when the arms are released.

Strategy
1. A scheme representing the steps to be taken, namely scanning each arm of the balance, to see which weight looks heavier.

Because these schemes appear in all the subsequent analyses I present, I shall list them in the following abbreviated form.

Executive Control Structure: Stage 0: (3–4 years)

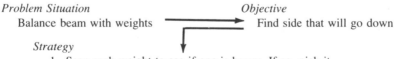

Problem Situation   *Objective*
Balance beam with weights   Find side that will go down

Strategy
1. Scan each weight to see if one is heavy. If so, pick it.

The executive control structure that children develop during the next stage may be represented in a similar format as follows.

Executive Control Structure: Stage 1 (4½–6 years)

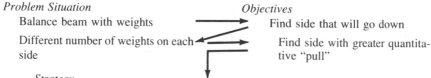

Problem Situation
    Balance beam with weights

Objectives
    Find side that will go down

    Different number of weights on each side

    Find side with greater quantitative "pull"

Strategy
1. Scan each weight to see if one is heavier; if so pick it (if not, go to 2).
2. Count weights on each side, label side with larger number as heavier (Return to 1).

Note that each component of the child's executive control structure now contains one additional element. In effect, a new "loop" has been added, consisting of a representation of a new problem feature, a representation of a new goal occasioned by this feature, and a representation of a new step or set of steps (subroutine) for reaching this goal. I have used an indented notation in listing the objectives to indicate a relationship of subordination. The child still has the same "top level" objective. However, he now has a lower level objective as well, which is subordinate to his initial one. In terms of the child's mental functioning, what this "stacking" of goals implies is that the child must store his top level objective in working memory,[1] while he devotes his attention to the subordinate one. Whatever the working memory load of the first strategy, then, the load of the second strategy must be higher. While the child is working toward the subgoal of determining which number of weights is greater, he must store a "pointer" indicating that his top level goal is to predict which side will go down. Once he has calculated the number of weights on the first side, he must also store this number briefly, while he counts the number of weights on the second side. The demand on his working memory is therefore to remember (1) 1 objective and (2) 1 number, while he is in the process of calculating a

---

[1]The term *working memory* is used by psychologists to refer to the intellectual resources that are available for (1) conducting mental operations (i.e., doing mental "work"), and (2) remembering the products of these operations for a short period of time. The human working memory capacity is quite limited, even in adults. As an illustration, the readers might wish to count five different sets of objects in a row and then try to remember the cardinal value of each set without recounting it. Although they may well be able to succeed at this task, they will find it quite challenging, due to the load that it will place on their working memory. Children experience this sort of task as even more challenging, and can remember even fewer cardinal values. The norms are 1, 2, 3, and 4 cardinal values remembered at 4, 6, 8 and 11 years of age.

second number. I call this a level 1 working memory demand. Consider next the control structure that emerges at the next stage.

Executive Control Structure: Stage 2 (7–8 years)

Problem Situation   *Objectives*
- Balance beam with weights ————————▶ • Find side that will go down
- Different number of weights on ◀——————— • Find side with greater quantita-
  each side   tive pull
- Each weight at a different distance ◀——————— • Find side with greater distance
  from the fulcrum.   from the fulcrum

   Strategy
1. Scan each weight to see if one is heavy. If so, pick it (if not, go to Step 2).
2. Count weights on each side, label one with greater number as heavy (if unequal, return to step 1. If equal, go to step 3).
3. Count number of distance pegs from fulcrum. Label weight at greater distance as having heavier pull. Return to step 1.

Note that this structure again preserves much of the preexisting structure but incorporates a new loop. This new loop consists of the representaion of a new problem feature, the representation of a new subgoal, and the representation of a new step or set of steps (subroutine) for reaching this subgoal. Once again, the addition of a new loop also adds an additional demand to the child's working memory. While the subject is counting the number of weights on the second side, he must remember everything he had to remember at the previous stage: namely (1) his general objective, plus (2) the number of weights just calculated on the first side. However, he must also remember one additional item: (3) his intention as to what to do next (count the distance pegs). Similarly, when he is counting the distance pegs on the second side, he must remember (1) his general objective, plus (2) the number of distance pegs just computed on the first side, plus (3) one additional item, namely the answer he just arrived at when he set himself the objective of determining which side had the greater number of weights. Both while he is counting the number of weights, then, and while he is counting the number of distance pegs, the demand on his working memory is one unit higher than it was at the previous substage. I call this a level 2 working memory demand.

A more formal analysis of the working memory demands of each control structure is presented elsewhere (see Case, 1978b; also Case, 1985). However, for the present, the general point is hopefully clear: The addition of a loop to an executive control structure entails a simultaneous addition to the child's working memory load.

If the foregoing analysis accurately reflects the changes that take place in the child's cognitive structure as he progresses from substage to substage, a question that naturally arises is what is responsible for producing these changes. One factor is obviously experience. A child needs experience with the domain in question, in order to encode the problem features of relevance, and to develop subroutines for dealing with them (cf. Siegler, 1976). Experience by itself, however, is not sufficient to explain why the process of development takes so long, or why it occurs at a similar rate across so many domains. To explain these latter data, one would have to postulate that experience with balances and teeter totters is quite rare, and that it is acquired at the same rate as experience in most other content domains. Both of these suggestions seem unlikely.

Piaget's answer to the preceding questions is well known. He suggested that development occurs by a mechanism of autoregulation, and that it leads to very general structures that he calls "structure of the whole." It is the need for auto-regulation that accounts for the slow rate of development. It is the structure of the whole that accounts for the cross-task linkage in performance. Over the last 20 years, however, the difficulties with this position have become increasingly apparent. Particularly important have been studies that have shown rapid training effects, substantial décalage, and low cross-domain correlations. Thus, in my own work, I have followed a suggestion made originally by Baldwin (1894) and more recently by Pascual–Leone (1970). Both suggest that the factors responsible for producing the high degree of cross-task linkage and the slow rate of development are: (1) the demand for a common size of working memory across tasks, and (2) the slow development of working memory with general experience and/or maturation.

In my laboratory over the last 10 years, we have conducted three basic types of studies to demonstrate that the Baldwin/Pascual-Leone hypothesis is correct: (1) We have developed tests of working memory and shown that children's working memory tends to match the level of structure that they employ. For example, children who use a level 1 structure on the balance beam tend to be able to remember one number, while they count a second, without losing hold of the task objective. As was mentioned earlier, this is precisely the demand that a level 1 structure entails; (2) the second type of study we have conducted is to train children in the use of novel structures, and to show that only those children who have the required working memory show much benefit from the training (see Case, 1985); (3) the final type of study we have conducted is to reduce the working memory of adults, and to expose them to the opportunity to assemble a new executive structure in a novel domain. Under these conditions, Jill Goldberg and I have shown that the level of structure that adults develop is predictable from a knowledge of their reduced working memory (Case, 1985).

I say more about these last two studies in a subsequent section. For the moment, however, my point is quite simple and may be summarized as follows: (1) Children's intellectual development can be represented a a series of executive control structures, with each successive control structure preserving much of the structure of the previous structure but incorporating one additional loop; (2) the acquisition of any new loop is dependent on specific experience in the domain to which the control structure is relevant; (3) the parallel across domains in the rate of loop incorporation, and the rather lengthy time it takes for a loop to be incorporated under conditions of spontaneous acquisition, can be explained by postulating a common working memory demand across structures and a slow rate of working memory development. I turn now to a consideration of the implications of this view of development for instruction.

EXECUTIVE FACILITATION AS A METHOD OF INSTRUCTION

If the previous view of development is correct, how might one facilitate children's progress, as they pass from one level of executive control structure to the next? Developmental psychologists have generally agreed that progress from stage to stage can best be facilitated by presenting children with tasks one level beyond their current level of functioning (see Turiel, 1972). They have disagreed, however, as to how much progress might be expected when this is actually done. This is because of the fact mentioned in the previous section, that there has been disagreement regarding the nature of the "linking" factor in development: i.e., the factor that ties together development in different domains. If one sees this linkage as being due to the existence of some underlying "structure of the whole," it is hard to see how any specific instructional intervention could have much impact. If one adapts the working memory view, however, then a different conclusion is reached: As long as one insures that the number of schemes (or "pointers") that a child must hold in mind does not exceed his available capacity, there is no reason to assume that there should be a limit to the number of loops that children can incorporate into their preexisting executive control structures. In short, "executive facilitation" should be a very reasonable instructional objective.

If one adopts executive facilitation as one's instructional objective, how might one proceed? What might the process of executive facilitation entail? As a minimum, I believe, it would have to entail the following three steps.

The Establishment of an Executive Hierarchy in the Problem Domain

The first step does not involve instruction at all. It involves analysis. The object of this step is to specify the sequence of executive structures that children bring to a domain spontaneously, and to arrange them in an executive "hierarchy." Unlike that described by Gagné (1968), an executive hierarchy that does not present a set of component skills on which the performance of some terminal skill is logically dependent. Rather, this hierarchy represents the naturally occurring sequence of executive structures that may be observed, as children come to represent some particular task in an increasingly sophisticated fashion. Each one of these structures will of course involve some set of component skills. However, these skills will not appear in one's analysis as a set of isolated entities, each one of which could conceivably be taught alone. Rather, they will appear as an integrated set of entities—a structure—whose nature is determined by the child's representation of the task situation and objectives.

Because the nature of the hierarchy is different, the method of analysis must be different as well. One cannot begin by conducting a rational "task analysis" and then proceed to develop tests for assessing each component that this analysis reveals. Rather, one must begin by giving the terminal task to children at several different levels of development and noting how they respond to it, what strategy they use spontaneously, how they justify its application, what errors they make, and so on. One must then generate a tentative description of the naturally occurring sequence of executive structures and invent a set of tasks that will permit this sequence to be specified more precisely. Because all these tasks will have the same "top level" goal, they will differ considerably in the features that must be represented to achieve this goal, and in the number of subgoals that must be set.

A more detailed procedure for generating such a set of tasks has been presented elsewhere (Case, 1978a, 1985). For the moment, however, the important point is that the results of the endeavor at this first step will be the description of an increasingly complex set of executive control structures on the one hand, and the description of a set of nested problems of increasingly empirical difficulty on the other. Siegler (1976) has provided an illustration of how this sort of analysis can be conducted for the balance beam task and has shown that the following four classes of problems form a well-ordered empirical scale: (0) problems where a weight is placed on only one side. These are passed at about the age of 3–5 years; (1) problems where two weights are placed at equal distances from the fulcrum, and one weight is composed of a slightly greater number of units than the other. These problems are passed at the age of 5–7 years; (2) problems where the weights are equal and placed at different distances from the fulcrum. These are passed at about the age of 7–9 years; (3) problems where both weight and distance vary, in opposite directions. These problems are first passed at the age of 9–11 years, at least for those cases where vector addition yields the same answer as vector multiplication.

Determination of Students' Current Level in the Executive Hierarchy

The second step is to determine the executive level of the students one will be teaching. Once a domain has been thoroughly mapped out, this may be done by presenting the children with a test that contains the various problem types identified and known to discriminate among various levels of executive structure.

To instruct children on the balance beam task, for example, one could precede the instruction by a test that contains the four problem types isolated by Siegler and determine the level at which the children consistently began to give incorrect answers. If a domain has been mapped out only tentatively, then the first and second steps may be combined. One can examine children's errors and interview them, simultaneously forming ideas of what sort of natural hierarchy exists, and of the level at which the majority of the children are functioning.

Facilitation of Progress from One Level of the Hierarchy to the Next

The final step is to facilitate children's progress from their existing level of functioning to the desired level by designing and implementing an appropriate instructional program. This third step may actually be broken down into a series of substeps, as follows: (1) design a situation where children will understand the top level goal of the task and can determine on their own the adequacy of their current strategy for reaching this goal; then, present them with a few problems that are solvable by means of the executive structure they currently have available; (2) advance to problems that are not solvable by means of the current executive control structure and that are one level above it; (3) help the students to notice the new feature of these problems, which they have not taken into account and which may lead them into error; (4) help the students to develop a new subroutine for dealing with this new feature; (5) make sure that the students understand the new subroutine and how it deals with the new problem feature; (6) provide a period of practice so that the students will no longer need to store the intention to execute this subroutine but consolidate it as an automatic part of their procedure; (7) reiterate the entire procedure for every subsequent level of the executive hierarchy.

As an illustration, suppose that students were assessed as having a level 1 executive structure on the balance beam task, and that the aim was to help them develop a level 2 structure. One might go about this in the following manner: (1) First, one might place a balance beam in front of the students and give them several example problems where the only factor that varied was weight. The students would succeed at these problems and realize that the behavior of the balance beam, once the arms were released, constituted a check on the adequacy of their strategy; (2) then one could introduce them to a level 2 problem, where the weight was the same but distance varied. Their prediction would be that the two arms would balance, and they could be shown that this prediction was not confirmed; (3) with a series of prompts, they could then be led to notice that the distance also varied; (4) with a series of further prompts, they could be led to incorporate a subroutine into their existing strategy to check for this feature; (5) finally, one could provide a practice period that would consist of a series of level 0, 1, and 2 problems intermixed. Once the children had consolidated a subroutine for checking distance from the fulcrum as well as the number of weights, one could introduce them to a level 3 problem, where the weight and distance both varied but acted in opposite directions. Once again, they could be led to see that their current strategy was inadequate, by being shown that it frequently led them to make incorrect predictions. Once again they could be led to a procedure for taking both dimensions into account simultaneously, perhaps by counting down the weights and along the distance on each side, thus in effect generating a total. Once again, a period of practice would be necessary, in which problems for levels 0, 1, 2, and 3 were intermixed.

Although it may not be obvious, the foregoing procedure should have the effect of reducing the working memory load of executing a level 3 strategy considerably. In the early phases, the instructor should function as an "external executive," removing some of the planning burden from the children. As the children become more familiar with the task, they should be able to take on this burden themselves, much as one does when one is learning to drive a car. Note, too, that the procedure of counting down the weights and along the distance pegs should act as an external memory aid for the children, removing the burden of having to store one number on each side for a few seconds, while they compute a second number.

I have actually tried out an instructional program such as tht just described, in collaboration with Rita Watson. The instruction was presented during two 15-minute sessions, on an individual basis, and the results were very encouraging. On a transfer test given 2 weeks after the instruction, by an experimenter who had not been present during the training, not one of the control subjects passed any of the level 2 or level 3 problems. By contrast, the experimental group passed 75% of these problems. Even their errors were encouraging, because they were no longer conceptual in nature, but rather mechanical (i.e., errors in counting). This was evident from the fact that errors were far more frequent when the totals on each side were close in magnitude than when they were widely discrepant, as is shown in Fig. 24.1.

We have used a similar method of executive facilitation with a variety of other developmental tasks, including maze tracing, quantity examination, conservation, and control of variables (Case, 1978a). In each case, the results have been the same: (1) Children have shown clear evidence of learning in a short period of time; (2) they have transferred what they have learned to new problems and new contents, as well as to new testers; (3) they have retained what they have learned over long periods of time. We have found treatment-control differences up to 1 year later.

A number of reasons might be suggested as to why we have obtained results like these across such a broad range of tasks. My own suspicion, however, is that the following four features of the method we have used are crucial, and that together they explain all three of the results: (1) The method places a strong emphasis on beginning with a task that children will have no difficulty in representing, given their current level of development; (2) the method specifies a natural sequence of progressively more complex tasks through which the children

Posttest
Item Differences on Weight & Distance x Item Errors

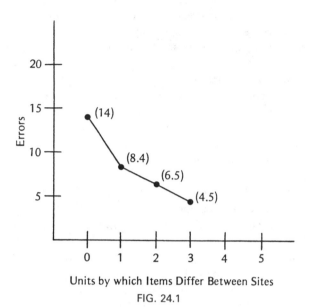

Units by which Items Differ Between Sites
FIG. 24.1

may be led; (3) the method maintains a close linkage between the way children represent these tasks and the strategies they are taught; (4) the method minimizes the load on children's working memory. In any scholastic domain where current curricula are not characterized by these features, and where results such as those that I have cited are not currently being obtained, the method of executive facilitation would appear to be an appropriate one to try out, at least on an exploratory basis.

EXECUTIVE FACILITATION AS APPLIED TO THE DESIGN OF CLASSROOM INSTRUCTION

There is one scholastic domain where the split between children's problem representations and the algorithms they are taught is often a serious one, and where problems of transfer, retention, and conceptual misunderstanding abound. That is the domain of mathematics (cf. Resnick, 1982). Gold (1978) has recently applied the method of executive facilitation to this domain with considerable success. One set of mathematics problems in which Gold was interested was ratio word problems, of the sort that are normally introduced in grade six. In setting up a curriculum to teach these problems, Gold went through all three of the phases mentioned earlier.

1. Establishment of an Executive Hierarchy.   In the first phase of his investigation, Gold identified the executive hierarchy shown in Table 24.1.

2. Determination of Students' Current Level of Functioning in the Hierarchy.   In the second phase of his investigation, Gold determined the executive level that his students had already reached. Gold worked with two different populations. The first were normal grades four and five students, in two California public schools. The second were math-disabled students in grades six and seven, who were drawn from the entire district. The majority of children in both groups had reached the first level in the hierarchy, and some had reached the second. None had progressed any further.

TABLE 24.1
Executive Hierarchy for Ratio Word Problems

Level	Description of Strategy	Example Items	
1	Given a unitary ratio, can match it to supply the missing value	$1/3 = 1/?$	$1/2 = ?/2$
2	Given a unitary ratio, can iterate to find the missing value for a nonunitary ratio	$1/2 = 3/?$	$1/3 = ?/9$
3	Given an integral ratio, can reduce to unitary ratio, then iterate to find the missing value for a nonunitary ratio	$3/6 = 2/?$	$2/4 = ?/10$
4	Given a nonintegral ratio, can reduce to a unitary ratio and iterate to find the missing value for a nonunitary ratio	$2/3 = 3/?$	$2/3 = ?/9$

3. Facilitation of Progress from One Level of the Hierarchy to the Next.   In the third phase of his investigation, Gold designed an instructional treatment that he felt would bring students through the preceding hierarchy.

First he designed a concrete situation by which he felt the students could appreciate the goal of the problem and decide on the adequacy of their current approach. This problem situation was the same for all levels and is illustrated in Fig. 24.2. The children were told that each box had pieces of gum in it, and

FIG. 24.2

the goal was to insure that each of the boxes had the same number of gum pieces in it. The first problems that Gold presented were at Level 1. Because this level was within the children's current competence, the problem of course presented no difficulty. Its function was to familiarize the children with the paradigm and to let them see that they could check their answers for themselves.

After the children had been introduced to the set of Level 1 problems, Gold moved on to the second level.

As he introduced the next set of problems, he pointed out their new feature; that is, he said, "Now I'm going to put several boxes in this side, instead of just one. But you still have to tell me how many pieces I will need, so that both sides will have the same number of pieces in each box."

For any student who did not develop a strategy for dealing with problems of this sort spontaneously, Gold modeled one himself. For example, he might say, "We have 3 pieces in this box on this side, so we want 3 pieces in the boxes on this side too. That means 3 here and 3 here and 3 here, so we need 9 in all." Note that this modeling also contained an explanation and that it made use of successive addition rather than multiplication.

At each level, Gold provided a number of practice problems, both of the type just introduced, and of simpler problems.

Finally, Gold recycled through the same six substeps for each of the levels in his hierarchy. Having done so for gum-and-box problems, he then repeated the entire procedure for problems using different materials, namely juice and water.

When he made the transition to a new level with either type of material, Gold introduced one additional feature. He "dropped back" to the lowest level in the hierarchy when he first introduced the new problem feature. For example, when introducting problems where more than one box was on the left, he "dropped back" to a simple matching situation at first and then worked up to one where the number of boxes on the right was greater than the number of boxes on the left. If the problem features associated with each level are labeled a, b, c, and d, the full set of problems that Gold presented could be labeled a, a + b, a + c, a + b + c, a + d, a + b + d, a + c + d, a + b + c + d. This sequence was maintained both for the "sum" problems, and for a parallel set of problems involving juice and water.

The rationale for the general sequencing of activities is no doubt obvious. It was to insure that each new activity was a direct and logical outgrowth of an activity that had immediately preceded it. Once again, however, it is worthwhile to stress that the procedure also had the effect of minimizing the load on children's working memory. First of all, the children had to deal with only one new feature at a time. Second, the teacher was there as a "coach" or "external executive" to begin with, so that they did not have to actively store a "pointer" to their new routine in memory. Third, when a new feature was introduced, all other complexities were stripped from the problem to begin with and only gradually built back in. Finally, a good deal of practice was presented at each level, in order to consolidate what had been learned, and to automize children's procedure as much as possible.

The success of Gold's approach was assessed with a posttest administered 1 month after the instruction that contained a variety of transfer problems. The various types of problems are shown in Table 24.2. As may be seen, only 6 of the 20 problems were of the sort actually presented in the curriculum. The other 14 involved situations differing to varying degrees. Given that many of the problems were quite remote from those used in the training, Gold decided to adopt a relatively weak criterion for success, namely 65% correct.

The results are presented in Table 24.3. As may be seen, the performance of the treatment groups was excellent. All the students passed the test, regardless of whether they were "normal" or "math disabled." The performance of the control groups was also of interest. As may be seen, two different control groups were included. The first control group was given a treatment that was based on the standard method in use in the California school system, a method based on cross multiplication. The second control group was also taught a cross-multiplication algorithm, but by a method based on an empirically validated learning hierarchy of the sort pioneered by Gagné (Anderson, 1976).

TABLE 24.2
Problem Used On Posttest

Problem Type	Example	Number of Problems
Juice equivalence[a]	I put 6 cans of water and 2 of lemonade in one pitcher. Then I put 18 cans of water in another pitcher. How much juice should I put in the second pitcher for the two mixtures to taste the same?	6
Juice concentration	One pitcher has 4 water and 3 juice. The other has 5 water and 4 juice. Which tastes more "juicy?"	6
Varied word problems	I can cook 2 pies with 5 big apples. How many pies can I cook with 12½ big apples?	5
Mr. Short and Tall (from Karplus & Peterson, 1970)	Here is a picture of Mr. Short. He is 3 big paper clips tall. If I measure him with small paper clips, he is 6 tall. I have a taller man in my office who is 4 big paper clips tall. How tall will he be if I measure him with small paper clips?	3

[a]These first six problems were of the exact type used in training. Only the numbers were changed.

As Table 24.3 shows, the performance of the first control group was poor. The majority of the subjects—both normal and math disabled—failed the test. The performance of the second control group was a good deal better. Interestingly enough, however, those children in this group who passed the posttests did not use the algorithm they had been taught. Rather, they used the "unitary method" that had been taught to the experimental group; that is, they first figured how many "1 unit" should get, then multiplied by the appropriate number to get the new value. One possible interpretation of the results, then, is as follows. The superior performance of the learning hierarchy group (Control 2) with respect to the conventional group (Control 1) was due to the careful sequencing and breakdown of the task into component skills. This enabled the children to come to some conceptual understanding of the problems and to develop a strategy of their own for dealing with them, because it lowered the working memory demands. The inferior performance of the same group with respect to the executive hierarchy group (treatment) was due to a related fact, namely that the children had to form this sort of conceptual representation and link it to an appropriate strategy, on their own. Although the normal subjects were capable of doing this, the math disabled were not.

Regardless of the precise mechanism by which the method of executive facilitation achieves its success, it seems clear that it *is* successful, both for the classic problems used in developmental research and for problems drawn from the conventional school curriculum. I therefore turn to a consideration of the conditions that must be met, if children's response to the method is to be optimized.

CONSTRAINTS ON THE METHOD OF EXECUTIVE FACILITATION

At least three conditions must be met if the method I have described is to be applied successfully.

The first is that the students who are to be taught should have sufficient working memory to assemble the lowest level control structure in the executive

TABLE 24.3
Percentage of Children Passing Posttest
(Criterion: 65% of Items Correct)
Number of Children Per Cell = 9

Population	Method		
	Executive Facilitation	Control 1	Control 2
Normal	100%	33%	78%
Math disabled	100%	11%	33%

hierarchy. In the balance training program, for example, the lowest level structure in the hierarchy was Level 1. For this structure subjects count the number of weights on each side of the beam and make their prediction according to which side has the greater number of weights. As was mentioned earlier, this entails a level 1 working memory. In the study that Rita Watson and I conducted, we included a small group of students who did not have a working memory of this size, as assessed by an independent measure. The results, presented in Table 24.4, indicate that the subjects in this group showed virtually no learning. The subjective impression of the teacher was equally interesting. Apparently, these children never really seemed to appreciate the nature of the activity in which they were being asked to engage, or what was being expected of them.

One possible method of insuring that students have sufficient working memory would be that employed in the aforementioned study. One could analyze the working memory demands of the most elementary task and assess the working memories of the students being exposed to it. Because this sort of analysis is still something of an art, however, a far simpler procedure is simply to pilot test the lowest level activity to determine the grade level for which it is appropriate. Particularly at the lower grade levels, the range of working memories is very narrow. The standard deviation is often not even as great as half a point. Thus, if the initial exercise were matched to the general level of a given grade, the program would be very apt to be appropriate for most of the children. Moreover, those children for whom it was *not* appropriate would be apt to be known to the teacher in any case, because they would have trouble with so much of the work at that grade level.

The second condition that must be met is that the basic operations that are entailed by the executive control structure must be thoroughly automatized. For the balance beam, the basic operation was counting, which is already quite automatic because children receive such a great deal of practice in it. In fact, we have found that, by giving students 20 minutes of additional practice in counting, twice a day, for a 3-month period, only marginal increments in counting efficiency are achieved (Kurland, 1981). For tasks such as ratio problems, how-ever, the basic operations are multiplication and division. These skills are much less likely to be automatic, with the result that valuable working memory may be diverted from higher level processing to lower level computation.

TABLE 24.4
Percentage of Subjects Showing Clear Evidence Of a Level 4 Control
Structure On the Balance Beam

Condition	Working Memory	Pretest	Posttest
Treatment	Level 0	0%	0%
	Level 1 or 2	0%	65%
Control	Level 1 or 2	0%	0%

All of us have no doubt had the experience of being unable to achieve our full potential in some higher order skill, because we have not yet automatized some lower level skill. This is a frequent experience, for example, in learning a new sport or in learning a foreign language. I do not think we realize, however, what a debilitating effect this can have on a young child who has less working memory to begin with. In order to demonstrate the power of the "poor-automatization" effect, we recently conducted an experiment in which we reduced adults' working memory by having them use a novel operation for quantification. One group was given massive training until they could remember 3 numbers while counting an additional set. Another group was given minimal training, after which they could remember only 1 number while counting an additional set. Both groups were then exposed to a new problem situation, which was formally identical to that of the balance beam problem.

The new situation for the adults was to predict which of three chutes a marble would roll down, given the clues provided by two cards with varying numbers of green and yellow dots on them. The subjects were told that they could only figure out which chute the marble would come down, if they quantified the arrays of dots on each trial, using the new operation. Note that under these circumstances the number of green dots on each card were analogous to the number of weights on each side of the balance beam, the number of yellow dots were analogous to the number of distance pegs from the fulcrum, and the three different chutes analogous to the three possible outcomes on a balance (tilt right, tilt left, balance). We discovered under these circumstances that the "well-automized" group (i.e., the group who had been given practice in counting until they could remember three numbers while counting another set) developed a level 3 control structure. By contrast, the poorly automized group (i.e., the group who had been given minimal practice and could only remember one number while counting an additional set) developed a level 1 control structure.

A third condition that must be met if the method of executive facilitation is to be applied is that the domain in which one is interested must be amenable to an executive hierarchy analysis. Because the examples I have presented have been from the areas of science and mathematics, it might be natural to assume that only "logical" skills can be analyzed in this fashion. In fact, however, this is not the case. The only requirement is that the domain involves skills that are of increasing complexity, and that are related to each other in a hierarchical fashion. Reading is a prime example of a content domain where the skills involved are not "logical," yet where the preceding two constraints are met. Biemiller (1970) and Marsh, Friedman, Welch, and Desberg (1981) have recently identified a developmental sequence of executive control structures in this domain, and these structures could quite easily form the basis for a curriculum of the sort I have described. Similar analyses could be made for any skill domain, including writing and sports. Even areas that are not normally considered to involve skills (e.g., social science, history) may ultimately profit from this sort of approach (cf. Biggs & Collis, 1982).

To summarize, in the present chapter I have tried to make six basic and closely related points. These are: (1) Intellectual development may be thought of as a process whereby children develop executive control structures of increasing complexity; (2) the factor that "ties together" the structures from different domains and that acts as a limit on the rate of structural development is the level of working memory that a structure requires; (3) executive development is a feasible instructural objective, and one that we have shown can be achieved. Our method of executive facilitation has been shown to be quite successful, not only in terms of the time required for learning and the length of retention, but in the scope of transfer; (4) this method can be applied to scholastic tasks as well as to standard "developmental" tasks, providing that the domain in question involves hierarchically related skills of increasing complexity; (5) the two major conditions that must be met if the approach is to be applied successfully in school are that the children should have sufficient working memory to assemble the lowest level executive in the executive hierarchy, and that sufficient concurrent practice in basic skills should be provided so that the children can use their working memory for high-level (conceptual) tasks rather than low-level (computational) ones; (6) the four key features of the method and those that we believe are responsible for its success are that it starts children out with a task they can represent quite easily, given their current level of development; that it then leads them through a series of progressively more complex tasks, which are presented in the natural order of acquisition; that it maintains a close linkage between children's representation of these tasks and the strategies they are taught for solving them; and that it minimizes the working memory load in making the transition from one level of task or executive structure to the next.

REFERENCES

Anderson, L. H. (1976). *Developmental effects in learning hierarchy structure for problems involving proportional reasoning.* Unpublished doctoral dissertation, University of California, Berkeley.
Baldwin, J. M. (1894). *Mental development in the child and in the race.* New York: McMillan.
Biemiller, A. J. (1970). The development of the use of graphic and contextual information as children learn to read. *Reading Research Quarterly, 6,* 75–96.
Biggs, J. F., & Collis, K. (1982). *A system for evaluating learning outcomes: The SOLO taxonomy.* New York: Academic Press.
Case, R. (1977). *The process of stage transition in cognitive development.* Final Report, Project #R01HD091Y8–01, NIMHCD.
Case, R. (1978a). A developmentally based theory and technology of instruction. *Review of Educational Research, 48,* 439–469.
Case, R. (1978b). Intellectual development from birth to adulthood: A neo–Piagetian interpretation. In R. Siegler (Ed.), *Children's thinking: What develops?* Hillsdale, NJ: Lawrence Erlbaum Associates.
Case, R. (1985). *Intellectual development: Birth to Adulthood.* New York: Academic Press.
Gagné, R. M. (1968). *The conditions of learning.* New York: Holt, Rinehart & Winston.
Gold, A. P. (1978). *Cumulative learning versus cognitive development: A comparison of two*

different theoretical bases for planning remedial instruction in arithmetic. Unpublished doctoral dissertation, University of California.

Inhelder, B., & Piaget, J. (1958). *The growth of logical thinking from childhood to adolescence.* New York: Basic Books.

Karplus, R., & Peterson, R. W. (1970). Intellectual development beyond elementary school. II: Ratio, a survey. *School Science and Mathematics,* LXX, 813–820.

Kurland, M. (1981). *The effect of massive practice on children's operational efficiency and memory span.* Unpublished doctoral dissertation, University of Toronto.

Marsh, G., Friedman, M., Welch, V., & Desberg, P. (1981). A cognitive-developmental theory of reading acquisition. In T. Gary Waller & G. E. MacKinnon (Eds.), *Reading research: Advances in theory and practice.* New York: Academic Press.

Pascual-Leone, J. (1970). A mathematical model for the transition rule in Piaget's developmental stages. *Acta Psychologica, 63,* 301–345.

Resnick, L. (1982). Syntax and semantics in learning to subtract. In T. P. Carpenter, J. M. Moser, & T. A. Romberg (Eds.), *Addition and subtraction: A developmental perspective.* Hillsdale, NJ: Lawrence Erlbaum Associates.

Siegler, R. S, (1976). Three aspects of cognitive development. *Cognitive Psychology, 8,* 481–520.

Siegler, R. S. (1981). Developmental sequences within and between concepts. *Monographs of the Society for Research in Child Development, 46,* (2, Serial No. 189).

Turiel, E. (1972). Stage transition in moral development. In R. M. Travers (Ed.), *Second handbook of research on teaching.* Chicago: Rand McNally.

25

Fostering the Development of Self-Regulation in Children's Knowledge Processing

Marlene Scardamalia
York University

Carl Bereiter
The Ontario Institute for Studies in Education

This chapter deals with ways to help children improve their strategies for handling complex knowledge-processing tasks. In a companion chapter (this volume), "Cognitive Coping Strategies and the Problem of 'Inert Knowledge'," we described a common strategy by which children reduce a number of potentially difficult tasks to a relatively simple task of "knowledge telling." Although this strategy has great coping value, enabling children to handle school tasks that would otherwise exceed their performance limitations, the strategy tends to defeat the educational purpose of much school work. There is a broad range of complex knowledge-processing activities in which the immediate consequences of deficient strategies are not definite enough to induce strategy change. In these activities, instruction therefore has an especially important role to play, but also an especially difficult one. Our research to date is still well short of providing instructional prescriptions, but we have identified two promising approaches that are described and explained in this chapter.

As in the companion chapter, we draw our material from work on expository writing. Expository writing is paradigmatic for a range of intellectual tasks occurring in everyday life. These are tasks in which the goal is at least partly emergent—your knowledge of what you are after grows and changes as part of the knowledge-constructing process—and in which there is a wealth of potentially applicable knowledge and potential routes to the goal. Tasks that have these properties fall within the category of what Greeno (1978) calls composition problems. We refer to the whole category as *compositional* tasks, to distinguish them from written *composition*, which is a subclass. Whether these are humble tasks of planning a weekend outing or grand ones of constructing a scientific theory, they all present formidable obstacles when it comes to teaching someone better strategies for doing them.

To get a general sense of these obstacles, one need only reflect on the conditions that favor rapid learning of new strategies. These are a clear-cut goal, against which to judge the efficacy of one's current strategy, and the opportunity to observe or be coached in a more effective strategy (cf. Case, this volume). In tasks that have emergent goals, however, the goal is in large part a product of actions taken in pursuing it, and so its value as a standard and as a motivator of change is ambiguous. This also means that the advantage of a more sophisticated strategy may not be obvious, because different strategies entail different goals, not merely different ways of pursuing the same goal.

There is a deeper difficulty with teaching new strategies for compositional tasks, however, which has to do with the level of specificity at which strategies may usefully be presented. A strategy for executing a task may be described at a range of levels of specificity, from the detailed level of production systems or computer programs to the level of very broad descriptive statements. Successful efforts at cognitive strategy teaching, such as those by Case (1975, 1978, this volume), have tended to use strategies of quite fine grain—strategies more or less at the level of specificity of computational algorithms. Teaching strategies at what we may accordingly call the algorithmic level is evidently powerful, but unfortunately it is practical only within a very restricted range of activities. It is restricted to activities for which algorithms can be written with a small enough number of rules that it is reasonable to expect that the rules can be learned. Such activities are largely confined to the realms of logico-mathematical problem solving. Outside that realm, most intelligent activity depends on context-sensitive rules (Bobrow & Norman, 1975). Grammar is a good example. A complete description of English grammar at the algorithmic level remains yet to be written, because each rule for a particular linguistic feature has many conditions attached to it relating to other feature combinations. Supposing an algorithmic description could be worked out, however, it is clear that it would be far too complex to teach. The same is true for any compositional tasks. In any tasks in which large amounts of propositional knowledge are relevant, choices of action become complexly contingent on the knowledge context. The result is that, even if it were possible to abstract and teach an algorithm for writing a good essay about dogs, there is no assurance that it would work for writing an essay about cats.

The obvious recourse is to move up to a more general level of strategy description. This is the level of heuristics (Polya, 1945) or tricks of the trade. A great deal of advice is given at this level pertaining to writing, ranging from the introspections and commonsense injunctions of innumerable books on the art of writing, to systematic schemes for developing compositions (e.g., Young, Becker, & Pike, 1970), and most recently to suggestions drawn from research on the composing processes of expert and novice writers (Flower, 1981). We have no doubt that strategy teaching at these levels can be helpful, having profited from it ourselves. But it is limited by two important presuppositions. First, it presupposes a high level of metacognition so that one is able to assess and consciously manipulate one's cognitive strategies. Second, it presupposes an existing executive strategy that is already highly enough developed to incorporate suggested new procedures as minor alterations or additional "loops" (cf. Case, this volume). We presume, in other words, that it is not possible to build or rebuild a complex executive strategy from the ground up through the use of verbal strategy descriptions. Thus strategy teaching at this level offers little hope for dealing with the kind of problem that motivates the present inquiry—the problem of students who use a "knowledge-telling" strategy that bypasses virtually all the problems that such high-level strategic advice is intended to help people contend with.

The strategy-teaching approaches we have just discussed, ranging from those that work at the algorithmic level to those that work at very general levels of description, may all be thought of as approaching strategy change through the implicit or explicit teaching of *rules*—rules that constitute principles or procedures of task execution.

We are convinced that rules of task performance do not represent the most promising objects of instructional effort when one is trying to upgrade immature strategies for complex knowledge-processing tasks, and that this is true regardless of the level of specificity of the rules and regardless of whether they are taught verbally or instilled through some more ingenious method. Instead, we believe that instructional efforts in this context are better directed at what Brown and Campione (1981) call "self-regulatory mechanisms."

As examples of self-regulatory mechanisms, Brown and Campione list *checking, planning, monitoring, revising,* and *evaluating.* We prefer to work with a somewhat more fine-grained specification than this, as is illustrated in the next section, but these examples nicely indicate the sort of cognitive entity we are talking about. Each one represents an information-processing skill or executive function amenable to improvement in its own right, a function that involves its own goal setting, knowledge retrieval, processing, and storage operations.

These self-regulatory mechanisms may be thought of in two ways. In one way, they may be thought of as building blocks or subroutines that can be assembled along with other subroutines to constitute a program for accomplishing some task. That is how they are treated, for instance, in Hayes and Flower's (1980) model of the composing process, where many of the same mechanisms mentioned by Brown and Campione are explicitly represented. The composing behavior of expert writers may in these terms be distinguished from that of novices by the greater frequency of use of regulatory mechanisms compared to the use of nonregulatory mechanisms such as generating and transcribing.

But there is another way of looking at self-regulatory mechanisms that has more long-range educational significance. It is to see these mechanisms as contributing not only to immediate performance but also as contributing to the further development of the cognitive system. When executive functions such as planning and evaluating are incorporated into the system of cognitive behavior, they generate information that may lead to strategic changes in behavior (Flavell, 1979). In other words, these self-regulatory mechanisms may constitute change-inducing agents that will have the effect of altering the rules by which the system operates. Thus, whereas introducing new self-regulatory mechanisms into children's cognitive behavior does not in itself constitute teaching new rules or strategies of task performance, it may result in the child's acquiring such new rules. In task domains where the rule systems are too complex to be teachable, it would seem that the best hope for promoting learning would be to promote self-regulatory functions that will help children acquire rules through their own activity (cf. Krashen, 1976).

The instructional methods that we propose in this chapter are, then, methods aimed at promoting more mature cognitive strategies through the action of the children's own self-regulatory mechanisms. The first method, *procedural facilitation,* consists of routines and external aids designed to reduce the processing burden involved in bringing additional self-regulatory mechanisms into use. The second method, *goal concretization,* uses substitute goals of a more concrete and stable type than those naturally occurring in compositional tasks. These goals serve as the basis for learning activities in which self-regulatory mechanisms can serve goal-directed functions that may later be transferred to natural tasks. Although these two methods can be—and we think should be—combined in practice, they are conceptually quite different, and so for clarity of exposition we treat them separately here.

Both of these instructional approaches are aimed at helping children apply self-regulatory mechanisms that are already in their repertoires. In a final section, we comment briefly on work in progress concerned with adding new mechanisms to children's repertoires.

PROCEDURAL FACILITATION

We start with the assumption that for any compositional task that might be presented to children they already have an executive procedure available for dealing with it—a procedure that will enable them to undertake the task and carry it through to some kind of completion. The situation is different with some kinds of logical or practical tasks, in which it is quite possible for a person confronted with the task to declare, simply, "I don't know how to do this." Thus, in the case of compositional tasks, instruction must always be brought to bear on a procedure that already works in some fashion and that the child may well believe to work perfectly.

Our instructional goal is to introduce an additional self-regulatory mechanism into this executive procedure, for instance, one for planning or for evaluation. Adding such a mechanism inevitably increases the information-processing load on the executive system. This occurs in two main ways. First, in order to bring the new mechanism into use, the executive system must switch attention to it at appropriate times and then switch attention back to the interrupted procedure. This requires active attention and recall of quite a demanding kind. One of the problems people have in incorporating new behavior into their habitual routines is that they simply don't remember to do it when they should (Wilkins & Baddeley, 1978). Second, the new mechanism itself requires processing capacity, possibly a large amount because of the newness of the function, and this may wipe out short-term stores of information needed for other parts of the task procedure that have been momentarily suspended. This would be experienced as losing one's place, forgetting what one was doing, etc.

One of the conjectures that led us to explore the technique we call *procedural facilitation* was that children might have appropriate self-regulatory mechanisms available and even know that they would be good to use and yet fail to use them because they were unable to place them in their existing executive procedures. Accordingly, we set out to design special supportive procedures that would (1) provide cues or routines for switching into and out of new regulatory mechanisms while keeping the executive procedure as a whole intact and (2) minimize the resource demands of the newly added self-regulatory mechanisms.

The main steps in designing a procedural facilitation are as follows:

1. Identify a self-regulatory function that appears to go on in expert performance but that does not go on or that goes on in an attenuated form in student performance: for instance, revision in writing (Nold, 1981).

2. Describe the self-regulatory function as explicitly as possible in terms of mental operations or functions. Thus, *revision* can be described in terms of the mental operations of *comparing, diagnosing, choosing a revision tactic,* and *generating* alternatives to previous phrasing and structuring of text (Scardamalia & Bereiter, 1983).

3. Design a way of cueing or routinizing the onset and offset of the process that makes minimal demands on mental resources. Thus, we may think of the four operations listed previously as a loop that is set in action when some mismatch has been detected between written text and intention. After that the output from each operation triggers the next until the comparison operation no longer detects a mismatch. Figure 25.1 shows a flowchart model of this process, which for brevity we call the CDO process (for COMPARE, DIAGNOSE, OPERATE). As a way of facilitating the onset and offset of this CDO process, for purposes of getting the function introduced into a child's executive procedure,

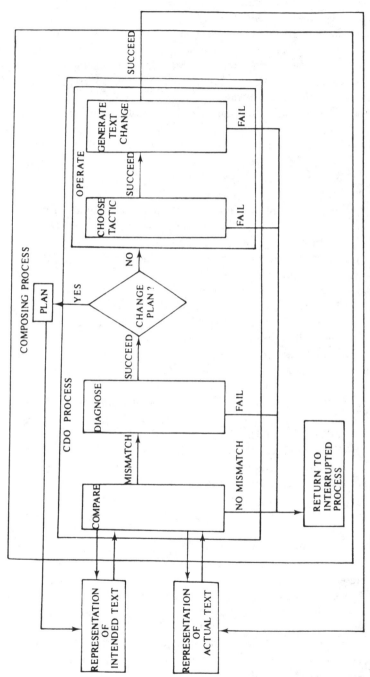

FIG. 25.1. Model of the CDO (COMPARE, DIAGNOSE, OPERATE) process in composition.

we may teach the child to initiate it routinely, at the end of every sentence, and to end the process after only one cycle.

4. Design external supports or teachable routines for reducing the information-processing burden of the mental operations. For instance, to facilitate *comparing* and *diagnosing,* we may reduce the task to a choice among a limited set of alternative evaluations ("This is good," "People may not understand this point," etc.). Similarly, we may reduce choosing a revision tactic to a finite choice (leave the text unchanged, delete, change wording, replace whole sentence, etc.). These choosing operations may be given external support by presenting the sets of alternatives on cards or in lists.

What we end up with, then, is a much simplified version of the self-regulatory function. The purpose of the simplifications is to enable children to start perfoming the self-regulatory function with as little additional burden on their processing capacities as possible. As they become practiced at it, the function should begin taking even less capacity, so that the simplifications can be withdrawn.

There is obviously a danger that in simplifying a self-regulatory function it will be so altered that practicing it will have no value in preparing children to carry out the normal function independently and might even interfere, by teaching bad habits. The likelihood that this will occur cannot be determined by surface appearances or commonsense assumptions. Indeed, it should be apparent that a procedural facilitation cannot be either constructed or evaluated except on the basis of a reasonably strong theory of the process—so that in the end testing the facilitation becomes a way of testing the theory.

We have conducted an experiment using a procedural facilitation of the CDO process along the lines just described (Scardamalia & Bereiter, 1983). To recapitulate, the onset–offset cueing problem was handled by having children go through the COMPARE-DIAGNOSE-OPERATE cycle once after each sentence. Several kinds of evidence, which we need not go into, suggest that if you want to break into the composing process with a minimum of disruption, sentence breaks are a good occasion for it (Matsuhashi, 1982; Woodruff, Bereiter, & Scardamalia, 1981). The COMPARE operation was simplified to a choice of 11 evaluations presented on cards. The DIAGNOSE operation was cued by the experimenter's asking for a justification of the evaluative choice. The CHOOSE TACTIC operation was simplified to a choice of six directives, also on cards. As a more general simplification, the focus of evaluations—and consequently the focus of the whole CDO process—was limited in range. Whereas in normal composing the CDO process might be applied to anything from doubtful spellings to a general sense that the composition was not turning out right, evaluations in this experiment were restricted, through the choices available on cards, to a middle range of concerns such as interest, clarity, and plausibility. The reason for this was to provide ample choices in this range, to direct attention away from the mechanical problems children are inclined to worry about already and at the same time to avoid high-level problems that might simply baffle them. This restriction, of course, is one that would gradually be relaxed and then removed as skill increased.

This procedure was tested in individual sessions with 90 children from grades 4, 6, and 8. Half used it while composing a first draft; half used it as a revision procedure applied to a previously written draft. None of the children had any trouble incorporating the procedure into their normal activity and most claimed it made their work easier—an indication that at least the effort to minimize information-processing load was effective. Virtually all the children stated in some way that the introduction of this new self-regulatory function allowed them to manage the composing process in a way that they were unable to do on their own. The following quotations are some of the more explicit ones:

Grade 8 child: If you could ask yourself the questions the cards have, then you could write something good.

Grade 8 child: You can use the cards to realize what you're saying. After a little while you wouldn't have to use the cards but could get it in your head and it would be faster. Right now I'd need to use the cards because I don't think of those questions.

Grade 4 child: They had all the things down on paper and you just look at it and you can think. The other way you have to get it out of your head. You can't think in your head sometimes.

This last Vygotskian sentiment, we might mention, is not unique. We keep running into children who express quite a detached view of their brain and its limitations, including some who seem to have a direct experience of limited working memory capacity.

Even though the children had only one session of experience with the procedure, so that little actual learning could have occurred, there was evidence of a positive effect on performance. They made more revisions than normal and changes for the better outnumbered changes for the worse—something that cannot be taken for granted in children of this age (Bracewell, Scardamalia, & Bereiter, 1978).

In experiments with procedural facilitations, we have consistently found that the effect on performance is limited to what one could expect to come directly from the regulatory function being facilitated. In one experiment, we provided a facilitating routine similar in form to the one described here but concerned instead with switching children back and forth between text generation and choice of abstract discourse elements (Bereiter, Scardamalia, Anderson, & Smart, 1980). The only observed effect on performance was an increase in the number and variety of discourse elements used. Such specific effects add plausibility to the theory behind the procedural facilitation. If, in fact, what has happened is that a particular self-regulatory function has been added to the child's executive procedure, the immediate effects should be limited to aspects of performance influenced by that function. As this new function became more fully integrated into the executive system and began to influence other functions, as well as the overall procedure, one would expect the effects to become more general.

In ending this section we want to underline the discriminative force of the adjective *procedural* in procedural facilitation. There is another much more common type of facilitation used in teaching, which we may call *substantive* facilitation. In substantive facilitation the overall executive burden is reduced by having the teacher or some other agent directly assume part of it and thus function as an active collaborator. With respect to the CDO process, for instance, a traditional school practice is for the teacher to do all but the last phase of it. Through comments on the student's composition, the teacher evaluates, diagnoses, and sometimes suggests the general type of remedy (to split up an overlong sentence, recast a paragraph, etc.), leaving GENERATE ALTERNATIVE as the only part of the process for the student to perform. In planning compositions, teachers sometimes collaborate in the selection of topics and content by asking questions and responding with encouragement to promising ideas. Substantive facilitation can no doubt be educationally worthwhile through freeing the student to attend to one function by taking over responsibility for others. It is not our intention to evaluate substantive facilitation here but only to point out that it is different from procedural facilitation. In procedural facilitation the facilitator, be it live teacher or inanimate set of cards, functions somewhat as conductor to soloist, but neither as puppeteer to puppet nor as partner in a duet.

CONCRETIZING OF GOALS

With the half-dozen different kinds of procedural facilitation in writing that we have investigated, we find in every case that a few children seem to use the added support as a way of tackling higher level goals. These are children who seem already to have a notion of what they would like to achieve in writing that exceeds their executive capabilities, so that any boost to these capabilities is exploited in the service of goals. Many elementary school children, however, appear to assimilate the new executive function to their established way of writing and exploit it as a way of making their job easier. In the case of one of our less successful facilitations this was true of almost all the children. Given sentence openers intended to facilitate more sophisticated choices of genre elements ("On the other hand . . . ," "This is like . . . ," and so on), they used them merely as cues to help think of something to say next.

As we have tried to show in our other chapter in this volume, children tend to approach expository writing as a task of telling what they know rather than a task of reaching some composition goal. Procedural facilitation cannot directly alter this tendency. But it also seems that a reorientation cannot be achieved by exhortation or other frontal means, because of the subtle and complicated nature of goal pursuit in compositional tasks. Accordingly, we have sought to devise some means whereby children who have not yet reached the point of formulating compositional goals for themselves could gain experience in pursuing such goals and begin to develop executive strategies for pursuing them.

A technique that seems promising is *concretizing of goals*. This technique is the stock-in-trade of developmental research with logico-mathematical problems. If the child cannot understand a problem formulated in abstract terms—a proportionality problem, for instance—then find a concrete representation of the problem with a goal the child can understand—like the goal of getting a balance beam to balance. In the logico-mathematical realm, concretizing of goals depends on being able to demonstrate the logical equivalence of semantically different problems. In other task realms, however, logical equivalence is either not demonstrable or it is not germane. What we need instead is psychological equivalence. Thus, what we seek with compositional tasks is a way to create concrete, stable goals that will evoke the same kinds of mental activity as the more abstract, unstable goals of real-life compositional tasks. This is not easy, but we believe it is possible. To illustrate, let us review the characteristics of goals in compositional tasks:

1. At the outset of a compositional task, the goal is global—to find a rewarding job, to have a good time, to write a good story, etc. To say that the goal is global is to say that it does not specify (or even necessarily suggest) the nature of the end state. Typically, there are many different end states that might satisfy the goal—for instance, many different rewarding jobs. This is in contrast to commonly studied logico-mathematical problems where there is only one satisfactory end state and it is fully specified by the goal statement and is therefore known from the beginning—all the cannibals and missionaries are across the river, the balance beam balances, etc.

2. Success in achieving the global goal is typically not all-or-none, and evaluation of success is hampered by not knowing what the alternatives might have been. Thus it is possible to be satisfied or dissatisfied with a range of outcomes.

3. The desired end state becomes increasingly specified as work proceeds. For instance, in exploring different job possibilities, more definite constraints on what constitutes a "rewarding" job are established.

4. Some of these constraints may have to be abandoned because they are later discovered to be incompatible with other desired conditions or practical limitations. For instance, inability to find a house meeting certain livability requirements might force the house hunter to reconsider an initial constraint that the house be near to work.

Starting with a global goal, there are basically two ways of proceeding, which for simplicity we may call the "high road" and the "low road" (Bereiter &

Scardamalia, 1983a). The high-road way requires that one keep reassessing partial solutions and goal constraints in the light of each other and of the global goal. Thus there is a great deal of forward and backward analysis, making for an intellectually demanding task. The low-road way is based on avoiding goal constraints. The global goal is retained and influences the choice of actions, but finally whatever end state is achieved will probably suffice because it will in some degree satisfy the global goal and one will be unaware of the alternative end states that might have been achieved. The low-road way is not necessarily thoughtless, but it is entirely forward moving, concerned only with what comes next, rather than with the more difficult problem of closing a gap.

What we want to achieve instructionally, then, is some concrete goal that will get the children who are accustomed to the low road to practice the kinds of mental operations required on the high road. Let us consider first a simple everyday task that illustrates how a concretized goal might induce high-road mental activity.

The task, let us say, is to take two small children for an outing. The global goal is simply that adult and children should have a pleasant time. The high-road thinker may begin by considering various alternatives and rejecting them because they are too costly, because they involve too much travel, because they are too commercialized, etc. Out of these trial solutions a clearer goal specification emerges—going someplace not too far away, not expensive, and of some "worthwhile" entertainment value. Search of the newspaper brings to light a free puppet show that will meet these goal requirements, but it promises to draw a big crowd, and so it will be necessary to go early to get a good seat. This, however, raises the prospect of waiting in line a long time, a problem with young children, and so that solution is also set aside, with "no waiting" added as a specification to the goal state. However, no better alternative can be found, so the puppet show is reconsidered along with the subgoal of finding a way to keep the children entertained while waiting to get in. A bag lunch, books to read, and games to play are added to a plan that finally conforms to the now-elaborate definition of the goal state.

The low-road way, of course, is to pack the kids into a car, ask them what they would like to do, and take it from there. We have no wish to argue that in this particular instance the high-road way is best, only that it involves a distinctly different mental process. Now how might one induce this mental process? The way we suggest is by giving someone a problem like the following: Plan an outing with two small children so that when it is over you could say, "It was worthwhile for the kids and I enjoyed it too. It was economical, and, because of my careful planning, the kids were kept happy all the time even though we had a long wait."

In order to solve that problem, it would seem that one would have to go through much the same mental process that our high-road thinker went through in arriving at the same end state. There is an important difference in that the high-road thinker had to construct this end state, whereas now we are specifying it at the beginning. But it still seems reasonable that practice with goal-specified tasks like this would induce the kinds of goal-directed processing that would help people develop toward becoming high-road thinkers themselves. Note, furthermore, that we have not fully specified the goal. The solution need not be the puppet show; it could as well be going fishing off a pier. The point, simply, is that enough specification has been supplied to induce the desired goal-directed processing. As we indicate later, the amount of specification required to do this is a researchable variable.

An essential property of the goal specification is that it set up interdependent constraints. In our example, a single activity must be found that meets the constraints of economy, value for children, interest for an adult, a long period of waiting, and the possibility of keeping children entertained during the wait. The instructional purpose would not be served by specifying a set of constraints that could be met by dealing with them one at a time. As we see, students tend to try to deal with constraints one at a time anyway.

We have experimented with this identical way of specifying end states in composition. Jacqueline Tetroe of our research group has done extensive work, designing ending sentences and monitoring children's composing strategies as they try to produce a composition that will lead up to the specified ending sentence. An example of a sentence she has used is, "So that is how Melissa came to be at a laundromat at midnight with one million dollars in her bag and a mob of angry people behind her." Thinking-aloud protocols have shown that children do, in fact, engage in more goal-directed processing when given an ending to work toward than they do in the more common task of working forward from a topic or initial statement (Tetroe, Bereiter, & Scardamalia, 1981).

There remain, however, high-road and low-road routes that children take in working toward these ending sentences. Children taking the high road keep assessing partial solutions in the light of the given constraints and of the additional constraints added by earlier decisions. They typically think their way well through to a solution before committing anything to paper. Children taking the low road will deal with one or two constraints (for instance, thinking of a reason for Melissa to go to a laundromat at night). Having committed themselves to a solution meeting the initial constraints, they may begin writing the story and then stop to think about how to meet the next constraint (for instance, how to account for the million dollars). As each additional constraint is considered, the problem of holding the composition together becomes more difficult. Sometimes this is handled by backing up and taking another tack, but more often by resorting to increasingly implausible or irrelevant connections.

It should be noted here that even when children are taking the low road they are still engaged in means–end analysis to an extent not found in their normal composing behavior. Moreover, on questioning they often show an awareness of the difficulties they have gotten into and when asked how they would proceed if they thought things out more, they describe the high-road strategy—and in some cases can switch to it. Tetroe is currently investigating to what extent children can adopt the high-road strategy by choice and to what extent their ability to do this depends on the number of constraints they must deal with. The "Melissa" sentence cited contains a heavy load of constraints. Reduced versions of it can be presented, for instance, by deleting "at midnight" and "angry."

We have so far been illustrating goal concretization that involves adding specifications to the end state. There is another kind of goal concretization that we have investigated casually, and for which we have designed a large number of learning tasks (Scardamalia, Bereiter, & Fillion, 1981). In this kind, the goal is made concrete but its specifications are left up to the learner to construct. Here, for instance, is an activity in which the global goal is to achieve realism in a narrative. This goal, however, is concretized in the following activity:

> Students are grouped into teams of three to discuss interesting personal experiences. They choose one person's experience, discuss it in detail, and each student goes off to write about it as if it happened to him or herself. The teacher may remind students that their stories should contain no real names. Each student in a team reads his or her story aloud and the class tries to guess which of the three stories was written by the person the experience actually happened to. The writer succeeds by convincing the class that his or her narrative is the true account.

Thus the abstract and intangible goal of realism is replaced by the concrete goal of producing a fictitious narrative that will pass for a true account. Yet the actual characteristics of the end state, the constraints that must be met in order for the concrete goal to be achieved, are left entirely to the student. Tasks of this sort, we believe, bring the student just one step short of the full act of dealing with emergent goals. The remaining step is to go from global goals to progressive goal specification without need for an intervening concrete goal. We turn to that as yet unsolved problem in the next section.

GOAL CONSTRUCTION

The two instructional approaches that we have described so far—procedural facilitation and goal concretizing—clearly need to be used in combination. One influences the cognitive means children employ but leaves the goals open, the other influences the goals they pursue but leaves the means open. Even in combination, however, they do not deal with the whole of what is involved in mature performance on compositional tasks. The missing element, as we have indicated, is movement from initial global goals—which are more or less in the nature of felt needs—to the specification of an end state that arises out of and further guides purposive behavior. This goal constructing activity is what spells the big difference between responding to impinging problems and contextually defined goals and what we have elsewhere described as *intentional cognition* (Bereiter & Scardamalia, 1983b).

We are currently experimenting with inducing goal construction and goal-directed planning in writing by using procedural facilitation of the planning process itself, rather than procedural facilitation of operations on text as in the example cited previously (Scardamalia, Bereiter, & Steinbach, 1984). In extended instructional work with a single sixth-grade class, it has become apparent that goal construction is the most difficult planning operation to induce, but that progress can be made. Procedural facilitation alone does not suffice. We have supplemented it by modeling the process through thinking aloud, by having individual students model the process in front of the class and receive comments, and by providing appropriately simplified presentations of such concepts as dialectic.

Moving to the "high road" of goal-directed processing in knowledge-rich domains is a complex and many-sided achievement. Many people in our culture appear to fall short of it. This achievement will not be brought about, we fear, by instructional approaches of either a technical or a romantic simplicity. As Whitehead (1929) said, "You are up against too skillful an adversary, who will see to it that the pea is always under the other thimble." It seems essential to enlist children's full support in the educational effort, to communicate to them somehow, through modeling or precept, an image of the psychological state they are to attain. Experience to date encourages us to believe that children become willing allies in the instructional process once they glimpse what it means to construct cognitive goals for themselves and to regulate their cognitive activity in light of such goals.

REFERENCES

Bereiter, C., & Scardamalia, M. (1983a). Does learning to write have to be so difficult? In A. Freedman, I. Pringle, & J. Yalden (Eds.), *Learning to write: First language, second language* (pp. 20–33). New York: Longman Inc.

Bereiter, C., & Scardamalia, M. (1983b). Schooling and the growth of intentional cognition: Helping children take charge of their own minds. In Z. Lamm (Ed.), *New trends in education* (pp. 73–100). Tel–Aviv: Yachdev United Publishing Co.

Bereiter, C., Scardamalia, M., Anderson, V., & Smart, D. (1980, April). *An experiment in teaching abstract planning in writing.* Paper presented at the meeting of the American Educational Research Association, Boston.

Bobrow, D. G., & Norman, D. A. (1975). Some principles of memory schemata. In D. G. Bobrow & A. Collins (Eds.), *Representation and understanding: Studies in cognitive science* (pp. 131–149). New York: Academic Press.

Bracewell, R. J., Scardamalia, M., & Bereiter, C. (1978, October). The development of audience awareness in writing. *Resources in Education.* (ERIC Document Reproduction Service No. ED 154 433)

Brown, A. L., & Campione, J. C. (1981). *Inducing flexible thinking: A problem of access.* In M. Friedman, J. P. Das, & N. O'Connor (Eds.) *Intelligence and learning* (pp. 515–529). New York: Plenum.

Case, R. (1975). Gearing the demands of instruction to the development capacities of the learner. *Review of Educational Research, 45,* 59–87.

Case, R. (1978). Piaget and beyond: Toward a developmentally based theory and technology of instruction. In R. Glaser (Ed.), *Advances in instructional psychology* (Vol 1, pp. 167–228). Hillsdale, NJ: Lawrence Erlbaum Associates.

Flavell, J. H. (1979). Metacognition and cognitive monitoring: A new area of cognitive-developmental inquiry. *American Psychologist, 34,* 906–911.

Flower, L. (1981). *Problem-solving strategies for writing.* New York: Harcourt Brace Jovanovich.

Greeno, J. G. (1978). Natures of problem-solving abilities. In W. K. Estes (Ed.), *Handbook of learning and cognitive processes* (Vol. 5, pp. 239–270). Hillsdale, NJ: Wiley.

Hayes, J. R., & Flower, L. (1980). Identifying the organization of writing processes. In L. W. Gregg & E. R. Steinberg (Eds.), *Cognitive processes in writing.* Hillsdale, NJ: Lawrence Erlbaum Associates.

Krashen, S. D. (1976, June). Formal and informal linguistic environments in language acquisition and language learning. *TESOL Quarterly, 10*(2), 157–168.

Matsuhashi, A. (1982). Explorations in the real-time production of written discourse. In M. Nystrand (Ed.), *What Writers Know: The language, process, and structure of written discourse* (pp. 269–290). New York: Academic Press.

Nold, E. W. (1981). Revising. In C. H. Frederiksen, & J. F. Dominic (Eds.), *Writing: The nature, development and teaching of written communication* (pp. 67–79). Hillsdale, NJ: Lawrence Erlbaum Associates.

Polya, G. (1945). *How to solve it.* Princeton, NJ: Princeton University Press.

Scardamalia, M., & Bereiter, C. (1983). The development of evaluative, diagnostic, and remedial capabilities in children's composing. In M. Martlew (Ed.), *The psychology of written language: A developmental approach* (pp. 67–95). London: Wiley.

Scardamalia, M., Bereiter, C., & Fillion, B. (1981). *Writing for results: A sourcebook of consequential composing activities.* Toronto: OISE Press. (Also, LaSalle, IL: Open Court Publishing Company, 1981.)

Scardamalia, M., Bereiter, C., & Steinbach, R. (1984). Teachability of reflective processes in written composition. *Cognitive Science, 8*(2), 173–190.

Tetroe, J., Bereiter, C., & Scardamalia, M. (1981, April). *How to make a dent in the writing process.* Paper presented at the meeting of the American Educational Research Association, Los Angeles.

Whitehead, A. N. (1929). *The aims of education.* New York: Macmillan.

Wilkins, A. J. & Baddeley, A. D. (1978). Remembering to recall in everyday life: An approach to absentmindedness. In M. M. Gruneberg, P. Morris, & R. N. Sykes (Eds.), *Practical aspects of memory* (pp. 27–34). London: Academic Press.

Woodruff, E., Bereiter, C., & Scardamalia, M. (1981). *On the road to computer assisted compositions. Journal of Educational Technology Systems, 10*(2), 133–148.

Young, R. E., Becker, A. L., & Pike, K. E. (1970). *Rhetoric: Discovery and change.* New York: Harcourt, Brace, & World.

26 Teaching Reasoning Skills

Allan Collins
Bolt Beranek and Newman Inc.

During this century, there has been a variety of movements to teach thinking skills along with domain-specific knowledge in the schools. These movements have not been altogether successful, but they have made some inroads. Today, our schools probably teach less by rote than in earlier centuries.

I view this volume as a symptom of another of these movements: this one specifically addressed to teaching thinking strategies. As a movement, it has two things going for it that the earlier movements clearly lacked:

1. *Research in the cognitive sciences:* With the vast amount of research on metacognition (Brown, 1978; Flavell, 1978), knowledge representation (Bobrow & Winograd, 1977; Minsky, 1975; Quillian, 1968), planning and problem solving (Hayes–Roth & Hayes–Roth, 1979; Newell & Simon, 1972), and language processing (Chomsky, 1965; Schank & Abelson, 1977; Winograd, 1972; Woods, 1970), there now exists a fundamental base of knowledge about cognitive processes that was outside the purview of the earlier behavioristic psychology.

2. *New technology:* With the invention of the computer and the accumulation of both computational capabilities and techniques, a new kind of educational technology is appearing (Goldstein & Brown, 1979; Sleeman & Brown, 1982). This makes it possible to embed cognitive theories into computer environments for children. It does not require direct reform of teacher education or the school systems, as did the earlier movements.

I see our work on inquiry teaching (Collins, 1977; Collins & Stevens, 1982, 1983) as a bridge between earlier attempts to teach cognitive skills and the current movement. We have been studying transcripts of a variety of teachers who use the inquiry, discovery, Socratic, or case methods derived from these earlier movements (Anderson & Faust, 1974; Davis, 1966; Sigel & Saunders, 1979; Silberman, Allender, & Yanoff, 1972). Among the teachers we have been analyzing are some of the most famous in the country, including Professor Max Beberman, Richard Anderson, and Robert Davis of the University of Illinois; Professor Arthur Miller of Harvard Law School; and Professor Roger Schank of Yale. Our analysis is built upon the formalisms that have been developed recently in the cognitive sciences. In particular, the analysis is cast in terms of the goals, strategies, and control structure that a computer could use to simulate the human teachers (Newell & Simon, 1972).

One of the major goals that the teachers we have analyzed pursue is to teach students the kinds of thinking skills required to be a scientist or mathematician. They do this in two ways: (1) by systematically questioning students to make them think about the relevant aspects of the problem they are working on and (2) by modeling the thinking skills they want the students to adopt.

The kinds of thinking skills we think the student learns from these methods are: forming hypotheses, testing hypotheses, making predictions, selecting optimal cases to test a theory, generating counterexamples and hypothetical cases, distinguishing between necessary and sufficient conditions, considering alternative hypotheses, and knowing the forms that rules and theories can take. These do not encompass all the cognitive skills one would want to include in a cognitive-skills curriculum. In particular, they omit metacognitive and planning skills we think are important. But these are important skills to learn, and the inquiry methods may be the most effective way to teach them.

In this chapter, we summarize the most important strategies of the teachers we have analyzed. These strategies are described in much more detail elsewhere (Collins & Stevens, 1982). In Collins and Stevens (1983), we show how they can be applied in such diverse domains as arithmetic, geography, and moral education.

EXPERT TEACHING STRATEGIES

Systematic Selection of Cases

In the dialogues, the most essential aspect of the case and discovery methods is the way the teachers choose cases. There are systematic patterns to the case selection strategies. We have identified 10 major strategies that characterize the way teachers select cases. We describe each of these in the following sections.

Positive Paradigm Case. A paradigm case is one where values of all the relevant factors are consistent with a particular value of the dependent variable. For example, in teaching about the factors that affect rainfall, teachers pick cases like the Amazon, Oregon, and Ireland where all the relevant factors have values that lead to heavy rainfall.

Negative Paradigm Case.   A negative paradigm case is one where all the factors have values going in the opposite direction. For rainfall, southern California, northern Africa, and northern Chile are negative paradigm cases, because all the relevant factors have values that lead to little rainfall.

Negative Exemplar for a Necessary Factor (a Near Miss).   If the teacher wants to highlight a necessary factor that the student has not mentioned, a case is selected where all but one of the necessary factors have values consistent with a particular value of the dependent variable. This is Winston's (1973) "near miss" strategy. For example, if the teacher wants to highlight the fact that you need good soil to grow rice, he or she might pick a case like Florida, where rice could be grown except for the poor soil.

Positive Exemplar for an Unnecessary Factor (a Near Hit).   If the teacher wants to highlight an alternative value for some factor that the students think must have a particular value, the teacher can pick a case that has the alternative value for the factor and the given value on the dependent variable (i.e., a near hit). For example, a teacher can illustrate that you don't need heavy rainfall for rice growing, by choosing a case like Egypt where rice can be grown by irrigation, even though there is little rainfall.

Generalization Exemplar for a Factor (a Maximal Pair).   Teachers often choose cases that have a specific relation to a previous case. One such strategy is to pick a case where the factors the teacher is focusing on and the dependent variable have the same value as in the previous case, but most other factors vary. For example, suppose the teacher has discussed why the Amazon has heavy rainfall. Then he or she might pick the Oregon coast, where less relevant factors like the latitude, temperature, and wind direction are different, but the underlying factors leading to heavy rainfall are the same.

Differentiation Exemplar for a Factor (a Minimal Pair).   Another comparison strategy is to pick a new exemplar that is as much like the previous example as possible except for differences on the focused factors and the dependent variable. This is the minimal pair strategy in linguistics (cf. Gleason, 1961). For example, a teacher might ask why Java has high population density, whereas a nearby island such as Borneo has low population density.

Exemplar to Show the Variability of a Factor.   Teachers sometimes illustrate the range over which a particular factor can vary without affecting the value of the dependent variable. For example, to illustrate the range of temperatures over which rice can be grown, a teacher might choose Japan at the cool end of the range and Java at the warm end.

Exemplar to Show the Variability of the Dependent Variable.   Similarly, it is possible to illustrate the range over which the dependent variable can vary for a given value of some factor. For example, to illustrate how temperature varies for a given latitude, a teacher might pick the Congo jungle at one extreme and the top of Kilimanjaro at the other extreme.

Counterexample for Insufficient Factors.   When a student explains the dependent variable in terms of insufficient factors, the teacher often picks a counterexample that has the given values for the factor but not for the dependent variable. For example, if a student attributed rice growing in Louisiana to the rainfall there, the teacher might pick Oregon, where there is heavy rainfall but no rice is grown.

Counterexample for Unnecessary Factors.   When a student explains the dependent variable in terms of unnecessary factors, the teacher often picks a counterexample that has the given value for the dependent variable but not for the factors. For example, when the student attributes rice growing to heavy rainfall, the teacher might pick Egypt as a counterexample, because they grow rice there without much rainfall.

These are not the complete set of case selection strategies (see Collins & Stevens, 1982, 1983). In particular, in law and moral education dialogues, teachers often construct hypothetical cases to test the students' reasoning. The hypotheticals can occur in all 10 of these forms.

These case selection strategies are teaching the students thinking skills in two ways. They model important strategies experts use to choose test cases. At the same time, they force the student to induce more refined theories. Students are learning how to refine their own theories by considering relevant cases.

Systematic Questioning of Students

Teachers use a variety of strategies to systematically question students in order to get them to reason about different cases. These strategies teach various reasoning skills: forming hypotheses, testing hypotheses, making predictions, considering alternative predictions, knowing the forms that rules or theories can take, knowing what questions to ask, etc. We describe eight of the most important strategies that teachers use to force students to learn these reasoning skills.

Asking Students to Form Hypotheses.   Teachers frequently probe students to formulate general rules relating particular factors to given values of the dependent variable. For example, in one dialogue, Anderson (see Collins, 1977) tried to get the student to formulate how average temperature depends jointly on distance from the ocean and latitude.

Asking Students to Test Hypotheses.   Teachers also ask students to test the hypotheses they have formulated. For example, Anderson tried to get the student to evaluate the hypothesis that winter temperature decreases as distance from the ocean increases by comparing cities at different distances from the ocean, while holding latitude constant.

Asking Students to Make Predictions.   Teachers ask students to make predictions about novel cases that have different values for particular factors. For example, in teaching about grain growing, the teacher might ask students to predict what grains can be grown in Nigeria or Argentina.

Asking Students to Consider Alternative Predictions.   Teachers sometimes propose alternative values of the dependent variable for the students to consider with respect to known factors. For example, if a student had suggested they grow rice in Nigeria, based on the warm temperature and heavy rainfall, the teacher might ask the student to consider whether wheat could be grown in that climate.

Entrapping Students into Revealing Their Misconceptions.   Teachers often pose questions designed to entrap students into proposing or agreeing to potential misconceptions. This teaches students to avoid certain kinds of pitfalls that are fairly common. A common entrapment strategy that Anderson (see Collins, 1977) and Davis (1966) use (the latter calls it "torpedoing") is to lead the student into an overgeneralization. For example, if a student suggests they grow rice in Louisiana because it rains a lot, the teacher might ask "Can they grow rice anywhere it rains a lot?"

Tracing Consequences to a Contradiction.   Sometimes a teacher will ask students to trace out the logical consequences of an answer until they see the contradiction between what they said and what they believe. This teaches students to "debug" their own theories. For example, if the student asserted that it was possible to grow rice anywhere it rained a lot, the teacher could point out that it rains a lot in the southern part of Alaska and ask the student a series of questions about the climate, terrain, and the possibility of growing rice there, until the student sees the difficulty.

Encouraging Students to Formulate Alternative Hypotheses.   In classroom settings, teachers often encourage the students to verbalize alternative rules or theories to the ones already formulated. For example, if a student formulated the rule that places further from ocean tend to be colder on the average, a teacher might ask another student if he or she thinks that is correct, or if he or she wants to formulate an alternative hypothesis.

Encouraging Students to Question Authority.   In several cases, teachers objected when students appealed to either the book or the teachers for correct predictions or hypotheses. Inquiry teachers clearly try to force students to formulate their own hypotheses. For example, if a student asked the teacher to say how temperature depends on distance from the ocean, the teacher would encourage the student to form a hypothesis and then test it out by considering different cases.

ADVANTAGES AND DISADVANTAGES OF THE INQUIRY METHOD

One important question is why the inquiry, discovery, and case methods we have described are rather infrequently used. In this section, we briefly discuss the costs and benefits of inquiry teaching and when it is most appropriate to use.

There are a number of advantages that the inquiry method has over other methods. It provides:

1. *Modeling of scientific thinking.*   The method teaches students strategies for dealing with any new problem. To the degree they learn to internalize (or model) the strategies the teacher uses, they have learned a powerful set of heuristics for dealing with the world.

2. *Involvement and motivation.*   The students are participants in formulating and evaluating theories. They may recreate theories the Greeks first developed or even create new theories. This gives them a personal stake in the ideas, and some of the kind of exhilaration a scientist feels.

3. *Individualization.*   The teacher is dealing with the students' ideas individually. Teachers thus can shape what they say to the specific knowledge and misconceptions of each student.

4. *Deep understanding.*   The method enables the teacher to probe students with difficult cases and entrapments to ensure that they learn the material well.

5. *Predictive thinking.*   The method ensures that the students not only learn specific rules and theories, but also how to use these to make predictions about novel situations.

But these advantages are not sufficient to make the method widely used. We think there are several disadvantages that make this so. They are:

1. *Low information-transfer rate.*   It is much faster to get information across to students by lectures or reading. For this reason, the inquiry method, where

used widely, is usually combined with extensive reading. The inquiry dialogues then are based on the readings.

2. *Negative reinforcement.* In a classroom, the inquiry method can lead to exposing the ignorance or misconceptions of particular students, which can make the students feel bad. This did not happen in any of the dialogues we analyzed, but clearly the potential is there. It takes a sensitive teacher not to turn the inquiry method into an inquisition.

3. *Uncertain participation.* In a classroom it is possible for the teacher to interact with whichever students offer ideas and suggestions. If a student cannot follow what is happening, the student will not say anything. So the teacher has to be careful to make sure everyone is participating.

4. *Reliance on the sophistication of the teacher.* To use the method successfully, the teacher must be able to think quickly, must avoid the pitfalls previously described, and must know the subject matter well enough to handle novel situations. Preparing for inquiry classes is not like preparing a lecture or lesson plan; in fact, the method requires less preparation time. It does not involve following a script in any sense, but rather choosing cases and problems wisely. We think difficulties arise because teachers are unfamiliar with the method and have not had practice using it.

5. *No evidence for the method's effectiveness.* As Anderson and Faust (1974) point out, there is no evidence that the method is more effective than lectures. This is not surprising because of the low information-transfer rate inherent in the method. If the method is effective, it is because it teaches students to think scientifically, to make predictions, and to have deep (as opposed to rote) understanding. But it is difficult to design tests to measure these abilities and there are very few that do. (An exception is the problem-solving test described by Frederiksen, 1979.) So the method may be a very effective way to accomplish the higher level goals of teaching, but we simply do not know that it is.

Our view then is that the inquiry method is likely to be most effective in teaching thinking skills and in teaching deep understanding of rules or theories. Where that is the teacher's goal, then the kind of strategies we have detailed in this chapter should be valuable.

ACKNOWLEDGMENTS

This research was sponsored by the National Institute of Education under Contract No. MS–NIE-C-400-76-0116 and, in part, by the Personnel and Training Research Programs, Psychological Sciences Division, Office of Naval Research and the Advanced Research Project Agency under Contract Number N00014-79-C-0338, Contract Authority Identification Number NR154–428.

REFERENCES

Anderson, R. C., & Faust, G. W. (1974). *Educational psychology: The science of instruction and learning*. New York: Dodd, Mead.

Bobrow, D. G., & Winograd, T. (1977). An overview of KRL, a knowledge representation language. *Cognitive Science, 3,* 3–46.

Brown, A. L. (1978). Knowing when, where, and how to remember: A problem of metacognition. In R. Glaser (Ed.), *Advances in instructional psychology* (Vol. 1). Hillsdale, NJ: Lawrence Erlbaum Associates.

Chomsky, N. (1965). *Aspects of the theory of syntax*. Cambridge, MA: MIT Press.

Collins, A. (1977). Processes in acquiring knowledge. In R. C. Anderson, R. J. Spiro, & W. E. Montague (Eds.), *Schooling and the acquisition of knowledge*. Hillsdale, NJ: Lawrence Erlbaum Associates.

Collins, A., & Stevens, A. L. (1982). Goals and strategies of inquiry teachers. In R. Glaser (Ed.), *Advances in instructional psychology* (Vol. 2). Hillsdale, NJ: Lawrence Erlbaum Associates.

Collins, A., & Stevens, A. L. (1983). A cognitive theory of interactive teaching. In C. M. Reigeluth (Ed.), *Instructional design theories and models: An overview*. Hillsdale, NJ: Lawrence Erlbaum Associates.

Davis, R. B. (1966). Discovery in the teaching of mathematics. In L. S. Shulman & E. R. Keisler (Eds.), *Learning by discovery: A critical appraisal*. Chicago: Rand McNally.

Flavell, J. H. (1978). Metacognitive development. In J. M. Scandura & C. J. Brainerd (Eds.), *Structural/process theories of complex human behavior*. Alphen a.d. Rijn, The Netherlands: Sijthoff & Nordhoff.

Frederiksen, N. (1979). Some emerging trends in testing. In *Testing, teaching and learning*. Washington, DC: National Institute of Education.

Gleason, H. A., Jr. (1961). *An introduction to descriptive linguistics* (rev. ed.). New York: Holt, Rinehart, & Winston.

Goldstein, I., & Brown, J. S. (1979). The computer as a personal assistant for learning. In J. Lochhead & J. Clement (Eds.), *Cognitive process instruction*. Philadelphia: The Franklin Institute Press.

Hayes-Roth, B., & Hayes-Roth, F. (1979). A cognitive model of planning. *Cognitive Science, 3,* 275–323.

Minsky, M. (1975). A framework for representing knowledge. In P. H. Winston (Ed.), *The psychology of computer vision*. New York: McGraw–Hill.

Newell, A., & Simon, H. A. (1972). *Human problem solving*. Englewood Cliffs, NJ: Prentice–Hall.

Quillian, M. R. (1968). Semantic memory. In M. Minsky (Ed.), *Semantic information processing*. Cambridge, MA: MIT Press.

Schank, R., & Abelson, R. (1977). *Scripts, plans, goals, and understanding*. Hillsdale, NJ: Lawrence Erlbaum Associates.

Sigel, I. E., & Saunders, R. (1979). An inquiry into inquiry: Question-asking as an instructional model. In L. Katz (Ed.), *Current topics in early childhood education*. Norwood, NJ: Ablex.

Silberman, M. L., Allender, J. S., & Yanoff, J. M. (1972). *The psychology of open teaching and learning*. Boston: Little, Brown.

Sleeman, D. H., & Brown, J. S. (Eds.). (1982). *Intelligent tutoring systems*. New York: Academic Press.

Winograd, T. (1972). *Understanding natural language*. New York: Academic Press.

Winston, P. (1973). Learning to identify toy block structures. In R. L. Solso (Ed.), *Contemporary issues in cognitive psychology: The Loyola Symposium*. Washington, DC: Winston.

Woods, W. A. (1970). Transition network grammars for natural language analysis. *Communications of the ACM, 13,* 591–606.

27

On Meeting the Challenge

Mary Carol Day
AT&T

The organizing question for the chapters of this group was "How can cognitive skills be taught?" Not only the chapters of this group, but all the chapters of these volumes present ideas and research that are pertinent to this question. Note that the way the question is phrased indicates the belief that cognitive skills *can* be taught. Indeed, many of the chapters presented offer not only that belief but evidence for its validity.

The belief that cognitive skills can be taught is not new. Alfred Binet, in his *Les Idees Modernes Sur Les Enfants* (1911/1962), expressed the same belief some time ago (see also Brown, this volume):

> Now if one considers that intelligence is not a simple indivisible function with a particular essence of its own, but that it is formed by the combination of all the minor functions of discrimination, observation, retention, etc., all of which have proved to be plastic and subject to increase, it will seem incontestable that the same law governs the ensemble and its elements, and that consequently the intelligence of anyone is susceptible of development. With practice, enthusiasm, and especially with method, one can succeed in increasing one's attention, memory, and judgment, and in becoming literally more intelligent than before; and this process will go on until one reaches one's limit.

> Having on our hands children who did not know how to listen, to pay attention, to keep quiet, we pictured our first duty as being not to teach them facts that we thought would be most useful, but to teach them how to learn. We have therefore devised what we call exercises of mental orthopedics. . . . In the same way that physical orthopedics straightens a crooked spine, mental orthopedics strengthens, cultivates, and fortifies attention, memory, perception, judgment, and will. (p. 143, p. 150)

Based on the chapters presented in this volume, an immediate answer to the question of how cognitive skills can be taught is the following: Cognitive skills can be taught in a great many ways, within various content areas, with varying degrees of success, and with varying degrees of transfer to other contexts. However, a more precise answer that reflects a *comprehensive* understanding of cognitive skills and their acquisition will require a great deal more research.

I think those of us interested in teaching cognitive skills are faced with what Scardamalia and Bereiter term a *compositional task*. They state:

> These are tasks in which the goal is at least partly emergent—your knowledge of what you are after grows and changes as part of the knowledge-constructing process— and in which there is a wealth of potentially applicable knowledge and potential routes to the goal. (this volume)

We have a goal that is generally stated—that of teaching cognitive skills—but that goal has not yet been made concrete in a way that satisfies us all. We have a large body of potentially applicable knowledge about the processes involved in reasoning and problem solving. We have solid demonstrations of a variety of instructional techniques that offer many potential routes to the still-emerging goal. At this point, then, the goal of teaching cognitive skills is a compositional task. As we conduct research on cognitive skills, as we teach and evaluate the effects of our instruction, and as we assess the transfer of specific skills and of metacognitive skills to new situations, we will probably change our current conception of the goal and of the optimal means of achieving it.

One likely consequence of engaging in the compositional task of teaching cognitive skills is increased specificity of both the question and its answer. The overarching question has at least three components that must specifically be addressed: (1) what particular cognitive skills, (2) taught to whom, and (3) using what instructional techniques? The answers to all three questions are obviously interrelated. In the remainder of my comments, I briefly address each component of this global question.

WHAT PARTICULAR COGNITIVE SKILLS?

Quite diverse sets of cognitive skills have been studied by the scientists and program developers represented in these volumes. The diversity of these skills has been a frequent topic of discussion, and special attention has been given to the location of skills on a specific-to-general continuum. Specific skills are those that are used in one content domain (and perhaps with that content domain in only one particular context). General skills are skills useful in a variety of content domains in a variety of contexts. Another distinction between types of thinking skills that has been mentioned frequently is that between cognitive and meta-cognitive skills. Flavell (1979) has defined the distinction as follows: "Cognitive strategies are invoked to *make* cognitive progress, metacognitive strategies to *monitor* it" (p. 909). Clearly the good problem solver possesses metacognitive skills, as well as both general and specific cognitive strategies. All contribute to making a good problem solver. To be a good problem solver in a particular content area requires substantial knowledge of that content area, i.e., a repertoire of content-related knowledge and strategies. Solving problems with the content-specific information requires somewhat more general strategies, and, in addition, appropriate deployment of the more general strategies requires strategies that fall under the rubric of self-regulatory mechanisms such as planning and checking (Brown & DeLoache, 1978). An important function of self-regulatory mechanisms may be not only to control cognitive activities but also to regulate anxiety and stress that may occur in attempts to solve difficult problems. The work that is presented in this volume by Case, by Collins, and by Scardamalia and Bereiter covers skills that range from the specific to the general.

In his research on a particular *executive control structure,* Case's focus falls near the specific end of the specific-to-general continuum. Many of the executive control structures he discusses have as components the particular problem situation and its objective. For example, in the first problem analyzed in his chapter, the problem situation is a balance beam (with a varying number of relevant features encoded) and the objective is to "find which side will go down." More-over, in his approach to instruction, Case refers specifically to a particular kind of content domain, i.e., the domain must involve skills that are of increasing complexity and that are related to each other hierarchically. Two implications of this point are noteworthy. First, teaching cognitive skills for domains that do not meet this criterion may require a different approach. Second, skills useful in one domain that meets the criterion may not be useful in other domains that meet the criterion.

However, there are undoubtedly some skills that are useful in a variety of domains and that would show up in more than one content-specific analysis. For example, one executive control structure used in various content domains is the *control-of-variables* strategy: In order to determine which of a set of factors influences an outcome, each factor must be tested while holding all other factors constant. (Note that this strategy can itself immediately become more complex if each factor is tested at every possible combination of the other factors.) The control-of-variables strategy is used widely in scientific investigation, offering prima facie evidence that it is generalizable across content domains. However, it should also be noted that its application in a particular content domain requires enough knowledge of content to identify potentially relevant factors. Thus, content-specific knowledge is necessary for optimal use of this particular executive control structure. Furthermore, one must realize when it is appropriate to use the particular strategy. This knowledge may involve use of a higher order skill, such as evaluating possible alternative approaches to problem solution.

The cognitive skills addressed by Collins are more general. They are "the kinds of thinking skills required to be a scientist and mathematician," and they constitute means to some particular goal. They include forming and testing hypotheses, making predictions, selecting optimal cases to test a theory, generating counterexamples and hypothetical cases, etc. These are skills that can be used across a wide range of particular content areas. Again, it should be noted that skills at both a more general and a more specific level are encompassed by the skills discussed by Collins. The optimal use of Collins' thinking skills requires some prerequisite knowledge of the content area being addressed, knowledge of more specific strategies involved in an activity like testing hypotheses (such as the control-of-variables strategy), and use of more general skills like planning and monitoring.

Scardamalia and Bereiter are concerned with strategies for "complex-knowledge processing tasks" or compositional tasks. They argue that specific algorithms for solving compositional tasks cannot be stated, because the strategies adopted are highly context dependent and the *specific* goal is often defined only through working on the problem. Scardamalia and Bereiter's research arena is expository writing, which they argue is paradigmatic for compositional tasks. The specific goal for a paper on a defined topic changes as writing progresses. Revision and the constant assessment of progress, in light of constraints on the global goal, are examples of self-regulatory mechanisms that are important in expository writing. Scardamalia and Bereiter move from the statement of these general, self-regulatory skills to a specification of particular cognitive activities that are components of the self-regulatory skills, such as revision. These more specific cognitive activities can then be taught, with the expectation that with practice, children will independently use these activities and perhaps other activities subsumed under the rubric of revision.

In sum, this set of chapters addresses cognitive skills that are intermediate in generality. The use of intermediate skills requires more specific skills as subcomponents. In addition, use of these skills outside of the contexts in which they were learned requires that more general skills invoke the intermediate skills when needed.

TAUGHT TO WHOM?

This question—to whom will cognitive skills be taught—is a critical one and deserves explicit consideration. The particular skills to be taught and the most appropriate means of teaching are likely to vary with the characteristics of the learners. Three characteristics that are particularly important are knowledge base, developmental level, and cultural background.

Knowledge base includes both substantive content knowledge and skill, or strategy knowledge. It has long been noted that the best instruction builds on what the learner already knows. Thus, the best instruction in cognitive skills would begin with some type of assessment of the learner's current mastery of the skills of interest and of the content area within which the skills are to be taught (and perhaps of the content area to which it is hoped the skills will be transferred).

The importance of *developmental level* is demonstrated by a wealth of data. In general, it has been found that children of different ages differ in the ease with which they learn cognitive skills (e.g., Case, 1974; Siegler, 1976; Stone & Day, 1978). As a correlate, the manner in which a specific skill should be taught is likely to vary with developmental level. In his chapter, Case made explicit the factors that he believes affect the learning of cognitive skills. They include working memory, mastery of the basic skills involved in executing the executive control structure, the current repertoire of strategies, and current content knowledge. The first is a developmental variable; the latter three are knowledge base variables.

Finally, the *cultural background* of the learner would probably influence the current knowledge base and, perhaps just as importantly, the manner of expressing that knowledge base and the attitudes that are brought to an instructional situation. (See De Avila's and Franklin's chapters, this volume.)

USING WHAT INSTRUCTIONAL TECHNIQUES?

Again I stress the interrelationship of all the components that are involved in the compositional task of designing instruction for cognitive skills. The most appropriate method of instruction will depend, to a large extent, on the particular skills being taught, on the characteristics of the learners, and on the goal of instruction (e.g., solution of a particular problem or use of the skill with a variety of problems). In his chapter, Case outlined a method of instruction that he terms executive facilitation; it involves an explicit consideration of all these factors. I think his approach would be quite useful for teaching a variety of cognitive skills. As Case himself notes, however, one constraint on the use of his instructional technique is that the skills in the domain must increase in complexity and be hierarchically related; that is, one must be able to state precisely the cognitive skills to be taught and the relationships among them. Scardamalia and Bereiter mention this constraint when they stress the difficulty of teaching strategies for compositional tasks, where a specific goal cannot be stated in advance, and thus specific, content-laden strategies cannot be directly taught. This contrast provides one example of the necessity for instructional method to vary with the particular cognitive skills being taught.

Rather than detailing the specific instructional approaches mentioned in each of the chapters, I emphasize a commonality that is especially striking—the provision of an external support for what is to become internal. Case notes that one effect of his executive facilitation is the reduction of the child's working memory load: "In the early phases, the instructor should function as an 'external executive,' removing some of the planning burden from the child." He also documents various procedures that serve as external memory aids. In Collins' Socratic approach to teaching reasoning skills, the teachers' primary techniques are "modeling the thinking skills they want children to adopt" and "systematically questioning students to make them think about the relevant aspects of the problem they are working on." Scardamalia and Bereiter's entire approach depends on providing supports for self-regulatory mechanisms so that these mechanisms can initially be implemented without overburdening the resources of the learner. For example, in their use of procedural facilitation, three primary supports help to make the skills involved in revision more concrete. First, the moment for children to stop reading and to evaluate what they have written is routinized (specifically, after each sentence). Second, the number of types of evaluations and the number of types of changes to be considered are limited. And, third, the specific evaluative comments and possible changes are written on cards, so that the children do not have to remember them. Scardamalia and Bereiter argue that as children become more proficient at the specific mental operations involved in revision, the need for the external supports will decrease.

Using the term *internalization,* Soviet psychologists have long emphasized the importance of external supports for cognitive activities that the child (or learner) cannot yet handle on his or her own. The following translation of Vygotsky (1981) reveals his emphasis on the role that more skilled individuals play in the learner's acquisition of skills.

> We could formulate the general genetic law of cultural development as follows: Any function in the child's cultural development appears twice, or on two planes. First it appears on the social plane, and then on the psychological plane. First it appears between people as an interpsychological category. This is equally true with regard to voluntary attention, logical memory, the formation of concepts, and the development of volition. We consider this position as a law in the full sense of the word, but it goes without saying the internalization transforms the process itself and changes its structure and functions.

According to the Soviet interpretation, the cognitive skills that the child can eventually use independently are first learned during interaction with others. During the interaction, the other person assumes many of the responsibilities that the child will later adopt. The other person may plan, direct attention, provide directions, etc; with this type of instruction, the child learns to handle the task alone. As it has been noted many times in these volumes, fine-grained analyses should be conducted so that we can more fully understand the process of internalization.

The processes that are involved in internalization are important, but another set of processes is equally important. Once certain skills have been learned by the child (i.e., have been internalized by the child), it is equally important that they are used by the child at appropriate times (i.e., that they are externally manifested). *Transfer* and *generalization* are terms often used to refer to the use of skills in contexts other than those of their initial use. Given a familiar context and a problem with familiar content, children can often use an appropriate strategy. Given an unfamiliar context or a problem that differs somewhat from the problem with which a strategy was learned, children may not even consider using the strategy. To some extent this may occur because the individual simply does not recognize the similarity in structure of the two problems; to some extent it may occur because the strategy itself has never been considered independent of the context and content of its initial use.

The ability to use strategies in a variety of situations may depend on extricating the strategy from its grounding and on reflecting upon the strategy itself. Simply modeling the use of a strategy probably will not result in the strategy's extrication from context. Most likely, there is a need to describe explicitly the nature of the strategy and to demonstrate or describe the variety of contexts in which it can be used. One approach may be to teach several strategies and to present problems that require determining which is appropriate for a particular problem.

Although we all tend to focus on the extent to which our schools are *not* teaching thinking and learning skills, there is some literature that suggests they are nevertheless on the right track. Comparisons between schooled and unschooled populations have revealed a set of somewhat related differences (reiewed by Day, 1980). For example, unschooled individuals do not spontaneously use mnemonic skills for deliberate memorization (Cole & Scribner, 1974; Wagner, 1974). When presented with a series of problems, unschooled populations tend to treat each problem as independent, whereas schooled populations are more likely to grasp a rule of solution and then transfer that rule from one problem to the next (Cole & Scribner, 1974; Scribner & Cole, 1973). Schooled populations seem better able to solve problems in the absence of concrete, empirical support (Cole & Scribner, 1974; Goodnow & Bethon, 1966; Luria, 1971). All these differences tend to suggest that schooled individuals use strategies in a less context- and content-bound manner than unschooled individuals; that is, schooled individuals tend to generalize their use of particular strategies.

In a similar vein, Vygotsky (1962) has argued that one of the main functions of schooling is to make one conscious of one's own cognitive activity. One of the ways schooling serves this function, he argued, is through its presentation of *scientific concepts*. In contrast to *spontaneous concepts,* which are built from everyday experience and often without thought about the concept itself, scientific concepts are typically introduced by verbal definition, frequently in the absence of concrete referents. They are presented as part of a system; the learner is immediately made aware of the relationships existing among the new concept and other concepts. It is this system that allows consciousness and deliberate control. Vygotsky (1962) asserts:

> School instruction induces the generalizing kind of perception and thus plays a decisive role in making the child conscious of his own mental processes. Scientific concepts, with their hierarchical system of interrelationships, seem to be the medium within which awareness and mastery first develop, to be transferred later to other concepts and other areas of thought. Reflective consciousness comes to the child through the portals of scientific concepts. (p. 92)

Research is needed both on how cognitive skills are initially learned and on how they should be taught so that they are used when they will be helpful. The work of Scardamalia and Bereiter demonstrates a way to make concrete a part of the writing process that has often been characterized quite vaguely, and it demonstrates the usefulness of such an approach. They turn, like many others, to the process of modeling to teach goal constructing activity, i.e., "movement from initial global goals—which are more or less in the nature of felt needs— to the specification of an end state that arises out of and further guides purposive behavior." Note that they do not use modeling alone; they also ask the student to identify the various approaches of the model and to practice these approaches themselves. This technique should lead the student to think about the processes explicitly. It would then be quite interesting to know if the students who learn from this approach can transfer the types of planning skills from expository writing to other compositional tasks.

PURSUING THE COMPOSITIONAL TASK OF TEACHING COGNITIVE SKILLS

Some of the factors that interact in the compositional task of teaching thinking and reasoning skills have just been described. It is clear that years of laboratory research could be conducted. But what can we say to Herb Ware of Arlington Virginia Public Schools and other educators in school systems?

In Ware's chapter (Volume 1), he documented the efforts of one public school system to implement a thinking skills curriculum. He noted a host of impediments to accomplishing the goal. "Program specialists found themselves expected to provide training to teachers in an area in which they had no explicit preparation. Teachers were in precisely the same position. Further, the journals of their own professional associations *were not,* and *still are not,* carrying articles which would provide direction for curriculum planners." In this same vein, Curtis Miles (Volume 1) of Piedmont Technical College noted that "practitioners are often informed more by desperation than by theory." Practitioners need to know how to teach thinking and reasoning skills *now*—not some years from now.

There is a tension, a justifiable and healthy tension, between the needs of the educators who are on the front lines of the classrooms and the caution of the academicians concerned with thinking and reasoning skills. On the one hand, educators cannot simply ignore thinking and reasoning skills until academicians and program developers concur in their judgments of the right way to teach children to think and to learn complex material. On the other hand, the caution of researchers and theoreticians is well advised for at least two reasons. First, we do not want to recommend any techniques that would be counterproductive or that would cause harm. Second, we do not want to oversell our product. We do not want to promise more than we can deliver; not only would this raise false hopes but also, when we all agree that we have something truly significant to deliver, we may have lost our credibility.

Nevertheless, even with a reasonable degree of caution, I think we can be helpful—helpful both to those of us doing research on teaching thinking skills and to those of us teaching thinking skills. When I asked Herb Ware what he had hoped to take home from the conference that resulted in these volumes, he mentioned reasonable and possible items: (1) references—so that he can be familiar with the type of research that is being conducted; (2) knowledge of the types of programs and curricula that are currently available so that school systems might select the one that best meets their needs; and (3) information concerning assessment techniques so that the educators can determine what they are and are not accomplishing.

There was little indication at the conference that educators expect a finished, perfect curriculum on thinking and reasoning skills. Instead, as several educators have noted, they look for some type of consensus among academicians concerning programs or approaches that are likely to be beneficial and that will not be harmful, and they look for a way to get started on their instructional mandate. It is important to keep their perspective in mind. Researchers might need to ask quite different questions of curricula when they consider what approach should be adopted *now* to teach cognitive skills and when they attempt to assess a curriculum or an approach as a researcher of thinking skills. Many of us would be quite hesitant, at this point, to engage in large-scale interventions heralded by promises of a new generation of excellent thinkers and problem solvers. However, I argue that efforts to teach thinking and reasoning skills (accompanied by reasonable claims) will be of benefit not only to educators who must take action now but also to researchers.

To some extent there has been an emphasis on how we as cognitive psychologists, as developmental psychologists, as instructional psychologists can provide help to educators. I think the benefits will go in both directions. Through our attempts to educate children in thinking and in learning skills, psychologists are likely to benefit as much as educators. A glance at the evolution of some of

the models of early childhood education during the 1960s and 1970s is informative. Some of the models were developed from clearly defined theoretical bases,
but the models were altered as they were actually implemented. There was a
tendency for programs with similar goals that were initially quite different to
become more alike. The child imposed a constraint that simultaneously led to
alterations in theory or in interpretation of theory and to changes in curricula.
What happened in the case of early childhood education is likely to happen in
education for thinking and learning skills. Feedback from the implementation
of instructional programs will lead to improvements both in the programs and
in our understanding of thinking and learning skills and how to teach them. In
a compositional task, one's understanding the goal and the costs and benefits of
alternative approaches to the goal develops as one actually works toward the
goal.

REFERENCES

Binet, A. (1962). [The nature and measurement of intelligence] (R. D. Tuddenham, Trans.). In L.
    Postman (Ed.), *Psychology in the making: Histories of selected research problems.* New York:
    Knopf. (Originally published, Paris: Flammarion, 1911.)
Brown, A. L., & DeLoache, J. S. (1978). Skills, plans, and self-regulation. In R. S. Siegler (Ed.),
    Children's thinking: What develops? Hillsdale, NJ: Lawrence Erlbaum Associates.
Case, R. (1974). Structures and strictures: Some functional limitations on the course of cognitive
    growth. *Cognitive Psychology, 6,* 544–573.
Cole, M., & Scribner, S. (1974). *Culture and thought: A psychological introduction.* New York:
    Wiley.
Day, M. C. (1980). *Adolescent thought: Theory, research, and educational implications.* Paper
    prepared for the National Institute of Education.
Flavell, J. H. (1979). Metacognition and cognitive monitoring: A new area of cognitive-develop-
    mental inquiry. *American Psychologist, 10,* 906–911.
Goodnow, J. J., & Bethon, G. (1966). Piaget's tasks: The effect of schooling and intelligence.
    Child Development, 37, 573–582.
Luria, A. R. (1971). Towards the problem of the historical nature of psychological processes.
    International Journal of Psychology, 6, 259–272.
Scribner, S., & Cole, M. (1973). Cognitive consequences of formal and informal education. *Sci-
    ence, 182,* 553–559.
Siegler, R. S. (1976). Three aspects of cognitive development. *Cognitive Psychology, 8,* 481–520.
Stone, C. A., & Day, M. C. (1978). Levels of availability of a formal operational strategy. *Child
    Development, 49,* 1054–1065.
Vygotsky, L. S. (1962). *Thought and language.* Cambridge, MA: MIT Press.
Vygotsky, L. S. (1981). The genesis of higher mental functions. In J. V. Wertsch (Ed.), *The
    concept of activity in Soviet psychology.* Armonk, NY: M. E. Sharpe.
Wagner, D. A. (1974). The development of short-term and incidental memory: A cross-cultural
    study. *Child Development, 45,* 389–396.

Two Perspectives

28 On Teaching Thinking: An Afterthought

Jerome Bruner
New School for Social Research

By any standard, this was a remarkable conference. We have had a tour of a large and bold frontier. It is a frontier that is of the first importance both in life and in theory. It is defined by a very practical set of questions that have now begun to find a theoretical formulation. In these chapters: participants have asked whether you can help people to think better, to plan better, to monitor and evaluate what they are doing more than they had done before? Indeed, can you lead them with benefit to reflect upon what they are doing and thinking in such away that they might formulate their goals better? All these questions are familiar in applied psychology. Now they have become part of mainstream psychology—under the rubric of metacognition. The shade of William James is at rest today!

David Perkins (this volume) urged that we "go for the stars." I think the work discussed does just that. It is not only ambitious, but compassionate. What could be more generous an idea than to help Everyman think for himself, no matter what his station, his ethnic background, his skin color, or his prior educational disadvantages? The presupposition is that man can help his fellow man to become his own thinker, and thereby to become more autonomous and self-determining. It is, I know, an ancient idea. But in the world climate of today, it is no less revolutionary than it ever was.

Looking at these volumes in the light of the history of psychology, it would seem that yesterday's new has, happily, become today's given. Many of us, in gloomier moods, worry that nothing cumulates in psychology, that, in Alan Allport's metaphor (1975), we dig such narrow and specialized research trenches that we are finally forced to abandon them more out of loneliness than disproof. In the present instance, this has not happened: Concepts that were being explored only tentatively a quarter of a century ago are now sufficiently operational and non specialized that they can be widely used and even taken for granted. When the physicist Robert Oppenheimer wrote a review of *A Study of Thinking* (Bruner, Goodnow, & Austin, 1956) in 1958, he reported seeing signs of change in psychology. It was at last, he reported, abandoning the units of the single stimulus and the single response and beginning to consider the complexities that stretch contingently between the formulation and the solution of a problem. Psychology was dealing with thinking, however modestly.

Not everyone felt so cheered by such proceedings. I recall giving a colloquium at Yale on strategies of problem solving. Midway through, the great Clark Hull began nodding assent and relaxing in his chair. When I asked him afterwards what had produced the sudden assent, he told me that it finally became clear to him that he could derive my idea of strategies from his habit-family hierarchy (Hull, 1952). Nor do I doubt that he could have, for he was a gifted man. But derivation was no longer the point. The problem had changed from learning and acquisition principles to problem-solving and performance principles. Nobody assumed any longer that strategies had to be learned *de novo*; strategies were, rather, generated or constructed from a knowledge base about the world and how to deal with it. That formulation of the problem stayed changed in just that way for the next quarter century with the result that the cognitive sciences have become richer and deeper and closer to real life.

I think that a confluence of many factors outside as well as inside psychology produced that change. One of them, ironically, was the development of computers—ironic because it freed us from the kind of radical behaviorism in psychology which banned all reference to mind or to mental activities as subjective and therefore regressive. How historically astonishing that we should find our way back to mind through the development of a thinking machine! But there is also a technological impetus behind psychology's return to mind generally and to problem solving particularly. It is almost the essence of the "post-industrial" revolution to place a high premium on the skills of the generalist, the trouble-shooter, and the problem solver. Once "mindful performance" becomes a practical necessity for the conduct of the technology, the issue of mind and its status ceases to be governed by philosophical or religious debates.

But new paradigms invariably create problems. They are eagerly propogated to new lands by their proponents. But they do not always fit the requirements of life there. And so it is with the computer-based model of the problem solver. Its design was for the land of the well-defined: solving problems in the White-head–Russell *Principia,* or trouble shooting circuit diagrams, or even characterizing how undergraduates solve concept-attainment problems. But is life like that?

And so, difficulties arise. Everyday problem solving does not reduce so readily to rational or even "satisficing" strategies or heuristics. Much of our ordinary problem-solving activity is directed to poorly defined problems with multiple goals and shifting standards, and the multiple goals may themselves be in a nested relationship with each other that changes with the course of attempted solution. Outside the glass house of the laboratory, multiple goals that change in passage are a structured fact of life. We want to succeed in solving *this* problem, but we do *not* want to get bogged down in a solution procedure that will bore us to death or take us forever. We want, shall I say, to be good problem solvers but not to the exclusion of all other graces. Jones (Volume 1) told us about Matrix Ordering strategies that can become so complex and time consuming that one might wonder whether to abort the whole problem rather than executing the next step, even though that next step might see us home and dry. That kind of decision depends, I suppose, on how one wants to spend the rest of the hour, or the day, or the week, or even the rest of one's life.

And very quickly the difference between "style" and "strategy" becomes hazy—and properly so. For perhaps style is, after all, just a specification about strategy preference, all other things being equal. Let me illustrate from a report in this volume. Perkins's poor problem solvers have just as many initial hypotheses as his good ones, only they quickly destroy them by a kind of Type II overkill. Well, I suppose the way to get them over their initial self-doubt is to cultivate arrogance. But you had better not succeed too well, for then they would become poor problem solvers again, this time by dint of having and holding on to premature hypotheses. So plainly then, there is some sort of stylistic balance operative in strategy construction about which we know very little. We had better know more about such matters. For if strategy is a useful concept in problem solving, it may be useful by serving as a constituent in theories of personality or motivation. What makes us cautious or bold? Why do we prefer one style of problem solving to another?

I think by now you rightly suspect that I am worried lest we make our accounts of problem solving too rational, more suited to the description of behavior in tasks whose objectives are clear, than to ill-formed behavior in general. For if one of our objectives is indeed to help people be good at problem solving, we had better keep well in mind how people would *like* to go at it, if they could get away with it.

But let me turn quickly now to the topic that was assigned to me.

DEVELOPMENTAL IMPLICATIONS

In reflecting upon the developmental implications of the theoretical and practical work reviewed in this volume, I shall group my remarks under three questions. These are: (1) What, if anything, must an information-processing model presuppose about development?; (2) What is the role of general or metacognitive skills in development?; (3) What is the role of social interaction and cultural milieu in the development of cognitive processes, particularly as seen in the perspective of information processing?

Developmental Models

We have just come through a period in developmental psychology dominated by a Stage Specific Model of the kind referred to by Carey (this volume) as Option 1: development in stages, each with its own format for problem representation, it own logic, its own set of concepts. This, of course, was the legacy of Piaget, and it has yielded great riches. By choosing a limited set of tasks or problems for study, the Genevan psychologists have given us a rare insight into how children deal with issues such as invariance of quantity across transformations, causality, probability, and classification.

But as Carey noted, the evidence does not support the view that there is qualitative discontinuity between stages. One has to choose one's experimental tasks with care to maintain the illusion of logically self-contained stages. Perhaps it is just as well that development did not, on close inspection, conform to her Option 1. For in fact, none of the extant theories has much by way of a mechanism to account for the child's progress from one self-contained stage to the next. The conditions that alter the equilibration between accommodation and assimilation, and thus permit or evoke change are left discreetly unmentioned by Piaget. Vygotsky (1962) did a bit better in describing the processes whereby the growing child is helped across the Zone of Proximal Development, but then it is doubtful whether he was in any proper sense a stage theorist. In those ancient years of the mid-1960s when I was a stage theorist—a bogus one really—I tried to deal with the shift from one stage to the next by introducing a notion of conflict in representations with resulting cognitive incompatibility. But to have conflict, the child must in some way be able to represent problems in different ways at any stage. So that made mine a rather half-baked stage theory, at that.

But whether the account of development as a series of unique, autonomous stages held up to scrutiny or not, the fact of the matter is that the search for stage theories *has* taught us some important things about cognitive growth. There may not be Great Big Stages, each with its own unique structure, but growth *is* characterized by *structural* changes. There are *paradigm* shifts in children's developing theories of the world, and although these may not be reducible to massive stage changes in basic axioms, neither are they matters of the simple accretion of information.

There are two things that convinced me that a stage theory could not be an appropriate account of development, and I want to mention them here for they help specify what an information-processing theory must take into account about development. The first was my own and others' data on development in early infancy. Whatever stages you may postulate, you can devise situations for testing young infants, once you get clever at it, that can easily bring the infants to a level way beyond where they are supposed to be developmentally. It is no great trick. If you make the testing task one that demands actions that they easily control, so that they have some surplus processing capacity to spend, you can bring off wonders.

Ilze Kalnins and I (1973), for example, were interested in the extent to which the 6-week-old infant could manage instrumental tasks involving a flexible or combinatorial deployment of means to achieve arbitrary or non-natural ends. Well, the 6-week-old does not have a large repertory. He can, we know, suck; he can look or avert his gaze—both quite expertly. He sucks for self-comforting and for nutriment, both quite naturally, quite expertly, and indeed even cannily (see Hillman & Bruner, 1972). It also happens to be the case, at that age, that infants prefer clearly focused pictures to blurred ones. Could we teach the infants in question to suck on a pacifier to produce a clearer focus in pictures they are viewing? The answer was a plain yes, and a trivial yes at that. Indeed, without additional prompting or training, the infants knew enough to keep their gaze averted until after they had sucked awhile and removed the blur from the displays. If sucking was made to produce blur, the same infants cannot suppress sucking entirely, however aversive its blurry outcome. But now they keep looking at the picture during the early phase of blurring, hanging on till the last aversive moment, when they finally look away.

It is hard not to conclude from this experiment, and many like it, that so long as you can get the problem translated into the child's processing space by honoring his limited attention span and leave some left over for combinatorial activity, then the child can solve problems "way over his head." What this means, I think, is that given the right support—you can call it tutorial support—the child will do much as Vygotsky suggested he would, given proper nurturing of his "zone of proximal development." The literature on infancy is rich in such demonstrations. They do not encourage much faith in a hard-line stage theory!

The same phenomenon occurs later in childhood, at school age. Children, given mathematical problems couched in the right embodiment and presented in a happy sequence, can also solve problems that are way over their heads and beyond their stage. Page (1960), using "box" notation, could produce surprisingly good intuitive algebraists among children not at all into Piagetian stage of formal operations. Again, it is a question of providing familiar instantiation of principles that are within the child's span and leaving some spare capacity over (see Shatz, 1978).

But this sounds, you will say, as if paradigm shifts are *not* involved in development at all. Indeed, *no* shift is needed, only an externalization of some sort of implicit, native knowledge, very much indeed like that evoked in the young slave "learning" geometry from Socrates in the *Meno*. Is it that Socrates is "merely" providing manageable representations for knowledge the slave already "possesses" in some way?

I suppose one could say that the first big paradigm shift consists of a representation or an instantiation for what was before only a mute and implicit intuition. After that, one encounters paradigm shifts to what might be called conceptually higher ground of the kind Carey (this volume) reports. There are also more gradual changes that are not so much paradigmatic as procedural, and these may be more like skill learning. We know from work on hypothesis development in children's problem solving that children come rather gradually to be more systematic in the application of such routines as "win–stay–lose–shift," that, bit by bit, they come to use feedback from attempted solutions to guide their decisions about whether to keep or jettison an hypothesis, etc. It is not that they start as nonproblem solvers and one day manage to get over the wall into problem solving. They are problem solvers from the start. What they are developing are workable strategies and modes for representing knowledge in some explicit, externalized way, for correcting that knowledge, and eventually for monitoring the whole process as it unfolds.

I agree with Gelman's account (this volume) of cognitive development: the older child tends to be more explicit, has a better grasp of how to access and manipulate structures and routines in order to get a job done or a problem solved. His recognition routines in looking for means are not only more explicit but tend to be driven increasingly by criteria of consistency and congruency. Markman (this volume) comments on the same matter: the younger child does not know explicitly enough what he knows, to be able to tell whether he is being consistent or not in organizing information. It may well be that the child deals successively with small chunks, until these become sufficiently routinized (or environmentally supported) for him to combine them into larger information structures. Then, and only then, can he be aware of consistency or even be able to know clearly what it is that he knows. It is at this point that metacognition begins to pay off—whether it is self-induced or evoked by a Socrates.

I think we can now begin to close in on the things that an information-processing theory must presuppose, and can safely presuppose, about development. It must presuppose that organisms are natural problem solvers who deploy means to achieve ends and use feedback increasingly well to control their deployment of means, etc. I think the evidence strongly supports this presupposition. The child from the start recognizes the means–end structure of problems and represents them in terms of such structures. He learns to use feedback and to develop greater regularity in his tryout of hypotheses, etc. The instantiations or "props" that he learns from the stored knowledge of the culture permit him not only to cope better with the problems he undertakes, but also to communicate with others in a common language so that he may learn more by vicarious means.

Metacognition and Development

I think that there is now sufficient evidence from work done by Brown and her colleagues (this volume), and others in this volume, to make it plain that children can assess their own performances and improve their procedures for remembering, for solving problems, and so on. It is not too far off the mark to say that this reflecting on one's own performance increases with age. We do not know for certain whether guided practice increases the likelihood of more appropriate and unprovoked reflection in the future, although the extant evidence suggests that this is the case, at least for memory strategies.

Work on the self-monitoring of speech (or on "linguistic awareness," as it is called) suggests that even the very young child has the capacity to reflect on his or her own speech flow and to correct it in the interest of being understood. Kasermann and Foppa (1981) have shown that such repairs are systematic even at 18 months. The literature has been reviewed recently by Eve Clark (1978), and it is simply not clear to what extent linguistic awareness is an accompaniment of or a factor in language acquisition. One study (Sinclair, 1981) suggests that, as far at least as "speech acts" are concerned, linguistic awareness is evoked not by errors in utterance form, but by errors in the behavior produced by the incorrect speech act form; that is to say, we become aware of what we are saying principally when we see through others' actions that our message has failed to convey its intended meaning.

I would like to raise a question now about childrens' play as a form of metacognition, possibly *the* form of early metacognition. I take metacognition to be reflection upon or monitoring of those acts that have to do with achieving, storing and retrieving, or using information. Its principal hallmark is its reflexivity. Play is not usually reflexive in this sense, but it represents nonetheless a form of activity from which the operator is more detached, better able to improvise. It is closer to a simulation than to a real thing. What is most characteristic of play is the manner in which it loosens the coupling between means and ends and allows for exploration of combinatorial possibilities among alternative means.

There is evidence that by getting children to play with materials that they must later use in a problem-solving task, one gets superior performance from them in comparison with those children who spend time familiarizing themselves with the materials in various other ways. The principal differences between the "players" and the other children may tell us something about the metacognitive function of play. For one thing, the players generate more hypotheses, and for another they reject wrong ones more quickly. Finally, they seem to become frustrated less and fixated less. They are going for feedback, one might say, rather than for self-esteem (Sylva, Bruner, & Genova, 1976). The playfulness fostered in the initial contact with the task seems to carry over into the problem-solving phase. Indeed, when you consider the matter, it should not be surprising. For play has the unique character of dissociating means and ends to permit exploration of their relation to each other. In "work," what one typically does is to hold an end or objective invariant while varying the means until one achieves it. In play, we uncouple the two in a different, more symmetrical way. We may hold the means constant while varying the end—the baby's typical routine of taking a block, for example, and achieving all possible outcomes with it: banging it, mouthing it, dropping it to the floor, etc. Or one holds the end invariant and varies the means, not with the object of achieving success but of exploring how many different routes one can use to get there. The infant bangs his or her cup, bangs a block, bangs any detachable object within reach. It may be a bit of an exaggeration, but may it not be the case that what we speak of as unprompted metacognition or monitoring, or reflection could be an internalized form of play?

After all, the commonsense way of referring to a metacognitve approach to a problem is to say that we are "playing around" with it a little.

One small aside before developing this point. There has been a good deal of analogizing in our discussions about how development is like going from being a novice to being an expert. Now that we have touched on play, I can tell you why I doubt it. Play is *the* business of childhood. Interestingly enough, when we try to impose the novice-to-expert regimen on children—which is principally what school is about—it very often produces a massive turning off of cognitive activity. Let me be very plain about it. I have (as I shall relate in a moment) studied hundreds of hours of play behavior. I have never, in all that time, seen a child glaze over or drop out or otherwise turn off while engaged in play. I wish I could say the same for the children I have observed in classrooms and even in one-to-one tutorials. This leads me to wonder whether play is not quite different from work, by which I mean the classical model of problem solving with the goal held constant and the means varied. Let me return to the main argument.

I want to pursue a problematic course. My colleagues and I have been engaged in an extended study designed to find out what conditions improve the "quality" of children's play (Bruner, 1981; Sylva, Roy, & Painter, 1981). Perhaps that can tell us something about how to improve their metacognitive activity as well. Let me not bore you with the details of how we compute quality or richness of play. Roughly, it consists of measuirng the number of contingent steps within a play sequence, their elaboration, the recruitment of objects or props in support of the play, and, finally, the sheer length of the play sequence which, of course, is highly correlated with its richness. In any case, in intensive observational studies of children aged 3–5 in playgroups, nursery schools, and kindergartens, we found four conditions that strikingly increase the richness and length of play. I want to describe the four conditions first and then to consider what they might tell us about the metacognitive side of play.

In no particular order, they are the following. First is the presence of *one* other child as a playmate: not two or none, but one. Two children in a shielded situation in which they can exchange and negotiate meanings, rules, etc. are the stuff of long and elaborated bouts of interactive play. The loner rarely plays long at one thing. As one would expect, two children will spend a great deal of time in deciding upon the procedures they will follow and how they may be instantiated. A second condition promoting long bouts of play is material that (a) has a clear-cut variable means-end structure, (b) has some constraints on the nature of the material that can be deployed, and (c) yields feedback that a child can interpret on his own without having to depend on authorities—i.e., direct rather than indirect feedback. Puzzles, building blocks, miniaturized versions of life activities, etc. all provoke longer and richer play bouts than the traditional quartet of water, sand, clay, and fingerpaint. These are the materials that provoke combinatorial exploration.

The third condition reminds one of *Lord of the Flies*. Play bouts are longer and richer among young children when there is an adult nearby who is buffering the situation, keeping it from getting out of hand, providing occasional comfort and response (Like: "See this airplane?" "Hm, what a nice plane."). The adult is not *in* the action, but a source of stability in the situation. The fourth and final condition is best called modeling. Those children who attended play-groups or nursery schools that spent some time each day in joint and compulsory high-level activity (e.g., school readiness games, so-called) were more likely to play longer and more elaborately than others when they were on their own.

In a word, then, negotiation, structure, stability, and a model of what is possible produces the richest play. I want to juxtapose with these findings one other observation, this time from Erik Erikson. He told me that, upon going back over the adult records from the California Growth Study, he had found that the most creative people were the ones with least separation in daily life between work and play. Now this could be an effect rather than a cause, and it doesn't matter much. That is to say, being creative and therefore not separating work and play may not be all that different from not separating work and play and therefore being creative. Like the Chinese and the structural linguists, I am not all that keen about establishing a temporal order for cause and effect. In linguistics, a verb phrase that follows in some sense causes the noun phrase that precedes it—or at least makes it possible for it to be a noun phrase. What I am saying, in effect, is that play at its best may be an early prototype, an *external* prototype of internal metacognitive activity in the more mature.

It is a hard case to establish, and I am not so much trying to establish it as to enter it into the lists for discussion. The argument is that all forms of external negotation of meaning, all external prods to reflection have the effect of *stimulating* internal negotiation, reflection, metacognition. Let me give some instances from the literature on the matter. In a recent study, for example, Tizard and Hughes (1980) show that the children who ask the most searching and deictically imbedded questions are the ones whose parents are most likely to give them full, intelligent, and elaborated answers to any questions they may ask. They become accustomed to negotiating interpretations and seeing alternative meanings. In a quite similar vein, Dunn and Beveridge (1980) have shown that children of mothers who concentrate during the second year on communicative intent, trying to explain to children what they and their siblings *intend* to express, regardless of what they *actually* say, show more sophisticated speech than the children of parents who do not. This is not strong evidence that earlier encouragement to go to higher ground produces greater likelihood of occupying higher ground when solving problems, but at least it is a start. Playful, negotiatory, flexible, mindful interaction early on may become a model later for what you do when you encounter problems. Having played around in fact, and with good effect, you may now feel encouraged to play around in your own head.

Culture and Cognitive Development

This brings me to my last topic: the impact of culture on cognitive growth. Let me begin with the Cultural Practice Model of Mike Cole and Warren Simmons, and I refer you to Simmons' chapter (this volume). He gives a striking example of cultural micropractice that fits the point I want to make. You recall the difference between the interpretation of a tutor's corrections made by a low-income, low-status kid and that made by his more privileged peer. The former takes the correction as punishment, the latter as feedback. There is an old finding from a study by Sroufe and Wunsch (1972) that I cite as often as I can, so important is it. They reported that those things most likely to make a young child laugh when done by a parent or familiar were the things most likely to make the child cry when done by a stranger. The tutored poor child is seeing his tutor as a stranger, as an adversary. But he, the child, has not *invented* the adversarial role of the tutor. It is a role established by a system in which poor children are defeated. An enormous amount of subtle rearranging of the social system is needed to bring the tutee into a position where he sees the tutor as a friend who gives him tips on how he is proceeding. I would add to this as well Virginia Shipman's finding. Those children in her study who early on are managed by a rationale rather than by physical coercive means do better in cognitive performance; that is to say, parents are not automatically in the category of allies whose response can be treated as feedback rather than punishment.

I have used the word "micropractices" to describe what a culture generates that affects the likelihood of particular kinds of cognitive activities developing in its members. It would be a mistake, however, to think of these as some sort of *list* of disparate elements. For the micropractices that shape cognitive growth, whether generated by parents, teachers, or adults in general, are highly patterned. They resemble what in linguistics is called a register (Snow, 1977): a patterned way of responding to another person's speech. As we know from the work of Cross (1977), these registers matter greatly for growth—even in language acquisition, where the received wisdom holds that everybody eventually learns to handle the language equally well. The cognitive register, so to say, is of a simple kind, I think. It consists of treating another as if they were of a certain kind or category of person. A good way of producing a dumbbell is to treat the person as a dumbbell. It is not surefire in its results, but it is a good beginning. It helps to get everybody else in that child's environment to treat him as a dumbbell too. If *you* didn't convince him, then perhaps a consensus will.

Rather than talking about how children can be shaped cognitively by the cultural micropractices of an environment, I will take older, indeed, aged subjects, and I refer to the experiments of Ellen Langer (Langer & Rodin, 1976). If old people in a nursing home are treated as if they are incapable of remembering and planning, they rapidly begin to perform accordingly. If now you introduce interventions so that old people are treated as if you expect them to be able to plan and to remember events as needed, then indeed there is a dramatic improvement in planning activity and in actual memory performance. One can wonder whether there may be something of this order operating in the Rosenthal effect as well.

Let me conclude by noting that the hidden agenda for middle-class children of well-educated parents is precisely to *expect* them to be reflective and meta-cognitively astute. And when their parents send them off to schools, the schools they go to are likely to expect just that of them. In a paper I wrote some years ago reviewing the literature of poverty and childhood (1975), I came to the conclusion that there was as discernible a pattern to be found among the fortunate as there was among those who were exploited by the society. Often, we signal our expectations about the use of mind subtly or not so subtly—whether we expect a person to be "stupid" or "impulsive" or "childish."

Bertrand de Jouvenal, the French philosopher, once tried to convince me that there was one sociological law that surpassed all others: "People do what you expect of them." I think he was not far off the track. I would end with one simple point, an extension of his. If you expect people to examine their thoughts, to be mindful about their use of mind, all of the evidence points to the fact that they can and will do so. If they have learned to play, perhaps, they can do it more readily, for they may be doing what comes naturally. But it would take a fair amount of rearranging of a society to assure that everybody has the opportunity to play richly. And it takes even more rearranging to see to it that we expect of each human being the best cognitive performance, the best and most mindful metacognitive performance of which he or she is capable, and that we make it worthwhile by rewarding him or her with the power and responsibility that their efforts deserve. That is what the challenge is about.

AFTER (AFTERTHOUGHT)

This conference, which would probably have been unthinkable a decade ago, is very nice testimony to the efficacy of metacognition. We have been talking and thinking about talking and thinking with great profit. In itself, it represents a very fine example of the importance of developing models that may guide one in repairing and reformulating the procedures by which we communicate with ourselves and with each other. I think that these volumes themselves, combining practical and theoretical concerns, bespeak the maturity of the study of cognition. When one looks at the models from which we borrow terms to formulate our cognitive activities, one reaches the point of recognizing that thought itself is not only about the world, but even more importantly, it is about thought itself.

REFERENCES

Allport, D. A. (1975). Critical notice: The state of cognitive psychology. A critical notice of W. G. Chase (Ed.), Visual Information Processing. *Quarterly Journal of Experimental Psychology, 27,* 141–152.

Bruner, J. S. (1975). Poverty and childhood. *Oxford Review of Education, 1,* 31–56.

Bruner, J. S. (1981). *Under five in Britain.* Ypsilanti, MI: High Scope Press.

Bruner, J. S., Goodnow, J. J., & Austin, G. A. (1956). *A study of thinking.* New York: Wiley.

Clark, E. (1978). Awareness of language: Some evidence from what children say and do. In A. Sinclair, R. J. Jarvella, & W. J. Levelt (Eds.), *The child's conception of language.* Berlin: Springer–Verlag.

Cross, T. (1977). Mothers' speech adjustments: The contribution of selected child–listener variables. In C. E. Snow & C. A. Ferguson, *Talking to children: Language input and acquisition.* Cambridge: Cambridge University Press.

Dunn, J., & Beveridge, M. (1981, September). *The effect of a sibling on mother–infant communication.* Paper delivered to Developmental Section British Psychological Society, Edinburgh, Scotland.

Hillman, D., & Bruner, J. S. (1972). Infant sucking response to variations in schedules of feeding. *Journal of Experimental Child Psychology, 13,* 240–247.

Hull, C. (1952). *A behavior system.* New Haven, CT: Yale University Press.

Kalnins, I., & Bruner, J. S. (1973). The coordination of visual observation and instrumental behavior in early infancy. *Perception, 2,* 307–314.

Kasermann, M. L., & Foppa, L. (1981). Self-repairs in early speech. In W. Deutsch, *The child's construction of language.* New York & London: Academic Press.

Langer, E. J., & Rodin, J. (1976). The effects of choice and enhanced personal responsibility for the aged: A field experiment in an instructional setting. *Journal of Personality and Social Psychology, 34,* 191–198.

Oppenheimer, R. (1958). Review of *A Study of Thinking. Sewanee Review, LXVI,* 481–489.

Page, D. (1960). Reported in J. S. Bruner, *The process of education.* Cambridge, MA: Harvard University Press.

Shatz, M. (1978). The relationship between cognitive processes and the development of communication skills. In C. B. Keasey (Ed.), *Nebraska symposium on motivation.* Lincoln: University of Nebraska Press.

Sinclair, A. (1981). Speech act development. In W. Deutsch, *The child's construction of language.* New York & London: Academic Press.

Snow, C. E., & Ferguson, C. A. (1977). *Talking to children: Language input and acquisition.* Cambridge: Cambridge University Press.

Sroufe, A., & Wunsch, J. P. (1972). The development of laughter in the first year of life. *Child Development, 43*(3–4), 1326–1344.

Sylva, K., Roy, C., & Painter, M. (1981). *Child watching at playgroup and nursery school.* Ypslanti, MI: High Scope Press.

Sylva, K., Bruner, J., & Genova, P. (1976). The role of play in the problem solving of children 3–5 years old. In J. S. Bruner, A. Jolly, & K. Sylvan, *Play: Its role in development and evolution.* Harmondsworth: Penguin Books.

Tizard, B., Hughes, M., Carmichal, H., & Pinkerton, G. (   ). Children's questions and adults' answers. *Journal of Child* 269–281.

Vygotsky, L. (1962). *Thought and language.* Cambridge, MA: MIT Press.

29 Learning and Instruction: A Letter for a Time Capsule

Robert Glaser
University of Pittsburgh
Learning Research and Development Center

Dear Men and Women of the 21st Century:

In the 1980's, distinguished scholars, scientists, and teachers attended a conference at the University of Pittsburgh entitled "Thinking and Learning Skills." The conference's purpose was the exchange of information among psychologists, educators, philosophers, and computer scientists. All present were attempting to understand and/or to teach thinking and learning skills; they were designing instructional programs or constructing theories of how these skills are acquired, and how they develop. Seeking a means of better understanding the circumstances that inspired the conference and the promises and limitations of our present resources, I found myself writing this letter to you of the 21st century.

This conference was held at a propitious time. Although older theories of learning and performance had proven effective in improving the fundamental literacy skills taught in our schools, newer advanced theories of human development and cognition had increased our knowledge of the higher level processes entailed in verbal comprehension, mathematical reasoning, the components of intelligence and aptitude, decision making, and problem solving. In addition, a number of school programs had appeared, based upon various theories and educational experience, that attempted to teach thinking, reasoned inquiry, and problem-solving skills. (Of course, these mental skills must be explicitly taught in your society.)

Most of the conference's research papers were heavily weighted toward theoretical descriptions of human performance and only fleetingly revealed their relevance to learning theory. A few research papers, however, did directly address an instructional problem. The reason for this was that cognitive psychologists

609

in the 1970s and 1980s had turned their attention to building precise methods of analyzing complex performance. When the conference convened, they were just beginning to return to experimental psychology's older emphasis on learning and the acquisition of knowledge and skill. Interest in cognition *and* learning *and* instruction was still rare, however, because theory integrating these three areas was only just emerging.

I hope to convey a sense of the participants' excitement about the conference in writing this letter to you. We all believe that our work can contribute to the attention given, in our time, to good thinking and to the development of proficient learners. Also, it is a faith of our era that such conferences can aid the advancement of science and human welfare. This conference was designed to encourage interaction between scientists and practitioners. We have no mandatory period of applied service for basic scientists or scientific service for practitioners in the behavioral sciences and in education, such as you must have instituted as an important stimulus to contributions to society.

Conditions in Education and Instructional Science in the 1980s

You may wonder why, in this period of nuclear energy, the grand tour of the solar system, the beginning of cloning and genetic engineering, and advancing decision theory and computer technology, we show deep concern about human intellectual functioning. Well, we are late in developing the cognitive and behavioral sciences and are very late in recognizing teaching as one of the most valued professions. One of the South American countries has established a ministry of human intelligence because it recognized this neglect. Of course, you can better understand this when I point out that although we have worldwide olympic competitions in physical sports, we do not yet have a cognitive olympics which you of the 21st century may well enjoy.

The 1980s are a challenging time. We have become interested in cognitive science and artificial intelligence, which encourages our concern with thinking, learning, and the augmentation of human problem solving, so that we can hope to understand and improve how humans use information. The information available to individuals through our proliferating means of communication is growing so rapidly that we must determine how to cultivate human abilities to filter it and to question it. We need the capacity to process information rather automatically, but still intelligently. Too many people, educators now realize, simply receive information with minimal processing; inert knowledge as opposed to generalizable forms of understanding is widespread.

In the latter part of this century, more and more children are attending our schools. We face problems of providing education for all—not only selecting and retaining the good learners. How can our schools adjust their programs to provide for universal literacy? This too encourages our interest in understanding as well as strengthening learning skills.

Schools have been somewhat incapacitated by a traditional selectivity whereby students dropped out for lack of the learning skills demanded by the system. Even now a subtle selectiveness causes absenteeism, failure, and helplessness. Fast learners also are among those fighting to break the mold. Our educators are, however, working on more adaptive forms of teaching in which instructional methods and environments for learning adjust to and challenge individual progress and strengthen the abilities required for students to profit from instruction and independent study.

The teacher's role has not changed very much in our century. While one still finds many marvelous teachers, teaching has lost prestige as a calling. In general, teachers carry out their work with few or very crude tools. Government-regulated industries supply physicians and engineers, but there is little attention given to supplying reliable, well-researched tools to teachers. At this conference, however, we found ourselves analyzing student-teacher dialogues and talking about more interactive, less exhortative student-teacher relationships. We have not yet learned (or only a few have) to study systematically what an expert teacher does; we find such expertise difficult to analyze. We focus the results of behavioral science primarily on the potential for improving instructional techniques and materials that teachers use. Less frequently, we consider applying our science to studying and explaining the performance of good teachers.

Schools are relatively isolated environments in our society. What students do with other parts of their lives is not well taken into account. And sometimes, thinking and learning skills courses are separate from the rest of school learning. At the time of the conference we had not yet learned, as I am sure you in future have, that the articulation of school and extraschool environments can encourage thinking skills and challenge learning, and can be a significant influence in accomplishing the task we had in mind.

At this meeting, some of our scientists reported attempts to apply our knowledge very directly. We were investigating cognitive strategies such as elaboration and were theorizing about the node–link structure of memory, so they built these ideas into instructional techniques. It seemed to me that behavioral and cognitive scientists did not yet understand how the art of the designer should assist in bridging scientific work and practical implementation. Furthermore, the newness and relative imprecision of our concepts about thinking and learning skills meant that we relied on the scientist as designer, and, at this time, application was most effective when scientists monitored the implementation of their ideas.

Certain scientist/program developers were especially ingenious in designing tasks that encourage students to manipulate their knowledge. A popular approach is to teach the self-monitoring skills that allow students to question and check their problem-solving activities. We call this metacognitive performance or metacognition. I suppose you will consider the term awkward, but it helps us to refine our incomplete understanding of learning and thinking by distinguishing between the performance processes involved in learning subject-matter knowledge and skill and the executive or control function of cognitive abilities used to assess and regulate learning. Because we were only beginning to construct theories about the automaticity of well-learned cognitive skills, I worried about "the centipede problem." Suppose a hundred-legged insect started to think about how he walked. If he applied metacognitive skills to improve his walking speed, all his legs would undoubtedly become tangled up.

We juxtaposed various conceptions of how learning and thinking skills could be acquired. In our science, a popular way of sorting out possibilities is pitting them against each other. For example, at the conference, we debated about theory and findings that indicate how thinking and learning skills might be taught either as content-free heuristics or as procedures in more content-specific contexts. At times, it seemed that with a content-free approach, it was possible to produce students who had all the good manners of understanding, who could ask metacognitive questions and who knew about general search procedures, but who had no well-developed knowledge structures at their command. But we were wary about content-specific strategies, because they might curtail abilities that fostered general transfer (an ill-defined term for us). We feared that we would produce contextually dependent, overly specialized students with little capacity for continued learning and problem solving in novel situations. If you bear with me, I will say more later about the contrast between content-free and content-specific approaches that was a significant issue at our conference.

When we met at Pittsburgh we were beginning to understand the following: (1) The ability to transfer one's skills and knowledge to new situations is not readily acquired in the course of learning but, like other abilities, must be practiced under appropriate conditions to develop. (2) Thinking and learning skills accrue as a person builds an informational and knowledge base. Initially, this knowledge base might be rudimentary, culturally different, or even inaccurate, but an identifiable knowledge structure could be used to develop thinking, first in the context of the information in that structure, and then in more formal subject-matter structures. (3) Sometimes, after much practice with problem structures in various domains and subfields, an individual develops more abstracted kinds of thinking, learning, and problem-solving skills. This is rare, however, because most people learn the strategic expertise and specific constraints of the fields in which they practice.

Difficulties We Face

Probably not to your surprise, we find it difficult to deal with affective and motivational matters; we call these "hot" cognition (too hot at least for us to handle systematically) but we have some leads in reinforcement and attribution theory.

We also find it difficult to handle individual differences for at least two reasons. First, schools do not have the flexibility necessary to cope with widely varied requirements for learning. The influences of family and social background that contribute to these differences are difficult to respond to in conventional school settings. Second, our experimental tradition has emphasized the discovery of general laws and deemphasized parameters of individual differences. The scientific study of individual differences has centered around the taxonomic goals of factor analysis and the psychometric techniques of test theory. Factor analysis has worked toward the identification of factor classifications as the end products of research but is less fruitful in explaining factors in terms of psychological processes. Test theory has centered on technological applications that promote models for accurate measurement of individual differences, with little emphasis on the nature of the psychological performance being assessed.

We are just beginning to develop measurement techniques that would assess the knowledge states and cognitive abilities with which a person starts a course of learning. For example, we are developing procedures with which we can first assess the performance rules that an individual uses to solve a problem and then use this information as a basis for developing higher level rules of performance. The general notion is that diagnostic testing for teaching and for fostering learning skills should involve means for detecting performance rules and strategies that define a person's current level of competence.

Please permit me to list a few more of our difficulties. In mentioning testing, I should say that we have developed primitive mastery-based learning systems with criterion-referenced (or domain-referenced) tests. But we have not yet discovered the cognitive dimensions along which the acquisition of subject-matter knowledge and skill can be measured. We are just beginning to appreciate what mastery in a field entails—particularly the characteristics of the powerful representations and encodings that competent individuals display when given problems to solve. Investigations of the nature of expertise in scientific and technical problem solving, in medical diagnosis, and in writing are beginning to be informative in this regard. (We are also, I believe, in danger of the "curriculum-test overlap problem," where success in schooling is artificially enhanced by maximizing the overlap between what is taught and what is tested.)

We are only beginning to consider the concept of optimization in instruction. What are the differential effects of various conditions for learning in guiding a learner from an initial state of knowledge to desired educational outcomes? For example, certain instructional procedures could maximize the retention of prose; others could maximize the understanding and comprehension of prose. We are just developing the theory to think about min–max effects and the interrelationships between basic and higher order processes in instruction.

Evaluating the effectiveness of thinking and learning skills programs is a major problem. Putting methodological details aside, deciding upon what attained outcomes to measure, and identifying and understanding the actual teaching and learning processes that occur in the course of instruction is extremely complex. We are only beginning to construct macrotheories (in contrast to the more microtheories of cognitive information processing) of the conditions of classroom learning and program implementation variables.

Learning theory, which should come to our aid, is working its way out of a recession. It has been well developed in the context of conditioning, S–R theory, and simple forms of learning and is now gearing up for theories about learning in rich knowledge domains and the acquisition of complex procedural skills. (The term *gearing up* must sound quaint to you; it refers to the expensive and polluting transportation on which we now depend.) Our current theories have discovered once again the cognitive world beneath the skin, so that we talk about influencing learning and thinking through changes in internal processing and in the organization of mental schemata.

It was of interest in the conference to notice the respect for clinicians shown by experimental psychologists in our discussions. Clinicians frequently are held in low esteem by experimentalists; at this conference, however, clinicians described certain conditions that enhance or retard change. They emphasized the power of their clients over their own performance and suggested that a good way to improve the effectiveness of teachers is to enhance the ability of their students for self-regulation. This requires understanding the strategies that students use to solve problems in learning and thinking and guiding this intelligence toward further development.

A Dilemma for Research and Practice

As I have indicated, the conference participants reflected upon disparate views of how to teach thinking and problem solving. Some emphasized instruction in general domain-independent rules and general heuristics, whereas others stressed the acquisition of domain-specific problem-solving skills. To resolve this dilemma, it appeared that we needed to have more information about the transferability of acquired knowledge and skill. Several outcomes were deemed possible. (I wonder what view your science and your instructional practices reflect.) First, you may have found that broad domain-independent knowledge and skill about thinking and problem solving are teachable in ways that make them useful in a variety of situations. Or, your research might have continued to show that people have limited capability to transfer skills from one context to another, and that expert skills are most apparent in the context of specific domains of knowledge. General heuristic methods are often weak because they are applicable to many situations and do not alone provide an evaluation of specific task features that enable a problem to be solved. Whereas, in contrast, skills learned in specific contexts are directly useful when they are accessed as part of an acquired knowledge structure but then may fail to transfer to new domains. How have you resolved that dilemma?

It became apparent from the discussions of our meeting that we were in the early, but potentially fruitful, stages of understanding and assessing the limits of generality and constraints of specificity in teaching thinking and learning skills. I personally permitted myself to speculate on this matter and would like to share my thoughts with you. Beyond the two possibilities just mentioned, it seemed to me and some others at the conference that a third possible outcome could be considered. Perhaps both generalizable and specific levels of thinking could be taught in the course of acquiring subject-matter knowledge and skill— particularly in interactive instructional situations, where there is an emphasis on active inquiry as learning occurs. Specific declarative knowledge and associated procedural knowledge would be learned, as well as the general processes involved in using one's knowledge for inquiry and new learning. This possibility, however, ran somewhat counter to most, not all, of the published programs described at the conference.

To date, most programs have emphasized the teaching of general processes, especially general heuristics and rules for reasoning and problem solving that might be acquired as transferable habits of thinking. Also, in large part, abstract tasks, puzzle-like problems, and informal life situations are used as content. An avoidance of the complexity of subject-matter information is typical, purportedly because teachers and students may find the combination of learning subject matter and thinking difficult to manage and inhibiting of general thinking processes that need to be acquired and practiced. The significant feature of this approach is that it makes little direct connection with thinking and problem solving in the course of learning cumulative domains of knowledge—that is, in the context of acquiring structures of knowledge and skill that comprise the subject matter of schooling.

The underlying reason for this separation of thinking and subject-matter learning, I believe, is a matter of theory on human thinking. The programs in use are based on early theories of human cognition. Some stem from psychometric notions of inductive reasoning and from concepts of divergent thinking in older theories of problem solving. Others derive from early information-processing theory, which explored knowledge-lean problems and concentrated on basic capabilities that humans employ when they behave more or less intelligently in situations where they lack specialized knowledge and skill. As you know, when faced with such novel situations, people resort to general methods. But in the context of acquired knowledge and specific task structures, these methods lack the focus of domain specificity, leaving the individual to search for procedures (which may or may not come to mind) to fit the given situation.

Although the general heuristic processes that humans use to solve problems were richly described by the pioneering work of the 1960s and early 1970s, this research used relatively knowledge-free problems and so offered limited insight into learning and thinking that requires domain-specific knowledge. In contrast, more recent work on problem solving, done in knowledge-rich domains, shows strong interactions between structures of knowledge and cognitive processes. Emerging findings and theory are forcing us now to consider teaching thinking not in terms of general processes primarily, but in terms of knowledge structure and process interactions. Indeed, it has seemed to me that thinking is best taught in the context of the "three R's" (I am sure that studies of the history of education make you familiar with this quaint term) and other knowledge and skill domains. As was pointed out in our conference, one has the feeling that for the students in our schools, there seem to be long periods when thinking and subject-matter learning are kept apart. The feasibility of a more integrated approach has been increased by the studies in developmental psychology and cognitive science reported at the meeting, in which attention was turned to cognitive process in the context of the acquisition of structures of knowledge and skill.

This emerging picture has bolstered my view of skill in reasoning, problem solving, comprehension, and related skills of learning as developing out of knowledge acquisition and use. People continually try to understand and think about the new in terms of what they already know. It thus seems best to teach thinking and learning skills in specific, familiar knowledge domains and in those that people are learning. Abilities to make inferences and to generate new information could be fostered by instructional methods that insure contact with prior knowledge, which is restructured and further developed as thinking and problem solving occurs. Learning and thinking skills would be acquired as the content and concepts of a knowledge domain are taught in learning situations that constrain that knowledge in the service of reasoning and inferencing that leads to new learning.

Instructional Theory

One of the questions asked at this conference was: What framework could theorists and practitioners share that would permit a dual attack on the problem both of understanding and of teaching thinking and learning skills? One answer that occurs to me (and that has been a focus of my own work for some time) is the development of an instructional psychology, a field that would bridge experimentation and theory to instructional design and technology. Earlier in this century, John Dewey had called for a "linking science"—a science that would fall between psychological theory and instructional practice. To my way of thinking, the instructional psychology of recent years displays the appropriate characteristics, ones that are typical of rational problem solving in many technological endeavors. These include (1) specification of a goal state (instructional objectives); (2) specification of an initial state of affairs (skills for learning and current knowledge); (3) admissable operations that would transform the initial state into the goal state (teaching techniques and instructional materials); and (4) assessment of the intermediate states that are subgoals that need to be monitored to provide information for the sequence of transition operations (achievement and diagnostic tests). Our present capability to develop instructional systems and environments for teaching thinking and learning skills might be assessed in terms of our progress with respect to these components of a systematic approach to fostering the acquisition of knowledge and skill.

To specify the goal state, we need to analyze the structures and processes of knowledge and skill that comprise the objectives of our instruction, and that characterize individuals with highly developed learning and thinking abilities. At our conference, it appeared that we were working on describing these skills in terms of information-processing theories and systematic analyses of knowledge structures. We seem less far along in theorizing about how these skills are acquired. We are nonetheless beginning to be able to identify the cognitive differences between skilled learners and problem solvers and poor ones. These findings serve as starting points for the development of programs that assist in teaching the skills involved. And the programs designed are being analyzed by researchers so that these skills and their acquisition can be better understood.

Progress has been made in specifying and understanding the initial state of the learner by identifying the abilities an individual brings to instruction that foster learning and thinking. We are reconsidering traditional intelligence and aptitude tests in order to design instruments for informing instructional decisions rather than providing only predictive validity. These new tests will not merely predict how well an individual will respond to academic demands (and hence relieve the school from assisting a student as much as possible). Rather, they will indicate the rules a student uses in displaying intelligence—rules that might be incorrect or incomplete but are nevertheless systematic performances that can be used as a basis for instruction. Research is also being encouraged in this area through cognitive theories that attempt to understand the information-processing requirements of intelligence and aptitude tests. New forms of dynamic assessments of performance level and learning abilities are being proposed.

The third component of the instructional problem—the operations that facilitate the transformation and development of an initial state into a goal state—is directly related to our knowledge of learning theory and developmental change. At this time, both areas are undergoing theory reconstruction, with interesting results. New learning theories seem compatible with the idea that knowledge organization significantly influences problem-solving processes. These theories describe how individuals acquire declarative and procedural knowledge, which intertwine and whereby an individual who becomes proficient in a field develops a declarative knowledge base, which becomes bonded to the conditions for using this knowledge effectively. Such understanding of the integration of knowledge and its conditions of applicability should help us avoid recapitulating the rote learning paradigms underwritten by older learning theories and can, instead, encourage learning and instructional theories that foster the attainment of knowledge that is accessible for problem solving.

Theories of human development are beginning to reveal the potentialities as well as the constraints of developmental levels. In fact, it seems that new learning theories will reflect new theories of development. An interesting idea about development in terms of theory displacements was presented at the conference: Because theories are what people think with, teaching might use rudimentary pedagogical theories that could be replaced with more complete theories as learning advances. The developmental psychologists at the conference showed great interest in study of the transition processes between stages, and how this knowledge could inform learning theory.

Of course, the psychological principles of behavior modification and reinforcement still offer techniques that can be applied to learning with interesting and effective results, and this was indicated at our meeting. We know how to reinforce and how to fade situational crutches but need to know more about the cognitive performances that we hope to reinforce. Our conceptions of motivation, attribution, and attitudes that foster learning skills remain very tentative, but we are increasingly convinced that cognitive skill and positive attitudes toward problem solving need to be encouraged side by side.

The fourth component of the instructional framework—the assessment and monitoring of attained performance that provides information for the effective guidance of learning—also appears to be showing progress. Instructional systems that provide performance criteria information to the teacher and the learner are being designed. We are teaching learners to monitor their own performance, on the basis of our increasing knowledge of metacognition and self-regulation. The systematic analysis of dialogues between student and teacher are showing how good teachers assess performance prior to instructional decisions, and I believe that we are seeing the beginning of dynamic forms of instruction that adapt to individual progress, so that the conditions of instruction selected to faciitate learning can respond to systematic differences between the student's current status and standards of competent performance. Most important, we are carrying out research that can lead to a theoretical basis for the measurement of competence founded on our knowledge of the acquisition of proficiency rather than primarily on an empirical technology of test design.

Finally, dear reader, I should emphasize that the participants in the conference at the Learning Research and Development Center at the University of Pittsburgh were strongly motivated to shape both science and practice in ways that would strengthen individuals' skills in interrogating and learning from the world around them. Some of the conference participants will continue to conduct research in their laboratories and on their computers. Some will conduct research in schools. Others will design curricula and work with students. All will be committed to the improvement of human knowledge, reasoning, disciplined inquiry, and intelligence. (Do you people of the future still use the word "intelligence"?)

I wish I could tell you more in this letter, but they will seal the time capsule in the morning.

Respectfully submitted,

Robert Glaser

Author Index

Subject Index